Christoph Witzenrath
The Russian Empire, Slaving and Liberation, 1480–1725

Dependency and Slavery Studies

―
Edited by
Jeannine Bischoff and Stephan Conermann

Volume 4

Christoph Witzenrath

The Russian Empire, Slaving and Liberation, 1480–1725

Trans-Cultural Worldviews in Eurasia

DE GRUYTER

Gefördert durch die Deutsche Forschungsgemeinschaft (DFG) im Rahmen der Exzellenzstrategie des Bundes und der Länder – Exzellenzcluster Bonn Center for Dependency and Slavery Studies (BCDSS) EXC 2036/1-2020, Projektnummer: 390683433

Funded by the Deutsche Forschungsgemeinschaft (DFG, German Research Foundation) under Germany's Excellence Strategy – Cluster of Excellence Bonn Center for Dependency and Slavery Studies (BCDSS) EXC 2036/1-2020, Project No.: 390683433

ISBN 978-3-11-152096-4
e-ISBN (PDF) 978-3-11-069643-1
e-ISBN (EPUB) 978-3-11-069658-5
ISSN 2701-1127
DOI https://doi.org/10.1515/9783110696431

This work is licensed under the Creative Commons Attribution-NonCommercial-NoDerivatives 4.0 International License. For details go to https://creativecommons.org/licenses/by-nc-nd/4.0/.

Creative Commons license terms for re-use do not apply to any content (such as graphs, figures, photos, excerpts, etc.) not original to the Open Access publication and further permission may be required from the rights holder. The obligation to research and clear permission lies solely with the party re-using the material

Library of Congress Control Number: 2022941852

Bibliographic information published by the Deutsche Nationalbibliothek
The Deutsche Nationalbibliothek lists this publication in the Deutsche Nationalbibliografie; detailed bibliographic data are available on the internet at http://dnb.dnb.de.

© 2024 with the author(s), published by Walter de Gruyter GmbH, Berlin/Boston
This volume is text- and page-identical with the hardback published in 2022.
This book is published open access at www.degruyter.com.

Cover image: St Nicholas of Mozhaisk, Inv. nr. 116-ДРС, with permission of Arkhangelsk District Museum.
Typesetting: Integra Software Services Pvt.

www.degruyter.com

Acknowledgements

Work at this book started when I perceived a gap between studies of Muscovite worldviews, in some regards arcane but accomplished scholarly field, and the social history of slave raids. It was the prescience, generous support and funding from the University of Aberdeen, Scotland, and the Leverhulme Trust's early career research fellowship allowing me to branch out for this study. Tony Heywood, Paul Dukes, William Naphy, Elisabeth Macknight, Andrew Dilley, Michael Brown, Karin Friedrich, Stefan Brink and Jackson Armstrong were supportive, perceptive and exhilarating. Robert I. Frost at an early stage opened my eyes to developments highlighted for the first time almost a year later by the usually well-informed feuilleton of Frankfurter Allgemeine Zeitung. My colleagues on both sides of the Atlantic have widened my vision in the process, particularly debates at panels organized by and with members of the Early Slavic Studies Association at ASEEES, Erika Monahan, Brian Boeck, Brian Davies, Peter Brown, and many more, at the conference on slavery in the steppe region and at the Casa de Velázquez, where Alessandro Stanziani introduced me to the scholars working on the Mediterranean, among many others, Fabienne Guillén, Youval Rotman, and later Ehud Toledano. Insights from Russian and Tatar angles respectively were graciously provided by Vadim Trepavlov and Bulat Rachimzyanov, who also gave a moving tour of Kazan. My debts to the Harvard Ukrainian Research Institute and its Eugene and Daymel Shklar Research Fellowship will not be forgotten; I gained much awareness and inspiration from people at the University and Widener Library, Don Ostrowski as a friend and mentor, and the helpful, discerning, and friendly Michael Flier, Lyubomir Hajdar, Serhii Plokhii, Mikhail Minakov and Natal'ia Sinkevych. The fellowship of the Gilder-Lehrman Center for the Study of Slavery, Resistance, and Abolition at Yale and the Petro Jacyk Visiting Scholarship awarded by the University of Toronto's Munk School of Global Affairs along with exchanges with Paul Bushkovitch, Victor Ostapchuk, and Maryna Kravets brought fresh and complementary acumen. Special thanks go to Nancy Shields Kollmann for encouraging and urging to write more wide-ranging. My interest in religious views of slavery in various communities was strengthened by exchange with Elisabeth and Joachim Schulze, Ludwig Steindorff and Marie-Luise Ehrenschwendtner, and Nicole Priesching, Heike Grieser and the wide range of accomplished researchers present at the conference on theology and slavery in Paderborn. Ludolf Pelizaeus was open to eastern extensions as rising awareness in Germany of the subject of slavery after antiquity went hand in hand with my studies. Angela Rustemeyer, Aleksandr Lavrov and Cornelia Soldat engaged in specialised debate. The German Historical Institute welcomed and furnished me in Moscow. Deutsche Forschungsgemeinschaft funded my projects twice, first at the University of Greifswald, where I benefitted from Matthias Niendorf's expertise in Polish-Lithuanian history and the congenial atmosphere among members of both his chair, Tilman Plath and Baiba Tetere, and the colloquia of the Interregional Graduate Research Training Group 'Baltic Borderlands' organized by Michael North. Exchanges with Stefan Rohdewald inspired involvement with the Priority Programme Transottomanica, and my affiliate project. The meetings and exchanges with members, Denise Klein, Veruschka Wagner, Robert Born, Suraiya Faroqhi, Albrecht Fuess, Dennis Dierks, Elke Hartmann, Andreas Helmedach, Yusuf Karabıçak, Jan Kusber, Nana Kharebava, Gül Şen, Johannes Pahlitzsch, and Markus Koller have done much to enhance my transregional outlook.

I have decided not to fully account for the tremendous and continuing range of stimulations and motivations afforded by membership in the Bonn Center for Dependency and Slavery Studies, which, sometimes implicitly and against my intention to finish up immediately, influenced last revision of the text and amendments during the eventful time since my arrival. However, this experience has rounded off some hard edges in the text. Stephan Conermann, Julia Hillner, Claudia Jarzebowski and Martin Aust gave important impulses and hints, partly as a result of debates with students when collaboratively teaching on the Center's Master courses. Finishing this book benefitted from the generous award of the Heinz Heinen Fellowship and the firm commitment of the University of Bonn.

Special mentions to Evgenii Evgen'evich Rychalovskii, Grigorii Efimovich Brodskii, Evgeniia Efimovna Lykova, and members of staff at the Russian Archive of Old Acts who have used their means to the utmost providing a working atmosphere and plenty of good advice.

Alexander Heinert, Iulia Vainzof, Patrick Tidball, Zhenia Danilevskaia, Mark Sweetman, Ingo Zirks, Ricarda deHaas, Kate Wilson, Heike Wippich, Carolin Leutloff, Uffa Jensen, Valentina Leonhard, Vera Urban, Rebecca Taylor, and Hannes Grandits kept company, gave good advice, involved in debates and kept up spirits during various stages of this project. Gabriele, Elias, and Malina have graced me with much empathy, perseverance, discernment, and curious and wide-ranging discussions.

Particular thanks go to Elena Smolarz and Marianne Stößl for liaising for copyright issues, as well as to Maria Ivanovna, Robert I. Frost, Don Ostrowski, the anonymous reviewers, Imogen Herrad, Angelina Vetter, Nataliia Voitko and Eva Locher at De Gruyter for helpful comments after reading parts or all of this book or earlier versions and tagging the index. It goes without saying that the whole text is my exclusive responsibility.

Contents

Acknowledgements —— V

List of illustrations —— IX

Maps —— XI

Introduction —— 1
    Slaving, ransom, and serfdom in western inner Eurasia, 1470s–1700s —— 7
        Muscovy and the steppe —— 7
        Serfs, slave raids, and border regime —— 8
        Slavery and Islam in Eurasia —— 13

Chapter 1
Trade Routes and Slaving Zones in Eurasia. Empire, Ideology and Framing Legitimate Human Merchandise —— 24
    (No-)Slaving zones —— 33
    Muscovy's counter dependency zone —— 35

Chapter 2
The Conquest of Kazan —— 43
    New Israel —— 46
    Liberation from slavery as justification —— 53
        The 1550s campaigns —— 58
        Liberation in the 'Chronicle of the Beginning of Tsardom' —— 59
        The 'Letter to the Ugra' —— 67
        From transfer to mobilisation —— 80
        From liberation to conquest —— 86
        Makarii's letters —— 92
    Conquest —— 95
    Conclusion —— 102

Chapter 3
Redemption, Ritual and Exodus —— 104
    Redemption —— 105
    The New Year's ceremony —— 113
    The Blessed Host —— 119

Chapter 4
Spreading Liberation Ideas —— 124
    Baptism and crossing the Red Sea —— 124
    The True Cross and purification by water —— 131
    Delivering saints —— 145
        St Sergius —— 145
        St Nicholas —— 148
        St George and the dragon —— 157
    Theatre and liberation —— 160

Chapter 5
Slavery, Ransom and Loyalty in Muscovy —— 168
    Petitions by returning slaves and captives —— 179
    Conclusion —— 190

Chapter 6
Slavery and Empire —— 193
    Intermediaries —— 195
    Honour and empire —— 199
    Saints' lives —— 205
        Saving heterodox subjects —— 206
        Joseph the Beautiful —— 209
    'Sons of Hagar' —— 216
    Wisdom, empire and liberation —— 224
        Light symbolism —— 230
        Love and wisdom in propaganda —— 236

Conclusion —— 247
    Outlook —— 254

Bibliography —— 259

Index —— 289

List of illustrations

Map. 1	Muscovite fortified line construction until the end of the seventeenth century —— XI	
Map. 2	Military colonization in the steppe until the end of the seventeenth century —— XII	
Map. 3	Changes to the northern Silk Routes, sixteenth to seventeenth centuries —— XIII	
Fig. 1	Icon 'Blessed Host of the Heavenly Tsar', 1550s, inv. nr. 6141, with permission of Tretyakovskaia Galereia —— 121	
Fig. 2	'St Nicholas of Mozhaisk', seventeenth century, Russia, inv. nr. 116-ДРС, with permission of Arkhangelsk District Museum —— 152	

Maps

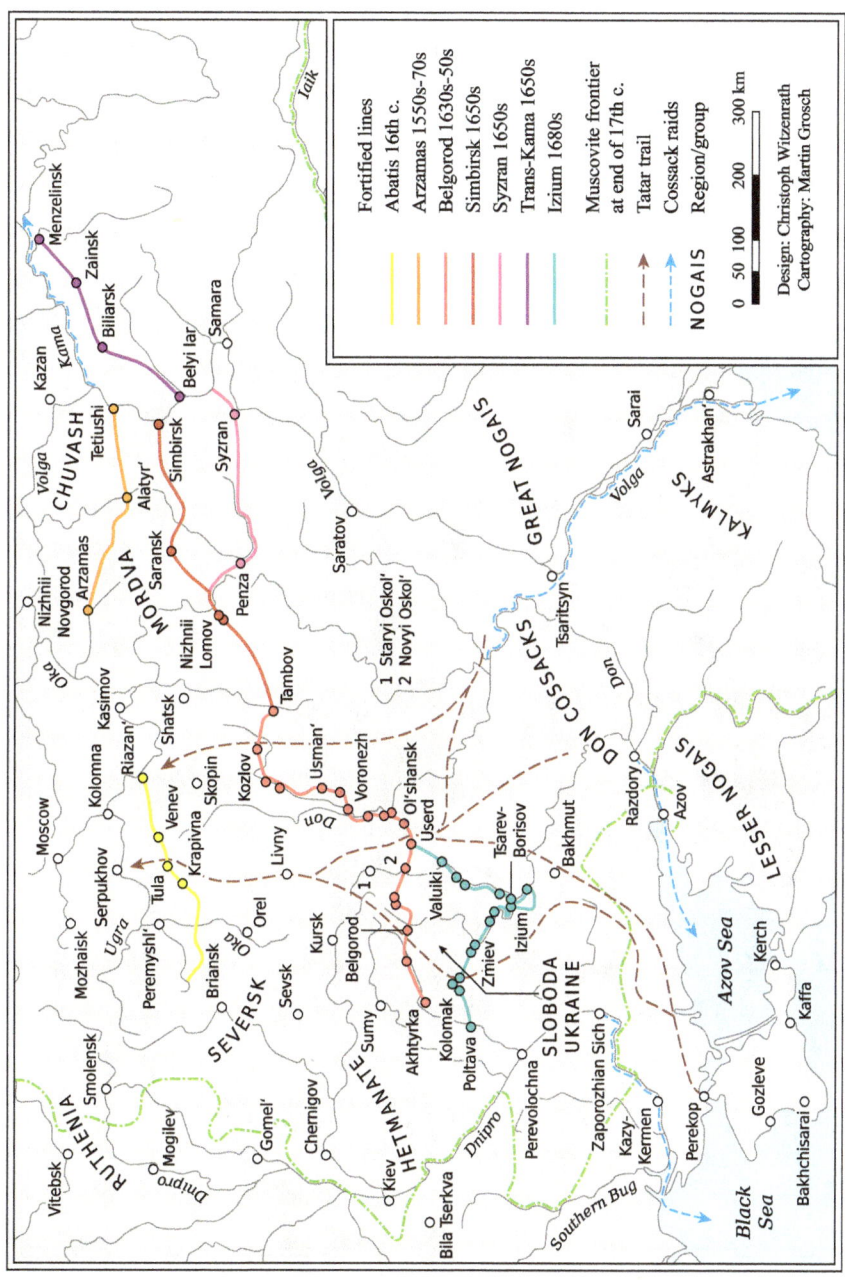

Map. 1: Muscovite fortified line construction until the end of the seventeenth century.

XII — Maps

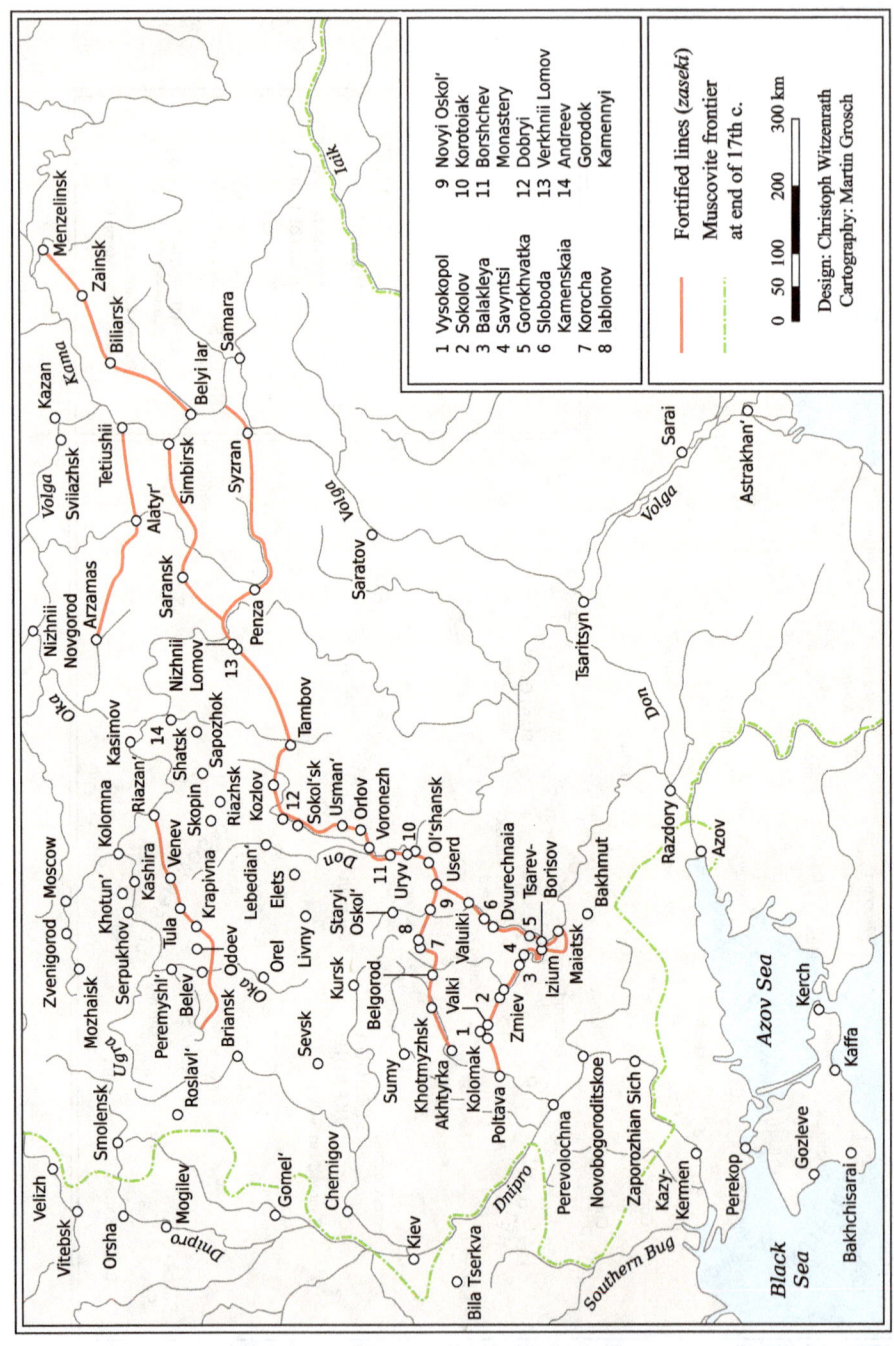

Map. 2: Military colonization in the steppe until the end of the seventeenth century.

Maps — XIII

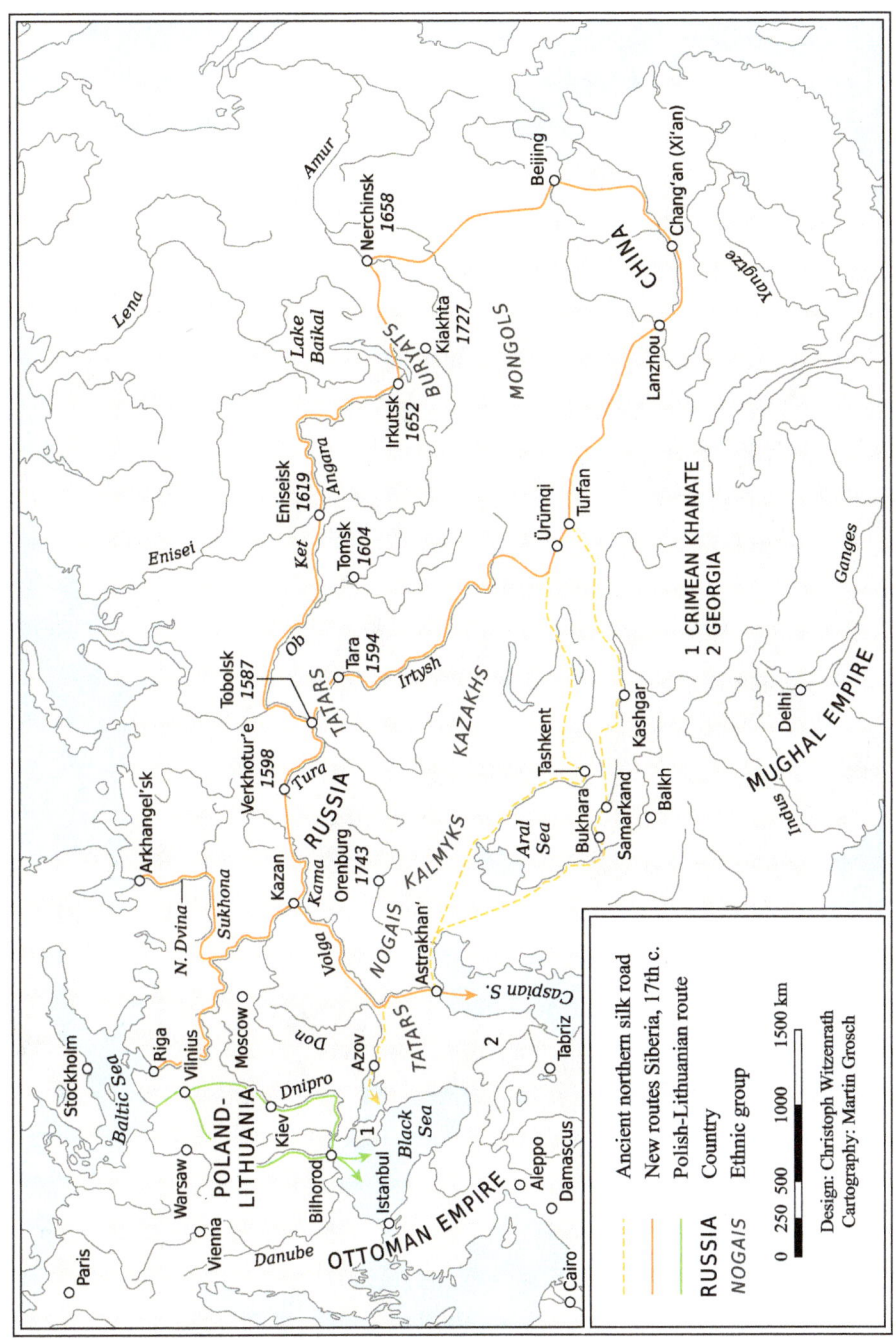

Map. 3: Changes to the northern Silk Routes, sixteenth to seventeenth centuries.

Introduction

> Paradox! The most insular people in the world managed to establish the largest empire the world has ever seen. No, not paradox. Insularity, like empire-building, requires superb self-confidence, a conviction of one's moral superiority.
>
> Paul Scott, A Division of the Spoils (The Raj Quartet [1975] 1977: 106)

> Old pirates, yes, they rob I
> Sold I to the merchant ships
> Minutes after they took I
> From the bottomless pit
> [. . .]
> Cause all I ever have
> Redemption songs
>
> Bob Marley

This book re-examines the role of slavery and the reactions to it in the political language of the Muscovite Empire – a topic sorely neglected by scholarship. It aims to reconnect the extant sources to the context that once was so obvious to most observers there seemed no need to mention it. Historians have approached this subject from two directions: many, foremost among them non-specialists, overlooked or denied the focus of the Muscovite worldview on being the New Israel, preferring other sources, barely related to the state sphere, from a teleological point of view of later imperial power. This interpretation originated during the heyday of imperial glory in the early nineteenth century, when Muscovite ideas might seem inglorious and even dangerous.[1] Others admit, even insist that Muscovite worldviews cannot be traced without focusing on New Israel imagery. However, these findings remain scarcely contextualised in politics and everyday life as semiotic, hagiographic, theological, or theatre studies, or again placed sub specie of later concerns, particularly theocracy.[2]

Recent debates about imperial ideologies have opened more questions than could be answered. One strand stresses the pragmatic character of imperial power, operating as it does mainly in discrete, often re-negotiated deals and reserving ideological discretion to the imperial centre which was configured in secular terms. These historians shifted attention from imperial expansion to more intricate questions of accommodating difference and sustaining order and cohesion in the imperial space. The predominant religion grounds imperial imagery and enjoys certain privileges over other creeds, especially those deemed heretical; however, toleration of the religions of subjected groups overrules those privileges. The focus on imperial repertoires and especially, on

---

[1] See chapter 2 for a more detailed historiographical discussion of the Third Rome historiographical myth and Muscovite self-representation as New Israel.
[2] For the latter: N.I. Efimov, *Rus' – novyi Izrail': Teokraticheskaia ideologiia svoezemnago pravoslaviia v do-Petrovskoi pis'mennosti* (Kazan' and Urzhum, 1912).

intermediaries as those who performed them rather than on ideologies, is at the core of Frederick Cooper's and Jane Burbank's account of empire.³ Even though they and others in this strand of the discussion include imperial imaginary in their notion of empire, they tend to downplay its import in day-to-day governance and the lives of subjects. This current of historiography suggests that empires are more about the humdrum business of governing and practices of accommodating difference in a narrow sense and a repertoire of practices beyond the discursive sphere in the broader sense of the meaning of imperial expediency. Ideas and flights of imagination are even regarded as perilous for imperial realism and its improvised policies – some would say that this is precisely the reason they decay and break down.⁴

Recent debate highlighted a second strand in imperial historiography which put forward a different perspective: empires appear as durable political formations that neither experience perpetual decline nor continually anticipate their end. Instead, this perspective appreciates imperial durability over millennia and asks what may explain it. It is doubtful that ad hoc practices that do not connect or cohere into a system can sustain complex polities over a long period. All empires, despite the purported continuity of their structures, underwent a series of ruptures and transformed themselves. Some of the questions raised may seem ambitious for this study of an early but formative period; however, they can be adapted to its needs: what could provide a vector of transformations and an opportunity for the renewal – or, in the case of the subject of this study, original installation – of imperial politics? Some comparative studies claim that without a mission there is no empire, and that therefore no account of a long-lived empire can omit discussing it.⁵ Moreover, the expansionist dynamism and resilience of the Russian Empire in crisis cannot be explained without giving imperial ideology its due.⁶

Within this approach, Kumar insists that imperial missions are always universalist, a quality that has often been attributed to the Muscovite Empire. However, such a broad generalization was clearly not contemporary but a teleology ('Third Rome') expanded in the nineteenth century without an adequate basis in the sources.⁷ There are

---

3 An early and defining start was made by A. Kappeler, *The Russian Empire: A Multiethnic History* (Harlow and New York, 2001 [German: 1992]). J. Burbank and F. Cooper, *Empires in World History: Power and the Politics of Difference* (Princeton NJ, 2010); K. Barkey, *Empire of Difference: The Ottomans in Comparative Perspective* (Cambridge, 2009); N.S. Kollmann, *The Russian Empire 1450–1801* (Oxford, 2017).
4 P.M. Judson, *The Habsburg Empire: A New History* (Cambridge MA, 2016); A. Semyonov, 'How Five Empires Shaped the World and How this Process Shaped those Empires', *Ab Imperio*, 4 (2017), pp. 27–51, here p. 45.
5 K. Kumar, *Visions of Empire: How Five Imperial Regimes Shaped the World* (Princeton NJ, 2017), p. 385.
6 Semyonov, 'How Five Empires Shaped the World and How this Process Shaped those Empires', here pp. 43–46.
7 D. Rowland, 'Moscow – the Third Rome or the New Israel?', *Russian Review*, 55, 4 (1996), pp. 591–614. Researchers of the documents citing the 'Third Rome' now concede that it does not claim the imperial power of the former Roman Empire for Muscovy: D. Khunchukashvili, 'Die

surely many empires with universalist missions, but we should not expect these to dovetail neatly across centuries or even millennia.[8] Muscovy hardly aspired to universalism, which was a cause for concern even for Greek Orthodox clerics, at least some of whom expressed their wishes to be rescued by the Orthodox tsar as an ethnic and religious group from the Ottoman Empire. Muscovite diplomats spent much of their precious time rebuffing these attempts and those of papal diplomats to persuade the Muscovites to reclaim their supposed 'Byzantine heritage' by military means.[9] More to the point, the Muscovite worldview could be particularistic but inclusive: this study traces how the Muscovite Empire combined a particularistic mission of liberating and ransoming mainly Orthodox believers with a concern for empire and its non-Orthodox subjects.

As a concern that partly arose in the course of planning and writing large parts of this book, the Cluster of Excellence 'Beyond Slavery and Freedom' aims to break out of binary models: there is more than slave and free, a whole continuum of dependency.[10] It has been fundamental to the design of this study not to ask whether Muscovites were free or slaves, but rather to enquire how the attempts to improve the lots of captives, slaves, and their relatives spared and left in Muscovy during raids were reflected in official and unofficial visions of empire, and trace the symbolical means of these attempts and their implications. This Introduction will therefore provide a brief overview of the different forms of dependency that existed in interconnected areas of inner Eurasia as requisite background information.

It is instructive to cross-reference two little-connected debates, namely about slavery and empire. The late John Calder Miller sought to synthesize approaches to slavery throughout historical periods in a highly influential and well received account. In Miller's terms, Kumar's cases – except for the Roman Empire which abandoned its captive citizens – would qualify first of all as monarchies, rather than merely empires. This differentiation may at first appear not to fit the concerns of historians of empire. Nevertheless, it makes sense to focus on the role of slaves in a polity, an aspect often neglected in the historiography of empire. A development from an early, conquering empire to later, monarchical one fits both epistemes and introduces a new quality into the debate. The import in world history of conquerors – chiefly from the steppe – has

---

heiligen Städte als eschatologische Legitimationssymbole der Zarenmacht unter den Rjurikiden', in Diana Ordubadi and Dittmar Dahlmann, eds., *Die 'Alleinherrschaft' der russischen Zaren in der 'Zeit der Wirren' in transkultureller Perspektive* (Göttingen, 2021), pp. 129–158, here p. 145.

8 J.C. Miller, *The Problem of Slavery as History: A Global Approach* (New Haven CT, 2012).

9 N.S. Chaev, "Moskva-tretii Rim' v politicheskoi praktike moskovskogo pravitel'stva XVI v.', *Istoricheskie zapiski*, 17 (1945), pp. 3–23; Rowland, 'Moscow – the Third Rome or the New Israel?', p. 595.

10 D. Eltis and S.L. Engerman, 'Dependence, Servility, and Coerced Labor in Time and Space', in D. Eltis and S.L. Engerman, eds., *The Cambridge World History of Slavery*, Vol. 3: *AD 1420–AD 1804* (Cambridge, 2011), pp. 1–21; C. Witzenrath, 'Introduction: Slavery in Medieval and Early Modern Eurasia: An Overview of the Russian and Ottoman Empires and Central Asia', in C. Witzenrath, ed., *Eurasian Slavery, Ransom and Abolition in World History, 1200–1860* (Farnham, Surrey, 2015), pp. 1–77.

been underrated in almost all historiography; only recently has it been highlighted by a growing number of studies.[11]

About 6,000 years ago,[12] when the new mounted nomadic lifestyle first expanded beyond the steppe, the empires often founded or supported by nomads were not interested in new subjects, whom they treated as expendable, cheap labour, but in further expansion and more spoils. At a later stage merchants began to extend credit to agricultural subjects and so created fast-growing numbers of debt dependents of their own. It took time until imperial elites and leaders in some cases reconsidered their relation to subjects who had become tax-exempt slaves of merchants. They restyled themselves redeemers of peasants, protecting them at no cost to themselves from creditors to salvage tax payments.[13]

Such a practice was inextricably linked to ideology, which found its expression in an entire field of terms in many world languages connecting debt, bondage, and ransom, among others in the Bible. Muscovites were particularly fond of drawing on these sources, as they found models fitting their situation almost perfectly; but they were far from the only ones to do so. This study will demonstrate that the role of the Muscovite state in redeeming its subjects from slavery formed the basis of the fundamental transcultural worldview of the empire. It sets out to challenge the assumption, still prevalent in historiography, that Moscow only developed a coherent imperial worldview under Peter I, even though the multi-faith empire dated back as far as the conquest of Kazan.[14]

Only sub-Saharan Africa surpassed Eurasia as a source of slaves during the sixteenth and seventeenth centuries. An estimated one to 2.5 million people were captured, mainly from the steppe, in the trans-Ottoman slave raids to meet the demand created in the common economic space of the Ottoman Empire and its neighbours from the 1470s to the late seventeenth century, when Ottoman expansion waned.[15] Periodic destructions and the constant drain of manpower made the capacity to stem the flow the inescapable rationale for any power which sought to establish itself in Eastern Europe. Muscovy employed ideological motifs similar to those of European powers who had to deal with slave raids on a much smaller scale. However, the fact that the main systems

---

[11] I.B. Neumann and E. Wigen, *The Steppe Tradition in International Relations: Russians, Turks and European State Building 4000 BCE–2018 CE* (Cambridge, 2018), Introduction.

[12] For a more recent timeline, starting 4200 years ago, see Librado, Pablo, et al. "The Origins and Spread of Domestic Horses from the Western Eurasian Steppes". Nature 598, no. 7882 (2021): pp. 634–40.

[13] Miller, *The Problem of Slavery as History*.

[14] Kappeler, *The Russian Empire*.

[15] For the concept of new regional studies focusing on mobility and transcending, but not abandoning, national boundaries and traditional regional limitations, see S. Conermann, A. Fuess and S. Rohdewald, eds., *Transottomanica: Osteuropäisch-osmanisch-persische Mobilitätsdynamiken: Perspektiven und Forschungsstand* (Göttingen, 2019). U. Freitag and A. v. Oppen, 'Translocality. An Approach to Connection and Transfer in Regional Studies', in: U. Freitag and A. v. Oppen (eds.), *Translocality – the Study of Globalising Phenomena from a Southern Perspective* (Leiden, 2010), pp. 1–21.

of slavery supported by European maritime empires were far away in the colonies facilitated the separation of the issue of slavery from debates about individual liberty.[16]

Russia could not do this because slavery was a different issue for the Russian Empire. Firstly, Russia had its own brand of slavery. Secondly, despite some basic differences the system of serfdom, which grew throughout the seventeenth and eighteenth centuries, bore some of the hallmarks of slave systems. Furthermore, Eastern Orthodox Christians themselves were victims of slave raiders and traders to an extent, in a way that was unknown among the metropolitan inhabitants of maritime European colonial empires.[17] Balancing these seemingly incompatible needs was paramount for imperial cohesion, as serfdom was an essential ingredient.

This study will show that religious elements shared throughout the history of faiths and confessions were particularly important for imperial cohesion. It turned out to be more important to construct loyal subjecthood as the empire grew increasingly multi-ethnic and multifaith, and expanded into the steppe and further frontier zones without clear borders. One central concern was to include those who served the tsar regardless of their background, but to exclude slavers – at least those who did not serve the tsar.

Throughout, I shall present Muscovy as embedded within the wider region of Eurasia. This is a useful concept in which to explore the wider perspectives of trade connections and related forms of slaving. However, Eurasia remains an ambiguous word in terms of definite territorial boundaries: it may refer to almost the whole of the Old World, sometimes including even northern Africa. Most pertinent for the present study is the Eurasian heartland or inner Eurasia[18] circumscribed approximately by the sub-arctic tundra, the Stanovoy, Tien Shan, Altai and Caucasus mountain chains, the Black Sea and the western borderlands of Eastern Orthodoxy; although I will largely leave out the Habsburg and Ottoman Slavic lands.[19] This area is characterised by a common continental climate and, except for a few narrow outlets on the Black and Caspian Seas, mountain barriers thwarting moderate or even sub-tropic influences. Common bands of climatic zones extend from west to east, desert in the south, various forms of

---

16 There are now some accounts of how this issue returned with a vengeance and influenced the movement to abolish the slave trade, for example during the struggle of publicists between partisans of the New England rebels and British rule: C.L. Brown, *Moral Capital. Foundations of British Abolitionism* (Chapel Hill, 2006). The underlying forces structuring the transatlantic slave trade shaped ideas of difference, race, commerce, and kinship: J.L. Morgan, *Reckoning with Slavery: Gender, Kinship, and Capitalism in the Early Black Atlantic* (Durham NC, 2021), p. 3.
17 L. Colley, *Captives: Britain, Empire and the World, 1600–1850* (London, 2002).
18 D. Ostrowski, 'The End of Muscovy: The Case for ca. 1800', *Slavic Review*, 69, 2 (2010), pp. 426–438; D. Christian, *A History of Russia, Central Asia and Mongolia*, vol. 1 (Oxford and Malden MA, 1998), p. xxi.
19 G. Dávid and P. Fodor, eds., *Ransom Slavery along the Ottoman Borders: Early Fifteenth – Early Eighteenth Centuries* (Leiden, 2007).

steppe grasslands, wooded steppe, deciduous forest, taiga and tundra in the arctic.[20] However, the history of slavery describes phenomena which, for most of the historical record, were entangled with trade and cannot be properly studied without the trade corridors that link inner Eurasia with China, Persia, India, the Ottoman Empire and Europe.

The predominance of continuities across the so-called Petrine divide has been demonstrated recently in various ways.[21] By referring to Muscovy as the Russian Empire in its title, this book highlights this continuity and questions the self-assured expectation that Muscovy did not matter after Peter. Nevertheless, in my Conclusion I will raise the question to which extent it is correct to speak of discontinuity with respect to the imperial world view, and its likely starting point.

This study focuses on worldviews; however, it aims to embed them in social history as a necessary background and interaction. Practices are related to ideas because they exist only with reference to patterns of the mind, while ideas can survive without any link to designated practices. Nevertheless, in most cases ideas that do not engender practices remain obscure. I will briefly introduce slaving in western Eurasia in order to provide a practical context for the Muscovite worldview. Chapter one skims recent approaches to empire and slaving for cues on how worldviews link both fields. It seeks to explain how liberation could become an ideology of empire in an area and period otherwise renown for enserfment. To this end it reformulates the recent and widely discussed proposal of the no-slaving zone, adding the concept of a counter dependency zone which accounts for enserfment. It will also be of interest for those studying empire on how recent advances in slavery studies might benefit this field. Chapter two delves into the nitty gritty details of how the ideology of liberation from slavery appeared in Muscovy, and how it was first formulated. It will mainly follow and analyse the narrative of an exceptional and widely admired source to demonstrate the focus on slavery in contemporary views of a defining event: the conquest of Kazan. This is a necessary limitation as this focus has been ignored or downplayed in topical studies so far. Moreover, the identification of Muscovy with the New Israel, widely acknowledged in recent studies, will be grounded in perceptions of slaving. Chapters three and four widen the circle by drawing on further chronicles, laws, murals, icons, hagiography, maps, as well as sources pertaining to ritual and theatre. These sources are scrutinized to establish the extent to which Muscovite worldviews were limited to a narrow elite in and around the Kremlin, or whether these views can be documented within the wider population. Some of the sources examined are among the most pervasive, giving access to widely shared beliefs and views in a period characterized far beyond Muscovy by a paucity of sources on the worldviews of ordinary, mainly illiterate

---

20 Kollmann, *The Russian Empire 1450–1801*, pp. 21–28.
21 Ostrowski, 'The End of Muscovy'. Recent introductions and overviews of the Muscovite period: Kollmann, *The Russian Empire 1450–1801*; M. Perrie, ed., *Cambridge History of Russia*, vol. 1: *From Early Rus' to 1689* (Cambridge, 2006); V.A. Kivelson and R.G. Suny, *Russia's Empires* (New York and Oxford, 2017).

men and especially women: some theatrical performances took over the streets, some of the saints are among the most revered and cross-kissing was the core ritual of confirming loyalty and subjecthood. These chapters explore how notions of salvation combined with the culture of liberation to exalt the image of the tsar. Chapter five studies the petitions and interviews recorded in Moscow chancelleries of returned former slaves and captives to explore notions of loyalty and competition for them in trans-Ottoman theatres of labour and service relations. They are placed near the end because many concepts resonating in them will have been established in the earlier chapters. Elite and common worldviews tend to be more connected than even those who aim to separate or reform them are aware, even though the forms taken by such connections may be complex and intricate. The last chapter goes beyond the views of Orthodox people to scrutinize relations of loyalty in the multi-faith empire. How could the culture of liberation and the counter-dependency zone contribute to mend relations between the tsar and the Orthodox and Tatar or other ethnic and confessional servicemen?

Slaving, ransom, and serfdom in western inner Eurasia, 1470s–1700s

Muscovy and the steppe

By the sixteenth century the neighbours of the Eurasian heartland south of the great mountain chains became 'gunpowder empires', stabilizing Islamic power after its previous decline in the fourteenth to sixteenth centuries.[22] Their armies, or those of their allies in the steppe and on the Atlantic seaboard, the Turkmens, Tatars, and Maghreb corsair states, carried off infidel captives on a grand scale from India to Eastern Europe, from the Sahara to the Balkans and from Newfoundland to Central Asia.[23] A Crimean Tatar army sacked Moscow outside the Kremlin walls in 1571, and 'harvested' up to 150,000 captives. They burned the suburbs of Moscow again in 1592, while Muscovite forces were busy fighting the Swedes. In the first half of the sixteenth century alone, Muscovy experienced forty-three major Crimean and Nogai attacks. Incursions intensified during the Time of Troubles in the early seventeenth century and the 1630s. More importantly, smaller armies led by members of the Girei dynasty or local dignitaries carried out annual stealth raids; hard to track on the steppe and sometimes financed by credit extended by Ottoman merchants, they took the majority of captives. The

---

[22] The following is a condensed and updated version of Witzenrath. 'Introduction: Slavery in Medieval and Early Modern Eurasia'.
[23] B.G. Williams, *The Crimean Tatars: The Diaspora Experience and the Forging of a Nation* (Leiden, 2001), pp. 49–51; R. Hellie, 'Slavery', in P.W. Goetz, R. MacHenry, J.E. Safra and D. Hoiberg, eds., *The New Encyclopaedia Britannica* vol. 27 (Chicago and London, 1993), pp. 288–300; H. İnalcık, ed., *An Economic and Social History of the Ottoman Empire* (Cambridge, 1997), pp. 284–285.

khan was often politically too weak to curb them. Even the larger attacks aimed more at raiding villages and capturing slaves than at crushing armed forces.[24] Still, many Tatars on the Crimean Peninsula lived as settled agriculturalists and were very reluctant to answer even the khan's call to arms.[25]

These advances of Islamic armies obscured structural flaws: newly conquered Christians and Hindus often refused to convert,[26] which increased pressures to rely on administrative and military slaves. Amongst others, Europeans shifted the balance of power in the Mediterranean further in their own favour; Ethiopia regained the upper hand in the late sixteenth century.[27] Muscovy relied on semi-independent Tatar retainers from the late fourteenth century onwards, and annexed the Tatar khanates of Kazan, Astrakhan and Sibir in the second half of the sixteenth century.[28] Cossacks from a variety of cultural and regional backgrounds who adopted sold boys or married local girls settled on Islamic frontiers while Tatars under Russian rule could no longer own Christian slaves after 1628.[29] Oirat Mongols adhering to Buddhism migrated westwards from 1608, displacing Muslim Tatars as far as the lower Volga while also raiding for, and selling, slaves.[30] From the seventeenth century onwards, discontent with slavery surfaced in gunpowder empires attempting to centralize power. Slavery was stagnant during the eighteenth century, as Muslim gunpowder empires lost their technological and cultural edge to Christian powers.

Serfs, slave raids, and border regime

Serfs and slaves are in many regards different, if linked, categories, and what serfdom exactly entailed has been questioned in recent studies, shedding new light on this old question. About half of the peasant population was still not owned by landlords in the eighteenth century; serfs regionally preponderated only in the mixed forest areas around Moscow and in the black soil areas closer to the steppe.[31] Many

---

[24] B.L. Davies, *Warfare, State and Society on the Black Sea Steppe, 1500–1700* (London, 2007), pp. 17–22; V.E. Vozgrin, *Istoriia krymskikh tatar: Ocherki ėtnicheskoi istorii korennogo naseleniia Kryma*, vol. 1 (Simferopol', 2013), pp. 440–454.
[25] Vozgrin, *Istoriia krymskikh tatar*.
[26] M. Hodgson, *The Venture of Islam*, vol. 2 (Chicago and London, 1974), pp. 59–133.
[27] S.C. Levi, 'Hindus beyond the Hindu-Kush: Indians in the Central Asian Slave Trade', *Journal of the Royal Asiatic Society*, 12, 3 (2002), pp. 277–288.
[28] Kappeler, *The Russian Empire*; D.G. Ostrowski, *Muscovy and the Mongols: Cross-Cultural Influences on the Steppe Frontier, 1304–1589* (Cambridge, 1998).
[29] R. Hellie, *Slavery in Russia, 1450–1725* (Chicago, 1982), pp. 73–74.
[30] P.B. Golden, *An Introduction to the History of the Turkic Peoples: Ethnogenesis and State Formation in Medieval and Early Modern Eurasia and the Middle East* (Wiesbaden, 1992), p. 327; Levi. 'Hindus beyond the Hindu-Kush: Indians in the Central Asian Slave Trade', p. 279.
[31] Overview: Kollmann, *The Russian Empire 1450–1801*, pp. 362–363.

hold that serfdom was close to or like slavery.[32] Others emphasize that, for the peasants, it was a way of living in climatic conditions severely limiting the fertile period. The harvest was often threatened by fluctuations in temperature, humidity and other factors the extent of which would have been minor in more moderate zones. The landowner's obligation to dispense aid in periods of famine provided a buffer against such effects. Sometimes peasants more easily accepted labour obligations for the owner of the estate than monetary contributions, since the former did not depend on climatic vagaries and the vicissitudes of the market, which was volatile due to climatic conditions and harvests.[33] Slaves were either raided or traded, while serfs were bound to the ground or the landowner and the community, but in Russia became increasingly tradable in the eighteenth century.

Recent studies of individual local estates looked closely at rights and obligations. Especially along the newly settled steppe frontier, they found harsh and restrictive conditions characterized by cooperation between the heads of households and the landowner to prevent over-exploitation of locally scarce resources such as wood.[34] The rebellions that included a serf element mostly erupted along the steppe frontier, but they were led by militarized cossacks and attracted non-Orthodox locals. However, complaints about serf flight came mainly from the owners of small estates. Their peasants fled to larger estates, monasteries, and even to the frontier and to the cossacks, where they found better conditions. This tells about the pressure on small landowners whose small and dwindling workforce increasingly struggled to provide for them during their frequent campaigns.[35]

Serfs on at least some of the larger estates were ruled by distinct, localized sets of administrative practices, property rights, judicial structures and customary norms to extract rents while peasants were flexibly allowed to engage in markets.[36] The limitations of this model of governance were on a different plane: they arose at the boundaries between these separate estate microcosms. Serfs could not rely little on institutions that spanned the whole of Russia, or considerable parts of it beyond the estate on which they lived and the landholder's office in the capital as a central authority. Imperial administration was run on a shoestring, occupying a poor third

---

32 P. Kolchin, *Unfree Labor: American Slavery and Russian Serfdom* (Cambridge MA, 1987).
33 R. Hellie, *Enserfment and Military Change in Muscovy* (Chicago, 1971); D. Moon, *The Russian Peasantry, 1600–1930: The World the Peasants Made* (London and New York, 1999); D. Khitrov, 'Tributary Labour in the Russian Empire in the Eighteenth Century: Factors in Development', *International Review of Social History*, 61, S24 (2016), pp. 49–70. On climatic conditions, see Kollmann, *The Russian Empire 1450–1801*, pp. 25–28.
34 S.L. Hoch, *Serfdom and Social Control in Nineteenth Century Russia: Petrovskoe a Village in Tambov* (Ann Arbor, 1983).
35 Hellie, *Enserfment and Military Change in Muscovy*.
36 E.K. Wirtschafter, *Russia's Age of Serfdom 1649–1861* (Malden MA, 2008), pp. 97–98; M.P. Romaniello, *The Elusive Empire: Kazan and the Creation of Russia, 1552–1671* (Madison WI, 2012). Cf. Kolchin, *Unfree Labor*, p. 41, 399 n. 74.

place after the military and concerns about stabilizing the tax base.[37] Peasant economic potential was both stabilized by serfdom and constrained by its limited range of influence.[38] However, many actually lived outside the estate in towns, while still paying their dues to the landowner.[39] In the Muscovite period at least, there were few middle-ranging institutions available to peasants beyond the reach of the estate; however, most peasants still lived in conditions of subsistence. The actual influence of the only overarching set of institutions – the tsar and the chancelleries – depended heavily on their local allies and therefore on the local balance of power.[40] This balance was partly determined by the power of landowners and heads of community to send peasants to Siberia, to the army or, from 1721 on, even to sell them.

Such a view of serfdom is upheld by a comparative overview of forms of the new serfdom in Central and Eastern Europe. It looks at the causes and degrees to which peasants lost their initial privileges and freedoms, which they were granted upon settlement both in Russia and in the West. The underlying factor that influenced the degree of loss was how recently settlement had begun or intensified before the state penetrated the countryside, taxing people directly or, as in serfdom, through the landowner. The ability of peasants to stabilize their agency depended on how securely intermediate agents, such as the church, monasteries, bailiffs, independent courts of minor rulers or towns and others, were established and how many diverse agents were available for interaction.[41]

Due to their close historical ties, serfdom and slave raiding contribute to understanding Russian history in its Eurasian setting. Serfdom as a form of bondage limiting mobility was introduced incrementally since the devastating Livonian War starting in 1558, when the tsar's forces relied on local servitors who petitioned to tie down their peasants. However, in the longer term, increasing opportunities for settlement in the more fertile and milder southern areas on the steppe frontier contributed to the growth of serfdom. These areas gradually became available for settlement as fortification secured them against incursions from the steppe, which had earlier impeded agriculture.

---

37 P.B. Brown, 'How Muscovy Governed: Seventeenth-Century Russian Central Administration', *Russian History*, 36, 4 (2009), pp. 459–529; Kollmann, *The Russian Empire 1450–1801*; B.L. Davies, 'The Politics of Give and Take: Kormlenie as Service Remuneration and Generalized Exchange 1488–1726', in A.M. Kleimola and G.D. Lenhoff, eds., *Culture and Identity in Muscovy, 1359–1584* (Moscow, 1997), pp. 39–67.
38 T. Dennison, *The Institutional Framework of Russian Serfdom* (Cambridge, 2011).
39 D. Brower and S. Layton, 'Liberation through Captivity', *Kritika*, 6, 2 (2005), pp. 259–279.
40 V.A. Kivelson, *Autocracy in the Provinces: The Muscovite Gentry and Political Culture in the Seventeenth Century* (Stanford CA, 1996); C. Witzenrath, *Cossacks and the Russian Empire, 1598–1725: Manipulation, Rebellion and Expansion into Siberia* (London and New York, 2007).
41 C. Schmidt, *Leibeigenschaft im Ostseeraum: Versuch einer Typologie* (Köln, 1997); P. Freedman and M. Bourin, eds., *Forms of Servitude in Northern and Central Europe* (Turnhout, 2005). On interagency, see chapter 5.

Lack of suitable implements for tilling the heavy, rich ground was a second limiting factor, which delayed full settlement until the eighteenth century.[42] For both strategic and economic reasons, as the next chapters will show, the tsar and the chancelleries were interested in stabilizing the frontier and legalized military settlement, which attracted many from among the enserfed peasantries. However, commitment in the interior depended on landlords for the same reason affected by loss of labour. While hardly anybody questioned the benefit of fewer raids from the steppe, the lower and middling service ranks clamoured about the loss of peasants to the 'strong people' – the boyars and monasteries whose estates were larger and therefore allowed their owners to be more lenient towards peasants.[43]

For the tsar, the dilemma was marked by the loss of agricultural labour for their military servicemen, dependable retainers at grassroots level. A slow evolution of countermeasures mainly based on state intervention and rule enforcement took until the mid-seventeenth century to somewhat reduce peasant flight. Under such conditions, border fortifications were intended not only to stop slave raids, but also to control in- and out-migration and to attract peasant migration. Moreover, border governors had instructions to pursue returning slaves fleeing the custody of slave traders. The traders brought the slaves closer to their homes and former master, the tsar. To do so, they often had paid for manumission of the slave or even pledged their own relatives as collateral to the slave's master. Such a transposition of dependency from slave master to tsar via the intermediary merchant was obstructed if the debtor and former slave fled to eschew repayment. It was in the interest of the tsar and the elite to keep this channel open.[44] However, neither peasants nor returning slaves could completely be stopped from uncontrolled moving in one direction or the other.

Fixing the ransom price was riddled with many uncertainties. Since Tatar captors brought captives to places hundreds of miles from home, they had few means of knowing captives' resources and social status to determine a proper ransom rate. The captor had the power over the captive's body, but little or no knowledge about

---

[42] The lack of a suitable plough allowing to cut through the heavy soil and grassroots clods of the steppe: B.J. Boeck, 'Containment vs. Colonization: Muscovite Approaches to Settling the Steppe', in N.B. Breyfogle, A.M. Schrader and W. Sunderland, eds., *Peopling the Russian Periphery: Borderland Colonization in Eurasian History* (London, 2007), pp. 41–60; W. Sunderland, *Taming the Wild Field: Colonization and Empire on the Russian Steppe* (Ithaca NY, 2004), pp. 55–95. I am grateful to Donald Ostrowski for bringing this to my attention.

[43] R. Hellie, 'The Economy, Trade and Serfdom', in M. Perrie, ed., *Cambridge History of Russia*, vol. 1: *From Early Rus' to 1689* (Cambridge, 2006), pp. 539–558, here p. 548; N.A. Gorskaia, *Krest'ianstvo v periody rannego i razvitogo feodalizma*, vol. 2 (Moskva, 1990), pp. 379–380; P. Smirnov, *Chelobitnaia dvorian i detei boiarskikh vsekh gorodov v pervoi polovine 17 veka* (Moskva, 1915), pp. 10, 38–41, 44.

[44] H. Hecker, 'Die Christenpflicht als Rechtsnorm. Der Loskauf der Gefangenen im Uloženie von 1649', in U. Halbach, ed., *Geschichte Altrusslands in der Begriffswelt ihrer Quellen: Festschrift zum 70. Geburtstag von Günter Stökl* (Wiesbaden, 1986), pp. 154–163.

them. On the one hand, the problem was overcome by the regularity of these cases – Russian envoys might receive blanket authorization to pay, as in the 1680s Crimea, 120 rubles for members of the service class, 80 rubles for male peasants and 60 rubles for women.[45] On the other hand, if captors and intermediaries suspected that captives hid their true status to either avert final sale overseas with moot chances to return, or alternatively downplay their value in case of high status, they might use torture to overcome this lack of knowledge. A good strategy for captives trying to avoid sale to the Ottoman Empire was to promise double the going price for slaves on the market.[46]

Michael Khodarkovsky has attributed imperial Russia's low level of urbanization to the drain on the labour force due to the raids and resulting expenses for tribute, ransom and fortifications.[47] This factor in Russia's slow development needs to be discounted for the newly founded, if small, towns in the south that ignited urbanization in areas formerly devoid of settled population. Earlier than in Ukraine and the Caucasus, fortifications curtailed slave raids in Muscovy by the second half of the seventeenth century. The resulting reallocation of resources increased the demand for labour at the frontier but constrained large-scale urbanization intermittently since the 1570s and more incisively since the 1630s. This further reduced the number of mid-range agents available to peasants, such as poor, unemployed jurists. In fifteenth-century Italy and France, redundant and migrant lawyers offered their services to peasants who faced challenges from landlords seeking to increase tributes, improving peasant interagency and their access to courts of law.[48] In Russia, there was a long-standing shortage of jurists because universities, which had first been projected under tsar Boris Godunov in the late sixteenth century, were in fact established only from the eighteenth century onwards, due to the economic exigencies of the Time of Troubles, steppe fortifications building and general warfare. Clearly, Muscovy was neither Europe nor the Ottoman Empire: 2–3% of the population could read

---

45 B. J. Boeck, 'Identity as Commodity: Tournaments of Value in the Tatar Ransom Business', *Russian History*, 35, 3–4 (2008), pp. 259–266, at 260. The 1649 law code stipulated for nobles and gentry 20 rubles per 133 acres, but a lower rate of 5 rubles if they were not caught in combat or during official assignments, 40 rubles for Moscow musketeers, 25 rubles for other musketeers and cossacks, 20 rubles for townsmen, 15 rubles for peasants and 'boiar's people' (*kholopy*). R. Hellie (ed.), *The Muscovite Law Code (Ulozhenie) of 1649*, vol. 1 (Irvine, CA, 1988), p. 18.

46 Ibid.; M. Broniewski, 'Opisanie Kryma (Tartariae Descriptio)', *Zapiski Odesskogo obshchestva istorii i drevnostei*, 6 (1867), pp. 333–367, at 363. On market prices: Z. Güneş-Yağcı, 'The Black Sea Slave Trade According to the Istanbul Port Customs Register, 1606–1607', in C. Witzenrath, ed., *Eurasian Slavery, Ransom and Abolition in World History, 1200–1860* (Farnham, Surrey, 2015), pp. 207–220.

47 M. Khodarkovsky, *Russia's Steppe Frontier: The Making of a Colonial Empire, 1500–1800* (Bloomington IN, 2002), p. 21.

48 Overview of the literature: Witzenrath, *Cossacks and the Russian Empire, 1598–1725*, pp. 73–74, nn. 93, 95.

and write, according to inconclusive studies of literacy even in the capital. However, the fact that of the cossacks in the eastern Siberian trade hub of Irkutsk at least eleven per cent had highly functional literacy – a measure for the level of literacy that remains impossible to prove for all European countries – is just one example of the interconnected island conditions that accounted for higher levels of education within some groups and localities.[49]

Slavery and Islam in Eurasia

As Islam came to be the dominant religion in one of the world's most developed and culturally advanced regions, the Middle East, Central Asia and the Mediterranean, it inherited whole sets of institutions and customs. They were not always easily compatible with what had taken root in the mind of Mohammed in an impoverished peninsula inhabited by herdsmen and some townspeople. Connected to civilization but remote in the desert, early Muslims combined an ancient local identity with a universal, monotheistic truth to create a momentum that kept them both apart from and connected to the cultures they conquered.[50] In these regions and beyond, one of the main institutions of the ancient world, slavery, proliferated and soon obtained its own, specifically Muslim flavour, understood here as a cultural vector rather than a purely religious one. The tensions inherent in the cultural adaptation of nomads to the remnants of antiquity lived on and may still be discerned in various forms in early modern Muslim perspectives on slavery.[51] There is consequently no one Muslim take on slavery: the various schools of religious law, laws promulgated by Muslim rulers, the locally strong admixtures of customs or regional, pre-Islamic laws and the diverse Sufi orders as well as individual Islamic scholars, all contributed to a rich and variegated patchwork of views. The tensions created by these overlapping texts, practices and customs could be exploited by slaves to some degree; therefore, the study of Islamic slavery presupposes a great deal of attention to details of law.[52]

There is no creed in history that can be singled out for slavery and the trade in slaves.[53] However, there were factors that set apart certain areas and periods in terms

---

[49] *Rukuprikladstvo* included a text of between one line and up to a paragraph which was changed according to several parameters in each signature: C. Witzenrath, 'Literacy and Orality in the Eurasian Frontier: Imperial Culture and Space in Seventeenth-Century Siberia and Russia', *The Slavonic and East European Review*, 1 (2009), pp. 53–77.
[50] Cf. R. Brunschvig, '''Abd', in P. Bearman et al., eds., *Encyclopedia of Islam* (Leiden, 1960), pp. 24–40.
[51] Cf. P. Crone, *Slaves on Horses: The Evolution of the Islamic Polity* (Cambridge and New York, 1980), pp. 18–26.
[52] E. Toledano, *As if Silent and Absent: Bonds of Enslavement in the Islamic Middle East* (New Haven CT, 2007), p. 16; W.G. Clarence-Smith, *Islam and the Abolition of Slavery* (London, 2006).
[53] J. Jomier, *Pour connaître l'Islam* (Paris, 1988), p. 102.

of the demand for slaves. Commerce, exchanges and wars in the Middle East, Central Asia and the Mediterranean between the early modern gunpowder empires and with expanding European powers generated a growing intake of involuntary labour. These factors are partly related to religion, partly to the establishment – or the survival – of a military regime, or to commercial and administrative competition that induced the elite to augment its economic potential by taking on human resources hitherto unrelated to their extended households, enterprises or the state.[54] Religion as part of the epistemological framework of culture and of institutions was basic to the definition of slavery, and for embedding in law and its practice.[55] Some ostensible believers also treated slaves as recruitment material for the cause of Islam. Nevertheless, Islam from early on called for the humane treatment of slaves.

Scholarly debate has centred on whether Muslim slavery was, as has often been claimed, 'milder' than the chattel slavery suffered by many Africans in the New World. Such claims are doubly dubious against the backdrop of recent and continuing enslavement in remote areas and sexual slavery in the modern world, and because of the more methodically bottom-up perspective of the latest scholarship on the early and middle periods of Ottoman history. Students of Islamic slavery are now less prepared to accept the good-treatment thesis created as a defensive concept by the late Ottoman elite in the face of Western abolitionists.[56]

Marshall Hodgson has put forward the paradox that an egalitarian and socially mobile society seemed to require slaves to balance those who had quickly risen to the top.[57] While this contention remains insufficiently explored, a sensible hypothesis is that, in Islam, slavery had a special edge because of its very egalitarian ideals and high social mobility. However, the military successes of strictly monotheistic egalitarianism brought about the creation of dominant social groups who expected political influence. Such broad enfranchised groups before long refused to serve in the military. Before industrialization, the only other source of military power for the sultan were slaves brought in from abroad.[58] Moreover, Islam quickly adapted to the social proviso of irrigated agriculture requiring a large workforce. Consequently the ubiquity of slave labour, drawn mostly from captives of wars or bought abroad,

---

[54] E. Toledano, 'Enslavement in the Ottoman Empire in the Early Modern Period', in D. Eltis and S.L. Engerman, eds., *The Cambridge World History of Slavery*, vol. 3: *AD 1420–AD 1804* (Cambridge, 2011), pp. 25–46.

[55] S. Peabody, 'Slavery, Freedom, and the Law in the Atlantic World', in D. Eltis and S.L. Engerman, eds., *The Cambridge World History of Slavery*, vol. 3: *AD 1420 – AD 1804* (Cambridge, 2011), pp. 594–630, here p. 609.

[56] Toledano, *As if Silent and Absent*, p. 17.

[57] M. Hodgson, *The Venture of Islam*, vol. 2: *The Expansion of Islam in the Middle Periods* (Chicago, 1974), p. 355.

[58] On exploring the relations between egalitarianism and slavery, see Clarence-Smith, *Islam and the Abolition of Slavery*, p. 19.

was a response to the inadmissibility of serfdom and forced labour by Muslims and subservient infidels.[59]

After the initial wave of conquests, rulers were no longer able to rely politically and militarily on Arabic tribes and the faithful who retreated to asceticism and local concerns; so they found a new pool of recruits in slaves. Elite slavery became a menace to public life, taking over political power in many places; concubines posed a parallel threat in the private sphere.[60] By the same token, however, slavery itself contributed to upward social mobility – characteristics that set Muslim societies apart from the social rigidities of European medieval social estates.

The definition of slavery was straightforward, except for the areas in which customary law was strong, which created numerous complex and conflicting gradations of slavery. According to the holy law of Islam, the sharia, slaves were chattels which could be resold, akin in many respects to livestock. However, unlike livestock they possessed certain cautiously marked-out rights, as their humanity was incontestable.[61]

The clear legal definition obscures a perplexing variety of social roles which obscures the scholar's view and puts obstacles in way of solidarity between those under the sway of slavery.[62] Rulers became dependent on household and military slaves and on eunuchs and concubines to such a degree that slaves sometimes seized power.[63] Singing-girls could become influential at court, and a concubine who bore a son to a mighty man wielded immense power, especially as a widow. The early seventeenth-century Ottoman Empire was even dubbed the 'sultanate of the women', many having originally come from Inner Eurasia as slaves.[64] Some female slaves successfully sued for mistreatment, especially if they were sold while pregnant.[65]

Early Ottoman court practice seriously undermined the sharia norms of family life. From the late fourteenth century, sultans restricted the succession to sons of concubines, who were permitted to have only one male child. After that, a concubine devoted her life to conspiring in favour of the boy, whose probable destiny was death at the hands of a rival, frequently a half-brother. If her son succeeded,

---

[59] Ibid. Cf. chapter 1.
[60] P. Crone and M. Cook, *Hagarism: The Making of the Islamic World* (Cambridge, 1977), p. 148.
[61] Clarence-Smith, *Islam and the Abolition of Slavery*, p. 2; Brunschvig, "Abd".
[62] Toledano, *As if Silent and Absent*.
[63] T. Miura and J.E. Philips, *Slave Elites in the Middle East and Africa: A Comparative Study* (London, 2000).
[64] E. Toledano, *Slavery and Abolition in the Ottoman Middle East* (Seattle, 1998), p. 44. On Roxelane/Hürrem L.P. Peirce, *Empress of the East: How a European Slave Girl Became Queen of the Ottoman Empire* (New York, 2017).
[65] L. Kurtynova-D'Herlugnan, *The Tsar's Abolitionists: The Slave Trade in the Caucasus and its Suppression* (Leiden, 2010), pp. 42–43; Toledano, *Slavery and Abolition in the Ottoman Middle East*, pp. 59–67.

she might become the veritable ruler of the empire. From the mid-fifteenth century, sultans even ceased to contract lawful marriages. The dynasty thereby dissociated itself from the masses of the believers and the powerful Turkic clans, controlling access to the throne as well as guaranteeing succession.

The harem system of the Ottoman court was extreme in comparison with other elite households. By having sexual relations with a handful of chosen women, a master denied a family life to many surplus concubines and in effect condemned them to a system of imprisonment, together with their female slaves.[66] Recent studies have revealed that concubinage was far from the ideal of good treatment in the intimacy of home, family or household depicted in late Ottoman defences of slavery and much of Western literature; these newer studies tend to privilege the view from within and bottom-up perspectives of the enslaved, yielding rather harsh pictures of realities in slavery.[67] The inclination to stay, especially among female slaves, has questionable value as an argument for the 'good treatment' hypothesis, as decisions were influenced by the 'horrors of the return journey', which were worse for non-military captives and those who could pay less.[68] Moreover, females in many societies were socialized to obey men unquestioningly and their reproductive capacity yielded new personal bonds in the receiving society – factors that tended to make them stay but are not connected to treatment. Finally, focusing on reproduction underestimates the productive work left to female slaves mainly by free women enjoying more leisure; gender segregation in Muslim society meant that they needed female slaves, and free women may have lost more than men during abolition.[69]

Yet this was not the lot of the vast majority assigned to menial tasks or who ended up as 'cannon fodder'. The lives of ordinary soldiers were cruel, brutish and short.[70] Slavery was also common on small and medium-sized landholdings, in Central Asian irrigation, in mining, transport, public works, proto-industry and large-scale construction.[71] Turkmen raiders made their slaves 'watch the flock, prepare the food, make felts and weave carpets'.[72] Singing-girls were prostitutes and courtesans. Sexual continence was imposed on abandoned sexual partners in harems, while their female attendants

---

[66] A.E. Elbashir, *The United States, Slavery and the Slave Trade in the Nile Valley* (Lanham MD, 1983), p. 127; N. Gervaise, *An Historical Description of the Kingdom of Macasar in the East Indies* (Farnborough, 1971), pp. 83–85; C.-L. de Montesquieu and P. Vernière, *Lettres persanes* (Paris, 1960), p. 241.

[67] J. Spaulding, 'Slavery, Land Tenure, and Social Class in the Northern Turkish Sudan', *International Journal of African Historical Studies*, 15, 1 (1982), pp. 1–20; Toledano, *Slavery and Abolition in the Ottoman Middle East*, pp. 14–19; Kurtynova-D'Herlugnan, *The Tsar's Abolitionists*, pp. 39–40.

[68] Toledano, *As if Silent and Absent*, p. 43.

[69] C.C. Robertson and M.A. Klein, eds., *Women and Slavery in Africa* (Madison, 1983), pp. 6, 8–9.

[70] D. Pipes, *Slave Soldiers and Islam* (New Haven CT, 1981); Crone, *Slaves on Horses*.

[71] Cf. Clarence-Smith, *Islam and the Abolition of Slavery*, p. 4.

[72] D. Cumming, ed., *The Country of the Turkomans: An Anthology of Exploration from the Royal Geographical Society* (London, 1977), p. 68.

suffered celibacy and drudgery; bad treatment might become more severe if it issued from a jealous mistress.[73] Prostitution of slaves was plainly forbidden in 24:33 of the Qur'an, commenting on pre-Islamic Middle Eastern custom.[74] However, the legal fiction of short-term sales covered its practice in Ottoman lands and probably elsewhere.[75]

Generalizations about treatment are risky since reports by slaves have commonly been removed from the historical record. Islamic law banned the molestation of wards, but control of such rules was restricted because the household fell under the private sphere. Less formal sources convey both vigorous exhortations for good treatment and alternative modes of operation: One Hadith – from the body of tradition linked to the prophet Muhammad – approved of corporal punishment, and a widely quoted Arab saying stated that 'slaves are beaten with a stick'. The twelfth-century Baghdad theologian Abu al-Faraj ibn al-Jawzi suggested that 'it is incumbent upon a wife to suffer her husband's ill-treatment as a slave should'.[76]

While there are several reports about mild-mannered masters, and some slaves enjoyed contractual independence in specific areas of activity, these are offset by less agreeable treatment that included social marginalization through frequent resale. An observer in nineteenth-century Istanbul noted that 'slaves pass through the hands of ten or twenty masters, who make them lead the life of cab-horses, beat them at intervals, and at last sell them'.[77] Two centuries earlier, dry-worded petitions to the Moscow chancelleries recorded that some returnees had been frequently resold, sometimes decades after their initial capture, doing menial work.[78] According to Christian and therefore potentially biased witnesses, the Crimean Tatar khanate was hardly better in the treatment of its captives.[79] The *ulama* prohibited mutilating slaves or filing their teeth, threatening severe consequences for the owners and manumission for the slaves.[80] However, sixteenth-century Crimean Tatars reportedly branded slaves on the forehead and Barbary corsairs marked

---

[73] Kurtynova-D'Herlugnan, *The Tsar's Abolitionists*, p. 39; L.P. Peirce, *The Imperial Harem: Women and Sovereignty in the Ottoman Empire* (New York, 1993), pp. 138, 141–142.
[74] Brunschvig, "Abd', p. 25.
[75] Y.H. Erdem, *Slavery in the Ottoman Empire and its Demise, 1800–1909* (Basingstoke, 1996), pp. 34–35; J. Forsyth, *A History of the Peoples of Siberia: Russia's North Asian Colony 1581–1990* (Cambridge, 1992), pp. 67–68, 73.
[76] Cited in Clarence-Smith, *Islam and the Abolition of Slavery*, p. 4. For a more detailed discussion of female slaves' treatment and rights, see Witzenrath, 'Introduction: Slavery in Medieval and Early Modern Eurasia'.
[77] J. Hunwick and E.T. Powell, *The African Diaspora in the Mediterranean Lands of Islam* (Princeton NJ, 2002), p. 124.
[78] For example, RGADA f. 210 (Razriad) d. 617, p. 5; ibid., d. 773, pp. 183, 185; ibid., d. 1194, p. 52; ibid., d. 1355, pp. 33, 34. Cf. Toledano. 'Enslavement in the Ottoman Empire in the Early Modern Period', pp. 37–38.
[79] Broniewski, 'Opisanie Kryma (Tartariae Descriptio)', pp. 355–366, here p. 357.
[80] Brunschvig, "Abd', pp. 27, 31.

them on the soles of their feet; this may sometimes also have been done to recaptured runaways.[81] While these observations rely on single sources, the recent scholar of the Crimean Tatars, E.V. Vozgrin of St Petersburg, insists that the sources that might contain material on slaves held by the Crimean Tatars have not been studied. However, it is unlikely that they kept many slaves, since the structures of their economy did not allow it.[82]

Enslavement depended on vicious raids, harrowing forced marches, dismal sales of the disenfranchised and perilous maritime voyages. It may be all too appealing to define away the issue by hinting at the interested nature of nineteenth- or even seventeenth-century European denunciations. However, some generally open-minded Islamic sources and the few first-hand accounts of slaves essentially describe the same horrors encountered elsewhere. Always a good read, the seventeenth-century traveller and *homme des lettres* Evliya Çelebi shows emotional attachment to his slaves with whom he usually travelled, but he also captured some on an expedition. While in Crimea, he quotes an Arab proverb, 'Whosoever sells a man, cuts down a tree, or breaks a dam, is cursed by God in this world and in the next'.[83] From the Prophet's own slave taken from the defeated Jewish Qurayza tribe, Rahaina, who may have tried to poison her – according to the Qur'an – divinely inspired master, to the recently studied Ottoman slaves who sought their own ways out in multiple everyday acts of petty assertion and resistance, there is every indication that Islamic slavery, despite the apparently broader spectrum of occupations and roles, was recognizably related to parallel phenomena in other cultures.[84]

The ways in which Islam promoted, but also decelerated, the agency of slaves can be briefly outlined as follows. The foundations of slavery in the original texts were weak, leading to a permanent tension between religious belief and social reality. Based on this tension, any interpretation that stipulates a single Islamic point of view on slavery must be rejected. Slavery was the clearest negation of the socially egalitarian vision of the faith. As it was embarrassing to many of the faithful, bondage promoted debates and differing interpretations.[85]

---

[81] A. Fisher, 'Chattel Slavery in the Ottoman Empire', *Slavery and Abolition*, 1, 1 (1980), pp. 25–45.
[82] Vozgrin, *Istoriia krymskikh tatar*, pp. 440–454. See also M. Ivanics, 'Enslavement, Slave Labour and Treatment of Captives in the Crimean Khanate', in G. Dávid and P. Fodor, eds., *Ransom Slavery Along the Ottoman Borders: Early Fifteenth – Early Eighteenth Centuries* (Leiden, 2007), pp. 193–220; L. Podhorodecki, *Chanat Krymski i jego stosunki z Polska w XV-XVIII w* (Warszawa, 1987), pp. 62–64; P.R. Magocsi, *A History of Ukraine: The Land and its Peoples* (Toronto, 2010), pp. 186–187.
[83] See Z. Abrahamowicz, ed., *Ksiega podróży Ewliji Czelebiego* (Warszawa, 1969), p. 308, referring to Turkish slave traders in the Crimean town of Karasu. My thanks go to Thomas M. Prymak for making his unpublished article available to me. R. Dankoff, ed., *An Ottoman Traveller: Selections from the Book of Travels of Evliya Çelebi* (London, 2011), pp. 338–340.
[84] Toledano, *As if Silent and Absent*.
[85] Clarence-Smith, *Islam and the Abolition of Slavery*, p. 19.

Sultan's law initially exacerbated slavery but began to rein in the institution from the sixteenth century. Once confronted by the strong and popular Western challenge to slavery in the nineteenth century, responses were still ambivalent. Mystics and millenarians, for example, explosively increased rates of enslavement when they chose the way of the sword. However, subversive millenarians, who claimed the right to abolish the law and reshape society, might oppose slavery. Peaceful mystics also did much to integrate former slaves into Islam.

Overall, a perplexing paradox remains: Islam was precocious in regulating slavery and encouraging the faithful to engage in manumission, and yet Muslim conservatives generally lagged behind those of other faiths in approving complete emancipation.[86]

A Sunni Consensus

The Qur'an neither approved of nor clearly banned slavery. Muhammad banned anybody but himself from taking slaves in battle and sanctioned no other method of acquiring them. Together with admonishments to manumit slaves, this could have led to the death of the institution. However, one Hadith, a tradition attributed to the Prophet, called for slaves to resign themselves to their faith. Moreover, appeals for good treatment of slaves in the Qur'an and Hadith were double-edged swords, for they presupposed the existence of slavery.

The details of a compromise were worked out by Sunni *ulama* around 800,[87] and disseminated in the *umma*, the community of Muslim believers. They upheld human freedom as the norm, without exceptions for orphans, debtors or criminals. One mode of enslavement was by capture of unyielding infidels in holy war, while others could be born to a slave mother and inherit the status, unless she was the concubine of a master who acknowledged paternity. Owners who wanted to marry one of their own slaves had to free her. Converting to Islam did not automatically confer liberty; but manumitting slaves, especially Muslim ones, was a pious act, even a binding one to propitiate for certain sins. Finally, religious law prescribed humane treatment in fine detail.[88] Rulings on slavery then came to be interwoven with the fabric of the holy law, making up about a third of the text of the *Hidayah* code, an important late twelfth-century Hanafi legal commentary.[89]

---

86 Ibid., pp. 19–21.
87 I. Schneider, *Kinderverkauf und Schuldknechtschaft. Untersuchungen zur frühen Phase des islamischen Rechts*. Habilitation (Universität Köln, 1996), pp. 349–351.
88 Brunschvig, "Abd'.
89 T.P. Hughes, *A Dictionary of Islam* (London, 1885), pp. 597–8; Hamilton, Charles and Standish G. Grady, *The Hedayah, or guide: a commentary on the Mussulman Laws* (London, 1870), p. xxxi.

Taking Infidels in Holy War

The Qur'an is silent on the ordinary believer taking slaves; nevertheless, seizing hard-bitten infidels in holy war came to be considered the most acceptable form of enslavement. While, according to many clerics, declaring holy war was the preserve of the caliph and justifications for taking slaves depended on it, there were many ways round these restrictions. The next stage in intensifying enslavement was to expand the category of the enslavable to the entire population of a conquered area. This allowed access to female slaves, which in turn opened the way to hereditary slavery and concubinage.[90]

From the ninth century on, jurists developed the concept of *Dar al-Harb*, the abode of war, which lay beyond the lands of the believers and whose inhabitants 'were all potential slaves'.[91] Moreover, as 'Abd al-'Aziz b. Ahmad al-Bukhari declared, slavery was a form of divine retribution for unbelief: 'Freedom is the attribute par excellence of a living being in a secular jurisdiction whereas slaves are in the category of the dead, for servitude is a vestige of obstinacy in refusing to believe in God, and this in the eyes of the law is death itself'.[92]

However, such religious sanctions did not prevail everywhere, as local custom might retain the upper hand: Chechen and Circassian clans in the Caucasus raided for slaves without religious sanction or leadership.[93] Mediterranean privateering, although it retained aspects of a contest between faiths, was also a business. It was rooted in economic relationships on, and sometimes even between, both sides of the Mediterranean. Joint slave raiding with infidels may have been the ultimate negation of the ideal of holy war, but it was common.[94] It was one of the mechanisms by which Russian tsars from Ivan IV onwards co-opted Muslim elites.[95]

There was a sophisticated body of Islamic jurisprudence regarding the treatment of slaves and well-established habits of persecuting religious outsiders, but the dissonance between theory and practice was plainly considerable. The extent of this disagreement increased directly proportionate to the distance from established religious centres such as Bukhara. Thus Khiva, without an established, politically powerful community of *ulama*, emerged as the hub of the Central Asian slave trade. The khanate's Uzbek ruling elite, who in the main owned and profited from oasis-irrigated cultivation, were the chief consumers of Persian and Indian slave labour.

---

90 Clarence-Smith, *Islam and the Abolition of Slavery*, p. 27.
91 J. Hunwick, 'Black Africans in the Mediterranean World: Introduction to a Neglected Aspect of the African Diaspora', in E. Savage, ed., *The Human Commodity: Perspectives of the Trans-Saharan Slave Trade* (London, 1992), pp. 5–38, here p. 11.
92 Clarence-Smith, *Islam and the Abolition of Slavery*, p. 28.
93 R. Majerczak, 'Le mouridisme au Caucase', *Revue du Monde Musulman*, 20 (1912), pp. 162–241, here p. 197; Erdem, *Slavery in the Ottoman Empire and its Demise, 1800–1909*, p. 46.
94 Clarence-Smith, *Islam and the Abolition of Slavery*, pp. 29–31.
95 Witzenrath, *Cossacks and the Russian Empire, 1598–1725*, pp. 24–26; Ivanics, 'Enslavement, Slave Labour and Treatment of Captives in the Crimean Khanate', p. 198.

Yet the nomadic Turkmen tribes inhabiting the trans-Caspian steppe were, as raiders, the main suppliers of that labour.[96]

Although ransom is specifically recommended in 47:4 of the Qur'an, the founder of the Hanafi School forbade this practice; later jurists even prohibited exchanges of captives.[97] Nevertheless, capturing people for the main purpose of offering them for exchange or ransom was frequently practiced – for example, by the Crimean Tatars. Establishing the price that could maximally be paid by a given captive under conditions of scarcity of information about their social whereabouts often entailed a liberal degree of torture, so these captives may have gone through worse ordeals than many slaves in Muslim lands.[98] Summarizing the prospect of travelling the steppe to escape Ottoman slavery approximated – notwithstanding the far better conditions many experienced – a journey out of the frying pan into the fire.

To ease ransoming, some people offered special services. Well-developed informal connections existed well into the nineteenth century on the North Caucasus frontier between cossacks and the indigenous population, who developed close relationships by fostering each other's children. These connections helped trade and forays into the mountains, but they could also help raiders seeking human and other booty. Moreover, these intermediaries, who knew where to find an open door in a generally hostile environment, acted as negotiators in ransoming disputes. While cossacks usually handed over their own captives to their superiors, if they felt browbeaten and exploited by ransom demands they resorted to a widespread customary right, called *barimta* or *baranta*, which allowed the taking of booty to compensate for losses and faults. So even on this unruly frontier there were certain mechanisms that allowed crossing from one side to the other, whether as captive, as intermediary or as trader. Such institutions provided rules for the game of raiding, rather than stamping it out.[99]

Tribute, Acquisition and Adoption

Infidels not directly ruled by Muslims offered tribute in slaves when they had little else of value. The Ottomans and the Crimean Tatars imposed levies of children on vassal states, including Christian Georgia and the Circassians.[100] Infidels might

---

96 B.D. Hopkins, 'Race, Sex and Slavery: "Forced Labour" in Central Asia and Afghanistan in the Early Nineteenth Century', *Modern Asian Studies*, 42, 4 (2008), pp. 629–671, here pp. 645–646.
97 A.A. Elwahed, *Contribution à une théorie sociologique de l'esclavage: Étude des situations génératrices de l'esclavage avec app. sur l'esclavage de la femme et bibliographie crit* (Paris, 1931), p. 131; Hughes, *A Dictionary of Islam*, pp. 597–598.
98 Boeck, 'Identity as Commodity', pp. 259–266.
99 T.M. Barrett, *At the Edge of Empire: The Terek Cossacks and the North Caucasus Frontier, 1700–1860* (Boulder CO, 1999), pp. 158–162, 174–179.
100 B.D. Papoulia, *Ursprung und Wesen der "Knabenlese" im Osmanischen Reich* (München, 1963), pp. 10, 14, 17, 57–59; D.M. Lang, *The Last Years of the Georgian Monarchy, 1658–1832* (New York, 1957), p. 22.

enter servitude with Muslims under a private contract. Deserters such as those fleeing harsh conditions in Russia's army or volunteers aiming to rid themselves of their serf status through legal loopholes were among them. However, Muslim slaves also fled in the opposite direction, joining the autonomous and, later, privileged cossacks.[101]

Disapproving attitudes towards Muslim slave traders who suffered from a generally poor reputation reveal some uncertainty as to whether purchasing slaves was acceptable. However, there is some evidence to the contrary, which points to the ties between the steppe, the Caucasus and the Mediterranean world maintained by the slave trade. Such was, for example, the lofty reputation of vendors supplying soldiers in Mamluk Egypt:[102] 'Strong ties of affection and veneration' bound successful Turkic soldiers to the men who had sold them.[103]

Purchasing child slaves in order to adopt them was rare in Islam compared to other civilizations.[104] Any kind of adoption was prohibited by the Qur'an. Furthermore, it contained a clear prohibition on enslaving 'people of the book' or scripturaries, which initially meant Jewish and Christian monotheists living peacefully under Muslim rule, who were required to pay special taxes.[105] However, one of the four prevalent sources of recruitment for the households of the Ottoman Empire was slavery. Since enslavement cut the social ties of the enslaved person, they could be reattached to a new social unit which would command their loyalties and thereby extend its social, political and economic capabilities and reach. This vertical flow of loyalty, patronage (*intisap*), was one of the basic resources of sociopolitically complex urban elite families, which connected the empire's provinces among each other and with the court – for example, by sending out their trusted slaves. The first among these units was the Istanbul court, where *kul* – elite slaves – regularly ran government business.[106]

Conversion, Manumission and Slavery

In 47:4, the Qur'an commands manumission after war. Jurists found reasons to nullify God's seemingly clear instructions to free prisoners in times of peace. The catch-all concept of 'public interest', drawn from repeated commands in the Qur'an to promote good and forbid evil, meant that men should not be released to fight

---

101 Erdem, *Slavery in the Ottoman Empire and its Demise, 1800–1909*, p. 52; Brower and Layton. 'Liberation through Captivity', pp. 259–279.
102 D. Ayalon, *L'esclavage du Mamelouk*, vol. 1 (Jerusalem, 1951), pp. 1–4.
103 A. Wink, *Al-Hind: The Making of the Indo-Islamic World*, vol. 2 (Leiden, 2003), pp. 197–198.
104 O. Patterson, *Slavery and Social Death: A Comparative Study* (Cambridge MA, 1982), p. 232.
105 For discussion of the *devşirme* as deviation from Islam, see Clarence-Smith, *Islam and the Abolition of Slavery*, pp. 36–39.
106 Toledano, 'Enslavement in the Ottoman Empire in the Early Modern Period', pp. 34–38.

again – an exegetical exercise that appears to mock the Qur'an.[107] From a practical perspective, the jurists feared that slaves would pretend to accept Islam to secure their release.[108] Piecemeal trans-imperial development led the Ottomans during the eighteenth century to treat their captives more and more as prisoners of war for exchange, alongside evolving European notions.[109]

A note on translations and transliteration

I have translated some terms situationally. Khan is the title of a legitimate supreme leader and Chinggisid dynast in Tatar. However, most of my sources are in Russian and they usually use the honorific title *tsar'* for khan. Until Ivan IV, the grand prince of Muscovy and the Mongol and Tatar tsars were easily told apart, but from his accession as tsar in 1547 onwards, there is some ambiguity. The full title used in the sources might help but would hold up the text flow. In many cases, translation as 'khan' is warranted, but in some, context is lost especially when characteristics of khan and tsar are contrasted. Moreover, the king of Israel and the Byzantine *basilios* translate as *tsar'*.

I have used the Library of Congress transliteration system throughout with some slight variations. Titles are spelled with lower-case initials, except where a specific person is indicated. Volitional (cossacks) and functional groups (musketeers, clerks, etc.) are also in lower case. For ease of reading, I have retained the more familiar English spellings for some common words (e.g. boyar, Kazan). Places of publication in footnotes are rendered in original spelling and transliteration.

---

[107] Clarence-Smith, *Islam and the Abolition of Slavery*, pp. 25–26; Hughes, *A Dictionary of Islam*, pp. 597–598.
[108] J.O. Hunwick, *Sharī'a in Songhay: The Replies of al-Maghīlī to the Questions of Askia al-Ḥājj Muḥammad* (Oxford, 1985), p. 123.
[109] W. Smiley, *From Slaves to Prisoners of War: The Ottoman Empire, Russia and International Law* (Oxford, 2018).

Chapter 1
Trade Routes and Slaving Zones in Eurasia
Empire, Ideology and Framing Legitimate Human Merchandise

Trade routes, slavery and ideology are mainstays of histories of empire, specifically of recent studies of the Ottoman and Russian empires. However, such studies are silent when it comes to the impact of worldview and religion on demarcating territories and eligible human groups for slaving, or on securing trade routes, and on how these are mutually interrelated. Fresh approaches derived from studies of slaving may benefit the historiography of empire in addressing these interrelations. Linked questions have recently opened up a new and growing field in slavery studies: the pragmatic and symbolic definition of the limits of slaving and the zones in which it was deemed legitimate, as well as the changes occurring in these relations over time.[1] The approach chosen in the present book connects two of the most thriving areas of research in previously largely untested ways: the history of slavery, and imperial ideologies. It looks at the interrelations of social history and cultural history with foreign relations, previously undertheorized and little researched. In addition, it offers an alternative approach to essentialist definitions of the imperial ethnic which have been highlighted in the study of empire as crippling remnants of methodological nationalism.[2] Looking at Muscovy, my study aims to refine a recent advance in this transdisciplinary and transregional area of study, the no-slaving

---

[1] Contributions to the debate include: H. Barker, *Egyptian and Italian Merchants in the Black Sea Slave Trade, 1260–1500* (PhD dissertation Columbia University, 2014), pp. 18–19, 36, 152, passim; J. Schiel, 'Sklaven', in M. Borgolte, ed., *Migrationen im Mittelalter: Ein Handbuch* (Berlin, 2014), pp. 251–265; Smiley, *From Slaves to Prisoners of War*; K. Vlassopoulos, 'Does Slavery Have a History? The Consequences of a Global Approach', *Journal of Global Slavery*, 1, 1 (2016), pp. 5–27; A. Rio, *Slavery after Rome, 500–1100* (Oxford and New York, 2017); J.A. Glancy, '"To Serve Them All the More": Christian Slaveholders and Christian Slaves in Antiquity', in J. Fynn-Paul and D.A. Pargas, eds., *Slaving Zones: Cultural Identities, Ideologies, and Institutions in the Evolution of Global Slavery* (Leiden, 2018), pp. 23–49; J. Fynn-Paul and D.A. Pargas, eds., *Slaving Zones: Cultural Identities, Ideologies, and Institutions in the Evolution of Global Slavery* (Leiden, 2018); S. Conermann, Review of Slaving Zones. Cultural Identities, Ideologies, and Institutions in the Evolution of Global Slavery, edited by Jeff Fynn-Paul and Damian Alan Pargas, Leiden, 2018', *sehepunkte*, 19, 1 (2019); J.M. Fontaine, *Slave Trading in the British Isles and the Czech Lands, 7th–11th Centuries* (PhD dissertation King's College, 2017). Critical appraisals by Rio, *Slavery after Rome, 500–1100*, p. 24, n. 17. A partly similar argument was proposed by Miller, *The Problem of Slavery as History*.

[2] Semyonov, 'How Five Empires Shaped the World and How this Process Shaped those Empires', pp. 47, 48, 50.

zone, by analysing the paradox of the fervent liberationist language in the sources and the reality of enserfment on the ground.

Recent synthetic accounts of the early modern Russian Empire offer comprehensive insights into the dynamics of slavery, as well as a complex framework for an analysis of empire. They focus mainly on internal structures and politics, the elite, administration, and law enforcement.[3] The hub-and-spoke model of empire underlines vertical integration and a lack of horizontal integration between local communities.[4] The genealogy of the ruling dynasty provided the main, if not the exclusive, focus of legitimacy until the Time of Troubles (1601–1613) pivoted on the issue of interrupted descent. The new Romanov dynasty restored it. This agenda reflects the praxeological focus in recent writings on empire.[5]

Others question the focus on genealogy as an exclusive Muscovite imperial ideology and legitimacy. The standard position, however, reveals deep-seated reasons for renouncing imperial ideology before Peter I. The 'Letter to the Ugra' (1480) has long been pronounced an early expression of Muscovite state ideology. However, it was written too early if we take seriously the dissonances in notions of the launch of 'de-facto empire' in the 1450s.[6] The launch of empire has also been detected on the eve of the conquest of Kazan in 1552, and of Siberia, as the first annexation of sovereign territory adhering to a different faith.[7] How can we explain the discrepancy in the timeline?

Before turning to the 'Missive', it is necessary to list the reasons given for discarding imperial ideology before Peter I, since they are as analytically pertinent as they are revealing and widely shared:

> Russia's first centuries of empire, roughly from mid-sixteenth century through the seventeenth, overwhelm [. . .] with their sheer energy and almost complete lack of self-reflective ideology describing the imperial project. Moscow's rulers did not define what they were doing; they simply expanded continuously. Sources such as chronicles, decrees, and bureaucratic correspondence form the meagre basis on which historians intuit conceptual attitudes. A crusading ideology was not characteristic of the Orthodox Church, although anti-Muslim rhetoric was a trope in chronicle writing. Even if the Orthodox Church had wanted a more energetic missionary role, the state did not support it. [. . .] Neither did an ideology of cultural

---

3 Kollmann, *The Russian Empire 1450–1801* offers wide-ranging access to the burgeoning, if circumscribed, field of Muscovite history. Comprehensive overview of the book's main themes and interpretations: O. Beilinson, Review of The Russian Empire 1450–1801 by Nancy Kollmann, Oxford 2017, *Review in History*, Review no. 2120, https://reviews.history.ac.uk/review/2120, (accessed 6 Sep. 2019). See the author's reply.
4 A.J. Motyl, *Imperial Ends: The Decay, Collapse, and Revival of Empires* (New York, 2001), chapter 1 Imperial Beginnings; Barkey, *Empire of Difference*; M. Aust, *Die Schatten des Imperiums: Russland seit 1991* (München, 2019).
5 Semyonov, 'How Five Empires Shaped the World and How this Process Shaped those Empires'.
6 Kollmann, *The Russian Empire 1450–1801*, p. 41.
7 Kappeler, *The Russian Empire*; Kollmann, *The Russian Empire 1450–1801*, p. 53.

> superiority drive conquest. Non-Russian subjects were recognized as different in language, religion and culture, but were not systematically described or discriminated against as inferior. [. . .] the Muscovite state revelled in the abundance of its subject peoples, regarding them as God's bountiful creation and evidence of divine favour on Russia.[8]

With supreme overview this defines the riddle to be solved – Muscovite imperial ideology, if it existed, did not conform to the usual Western models, or at least not what is expected from them. If Muscovite ideal attitudes to diversity remotely and eerily, if unintentionally, remind us of those held today in, say, the European Union; what were the differences between these historical figurations and what were the conditions that bring to the fore such apparent similarities, yet, surely, also apparent gulfs between them? Notably, early modern colonial maps from Western European empires contain not even remotely the same positive attitude towards diversity as do Muscovite maps; instead they hide colonialised peoples and slaves.[9] Since this book focuses not only on slavery and dependency, but also on empire, the question about differences has already been answered. Difference is constitutive of empire. This raises yet another question: what could realign such Muscovite attitudes which seem to modern sensibilities so utterly incommensurable? How to realign a highly differential concern with inclusive diversity shared by all recent accounts of Muscovite Empire with the equally pervasive stress on the absence of a consistent imperial ideology?

It might seem that the explanation is that it was simply an inherited Mongol tradition, since the Mongol Empire already tolerated different faiths in its subject peoples. But that was not the way in which Muscovite political culture formed. The 'Letter to the Ugra's' little known history as an underground text has recently been investigated by M. Pliukhanova. According to her detailed textual comparison and background research, it was influenced by a post-Byzantine, early Renaissance academy in Rome and written by Greek monks in Moscow under Ivan III in 1480 or at the turn of the sixteenth century. Yet the court deemed it too extreme against the background of an essential alliance with the Crimean khan. The 'Letter' controversially asserted that the first Mongol khan of the Golden Horde, Batu, was a robber baron and, as we will see, a slaver who could not be tsar. So, the Moscow grand prince, impetuously named 'tsar' in the 'Missive', did not owe allegiance to Batu's heirs. Therefore, rather than influenced by the Mongols, the 'Missive' opposed them, citing slave raids as a reason.

Since Muscovy was still deeply entangled in the post-Mongol steppe world, Chinggisid legitimacy was paramount and the 'Letter' was kept under wraps for decades. Only in the 1540s–1550s was it eventually integrated into the canon of

---

8 Kollmann, *The Russian Empire 1450–1801*, p. 55.
9 V. Kivelson, *Cartographies of Tsardom: The Land and its Meanings in Seventeenth-Century Russia* (Ithaca NY, 2006).

sanctioned Muscovite literature.[10] The extension of Muscovite power over its former masters, the three legitimate crowns of the *tsars* or, in Tatar: the Chinggisid khans of Kazan, Astrakhan and Sibir, necessitated this new approach to authority. It was also time to assert the highest authority for often underestimated reasons which will be central to this book: these were unruly, rebellious times in the newly conquered middle Volga. However, in current studies the process by which parts of the 'Letter' became imperial ideology remains murky. After all, it is part of what is supposed to be the radical, religious mindset prevailing in politics only during the conquest of Kazan but discarded soon after.[11] This adds to the questions posed here: Was there indeed an extremist clerical mindset of some import that differed from the more pragmatic, imperial point of view? What was the contribution of the 'Letter to the Ugra' to such debate? Finally, the question not yet raised in these debates about empire: What is the contribution of the 'Letter' and the contemporary wider literature on imperial worldview to questions of slavery and liberation?

This chapter will highlight, first, the connections between trade, slaving, empire and worldview; second, it will introduce contributions to the historiography of empire little noticed even by the new imperial historiography, which have surfaced in debates on slavery; third, in an attempt to highlight a way forward I shall return to the riddle sketched out above. Finally, these questions will be examined by close scrutiny of the sources in the next chapter.

Recent accounts of empire building most productively centre on global interconnections, whereby the Afro-Eurasian zone from China to Northern Africa had been linked for millennia by the fabled east-west Silk Roads. They developed as a changing network, eventually favouring Russia. Analysis so far centred on states but recognized the significance of what once was called the periphery, focusing on the waxing and waning of especially nomadic federations. The impact of internal steppe strife on trade routes meant that Central Asia was blocked in the sixteenth and first half of the seventeenth centuries. Contrary to standard Eurocentric accounts in global history, and following Morris Rossabi and Scott Levi, new trade routes opened not only on the seas but also to the north, connecting Europe via the Volga to Iran and via Siberia to China.[12] This development was part of the emergent early modern global economy, in which Russia participated and from which it benefitted. According to J. Bentley, this

---

[10] For the complex court intrigues that led to this outcome, which involved the *tsaritsa* Zoe (Sofiia) Palaiologina, niece of the last Byzantine emperor, see chapter 2; see also M.B. Pliukhanova, '"Poslanie na Ugru" i vopros o proiskhozhdenii moskovskoi imperskoi ideologii', *Trudy Otdela drevnerusskoi literatury*, 61 (2010), pp. 452–488.

[11] Kappeler, *The Russian Empire*; Cf. I. Giliazov, 'Islam i pravoslavie v Srednem Povolzh'e posle 1552', in A. Kappeler, ed., *Die Geschichte Russlands im 16. und 17. Jahrhundert aus der Perspektive seiner Regionen* (Wiesbaden, 2004), pp. 310–321.

[12] Kollmann, *The Russian Empire 1450–1801*, p. 36; M. Rossabi, 'The "Decline" of the Central Asian Caravan Trade', in J.D. Tracy, ed., *The Rise of Merchant Empires: Long Distance Trade in the Early Modern World 1350–1750* (Cambridge, 1991), pp. 351–370; S. Levi, 'India, Russia and the

global world began to emerge from 1400 onwards.[13] The costs of the early modern global economy were high, and Russia did not escape them. The production of consumer goods and specie from Asian and American markets was built on the backs of slaves. Moreover, in Russia enserfment, instituted to support the army, brought such human suffering.[14] These phenomena were linked in complex ways by economic mechanisms, through political decisions and by religion and ideology, raising the question of how these links can be conceptualized.

The two empires at the western end of the Silk Roads, the Ottoman and the Muscovite Empires, and their interrelations, were to considerable degrees shaped by and for trade and slaving. They were distinguished by geographically separate trade routes between Europe and Asia. It is beyond the scope of this book to look into Silk Road trade with terminus at the Ottoman Mediterranean ports. Yet in the seventeenth century a new Siberian arm of the Silk Road network opened running from China and India through Nerchinsk, Irkutsk, Tara and Tobolsk to Moscow.[15] It re-routed long-running Central Asia tracks: Increased security and communications in these new Siberian outposts swayed well-connected Bukharan transcontinental merchants to move from Central Asia to Tobolsk, the capital of Siberia. They sought to evade the growing internal troubles in Central Asia brought about by the slow dissolution of the Mongol Empire. Meanwhile, Armenian and Indian traders set up at Astrakhan.[16] Growing transcontinental trade was the medium-term outcome of sixteenth century conquests along and beyond the Volga: the capital of the Volga Tatars, Kazan (1552), Astrakhan (1556) near the estuary, and Sibir. Attempts to expand to the Baltic in the Livonian War 1558–83 at first hampered trade, but led to the opening of the Arctic route in cooperation with the Dutch and English via newly founded Arkhangelsk.[17]

However, the main trade artery from Northern Europe to the Ottomans led through Poland, a frequent and long-term Ottoman ally and competitor of Muscovy.[18] After the Muscovite conquests along the Volga threatened Ottoman trade and pilgrim routes along the Northern Caucasus, the Ottomans attempted to cut a channel through the isthmus between the Don and Volga. They failed in 1569, to some extent because their

---

Eighteenth-Century Transformation of the Central Asia Caravan Trade', *Journal of the Economic and Social History of the Orient*, 42, 4 (1999), pp. 519–548.
13 J.H. Bentley, 'Early Modern Europe and the Early Modern World', in C.H. Parker and J.H. Bentley, eds., *Between the Middle Ages and Modernity: Individual and Community in the Early Modern World* (Lanham MD, 2006), pp. 13–31.
14 Kollmann, *The Russian Empire 1450–1801*, p. 33.
15 E. Monahan, *The Merchants of Siberia: Trade in Early Modern Eurasia* (Ithaca NY, 2016).
16 G.L. Penrose, 'Inner Asian Influences on the Earliest Russo-Chinese Trade and Diplomatic Contacts', *Russian History*, 19, 1–4 (1992), pp. 361–392, here pp. 388–392.
17 Kollmann, *The Russian Empire 1450–1801*.
18 A. Fuess, 'Handel und Waren', in S. Conermann, A. Fuess and S. Rohdewald, eds., *Transottomanica: Osteuropäisch-osmanisch-persische Mobilitätsdynamiken: Perspektiven und Forschungsstand* (Göttingen, 2019), pp. 105–134.

Crimean Tatar guides led the campaign astray. This defined a common point of interest between Moscow and a number of changing Tatar hordes, who were unwilling to let their suzerain bypass the Caucasus, appear by waterborne transport in force at the northern domains of its adversary – Safavid Iran – and cut out the nomadic Tatar intermediaries and Muscovy on the steppe from eastern trade.[19] Mountain routes from the Ottomans to Persia were noted for their inaccessibility, as was its southern desert. It was not until disaster befell Istanbul's long-time ally Poland-Lithuania and threatened the balance of power in Western Eurasia that the Ottomans themselves attacked beyond the Black Sea steppe.[20] The Muscovite-Ottoman war of the 1670s brought a new, uneasy balance that emptied Right-bank Ukraine to the west of the Dnipro, but allowed Muscovy to populate its newly-won steppe possessions east of the river.[21]

To sum up trade relations: north-south Muscovite-Ottoman trade was alive but limited.[22] The two empires remained distant on two sides of the Pontic or Black Sea steppe, competitors for predominantly east-west transcontinental trade on mostly parallel routes. Income flows had changed from the earlier situation in the Mongol Empire, uniting the Silk Road routes as the Chinese route was diverted through Siberia. From the late fifteenth century onwards nomads, especially in the Pontic or Black Sea steppe, were often compelled by their meagre earnings as herders and the increasingly river-based transport to seek additional sources of income, which they found in slave raiding and highway robbery. The middle and lower Volga, rival trade artery to caravan trade, was well-known for this phenomenon in the later 1500s and Siberia into the eighteenth century.[23]

Demand for labour was high in the economically thriving Ottoman Empire, and access to human resources by raiding was easy for nomads who remained militarily superior in pitched battle until the eighteenth century. Slave raids north across the steppe, often several times a year, yielded large numbers of captives:[24] Between the 1470s and 1700, Eastern Europe from the Caucasus to Poland was the second largest source of enslaved people after sub-Saharan Africa.[25] The reverse phenomenon existed,

---

19 Davies, *Warfare, State and Society on the Black Sea Steppe, 1500–1700*; Monahan, *The Merchants of Siberia*; Kollmann, *The Russian Empire 1450–1801*.
20 Eurasia in this sense denotes the area north of the major mountain ranges and west of the Carpathian arc: J.P. LeDonne, 'Poltava and the Geopolitics of Western Eurasia', *Harvard Ukrainian Studies*, 31, 1/4 (2009–2010), pp. 177–191; Ostrowski, 'The End of Muscovy'.
21 Davies, *Warfare, State and Society on the Black Sea Steppe, 1500–1700*.
22 Ibid., pp. 26–27.
23 Khodarkovsky, *Russia's Steppe Frontier*.
24 C.L. Wilkins, 'A Demographic Profile of Slaves in Early Ottoman Aleppo', in C. Witzenrath, ed., *Eurasian Slavery, Ransom and Abolition in World History, 1200–1860* (Farnham, Surrey, 2015), pp. 221–246.
25 Estimates based on various sources confirm the larger picture: İnalcık, *An Economic and Social History of the Ottoman Empire*, pp. 32–37; A. Fisher, 'Muscovy and the Black Sea Slave Trade', *Canadian-American Slavic Studies*, 6, 4 (1972), pp. 575–594, here p. 579; A.A. Novosel'skij, *Bor'ba Moskovskogo*

in which cossacks raided coastal areas; but on balance slaving until the latter part of the seventeenth century ran north to south, less so in the opposite direction.[26]

Connectivity was central to this nomadic extra income: Muscovite and Ruthenian slaves could be found in large numbers in places as far removed as Aleppo, Istanbul or Bursa, as well as in Central Asia. For most, this was a one-way trip: they never returned. Not all remained unwillingly and out of sheer necessity in their new places due to the Ottoman Empire's attraction. Others stayed, hemmed in by intervening steppe where the slavers lay in wait.[27] In the seventeenth century, slaves in Central Asia were unlikely to reach the other side of the Hungry or Caspian steppe; Turkmen slavers roamed there and were likely to intercept them, paying no heed to manumission documents.[28] Slaves were usually manumitted after between seven and twelve years, and continued to live in the vicinity of their former master as clients; however, not all benefitted from this custom and some were sold on before they had been manumitted. Some slaves reached the heights of the Ottoman hierarchy, epitomized by Hurrem (1500/1506–1558), a slave girl from Ruthenia whom foreigners therefore called Roxelana. She was the first after generations of slave consorts to lawfully marry the sultan. Suleyman the Magnificent, or the Lawgiver in Ottoman parlance, broke with tradition by writing love poems to her. Regent to her son after a biting round of Ottoman throne succession fights, she had already begun to increase the harem's influence in politics and culture.[29]

Other captives returned to their homes after months, years or even decades – ransomed, fled, or manumitted. Many were much less fortunate, finding themselves on galleys as rowers. From the Ottoman silver mines no slave returned, according to

---

gosudarstva s tatarami v pervoj polovine XVII veka (Moskva, 1948), p. 436; G.A. Sanin, *Otnosheniia Rossii i Ukrainy s Krymskim Khanstvom v seredine XVII veka* (Moskva, 1987), p. 243; D. Kołodziejczyk, 'Slave Hunting and Slave Redemption as a Business Enterprise: The Northern Black Sea Region in the Sixteenth to Seventeenth Centuries', *Oriente Moderno*, 25, 86 (2006), pp. 149–159, here p. 151; M. Kizilov, 'Slave Trade in the Early Modern Crimea from the Perspective of Christian, Muslim, and Jewish Sources', *Journal of Early Modern History*, 11, 1–2 (2007), pp. 1–31, here pp. 6–7.

26 V. Ostapchuk, 'The Human Landscape of the Ottoman Black Sea in the Face of the Cossack Naval Raids', *Oriente Moderno*, 81, 1 (2001), pp. 23–95.

27 B.L. Davies, 'The Prisoner's Tale: Russian Captivity Narratives and Changing Muscovite Perceptions of the Ottoman-Tatar Dar-Al-Islam', in C. Witzenrath, ed., *Eurasian Slavery, Ransom and Abolition in World History, 1200–1860* (Farnham, Surrey, 2015), pp. 279–294; A. Lavrov, 'Captivity, Slavery and Gender: Muscovite Female Captives in the Crimean Khanate and in the Ottoman Empire', in C. Witzenrath, ed., *Eurasian Slavery, Ransom and Abolition in World History, 1200–1860* (Farnham, Surrey, 2015), pp. 309–319; A. Lavrov, 'Rapatriement, genre et mobilité sociale. La liste des captifs rapatriés de Crimée par Timofej Hotunskij (1649)', *Cahiers du monde russe*, 57, 2–3 (2016), pp. 667–685.

28 A. Burton, 'Russian Slaves in Seventeenth-Century Bukhara', in T. Atabaki and J. O'Kane, eds., *Post-Soviet Central Asia* (London, 1998), pp. 345–365; A. Burton, *The Bukharans: A Dynastic, Diplomatic and Commercial History, 1550–1702* (Richmond, Surrey, 1997); V. Mikhailov, *Adventures of Michailow: A Russian Captive among the Kalmucs* (Bloomington IN, 1996).

29 Peirce, *Empress of the East*; Peirce, *The Imperial Harem*.

the records. Nevertheless, far from all miners were slaves and for both slaves and free miners death was not uncommon, even in Christian empires.[30] Some were manumitted after a period of years, according to a contract or after buying their own liberty from their earnings as their masters' trade agents. Others were ransomed by Muscovite envoys, merchants, foreign ambassadors or intermediary steppe groups, such as cossacks. Some cossacks on the steppe frontier intermarried with Tatars or mountaineers; others, including some Muscovite Tatars, returned from slavery to become interpreters for the Muscovite foreign (or 'Ambassadors') chancellery.[31] The resulting networks were instrumental in arranging the exchange of captives or ransom, including even boyars.

Historians have highlighted the peculiar context of the links between the Muscovite and Ottoman Empires. Land, people, and culture have been looked at in a global context. Yet as a part of global trade and conflict, slaving has been mentioned, but not contextualised in Muscovite culture. An early modern empire living off global trade to a significant degree needed security from slave raids, especially if in a contiguous land empire this was not guaranteed by exclusive technologies such as those available at the time for shipping on the high seas far beyond any pirate's reach.[32] In a political environment characterised by numerous contiguous and insecure land powers, soft power initiatives could seem just as promising as military forays for securing transcontinental trade.[33] Cultural expression was relevant to trade security for its mobilizational and integrating qualities in a land based empire.

Current scholarly approaches to Muscovite ideology correctly underline the 'broadcasting' of legitimacy. Nevertheless the question arises where legitimacy derived from, beyond the dynastic link which broke down at the end of the sixteenth century. The current solution is reductive, but elegant: Muscovites had no mechanism of transferring legitimacy beyond the dynasty, which explains the numerous pretenders during

---

30 Witzenrath, 'Introduction. Slavery in Medieval and Early Modern Eurasia'.
31 M. Khodarkovsky, *Bitter Choices: Loyalty and Betrayal in the Russian Conquest of the North Caucasus* (Ithaca NY, 2011); Boeck, 'Identity as Commodity'.
32 J. Law, 'On the Methods of Long-Distance Control: Vessels, Navigation and the Portuguese Route to India', in J. Law, ed., *Power, Action and Belief: A New Sociology of Knowledge?* (London, 1986), pp. 234–263. C. Witzenrath, 'Orthodoxe Kirche und Fernmacht: Das Moskauer Reich, Kosaken und die Gründung des Bischofssitzes von Tobolsk und Sibirien 1620–1625', in C. Hochmuth and S. Rau, eds., *Machträume der frühneuzeitlichen Stadt* (Konstanz, 2006), pp. 309–332.
33 Even today, a soft power approach to Inner Eurasian trade seems promising: E. Fels, ed., *Power in the 21st Century: International Security and International Political Economy in a Changing World* (Berlin, 2012); J. Garlick, *The Impact of China's Belt and Road Initiative: From Asia to Europe* (London, 2020); N. Chitty, L. Ji, G.D. Rawnsley and C. Hayden, eds., *The Routledge Handbook of Soft Power* (London, 2017); J.S. Nye, *Soft Power: The Means to Success in World Politics* (New York, 2004).

the Time of Troubles.³⁴ But the dynastic link was already broken at the death of Fedor Ivanovich in 1598. Boris Godunov, whose claim to dynastic continuity was at best flimsy, relied on the abdication in his favour of his sister, the late tsar's widow. The first pretender succeeded only because of Godunov's untimely death, leaving an infant heir who was not seen as legitimate. It is therefore an open question why Godunov's son was less legitimate than his father, if the rather overt construction of a dynastic link was truly seen as overriding any political considerations, let alone the accomplishments of Boris Godunov, the capable regent during the reign of the incapacitated but 'pious' Fedor Ivanovich (1584–1598). Boris sidelined all competing boyar clans during a crisis of his regency in 1591. Although there was mounting tension in the dynamic frontier region, he was not challenged until catastrophic famines in successive years from 1601 cast a pall over his reign. Few could have bettered Godunov's attempts to avert it before his untimely and unexpected death.³⁵

Could legitimacy in Muscovy have been a more accommodating process than the focus on dynasty suggests? Muscovite rulers from the mid-sixteenth century onwards were eager to engage with at least one of the main associated foreign policy issues, the Tatars or Poland-Lithuania. Those who were not in a position to live up to this expectation were either sidelined by regents – Boris Godunov, Filaret and Sofiia – or they did not last, as the abortive campaigns against Crimea show, which did not help Sofiia in her final bid for sovereign power.³⁶ Ivan IV abolished the fearsome *oprichnina* in 1572, right after its troops proved ineffective against a devastating Tatar slave raid on Moscow.³⁷ Even after the fall of Kazan, Chinggisid legitimacy was strong enough to impel Ivan IV to raise Simeon Bekbulatovich to the Moscow throne in 1575. After a year, he demoted him step by step, until he was a mere grand prince of Tver'. Simeon was the last of the Chinggisid princes in Muscovite services, baptized but still important in conditions of repeated Tatar rebellions in the middle Volga. Ivan had bestowed the title of tsar on him in the second half of the 1560s. He had been the khan of Kasimov, a Muscovite territory often given to Tatar princes, and thus *tsar'* for reasons of title and pedigree. This made Simeon a potentially legitimate pretender for the Muscovite throne. The use of violence against him to thwart such an attempt might have offended the idea of the tsar's

---

34 M. Hildermeier, *Geschichte Russlands: Vom Mittelalter bis zur Oktoberrevolution* (München, 2016), pp. 286–287. Cf. Kollmann, *The Russian Empire 1450–1801*, pp. 279–280.
35 C.S.L. Dunning, *Russia's First Civil War: The Time of Troubles and the Founding of the Romanov Dynasty* (University Park PA, 2001), pp. 119–137.
36 If Boris Godunov was extolled during the Time of Troubles, he was put on a par with Ivan IV in regard to activities in the southern border regions: C. Witzenrath, 'Versklavung, Befreiung und Legitimität im Moskauer Reich: Avraamij Palicyn und die "Zeit der Wirren"', in D. Ordubadi and D.Dahlmann, eds., *Die "Alleinherrschaft" der russischen Zaren in der "Zeit der Wirren" in transkultureller Perspektive* (Göttingen, 2021), pp. 13–44.
37 Due to the omissions in the archival sources and the heated scholarly debate, discussing the short history of the *oprichnina* in any detail would overextend the brief of this book.

God-given power, or it might not; but it was hardly advisable given the volatile situation in the middle Volga.[38] The power of the Muscovite tsar was in fact still smaller than the conquest of Kazan might suggest. By the early seventeenth century it had resulted in an 'elusive empire' unsure of itself, as M. Romaniello has underlined. It existed de facto in a web of closely connected post-Mongol states and groups whose partial support it needed to achieve this conquest in the first place.[39] The Moscow grand princes and tsars needed the raiders, who were all part of this evolving, politically disorganized slaving zone. Yet for the same reason they needed a worldview that set Moscow apart from the pack.

This outlook was supported by the main aspects underlying the rise of Moscow. Consciously recounting the traditional story of Muscovy's rise as first devised by V.O. Kliuchevskyi, there were four factors contributing to its growth: Mongol patronage, securing the see of the Orthodox metropolitanate by the 1320s; the dynasty's de facto primogeniture in the face of the partible inheritance practiced by its rivals; and, finally, its advantageous geographic position.[40] These factors were important, except for Moscow's location which was hardly better suited for trade than that of its rival Tver';[41] it was, however, closer to the steppe frontier.

Since Lawrence Langer's investigation it has become harder to overlook, first, the role of internal slaving by the Rus' principalities and their selling of slaves. Second, an initial no-slaving zone was set up – although Langer wrote just as this label was invented – by Moscow in its as yet limited territories, especially during the period of internal wars within the Golden Horde during the 1360s and 1370s.[42] So it might be asked whether a no-slaving zone and the detrimental effects on its environment might be the fifth – or new fourth – factor of Moscow's rise.

(No-)Slaving zones

Although the concept of slaving zones and no-slaving zones is increasingly being used by scholars of slavery, it was initially concerned with empire building.[43] Since

---

38 S. Bogatyrev, 'Ivan IV (1533–1584)', in M. Perrie, ed., *Cambridge History of Russia*, vol. 1: *From Early Rus' to 1689* (Cambridge, 2006), pp. 240–263, here p. 260.
39 Romaniello, *The Elusive Empire*; B.R. Rakhimzianov, *Moskva i tatarskii mir: Sotrudnichestvo i protivostoianie v ėpochu peremen, XV-XVI vv.* (St Peterburg, 2016), p. 229.
40 Kollmann, *The Russian Empire 1450–1801*, pp. 44–53.
41 M. Krom, Review of The Russian Empire 1450–1801 by Nancy Shields Kollmann, Oxford 2017, *Ab Imperio*, 4 (2017), pp. 295–302.
42 L.N. Langer, 'Slavery in the Appanage Era. Rus' and the Mongols', in C. Witzenrath, ed., *Eurasian Slavery, Ransom and Abolition in World History, 1200–1860* (Farnham, Surrey, 2015), pp. 145–170.
43 J. Fynn-Paul, 'Empire, Monotheism and Slavery in the Greater Mediterranean Region from Antiquity to the Early Modern Era', *Past & Present*, 205, 1 (2009), pp. 3–40.

then, it has undergone some revision, but has been embraced and its basic tenets accepted by a growing number of international scholars who mainly study slavery in the Greater Mediterranean – including the Genoese Black Sea trade as well as Gypsy slaves in Romania –, medieval Europe, and the colonial world.[44] Despite some helpful generalizing comments beyond these regions, the concept has not yet elicited much work among students of the inner Eurasian regions.[45] However, there are shortcomings to the concept, namely its treating all no-slaving zones, especially the monotheistic varieties, under the same heading: within some, for example in Muslim territories, subjects could be treated legitimately neither as slaves nor as serfs, in sharp contrast to medieval and early modern Europe and Muscovy.

The main characteristics of the no-slaving zone were originally enumerated as six pillars. They may be summarized as follows, cutting across disciplinary boundaries of social, economic and cultural history as well as foreign relations:

1) Political organization frequently protected people from enslavement, while political disorganization can have the opposite effect.
2) Many societies designated geographical areas that can be described as 'slaving zones', i.e. places from which slaves could be captured or purchased.
3) Many societies created 'no slaving-zones' using various terms which were (theoretically) off limits to slaving.
4) Non-monotheistic societies often had more permeable 'no-slaving zones', while monotheistic societies tended to create more absolute bans on the enslavement of co-religionists. Thus, religious boundaries in many cases influenced boundaries of slaving zones.
5) Slaving zones can represent fractures within a given society. For example, some 'classes' of people, such as criminals, or the poor, or people of a certain race, creed, or ethnicity might be legitimate slave targets, while others are off limits.
6) Thus, worldview plays a key role in determining the actual boundaries of slaving zones, often just as much or more than political and economic organizations.[46]

One of the most interesting points is that the slaving zones of politically organized states might be more thoroughly exploited than those of politically disorganized states, due to their potentially being 'long-term' slaving zones; and also due to the increased economic sophistication that might come with political organization, increasing effective

---

44 Ibid; Fynn-Paul and Pargas, *Slaving Zones*.
45 Schiel, 'Sklaven'; Fynn-Paul and Pargas, *Slaving Zones*, p. 2 focus on Rus' prior to 1100. On the Crimean Khanate: N. Królikowska-Jedlińska, 'The Role of Circassian Slaves in the Foreign and Domestic Policy of the Crimean Khanate in the Early Modern Period', in S. Conermann and G. Şen, eds., *Slaves and Slave Agency in the Ottoman Empire* (Göttingen, 2020), pp. 355–372.
46 Fynn-Paul, 'Empire, Monotheism and Slavery in the Greater Mediterranean Region from Antiquity to the Early Modern Era', pp. 3–4.

demand for slaves. Fynn-Paul nods to Africa and Russia, though the latter largely in the medieval period, as prime but by no means exclusive examples.[47] This allows for a more rigorous evaluation of the historical record, as the terms used are analytical and less essentializing than the usual ethnic and religious markers for raiders and raided with their inherent potential to stigmatize their modern-day descendants.[48]

Concepts often discussed as identity markers that might render a person eligible for slavery can be extended to a point that the interaction of economic and political interests become discernible. 'Caribs' are to a considerable degree those whom the Spanish Crown designated enslavable for a certain period and in an area deemed less economically important. Sometimes specific fees had been paid by traders and raiders leading up to the decision; the precise area was changeable according to these factors. Between the era of religion and that of race there were multiple intermediate markers of eligbility – citizenship, religion, ethnicity, race, tribal affiliation and kinship, political priorities, gender, as well as geographical: all have been used at various times and places around the globe to delineate enslavable people.[49] No-slaving zones, therefore, provide a framework broadening the almost exclusive focus on ethnic markers in current studies of empire.

Many examples from a wide variety of regions clarify that different power regimes and ideological systems can compete over a given region at a given time, which can cause conflict or competition inside slaving zones.[50] This is especially pertinent to inner Eurasia where core areas developed no-slaving zones, such as Central Asia or Persia, but where there were also numerous 'shatter zones', politically fragmented and competed-over areas in which the impact of differing empires was felt and rival slaving zones overlapped.[51]

Muscovy's counter dependency zone

Fynn-Paul's concept of no-slaving zones allows us to describe the interrelated dynamics between no-slaving zone and slaving area, but focuses on metropolitan areas with broad groups exempt from enslavement and other forms of strong asymmetric dependency.

---

[47] J. Fynn-Paul, 'Introduction: Slaving Zones in Global History: The Evolution of a Concept', in J. Fynn-Paul and D.A. Pargas, eds., *Slaving Zones: Cultural Identities, Ideologies, and Institutions in the Evolution of Global Slavery* (Leiden, 2018), pp. 1–19, here p. 3.
[48] On stigmatization of descendants, which is usually only discussed regarding descendants of the enslaved: Toledano, *As If Silent and Absent*, pp. 2–8, 19–20.
[49] Similarly, Stanley Engerman and David Eltis have pointed out that eligibility for slavery is a major neglected issue: Eltis and Engerman, 'Dependence, Servility, and Coerced Labor in Time and Space', pp. 15–21.
[50] Fynn-Paul and Pargas, *Slaving Zones*, p. 7.
[51] Cf. A.J. Rieber, *The Struggle for the Eurasian Borderlands: From the Rise of Early Modern Empires to the End of the First World War* (Cambridge, 2014).

In ninth to eleventh century Francia and in Muscovy, the exemption did not extend to these other forms of dependency, as enserfment there thrived.[52] Dependencies of people outside the tiny elite on their superiors ranged from mutually dependent to strongly asymmetrically dependent.[53] But political discourse and policies were directed against outside slavers targeted as competitors for labour or subjects.

The existence of serfdom means that Russia cannot be generally called a no-slaving zone: Fynn-Paul's terms do not work there. To overcome this obstacle, I first considered the term 'counter slaving zone', i.e. a zone protecting its inhabitants against outward but not against internal predation. This seemed open to criticism as a euphemism. Later I changed this to 'counter dependency zone' for an area that is not a slaving zone, but a zone of asymmetrical social dependency which provided protection against slave raids. 'Dependency counter slaving zone' would be more precise but is just awkward. What is meant is strong asymmetrical dependency, since dependency in a strict sense allows for mutual relations.[54]

'Counter dependency zone' matches all these criteria: dependency includes slaving, so counter dependency means counter slaving. The term also contains dependency zone, meaning serfdom and enslaved Tatar captives. It refers to mutually dependent relations such as those with some ethnic groups and cossacks guarding the frontier. Moreover, the unenserfed half of the peasant population tended to live in the North, in Siberia and those paying quitrent and allowed more mobility lived closer to urban centres, farther from the steppe.[55]

---

52 Rio, *Slavery after Rome, 500–1100*.
53 R. Stichweh, 'How Do Divided Societies Come About? Persistent Inequalities, Pervasive Asymmetrical Dependencies, and Sociocultural Polarization as Divisive Forces in Contemporary Society', *Global Perspectives*, 2, 1 (2021).
54 J. Winnebeck, O. Sutter, A. Hermann, C. Antweiler and S. Conermann, *On Asymmetrical Dependency* (Bonn, 2021), https://www.dependency.uni-bonn.de/images/pdf-files/bcdss_cp_1-_on-asymmetrical-dependency.pdf (accessed 9 May 2022).
55 There were more areas and periods in Europe with attributes that match. Prevailing east-west dichotomies have been questioned especially with regard to burdens. Serfdom spread in Europe east and west very unevenly and in extremely patchy, localized patterns: M. Cerman, '"Serfdom" and Slavery in European History since the Middle Ages: Identifying Common Aspects for Future Research. Contribution to the Final Round Table', in S. Cavaciocchi, ed., *Schiavitù e servaggio nell'economia europea, secc. XI–XVIII/Serfdom and Slavery in the European Economy, 11th–18th Centuries*, vol. 1 (Firenze, 2014), pp. 665–676. On 'free', tax-paying peasants in Muscovy, see Introduction. Meanwwhile slavery, not least of Slavs and Tatars, spread in Renaissance Europe. See e.g. J. Fynn-Paul, 'Tartars in Spain: Renaissance Slavery in the Catalan City of Manresa, c. 1408', *Journal of Medieval History*, 34, 4 (2008), pp. 347–359; R.v. Mallinckrodt, 'There Are No Slaves in Prussia?', in E. Rosenhaft and F. Brahm, eds., *Slavery Hinterland: Transatlantic Slavery in Continental Europe, 1680–1850* (Woodbridge, 2016), pp. 109–131. Tatars were called *Tartars* in Western Europe with derogatory overtones. Moreover, no comparison of Eurasia and Europe is complete that excludes European colonies, slaveries and indentured labourers.

Muscovy established a ransom regime and the fortified steppe border to counter the slave raids from the steppe, while the the steppe border also held in serfs fleeing their landowners.[56] There is a debate among scholars about the pragmatic value of steppe fortifications: they may be considered detrimental to the Tatar nomads as they protected the new Russian settlers, although there were both nomadic and settled Tatars, the latter especially in the middle Volga region. Matthew Romaniello, who discusses the early, 'elusive' empire in the middle Volga, notes that the singular effective change that put an end to local rebellions of the Tatars, Mordvins, and Cheremis after conquest was the fortified steppe border which had been constructed since the 1570s to protect the area from steppe raids and political influence.[57] Less often noted are the fundamental military contributions of Tatar cavalry to the ensuing Livonian war. Tatar units also gained a deserved reputation for enslaving and selling off the population in large numbers. Ivan IV used the shock value of enslavement to force Livonian communities to surrender. Moreover, this policy deflected Kazan Tatar slave raiding from peasant populations under Moscow's sway without hurting Tatar economies. Neighbouring Baltic areas were thus opened to slaving.[58] External slaving zones and fortifications could be utilized to pacify the empire.

Relations between steppe nomads and Moscow were mostly guided by a pragmatic approach which brought Moscow the stability it required in the borderlands.[59] And not only there – without border protection, raids reached deep into the interior. This pragmatic approach fits the counter dependency zone, which tolerates or utilizes dependency even of the protected workforce, as long as it helps to thwart outside slave raids. This is tantamount to a value-led decision to manipulate relations with the nomads according to the aim of protecting mainly peasants, as well as settled and semi-nomadic populations.[60] An important aspect of the counter dependency zone are thus re-negotiable counter slaving relations with particular members of ethnic and religious groups on the new periphery. Can such decisions be taken and implemented effectively without expressing clear values and a coherent worldview broadcast to different populations?

---

56 Davies, *Warfare, State and Society on the Black Sea Steppe, 1500–1700*, chapter 1; Kollmann, *The Russian Empire 1450–1801*, pp. 66–67.
57 Romaniello, *The Elusive Empire*.
58 J. Martin, 'Tatars in the Muscovite Army during the Livonian War', in E. Lohr and M. Poe, eds., *The Military and Society in Russia, 1450–1917* (Leiden, 2002), pp. 365–388, here pp. 380–382.
59 Kollmann, *The Russian Empire 1450–1801*, pp. 70–71.
60 Conflict between Moscow and the Smolensk *szlachta* ensued over kidnapped rebellious populations on the lower Volga when they helped to quell the Razin rebellion. Moscow declared an amnesty for all but a few villages on the grounds that ordinary rebels had been 'misled' by Razin: A. Rustemeyer, 'Szlachta, Bauern und Majestätsverbrechen in Smolensk 1654–1764', in A. Kappeler, ed., *Die Geschichte des Moskauer Reiches im 16. und 17. Jahrhundert aus der Perspektive seiner Regionen* (Wiesbaden, 2004), pp. 137–158.

The semi-nomadic and, in the more southernly parts of their territories, nomadic Bashkirs were persuaded to man the fortified lines built across their territory. Rebellions in which Bashkirs joined were met with harsh reprisals, including permission to the Mongol Kalmyks to raid the Bashkirs: in other words, by setting up or temporarily permitting a slaving zone. On the other hand there were conciliatory gestures which included lowering the tribute and banning Russians from settling in the Bashkir lands. Moscow thereby cut a deal which was, on the surface, unfavourable to Russian ethnic expansion.[61] The unspoken reason behind it was the protection of taxable populations living in the counter dependency zone, whether Russian, Orthodox or any other marker. What counted was only the requirement of being a loyal subject.[62] Those who could not be persuaded to accept protection were abandoned and transformed into someone else's slaving zone, effectively enforcing the strong asymmetrical dependency in which they had lived under Muscovite rule. As a result of the Muscovite-Ottoman war in the 1670s, this fate of groups fractured into slaving and counter dependency zones eventually befell some of the rebellious Dnipro cossack groups to the west of the river. The Right Bank became Polish territory after it had been depopulated, while the Left Bank's population increased due to migration.[63]

So interpreting inter- and internal imperial social and political dynamics along the lines of counter dependency areas and the associated ideology allows us to overcome a typical residual notion of methodological ethno-nationalism, the interplay of essentialized 'imperial nations', Tatars and Russians, Bashkirs and more. In this way, the concept of interrelated slaving, no-slaving, and counter dependency zones responds to recent calls for removing the analytical boundary between the inhabitants of the empire's heartland and the rest of empire, and to situate imperial visions in the dialogic space of imperial diversity.[64]

In the case of serfs fleeing to the steppe border, Moscow valued security even above the interests of the elite, especially the gentry who formed just 3–4% of the population. Peasants fleeing to the steppe fortifications were very often not returned. They were needed to feed soldiers, but mainly to man the new fortifications as soldiers themselves.[65] These fractures within society, characteristic for the counter dependency zones approach, take up the statement made in discussing the internal colonization hypothesis and bring it to its logical conclusion: Neither was it just the elite

---

[61] Kollmann, *The Russian Empire 1450–1801*, pp. 69–70. Etkind omits the Bashkirs and similar cases in his account of "internal colonization": A. Etkind, *Internal Colonization: Russia's Imperial Experience* (Cambridge, 2011), pp. 6, 69.
[62] For loyalty see chapters 5 and 6.
[63] B. Davies, 'The Second Chigirin Campaign (1678): Late Muscovite Military Power in Transition', in E. Lohr, ed., *The Military and Society in Russia 1450–1917* (Leiden, 2002), pp. 97–118.
[64] Semyonov, 'How Five Empires Shaped the World and How this Process Shaped those Empires', p. 47.
[65] Kollmann, *The Russian Empire 1450–1801*, pp. 222–231.

who benefited from Moscow's policies, nor did Moscow betray the Russians to privilege the non-Russians.[66] A recent game-changing reformulation of the history of slavery notes that a characteristic feature of monarchy ever since its invention in the early empires since c. 500 BCE was the protection from slaving it provided for the taxable population, whether in the form of raids or debt slavery, as such people would not pay taxes. New-fangled monarchs invented a personal relation to their subjects to squeeze out merchant owners of slaves at no cost.[67] Characteristically, the 1649 law code twice stipulates for different categories of the population that captives returning from foreign countries are to be liberated (*svobodit'*) from their tax obligations and allowed to go wherever they want to go. Both these markers, townspeople and *kholopy* (bond people and slaves) are discussed in a context of raising and ordering the tax basis.[68] Again, the specific characteristic of the counter dependency zone, whether individuals or groups were concerned, hinges on the re-negotiable relation to the tsar. Status was less community-based than determined by service, experience and kin.

Since a slaving zone – in the Muscovite case, steppe nomad raids feeding demand for labour on external markets by raids in Muscovy and neighbouring areas – meant that the tsar lost taxable subjects, protection was justified. This amounted to various conscious choices in need of a moral compass to gain traction. Sometimes individual petitions by serf owners who asked for the return of their peasants from the border were granted. Patterns of situated decisions changed over time and may therefore have been influenced by pragmatic considerations appropriate to a changeable counter dependency zone. However, the very decision to set up steppe fortifications and to strengthen and enlarge them over time was, in the language of the time, justified by protecting the population from slave raids. In the messages exchanged between Moscow and Belgorod administration the setting up of new frontier towns was called a measure 'to free the Orthodox peasants from the clutches of the *busurmany* [Muslims]'.[69] Russia's urbanization was slowed down by the raids and the huge costs of hundreds and ultimately thousands of kilometres of steppe fortifications, as well as tribute paid to the Tatars. It was a value-oriented rather than pragmatic decision to build the fortified lines requiring a coherent worldview to back up the counter dependency zone.[70] Political gains entered

---

66 Ibid., pp. 80–81. Etkind, *Internal Colonization*.
67 Miller, *The Problem of Slavery as History*. See below for further elaboration.
68 R. Hellie, *The Muscovite Law Code (Ulozhenie) of 1649*, vol. 1 (Irvine CA, 1988), XIX § 33 (p. 159) and XX § 34 (p. 172); Khodarkovsky, *Russia's Steppe Frontier*, p. 23.
69 However, evaluation takes the cue from a Eurocentric view: a 'coherent pan-Slavist and anti-Islamic reconquista propaganda linking [. . .] to the larger struggle of Christian Europe against the Turks would not emerge until the 1670s': Davies, *Warfare, State and Society on the Black Sea Steppe, 1500–1700*, p. 13. Indeed, that was not what Muscovites needed from the mid-sixteenth to mid-seventeenth centuries.
70 C. Witzenrath, 'Sklavenbefreiung, Loskauf und Religion im Moskauer Reich', in H. Grieser and N. Priesching, eds., *Gefangenenloskauf im Mittelmeerraum: Ein interreligiöser Vergleich* (Hildesheim, 2015), pp. 287–310; C. Witzenrath, 'The Conquest of Kazan' as Place of Remembering the Liberation

into the bargain, but pragmatic gains were not a priori self-evident: they required cultural mediation such as the church and religion could offer.

It cannot be overlooked that most of the members of the Russian ethnic were more disadvantaged in absolute material and status terms than most of those living on the periphery. *Iasak* tribute was lower on the periphery than tax burdens in the 'centre', as were service obligations.[71] One attempt to answer this contradiction is the concept of internal colonization, developed by the intellectual historian Alexander Etkind. His most salient point is the fundamental amorality of imperial policy: Russian Orthodox serfs were exploited while members of the non-Russian ethnics were not, or less so.[72] Such interpretations, as well as those that claim that there was no sense of a contractual relationship between landowners and serfs,[73] overlook the practical contribution toward security from slave raids of the fortified steppe lines and generally the Muscovite military, made up of forces from many ethnic groups, and in some steppe frontier areas especially non-Russians or cossacks.

Etkind's notion of the irony of an additional burden on the Russian peasantry and privileges for other ethnic groups is at the core of his interpretation of Russian history as a process of internal colonization. But it misses the point, at least for the period between the sixteenth and mid-eighteenth centuries, since empires made decisions that sustained existing power structures, rather than protect an at best evolving nation.[74] However, this does not exclude that the centre ruled in a way that was intended to protect Russians. By not protecting their workforce, the elite would have acted against the logic of the counter dependency zone, which meant risking a return to the dynamics of the slaving zone still effective to the west in Ukraine and to the east along the Caucasus. In the no-slaving zone it was the monarch's intention to protect the taxable population against encroachment by illegitimate interests. That is, illegitimate from the perspective of the monarch and the ideology of legitimacy propagated by the monarch and the elite. However oppressed and exploited by its elite, the population in the counter dependency zone escaped double taxation or double raids in overlapping slaving zones, as well a loss of other taxpayers, which made the overall burden lighter. Highlighting the dynamics of the counter-dependency zone, Muscovites often expressed concern about losing fellow taxpayers, since taxes were

---

of Slaves in Sixteenth- and Seventeenth-Century Muscovy', in C. Witzenrath, ed., *Eurasian Slavery, Ransom and Abolition in World History, 1200–1860* (Farnham, Surrey, 2015), pp. 295–308.
71 Kollmann, *The Russian Empire 1450–1801*, p. 80.
72 Etkind, *Internal Colonization*, p. 14.
73 Eltis and Engerman, 'Dependence, Servility, and Coerced Labor in Time and Space', p. 6.
74 Cf. Kollmann, *The Russian Empire 1450–1801*, p. 81; Kivelson and Suny, *Russia's Empires*, pp. 53, 72. Val Kivelson stresses the benefits of the tsarist system for peasants, beyond the well-known drawbacks, although protection from slave raids is not mentioned: Kivelson and Suny, *Russia's Empires*, pp. 53, 72.

assessed collectively and the institutional structure thus impelled them to make up for lost taxes by increasing their share.[75]

One question looms large over these issues: since legitimacy was promulgated and therefore readily available, where are the remnants of the concomitant monarchical worldview of the counter-dependency zone? This will be the main question studied in this book.

Development of the counter dependency zone

To what extent was the Muscovite Empire created by devising a counter-dependency zone? The development of an incipient no-slaving zone commenced in the late fourteenth century, when the gradual disintegration of the Mongolian Empire increasingly produced slave raiders who supplied human chattels to the burgeoning markets in the arc from the Greater Mediterranean to Central Asia. Initially, this no-slaving zone did not extend to all territories inhabited by Eastern Orthodox Christians, which meant that less organized territorial entities such as the 'trampled-over district' of Riazan' on the south-eastern approaches to the steppe, or Kyiv in the south-west, succumbed to the market forces exerted by the Muslim no-slaving zones. We may surmise that there were several phases leading up to the fully developed counter dependency zone. The initial internal Tatar war of the 1360s and 1370s gave way to a new phase of Tatar consolidation in the early fifteenth century, until the 1440s, when the Golden Horde began to split up into many smaller hordes and khanates. Beyond the oft-mentioned effect of close Muscovite-Tatar cooperation on taxation during these phases until the mid-fifteenth century, the Muscovite no-slaving zone probably indirectly strengthened emerging Muscovy vis-à-vis its Orthodox competitors in North-Eastern Rus. Note that paying taxes to the Tatars was initially not part of setting up a no-slaving zone, which at this time was directed mainly against competing east Slavic principalities, since many towns revolted over tax rate increases in the 1260s.[76] Later, Moscow grand princes received the help of Tatar troops, and the rebellious spirit subsided.

In a third phase, Muscovy faced a far greater threat as the political fragmentation of its steppe neighbours and erstwhile suzerain, the Golden Horde, progressed. Some regions rather typically turned into slaving zones themselves as political organization fragmented and Tatars sold Tatars. Meanwhile the Ottomans, after a period of disintegrating Muslim polities, established their new centre of power and a new and growing no-slaving zone in the wider region. Ottoman and Safavid power, market capitalization, and demand for human resources in the Muslim no-slaving

---

[75] Kivelson and Suny, *Russia's Empires*, pp. 53–54; H.W. Dewey and A.M. Kleimola, 'From the Kinship Group to Every Man His Brother's Keeper: Collective Responsibility in Pre-Petrine Russia', *Jahrbücher für Geschichte Osteuropas*, 30, 3 (1982), pp. 321–335.
[76] Langer, 'Slavery in the Appanage Era'.

zones was at its height. Muscovy re-formulated border policies and invested considerable resources that helped to change local and regional population dynamics. However, it also faced a different kind of highly sophisticated no-slaving zone in the Union of Poland-Lithuania, one of the wealthiest states in Europe, which combined high rates and degrees of political enfranchisement with adequate military organization. In the long run, however, out-migration and rebellion of less privileged Ukrainians (Ruthenians), who were also much less secure from Tatar slave raids, helped Moscow reverse the regional power balance.[77]

The currently prevailing approach to the history of empires highlights their politics of difference towards ethnic and religious groups. To interrogate this approach with the role played by slaving zones in empire building and delimiting boundaries implies asking whether the latter was an effect of the former? Or should the politics of difference be understood as a way of dealing with the economic and social effects of the slave trade resulting from the large Muslim no-slaving zone? Seen in this perspective, the greatest omission in the historiography of the Muscovite empire so far is the question of how the discursive articulation and practice of the Muscovite and later imperial counter dependency zone affected the structure of empire. How did slaving zones influence social relations in Muscovy and the Russian Empire?

---

77 R.I. Frost, *The Northern Wars: War, State, and Society in Northeastern Europe, 1558–1721* (Harlow, 2000); Davies, *Warfare, State and Society on the Black Sea Steppe, 1500–1700*, p. 84. The degree to which Poland-Lithuania based its claims of legitimacy on protection from slave raids remains to be determined.

Chapter 2
The Conquest of Kazan

In the wake of the 1552 conquest of the city of Kazan, the capital of the Tatar khanate on the middle Volga, Muscovy suddenly appeared on the mental map of European powers.[1] Whether or not showing off the conquest to visitors and foreign embassies made an impact on the European public, an attempt was made to boost the positive image at home.[2] In the decades following the conquest and the consolidation of imperial rule in the middle Volga, however, it swiftly gained access to the whole of Northern Asia, limited only by the rate by which it could absorb these enormous expanses. It was an unfolding story of vast dimensions, not entirely uncommon in this era of newcomer empires on a world scale, but with its own specific features. Until recently Muscovy had been dominated by the Mongol Empire and its successors. It supplied tribute and slaves, but during the period of Golden Horde domination gained access to transcontinental trade. After the failed campaign of 1480, however, the Tatar successor khanates of the Mongols had lost direct access to their former Rus' subjects whose princes no longer paid homage, although Muscovy continued to deliver tribute to the Crimean khan until the late seventeenth century. It was easier to pay off the Tatars than to suffer their recurrent slave raids. These were second in scope only to raids in sub-Saharan Africa and remained a significant threat to individuals, families, and entire communities, if not the whole grand principality. If most of the – according to various estimates – between one and 2.5 million captives taken during raids in Eastern Europe from c. 1500 to 1700 did not originate in Muscovy but in Ukraine and the Caucasus, this was due largely to decisive action on the intertwined practical and symbolical levels: after the alliance with the Crimean khanate in 1521 had finally ended, practical action saw the building and maintaining, at enormous expense, of forts and continuous fortified lines across the steppe; this effectively kept raiders out from the mid-seventeenth century onwards and simultaneously strengthened the tsar's administration.[3] The second type of action, symbolic politics, is the main subject of this book.

---

[1] Kappeler, *The Russian Empire*. Herberstein's fundamental study of Muscovy (see n. 3) was first published in Latin in 1549 and saw seven editions in various translations until 1563 alone, mostly in the years immediately after the conquest.
[2] M. Obolenskii, ed., *Sobornaia gramota dukhovenstva pravoslavnoi vostochnoi tserkvi, utverzhdaiushchaia san tsaria za velikim kniazem Ioannom IV Vasil'evichem, 1561*, (Moskva, 1850), p. 33. J. Pelenski, *Russia and Kazan: Conquest and Imperial Ideology (1438–1560s)* (The Hague, 1974), p. 300. M.N. Tikhomirov, ed., *Letopisets nachala tsarstva* (Moskva, 1965), pp. 75–76.
[3] Overview of the slave raids and military history: Davies, *Warfare, State and Society on the Black Sea Steppe, 1500–1700*.

The underlying change that facilitated this slow but sustained and successful long-term rise of Muscovy from a minor to a regional and ultimately a global power was the expansion of Western Europe. From the late fourteenth century onwards it had gradually and slowly replaced China, the former leader in terms of cultural influence, technical inventions and power ever since the demise of Latin antiquity.[4] In Eurasia, this process created turmoil and new opportunities, which the grand princes of Moscow seized and turned to their advantage:[5] They profited from trade flows along the northern branches of the Silk Road re-routed to Astrakhan, the Volga and southern Siberia, and adjusted their symbolic representation to the turmoil and to their new European suppliers of weapons, technology and expertise.[6]

One of the driving forces behind the earliest European maritime explorers was exchange and conflict with the growing Ottoman Empire: some players sought resources in their own or other powers' hinterland: the Portuguese, blocked from trading directly with India, found an alternative while exchanging African slaves for gold from West African mines and went around the Horn of Africa to cut into the profitable Muslim trade in spices in the Arab Sea. Such limited enterprises eventually evolved into an entire, highly profitable, new area of world trade, the triangular Atlantic trade, exchanging wares from Europe, the Americas and Africa. This trade triangle included slaves as an essential means of exchange and production.[7] The Ottomans sought rowing slaves whom they needed in growing numbers to fill their galleys, to protect the essential grain trade connecting Egypt and Constantinople/Istanbul, the metropolis revived after the 1453 Ottoman conquest. Galleys remained more navigable in the unpredictable winds of the island-studded eastern Mediterranean for some time, even though occidental maritime powers cruising the open oceans increasingly replaced rowers with sails. Thus, beyond easy access to labour, there was a second force driving the slave raids in the steppe after 1453 and more so after the 1475 conquest of the Crimean port cities: burgeoning Ottoman demand in a context of Mediterranean conflict and European expansion as the sultan fitted major fleets, which sometimes resulted in astronomical prices for slaves.[8] Among the suppliers were the Tatar khanates and *ulus*[9] of Crimea, the Northern Black Sea Coast and of Kazan.

---

4 Ostrowski, 'The End of Muscovy'.
5 Penrose, 'Inner Asian Influences on the Earliest Russo-Chinese Trade and Diplomatic Contacts'.
6 Monahan, *The Merchants of Siberia*. Kollmann, *The Russian Empire 1450–1801*.
7 Eltis and Engerman, 'Dependence, Servility, and Coerced Labor in Time and Space'.
8 Davies, *Warfare, State and Society on the Black Sea Steppe, 1500–1700*; N. Sobers Khan, *Slaves Without Shackles: Forced Labour and Manumission in the Galata Court Registers, 1560–1572* (Berlin, 2015). Still a factor in the 1650s: Sanin, *Otnosheniia Rossii i Ukrainy s Krymskim Khanstvom v seredine XVII veka*, p. 194.
9 Often called hordes: *orda* is the ruler's tent.

The need to turn to the west and its increasing technical knowledge was especially evident at Kazan: miners sent by the Habsburg emperor with skills otherwise unavailable in Muscovy were central to collapse the city's walls, which in earlier campaigns had proved impregnable. This was only one aspect of the growing reliance on Europe, and Muscovy embraced this new trend, albeit fitfully and with major setbacks, by appealing to the common heritage, Christianity. The Orthodox Church had survived due to the tolerant, even supportive, attitude of the Mongols. Nevertheless, the Church resolutely changed its views against its former benefactors, starting intermittently from 1449 – the date of the Muscovite Church's autocephaly and its independence from Byzantine requirements in chronicle writing – and increasingly so in the century following the 1550s, while religious writing and the copying of manuscripts flourished.[10] Orientation to the West did not mean wholesale transfer, let alone official acceptance of Latin or Protestant precepts. As it relied on the untapped economic and political potential of Northern Rus' and, increasingly, Eurasian lands, as well as trade contacts, Moscow sought a specific angle in Byzantine teachings. Besides the haphazard older Slavic Orthodox tradition, it was the Byzantine experience of frontiers in Asia, the long history of alliance with the Mongol Empire, of confrontation and cohabitation with the Seljuq sultanate that conditioned Muscovy's return to its origins. Muscovy saw potential in learning from a world that resembled its own in many ways, and soon experienced a renaissance of Byzantine thought in the teachings of the Church Fathers. However, virtually nobody spoke or read Greek in Muscovy after the incomplete translation of the Bible and other Byzantine literature into Slavonic in the Kievan period. Muscovy relied on Western monks for its first full Bible translation using the Latin Vulgate as supplement under archbishop Gennadii of Novgorod in 1499. Greek Orthodox monks such as Maxim the Greek introduced textual criticism and biblical hermeneutics: European methods. Nevertheless, Muscovy stuck to autocephaly and renewed the patristic tradition.[11] These became markers of difference to the Latin churches and emphasized Muscovy's affiliation with the Orthodox churches of the eastern Mediterranean, Africa and Asia, with a view to its potential in Eurasia.

The evolving orientation to the European west also meant that new concepts were transferred via the western parts of former Rus' lands such as Novgorod or

---

10 A. Kleimola and G. Lenhoff, eds., *The Book of Royal Degrees and the Genesis of Russian Historical Consciousness/"Stepennaia kniga tsarskogo rodosloviia" i genezis russkago istoricheskogo soznaniia* (Bloomington IN, 2011); D. Ostrowski, 'The Mongols and Rus': Eight Paradigms', in A. Gleason, ed., *A Companion to Russian History* (Malden MA, 2009), pp. 66–86; C.J. Halperin, 'Paradigms of the Image of the Mongols in Medieval Russia', in V. Rabatzii, A. Pozzi, P.W. Geier and J.R. Krueger, eds., *The Early Mongols: Language, Culture and History. Studies in Honor of Igor de Rachewiltz on the Occasion of His 80th Birthday* (Bloomington IN, 2009), pp. 53–62.
11 A.I. Negrov, *Biblical Interpretation in the Russian Orthodox Church: A Historical and Hermeneutical Perspective* (Tübingen, 2008).

Ruthenia[12] to the centre of Muscovite power, where they initially created misunderstandings and controversy in the elite but in some cases became part of accepted culture and reached out to the wider population.[13]

This complex religious renaissance was, moreover, fed by frequent transottoman contacts with clerics from the Greek Orthodox mother church, now under Ottoman control, who were often educated in Padua at the Orthodox university in exile.[14] But while historians have commented on the revival's religious expressions for a long time, what moved Muscovites above all has been lost almost entirely to modern historiography, not to speak of public opinion or modern Russian historical consciousness. A new political culture emerged after the success at Kazan and it did so because it appealed to many people across Muscovy; just how wide that appeal was and what forms it took shall be studied here. This appeal held its own because the language used in the immediate run-up to Kazan and during the suppression of Tatar rebellions answered to one of the main grievances of many people living in Eastern Europe north of the steppe – namely the slave raids. Moreover, it was framed in an accessible Orthodox political language and imagery drawing on narratives of the Old Testament and popular saints' and miracle cults.

New Israel

Recent studies of the political and religious culture of Muscovy are definite about the prevalence of the New Israel theme.[15] They note that Muscovite sources defined their

---

12 Now part of Ukraine.
13 D.B. Miller, 'The Viskovatyi Affair of 1553–54. Official Art, the Emergence of Autocracy, and the Disintegration of Medieval Russian Culture', *Russian History*, 8, 3 (1981), pp. 293–332. For an example of the limits of reception: R. Romanchuk, 'The Reception of the Judaizer Corpus in Ruthenia and Muscovy: A Case Study of the Logic of Al-Ghazzali, the "Cipher in Squares," and the Laodicean Epistle', in V.V. Ivanov and J. Verkholantsev, eds., *Speculum Slaviae Orientalis: Muscovy, Ruthenia and Lithuania in the Late Middle Ages* (Moscow, 2005), pp. 144–165.
14 E. Wimmer and J. Henning, *Novgorod – ein Tor zum Westen?: Die Übersetzungstätigkeit am Hofe des Novgoroder Erzbischofs Gennadij in ihrem historischen Kontext (um 1500)* (Hamburg, 2005), pp. 113–116; E. Kraft, *Moskaus griechisches Jahrhundert: Russisch-griechische Beziehungen und metabyzantinischer Einfluss 1619–1694*, (Stuttgart, 1995); N.A. Chrissidis, *An Academy at the Court of the Tsars: Greek Scholars and Jesuit Education in Early Modern Russia* (DeKalb IL, 2016).
15 J. Raba, 'Moscow – the Third Rome or the New Jerusalem', in Osteuropa-Institut, ed., *Beiträge zur 7. Internationalen Konferenz zur Geschichte des Kiever und Moskauer Reiches* (Wiesbaden, 1995, pp. 297–308); Rowland, 'Moscow – the Third Rome or the New Israel?'; S. Goncharov, 'Moskau neues Jerusalem (Moskva, novyj Ierusalim)', in N. Franz, ed., *Lexikon der russischen Kultur* (Darmstadt, 2002); M.V. Dmitriev, 'Predstavleniia o "russkom" v kul'ture Moskovskoi Rusi XVI veka', in *Obshchestvo, gosudarstvo, verkhovnaia vlast' v Rossii v Srednie veka i rannee Novoe vremia v kontekste istorii Evropy i Azii (X–XVIII stoletiia): Mezhdunarodnaia konferentsiia, posviashchennaia 100-letiiu so dnia rozhdeniia akademika L.V. Cherepnina. Moskva, 30 noiabria – 2 dekabria 2005 g.*

people as the New Israel and that the tsar was praised as a new Moses. These mostly recent, as well as a very few older, studies prove that these expressions occurred much more frequently than the few times Muscovite sources called the grand principality or, after 1547, the Tsarist Empire, the 'Third Rome'. Since the schism of the 1660s, the latter notion was exclusively cherished among sectarians. It only became popular in late imperial Russia, when it was promoted by Neo-Romantic scholars and idealist philosophers of the late nineteenth century and the 'Silver Age', among whom most notably Vladimir Solov'ev and the émigré Nikolai Berdiaev, who perceived Communism as a new Russian Messianism. This interpretation was revived during the first decade of the Cold War, since it seemed to furnish an enemy stereotype of an empire bent on grasping world power.[16] For a time this erroneous notion almost superseded knowledge of Muscovy's more pervasive political ideas. Thus, in 1935 R. Stupperich in an article about Kyïv went, tongue in cheek, as far as claiming that, 'in any case, there is never talk of Moscow as the Third [sic] Jerusalem'.[17] The notion of the Third Rome has led numerous commentators to speculate that Muscovy was on a universalist quest to conquer the world, based on the idea that it was a new Roman Empire bringing salvation to an apocalyptic world.[18] Such a notion caters to Russian imperial and later, Cold War and specifically Stalinist National-Communist sensibilities.[19] But for a relatively small, all too often starved, and remote principality in the forests of Northern Eurasia, which

---

(Moskva, 2005), pp. 182–187; G. Lenhoff, 'The Tale of Tamerlane in the *Royal Book of Degrees*', in G. Svak, ed., *Mesto Rossii v Evrazii/The Place of Russia in Eurasia* (Budapest, 2001), pp. 121–129. For the Time of Troubles: I. Gruber, *Orthodox Russia in Crisis: Church and Nation in the Time of Troubles* (DeKalb IL, 2012).

16 H. Schaeder in 1929 wrote with idealistic hyperbole: 'The idea of Moscow as the Third Rome associates to the first political relations between the Moscow state and the world of European states a first intellectual classification [*geistige Einordnung*] of Russia within world history, which it detonates'. H. Schaeder, *Moskau das dritte Rom: Studien zur Geschichte der politischen Theorien in der slavischen Welt* (Darmstadt, 1957), p. 77. It remains a global classification and association to foreign relations which rates artistic rareness, achievement and completion above reception in extant Muscovite sources.

17 R. Stupperich, 'Kiev – das zweite Jerusalem: Ein Beitrag zur Geschichte des ukrainisch-russischen Nationalbewusstseins', *Zeitschrift für slavische Philologie*, 12, 3–4 (1935), pp. 332–354.

18 In textbooks, e.g. P.N. Stearns, M. Adas, S.B. Schwartz and M.J. Gilbert, eds., *World Civilizations: The Global Experience* (Boston, 2011), p. 506; O. Figes, *A People's Tragedy: The Russian Revolution 1891–1924* (London, 1996), p. 62; W.H. McNeill, *Europe's Steppe Frontier, 1500–1808* (Chicago, 1964), p. 521. H.N. Kennedy, 'Review of Byzantium. The Decline and Fall by John J. Norwich, London 1995', *The New York Times Book Review* (07 Jan. 1996); *The New York Times*, 16 Sep. 1984. Some Western leaders picked up the notion: e.g. Helmut Kohl, quoted in *The New York Times*, 16 September 1984. For a more cautious approach to the 'Third Rome' notion in a grand synthesis with a blind spot for the context of New Israel see Hildermeier, *Geschichte Russlands*, pp. 213–214, 386.

19 On parallel developments of Roman imperial imagery in the late nineteenth-century Russian and British empires, see M. Poe, 'Moscow the Third Rome: The Origins and Transformations of a "Pivotal Moment"', *Jahrbücher für Geschichte Osteuropas*, 49, 3 (2001), pp. 412–429; E. Hausteiner, *Greater than Rome. Neubestimmungen britischer Imperialität 1870–1914* (Frankfurt am Main, 2015);

for much of the time was beset by stronger forces and often enough survived only due to its remoteness, it would have been utter nonsense.

Recent studies and overviews have left no doubt that our extant sources do not allow for such an interpretation of aspiring universal power in Muscovy, most certainly not as the centre of its worldview. Very few sixteenth-century sources mention the concept of the 'Third Rome'. Even these few are almost exclusively concerned with the church defending its privileges against the grand prince, or the Muscovite Orthodox Church announcing its pretence to prestige. In some early manuscripts, the abbreviation $r^{sl}m$ (Jerusalem: [E]$r^{[u]s[a]l[i]}m$) is found in the place where a later copyist misread *rim* (Rome). Early documents refer to the protection of the Novgorod Church against Muscovy rather than to Moscow. Where sources refer to Moscow as the 'Third Rome', they relate to the church and never primarily to the state, except for the founding of the Moscow Patriarchate in 1598.[20] Only twice official documents mention the 'Third Rome' theory in rather specific contexts: first, referring to the 1589 foundation of the Moscow Patriarchate and second, when the doctrines of *translatio imperii* it implies were banned by church council in 1666/67, intended as a remedy against the Old Believers sect.[21] The 'Third Rome' as a concept of empire was projected backwards to the sixteenth century by historians of the state school and by Russian nationalists in the late nineteenth century.[22] Before the reforms of the metropolitan Nikon in the second half of the seventeenth century, references to the 'Third Rome' even as it concerned the Church were one small cluster among a large array of church statements seeking to dignify Muscovite Orthodoxy and enhance unity in a situation of increasing external chaos, as Muscovy threatened to become a slaving zone.[23] The most important in scope of meaning, its closeness to politics, and frequency in the sources was the idea that Muscovy was the New Israel.

Semyonov, 'How Five Empires Shaped the World and How this Process Shaped those Empires', p. 44.

20 P. Bushkovitch, Review of Tretii Rim: Istoki i evoliutsiia russkoi srednevekovoi kontseptsii (XV–XVI vv.) by Nina V. Sinitsyna, Moscow 1998, *Kritika*, 1, 2 (2008), pp. 391–399. F. Kämpfer, 'Die Lehre vom Dritten Rom – pivotal moment, historiographische Folklore?', *Jahrbücher für Geschichte Osteuropas*, 49, 3 (2001), pp. 430–441; Raba, 'Moscow – the Third Rome or the New Jerusalem'; D. Ostrowski, '"Moscow the Third Rome" as Historical Ghost', in S.T. Brooks, ed., *Byzantium: Faith and Power (1261–1557): Perspectives on Late Byzantine Art and Culture* (New York, 2007), pp. 170–179, here pp. 173–175. Historians researching the 'Third Rome' notion now agree that it did not pertain to imperial power and expansion, but to protecting the church: Khunchukashvili, 'Die heiligen Städte als eschatologische Legitimationssymbole der Zarenmacht unter den Rjurikiden', p. 145.

21 Poe, 'Moscow the Third Rome', p. 418.

22 Ibid., pp. 419–425.

23 On changing perceptions of the Mongols by ecclesiastical writers see Ostrowski, 'The Mongols and Rus'"; Rowland, 'Moscow – the Third Rome or the New Israel?', p. 614. Against this background, metropolitan Makarii included the letters of Filofei of Pskov in his *Velikie Minei Chet'i*, a vast collection of church documents for internal use that was never printed in Muscovy. In the 'History of Kazan', the

Recently, Gail Lenhoff went one step further: she demonstrates that one of the main documents propagating this theme, the 'Book of Royal Degrees', was motivated by the conquest of Kazan. In other words, it was related to political culture and contemporary historical events. Even so, in Lenhoff's interpretation it was mainly religious in content and provenance.[24] This was first highlighted in recent historiography by Joel Raba, who noticed that in an overwhelming number of contemporary sources Moscow is called the Second Jerusalem and Muscovy the New Israel. However, in his reading this 'cornerstone of Muscovite self-definition' belonged entirely to the 'sphere of ideal, abstract notions'. The resources of the Muscovite state did not allow it to challenge the Ottomans militarily by posing as an heir of the New Jerusalem or the New Rome, two names given to their city by the inhabitants of Constantinople. Actual activity was therefore limited to financial support for the Greek Orthodox Church and its clerical emissaries, though this form of almsgiving increased over time. Thus, the concept of Muscovy as the New Israel did not in Raba's interpretation mean a political mission, which he defined rather narrowly as one involving liberation of Greek Orthodox believers. Even so, in his view the idea of the New Israel mysteriously but strongly 'influenced the political thinking of Muscovite Russia'.[25] This thinking informed subsequent studies of Muscovy as the New Israel, which mention the connection with the liberation of slaves only briefly, if at all.[26] Muscovite religious-political ideas have been chalked down too easily to eschatological thinking that urged the tsar to lead the people to salvation, while the historical dimension has been neglected, although Muscovites at the time had no trouble reading historical events as prefiguration.[27]

In a recent re-investigation of the conquest of Kazan, Matthew Romaniello convincingly demonstrates that Muscovite rule immediately went into crisis mode and

---

third Rome 'really a second Kyiv' promises 'a bright future [. . .] in this country' after the fall of the Great Horde, which is definitely not the idea of aiming at global power. T.F. Volkova, *Kazanskaia Istoriia*, 2006–2011, http://www.pushkinskijdom.ru/Default.aspx?tabid=5148 (accessed 8 July 2017), chapter 5; Poe, 'Moscow the Third Rome', pp. 417–418.

24 G. Lenhoff, 'Politics and Form in the Stepennaia Kniga', in G. Lenhoff and A. Kleimola, eds., *The Book of Royal Degrees and the Genesis of Russian Historical Consciousness/"Stepennaia kniga tsarskogo rodosloviia" i genezis russkago istoricheskogo soznaniia* (Bloomington IN, 2011), pp. 157–174. C.J. Halperin, '*Stepennaia kniga* on the Reign of Ivan IV: Omissions from Degree 17', *The Slavonic and East European Review*, 89, 1 (2011), p. 63.

25 Raba, 'Moscow – the Third Rome or the New Jerusalem', p. 307.

26 M.S. Flier, 'Golden Hall Iconography and the Makarian Initiative', in V. Kivelson, M. Flier, N.S. Kollmann and K. Petrone, eds., *The New Muscovite Cultural History: A Collection in Honor of Daniel B. Rowland* (Bloomington IN, 2009), pp. 63–76, here pp. 72, 73; Rowland, 'Moscow – the Third Rome or the New Israel?', here p. 600 at n. 22; A.P. Pavlov and M. Perrie, *Ivan the Terrible* (London, 2003), pp. 48–49.

27 Prefiguration as a principle of salvation history will be discussed in chapter 3.

required more than forty years to achieve peace.[28] Although the new territory remained predominantly Muslim and animist, analysis of propaganda texts and ritual has so far hardly strayed from the traditional reading that these sources interpreted events mainly in religious terms, as the victory of triumphant Orthodoxy over Islam. Such was also the gist of the only Russian (post-)imperial author who looked at the sources on the New Israel: N. I. Efimov's short study frames these motifs as an exclusionary 'theocratic ideology', which he claims was established with the baptism of Rus'. On the one hand, his source basis is broad, covering all periods until the end of the seventeenth century. On the other hand, it is restricted to – mostly – sacral texts of often limited exposure beyond the church. He presents his sources in a very narrow fashion and without context, significantly exaggerating the theocratic ideal. Indeed, he claims that theocracy was the basic principle of the various forms in which New Israel imagery was assimilated by the Muscovites.[29] He leaves unanswered the question of whether there was any attempt to overcome the imaginary and practical lines that separated, on the one hand, Christian Orthodoxy from Islam, and on the other, elite from ordinary Muscovites. In effect, recent as well as a few earlier studies stop short of studying the popular acclaim enjoyed by casting Muscovy as the New Israel. Moreover, the symbolic or real connections between the slave raids and these concepts have so far not been appreciated.

Moreover, if Muscovy had not developed a political culture with widespread appeal that derived from these representations, it would be seriously at odds with all standards of contemporary European thought. Early modern European political philosophy was firmly convinced of the special leadership model contained in the common Christian literature on the Old Testament. Moses appeared to these thinkers as the model of a successful political leader, because he led his people out of slavery in Egypt to the Promised Land and managed to forge a state out of tents.[30] These ideas circulated widely in medieval and early modern Europe,[31] and it would require an explanation if Muscovy, increasingly seeking contact with this never completely forgotten world,[32] had not seized on it.[33]

---

[28] Romaniello, *The Elusive Empire*.
[29] Efimov, *Rus'–novyi Izrail'*.
[30] D.C. Rapoport, 'Moses, Charisma, and Covenant', *The Western Political Quarterly*, 32, 2 (1979), pp. 123–143.
[31] A. Hastings, 'Holy Lands and their Political Consequences', *Nations and Nationalism*, 9, 1 (2003), pp. 29–54; G. Murdock, *Calvinism on the Frontier, 1600–1660. International Calvinism and the Reformed Church in Hungary and Transylvania* (New York, 2000); C.W. Prior, 'Hebraism and the Problem of Church and State in England, 1642–1660', *The Seventeenth Century*, 28, 1 (2013), pp. 37–61.
[32] Ostrowski, 'The End of Muscovy'.
[33] On cultural transfers: D. Ostrowski, 'Towards the Integration of Early Modern Rus' into World History', in C. Witzenrath, ed., *Eurasian Slavery, Ransom and Abolition in World History, 1200–1860* (Farnham, Surrey, 2015), pp. 105–143, here pp. 111–112.

One widespread paradigm which scholars only recently began to question stood in the way of a broader conceptualization and study of these questions. Muscovites were believed to have valued autocracy above freedom due to Mongol influence. This Orientalist interpretation depicts a remote culture as an incomprehensible and dangerous 'other' without bothering to explain why it was the way it was.[34] Although numerous popular books and frequently even textbooks of Russian history contain the claim that Mongol influence led to autocracy, it is no longer tenable. Despite the persistent prejudice the Mongols were not inherently despotic. The most recent works by historians of the Mongols and the Turkish people of Central Asia that look at traditions of political rule and state structures of the Mongol khanates show that except for very few outstanding military leaders such as Chinggis Khan, the most influential figures in the successor states to his empire were not autocratic khans, but rather the council of four *qarachi* beys, the heads of the four leading clans in the realm.[35] During one defining event in 1432, the khan of the Golden Horde tried to install a strong grand prince in Moscow as an ally, Iurii Dmitriev, brother of Dmitrii Donskoi and next in line according to the senioral principle. However, in alliance with the three weaker members of the khan's council, the Muscovite boyar Vsevolozh told the khan that this plan would put Iurii's ally, the most influential of the beys, Shirin-Teginia, in an unassailable position which threatened the khan himself. The khan changed his mind and put the weaker, underage candidate on the Muscovite throne. Vsevolozh's interference replicated Mongol structures of power in Rus', which were more durable and flexible than the sheer dominance of one person over all other dignitaries. As an important side-effect, the boyar's intervention and the khan's decision strengthened a recent trend in Muscovy towards primogeniture at the very point of its most severe crisis during internecine warfare caused by the succession dispute; a trend which was to become a pillar of Muscovy's strength.[36]

Such post-Mongolian practices eventually prepared Muscovy to assimilate exile Tatars as well as to accommodate the needs of the growing multi-faith state.[37] This

---

34 E. Adamovsky, 'Euro-Orientalism and the Making of the Concept of Eastern Europe in France, 1810–1880', *The Journal of Modern History*, 77, 3 (2005), pp. 591–628; M. David-Fox, P. Holquist and M. Martin, eds., *Orientalism and Empire in Russia* (Bloomington IN, 2006); D. Schimmelpenninck van der Oye, *Russian Orientalism: Asia in the Russian Mind from Peter the Great to the Emigration* (New Haven CT, 2010); V. Tolz, 'Orientalism, Nationalism, and Ethnic Diversity in Late Imperial Russia', *The Historical Journal*, 48, 1 (2005), pp. 127–150; A. Jersild, *Orientalism and Empire* (Montreal, 2002).
35 D. Sneath, *The Headless State: Aristocratic Orders, Kinship Society, and Misrepresentations of Nomadic Inner Asia* (New York, 2007); C. Atwood, 'Ulus Emirs, Keshig Elders, Signatures, and Marriage Partners: The Evolution of a Classic Mongol Institution', in D. Sneath, ed., *Imperial Statecraft: Political Forms and Techniques of Governance in Inner Asia, Sixth–Twentieth Centuries* (Bellingham WA, 2006), pp. 141–173.
36 Kollmann, *The Russian Empire 1450–1801*, p. 48.
37 C. Woodworth, 'The Birth of the Captive Autocracy: Moscow, 1432', *Journal for Early Modern History*, 13, 1 (2009), pp. 49–69.

model of the 'king in council', sometimes called *monarchia mixta*, resounded in Europe as a way of counterbalancing the various drawbacks of available forms of government, something already pointed out by Aristotle. It predominated in Eurasia during the early modern period, albeit with various degrees of the council's power and its institutionalisation in legal, codified form. This book aims to contribute to unravelling the question of why the latter was slowly degrading in Muscovy.[38]

The myth of the all-powerful Muscovite tsar in historiography was based on the traditional interpretation of the *pomest'e* land grant to servitors as a conditional, temporary, and non-inheritable endowment. Russian nobles are therefore often perceived as dependent on the tsar, without their own economic basis. Contrary to prevailing interpretations, recent studies have demonstrated that the 'conditional land grant' was inheritable and exchanged for other landed property from the start: it was donated and even 'sold' in the practice of unequal exchange.[39] Its value as evidence of increased asymmetrical dependency on the tsar is limited. Valerie Kivelson's landmark study of the provincial servitors asked 'how the Muscovite autocracy, with its seemingly impracticable combination of absolutist pretensions and chronic shortages of bureaucratic and disciplinary might, managed to govern its ever-growing territories so successfully'.[40] It was achieved with the participation of the provincial gentry. Studies of the expansion into Siberia and the middle Volga, where the cossacks were in an analogous position and even Tatars negotiated certain privileges, have produced similar results.[41]

Recent reassessments of the cultural aspect of Muscovite politics and empire have insisted on the incongruous character of its statements, which, together with the accompanying pictorial and ritual programme, had the status of political imagery rather than that of an ideology. The elements of this imagery were the role of boyars as advisors and of the tsar as accepting such righteous advice to generate the required support. Since the tsar was in a position unlike God, but analogous to God, he was to be humble, pious, and a protector to his people. The people saw themselves

---

[38] D. Ostrowski, 'Muscovite Adaptation of Steppe Political Institutions', *Kritika*, 1, 2 (2000), pp. 267–304.

[39] D. Ostrowski, 'Early *Pomest'e* Grants as a Historical Source', *Oxford Slavonic Papers*, 33, 2000, pp. 36–63; V.E. Hammond, *State Service in Sixteenth Century Novgorod: The First Century of the Pomestie System* (Lanham MD, 2009); C.B. Stevens, *Russia's Wars of Emergence, 1460–1730* (Harlow, 2007); Hellie, *Enserfment and Military Change in Muscovy*; A. Stanziani, *Bâtisseurs d'empires: Russie, Chine et Inde à la croisée des mondes, XVe-XIXe siècle* (Paris, 2012).

[40] Kivelson, *Autocracy in the Provinces*, p. 2.

[41] Romaniello, *The Elusive Empire*; Witzenrath, *Cossacks and the Russian Empire, 1598–1725*. See also S. Bogatyrev, 'Localism and Integration in Muscovy', in S. Bogatyrev, ed., *Russia Takes Shape: Patterns of Integration from the Middle Ages to the Present* (Helsinki, 2005), pp. 59–127; B.J. Boeck, *Imperial Boundaries: Cossack Communities and Empire-Building in the Age of Peter the Great* (Cambridge, 2009). On the central practice of imperial elites negotiating deals for discrete groups, see now Kollmann, *The Russian Empire 1450–1801*.

as led by the tsar on a path towards salvation, while living in a bright place.[42] Scholars understand all of these images to be part of the New Israel imagery, but why and how this concoction occurred and interrelated has scarcely been investigated. It is one of the aims of this book to provide a new angle on this Muscovite worldview and to appreciate its internal coherence.

Liberation from slavery as justification

The political language of the Muscovite conquest of Kazan has been intensely studied in the 1960s. Owing to the nature of the sources, the pages of these studies are sprinkled with – often oblique – references to slavery, but in their conclusions and partly also in the text, authors either play down this element of Muscovite perception or manage to sidestep it entirely. Anyone with a general interest in the rhetoric of slavery will ultimately be frustrated with these contradictory studies. One example is Frank Kämpfer, who in his otherwise solid and insightful study admits only in passing that the conquest of Kazan 'was undertaken above all for the benefit of the captives, or so [the sources] emphasize time and again', and generally evades the issue altogether.[43] He commendably sides with the victims at the time of conquest – the Tatars – but downplays the large number of sufferers on the Muscovite side; he also overlooks the parts played by Tatars in the service of the tsar. Ultimately, this becomes a blame game. With a mental leap, the Muscovite legitimation for the conquest, namely the fate of captives urgently awaiting liberation, becomes instead

> a habitual pattern of thought, for the conquest of Kazan cannot be explained as an act of defence. The prisoner motif, which covered this fiction, was subsequently demonstrated plainly by lining up the prisoners along the way forming speaking choirs. The real event, the conquest of foreign territory, was wrapped in euphemistic formulae.[44]

Such implicit and unhistorical comparison with Stalinist festivals is not warranted by the source, which merely says that 'the boyars and all Orthodox people met the tsar' and praised him.[45] Kämpfer's interpretation presupposes an all-powerful state and a coercive Stalinist festive culture, which did not exist in the sixteenth century. Moreover, he diminished the import of captivity by selectively emphasizing those

---

42 D. Rowland, 'The Problem of Advice in Muscovite Tales about the Time of Troubles', *Russian History*, 6, 2 (1979), pp. 259–283; Kivelson, *Cartographies of Tsardom*; Kollmann, *The Russian Empire 1450–1801*.
43 F. Kämpfer, *Die Eroberung von Kasan 1552 als Gegenstand der zeitgenössischen russischen Historiographie* (Wiesbaden, 1969), pp. 92, 100–101.
44 Ibid., p. 96.
45 Tikhomirov, *Letopisets nachala tsarstva*, pp. 109, 112.

who stayed on after manumission.[46] It is likely that many stayed, but had no impact on the perceptions of Muscovites. In his blow-by-blow discussion of the campaigns against Kazan, Kämpfer relegated the motivation of liberation from captivity to the second plane where he mentioned it at all. But it was clearly uppermost on the mind of the scribe, as I will show below.[47]

Kämpfer mentioned the concept of the New Israel as self-description of Muscovites. However, in his reading its most important underlying idea is the 'inner link between past and future events' within the framework of salvation history, which is relegated to the religious expectations of the Second Coming of Christ. In its transcendental, eschatological fixation, this is a rather lofty claim left unsubstantiated.[48] Limited to general statements about the importance of religion and salvation history, Kämpfer's conclusion leaves unexplored the complex web of meaning woven from notions of slavery, redemption and biblical Exodus motifs in Muscovite sources about the conquest, some aspects of which he scattered in the body text.[49] The image of the tsar as liberator, however limited or broad its following may have been, was unlikely to persist during the existence of the Soviet Union: Soviet historians were not allowed to mention it, and to their Western counterparts such a view was beyond the widely unquestioned, orientalist depiction of Russia current among most historians and intellectuals.[50]

Another important analysis of the Kazan events was Jaroslaw Pelenski's interpretation, first published in the 1960s–1970s. His ascription of nationalising intentions to metropolitan Makarii and Ivan IV[51] was, with some justification, rejected as too overtly based on teleological theories borrowed from the sociology of modernisation. Due to the nature of the sources, Pelenski could not avoid describing the ideology of liberation from slavery.[52] However, it is no coincidence that this went almost unnoticed, while debates were concerned with his overall conclusions about the national and the religious motivations of the conquest.[53] Pelenski claimed a

---

46 Kämpfer, *Die Eroberung von Kasan 1552 als Gegenstand der zeitgenössischen russischen Historiographie*, p. 117.
47 Ibid., p. 35.
48 Ibid; Kämpfer, *Die Eroberung von Kasan 1552 als Gegenstand der zeitgenössischen russischen Historiographie*, p. 63. See also chapter 4.
49 Cf. Kämpfer, *Die Eroberung von Kasan 1552 als Gegenstand der zeitgenössischen russischen Historiographie*, p. 37. See chapter 3 for a discussion of the implications of redemptionist imagery in this world and in the hereafter.
50 David-Fox, Holquist and Martin, *Orientalism and Empire in Russia*; E.W. Said, *Orientalism* (New York, 1978).
51 E.L. Keenan, 'Muscovy and Kazan': Some Introductory Remarks on the Patterns of Steppe Diplomacy', *Slavic Review* 26, 4 (1967), pp. 548–558.
52 Pelenski, *Russia and Kazan*, pp. 232–250.
53 Lately, Romaniello, *The Elusive Empire*, p. 32. For a critique of the modernist assumptions about a national ideology in Pelenski's book about Muscovy and Kazan, see E.L. Keenan, Review of Russia

'national' justification for the conquest of Kazan besides the historical and religious arguments and dynastic claims. His topical chapter is almost entirely built on the 'History of Kazan', a complex, literate and re-edited source which was, however, widely distributed in the seventeenth century.[54] The 'History's' main argument that Pelenski interprets as 'national' is that there was a dragon living in Kazan, an allegory of the Tatars, who kidnapped Orthodox Russians. Moreover, this land is 'flowing from milk and honey' (Joshua 5:6), the promised land of the New Israel during the exodus from slavery.[55] In the last two paragraphs of the chapter on liberation and particularly in the Conclusion he played down the motif of liberating captives and barely mentioned its connection to the language of the Israelite Exodus employed in many of the sources. He artificially separated the captivity motif in a chapter and de-contextualised religious motivations, an analytical device which allowed for such a finale.[56]

Another serious allegation is that Pelenski's chosen body of sources does not stand up to scrutiny, as the date for many is unknown and their status as sources for the period of the conquest of Kazan is therefore questionable.[57] This may be true for some of them, particularly the 'History of Kazan', which was written, even according to the most optimistic investigators, several years after the conquest. Moreover, all available copies for the 'History' date from the seventeenth century. Therefore this text pertains to another part of our argument; it should not be mixed with the sources from the mid-sixteenth century; at least not until earlier manuscripts may be found.[58]

Because Pelenski's analysis was of uneven quality, many of his results need further testing. In particular the '*Letopisets nachala tsarstva* (The Chronicle of the Beginning of Tsardom)' and the '*Stepennaia kniga* (The Book of Royal Degrees)' contain a wealth of information about official Muscovite views, which can be corroborated by other sources, in particular the murals of the tsar's throne and ante rooms in the Golden Palace.[59] The period during which the murals were painted is established by the fire of 1547, which destroyed the earlier throne room, and the controversy spawned

---

and Kazan: Conquest and Imperial Ideology (1438–1560s) by Jaroslaw Pelenski, The Hague 1974, *Slavic Review*, 34, 3 (1975), pp. 585–588. Günther Stökl, quoting Keenan, pointed out that Makarii created a very complex, comprehensive ideology: G. Stökl, Review of The Velikie Minei Chetii and the Stepennaia Kniga of Metropolitan Makarii and the Origins of Russian National Consciousness by David B. Miller, Wiesbaden 1979, *Jahrbücher für Geschichte Osteuropas*, 29, 2 (1981), pp. 264–266.

54 E.L. Keenan, 'Coming to Grips with the Kazanskaya Istoriya: Some Observations on Old Answers and New Questions', *Annals of the Ukrainian Academy of Arts and Sciences in the U.S.*, 11, 1–2 (1964), pp. 143–183. On the *Kazanskaia Istoriia* see chapter 6.

55 The whole passage has been translated: Pelenski, *Russia and Kazan*, pp. 119–120, for the national argument see pp. 104–138. On dragons, see chapter 4.

56 Ibid., p. 292.

57 Keenan, Review of. Russia and Kazan: Conquest and Imperial Ideology (1438–1560s)'.

58 Qualifications, particularly regarding internal evidence in chapter 6, discussing Shah Ali.

59 On the role of the cross in the *Letopisets*, see chapter 4.

by them, settled in 1553.⁶⁰ However, the value of these sources for the political culture of Muscovy extends far beyond these narrow dates, as the 'Chronicle of the Beginning of Tsardom' was incorporated into all later chronicle projects.⁶¹

A few authors mention Muscovite ideas about the exodus and the liberation from slavery in passing. Charles Halperin, for example, who expertly deals with the period up to the early sixteenth century, claims that these ideas were

> of course conventional; [. . .] [The Mongols are] said to have "enslaved" Rus', the common sixteenth century Muscovite extravagance that resonated with the imagery of Exodus [. . .] and with the larger system of metaphors and ideas of Russia as the New Israel.⁶²

They are extravagant from the perspective of a scholar of medieval Muscovy, but this does not answer the question of how extravagance and conventionality fit together. Such evaluations beg the question whether there is a new quality in these sources which was absent in earlier centuries. When Halperin discusses the '*Skazanie o Mamaevom poboishche* (Tale of the Battle with Mamai)', of which hundreds of mainly seventeenth-century copies survive, he acknowledges that

> the concept of slavery (*rabota*) regarding Russo-Tatar relations started to appear after the 1480 "Stand on the Ugra River", especially in sixteenth-century Muscovite works associated with the metropolitan Makarii.⁶³

Despite this perceptive observation, albeit made in passing, Halperin's focus is on the question of whether Muscovite bookmen admitted to the 'reality' of Mongol and Tatar suzerainty over Muscovy in the period after the Mongol conquest until the fifteenth century. This leads him to dismiss the repeated claim in the sources of Tatars enslaving Rus' people as 'logical contradiction' and implicitly accuse the Muscovites

---

60 Rowland. 'Moscow – the Third Rome or the New Israel?'. M. Flier, 'Political Ideas and Ritual', in M. Perrie, ed., *Cambridge History of Russia*, vol. 1: *From Early Rus' to 1689* (Cambridge, 2006), pp. 387–408.
61 Major chronicles included the 'Chronicle of the Beginning of Tsardom': the 'Nikon Chronicle', the 'Illustrated Chronicle' and the 'L'vov Chronicle' and their manuscript copies. D.S. Likhachev and D.M. Bulanin, eds., *Slovar' knizhnikov i knizhnosti drevnei Rusi*, vol. 2: *Vtoraia polovina XIV – XVI v.*, pt. 2: *L – Ja* (Leningrad, 1989–2017). A.A. Shakhmatov, *Razbor sochineniia I.A. Tikhomirova "Obozrenie letopisnykh svodov Rusi Severo-Vostochnoi"* (Sanktpeterburg, 1899); A.A. Zimin, *I.S. Peresvetov i ego sovremenniki: Ocherki po istorii russkoi obshchestvenno-politicheskoi mysli serediny xvi veka* (Moskva, 1958), pp. 29–41; B.M. Kloss, *Nikonovskii svod i russkie letopisi XVI-XVII vekov* (Moskva, 1980), pp. 195–196; I.S. Lur'e, 'Genealogicheskaia skhema letopisei XI–XVI vv., vkliuchennykh v "Slovar' knizhnikov i knizhnosti Drevnei Rusi"', *Trudy Otdela drevnerusskoi literatury* (TODRL), 40 (1985), pp. 190–205.
62 C.J. Halperin, *The Tatar Yoke: The Image of the Mongols in Medieval Russia* (Bloomington IN, 2009), p. 186.
63 Ibid., pp. 127–128.

of false consciousness: khan Akhmat in 1480 could not have aimed to repeat what Batu had already accomplished more than two centuries earlier, except if the bookmen 'shunted aside questions of political suzerainty in favour of hostile religious rhetoric'.[64] Enslavement here and in much of specialised literature is understood merely in terms of foreign relations, as establishing suzerainty; moreover, expressions in contemporary texts are reductively understood as a 'calculated metaphorical "yoke of slavery"', which had no political content.[65] Regarding suzerainty, the Rus' principalities in the period of Mongol rule were not states in the modern sense, nor were they like European medieval princedoms owing oaths of fealty to a king or emperor. Princes asked the khan to be instated as grand prince to gain the backing of the Tatars. Meanwhile, Tatar slave raids were a recurring fact of life in the medieval period as Tatars sided with individual power-hungry Rus' princes, not a matter of bookish propaganda.[66] As the first chapters of this book have shown, these raids became more frequent in the last part of the fifteenth and throughout the sixteenth centuries as the Tatar realms disintegrated, discipline slackened, and demand for slaves in the sprawling Ottoman and Persian gunpowder empires increased. So it was not only the church that had an urgent and renewed reason to be concerned for its flock which was increasingly being taken away in droves, but also the princes of Rus', formerly beneficiaries of slave raiding and trading.

The analytic slant of earlier studies of the language employed in the accounts of the conquest of Kazan underestimated the narrative qualities especially of the admired 'Chronicle of the Beginning of Tsardom'.[67] What to these scholars appeared merely to be the repetitive use of the same motif in fact builds up to climax, starting slowly from an exposition towards the triple apex of the peace conditions and liberation of slaves, the conquest, and the festive return to Moscow.[68] This chapter will therefore present the narrative of the 'Chronicle' and focus on its integration of liberation imagery into the presentation of these events.

---

64 Ibid., p. 175.
65 Kämpfer, *Die Eroberung von Kasan 1552 als Gegenstand der zeitgenössischen russischen Historiographie*, p. 131; Halperin, *The Tatar Yoke*, p. 199; see also 180.
66 Langer, 'Slavery in the Appanage Era'. On raids by the Kazan Tatars: Pelenski, *Russia and Kazan*, pp. 233, 235–236.
67 D. Weber, *Erzählliteratur: Schriftwerk, Kunstwerk, Erzählwerk* (Göttingen, 1998).
68 Kämpfer questionably avers, 'A conquest that is justified [*begründet*] in itself and is seen as a matter of course does not need such a compilation of ever-repeated motifs'. Kämpfer, *Die Eroberung von Kasan 1552 als Gegenstand der zeitgenössischen russischen Historiographie*, p. 114.

The 1550s campaigns

Was the slave rhetoric of the sixteenth century, and its imagery of the New Israel, indeed 'religious rather than political'?[69] The '*Letopisets nachalo tsarstva*' is a suitable launch pad for answering this question. As mentioned above, the text has been studied before, but so far the interlocking motifs in the discourse of liberation from slavery have only been analysed separately, not in their narrative context.

The 'Chronicle of the Beginning of Tsardom' contains several parts which are connected by the overarching theme of the first years of Ivan IV's reign as tsar. The main portion describes the conflict with Kazan and the capture of the middle Volga Tatar capital. Its oldest part is identifiable by a heading at the start of this portion concealed in the text. The heading covers only the first, limited campaign of the young tsar against Kazan and the subsequent building of the mountain fortress of Sviiazhsk as a challenge and permanent presence on the lands of the Kazan Tatars, and a launch pad for his campaigns there. So the heading was written before the final conquest of the city, in the assumption that it was telling a completed story.[70] The title sets the tone for the whole of the remaining, larger part of the Chronicle:

> 'The Beginning of the Tale of How the All-Merciful and Man-loving God Performed the Most Famous Miracles Among Us Through Our Orthodox, Pious Tsar, Grand Prince Ivan Vasil'evich, the Sovereign and Autocrat of All Rus' [Liberating] the Orthodox Christians from Muslim Captivity and from the Slavery of the Godless Kazan Tatars, and About the Foundation of the Town of Sviiazhsk [. . .] in the Year 1551 [. . .]'.[71]

Assuming for a moment that Muscovites should not be taken too seriously when talking about liberating slaves, as Kämpfer and Pelenski concluded,[72] it is hardly possible that the 'Most Famous Miracles' should have been reserved for such relatively modest events by any Muscovite literate enough to write down this title – modest, that is, in comparison to the conquest in the following year which is not covered by the intra-textual caption. This mismatch and the later additions which were inserted at the end without editing the whole text and the caption contribute to the impression that at least the author or authors and the later copyists placed a high value on the aim of liberating captives. As will be shown below, this aim was seen as already achieved before the final conquest of Kazan in 1552.

This interpretation is supported by the very next lines of the 'Tale', in which Ivan is shown contemplating the situation of the country. His virtue as his people's

---

[69] Halperin, *The Tatar Yoke*, p. 128. Cf. Kämpfer and Pelenski above.
[70] Pelenski, *Russia and Kazan*, p. 205 agrees on the date of composition. He discusses this passage under the heading 'religious struggle'.
[71] Tikhomirov, *Letopisets nachala tsarstva*, p. 59.
[72] Kämpfer, *Die Eroberung von Kasan 1552 als Gegenstand der zeitgenössischen russischen Historiographie*; Pelenski, *Russia and Kazan*, p. 292.

shepherd is demonstrated by the fact that he finds the captivity and slavery of his fellow countrymen among the Tatars intolerable:

> Tsar [. . .] Ivan [. . .] saw the captivity of Christians [. . .], unbearable evils. [A]ll this evil was done by the godless Kazan Saracens.[73]

Therefore, the Chronicle in general and particularly this title and the ensuing portions of the text bear internal evidence that Muscovite writers applied the legitimating concept of liberating captives to the campaigns – even before the actual conquest of Kazan. This questions Pelenski's allegation that

> only when the struggle [over Kazan] reached its final stages, did the problem of captives come to be included in the ideological program.[74]

Since internal strife had plunged the country into disarray during Ivan IV's minority, and invited Kazan Tatar slave raids, it is hardly pertinent to argue that his first steps to close the slaving zone were 'late'. To underline Pelenski's conviction that religious concerns were not only more important but also different from concerns over the captives, in his Conclusion he cites in full length an ecclesiastical eulogy written in the early 1560s, 'In Praise of Ivan IV and His Host for the Victory Against the Kazan Tatars', which according to Pelenski 'summarizes [the religious motivation] well'. At variance with his usual treatment of sources, which he translated throughout his book, here in the Conclusion only the original Russian is quoted, confined to the footnote. It betrays Pelenski's confusion about his own interpretation and categorization of motives for the conquest that the eulogy compares Ivan's accomplishments to those of great rulers of the past and emphasizes deliverance from slavery in a way that is most relevant:

> And you, o sovereign, god-crowned, with God's help have destroyed the ungodly sons of Hagar and liberated Orthodox Christians from slavery and captivity.[75]

Liberation in the 'Chronicle of the Beginning of Tsardom'

The interconnected themes of religion, slavery and liberation in the 'Chronicle of the Beginning of Tsardom' cannot be disentangled – something the above-mentioned scholars tried in vain – without losing some of the meaning of the source; they form one closely interrelated programme. Religion forms part of and informs the thinking about liberation. The first sentence after the internal title already mentioned sets the scene for most of the text:

---

73 Tikhomirov, *Letopisets nachala tsarstva*, pp. 59–60.
74 Pelenski, *Russia and Kazan*, p. 292.
75 Ibid. On Hagarites, see chapter 6.

> Tsar [. . .] Ivan [. . .] saw the captivity of Christians, streams of Christian blood and numerous holy churches destroyed, which are unbearable evils. As I say, all this evil was done by the godless Kazan Saracens. Thus, the honourable soul of our tsar, chosen by God, could not bear these hardships of Christianity in captivity, and he said to himself: "Merciful God [!] By the prayers of your pure mother, by those of the saints and our Russian miracle workers I was put before these Orthodox lands and all people as tsar and shepherd, leader and ruler, to rule these people steadfastly according to Orthodoxy, guard them from all ills and all hardships befalling them. Lord, help me and redeem [izbavi] your captured slaves (plennykh rab)[76] from the heathens. For he is truly the good shepherd who gives his soul for [his] sheep.[77]

The task put before Ivan in this text is to save both his subjects – at this stage we can assume, the Christian subjects – and simultaneously the Church. The text interlaces mundane duties with spiritual care in the quote from the 'Letter to the Ugra' about the tsar as a good shepherd.[78] It stresses care for his subjects, who are to be liberated from foreign bonds just in the way attributed to Moses as a link between the spheres of politics and religion.[79]

At the beginning of Ivan's first decisive measure in foreign relations as recently crowned ruler, with the fresh title of tsar added to the grand princes' list of designations in 1547, the author or authors of the 'Chronicle of the Beginning of Tsardom' deployed this programmatic speech as a literary device framed as introspection. It links the obligations and expectations directed at the God-chosen tsar to the plan of liberating the Muscovite slaves in Kazan. The immediate background to this decision were several large-scale Kazanian slave raids during the prolonged, politically instable period of Ivan's minority, as well as the more regularly occurring, devastating Crimean raids and the failed attempts to place Kazan firmly under Muscovite suzerainty.[80] Rather than mere pretext or an outrageous break with the conventions of steppe politics,[81] the tsar thus addressed the spectre of the war on three fronts which Moscow had faced when Ivan was underage. These raids were part of a major overhaul of Crimean foreign relations, aiming to preserve stability and the balance of forces, grind down an ascending Muscovy and prevent it from taking over Eastern Europe.[82] In turning against this Crimean policy and fighting the

---

[76] 'Slave' here denotes the biblical reference of the believers to themselves before God, whereas 'captured' underlines the notion of mundane captivity, recalling the Mosaic paradigm.
[77] Tikhomirov, *Letopisets nachala tsarstva*, pp. 59–60.
[78] See below.
[79] Rapoport, 'Moses, Charisma, and Covenant', pp. 123–130.
[80] Davies, *Warfare, State and Society on the Black Sea Steppe, 1500–1700*, pp. 14–15; Pelenski. *Russia and Kazan*, pp. 233, 235–236.
[81] Kämpfer, *Die Eroberung von Kasan 1552 als Gegenstand der zeitgenössischen russischen Historiographie*, p. 117; Keenan, 'Muscovy and Kazan', pp. 548–558.
[82] M. Arens and D. Klein, 'Neues Forschungsprojekt am Ungarischen Institut München: "Das frühneuzeitliche Krimkhanat zwischen Orient und Okzident: Dependenzen und autonome Entwicklungsmöglichkeiten an der Schnittstelle zwischen orthodoxer, lateinischer und muslimischer Welt"', *Ungarn-Jahrbuch*, 27 (2004), pp. 492–498.

concomitant, smaller, demand-driven slave raids, Ivan may not have served world peace, but this was realpolitik. The religious argument was key to organising the desired no-slaving zone.[83] Moreover, the 'Chronicle' does not spell out the aim of conquering Kazan from the outset. The aim it presented is the challenge to the predators on human beings: an aim consistent with a no-slaving zone.

In the description of the campaign of 1551, the chronicle several times calls attention to the motivation of liberating captives, underlining the main theme of justification of the campaigns. Right after the initial introspective speech, Ivan assembles his advisors, among them Tatars from Kasimov and elsewhere, and calls on his retainer Shah Ali, a Chinggisid with a claim to the throne of Kazan. For strategic reasons, they decide to set up a new fortress in a strategic position on the hill at the confluence of the river Sviiaga and the Volga, close to Kazan. Directly afterwards, Ivan proceeds to the cathedral, where he meets metropolitan Makarii and the higher clerics. He entreats the metropolitan to pray continuously and engage in pilgrimages to 'holy places', so that

> Christ will send his mercy, [. . .] [and] offers to poor Christianity the liberation from Kazan slavery.[84]

Just about two months later, in May 1551, the Muscovite army took the Kazan suburbs. This was just a brief episode, a surprise attack early in the morning, but the chronicle mentions specifically that they 'liberated many Russian captives'.[85] After thus confirming the ideological justifications of deliverance from slavery and arousing awe in the Kazanians, the advance troop met up with the tsar's main army. They had moved more slowly down the Volga to the mouth of the river Sviiaga, where they swiftly set up the new fortress on a steep hill. As one of their first measures, they made forays to subdue the locals. The conditions put before the Cheremis and Chuvash during negotiations, people heretofore subservient to Kazan, emphasize that everything remained as it was, including the tax payable to the Tatars, the *iasak*. However, in one specific regard conditions diverged from Kazanian rule: they were not allowed to capture Russians and had to release all captives: 'and they are not to keep any Rus' captives, they must all be liberated (*oslobozhati*)'.[86]

---

[83] See chapter 1 for the analytic concept of the slaving zone.
[84] Tikhomirov, *Letopisets nachala tsarstva*, p. 60.
[85] Ibid., p. 61.
[86] Kämpfer, *Die Eroberung von Kasan 1552 als Gegenstand der zeitgenössischen russischen Historiographie*, pp. 61–62. See chapter 4 on this episode. Alternative translation: 'returned to their homes': E. Smolarz, 'Speaking about Freedom and Dependency: Representations and Experiences of Russian Enslaved Captives in Central Asia in the First Half of the 19th Century', *Journal of Global Slavery*, 2, 1–2 (2017), pp. 44–71. However, placing this early form of freedom on a qualitatively different level than individual freedom ignores complexities on two counts: First, it is a common observation in premodern societies. '(To) free/*freien*/*vrijen*' and further variations in Germanic languages derive from the Indo-European root *pri-*, to treat in a friendly manner, to delight, to

During the campaign, the tsar treated all servitors and auxiliaries extraordinarily well and spent huge sums on provisions and salaries, so that all his servitors were fully contented. Such spending was unheard of in earlier chronicles, the authors of the 'Chronicle' remarked:

> In earlier chronicles there are no records about such expenditure, which the ruler extends to all his soldiers and those who have recently arrived [i.e. Tatars, Cheremis]. God may invest him to have mercy on the Christian people and redeem them from Barbarian assaults and liberate the[m] forever from the Tatars.[87]

The explanation given by the 'Chronicle' for Ivan's largesse is that he wanted to liberate 'the Orthodox people' from captivity. It is the monarchical programme of squeezing out competitors for taxable population, here the Tatars, by claiming a special, personal link to subjects; its mode is disruptive.[88]

As a result of the 1551 Muscovite campaign, Kazanian Tatars started to squabble with the Crimean Tatars who lived among them. Moreover, their former auxiliaries, the Chuvash of Arsk, 'quarrelled with the Crimean Tatars living in Kazan: "why don't you bow to the tsar [?]"', they asked their opponents provocatively.[89] Soon, Kazanians sought peace and the 'Chronicle' spells out repeatedly at length in the negotiations that they must liberate Muscovite captives. Already in the peace offer delivered by the noble *mirza* Enbars on behalf of the Kazanians, they proposed to deliver all captives and representatives of the Crimean khan remaining in the city:

---

please, to love, which returns in Old Church Slavonic *prijati*: *Oxford English Dictionary: OED online* (https://www.oed.com), 'free – v.' and etymology (accessed 11 Aug. 2021). Thus, 'to free someone' originates in wooing, courting, marrying and an array of denotations related to founding a family, an act of dependence, mutual or asymmetric, and the conferral of rights associated with affiliation to which '*osvobozhdati*' likewise refers. The same argument about older layers of meaning involving affiliation could be made regarding 'liberty'. See C. Schmidt, 'Freiheit in Russland. Eine Begriffshistorische Spurensuche', *Jahrbücher für Geschichte Osteuropas*, 55, 2 (2007), pp. 264–275, who revises earlier approaches denying the existence of freedom in Russia: G.P. Fedotov, 'Rußland und die Freiheit', *Merkur*, 5, 40 (1951), pp. 505–523; R. Wittram, 'Das Freiheitsproblem in der russischen inneren Geschichte', *Jahrbücher für Geschichte Osteuropas*, 2, 4 (1954), pp. 369–386; D. Geyer, 'Die Idee der Freiheit in der osteuropäischen Geschichte', in D. Geyer, ed., *Europäische Perspektiven der Perestrojka* (Tübingen, 1991), pp. 9–22; M. Hagen, '"Volju nevolja učit" – Die russische Freiheit', in M. Hagen, ed., *Die Russische Freiheit. Wege in ein paradoxes Thema* (Stuttgart, 2002), pp. 9–22. Second, while contemporary forms of institutionalised individual freedom have expanded beyond the family, community and parish, what remains common to all forms is the reliance on social, knowledge, symbolical, and material network nodes in a continuum ranging from strong asymmetric dependencies to mutual dependencies, also called freedom. Among these nodes prominently count constitutional guarantees and related worldviews. Cf. Winnebeck et al., *On Asymmetrical Dependency*.

87 Tikhomirov, *Letopisets nachala tsarstva*, p. 63.
88 See chapter 1. Miller, *The Problem of Slavery as History*.
89 Ibid. Question mark added by author.

[. . .] all the Kazan people bow to you, o Lord, so that the Lord show mercy [and] may his wrath be allayed, that he gives them tsar Shah Ali on the throne [of Kazan], take Utemesh-Girei [the incumbent underage scion of the Crimean dynasty] and his mother captive and [then Kazanians] will liberate all Russian captives. The Lord may decree that no-one will further be kept as a slave, and the remaining Crimeans and their wives and children will be delivered to the Lord. This is how the Lord may show us mercy, this is what we ask humbly.[90]

In Ivan's reply to their petition, liberation of all slaves is again the main concern; its implementation is decreed step for step:

[. . .] he ordered to answer Enbars that the Lord wants to show mercy to all Kazanians, only they should hand over the khan, his mother and all remaining Crimeans, their wives and children. They must not by any means keep Rus' captives against their will (*a polonu Ruskovo ni v kotoroi im nevole ne derzhati*). All princes shall lead the captives to the mouth of the Kazan River and hand them over to the boyars [right away], while the remaining captives [of rank-and-file masters] shall be liberated as soon as tsar Shah Ali will be enthroned. Kazanians must let everyone take leave, and nobody shall be kept as slave.[91]

After Enbars accepted, a dismayed Shah Ali learned from Ivan that as khan of Kazan he would not rule over the High Bank, the western parts of Kazan territory that were to be attached to Sviiazhsk, citing as reason that these areas were won by the 'right of the sabre'. Nevertheless, Shah Ali praises the decision to make him khan of Kazan. Subsequently, he delivers the Lord's speech of mercy at Sviiazhsk to a second Kazanian delegation, presumably including the complete set of conditions. On this occasion, the Kazanians are concerned and the 'Chronicle' seizes the occasion to talk extensively about their 'cunning customs', as well as mentioning that the accompanying boyars 'did not accede to any of their cunning manoeuvres'. There is no further mention of the division of Kazan's territory, whereas the 'Chronicle' instantly engages in another discussion of the requirement to liberate slaves, adding some threats:

they must liberate all Rus' captives and the princes shall take all captives to the estuary of the Kazan river. Should the ruler [of Moscow] learn afterwards that there are [remaining] captives among the Muslims then he will stand steadfastly to the conditions of this contract, and all Kazanian people must meet the tsar.[92]

The Kazanian nobles are shown aiming to fulfil these conditions, to which they and their new khan swore oaths. They manumit the captives in their households and swear a second oath to release all remaining slaves:

The princes of Kazan brought many Rus' captives, those whom they held, to the appointed place; moreover, all administered an oath to liberate the rest of the captives.[93]

---

90 Ibid., p. 64.
91 Ibid.
92 Ibid., p. 65.
93 Ibid.

The *Chronicle* takes care to add that anybody who thereafter is found keeping Muscovites enslaved may be punished by death:

> If the [Moscow] ruler learns about Christian captives in Muslim slavery and confiscates them, their owner will suffer the death penalty. If the Kazanians refuse to liberate all captives, the ruler will mete out [just] punishment as God may help him.[94]

The Muscovite tsar reserves the right to punish the Kazanians if they do not meet the condition of releasing all captives. For three days, Kazanians of all ranks went to the mouth of the river Kazan to deliver these oaths.[95]

Shah Ali, accompanied by the boyars Iurii Mikhailovich Golitsyn and Ivan Ivanovich Khabarov, the secretary Ivan Gregor'ev Vyrodkov and three hundred Tatar nobles and cossacks in the Moscow tsar's service from the steppe frontier settlement Gorodets as well as 200 musketeers, entered the city and took quarters in the khan's court. The very next day, on 17 August 1551, the boyars and the secretary reminded the new khan of the obligations he had accepted; it seems as if the concern for the slaves was now uppermost in their minds, too:

> the boyars princes Iur'i and Ivan went to the khan and told him: "The Kazanians have delivered an oath to liberate the captives and it is your obligation to order that they are all taken wherever they are in town and liberate them".[96]

The 'Chronicle' stresses that the boyars took their obligation to liberate the captives very seriously and that Ivan IV took their fate to his heart. It was the Kazanians' foremost obligation to set the captives free. Shah Ali sent out guards to assemble all the khan's captives in his court:

> The khan sent guards to assemble all captives in his court; when he had assembled many captives, the very day khan Shah Ali handed over to the boyars 2700 people and later, he liberated others.[97]

As a narrative device, expanding the description of the deliverance of the slaves ensures that readers pay due attention to the topic of liberation. Its importance is heightened by the observation that the tsar rejoiced upon receiving the news. A new era had just started as

> the Lord [of Muscovy] was immensely happy about the rescued Christians, that God had liberated the Christian gens from captivity and punished Kazan as never before under his predecessors. [Until 28 August,] 60,000 former Orthodox Christian captives left the High Bank, Kazan

---

94 Ibid.
95 Ibid.
96 Ibid., p. 66.
97 Ibid.

and the Kazan Bank. They were registered in Sviiazhsk, received the Lord's sustenance and were taken upstream on the Volga [. . .].[98]

In this new era, the 'Chronicle' praised the liberated captives' new-found ability to return to their homes, valuable and popular in Muscovy.[99] The 'Chronicle' continues:

> [. . .] except for those captives who left Kazan directly to go to their [former] places, the Viatkans and Permians to their places, the Ustiugians and Vologdians to their places, the Murom and Meshcherians and Taletsians and Kostromians, all of them to their own places, for whomever it was nearest, they went straight [back home].[100]

The 'Chronicle' thus directly comments on the Muscovite concept of liberty, opposed primarily to the *volia* or unbridled wilfulness attributed to the steppe, the 'crafty and cunning ways' of the 'Hagarites'.[101] From the point of view of the 'Chronicle', the way out of slavery is one which will lead an Orthodox Christian straight back to the close attachment to the place where they were born or lived before captivity. This attachment appears preferable to boundless mobility, framed in the stark words of the 'Chronicle' or, if the author is to be believed, of the metropolitan Makarii on the occasion of the glorious entry of the victorious Ivan into Moscow as 'captives [sold as] spoils of war who were then scattered over the face of the whole earth (*v plen raskhishcheny, i razseianny po litsu vsea zemli*)' by the forces of slave raids and the trade in human beings.[102]

In the sentence directly following this reflection about liberation and one's own place, the 'Chronicle' intensifies the imagery to compare Muscovy to Old Testament Israel during Exodus:

> Long ago, the old creator led the Israelites out of Egypt by his hand Moses, so today Christ by the instrument of our Orthodox tsar leads a plethora of Christian souls out of Kazan slavery.[103]

Diverging from established models of representing slave raids, in which Orthodox Russians appear invariably as people punished for their sins, there is a new reading inherent in this interpretation of the prefiguration of the Biblical Old and New Covenant. The Orthodox tsar, inspired by Christ, leads a throng of Christian souls out of Kazan slavery, just like Moses in days of old led the Israelites out of Egyptian slavery.[104] This implicit concept of a new covenant, a new care of Christ for his Russian

---

98 Ibid.
99 V. Kivelson, 'Bitter Slavery and Pious Servitude: Muscovite Freedom and its Critics', in R.O. Crummey, ed., Russische und ukrainische Geschichte vom 16.–18. Jahrhundert (Wiesbaden, 2001), pp. 110–119; Smolarz, 'Speaking about Freedom and Dependency'.
100 Tikhomirov, *Letopisets nachala tsarstva*, p. 66.
101 On Hagarites, see chapter 6.
102 Tikhomirov, *Letopisets nachala tsarstva*, p. 113. On this event and Makarii's letters and speech in further detail, see below.
103 Ibid., p. 66.
104 On the imagery, see chaper 3, The Blessed Host.

flock in the person of Ivan, is then enhanced and made explicit, first by reverting to the old image of God's wrath, and then by repeating once again in the following sentence the bright, new age imagery of liberation from Tatar enslavement 'forever':

> Nowadays the Christians are set free by God's grace and through our Orthodox ruler and his wisdom. This has been achieved by order of the ruler and the service of the commanders and the whole army, so that not one subject (*chelovek*) of our ruler was lost.[105]

The whole hierarchy of the army down to the last soldier is thus praised, since the 'Lord's work' of liberating the slaves was achieved by their collaboration and diligent service. The care inspired by Christ in Ivan and his army is stressed by the claim that 'not even one human being perished'.

Just to drive home the concept that every detail of the campaign was preordained by Christ's care for his captive Orthodox flock, Kazan Tatars and 'many [Orthodox] peasants who had been captured' saw signs and heard bells ringing on the hill later to be chosen by the tsar's advisors as the site of Sviiazhsk. These signs were brought to Tsar Ivan's attention, who was pleased to hear that the site he selected shone with holiness.[106]

Pelenski questioned the high numbers of captives given in this source and more so, in the 'History of Kazan' on the grounds of the khan's tax. The khan held less than his share of five per cent of the captives, if the numbers given in the chronicle are correct, and if the tax was the same for Kazan as it was for Crimea.[107] As far as medieval hyperbole and the surviving, one-sided information goes, this doubt may well be justified; however, Pelenski did not take into account the thriving trade in slaves, as well as conditions in Crimea, the ally of Kazan.[108] Any number of captives might have been sold off into slavery and, as already mentioned, this is indeed one of the claims the 'Chronicle' makes.[109] It is quite possible that the rank-and-file Kazanians had made a profit, while the khan had ostentatiously kept the captives, to bolster his power; or vice versa. The discrepancy in numbers could also be down to changes of ruler, which frequently occurred in the years leading up to 1552.[110] The sources just do not allow us to draw any firmer conclusions. In any

---

105 Ibid.
106 Ibid.
107 Pelenski, *Russia and Kazan*, p. 239. The stability of the tax is more doubtful than Pelenski allows, as various customs across the Islamic world show: see R.T. Ware III, 'Slavery in Islamic Africa, 1400–1800', in D. Eltis and S.L. Engerman, eds., *The Cambridge World History of Slavery*, vol. 3: *AD 1420–AD 1804* (Cambridge, 2011), pp. 47–80, here p. 69.
108 Cf. chapter 1.
109 Tikhomirov, *Letopisets nachala tsarstva*, p. 114.
110 S. Papp, 'Die Inaugurationen der Krimkhane durch die Hohe Pforte (16.–18. Jahrhundert)', in D. Klein, ed., *The Crimean Khanate between East and West (15th–18th century)* (Wiesbaden, 2012), pp. 75–90.

case, despite Pelenski's assertion[111] the question of whether or not there were as many captives as claimed does not concern the quotations under discussion; the Muscovite writer represented events as the dawn of a new era in which Orthodox Russians were free from external enslavement. Although it took roughly another ninety years until the steppe fortifications reliably stopped the slave raids from Crimea, this speaks for itself. The topic at hand concerns the Muscovite worldview, rather than numbers.

I have already drawn attention to the 'Chronicle's' elevation of these events by comparing them to Israel's Exodus from Egyptian slavery. Distinctly summing up the optimism of Muscovite self-identification as New Israel, the 'Chronicle' relates the continuum of salvation history[112] to its origins in a narrative about liberation from slavery in Egypt. In the chronicle's timeline, if not the time in which they were actually written, these words occur before the conquest is even planned or imagined. This is in keeping with its model, since the Israelites did not invade Egypt, nor was Christ known for wielding the secular power of a king. The quotation marks the point at which the motivation, i.e. liberation from slavery and slave raids, gains the upper hand over received tradition: Christ is imagined as the spiritual leader of a campaign even before the war has reshaped traditional steppe politics in the Muscovite image. This jubilation about the new era is the logical conclusion to the connection introduced by the internal heading: 'The [. . .] Tale of How [. . .] God [. . .] Through Our [. . .] Tsar [. . .] [liberated] the Orthodox Christians from Muslim Captivity [. . .]' While one of the two military leaders returns to Moscow with the good news, the second, boyar Ivan Khabarov, and the secretary remain with khan Shah Ali in Kazan 'attending to the slaves and other administrative affairs [. . .]', which underlines the importance given to liberation. In the dramaturgy of the 'Chronicle's' narration, this heightened attention to a single issue foreshadows things to come.

The 'Letter to the Ugra'

This jubilation and the reference to the biblical book of Exodus not only occurs late in this account of Ivan's first campaign and his intention to liberate the slaves. It also marks the moment when the identification of Muscovy with the New Israel came to be an obligation of the tsar to liberate slaves, an idea which was subsequently widely used in Muscovite literature and art as justification for expansion. Before the 1550s, it

---

111 Pelenski, *Russia and Kazan*, p. 292.
112 D.K. Prestel, 'Creating Redemptive History: The Role of the Kievan Caves Monastery in the Stepennaia Kniga', in G. Lenhoff, ed., *The Book of Royal Degrees and the Genesis of Russian Historical Consciousness/"Stepennaia kniga tsarskogo rodosloviia" i genezis russkago istoricheskogo soznaniia* (Bloomington IN, 2011), pp. 97–110 focuses on the history of salvation; there is no sense of linkage to ransom.

had been almost inexistent in Muscovite chronicles, art and letters.[113] The prominent exception is the 'classic' formulation of the theme 'Muscovy the New Israel' in a letter addressed – according to the accompanying documents – to Ivan III during the stand-off at the river Ugra between the forces of the grand prince and the khan of the Great *Ulus*, Akhmet in 1480; it is ascribed to the archbishop of Rostov, Vassian Rylo. The 'Letter' was most likely written in that very year and already contained many salient features of later Muscovite political representations, especially regarding the empire, which will be discussed in chapter six.[114]

The 'Letter' has been analysed from the perspective of European theories of sovereignty, and Charles Halperin has aptly remarked that its phrasing does not fit these theories. He highlights this where he emphasizes the repeated character of Tatar 'incursions', which invalidate assertions of Tatar supremacy. However, from this perspective the repeated 'incursions' render the recurrent claim of 'liberation' in the source text pointless.[115] Quite contrary, the Tatar *nakhozhdeniia* were not so much wars of conquest as repeated slave raids.[116] In part this difference in interpretation hinges on the

---

[113] Rowland, 'Moscow – the Third Rome or the New Israel?', p. 602. Cf. Halperin, *The Tatar Yoke*, pp. 180, 183, 186 focuses on the refusal of Russian bookmen to accept Mongol suzerainty and 'political' liberation. His account closes in the early sixteenth century. See also ibid., pp. 127–128.

[114] Pliukhanova, '"Poslanie na Ugru" i vopros o proiskhozhdenii moskovskoi imperskoi ideologii'. Some researchers point to the earliest extant copy, which was written before 1499, and the struggle for succession at the turn of the century: I.M. Kudriavtsev, '"Poslanie na Ugru" Vassiiana Rylo kak pamiatnik publitsistiki XV v', *Trudy Otdela drevnerusskoi literatury*, 8 (1951), pp. 158–186; N.V. Vodovozov, *Istoriia drevnei russkoi literatury* (Moskva, 1966), pp. 200–202; K.V. Bazilevich, *Vneshinaia politika russkogo tsentralizovannogo gosudarstva: Vtoraia polovina XV veka* (Moskva, 1952), pp. 155–163.

[115] Halperin, *The Tatar Yoke*, pp. 171–189. Debates before Pliukhanova and Halperin mainly revolved around the question whether the 'Letter's' tendency is more conservative or expresses hopes for reform: A.A. Shakhmatov and M.D. Priselkov, *Obozrenie russkikh letopisnykh svodov XIV -XVI vv* (Moskva and Leningrad, 1938), pp. 295–296; Kudriavtsev, '"Poslanie na Ugru" Vassiiana Rylo kak pamiatnik publitsistiki XV v'; I.M. Kudriavtsev, '"Ugorshchina" v pamiatnikakh drevnerusskoi literatury: Letopisnye povesti o nashestvii Akhmata i ikh literaturnaia istoriia', in Institut mirovoi literatury imeni A.M. Gor'kogo, ed., *Issledovaniia i materialy po drevnerusskoi literatury* (Moskva, 1961), pp. 23–67; P.N. Pavlov, 'Deistvitel'naia rol' arkhiepiskopa Vassiana v sobytiiakh 1480 g.', *Uchenye zapiski Krasnoiarskogo pedagogicheskogo instituta*, 4, 1 (1955), pp. 202–212; I.S. Ganelin, 'Ob umeniii chitat' raznochteniia', *Trudy Otdela drevnerusskoi literatury*, 16 (1960), pp. 637–638; L.V. Cherepnin, *Obrazovanie russkogo tsentralizovannogo gosudarstva v XIV-XV vekakh: Ocherki sotsial'no-ėkonomicheskoi i politicheskoi istorii Rusi* (Moskva, 1960), p. 882; I.S. Lur'e, 'Novonaidennyi rasskaz o "stoianii na Ugre"', *Trudy Otdela drevnerusskoi literatury*, 18 (1962), pp. 289–293; I.S. Lur'e, *Obshcherusskie letopisi XIV-XV vv* (Leningrad, 1976), pp. 218–219, 233, 244–247; A.N. Nasonov, *Istoriia russkogo letopisaniia XI – nachala XVIII veka: Ocherki i issledovaniia* (Moskva, 1969), p. 320; I.G. Alekseev, 'Moskovskie gorozhanie v 1480 g. i pobeda na Ugre', in I.I. Froianov, ed., *Genezis i razvitie feodalizma v Rossii: Problemy social'noj i klassovoj bor'by: Mevuzovskij sbornik* (Leningrad, 1985), pp. 118–119; B.M. Kloss and V.D. Nazarov, 'Rasskazy o likvidatsii ordynskogo iga na Rusi v letopisanii kontsa XV v.', in O.I. Podobedova, ed., *Drevne-russkoe iskusstvo XIV–XV vv* (Moskva, 1984), pp. 283–313.

[116] Langer, 'Slavery in the Appanage Era'.

verb *pleniti*, which occurs frequently in the sources: its two most widespread meanings are to take captives; secondly, to take spoils of war. Only the late, third most common meaning is 'to conquer', which requires further contextual markers.[117]

The text is both closer to European occurrences of the New Israel ideology, and at the same time to Muscovite needs of containing slave raids, than has been noticed so far. The 'Letter' uses the imagery of Exodus to depict the defence of Christians from Tatar slave raids as active repentance. This is ample grounds for divine help in overcoming the 'predatory' slaver, khan Akhmet, who like his forefather Batu khan arrogated to himself the title of *tsar'*, whereas the 'Letter' asserts that he is not of imperial descent since there are only Christian emperors. 'Vassian' thus denies the primacy of Chingissid descent, which had been accepted as a rule in the steppe and in Muscovy, while underlining their role as despicable slave raiders. Consequently, the grand prince is to be absolved from his forefathers' supposed oath because he saved the New Israel:

> If you will thus dispute and say: "We are under the oath of the forebears not to raise hands against the tsar [khan; C.W.], how can I break the oath and rise against the tsar?" Listen, oh tsar, you are God's blessed, if an oath has been forced on [your forefathers], you may be released from it [. . .]: it was not given to a tsar, but to a raider, a predator fighting against God [. . .] he arrogated the title tsar to himself [. . .] The cursed Batu khan attacked our whole land in the manner of a robber and raided all our people (*popleni vsiu zemliu*) and enslaved them, and he made himself our tsar, although he was not the son of a tsar, not from a tsar's lineage. [. . .] It was then just like now and forever that God drowned pharaoh and delivered Israel.[118]

Such a forceful denial of the rights of the Chingissid dynasty on the grounds of slave raiding could never be a focal point of Muscovite representation as long as it sought the Crimean khanate as its ally. Thus, although the 1480 'Letter to the Ugra' for the first time contains many features of the ideology of liberation from slavery which became standard in the mid-sixteenth century, Muscovy's political and strategic position in the inervening decades meant that this ideological position remained almost entirely isolated; even among clerics scorning Tatars it was not approved due to the denigration of the Chingissid khan. Until that time, it was copied in only four chronicles, all maintaining a distance to the Moscow grand prince and some of them based on a compilation of sometimes contradicting sources.[119]

---

[117] S.G. Barkhudarov, *Slovar' russkogo iazyka XI–XVII vv*, vol. 15 (Moskva, 1975–); Cf. Halperin, *The Tatar Yoke*, pp. 193 and passim.

[118] *Poslanie na Ugru Vassiana Rylo: Podgotovka teksta E.I. Vaneevoi, perevod O.P. Likhachevoi, kommentarii Ia.S. Lur'e*, http://lib.pushkinskijdom.ru/Default.aspx?tabid=5070 (accessed 7 Sep. 2018). B.M. Kloss, ed., *L'vovskaia letopis'* (Moskva, 2005), pp. 342–343. The textual tradition of the 'Letter to the Ugra' is generally very stable. Another lengthy passage of the 'Letter' focuses on enslavement, not translated here.

[119] I.S. Lur'e, *Dve istorii Rusi XV veka: Rannie i pozdnie, nezavisimye i ofitsial'nye letopisi ob obrazovanii Moskovskogo gosudarstva* (Sankt-Peterburg, 1994), pp. 181–182, 185. Among these chronicles, the 'Voskresenskii letopis'' in its earliest redaction ends 1533; it was compiled between 1542

Even the author's identity is doubtful, since the '*Tipografskii*' chronicle, another important source for the events of 1480, omits the 'Letter'. However, this chronicle unlike the 'Letter' itself was closely associated with Vassian's Rostov archbishopric until his death.[120]

The conception of Muscovy's role in history in the 'Letter' initially appears even more isolated in the light of attempts by copyists in a later period to interpolate Exodus references and quotations into traditional accounts of earlier episodes that appeared to lend themselves to re-interpretation along the lines of the 'Letter to the Ugra'. As a rule, the earlier accounts onto which this interpretation was grafted did not focus on liberation from slavery. Such changes were grafted, for example, by the editors of the *Stepennaia kniga* onto the story about the campaign of the Central Asian ruler Tamerlane (Amir Timur or Timur the Lame; in the chronicle, Temir Aksak) in 1395, whose 'heart was hardened', which in the Biblical idiom implies: hardened against allowing Muscovy to leave captivity, or simply, against sparing them from slave raids. In this mid–sixteenth-century interpolation, the steppe was likened to the Red Sea:

> [. . .] just as pharaoh of old, whose heart was hardened against Israel, wanted to capture and harm them, but God led them through the sea on dry land, then drowned pharaoh and his entire army. Similarly, Temir Aksak again hardened his heart [. . .] The merciful God did not

---

and 1544 by a partisan of the princes Shuiskii, but work hypothetically may have started before 1533: S.A. Levina, 'Letopis' Voskresenskaia', in Likhachev and Bulanin, eds., *Slovar' knizhnikov i knizhnosti drevnei Rusi*, http://lib.pushkinskijdom.ru/Default.aspx?tabid=4278. The 'Novgorodskaia 4-ia Chronicle (NIVL)' diverges from Moscow chronicles depiction of, among other things, Ivan III's conquest of Novgorod in 1471 by a much more detailed report about internal Novgorod conflicts: Ia. S. Lur'e, 'Letopis' Novgorodskaia IV', in Likhachev and Bulanin, eds., *Slovar' knizhnikov i knizhnosti drevnei Rusi*, http://lib.pushkinskijdom.ru/Default.aspx?tabid=4288. The version known as 'Letopis' Novgorodskaia Dubrovskogo' was 'apparently compiled by order of Makarii, archbishop of Novgorod and later metropolitan of Moscow' on the basis of NIVL: Ia. S. Lur'e, 'Letopis' Novgorodskaia Dubrovskogo', in Likhachev and Bulanin, eds., *Slovar' knizhnikov i knizhnosti drevnei Rusi*, http://lib.pushkinskijdom.ru/Default.aspx?tabid=4289. It is therefore already part of the Makarian initiative. The 'Sofiiskij II chronicle (SIIL)' contains events from 1471–1539; it has an 'unofficial character and was written in a monastery': Ia. S. Lur'e, 'Letopis' Sofiiskij II', in Likhachev and Bulanin, eds., *Slovar' knizhnikov i knizhnosti drevnei Rusi*, http://lib.pushkinskijdom.ru/Default.aspx?tabid=4296. The 'L'vovskaia letopis'' was compiled not before 1533; it features identical entries with SIIL between the end of the 14th century and 1518: Ia. S. Lur'e, 'L'vovskaia letopis'', in Likhachev and Bulanin, eds., *Slovar' knizhnikov i knizhnosti drevnei Rusi*, http://lib.pushkinskijdom.ru/Default.aspx?tabid=4283. All links in this note last acc. 11 Sep. 2021. The Nikon chronicle was compiled already at the court of Ivan IV: Ostrowski, *Muscovy and the Mongols*, pp. 147–149. See also C.J. Halperin, 'The East Slavic Response to the Mongol Conquest', *Archivum Eurasiae Medii Aevi*, 10 (1998–1999), pp. 98–117, here p. 114, points to the exceptional position of the 'Letter' in East Slavic literature. He dismisses the mid-sixteenth century sources, esp. *Letopisets nachalo tsarstva*, as discussed above.

120 Pliukhanova, '"Poslanie na Ugru" i vopros o proiskhozhdenii moskovskoi imperskoi ideologii', p. 458, dismisses Kloss and Nazarov, 'Rasskazy o likvidatsii ordynskogo iga na Rusi v letopisanii kontsa XV v.', pp. 303–313.

permit him to harm the Russian land, but destroyed the life of this blood drinking Temir Aksak with a terrible death [. . .] Just as pharaoh [drowned] in the sea, so Temir Aksak vanished in a desolate field [i.e. the steppe]. And his kingdom swiftly was destroyed [. . .] and just as of old God's glory was manifested in [the drowning of] pharaoh and his chariots and his armies, so his glory was manifested in [the perishing of] Temir Aksak.[121]

Identification with the New Israel in the 'Letter to the Ugra' will be discussed below. It may have built on early Kievan traditions fragmentarily reported in the Primary Chronicle; however, most recently scholars have regarded the latter text no longer just as mythologized history, but as outright historicised myth, adapted from common European travelling motifs, which makes it hard to relate it to specific historical events.[122] Moreover, such earlier quotations from Exodus were limited to praising a Rus' prince by setting him next to a biblical leader, to the cyclical succession of Rus' and Jewish rulers and that of their foes, or to identifying Turks and other nomads in the vicinity of Rus' principalities with Israel's foes.[123] Interpolations that draw on anti-slavery sentiments were made from the late fifteenth and especially frequently from the mid-sixteenth century on, for example in the Vita of Aleksandr Nevskii in the Nikon Chronicle, a large-scale collation of East Slavic chronicles continued until 1558.[124] The interpolation underscores the virtue of princely rulers who ransom and protect their subjects, but remains vague:[125]

> He was most merciful [. . .] spending much gold and silver on captives, which he sent to khan Batu in the Horde on behalf of captive Rus' [people] who had been seized by godless Tatars, and whom he redeemed and saved from slavery (*liutyia raboty*) [. . .][126]

---

121 Lenhoff, 'The Tale of Tamerlane in the Royal Book of Degrees', p. 128, with an additional omission by the author.
122 E. Levin, 'Muscovy and Its Mythologies: Pre-Petrine History in the Past Decade', *Kritika: Explorations in Russian and Eurasian History*, 12, 4 (2011), pp. 773–788, here p. 778.
123 I.N. Danilevskii, 'Bibliia i povest' vremennykh let (k probleme interpretatsii letopisnykh tekstov)', *Otechestvennaia istoriia*, 1 (1993), pp. 78–94; P. Jackson, 'The Testimony of the Russian "Archbishop" Peter Concerning the Mongols (1244/5): Precious Intelligence or Timely Disinformation?', *Journal of the Royal Asiatic Society*, 26, 1–2 (2016), pp. 65–77; A.V. Laushkin, 'Nasledniki praottsa Izmaila i bibleiskaia mozaika v letopisnykh izvestiiakh o Polovtsakh', *Drevniaia Rus': Voprosy medievistiki*, 4, 54 (2013), p. 76–86; L.S. Chekin, 'The Godless Ishmaelites: The Image of the Steppe in Eleventh–Thirteenth-Century Rus'', *Russian History*, 19, 1–4 (1992), pp. 9–28.
124 More on interpolations which focus on slavery and liberation in chapter 4.
125 I am grateful to Donald Ostrowski for pointing out this interpolation. See I.K. Begunov, *Pamiatnik russkoi literatury XIII veka 'Slovo o pogibeli Russkoi Zemli'* (Moskva, 1965), pp. 158–180 for an edition of the text. D. Ostrowski, 'Dressing a Wolf in Sheep's Clothing: Toward Understanding the Composition of the Life of Alexander Nevskii', *Russian History*, 40, 1 (2013), pp. 41–67 for earlier versions and interpolations layered in the text.
126 N.N. Pokrovskii and G. Lenhoff, *Stepennaia kniga tsarskogo rodosloviia po drevneishim spiskam: Teksty i kommentarii*, vol. 1 (Moskva, 2007), p. 517; A.F. Bychkov, ed., *Letopisnyi sbornik, imenuemyi Patriarsheiu ili Nikonovskoiu letopis'iu*, vol. 2 (Sanktpeterburg, 1885), p. 119. For a version

In the period prior to Muscovy's conquest of Kazan, let alone before the change of steppe alliances of 1503/1521 which deprived emboldened Muscovy of the powerful backing of the Crimean khan,[127] the very few but nevertheless existing references to liberating the New Israel from slavery are best explained by Greco-Italian influences. They were brought to Muscovy by the niece of the former Byzantine emperor and wife of Ivan III, Zoe-Sofiia and her suite, whom I referred to earlier.[128] This argument is not an attempt to revive the doubtful assertion that her marriage to Ivan III, grand prince of Moscow, marked a high point of Byzantine influence in Muscovy whose time had not yet come. The actual paths of cultural transfer were much more intricate and beset by mishaps and setbacks.

Zoe was the orphaned daughter of the *despotes* of Morea (Greece) after its conquest by the Ottomans. She became the disciple of her protector, the propagator of the idea of a renewed crusade uniting all of Christianity against the Muslims, the Uniate cardinal, former Greek Orthodox metropolitan of Nicaea and, a decade after the Ottoman conquest of Constantinople, its titular patriarch (1463–1472), Basilius Bessarion. A trailblazer of Italian Renaissance learning and knowledge of ancient Greek texts, Bessarion had many of them translated in his palazzo-academy in Rome. Zoe-Sofiia's marriage was sponsored by a papal fund intended to promote the twin aims of Christian unity and war against Islam. The mission of her entourage in Muscovy was twofold: the propagation of a joint crusade to recover Constantinople and the revitalization of Orthodoxy. The second aim, the union of Christian churches, was never very popular in Muscovite Orthodoxy – Zoe-Sofiia had to renounce the Latin rites in Pskov before her marriage – and the political aim of all-out war against an indiscriminate 'Muslim foe' was hardly in Moscow's best interests, let alone in line with its policies. The *'Poslanie'* only became part of the main body of Muscovite chronicles towards the end of the reign of Vasilli III and even more so in the 1550s, during the tenure of the erstwhile archbishop of Novgorod and subsequently metropolitan Makarii, when it was included in three important chronicles. Insertion into chronicles which were held at court indicates that a text was central and meaningful at least in the Kremlin. Moreover, one of these works was the 'Illustrated Chronicle', a representative large-scale undertaking at Ivan IV's court. It is suggestive of the career of the 'Letter' that a line was added to the text indicating the high esteem in which its recommendations were held in the second half of the sixteenth century: 'This letter will invigorate and benefit many, as to the

---

predating the 1530s, see *Pskovskiia i sofiskiia letopisi* (Sanktpeterburg, 1851), p. 3; Ostrowski, 'Dressing a Wolf in Sheep's Clothing', p. 46.

127 Davies, *Warfare, State and Society on the Black Sea Steppe, 1500–1700*; D. Kołodziejczyk, *The Crimean Khanate and Poland-Lithuania: International Diplomacy on the European Periphery (15th–18th century): A Study of Peace Treaties Followed by Annotated Documents* (Leiden, 2011).

128 Pliukhanova, '"Poslanie na Ugru" i vopros o proiskhozhdenii moskovskoi imperskoi ideologii', pp. 458–459.

pious autocrat, so to all of his army [. . .]'[129] Despite its spectacular success in the middle of the sixteenth century, there had been almost complete silence about it previously, punctured only by copies in two marginal chronicles of 1499 and 1518, both of which are generally deemed unreliable.[130]

Earlier scholarly researchers into the 'Letter' who follow Shakhmatov almost entirely overlooked this gap in the tradition, which might even suggest that the text was not contemporary. Referring to the similarity of these texts, they accepted the hypothesis that Vassian was the author of both the '*Tipografskii* chronicle' of the Rostov school and the 'Letter'.[131] However, Maria Pliukhanova has established that in the narrative of the Rostov-based chronicles there is not even a hint to the existence of 'Vassian's' 'Letter', which would indeed be contrary to the chronicle's intentions. Moreover, the '*Tipografskii* chronicle' is contemporary with the events discussed, ending with the death of Vassian.[132]

It can be a daring enterprise to reconstruct the transmission of texts in early Muscovy, because establishing the authorship of usually anonymous texts often relies on circuitous evidence. Based on a more nuanced reading of the available evidence, Pliukhanova advanced the well-founded hypothesis that several circles of literate courtiers were involved in writing and translating the 'Letter to the Ugra', mainly clerics, the Greeks in the Kremlin and monks at Kirillo-Belozerskii monastery in league with metropolitan Gerontii, who for several reasons clashed with Ivan III in the 1480s. Therefore, the chronicle entry about Akhmat's campaign and the two related messages which urge the panic-stricken Ivan III to go to war, ascribed to Gerontii and Vassian Rylo, surfaced in the Vologda-Perm chronicle of the bishopric that includes Belozero. Vassian's or, rather pseudo-Vassian's, letter first appeared in this chronicle only in 1499 because of the recent victory of Zoe-Sofiia's party in court intrigues in the same year, when Ivan III accepted her son Vasilii as heir to the grand princely throne.[133]

Comparison of the chronicles that include the 'Letter to the Ugra' and those that did not reveals a typical cleavage of this period:[134] the latter did not agitate against

---

129 Ibid., pp. 453–454. Published manuscript copies of the 'Letter to the Ugra': PSRL 4 (1925), pp. 517–523; 6 (1856), pp. 225–230; 8 (1859), pp. 207–213; 20 (1910), pp. 340–344; 26 (1959), pp. 266–273; PLDR 2-ia pol. XV v. (M., 1982), pp. 521–537.
130 Ibid., p. 454.
131 A.A. Shakhmatov, 'Ermolinskaia letopis'' i Rostovskii vladychnyi svod', *Izvestiia Otdeleniia Russkago Iazyka i Slovestnosti imperatorskoi Akademii Nauk*, 9, 1 (1904), pp. 366–423, here pp. 422–423 n. 3; B.M. Kloss and V.D. Nazarov, 'Rasskazy o likvidatsii ordynskogo iga na Rusi v letopisanii kontsa XV veka', pp. 303–313. Accepting a later date of occurrence, but also placing the 'Letter' within the context of 'official' chronicle writing: Lur'e, *Dve istorii Rusi XV veka*, p. 180.
132 Pliukhanova, '"Poslanie na Ugru" i vopros o proiskhozhdenii moskovskoi imperskoi ideologii', p. 458.
133 Ibid., pp. 467–472. P. Nitsche, *Grossfürst und Thronfolger: Die Nachfolgepolitik der Moskauer Herrscher bis zum Ende des Rjurikidenhauses* (Köln, 1972), pp. 168–169.
134 Ostrowski, 'The Mongols and Rus''.

the Tatars. The great majority of chronicles, based on the afore-mentioned Rostov tradition, is level-headed about the performance of the Muscovite and Tatar armies in 1480: during a show of force which included some diplomatic element of negotiating the tribute, they did not expect to get access to each other and were not prepared for battle when the River Ugra suddenly froze. Both armies backed off avoiding inadvertent clashes and the Muscovites received a hefty deduction from the tribute. Thus, in the version that initially won the day, it was not divine intervention, the bishop's letter or outstanding bravery that dispelled Tatar power over Muscovy, but a fortuitous natural phenomenon at an already low point of Tatar influence. Although this is still a simplified version of historical events, the accepted, contemporary narrative thus eschews divine interference in favour of a more 'secular' explanation.

The Rostov-based account rebukes not so much Ivan III as Zoe-Sofiia, who flees traitorously from the mere scare of a Tatar attack on Moscow to Belozero. This accusation forms the core of an account which in its very emotional quality is uncharacteristic of Muscovite chronicle writing. While the Tatars seem beyond reprieve, this text names the enemies of Orthodoxy and those who put it in danger: it is the ruler's family who tend to flee and whose Orthodoxy is not above doubt. They are connected to the countries that succumbed to the Ottomans, so the fact that Sofiia has taken to flight is seen in analogy to a root cause for the end of their power, and therefore, a danger to Moscow's might and security, too.[135] Moreover, the arrival of Andrei Palaeolog, brother of Sofiia 'from Rome in Moscow'[136] is taken as bad omen; it occurs immediately before the description of Akhmet's 'incursion'.[137] Political and religious resiliency are considered twin roots of dynastic survival, which is in good accord with the principles of the evolving no-slaving zone.

Not by chance, Sofiia's flight route via Dimitrov to the Kirillo-Belozersk monastery coincides with another conflict that put Sofiia and Vassian at loggerheads: the archbishop of Rostov wanted to subjugate the monastery; the Rostov chronicle complains about the monks' refusal to submit.[138] The appanages of Vereia and Belozersk were linked to the *tsaritsa* by marriage of the appanage prince's son, Vasilii, to Sofiia's niece, Maria Palaeologina. In 1483, the couple had to flee to Lithuania when Ivan III claimed jewellery he had given to Sofiia but which she had bestowed on her niece. Apparently Sofiia never expected to have to return them, but Ivan claimed them now on the occasion of the birth of Ivan the Younger's son by Elena of Moldova.[139] Two years

---

135 M.N. Tikhomirov, ed., *Polnoe sobranie russkikh letopisei*, vol. 26: *Vologodsko-Permskaia letopis'* (Moskva and Leningrad, 1959), pp. 201–202.
136 In other words, a suspected heretic.
137 Pliukhanova, '"Poslanie na Ugru" i vopros o proiskhozhdenii moskovskoi imperskoi ideologii', p. 460.
138 S.P. Rozanov, ed., *Tipografskaia letopis'* (Petrograd, 1921), p. 197.
139 Nitsche, *Grossfürst und Thronfolger*, p. 121; J.L.I. Fennell, *Ivan the Great of Moscow* (New York, 1961), p. 324.

later, Maria's father-in-law died and his heir not only lost the lands of the appanage of Belozersk, but in breach of the contract of 1482 also those of Vereia, which Ivan III had formerly granted to Vasilii.[140] These events are part of the conflict within the grand princely family and emblematic of the general tendency of Rostov-based chronicle writing and Vassian's stance, opposing Sofiia and Greek influence.

The different and confusing interpretations of the events on the Ugra make sense against the backdrop of Sofiia's fateful clashes with her rival, Elena of Moldova,[141] the wife of the heir apparent, Ivan the Younger, who died in 1490. As their courtly rivalries evolved in the 1490s, they were connected to war plans against Lithuania which involved an abortive alliance with Elena's father, the ruler of Moldova, as well as to Elena's support for the so-called 'heresy of the Judaizers', a heterodox movement that for some time enjoyed the support of the grand prince.[142] The preservation and revival of Orthodoxy after the fall of Constantinople, possibly in close alliance with Catholicism, if not an actual union, remained the aim of Sofiia and the Greek members of her entourage following the abortive 1439 Union of Florence between the papal church and Greek Orthodoxy, which Moscow had repudiated. Her links to the Union and to Lithuania made her vulnerable while Moscow planned for war, culminating in her and her son's temporary banishment and the announcement of Elena's son Dmitrii as heir apparent in 1498. However, in 1499 Ivan III crowned their son Vasilii grand prince of Novgorod and Pskov and heir apparent. Muscovy now faced closer collaboration of Poland and Lithuania, so the change of heir was most likely a first step to pacify the grand princely family. Elena's partisans were subsequently executed and the 'heretics' in Novgorod and Moscow persecuted.[143]

The narrative in the two collections of manuscripts that contain the 'Letter' comprises details about relations to the Tatars which are not otherwise found in chronicles, but have been preserved in an entirely unrelated source, Herberstein's *Notes upon Muscovy*. Both claim that Sofiia was infuriated by the 'slavish' habits of the mighty grand prince who addressed the mounted khan on foot. The two chronicle manuscripts cite her opposition as a reason for the grand prince to fall out with the Tatars. Herberstein is generally a reliable source as he spoke Slavic languages. Nevertheless, in this case both his inclination as imperial ambassador and his likely source, George Trakhaniot the Younger, from Sofiia's Greek entourage, point towards

---

140 Cf. Nitsche, *Grossfürst und Thronfolger*, p. 107. On the disposition of Vereia after the appanage prince's death: L.V. Cherepnin and S.V. Bakhrushin, eds., *Dukhovnye i dogovornye gramoty velikikh i udel'nykh kniazei XIV–XVI vv.* (Moskva and Leningrad, 1950), p. 281. Pliukhanova, '"Poslanie na Ugru" i vopros o proiskhozhdenii moskovskoi imperskoi ideologii', pp. 461–462.
141 In Russian, Elena Voloshanka (of Wallachia).
142 J. Martin, *Medieval Russia: 980–1584* (Cambridge, 2007); Pliukhanova, '"Poslanie na Ugru" i vopros o proiskhozhdenii moskovskoi imperskoi ideologii', p. 463.
143 J.V.A. Fine, 'The Mucovite Dynastic Crisis of 1497–1502', *Canadian Slavonic Papers/Revue Canadienne des Slavistes*, 8 (1966), pp. 198–215.

tendentiousness and indicate the unreliability of the version that puts Sofiia at the helm of the fight against the Tatars and Muscovite slavishness.[144]

The narrative framing of the 'Letter' in early documents seeks to demonstrate the unity of Sofiia and the Muscovite clergy by introducing 'Vassian's' letter as one of two or three letters sent by clerics intended to convince the still wavering grand prince to confront the Tatars, whereas his 'bad' advisors sought to hold him back from the river bank and offending the khan.[145] This sets the scene for the trenchantly anti-Tatar, erudite speech of the 'Letter to the Ugra' and its culminating theme, liberation from slave raids, which could not be part of grand princely politics while the alliance with the Tatars continued. This theme was still employed, but with the opposite intention, i.e. to explain acceptance of Tatar demands, during a setback of Muscovite policies in the reign of Vasilii III.[146]

The 'Letter to the Ugra' has its origins in the joint writing exercise of Greek and Muscovite scribes in Moscow and Belozero, who were connected to archbishop Gennadii's Bible translation activities in Novgorod. The writing process also links it to the Slavic version of the 'Letter of the Eastern Patriarchs to Emperor Theophilos'. Its Greek original version was written in the fourth century, while we know of the earliest manuscript copies of the Slavic version in the fifteenth and sixteenth centuries. Its importance is indicated by the fact that it was read out during the Sunday of Orthodoxy, praising the Muscovite faith. In the process of translation, only the introductory parts of the Greek original were left largely unchanged; it is on these parts that the 'Letter to the Ugra' draws. However, there is one major omission, which pertains to praise for liberating slaves, which is entirely absent in the Greek version. In one and the same place in the texts the 'Letter to the Ugra' and the Slavic version of the 'Letter of the Eastern Patriarchs' contain a passage on the creation of the world and the dry path beneath the waves, taken from the *Wisdom of Salomon* 14:3, which references Exodus.[147] In the latter text, it reads (I have italicized variations between the Greek and Slavic versions):

> The Lord created the heavens and approved it. He founded earth on the main and breathed life into people and animals and everything that moves there, and he made way in the sea, making it firm in the water without distress, *he destroyed the weapons, the [pursuers] and the horses.*[148]

---

144 B.N. Floria, 'Greki-emigranty v Russkom gosudarstve vtoroi poloviny XV-nachala XVI v.: Politicheskaia i kul'turnaia deiatel'nost'', in P. Rusev, ed., *Rusko-balkanski kulturni vrazki prez srednevekovieto* (Sofiia, 1982), pp. 122–138, here p. 134; Pliukhanova, '"Poslanie na Ugru" i vopros o proiskhozhdenii moskovskoi imperskoi ideologii', p. 463.
145 Tikhomirov, *Vologodsko-Permskaia letopis'*, p. 266.
146 Pelenski, *Russia and Kazan*, p. 233.
147 Pliukhanova, '"Poslanie na Ugru" i vopros o proiskhozhdenii moskovskoi imperskoi ideologii', p. 484.
148 First printed: *Kniga slova izbrannyia sviatykh otets o poklonenii i o chesti sviatykh ikon* (Moskva, 1642).

In the 'Letter to the Ugra' this short interpolation is missing, but a much longer passage, inserted immediately preceding the cited paragraph, continues the line of the biblical Exodus narrative up to taking the Promised Land, which is identified as that of the Tatars. It starts with the text already quoted above and continues:

> For if we repent, our gracious God will not only have mercy, will not only deliver and save us like the old Israelites from proud and evil pharaoh, so now from the new pharaoh the heathen son of Ishmael, Akhmat, but he will even make them our slaves. When the ancient Israelites sinned before God, He enslaved them to foreigners, and when they repented, He set them judges from one of their tribes and delivered them from the slavery of strangers [. . .] When they slaved in Egypt, God liberated them by the hand of Moses from slavery in Egypt. Then God gave them Joshua, who led them to the promised land where he took 20 and 9 kingdoms and they settled down there. Later the sons of Israel transgressed, and the Lord God enslaved them in the hands of their enemies.[149]

The narrative consecutiveness of these two interpolations in adjacent places in these texts shows intention; an intention which is not explained in the texts, but which may be inferred from their internal and external logic. The passage about the dry crossing of the Red Sea was assigned to the text that was to be read in church, highlighting liberation and rescue from slavery and slavers: ordinary Orthodox believers were mainly told about the liberation. Meanwhile the parts identifying Muscovy with the New Israel and the steppe with the promised land were assigned to the 'Letter to the Ugra', as befits the more political, imperial message transported in it, to inspire speeches to the tsar's military retainers. At the present stage it seems that the sweetener for the general population – protection and liberation from slavers – was added in the Slavic version, or at least made more explicit: the part of the Greek 'Letter of the Three Patriarchs' that transferred the protective role of the bishop to the ruler was accepted wholesale; however, the role of bishops in the Byzantine Empire in ransoming and liberating of captives was not explicitly mentioned.[150]

Internal textual evidence therefore points to an early date: if the 'Letter to the Ugra' had indeed already been written in 1480, it was likely preserved at Kirillo-Belozero monastery and, due to the literary and political connections between Moscow, Belozero and Novgorod reflected in the miscellanea, the archival convoy of the Vologda-Perm documents, would have surfaced there and was copied – if not actually written in its original version – in 1499 to bolster Sofiia's recovering fortunes.[151] At least some of its concepts seem to have been put to good use already by her opponents: during the coronation ceremony in February 1498, the metropolitan asked God for Dmitrii Ivanovich, Elena's son, to be anointed as tsar just as David had been 'anointed over the people of Israel'.[152] Although he expressed his hope that God 'subdue to [Dmitrii] all

---

149 Kloss, *L'vovskaia letopis'*, p. 343.
150 Cf. chapter 5.
151 Pliukhanova, '"Poslanie na Ugru" i vopros o proiskhozhdenii moskovskoi imperskoi ideologii', p. 457.
152 Raba, 'Moscow – the Third Rome or the New Jerusalem', p. 303.

Barbarian tongues', there is not a trace yet of the biblical Exodus or the liberation from slavery in the coronation account.[153] These textual relations therefore support the observation that between 1480 and sometime in the first half of the sixteenth century the ideas of the 'Letter to the Ugra' were not well received; specifically, the nexus between self-identification as the New Israel and liberation from slave raids did not stick yet.

It is not possible to demonstrate textual contact of Bessarion's book and the 'Letter to the Ugra'; but for our purposes it is not necessary to show that it was directly influenced by contact with Greco-Italian texts. However, the early tradition of the 'Letter to the Ugra' is connected by its miscellanea to the Slavonic translation of the 'Letter of the Three Eastern Patriarchs', originally a Greek text which was changed in the process of translation. As detailed above, these two sources shared quotations in a particularly intricate, almost playful way, alternatingly starting in places in the Greek text at which the other had stopped. In some parts, the 'Letter to the Ugra' is closer to the Greek than the Slavonic 'Letter of the Three Patriarchs'; so the writer must have had direct exposure to Greek texts.[154] Given that the only capable translators were the Greeks who arrived with Sofiia, like her acolytes of Bessarion, the influence of his ideas on the 'Letter to the Ugra' needs no further explanation, even if it was indirect, that is, through the teachings which they had imbibed as pupils. Thus, Muscovy's new political culture emerged in contact – albeit indirectly – with the sources of the Italian Renaissance at its inception. This is an extraordinary finding even though, in its singularity, it does not invalidate the general reading that Muscovy did not experience the Renaissance; especially as an epoch of scholarly erudition that highly valued ancient authors, sciences and arts.

The tribulations of Sofiia and the incubation period of the ideas in the 'Letter to the Ugra' leave no doubt that practical diplomatic considerations as well as the low esteem for the Greeks, who in 1453 had finally lost their empire and their independence, impeded for the time being the consolidation of these influences. There were formidable obstacles before any more could be done in Moscow than what was done under Ivan III: to rebuild the Kremlin with the help of Italian architects, reform the military, establish an administration, reduce internal subdivisions, and translate and illuminate a few religious books according to Latin fashions. The chief obstacles were the slave raids that depleted the empire, the lack of education in all but the very top of the elite and the continuing need to ally with the Crimean khan to build and extend a power base in the Russian principalities. Practical foreign policy concerns trumped any substantial engagement on behalf of captives or the fighting of religious wars; these were not ends in themselves.

---

153 K.N. Serbina, ed., *Letopisnyi svod 1518 (Uvarovskaia)* (Moskva and Leningrad, 1962), p. 330.
154 Pliukhanova, '"Poslanje na Ugru" i vopros o proiskhozhdenii moskovskoi imperskoi ideologii', pp. 475–488.

Closely connected to the vicissitudes of alliances and court politics, isolated and partial applications of these ideas can be observed. The oath (*shert*) of the Chingissid Abd-al-Latif to Vasilii III in 1508 occurred nine years after the resurfacing of the 'Letter to the Ugra' and the reversal in Sofiia's favour with the grand prince, during the reign of her son. This oath was unusual in length and detail, containing the first requirement of a Chingissid prince at the court of the ruler of Moscow to allow captives who returned from the hordes pass unharmed:

> If a *Rusin* flees from whichever horde and takes refuge to our [Abd-al-Latif's] cossacks [*kozaki*, i.e. Tatars], our cossacks may neither hold nor rob those people and let them leave on their own accord for your [grand princely] lands.[155]

Abd-al-Latif had fallen into disfavour when Ivan III replaced him with his brother as khan of Kazan in 1502, the same year the alliance with the Crimean khan was jeopardized by the victory over the Great Horde, raising the Gireys of Crimea to the status of exclusive heirs of the *Ulus* of Jochi. His mother was Nur-Sultan, prominent widow and mother of Kazan khans and a wife to Mengli-Girey. She used her considerable influence for peace-making efforts during the transitional period before the Crimean khan led the first outright attack against Muscovy in 1521.[156] One of her aims was to liberate her son from arrest and reinstall him as Vasilii's retainer and khan in Iur'ev, later in the larger Kashira. Special efforts were made to ensure that Abd-al-Latif's status was considered equal to that of the grand prince – he was to be called Ivan's 'brother' who 'obeyed' the grand prince rather than serve him.[157] In an uncertain, transitional period this added to Muscovite leverage in negotiations, opening a window for new demands. The above quotation shows the strenuous effort of the Muscovites to differentiate Moscow's Chingissid retainers from its enemies – or simply from outlaws slaving[158] – during a crisis of alliance by finely grained treaty requirements. This instance of an obligation to deliver and help captives and slaves was a prelude to its later vital role in imperial culture.

The temporary failure of Bessarion's tireless attempts to encourage European and Italian powers to confront the expanding Ottoman Empire shows them united with Muscovy in this sentiment. However, they remained politically divided in what

---

155 Abdyl-Latif, Shertnaia gramota byvshago Kazanskogo tsaria Abdyl-Latifa velikomu kniaziu Vasiliiu Ioannovichu po pozhalovanii emu goroda Iur'eva. 1508 dekabria 29, *Zapiski Odesskogo Obshchestva Istorii i Drevnostei*, N 5 (1863), pp. 399–401, here p. 400; B. Rakhimzyanov, 'The Muslim Tatars of Muscovy and Lithuania: Some Introductory Remarks', in B.J. Boeck, ed., *Dubitando: Studies in History and Culture in Honor of Donald Ostrowski* (Bloomington IN, 2012), pp. 117–128, here p. 127.
156 I. Mirgaleev and R. Khakimov, eds., *The History of the Tatars since Ancient Times*, vol. 4: *Tatar States (15–18th Centuries)* (Kazan, 2017 [Russian: 2014]), pp. 9, 298, 302, 365, 561, 737, 742.
157 Rakhimzianov, *Moskva i tatarskii mir*, pp. 101–105.
158 See chapter 1.

to modern eyes, before the critique of Orientalism, often appeared as a lapse, but at the time may suitably be referred to as realpolitik.[159]

Despite Bessarion's striving and his apparent influence on Muscovy in the long term it would be a mistake to portray him as a fundamentalist. Not only was he a humanist, he also avoided religious parochialism and bigotry, possibly due to his peculiar position as a cardinal whose prospects to become pope were at times hampered by being Greek. When he was a papal legate, he tried to inflame Venetians for a war against the Ottomans at the instigation of the Doge in 1463. At the same time he restored to Venetian Jews their rights which had been taken from them by the previous pope, so they could once again go about their business legally.[160]

The genesis of Muscovy's political culture demonstrates that its mode of absorbing transfers from Europe and Byzantium, particularly in the early stages, was determined by political conditions in the steppe. The idea of using the moral capital of liberating slaves in order to enhance the authority of the ruler was transmitted almost immediately to Moscow when Bessarion used it to influence European princes.[161] While there was a time lag between reception and broader application attributable to steppe politics, it was nonetheless shorter[162] than in many other European cases, for the challenge of slave raids was more pressing on the edge of the steppe than it was even in Southern Europe, at least once the Muscovites had forfeited the countervailing alliance with the Crimean khanate.

From transfer to mobilisation

It is almost commonplace to comment on the fanaticism expressed by metropolitan Makarii during the conquest of Kazan. He allegedly abandoned the formerly moderate Muscovite approach to steppe politics and put the aim of converting Muslims centre stage, only to return to a more tolerant policy shortly after the conquest.[163] But it is doubtful that the 'religious motivation' identified by Jaroslav Pelenski in

---

159 L. Mohler, *Kardinal Bessarion als Theologe, Humanist und Staatsmann: Funde und Forschungen* (Paderborn, 1967), pp. 269–304, 416–424; E. Konstantinou, *Der Beitrag der byzantinischen Gelehrten zur abendländischen Renaissance des 14. und 15. Jahrhunderts* (Frankfurt am Main, 2006); G. Podskalsky, *Von Photios zu Bessarion: Der Vorrang humanistisch geprägter Theologie in Byzanz und deren bleibende Bedeutung* (Wiesbaden, 2003).
160 Mohler, *Kardinal Bessarion als Theologe, Humanist und Staatsmann*, p. 314.
161 J. Kane, *The Politics of Moral Capital* (Cambridge and New York, 2001), p. 7; Brown, *Moral Capital*, p. 457.
162 Hungary: G. Murdock, *Calvinism on the Frontier, 1600–1660: International Calvinism and the Reformed Church in Hungary and Transylvania* (New York, 2000).
163 Reasons for Moscow to conquer Kazan – as opposed to how this event was represented – are discussed in A. Kappeler, *Russland als Vielvölkerreich* (München, 1992), p. 31 (trans.: Kappeler, *The Russian Empire*).

the sources on the conquest of Kazan really represents the victory of a clerical party. Most of the sources that highlight religious motives in their attempts to justify the conquest are markedly secular in origin: such as the 'Chronicle of the Beginning of Tsardom', although it copied the major speeches and letters of Makarii; or Kurbskii's letters and his 'History'. Even the starkly religious 'Book of Royal Degrees' is addressed to the dynasty, aiming to educate the heir to the throne. The 'Chronicle' attributes the initiative for the Kazan campaigns to Ivan IV and stresses practical concerns. Even the Tatars – many of whom were Muslims – who served him were included in deliberations from the first moment, and continued to play a major role in the unfolding conquest, which sits ill with a purely religious motivation. A closer and more detailed reading of the sources reveals that religious issues were voiced in relation to concerns about slavery. As already mentioned, tsar Ivan is portrayed as deeply apprehensive about slave raids in the initial interior monologue as he gathers his resolve for the first campaign. When supplies for war were ready, Ivan went to the Kremlin Cathedral of the Annunciation to pray, to receive the blessings of the metropolitan Makarii and the other clerics, and to 'share his thoughts' with them, which changed prevailing patterns of representing raids:

> [. . .] pray and set up processions to the holy places with all clerics to ensure Christ sends his grace and overlooks our sins and ignorance and redeems the poor Christians from Kazanian slavery; [we] may be sinful, but [we] are his creation, and so that His holy name will not be tainted with our sins, he will liberate (*izbavit*) the poor Christianity, tortured by Muslims (*besermenstvo*), as the Lord redeemed (*iskupi*) [humanity] by his honourable blood, and His name and His holy resolve will be praised among us.[164]

With these words, put in the mouth of Ivan IV, Muscovy turns its back on the tradition of centuries. Slave raids used to be represented only as punishment 'for our sins' in eastern Slavic sources, and if Muscovites managed to overcome a Tatar army, it was by the grace of God that they won.[165] That used to be the whole commentary given. Apart from the triumphant tone already mentioned, the 'Chronicle' engages with this earlier convention, but turns it on its head by citing an innate entitlement to be redeemed, for 'we are [God's] creation'. While the 'Chronicle of the Beginning of Tsardom' in general focuses on secular concerns and tends to omit church events, here it engages with similar ideas as the 1551 Hundred Chapters Synod: redemption in the secular sense, i.e. the liberation of slaves, is closely aligned to the spiritual redemption of humankind by Christ.[166] Muscovite culture

---

[164] Tikhomirov, *Letopisets nachala tsarstva*, p. 60. Cf. chapter 3.
[165] Pelenski, *Russia and Kazan*, p. 183.
[166] See chapter 3.

has been berated for being 'silent', yet this text eloquently speaks to modern-day sensitivities rather than explaining the events by reference to the past.[167]

Makarii echoes Ivan's sentiment in his letter to the ruler during the campaign of 1551, again stressing that the captives were 'innocently' enslaved: that is, not for their sins, as older sources had it:[168]

> We pray to God [. . .] about your present campaign [. . .] against your foes, the godless Kazanian Tatars, your traitors and apostates, who incessantly shed innocent Christian blood and befoul and destroy the holy churches. The more so it befits you, O pious tsar Ivan [. . .] with all your Christ-loving host, to struggle firmly [. . .] for all Orthodox Christians, innocently led away into captivity, robbed and tormented by them [Kazanians] with every possible calamity, and defiled with various passions and because of these misfortunes it is appropriate for you to struggle for our holy, pure and most honourable Christian faith [. . .][169]

While innate rights are not exactly what one would usually expect in medieval Russia and certainly in Muscovy, the argument is contemporary. This letter is among the texts that Pelenski thought especially imbued with religious fervour. While there is a religious dimension here, even the omissions for the sake of brevity take nothing away from the underlying idea that it is 'befitting the tsar' to 'struggle firmly for' those 'innocently led into captivity' and effectively enslaved; therefore Ivan should campaign for Orthodoxy.[170] This is also a departure from the metropolitan's or earlier, the Byzantine bishop's obligation to redeem captives, towards the ruler assuming this role and consequently an antislavery aspect in imperial policy.[171] It adopts Bessarion's ideas on the ruler's obligation to liberate subjects, but was de-emphasized in the original 'Letter to the Ugra'.[172] In this way, it fits together with setting up a counter dependency zone in which secular policies backed up by religious prescriptions would keep Orthodox Russians safe from slave raids.[173]

While the 'Chronicle of the Beginning of Tsardom' does not depart from tradition everywhere, it does so in the main sections which are central to this argument. This is not restricted to symbolic representation. As a novelty in Russian literature and particularly the chronicles, the Kazan campaign 1552 is described in detail, complete with reports on technical details of the movement of troops, names of commanders and their concrete actions in the various conditions of siege and

---

167 Cf. V.V. Morozov, *Litsevoi svod v kontekste otechestvennogo letopisaniia XVI veka* (Moscow, 2005), p. 138.
168 On the older paradigm: Halperin, 'Paradigms of the Image of the Mongols in Medieval Russia'.
169 Tikhomirov, *Letopisets nachala tsarstva*, pp. 87–88.
170 Cf. Pelenski, *Russia and Kazan*, p. 199. On the following remarks about the sun of Orthodoxy see the last chapter about Wisdom; and about the 'dragon' or 'snake' symbolism, see St George in chapter 4.
171 See chapters 4 and 5.
172 Pliukhanova, '"Poslanie na Ugru" i vopros o proiskhozhdenii moskovskoi imperskoi ideologii', p. 465.
173 See chapter 1.

attack; motivations are also ascribed to central personages. Moscow's actions are described in documentary form: the council held by the tsar, the metropolitan and boyars, the leave-taking of the tsar from the *tsaritsa*, the messages Makarii sent to Ivan and so forth. In this way, the longest narration in early Russian literature was constructed – the so-called 'Tale about the conquest of Kazan'.[174]

Unlike many Muscovite sources of the sixteenth century, the 'Chronicle' can be dated with great confidence, and its internal data about its author point in a clear, if general, direction. The selection of events highlights the actions of Aleksei Adashev, from the rather unimportant embassy to Istanbul in which he took part as a youngster with his father, a well-versed diplomat, to the detailed treatment of the Kazan campaigns. Adashev's role in the latter is emphasized, including his missions to Kazan as a negotiator and in organizing the mining operation that collapsed the city wall. Updated versions of the chronicle up to 1560 give greater prominence to his actions while suppressing events that might cast a shadow on his role in the conquest of the city. In his role as *kazna*, the de-facto head of the tsar's treasury who signed its documents, he had access to the letters sent by metropolitan Makarii to Ivan IV. These letters are quoted in the chronicle. While major church events are omitted, matters of state and the military are usually treated in detail and with great competence, as befit Adashev's profile of administrator, diplomat and military leader. Moreover, he engaged in chronicle writing, keeping a copy of the Nikon chronicle for reference. Throughout the extant copies, several phases of chronicle writing can be traced between the early 1550s and 1560. These stages are in good accord with records about Adashev's own engagement in writing the 'Chronicle of Recent Years', the continuation of the 'Chronicle of the Beginning of Tsardom' up to 1560, which was preserved as part of the 'L'vov Chronicle'. Finally, the late husband of Adashev's daughter left 'many Latin and German books'.[175] Although more detailed information about these books is not available, they may have added to the sources of Adashev's ideas about Moses and the liberation of slaves. Thus, while the nature of the sources does not allow us to determine the exact history of reception, it is possible to identify the general paths along which ideas of an innate right to liberation travelled to Muscovy, as well as the likely date and authorship of the 'Chronicle of the Beginning of Tsardom'. Moreover, its omission even of major church events such as the Hundred Chapter Synod and the general administrative and military-minded character of this source raise questions

---

[174] D.S. Likhachev, *Russkie letopisi i ikh kul'turno-istoricheskoe znachenie* (Moskva, 1970), pp. 367–370.
[175] Zimin, *I.S. Peresvetov i ego sovremenniki*, pp. 29–41. A summary of recent debates on the *Letopisets*'s origins: B.M. Kloss, 'Predislovie', in *Letopisets nachala tsarstva tsaria i velikogo kniazia Ivana Vasil'evicha – Aleksandro-Nevskaia letopis' – Lebedevskaia letopis'* (Moskva, 2009). Lenhoff, 'Politics and Form in the Stepennaia Kniga'. The question whether it was indeed Adashev who wrote the chronicle, or someone close to him, is irrelevant for the task at hand.

about the exact nature of the 'religious' statements and motivation for conquering Kazan, which are emphasized by much of scholarly literature.[176] Such a combination seems unlikely.

This aligns with the question of how practical, 'realist' foreign policy issues were balanced by the Exodus narrative and the concern for liberating captives. Was this concern merely a cloak, a veil pulled over events to mask the real motives,[177] or was it part of the events, did it perhaps even contribute to them? And if so, in what way?

As shown above, in the immediate context of the stand-off at the Ugra the new ideas expressed in the letter ascribed to Vassian Rylo had little effect. These ideas had just been transferred from the post-Byzantine milieu in Renaissance Italy into the cultural environment of Muscovy, where some may have noted them as a remarkable, though seriously deviating new point of view, but without much immediate political value. However, after an incubation period, the 'Letter to the Ugra' was promoted in the mid-sixteenth century to core reading for educated Muscovites: it was included in a range of chronicles, the 'Novgorod Chronicle', the 'Voskresenskii Chronicle' and the 'Illuminated Chronicle', as well as metropolitan Makarii's 'Great Reading Meneae'.[178] This is a well-known fact but mostly quoted out of context. Yet it brings out some central concepts at an early stage that shaped Muscovite political culture.

While the dynastic legitimation for the conquest of Kazan is often taken for a distinct motive,[179] the 'Letter' makes already clear that the dynasty was to be seen in the context of their deeds of liberation:

> For your known rakes still whisper false advice into your ears not to stand against the heretics, but to quit and deliver the speaking herd of Christian sheep to the wolf. [. . .] "[B]lessed be the man who gives his soul for his people", for we hear that the ungodly language of the Sons of Hagar closes in on our country and your [i.e. the tsar's] inheritance. They have already captured many intermediary peoples and lands and move towards us. Set out, therefore, quickly to oppose them [. . .] Follow the example of your grand princely ancestors who [. . .] defended the Russian [people and] land from the heathens, [. . .] such as the feats of Igor and Sviatoslav, and Vladimir [. . .] Later, Vladimir Monomakh battled with the accursed Polovtsians for the Russian land [. . .][180]

---

176 Cf. Romaniello, *The Elusive Empire*, p. 32.
177 Pelenski, *Russia and Kazan*, pp. 249–250; Kämpfer, *Die Eroberung von Kasan 1552 als Gegenstand der zeitgenössischen russischen Historiographie*, p. 117.
178 Pliukhanova, '"Poslanie na Ugru" i vopros o proiskhozhdenii moskovskoi imperskoi ideologii', pp. 453–454; D.B. Miller, 'The Velikie Minei Chetii and the Stepennaia Kniga of Metropolitan Makarii and the Origins of Russian National Consciousness' (Wiesbaden, 1979), pp. 263–382.
179 Pelenski, *Russia and Kazan*, pp. 94–103.
180 M.N. Tikhomirov, ed., *Vologodsko-permskii letopisets* (Moskva and Leningrad, 1959), p. 269.

The 'Book of Royal Degrees (*Stepennaia kniga*)' corroborates this redemptive view of genealogy as not only a central ideology of justification, but as validation of the tsar's task to liberate Orthodox Christians. It deals extensively with this theme after an introduction which promotes identification of Muscovy with the New Israel as one of the book's defining subtexts. Throughout the genealogical part, there are clues pointing forward to fulfilment of the promise inherent in the covenant with God in the book's last 'step' – i.e. the last generation – portraying the reign of Ivan IV as a blessed leader.[181] In step 17, the last, which never went beyond the year 1555 in describing Ivan's reign, this line of thought culminates in the description of the deliverance of 'uncountable male and female Christian captives' during the conquest of Kazan. The 'Book of Royal Degrees' compares this feat, using the image already applied to Tamerlane, with those of

> God [who] through the agency of Moses liberated the Hebrew lineage from pharaoh's slavery, who despite many premonitions due to his hardened heart drowned in the sea with his whole army, while [Moses] led Israel on dry ground through the sea. Likewise, the same God sent the pious and honourable tsar Ivan [IV] to liberate by his own hand the New Israel of Christian people from Tatar captivity, while the Kazanians had hardened their hearts.[182]

Thus, the saintly members of the dynasty become a precondition for deliverance from slavery and settlement of the promised land while their rule is dignified and legitimised by Ivan's conquest. This idea adapts the claim in the 'Chronicle of the Beginning of Tsardom' to innate rights referred to above: that it would be disgraceful to God to keep the New Israel in captivity any longer, as man was created by God and in His image. The 'Book of Royal Degrees', composed in the 1550s to instruct the royal successor, aims to inflect this idea to the greater praise of the dynasty.[183] This later interpretation already recognizes the inherent danger: it differed

---

[181] N.N. Pokrovskii, ed., *The Book of Degrees of the Royal Genealogy: A Critical Edition Based on the Oldest Known Manuscripts. Texts and Commentary*, vol. 2: *Degrees XI–XVII. Appendices, indices* (Moskva, 2008), pp. 30, 115–116, 239, 294, 299–300, 569, 584, 605–609, 623, 626–627. Gail Lenhoff argues that the work was structured 'to project the triumph of Ivan's eastern policy onto Russia's past and to interpret that past as a new triumph of Orthodoxy:' Lenhoff, 'Politics and Form in the Stepennaia Kniga', p. 174; G. Lenhoff, 'The Construction of Russian History in Stepennaia Kniga', *Revue des études slaves*, 76, 1 (2005), pp. 31–50, here pp. 40–41. 'Stepen' is sometimes translated as 'degree', although in this title it designates the symbolic confluence of generations of the dynasty and steps on a ladder. Cf. V.A. Kivelson, 'Diskussion: Papers of a Conference Complementing the New Edition of the "Stepennaia Kniga"', *Jahrbücher für Geschichte Osteuropas* 61, 3 (2013), pp. 444–446.
[182] Pokrovskii, *The Book of Degrees of the Royal Genealogy*, p. 365.
[183] On dating the Tomsk ms. which was written on paper produced and otherwise used in Moscow in the mid to late 1550s: A.J. Usachev, *Stepennaia kniga i drevnerusskaia knizhnost' vremeni mitropolita Makariia* (Moskva, 2009), pp. 125–175; G. Lenhoff, 'Neue Literatur zur "Stepennaja kniga": Current Research on the Stepennaja kniga: Consensus, Controversies, Questions', *Jahrbücher für Geschichte Osteuropas*, 61, 3 (2013), pp. 438–443, here p. 441.

from the account given by the administrators, where the right to be liberated was first seen as innate to Orthodox Christians. In the 'Book of Royal Degrees', the moral capital of liberating slaves is firmly associated with the dynasty – not with the people, de-emphasizing potential oppositional interpretations.

From liberation to conquest

Just a month after Shah Ali's celebrated inauguration in Kazan, events took a sharp reversal – at least from the point of view of the 'Chronicle of the Beginning of Tsardom'. In September 1551, the khan sent a delegation of Kazan nobles headed by the *mirza* Muralei to reclaim the High Bank, Kazanian territory on the western bank of the Volga. Ivan IV stuck to what he saw as his right of conquest, as he had taken the High Bank before peace was signed. At the same time, the boyar and Muscovite military commander at Shah Ali's court, Ivan Khabarov and secretary Ivan Vyrodkov reported that

> The Kazanians do not keep their written oath to the ruler about captives; khan Shah Ali indulges them due to [the threat of] rebellion.[184]

Shah Ali may have feared an insurrection that would topple him from the throne. Whether concern over captives was indeed at the centre of Kazanian claims or only intended as a bargain chip in exchange for the High Bank[185] remains uncertain. However, Muscovites in no uncertain words linked treason to a delay in liberating slaves.

Ivan reacted swiftly and sent back prince Muralei to Shah Ali; he separately dispatched the new governor Dmitrii F. Paletskii and secretary Ivan Klobukov, the latter two with a clearly stated task. They carried great gifts for Shah Ali and the dignitaries of Kazan and Gorodets. Their task was to talk to the Kazanians and warn them:

> He ordered to give a formal speech of grace to the khan and all people of Kazan for their service. About the captives he gave orders to liberate all Rus' captives according to the written oath. If they do not release the captives and the ruler sees Christians in fetters, he will not suffer this, as God may help him. He reminded the khan about the grants obtained from his father the grand prince and from tsar and Grand Prince Ivan, to rule in Kazan according to the written oaths and set free all Rus' captives.[186]

---

184 Tikhomirov, *Letopisets nachala tsarstva*, p. 67.
185 Kämpfer, *Die Eroberung von Kasan 1552 als Gegenstand der zeitgenössischen russischen Historiographie*, pp. 119–120.
186 Tikhomirov, *Letopisets nachala tsarstva*, p. 67.

Once more the 'Chronicle' insists on the significance of liberating all slaves in Kazanian hands. Any omission is considered 'unbearable' by Ivan. The tsar already spoke sharply and uncompromisingly, on an elevated moral plain. From Moscow's perspective, liberation from slavery was the crucial point; the issue of territory, which the Kazanians wished to discuss, was not open to discussion. The 'Chronicle's' choice of words remains factual where it speaks about captives, but where the issue of liberation and the oath of Kazanians is touched, it evokes the morally apprehensive condition of slavery or 'unfreedom', deprivation of mobility (*nevolia*) of Rus' people (*ruskii*) by a foreign power.[187]

It is unfortunate that the perspective of the other side, the points of view of the Kazan and Crimean Tatars, have not come down to us. They might have revealed hidden agendas. However, if we grant Keenan's hypothesis of a special practice of steppe politics, which claims that diplomacy in the steppe was used only to construct temporary alliances which could be revoked as soon as conditions changed and that nomads as well as Kazanians did not accept the concept of suzerainty and limitation of sovereignty implied in Muscovite rule,[188] the 'Chronicle' still conveys a clear message. The war was about liberating captives; if this demand was not met, at least in a binding statement, territorial aggrandizement was acceptable. Moreover, the obligation to manumit all captives was used to defend an unassailable moral high ground and to offset all Kazanian complaints about what might be called colonization. The 'Chronicle' exhorts Shah Ali

> [. . .] to rule in Kazan according to the written oaths and set free all Rus' captives. Moreover, he shall make Kazan safe (*ukrepil*) for the ruler and for himself as he did in Kasimov; so that it may never again be inclined to move away [from its oath] and blood will not be spilled on both sides for many ages.[189]

Since 1447, the newly created khanate and Muscovite district of Kasimov had been the station of many Chinggisids in Muscovite service, the place Shah Ali had been first awarded in 1516. It was an appanage princedom, which meant the Moscow ruler decided who received it, although this might be an issue of diplomatic negotiations with Chinggisid rulers outside of Muscovy. Kazan was to be 'strengthened', tied to Moscow in the same way as Kasimov to guarantee an end to bloodshed in future.[190] Slave raids and the liberation of slaves who were to have the right to be set free and being with their families served as litmus test of unshakable loyalty and as a kind of moral capital, levelled against the legitimate claims of Kazanians to rule their territory and change alliances.[191]

---

187 Kivelson, 'Bitter Slavery and Pious Servitude'.
188 Keenan, 'Muscovy and Kazan''. Cf. Rieber, *The Struggle for the Eurasian Borderlands*, p. 37.
189 Tikhomirov, *Letopisets nachala tsarstva*, p. 67.
190 Rakhimzianov, *Moskva i tatarskii mir*; Tikhomirov, *Letopisets nachala tsarstva*, p. 68.
191 Brown, *Moral Capital*; Kane, *The Politics of Moral Capital*.

The 'Chronicle of the Beginning of Tsardom' repeatedly and vehemently drives home this point. In the following paragraph, the next Kazan envoys, who had been sent by Shah Ali in the autumn of 1551 and included a prominent member of the Divan, the great *karachi bey* Shirin-Muralev, repeat their request to return to Kazan the territories or at least the associated revenues. The tsar flatly denies. He then continues with a much longer answer about the oath they gave to the Moscow ruler, which they apparently considered mutually binding. In the Kazanian's voice reported by the 'Chronicle':

> that the ruler be merciful and consider his word binding: give the khan and all Kazanians, for what they had given their oath to the ruler.[192]

Ivan was concerned about a rebellion against his and Shah Ali's rule, since there was already a long history of mutual disputes and depositions of rulers of Kazan, in which Moscow's influence waxed and waned and, over long periods, had entirely broken down.[193] The tone therefore became even more strident, and the subject of slavery proved an inexhaustible reservoir of distraction from negotiation over territory:

> Ivan IV had listened to their petition and ordered to answer that Kazan would not see even one coin from the High Bank. About the oath the ruler said: Kazanians swore an oath to set free all Orthodox Christian captives to the last man. However, today they keep many captives. Once the khan and all Kazanians release all Rus' captives they may remind him of the oath. The envoys petitioned the ruler that he may send a letter to the khan and all people about the captives, and they would wait it out, until all captives are liberated.[194]

Demonstrative concerns of this kind are swiftly justified, as Khabarov and Vyrodkov arrived in Moscow, the boyar and the secretary who, as already mentioned, had stayed with Shah Ali in Kazan to oversee the liberation of the slaves. They reported that things were not at all well:

> The Kazanians have released few captives so far, they shackle and put them into pits. The khan does not look after the captives as he should since he refuses to execute those on whom captives are confiscated according to the written oath excusing himself by the threat of rebellion.[195]

As we have no Tatar sources, we cannot prove conclusively that Kazanians were unwilling to fulfil their pledge, or that some of them shackled and 'buried' (*khoroniat*) slaves in earth holes. This practice was reported in Crimea and later in the Caucasus, where guards slept on planks laid across pits to stop slaves from escaping

---

192 Tikhomirov, *Letopisets nachala tsarstva*, p. 68.
193 Pelenski, *Russia and Kazan*, pp. 23–61; M.G. Khudiakov, *Ocherki po istorii Kazanskogo khanstva* (Moskva, 1991), pp. 106–109; V.V. Vel'iaminov-Zernov, *Izsledovanie o Kasimovskikh tsariach i tsarevichakh*, pt. 1 (Sankt-Peterburg, 1863); Rakhimzianov, *Moskva i tatarskii mir*, pp. 92–107.
194 Tikhomirov, *Letopisets nachala tsarstva*, p. 68.
195 Ibid.

during an emergency.[196] However, the 'Chronicle' has Moscow use these arguments to counter Kazanian demands that lost territory on the western bank of the Volga be returned, applying them to both the situation during campaign and after the conquest of Kazan, when the Tatars of the middle Volga were still in open rebellion.[197] The Tatars are portrayed here as being prepared to risk offending the tsar rather than relinquishing their slaves; Shah Ali is even forced to claim that his subjects were in a rebellious mood. Such a stance is damning in the context of their oath and the much-repeated policy of the Muscovites, adding to Muscovite moral capital. The 'Chronicle' works hard to establish an image of the Tatars as recalcitrant slavers, but might be inclined to overstate the importance of slavery in Kazan.

The issue of slave liberation was important enough to be repeated: it is next taken up against Shah Ali when for the third time he complains that he will not be able to serve the Muscovite ruler in Kazan if he fails to recover the High Bank for Kazan. Prince Dmitrei F. Palitsei again denies this request, stressing that God granted these territories to the tsar by the right of the sword. He then adds to this argument of customary law of nations based on naked violence the repeated accusation that the Kazanians refused to liberate slaves, thus showing the Muscovites in a more favourable light:

> You know best about the excess of disgrace and loss caused by Kazanians to our ruler. Nowadays they keep Christian captives in slavery (*polon krestiianskoi u sebia derzhiat v nevole*), and they lie to our ruler despite their oath. Many Gorodetsk [Tatars] who arrived with you keep Christian captives as slaves, as you know. Kazanians will continue to act in this way, but how can our ruler bear to watch Christians in slavery (*v rabote*)? When you, ruler [Shah Ali] were enthroned in Kazan by the great prince's boyar and prince Iur'i Golitsyn, all people swore an oath that they will manumit all captives. Yet they have not set free even one person. The ruler should stand up for his Christianity with the aid of the gracious God. If, ruler, you do not protect them on behalf of our ruler, then he, the [Muscovite] ruler, will have to answer God for this.[198]

These repetitions are dramaturgical hyperbole, adding urgency to the Muscovite quest. It puts the issue of slavery and liberation centre-stage, enhancing the image of the ruler. Slaving is portrayed as almost contagious, a motif soon echoed in Makarii's 'Letter', although the precise way in which the Gorodets cossacks, themselves Tatars in the Moscow tsar's service, were contaminated by taking slaves, is left to anyone's guesses. After all, it was in keeping with the precepts of the counter dependency zone that not until 1627 was it prohibited for Muslim subjects of the Muscovite tsar to keep Orthodox slaves; even thereafter there were plenty of loopholes.[199] Liberating

---

196 Sanin, *Otnosheniia Rossii i Ukrainy s Krymskim Khanstvom v seredine XVII veka*, pp. 195–196.
197 Romaniello, *The Elusive Empire*.
198 Tikhomirov, *Letopisets nachala tsarstva*, p. 69.
199 See Introduction. Hellie, *Slavery in Russia, 1450–1725*, pp. 73–74. However, consider the oath of Abd-al-Latif, above.

the slaves is seen as God's command with severe consequences for the shirker, even if he was elevated to *tsar'*. These events lead up to the decisive confrontation, explained in terms of the Muscovite motivation to set the captives free. Let us not forget that the decision to found Sviiazhsk had already been framed in these terms.

Khan Shah Ali, who understood that these were final words, replies to Prince Dmitrei that this will put him at odds with the Kazanians. Aiming to remain faithful

> to Ivan, he will do everything to weaken Moscow's adversaries in Kazan, including spoiling powder and leading ringleaders of the anti-Moscow party astray to deliver them to Ivan. Nevertheless, he insists that he will not become apostate (*stati na svoiu veru*), that is in this case [not] allow the Muscovite army clandestinely into town.[200]

In the meantime, some Kazanians decided it was better to become full subjects of the tsar of Moscow than to fight on: Ivan received such a document from Tatar dignitaries in January 1552. When some had taken the oath of fealty to Ivan in March, others raised the alarm and claimed that the approaching Muscovite troops intended to massacre the population. Since Shah Ali had left the town, gates were closed and Kazan seceded from Muscovy again.[201] Kazanian dignitaries dispatched a letter to the Nogais asking for a Chinggisid prince to be put on their throne. To the 'Chronicle' this constituted treason, along with a Tatar attack on the High Bank which was repelled by locals loyal to Moscow. On hearing about it, Ivan again turns to God for support, unfailingly calling for liberation of the slaves:

> The ruler was astounded about this, called on God's aid and [. . .] on metropolitan Makarii and the whole holy assembly to pray to God for the liberation of Orthodox Christians and the victory over enemies.[202]

Shah Ali originally advocated delaying the campaign until winter when conditions would be better, but Ivan had already started the army's advance. The khan of Kazan, who had left his throne and city due to accusations and threats from the locals, thereupon extolled Ivan:

> It is your right, ruler, since the beginning; and they betrayed you. Thus, God be with you, ruler.[203]

Ever since the works of Kämpfer, Pelenski and Keenan appeared, scholars have openly or indirectly doubted the sincerity of this statement, which amounts to a full endorsement of the Muscovite position by a Chinggisid who insists on punishment for thwarting the full liberation of all captives demanded by the oath. This position is based on Edward Keenan's notion of 'steppe politics' in loose confederations of tribes

---

200 Tikhomirov, *Letopisets nachala tsarstva*, p. 69.
201 Pelenski, *Russia and Kazan*, pp. 45–46.
202 Tikhomirov, *Letopisets nachala tsarstva*, p. 73.
203 Ibid., p. 78.

and alliances which could be foregone almost instantly if conditions changed. Consequently, Moscow had applied its own, sedentary rules to conquer and annex Kazan.[204] However, such statements are somewhat beside the point. To Muscovites, the oath taken the year before was decisive, but this may not have been accepted as binding on both sides. It should not be forgotten that republican, urban politics in Europe were changeable enough to inspire Machiavelli's *Il Principe*, which stresses the need to act swiftly and decidedly at the beginning of one's reign, to unsettle and exile opponents. Obviously, the sources do not allow us to probe Shah Ali's validation of the Muscovite view. However, if his statement was forged, it remains a forgery well informed by contemporary European and worldwide norms for treating traitors. If a city or vassal was disloyal to king or emperor, a variety of norms applied. However, even in Europe legitimate harsh treatment was reserved for those who transgressed repeatedly.[205] Outright terror was a means of internal politics even in early modern England's policies towards Ireland. It was not alone in doing so, as Spanish measures against rebellious Dutch subjects prove.[206] The Mongol practice of swift and devastating retribution even to those who resisted initial conquest set a precedent hardly likely to be forgotten by falling into disuse – and certainly not by Muscovite chronicle writers. Moreover, Lhamsuren Munkh-Erdene recently showed that already in the pre-Mongol period there existed a commonly accepted norm (*cimar*) requiring sanctions for breaking an oath of alliance. Given the propensity to yield to a raiding economy, it might have to be enforced by armed means, as Temüjin did who in due course became Great Khan of the Mongols. However, punishment for oath-breaking was a Mongol norm. Consequently, the *Secret History of the Mongols* consecrates a lengthy passage to establishing Temüjin's multifarious rightful grievances towards his erstwhile partners and foes. In recent decades, the 'steppe politics' paradigm – essentially an Orientalist reminiscence – appears to have stalled the study of these and more general questions of Mongol and steppe statecraft.[207] While misnamed and essentialised 'steppe politics' was the outcome if norms could not be enforced during the shatter period of empire, which resulted in a slaving zone, empire builders could rely on notions that were shared beyond settled,

---

204 Keenan, 'Muscovy and Kazan'. In its own time, this was a visionary formulation of relations between Moscow and the steppe.
205 T. Broekmann, *Rigor iustitiae: Herrschaft, Recht und Terror im normannisch-staufischen Süden (1050–1250)* (Darmstadt, 2005). See also: Kämpfer, *Die Eroberung von Kasan 1552 als Gegenstand der zeitgenössischen russischen Historiographie*, p. 123.
206 J. Israel, *The Dutch Republic: Its Rise, Greatness, and Fall 1477–1806* (Oxford, 1995), pp. 159–160.
207 L. Munkh-Erdene, 'The Rise of the Chinggisid Dynasty: Pre-Modern Eurasian Political Order and Culture at a Glance', *International Journal of Asian Studies*, 15, 1 (2018), pp. 39–84, here pp. 47–50. After the conquest of Kazan and Astrakhan, Moscow allowed itself for the first time to install a khan (*tsar*) in the khanate of Kasimov instead of a sultan (*tsarevich*), or prince. This indicated that the tsar of Moscow ranked higher than the khan: Rakhimzianov, *Moskva i tatarskii mir*, pp. 124–126. Whether Moscow changed this rule due to its victory in battle or because Ivan IV had acted like Chinggis khan remains an open legal question.

agricultural Muscovy. The 'Chronicle of the Beginning of Tsardom', written under the constant threat and reality of rebellion in the middle Volga region, was well-advised to give much attention to such details of legitimation. It attests to the fact that Muscovy was still part of the steppe world although it had extended its position, penetrating Chinggisid realms step by step and using all means available.[208]

Makarii's letters

As Ivan IV set out for the decisive campaign in May 1552, his commanders repelled the incursion of the Crimean khan as they crossed the steppe. Meanwhile Ivan proceeded further north, never forgetting to stop and pray at local shrines and in monasteries, which turned the campaign into a sort of pilgrimage.[209] Already at Sviiazhsk, the 'Edifying Letter' of metropolitan Makarii reached them and was read aloud.[210] At the outset it praises the liberation of slaves who joyously returned to their homes. This is part and precondition of a great celebration of a *pax Rossica* using biblical imagery. Envoys from 'all ends of the world' arrive with gifts, and formerly slave-raiding foes pledge allegiance to the tsar:

> Our pious tsar and ruler handed the city of Kazan over to his khan (*tsar'*) Shah Ali with all Kazanian districts (*ulus*) and the Cheremis high bank was attached to the new town of Sviiazhsk thanks to our ruler, tsar and grand prince. The abundant Christian captives, male and female, youths and maidens and children, happily returned to their own (*vo svoiasy*) insulted by nobody, due to our [army's] manly bravery, aided by God's grace and [our] ruler's free will and independence (*gosudarskoiu svobodoiu*). The Crimean khan and the Nogai princes, many nomads (*ordy*), the [Polish-]Lithuanian king and foreign kings sent ambassadors with presents and letters for love and peace to our tsar and ruler, and all ends of the world were awed. Many countries sent presents and Chingissid princes (*tsarevichi*) and scions of other great powers flocked to the court of our tsar and ruler by their own initiative and wished to serve him due to his broadmindedness and great recompense. Our cities and country live in peace and without inner turmoil and the Kazanian princes, *murzes*, *seitans*, *ulans* and people of all ranks came and wished to serve our pious tsar by their own will, due to God's aid and fear of our pious tsar, and they did not turn away from him.[211]

The 'Chronicle's' statement here about the emotions of the returnees from slavery amounts to an assertion that the court of the tsar was concerned about its subjects' happy return to their homes, safe from insults. Next in the Letter, Makarii included liberation from slavery in his list of the virtues of good government:

---

208 Rakhimzianov, *Moskva i tatarskii mir*, pp. 391–393.
209 See chapter 4.
210 His first of three written in 1552: Pelenski, *Russia and Kazan*, p. 197.
211 Tikhomirov, *Letopisets nachala tsarstva*, pp. 75–76.

> About all the ineffable virtues we owe to the Lord our God. [. . .] Remember what God demands from us in return: Nothing but to observe His Commandments. The Commandments are not hard to observe, since they are no more than true, righteous, unflinching and warm belief in almighty God and mercy, peace and love without falsehood for all, and righteous justice, aiding the poor and speedy administration and liberation of captives [. . .][212]

This line of thought continues, as God's commandments are not exhausted with recommendations on good government; general moral and canonical rules are to be observed to satisfy God much in the way of the biblical covenant between God and the Israelites. Among these, one in particular concerns captives and their treatment:

> By their disrespect and lawlessness they have ruthlessly and shamelessly committed fornication with young boys, sodomite defilation and unholiness. Even less will I keep silent about the insolence of those who do not shy away from annoying God by defiling and destroying captives only just liberated by God from heathen hands, virtuous women and virgin girls, as I have heard many times.[213]

Following middle Byzantine changes to established Roman models,[214] returned and ransomed captives and slaves are included as part of the community of God's covenant, and must therefore be treated respectfully. Makarii espouses principles of communal life that treat captives and former captives as both a blessing and a threat to community. He cites Phinehas, son of Aaron, the high priest during the Exodus from Egypt as an example to those who mix with captives or captors: his zeal for purity of belief in the one and only God allegedly ended the plague that had befallen Israel as punishment for falling from Judaic monotheism. Phinehas' zeal brutally ended the life of a Midianite princess and an Israeli man on their bed with his lance.[215] Makarii spares no effort to make it clear that such mixing was reprehensible and led to exclusion from church and community:

> [. . .] See and know the sword and wrath of God. [. . .] Under the prophet Moses, when the Israelites wandered the desert, the grace of God was with them and the Lord gave them victory over their enemies; likewise, He has shown it to you in our time. [But] if you start to fornicate [with captives] you will not be able to overcome your enemies but will always succumb to them.[216]

The Christian community is imagined as pure and valiant as long as it abstains from carnal pleasures both with weaker members of the community, for whom returned captives are used as an evocative example, and with Muslims who as so-called 'pagans' – despite adhering to a religion of the book – are depicted as a threat to the covenant

---

212 Ibid., p. 76.
213 Ibid.
214 Y. Rotman, *Byzantine Slavery and the Mediterranean World* (Cambridge MA, 2009).
215 5 Moses 25.
216 Tikhomirov, *Letopisets nachala tsarstva*, pp. 76–77.

and liberation. Sexual relations across the invisible line that Makarii would like to separate Muslims and Christians, and especially homoerotic, is seen as weakening the militant spirit of Muscovites and as a threat to its new-found liberty. As a 'foreign custom', even 'indulging women' by shaving off beards is portrayed as an enemy of Orthodoxy, something that defines Latin culture and the South. Makarii singles out intercourse with formerly enslaved women and virgins, imagined as pure and unpolluted, as particularly inappropriate in his eyes. His loud warnings betray a sense of the Church's insecurity much like that of the Hebrew writers of the Pentateuch surrounded by polytheists to whom they often succumbed, as well as to their rituals. His aim is to graft an Old Testament sense onto the Muscovite expressions of honour, which formed a central ligament of society, or at least of the warrior elite.[217] He threatens excommunication and the tsar's disgrace to all who transgress:

> [. . .] those who commit adultery and fornication with captive women and girls and who are then accused will fall in disgrace of the pious tsar and will be [. . .] excommunicated.[218]

Makarii misses no opportunity to link this to overall ideas about the New Israel:

> When Moses was the prophet, when the Israelites wandered [forty years] through the desert, he gave the victory over their enemies as he gives it to you today.[219]

With all due reservations owing to the pre-modern elements in Makarii's worldview, here is an attempt to define the covenant through the procreative cycle of human fertility, idealising the captive body as something particularly holy and pure, which needed to be set free, to enjoy being able to return back home unblemished. To this purported end, the militant spirit of Muscovites needs to be enhanced. Makarii spares no strong words to pour scorn on the Tatars opposing Ivan in Kazan. To what extent his ideas were accepted in wider Muscovite society cannot be gleaned solely from this text, although its inclusion and the creation of further copies along with the 'Chronicle' are indications of its distribution.[220] Such an idealised differential treatment of Muslim slaving and strong asymmetrical dependency in Orthodox Muscovy underlines the role of religion in the counter dependency zone, differentiating between insiders and outsiders, rather than victors and vanquished.

In his second letter during the last Kazan campaign, which Ivan received on or after 13 July 1552, Makarii reiterates his admonition to behave piously. He again justifies the war against Kazan with the need to forcibly liberate the slaves after Kazan broke oath:

---

[217] N.S. Kollmann, *By Honor Bound: State and Society in Early Modern Russia* (Ithaca NY, 1999).
[218] Tikhomirov, *Letopisets nachala tsarstva*, p. 78.
[219] Ibid., p. 77.
[220] This will be discussed in chapter 4 on popular attitudes to liberating slaves. Multiple copies of the 'Chronicle' in later records and Remezov's writings amongst others suggest a lasting and, for Muscovite conditions, rather widespread reception.

against your ungodly enemies, the Kazan Tatars, your traitors and insubordinates, who have always shed the blood of innocent Christians, defiled and destroyed holy churches. For this reason, it is incumbent upon you, pious and honorific tsar, and on your brother prince Vladimir Andreevich and all your Christ-loving army, to rise manfully with God's help for the holy Church and for all Orthodox Christians who were innocently led into captivity and taken away and tortured and defiled by all manner of malice and lust.[221]

Makarii underscores the wrongfulness of enslavement and the bad and 'defiling' treatment slaves purportedly received at the hands of Kazan Tatars. Due to their hard lot and Kazanian treason, he repeats, piety calls for taking up arms against Kazan.[222]

Conquest

At every step during the preparations and the army's march towards Kazan, the 'Chronicle' brings up the role of liberated captives and those taking the opportunity of the approaching army to flee. Thus, at Tula, where the passing army repulses the onslaught of the Crimean khan, the liberation of 'many' captives driven by the Crimean Tatars is mentioned.[223] At Kazan, the tsar calls on captives and recent defectors who had fled from the city at the approach of the Muscovite army to find out about the city's secret water supply.[224] When during the fighting khan Ediger-Mahmet advances daringly and at least partly successful, he is depicted as a hardened enemy who with all people in Kazan swore to fight to the death, averse to submit to the Muscovite ruler. Such a stance is explained by citing the biblical Exodus motif of pharaoh refusing to let the slaves leave Egypt until the plagues imposed God's will on him: 'God hardened their hearts, as he did with pharaoh'.[225] This in turn serves to reconfirm the claim that Kazanians had broken their oath by refusing to manumit the slaves. The beneficial role of Ivan's army for the slaves as well as its support to the common effort of liberation is underscored wherever possible and by whatever means at hand. Thus, the 'Chronicle' maintains its general line and emphasis on slavery and liberation throughout passages that are basically technical, military and administrative in nature. The well-informed and pointed use of such sources and voices demonstrates that these ideas penetrated deep within the chancellery structure.

Once it had been made abundantly clear that the tsar wished to see the slaves liberated, and obligations fulfilled, the narrative climaxes when the besieging troops

---

[221] Tikhomirov, *Letopisets nachala tsarstva*, pp. 86–87.
[222] Cf. I. Izmaylov, 'Conquest of the Middle Volga Region and Sociopolitical Consequences. §1. Conquest of Kazan: Reasons, Course, Consequences', in R. Khakimov, I. Gilyazov and B. Izmaylov, eds., *The History of the Tatars since Ancient Times*, vol. 5: *Tatars in Russia (Second Half of the 16–18th Centuries)* (Kazan, 2017 [Russian: 2014]), pp. 60–70, here p. 61.
[223] Tikhomirov, *Letopisets nachala tsarstva*, pp. 83–84.
[224] Ibid., p. 100.
[225] Ibid., p. 99.

stand under the walls and climb them. The Kazanians are given a last opportunity to deliver themselves to the tsar, who is portrayed as a good, honourable Christian ruler wishing to avoid spilling blood and therefore generously offers subjecthood and no reprisals to his adversaries:

> The pious and honourable lord [and] Christian tsar wanted to avoid human bloodletting and sent Kamaia-*murza* the Kazanian and [a delegation of] mountain people to the city to [tell them to] petition the ruler. If the khan's people see God's grace, petition and give themselves into the hand of the tsar and extradite the traitors, then the Lord will forgive them and will not avenge himself on them. However, the Kazanians in the city said with one voice: "We will not petition, [even if] Rus' was on the walls and in the tower; we will just build another wall. We will all die or wait out the siege". They answered like doltish hardheads, as God had deafened their enmity to make them misunderstand how the tsar properly applied the rules just in front of them. The Orthodox tsar said: "All-merciful God, look [into] our heart[s], although I sent to them with all humility, they chose blood rather than peace and directed their illness at their heads and there will be blood over them and their sons".[226]

The whole point of the campaign is to subjugate firmly those who previously had been able to choose their ruler themselves and sought to preserve their liberties. Nevertheless, the liberation of slaves helps to portray the conquest as a choice between, on the one hand, serving bonds and oaths, and, on the other hand, becoming obstreperous traitors who deserve their lot. Insistence on 'the rules' stresses the background in Mongol law without naming it. Stressing the Christian ideal of humility serves to distance Ivan from Mongol customs. This image conforms to the counter dependency zone by identifying Muscovy with the New Israel, a theme which recurs more frequently in the text from this point on. As mentioned above, khan Ediger's advance attracted comments about the plagues that beset Egypt when pharaoh's heart hardened against the slaves. This point is taken up here at the tsar's last offer to the besieged Kazanians, which they decline 'like doltish hardheads'. They refuse to listen to God's and Ivan's 'new Moses" warnings and to his offer; it is seen as a hardening of the soul similar to that which befell pharaoh during the plagues, stressing the biblical theme of liberation from slavery.

Just how very central this issue is to Muscovite religiosity and political culture can be seen from the explanation of related terms which are usually considered to be far apart, that is, a 'slave of God' (*rab bozhii*), and a worldly slave or, in this case, a captive (*plenennyi*). In Ivan's prayer during the final conquest of the city, he implores God by emulating Moses during battle with the Amalekites, who prayed behind the lines on behalf of his people:

> Oh, gracious Lord Christ, show mercy to your slaves. This time let your mercy come over us, this one time. Give strength to your slaves against the enemy. Have mercy, have mercy for your fallen slaves, loving humankind [as you do], liberate the wretched captives and restore

---

[226] Ibid., p. 104.

> them to your grace, send your mercy of old from high, and those heathens will realize that you are our God and relying on you we will be victorious.[227]

As during Exodus in Sinai, the profane slave becomes the slave of God by His mercy, reprieving His slaves who have turned away from him. In this sense, the resurrection or redemption of the Lord, the Son of Man, is seen as part of the same action of liberating captives.[228]

If reluctance to part with slaves according to a sworn oath was the stated reason for punishment and an excuse for conquest, then by ancient biblical logic – one cannot keep the slaves of God in captivity to anybody else – the punishment was that the entire city of the captors was to be taken captive themselves, and the combatants killed:

> The tsar gave orders to take women and small children captive (*imati v polonu*), but to kill all warriors for their betrayal. So many Tatars were taken captive that the whole Rus' army received their share, every Rus' man had a Tatar captive. Meanwhile many thousands of Christian captives were liberated and went home (*svobodili*).[229]

This follows the emic logic of the Biblical books of Isaiah and Leviticus, which call on the faithful to liberate or ransom a brother, a relative or the people of God because they are His servants, while foreigners may be sold off as slaves.[230] The Russian armies are recompensed with captives, while by the same worldview the line is upheld that they liberated many thousands of Christians. Just like Moses, who did not fight personally during the battle with the Amalekites, Ivan raises his arms to thank God for this victory and the liberation of slaves:

> The tsar praised God. When the honourable tsar and great prince Ivan Vasil'evich of all Rus' saw such mercy on himself and all his Christ-loving army, he raised his hands to God.[231]

After seizing the fortress and city, Ivan's cousin, prince Volodimir Andreevich Staritsky, all boyars and army commanders joined the tsar to praise the conquest:

> Rejoice, Orthodox tsar, the enemies have succumbed to you with God's help. Be healthy for many years in your God-given tsardom of Kazan. Truly you are our intermediary to God [guarding] against the godless Hagarites. By your agency today the poor Christians are liberated forever, and the dishonourable and impious place will be purified by [God's] grace. And in future we ask God for his grace, for many years added to your life, all enemies succumbing under your feet and may He give you sons as heirs to your tsardom, so we will live in peace and quiet.[232]

---

227 Ibid., p. 106.
228 For more, see chapter 3.
229 Tikhomirov, *Letopisets nachala tsarstva*, p. 108.
230 Lev. 25:35–55; Ex. 21:1–11.
231 Tikhomirov, *Letopisets nachala tsarstva*, p. 108.
232 Ibid., p. 109.

Again, liberating 'poor Christians' appears as the tsar's main merit, making him the true intermediary with God for help against the affliction of the 'Hagarites', or in the Muscovite view the descendants of a slave, implying that they were at least aspiring slavers. For this reason they were reprehensible unless they served the Muscovite tsar.[233] The 'Chronicle' unambiguously expresses motivation for loyalty to the tsar: he gave hope that from now on, all could live peacefully and unmolested by slave raids.

The remainder of Ivan's triumphant sojourn in Kazan is reserved for ritual and symbolic acts, which will be investigated in chapters three and four. The focus remains on slavery and its supposed ills throughout, even where it is not mentioned directly:

> Earlier in this very palace the dishonourable and impious *tsar'* [i.e. khan] held court and throughout the years they spilled much Christian blood and did much evil to Christians, but now shines forth over it the righteous sun, which is the life-giving wood, the life-giving cross and the icon of our Christ.[234]

During a stopover in Nizhnii Novgorod on the return journey, Ivan is told about his merits in yet a different image:

> Extend, merciful God, the years of [Ivan's] life, as he saved us from such venomous serpents, from whom we suffered evil for so many years. Endorse him for many years to come.[235]

The symbolical connections between slavers, Tatars and the serpent or dragon will be explored in chapter four. At another halt at the Trinity monastery, which was fast becoming Muscovy's largest and most influential monastery, Ivan prayed to the relics of the founder St Sergii and the former metropolitan Ioasaf tearfully paid him homage, praising the liberation of Christians.[236]

The capital celebrated the success of the tsar's armies liberating slaves with boundless outpourings of joy. During the triumphal entry into Moscow, the tsar appeared before his subjects 'shining with the great victories'. As the 'Chronicle' relates, his subjects responded by hailing him as saviour, a title related to slave redemption further discussed in chapter three:

> Countless people stood along both sides of the roads, from the river Iauza to the city and within the Kremlin, young and old, crying loudly, and there was nothing to be heard but "many years to the honourable tsar, victor over the barbarians and Christian saviour".[237]

---

233 Chapter 6.
234 Tikhomirov, *Letopisets nachala tsarstva*, p. 109.
235 Ibid., p. 111.
236 Ibid., p. 112.
237 Ibid.

The metropolitan, the archbishops, bishops 'and all clerics' waited at the Sretenskyi monastery for the tsar, all carrying crosses and icons. The tsar praised their spiritual caretaking of the land and the army's exploits in the cause of liberating the slaves.[238] Ivan stressed that they had been a reason to act for his forebears, repeating his view that many Christians were killed by Kazanians breaking their oaths, who enslaved many more and dispersed them in many countries:

> You prayed to the merciful God [. . .] to save [my subjects] from barbarous raids [. . .] Moreover we took advice from you on how to deal with the Kazanians who for many years in spite of our stipend betrayed us and robbed Christians and raided many towns and villages, our God-granted Rus' domain [. . .] and [. . .] enslaved (*v plen raskhishcheny*) a great many Christian people, clerics, nuns, princes and boyars, the young and children, male and female, and scattered them over the face of the earth.[239]

Later in his speech, the tsar in his address to the clergy again emphasizes the link between the liberation of slaves, Orthodoxy, mobilisation and success in war:

> We achieved our aim with God's help [. . .] and your great holy works [. . .] and prayers and by the bravery and manliness of our brother Volodimir Andreevich and all our boyars, and all our Christian army's eagerness and zeal [. . .] for our brethren, the Orthodox Christians.[240]

Ivan then recounts the ceremonies of taking possession of the city, how all the Tatars in it fell in one hour by God's judgement, and how all Tatars of the middle Volga came to bow to the tsar of Moscow. As Kämpfer and Pelenski correctly pointed out, this glosses over the dispute about the right to expand into heterodox territories denying their non-Rus' status. This is even amplified by expressing hopes that Kazan Tatars may eventually convert to Christianity.[241] Nevertheless, any consideration of the actual reasons for conquering Kazan or the way Kazanians were treated in the short term does not change the fundamental argument of the tsar's speech, its propagandistic content – that Kazan was conquered to save and liberate Rus' slaves, irrespective of how realistic that may have been.

Finally, in front of metropolitan Makarii and the congregation of high-ranking clerics, the tsar, his cousin, and the whole army 'bowed down to the face of the earth'. They explained their success in terms of the heading incorporated in the text at the start of the narrative about the Kazan campaigns, the miracle that first referred only to liberating slaves and establishing Sviiazhsk:

---

238 Kämpfer called this 'the well-known topoi', without specifying, or quotation: Kämpfer, *Die Eroberung von Kasan 1552 als Gegenstand der zeitgenössischen russischen Historiographie*, pp. 100–101.
239 Tikhomirov. *Letopisets nachala tsarstva*, p. 112. V.N. Tatishchev, *Istoriia rossiiskaia v semi tomakh*, vol. 5 (Moskva and Leningrad, 1965), pp. 179–180.
240 Tikhomirov, *Letopisets nachala tsarstva*, p. 113.
241 Pelenski, *Russia and Kazan*, pp. 249–250; Kämpfer, *Die Eroberung von Kasan 1552 als Gegenstand der zeitgenössischen russischen Historiographie*, pp. 100–101.

> And I with my brother Volodimer Andreevich and all our army beat our foreheads to the face of the earth to you, my [spiritual] father and intercessor and to the whole holy synod for your works and prayers [since] your prayers won God over to work these great miracles.²⁴²

The tsar, rising, gives his hopes for the future of the 'flock of Orthodox Christians, entrusted to us by God' and rescued in terms of the history of religious salvation and 'the rebuilding of the land':

> Today I bow to the ground for you [clerics] to grant your prayers to God about our sins and the rebuilding of the land, for through your prayers the gracious God may send mercy to us and the flock of Orthodox Christians entrusted to us, whom Christ redeemed by his honourable blood from the curse of sin [in paradise], inspired with all good faith and purity and put us on the path to salvation, saving us from the enemies. May He save for His holy name the newly enlightened city of Kazan, which was given into our hands by his holy will and fortify Orthodoxy in it, true Christian rule, and convert the faithless to the true rules of Christianity. [. . .] Amen.²⁴³

While the tsar thus ends his speech with a reference to the religious side of salvation, metropolitan Makarii replies in just another long speech, stressing the secular side of redemption and the tsar's recent successes in freeing slaves. He eloquently repeats the phrase from the 'Letter to the Ugra' about the sacral duty to redeem captives from among his flock from the slavers and slave traders, the 'abusive Sons of Hagar'. This duty had been transferred from the bishop to the ruler, all to the greater glory of God and Ivan's and his army's deeds, which were unheard of among previous generations despite their great merits. This long speech is worth quoting in full, since it refers to the motivation of liberating slaves throughout, deriving from it the legitimation for conquering Kazan:

> God effected these miracles, showing His glory to you, honourable tsar, giving you splendid victories over the impious and dishonourable Crimean Tatar khan and rescuing us, His Christ-named flock, from the raids of the foreign Hagarians by your agency, our Lord. You, our lord, with the aid of such divine mercy and your cousin prince Volodimir Andreevich's and all of the Christ-loving army's great works fighting manfully for honour with God's help and protection, you, o tsar, have campaigned like a good tsar against your enemies the dishonourable and heathen *tsary* [khans] and oath-breaking Kazanian Tatars, who always shed innocent Christian blood, desecrated and destroyed the holy church of God and enslaved Orthodox Christians (*v plen raskhishchaia*) and scattered them over the face of the whole earth. You, honourable tsar strong in battle, put your steadfast hope and faith in almighty God and showed great works and strength of the soul, and you have increased the talent given to you and have liberated from slavery (*razkhishchenoe stado* [. . .] *svobodit' ot raboty*) the flock that was robbed from your pasture. When the Lord saw your unwavering faith and purity and steady love and wise decisions and your audacity, which did not hesitate to suffer to the blood, in other words: you would have laid down your soul and body for the holy honourable Christian faith and for the holy Church and for the Orthodox Christian flock entrusted to you

---

242 Tikhomirov, *Letopisets nachala tsarstva*, p. 113.
243 Ibid., pp. 113–114.

for shedding their blood, and those who were led into slavery and the abuse and manifold tortures they endured from [slavers]. For your faith and great unspeakable works God gave you this benefit: the town and tsardom of Kazan handed over to you, and His gratitude shines over you.[244]

The increased talents refer to Christ's parable about the bags of gold or talents (Mat 25:14–34), in which the master is grateful to the servants who made another talent from each he had entrusted to them during his absence. In the context of this speech, Makarii invokes the economic benefits of founding and implementing a no-slaving zone, saving the population from the havoc and displacement of foreign and mutual internal enslavement and trade.[245]

Makarii then compares Ivan to the Roman emperor Constantine, and to his most illustrious forebears such as Vladimir, Dmitrii Donskoi and Aleksandr Nevskii. However, Ivan's great deeds of adding Kazan to the realm and liberating the captives from slavery outshine all former gains. He is therefore worthy of the unrestrained adulation of the clerics and all people. Most of the subsequent parts of this speech need further analysis of the symbolism employed, such as will be furnished in the following chapters to appreciate its significance for liberation ideology. Nevertheless, Makarii made sure to insert another clear statement about slavery and liberation even into this passage, which appears obscure only at first sight. He employs the term *rabota* to underline the parallel with Israel's Exodus, and he leaves no doubts about the intentions of his speech:

> We beat our foreheads to you as we can and praise you. You have with God's help saved us from the barbarous raids with your grace, destroyed their dwellings to the foundations and liberated our poor, captured brothers from slavery (*ot raboty svobodi*). With our saved (*izbavlennoiu*) brethren, we say to you: Rejoice, pious tsar.[246]

The 'Chronicle' thereby not only establishes the theme of liberation from slavery in Muscovite literature, it uses it in a straightforward way to enhance the position of the tsar in the eyes of the world and of his people, and raises it to sacral heights. The tsar becomes the secular likeness of the bishop and Christ, the shepherd of his people by liberating slaves from the clutches of the unbelievers who enslaved and scattered them across the face of the earth. In this text the reference to 'the face of the earth', which occurs twice, in relation to slaves scattered by raid and trade; and the reference to the ritual bowing to the tsar or his sacral *alter ego*, the metropolitan, is in each case contextualised by liberation from slavery. This amounts to a justification of autocracy utilising the hopes for liberation and binding autocracy to its promises of liberation.

---

[244] Ibid., p. 114.
[245] Chapter 1.
[246] Tikhomirov, *Letopisets nachala tsarstva*, p. 115.

Conclusion

Some scholars attempted to justify the conquest of Kazan, while others criticized it, trying to show that both sides were equally oppressing the populations on both sides, or, as in the still little-known work by Mikhail Khudiakov, that actually the Muscovites caused more havoc than the Kazanians ever did.[247] Some of these studies are impressive analyses of the apologetical tendencies inherent in Muscovite sources, which are the only extant ones for the period – although there are also a few preserved kernels of a different, and possibly non-Muscovite, consciousness. This chapter did not attempt to add weight either side in these disputes. It looked at the worldview for its own sake, as a tool of legitimization, mobilization, and outreach to populations under Muscovite rule.

The reasoning behind this form of presentation is that the whole weight and narrative coherence of the liberation ideas in the 'Chronicle of the Beginning of Tsardom' should be appreciated independently of the merit of its purpose. This exercise has shown that most, if not virtually all, ideological content in this source is related in various ways to this idea. Moreover, it was echoed or downright copied into a host of other manuscripts and texts. Irrespectively of how the political system of Muscovy is judged and classified in its entirety today, this is a crucial factor of its policies.

Kazan was not a great danger at the time of its final conquest – apart from the in no way trivial spectre of a war on two or even three fronts facing Muscovy. The claims that there were tens of thousands or, as the 'History of Kazan' claims, even a hundred thousand abused slaves in Kazan who were liberated by Ivan's army have been exposed as exaggerations, although it remains difficult to gauge just how many there really were, or how many were happily rescued. Kazan was a convenient and just attainable target for Moscow, whether the latter's aims were aggressively-defensive in securing its flank or outright expansionary.

Be that as it may, not only Ivan IV and the metropolitan, but also those at mid-managerial level who ran Muscovy and the campaigns on a day-to-day level, seem to have believed that an ideology of liberation and the New Israel was beneficial.[248] They partly unearthed it from the archives or carried it to Moscow from Novgorod, spreading it throughout the surviving sources. The success of Ivan's final campaign gave them reason to feel emboldened, irrespective of whether today this campaign seems appropriate or legitimate.

---

247 Khudiakov, *Ocherki po istorii Kazanskogo khanstva*; Brown, *Moral Capital*. See now: R. Khakimov, I. Gilyazov and B. Izmaylov, eds., *The History of the Tatars since Ancient Times*, vol. 5: *Tatars in Russia (Second Half of the 16–18th Centuries)* (Kazan, 2017 [Russian: 2014]), pp. 60–82.

248 See also Tikhomirov, *Letopisets nachala tsarstva*, p. 89, and the analogy of 'God's wrath' towards the Egyptians and Crimean Tatars on p. 113.

Conclusion

Nevertheless, the apparent success itself of the steps taken is not evidence that the propaganda of liberation was positively received and made an impact on peoples' minds. While it is evident that the measures as a whole were successful, it is less obvious whether ideology contributed to a significant degree. The 'Chronicle' claims that Ivan was received in Moscow by huge crowds calling him a saviour, which demonstrates that the authors placed a premium on the population's support based on ideas of liberation. However, the sources analysed so far by themselves can do little to prove that the ideological device ever reached beyond the tiny elite circles of Moscow, or whether its influence simply remained wishful thinking, except for the significant degree to which they were copied. The remaining chapters will investigate how these concepts were communicated and shared, to estimate their potential appeal to the wider population.

Chapter 3
Redemption, Ritual and Exodus

Any consideration of liberation in the history of Muscovy cannot bypass the question of authority, the role of the tsars and the myths associated with them. Boris Uspensky and Victor Zhivov have forcefully argued that the rhetoric of the Church raised the sacred stature of the tsar just around the time of the conquest of Kazan, in the mid-sixteenth century.[1] This chapter will ask whether this was mere coincidence, or whether the sacralisation of the sovereign was linked to the ideas about the New Israel and the liberation of slaves which are expressed in the texts related to this event.[2]

The previous chapter has demonstrated that ransoming and liberation from slavery were among the main aims named in the Muscovite sources on the conquest of Kazan. These objectives were formulated in a Biblical language based on Israel's Exodus from slavery in Egypt and other places. These ideas were broadly linked to Christian literature, to the frequently cited texts from the New Testament, to saints' vitae and petitions: types of sources that were widely disseminated. This and the following chapters trace how Muscovite political culture, particularly the culture beyond the tiny boyar and chancellery elite, was pervaded by an expectation and promise of being redeemed from slaving – not just at the end of times, as historians routinely notice, but also – and perhaps even primarily – in the here and now. Detectable links between ransoming and liberating slaves and the history of salvation imagery in the religious, even eschatological, sense add to the evidence that the main religious resources of legitimation available to the tsar were intimately linked to the subject of this book.[3]

The import as well as the limitations of such an undertaking may be fathomed in comparison to a later development in a commonly, and rightly, deemed incomparable setting, i.e. the British Empire in the lead-up to the abolition of the slave trade in the North Atlantic in 1807. Certain aspects of the British evangelical approach to Scripture do much to explain the anti–slavery dynamism of evangelicalism. One might sum up the latter approach by saying that the Bible was interpreted from significant new perspectives.

---

1 B.A. Uspenskii and V.M. Zhivov, 'Tsar and God: Semiotic Aspects of the Sacralization of the Monarch in Russia', in B.A. Uspenskii, V.M. Zhivov and M.C. Levitt, eds., *"Tsar and God" and Other Essays in Russian Cultural Semiotics* (Boston, 2012), pp. 1–112; Kollmann, *The Russian Empire 1450–1801*, p. 135.
2 In this regard, the design of the chapter to an extent parallels Marcel Mauss' renowned study of the ambivalences of the term *gift* and related concepts. M. Mauss, *The Gift: Forms and Functions of Exchange in Archaic Societies* (London, 1954). My thanks go to Klaus Weber for reminding me how this helps to put in perspective the approach taken here.
3 Flier, 'Political Ideas and Ritual', p. 390; Kollmann, *The Russian Empire 1450–1801*, p. 135.

Redemption

The first perspective among evangelicals was the metaphor by which they apprehended the core doctrine of salvation. The study of Wilberforce's *A Practical View* (1797) and the Rev. Thomas Scott's *Commentary on the Holy Bible* (1791), both key statements of evangelical theology and immensely influential, make clear that while they speak of justification, propitiation and the other salvation concepts, the bedrock concept is redemption. Moreover, both Scott and Wilberforce frequently use 'redemption' as a synonym of 'salvation', and 'Redeemer' as a synonym of 'Saviour'.

The second perspective was the vital Old Testament analogy of the redemption experience:

> I am the Lord your God, which brought you forth out of the land of Egypt, that ye should not be their bondmen; and I have broken the bands of your yoke, and made you go upright.
> (Lev 26:13)

Such assertions are repeated time and time again in the Old Testament, not least during the Babylonian captivity, underlining the pattern of God's redemption of His people from slavery. God's whole redemptive purpose is placed firmly in the context of physical slavery and liberation.[4]

This is not to say that evangelical approaches to slavery and redemption were the same as in Muscovy. As this chapter will show, there were indeed considerable differences between them. Nevertheless, the foundations were close, and the path taken was remarkably similar up to a certain, but important point – the Muscovite approach always emphasized the redemption of the Chosen People, in other words the subjects of the tsar, whereas the British evangelicals tended to include all of humanity, albeit not wholly consistently. The generalisation of these concepts was advanced in the Enlightenment, so Muscovy was not alone in its time.

Redemption and liberation from slavery are central and related terms in the Muscovite period. In their complex evolution they are still vastly underestimated. This was due not least to the urge of Russian romantic nationalists in the nineteenth century to define a 'mission' for the Russian nation, which according to the ideas of their time ought to be applicable both to an imagined past and to the confident imperial present.[5] The need to defend and recuperate slaves who had been captured by a much stronger enemy receded to earlier periods. The new opposition between liberals and conservative monarchists reattached ideas about liberation to new contents, such as the increasingly obsolete serfdom. Ideas that once had been

---

[4] R. Anstey, Review of The Problem of Slavery in the Age of Revolution, 1770–1823 by David Brion Davis (Oxford 1999), *The English Historical Review*, 91, 358 (1976), pp. 141–148, here pp. 144–145.
[5] Kumar, *Visions of Empire*; Semyonov, 'How Five Empires Shaped the World and How this Process Shaped those Empires'; Poe, 'Moscow the Third Rome'.

connected to the dynasty despite their broadly emancipative content were misjudged and consigned to oblivion, as they seemed to fit neither of these new political groups.[6] These misconceptions about Muscovy gave rise to grandiose schemes of Russia's role in the world and of the exalted expectations of the dynasty allegedly cherished by ordinary Russians. This urge overshadowed the historical record, which was misrepresented perhaps even more sweepingly than by other contemporary nationalisms: the link that connected Muscovite tradition to the present was broken, not just as a consequence of the westernizing pathos associated with Petrine reform and propaganda, something frequently highlighted by historians. It was the whole dynamic of competing with European imperialisms that tended to de-emphasize the concepts of the Muscovite period. This hiatus has only begun to be mended by historical inquiry.[7]

Muscovy has often been portrayed as 'silent': it was remote from the Atlantic seaboard, the rising early modern economic and cultural powerhouse; separated by vast forest and bog areas even from its nearest western neighbours, the Ruthenians in Poland-Lithuania. It is true that its book culture cannot compare to the advanced contemporary Western theoretical or theological literature. But Muscovites were not entirely disconnected from Europe. There had been connections in the Middle Ages, and despite intermittent Mongol influence, these were only intensifying after the eclipse of the Byzantine Empire.[8] Therefore, ideas about the deliverance of captives by the tsar and God's chosen New Israel might have been new to a considerable degree in fifteenth- and still in sixteenth-century Muscovy, but they were not entirely out of context.

As the biblical, Exodus language analysed in the last chapter already indicates, an important nexus for such views was the religious-political symbolic interface. There existed some deep-rooted links between the political and religious symbolical worlds. As in the English word 'redemption', the very term signifying the ransoming of a slave in Russian also means salvation: *iskuplenie* in Church Slavonic and the closely related *otkup* or *vykup* in the more mundane chancellery language of the seventeenth century. All of these terms were also used in later periods.[9] This was highlighted in the Muscovite law code of 1649, stipulating annual levies for the ransoming of captives[10] at the

---

[6] Such an approach is evident in Efimov, *Rus'–novyi Izrail'*, the first but short approach to the sources on Moscow the New Israel during the imperial period; see chapter 2 for evaluation.

[7] Hausteiner, *Greater than Rome*; E. Hausteiner, 'Selbstvergleich und Selbstbehauptung: Die historische Imagination imperialer Eliten', in H. Münkler and E. Hausteiner, eds., *Die Legitimation von Imperien: Strategien und Motive im 19. und 20. Jahrhundert* (Frankfurt am Main and New York, 2012), pp. 15–33.

[8] Ostrowski, 'Towards the Integration of Early Modern Rus' into World History', pp. 111–113 for a recent overview of influences from western sources. E. Kraft, *Moskaus griechisches Jahrhundert: Russisch-griechische Beziehungen und metabyzantinischer Einfluss 1619–1694* (Stuttgart, 1995).

[9] Barkhudarov, *Slovar' russkogo iazyka XI–XVII vv. Kupit'* translates as 'to buy'.

[10] Etymologically, the term used in the 1649 *Ulozhenie*, '*polonianik*', is close to booty, fitting to small-scale steppe warfare and nomadic raids. See M. Fasmer, O.N. Trubachev, and B.A. Larin.

rate of 0.2 roubles from peasant or *posad* homesteads, service landholdings and hereditary estates. Lower-ranking servitors, such as cossacks, musketeers, artillerymen, gunners, gatekeepers, and others, who were most susceptible to captivity, were taxed at half the rate. In return, the code also stipulates rates to be paid for ransom, in a progression according to rank and the circumstances of captivity.[11] These monies were to be collected annually in the Foreign Affairs chancellery based on new census books:

> So that no one will be omitted from that cash levy because such ransoming is a common act of mercy [for all]. The pious tsar and all Orthodox Christians will receive great recompense from God, as the righteous Enoch said: "Do not spare gold and silver for your brother, but redeem him, and you will receive a hundred-fold from God".[12]

The original reads both times: '*iskuplenie* [. . .] *iskupite ego*': to ransom, respectively to redeem are two meanings of the same word. They were commonly used in a slightly different context for 'the Lord, your redeemer (saviour)', among others, in the apocryphal biblical Book of Enoch. Moreover, this passage o the Law Code was the only one using religious concepts. It was copied unchanged from canon law in the Hundred Chapter Synod (*Stoglav*) of 1551 into the otherwise remarkably pragmatic 1649 law code, which was written in a down-to-earth, chancellery style.

Both the *Stoglav* and the *Ulozhenie* underline that these ideas were widely distributed: until the early nineteenth century, the codification of 1649 was the only code of law commonly available in all provincial courts, printed in its first edition with a press run of 1,200 copies, with further imprints and translations following.[13] Moreover, it was the last law of the Russian Empire that owed its existence to a dual process of law making rather than the top-down style of decrees. It was codified by a commission of boyars in reaction to the 1648–49 Moscow rebellion, including much of the chancellery law of preceding decades.[14]

The eschatological political culture of the Muscovite tsardom was not merely oriented towards salvation in the end times. It was much more open to practical requirements than scholarly debate has allowed so far.[15] This holds true for the two basic

---

Ėtimologicheskii slovar' russkogo iazyka. 4 vols. Moskva, 1971, vol. 2: entry '*polon*'. Barkhudarov, *Slovar' russkogo iazyka XI–XVII vv.*, vol. 16: entry '*polonianik*'. Cf. Hellie, *The Muscovite Law Code (Ulozhenie) of 1649*, p. 17.

11 Hellie, *The Muscovite Law Code (Ulozhenie) of 1649*, pp. 17–18. Discussion of going ransom rates, which depended on personal negotiation and differed from state expenditure: Boeck, 'Identity as Commodity'.

12 Hellie, *The Muscovite Law Code (Ulozhenie) of 1649*, p. 17; Hecker, 'Die Christenpflicht als Rechtsnorm', p. 156.

13 Another print run of 1,200 probably in 1649, translations into Latin 1663, French 1688, German 1723, possibly Danish: A.G. Man'kov, *Ulozhenie 1649 goda: Kodeks feodal'nogo prava Rossii* (Leningrad, 1980), pp. 54–55.

14 C. Schmidt, *Sozialkontrolle in Moskau: Justiz, Kriminalität und Leibeigenschaft 1649–1785* (Stuttgart, 1996).

15 Hecker, 'Die Christenpflicht als Rechtsnorm'.

modes of policy: on the one hand, a pragmatic style, accommodating various ethnic groups. On the other hand, the brutal deportations and forceful conversion of Muslim Tatars were based on aggressive crusading ideas during the fall of Kazan in 1552. Andreas Kappeler rightly emphasizes that deportations gave way to greater pragmatism shortly after the conquest.[16] However, the sources themselves attest to a more nuanced stance of the conquerors already during the initial phase of conquest, albeit no less violent. The closest text in terms of time and confirmed knowledge about contemporary events, which originated in the administration and military, the detailed 'Chronicle of the Beginning of Tsardom', explains the conquest at the beginning of the text in an intra-textual caption setting the eschatological tone to 'mundane' if miraculous:

> The Beginning of the Tale of How the All-Merciful and Man-loving God Performed the Most Famous Miracles in Our People Through Our Orthodox, Pious Tsar [. . .] Ivan Vasil'evich, [. . .] [by Liberating] the Orthodox Christians from Muslim Captivity and from the Slavery of the Godless Kazan Tatars [. . .] in the Year 1551 [. . .][17]

Performing – actually '*sotvori*', creating – miracles clearly indicates an eschatological mode, although not by invoking the Final Judgement or the end of times. The participants in the lively debate about the role of the apocalypse in Muscovite culture are split into two opposed camps. According to a still widespread interpretation, Orthodox eschatology, especially of the sixteenth and seventeenth centuries, is fraught with 'tragical extremism', even 'eschatological psychosis', amplified by presuming the 'terrors of the apocalypse, if Moscow failed its mission'.[18] Thus it was Moscow's divine mission to counter every kind of heresy; if any were detected, it had failed and the last bastion of the true faith fell:

> In the popular imagination as well as the monastic chronicles, all history was permeated with God's presence. God's silence and withdrawal from present history, therefore, could mean only that history was at or near its end. Those who looked desperately for some final, tangible way to fulfil His will in this unprecedented situation could find but one act left to perform: the committing of oneself to the purgative flames which, according to tradition, must precede the Last Judgement.[19]

This interpretation overlooks central tenets of medieval and early modern eschatologies that pertain to Orthodox and Latin views alike: eschatology is based on precedent.

---

16 Kappeler, *The Russian Empire*, p. 31.
17 Tikhomirov, *Letopisets nachala tsarstva*, p. 59.
18 E. Hurwitz, 'Metropolitan Hilarion's Sermon on Law and Grace: Historical Consciousness in Kievan Rus'', *Russian History*, 7, 1 (1980), pp. 322–333, here pp. 332–333; G. Florovsky, *Ways of Russian Theology*, vol. 1 (Belmont MA, 1966), pp. 86–114; F.J. Thomson, 'The Intellectual Difference between Muscovy and Ruthenia in the Seventeenth Century: The Case of the Slavonic Translations and the Reception of the Pseudo-Constantinian Constitution (Donatio Constantini)', *Slavica Gandensia*, 22 (1995), pp. 63–107.
19 J.H. Billington, *The Icon and the Axe: An Interpretive History of Russian Culture* (London, 1966), pp. 139–140.

The whole procession of salvific history – which was thought to foreshadow and even contain all of history – was believed to be prefigured in Biblical sources. For medieval man there was no such thing as a lack of precedent, and Muscovite sources convey this sense at every step.[20] Muscovites expressed their ideas about the world in property litigation maps by numerous symbols and exuberant ornaments. They thereby insisted that God was present in the smallest and most trivial details of His creation, resulting in a beautiful image that inspired hope despite the prosaic purpose of the map.[21] Similarly, the sources on the liberation of captives confirm God's presence and his activity in the present, as will be shown below.

Recent studies stress that Muscovite eschatology as it was expressed at court and beyond praises God's creation. The sources optimistically emphasize the perfection of the human being created in God's own likeness whose sins were redeemed by His son's incarnation. On their way to Judgement Day, Muscovites imagined themselves safely harboured in the New Jerusalem, the city of Moscow, waiting for salvation.[22] Mostly, the elite in the capital and considerable parts of the local gentry disregarded the grim notions of marginal apocalyptical sects who gained some attention in the late seventeenth century, as well as their ideas about the coming terror, the destruction in the cataclysmic battles of Armageddon presaged in the Book of Revelation. Muscovites instead concentrated faithfully on the promise of redemption in a broad variety of meanings.

The loaded, ambiguous term redemption (*iskuplenie*) marks the connecting point of the two current interpretations of Muscovite political culture, which so far appeared entirely unconnected. This term puts the idea of precedent in salvation history and the Final Judgement prefigured in Israel's Exodus from slavery in Egypt in the limelight. In the three original languages of the Bible, this term and its equivalents have been borrowed consistently from the usage of the slave market. It refers metaphorically to salvation history and pragmatically to ransom.[23] This mode of speaking is grounded in the classic, dramatic or ransom theory of Christ's salvific sacrifice. It represents God triumphant over the enslaving spiritual powers and dominated soteriological theology in the first period of Church history and in Orthodoxy. This interpretation was widespread among early Christians as they saw themselves surrounded by oppressive 'satanic' activities in their contemporary heterodox environment.[24]

---

20 See chapter 2 for more of these expressions involving mainly Old Testament tales.
21 Kivelson, *Cartographies of Tsardom*, pp. 106–108. See also below, on trees and the symbol of the cross.
22 Flier, 'Golden Hall Iconography and the Makarian Initiative'.
23 In this and the following paragraphs on redemption and the language of the slave market as used in the Bible, I follow B.A. Demarest, *The Cross and Salvation: The Doctrine of Salvation* (Wheaton IL, 1997), pp. 176–179, which provides a rare and useful overview of soteriology and theories of atonement.
24 The metaphor of slavery was actively used by early theologians to instill obedience among the faithful to Christian and heterodox masters. J.A. Glancy, 'Slavery and the Rise of Christianity', in

This theory does not emphasize that Christ takes over expiation for the sinful in the afterlife, but his active liberation of the faithful from the hands of enslaving powers. It takes two main forms: some interpreters follow Mark 10:45 considering Christ's death on the cross as a ransom price (Greek: *lytron*; Russian, RSV: *iskuplenie*[25]), which was paid to the devil. Humanity had succumbed to the devil as a result of sin. At the cross God delivered Jesus to the devil in exchange for the souls whom the latter held captive. However, Satan could not keep Jesus prisoner forever and the son of God was resurrected from the grave. Moreover, the noun *lytron*, 'ransom price', was commonly used in classical Greek in the sense of 'payment to free a slave'. Paul wrote that 'the man Christ Jesus [. . .] gave himself as a ransom [*antilytron*] for all men'. The compound *antilytron* means literally 'substitute-ransom' and denotes 'what is given in exchange for another as the price of redemption'. The English word 'redemption' derives from Latin *redimere*, to repurchase or buy back used in place of *lytron*. Redemption focuses on the release of persons detained in bondage. The Aramaic verb *ga'al*, to 'redeem', 'avenge', 'do the part of a kinsman'

K. Bradley and P. Cartledge, eds., *The Cambridge World History of Slavery*, vol. 1: *The Ancient Mediterranean World* (Cambridge, 2011), pp. 456–481, esp. pp. 457–461. A focus of debate is the question whether early asceticists, hermits and monks in the east of the Roman Empire were precursors of later abolitionists: I. Ramelli, *Social Justice and the Legitimacy of Slavery: The Role of Philosophical Asceticism from Ancient Judaism to Late Antiquity* (Oxford, 2016). C.L. de Wet, *The Unbound God: Slavery and the Formation of Early Christian Thought* (London and New York, 2018) maintains that early Christian writings were fundamentally shaped by a discourse of slavery. However, views of liberation from the enemy changed in the Byzantine period: see chapter 4 and 6 on St Nicholas. Muscovite discourse on liberation from foreign captivity and ransom as redemption is closer to the Old Testament than early Christianity. Moreover, Muscovy was a very different environment from the great income disparity and affluence of the elite in the late Roman Empire coinciding with 'doulology' as discourse of domination, while early theologians de-emphasized the Exodus narrative (Julia Hillner in discussion with Elisabeth Herrmann-Otto at the BCDSS, Joseph C. Miller memorial lecture, 8 November 2021). See chapter 1 for background on these shifts.

25 The Russian Synodal Version of the bible counts 58 instances of 'iskup': Pitirim, mitropolit Volokolamskogo i Jur'evskogo, ed., *Simfoniia ili slovar'-ukazatel' k Sviashchennomu Pisaniiu Vetkhogo i Novogo Zaveta*, vol. 2 (Moskva, 1988), pp. 864–865, entry 'iskuplenie'. See also https://www.biblegateway.com/quicksearch/?quicksearch= (accessed 22 Aug. 2021; enter the term искупление and set version as RUSV). This translation, based on the Masoretic text and Greek editions of the New Testament, was initiated in 1816 and halted in 1826, by which time most of the text had been translated. Its language borrows heavily on Church Slavonic. See the introduction by the Russian Bible Society, the re-kindled organisation which initiated the project: https://biblia.ru/AboutBible/TranslationsInRussia/ (accessed 22 Aug. 2021). Cf. the first full printed bible in the eastern Slavic area, based on the translation ordered by archbishop Gennadii in 1499, on Greek texts, and Czech, Polish, and Ruthenian translations: *Biblia sirech knigi Vetchago i Novago Zaveta po iazyku slovensku* (Ostrog, 1581). The modern Russian Synodal version (RUSV) uses *iskup* in some places in which the Ostroh Bible translated by synonyms. Cf. R.K. Tsurkan, *Slavianskii perevod Biblii: Proiskhozhdenie, istoriia istoriiǎteksta i vazhneishie izdaniia* (Sankt Petersburg, 2001); F.J. Thomson, 'The Slavonic Translation of the Old Testament', in J. Krašovec, ed., *The Interpretation of the Bible: The International Symposium in Slovenia* (Sheffield, 1998), pp. 605–920.

emphasizes the release obtained. God redeemed the Israelites by freeing them from Egyptian slavery (Ps 74:2; 77:15; cf. Exod 6:6; 15:13; Isa 63:9), by delivering his people from captivity in Babylon (Mic 4:10), and by rescuing persons in a worldly sense from the consequences of sin. Therefore the Lord is known as Israel's 'Redeemer'. The mission of the Messiah will be 'to free captives from prison and to release from the dungeon those who sit in darkness' (Isa 42:7; cf. 61:1). In the New Testament, Christ's death on the cross brought redemption (*lytrosis*), 'deliverance' or 'release'. In the synagogue at Nazareth, Jesus read from the salvation passage in Isaiah, the 'Year of the Lord's Favour' (Isa 61:1–2).[26] In fulfilment of this prophecy, Jesus stated that the Lord had sent him 'to proclaim liberation (*aphesis*) for the prisoners' and 'to release the oppressed' (Luke 4:18). *Aphesis* sometimes means 'forgiveness of sins', but Luke uses it in the sense of 'release from captivity'. Ransom and redemption represent God's merciful answer to the many forms of bondage that enslave men and women.[27] In short, the context of the words used in the Bible to express salvation is the slave market. This aligns closely with the results of recent studies of the connections between debt bondage, monarchy, and monotheism which at all times depended on political fiat.[28]

Metropolitan Makarii expresses the close connection between redemption in this life and in the hereafter in his letter to the tsar shortly before the final assault on Kazan. The letter starts with concerns for slaves held by the Tatars, followed by exhortations to the brave and pious Christian soldiers about proper behaviour. Then it turns again to the subject of redeeming slaves by military means, lifting it on a higher symbolic level and promising forgiveness of sins:

> If someone from among the Orthodox Christians should suffer to death in this battle for the holy church, for Christian belief and for the countless Orthodox people (*mnozhestva naroda liudei pravoslavnykh*), whom Christ redeemed from the torments of hell by his honest blood, they will fulfil the word of Christ: 'There is no greater love than to lay down your soul for your brother.[29]

Makarii went on to promise rewards both in the eternal and, for those who fought without sparing themselves, already in this life, such as greater lifespan and earthly bliss. Those who died in battle enter the 'elevated city of Jerusalem'. The quote from John 15:13 denotes Jesus' death as substitutionary sacrifice for sins, which John also represented as spiritual food in the context of the manna given to the Jews in the desert during their exodus from Egypt: 'This bread is my flesh which I

---

[26] Sometimes also called the fifth servant passage, although the term 'servant' does not occur. 'Propovedati plennikom proshchenie': *Biblia sirech knigi Vetchago i Novago Zaveta po iazyku slovensku*. Identical in the Moscow Bible, 1663. These are the official bible editions until the 1740s.
[27] Demarest, *The Cross and Salvation*, pp. 137–138. Note that Christianity did not necessarily mean release of slaves: D.B. Davis, *The Problem of Slavery in Western Culture* (Ithaca, NY: 1988 [1966]), pp. 84–90. On transitions: Rotman, *Byzantine Slavery and the Mediterranean World*.
[28] Miller, *The Problem of Slavery as History*. See chapter 1.
[29] Tikhomirov, *Letopisets nachala tsarstva*, p. 89. Cf. John 15:13.

will give for the life of the world'. (John 6:51). Worldly ransom and eternal salvation, the liberation of the Jews in the sense of dissolution of the bonds to the Egyptians and atonement are clearly and explicitly linked.[30] Just as Jesus made full payment for all human failures and misdeeds by dying in the place of sinners, the tsar as another good shepherd is said to accept the risk to die in battle. Vicarious death in battle was strongly promoted in the 'Letter to the Ugra', allegedly to embolden grand prince Ivan III and his army facing the Tatars:

> Be brave and strengthen yourself as a good warrior for Christ, according to the Lord's word: 'You are the good shepherd who lays down his life for the sheep, but he who is a hired hand, and not a shepherd, who does not own the sheep, sees the wolf coming, leaves the sheep and runs away. So, the wolf catches the sheep and scatters them, and the hired hand flees, since he is hired and does not own the sheep'. So you, lord [Ivan III], should not act like a hired hand, but as a real shepherd, who unfalteringly saves from the threatening wolf the herd of the word (*slovesnoe stado*) entrusted to you by God.[31]

Ownership is linked to vicarious death in a battle for liberation of captives in this transfer of duties from bishop to ruler, stressing the centrality of the redemptive obligation for legitimate rule.

To fully inculcate this idea, it is repeated in a similar context two pages further on: '[B]lessed is he who lay down his soul for his people'.[32] In precisely this sense, other church authorities, guided by Col. 2:15, declared that God was warring with Satan, triumphed over Satan once and for all and delivered the captives of the powers of darkness. For early Church Fathers, the subjects of ransom, victory and liberation were therefore seamlessly connected. Thus, Irenaeus of Lyons (†200) wrote:

> Redeeming us with his blood, Christ gave himself as a ransom for those who had been led into captivity.[33]

Christ's great victory over the powers of darkness, predicted in Gen. 3:15 and foretold by Christ himself in Matt. 12:29, is represented in the image of the slave market or, alternatively, the victorious commander proceeding to liberate the captives. This perspective served the needs of the Muscovite Empire and it was expressed in the displays of its foreign relations and legitimating ideology. This view correlates with Orthodox insistence that the true faith cannot have evolved after the teachings of the early Church Fathers. The close link between salvation in the beyond and redemption of slaves in this life is specific to early interpretations and underlines the concern of monarchy and church for ransoming and liberating captives.[34]

---

30 Demarest, *The Cross and Salvation*, p. 175. Rapoport, 'Moses, Charisma, and Covenant', p. 123.
31 Tikhomirov, *Vologodsko-permskii letopisets*, p. 267. Cf. John 10:12–13.
32 Ibid., p. 269. Pliukhanova, '"Poslanie na Ugru" i vopros o proiskhozhdenii moskovskoi imperskoi ideologii', p. 464.
33 Demarest, *The Cross and Salvation*, pp. 149–151.
34 Ibid. See chapter 1.

The New Year's ceremony

These complex meanings can be found in one of the central monuments of sixteenth century representative political culture, the murals of the Kremlin's Golden Palace. They were painted during the period of the conquest of Kazan, after the great fire of 1547. The palace was demolished in the eighteenth century, but the inscriptions were copied in full and preserved along with descriptions of the murals during reconstruction work in the 1670s. In the antechamber those waiting for an audience encountered martial scenes borrowed from the biblical Exodus and the conquest of the Promised Land. In the adjacent throne room motifs of Divine Wisdom and the harmonious themes of the annual cycle dominated.[35] Moreover, the antechamber displayed Exodus imagery of a more miraculous nature, such as Aaron's staff turning into a serpent when he goes to warn pharaoh to let the Israelites go, Moses dividing the waters of the Red Sea, or making the bitter waters of Marah sweet for the thirsty during the journey through the Sinai desert.[36]

Michael Flier found that the three quotes that circled the central figure in the throne room were taken from the missal for the New Year's service on 1 September. This was a major ritual involving the tsar, clerics and his courtiers.[37]

At least two of the three texts taken from the missal have something in common beyond the New Year theme: the quotes refer to Biblical passages that explicitly speak about the liberation of captives and slaves. The service is absent from the missals before metropolitan Makarii. This observation adds to the sharpening of the ideology of slave liberation instigated by this strategic thinker. His influence is palpable in most of the documents of the middle of the sixteenth century – or by default his contemporaries due to uncertainties in attributing the texts.[38]

Right after the first introductory sentences of the New Year mass – held out in the open on the Kremlin's Cathedral Square to mark the special occasion – follows the extensive text from Is 61:1–9. This passage gained prominence in the late eighteenth and early nineteenth century, when Protestant abolitionists re-interpreted it

---

[35] F. Kämpfer, '"Rußland an der Schwelle zur Neuzeit": Kunst, Ideologie und historisches Bewußtsein unter Ivan Groznyj', *Jahrbücher für Geschichte Osteuropas*, 23, 4 (1975), pp. 504–524, here pp. 507–518.
[36] O.I. Podobedova, ed., *Moskovskaia shkola zhivopisi pri Ivane IV: Raboty v Moskovskom Kremle 40-kh–70-kh godov XVI v* (Moskva, 1972), pp. 20–24.
[37] Michael Flier asks how these motifs are linked and which iconographic and conceptional programme informs this elaborate composition: Flier, 'Golden Hall Iconography and the Makarian Initiative', pp. 70–71. I.E. Zabelin, *Materialy dlia istorii, arkheologii i statistiki goroda Moskvy*, vol. 1 (Moskva, 1884), pp. 1238–1255.
[38] Cf. M.N. Speranski, 'Sentiabr'skaia mineia-chetia do-Makar'evskago sostava', *Sbornik otdeleniia russkago iazyka i slovesnosti Imperatorskoi Akademii Nauk*, 64, 4 (1896), pp. 1–23, here p. 11. Flier, 'Golden Hall Iconography and the Makarian Initiative', pp. 67, 70.

to underline their view that slavery is not a punishment for sin, but itself a sin, so that consequently all slaves had to be liberated.[39] The biblical context mixes Babylonian captivity with the monarch's claims to debt slaves in favour of reclaiming taxpayers, expropriating private property of merchants:[40]

[The Year of the Lord's Favour]
1   The Spirit of the Sovereign Lord is on me,
    because the Lord has anointed me
    to bring good news to the poor.
    He has sent me to proclaim liberation[41] for the captives [. . .]
2   to proclaim the year of the Lord's favour
    and the day of vengeance of our God, [. . .]
3   and provide for those who grieve in Zion [. . .]
5   Strangers will shepherd your flocks;
    foreigners will work your fields and vineyards.
6   [. . .] You will feed on the wealth of nations,
    and in their riches you will boast.

---

39 Clarence-Smith, *Islam and the Abolition of Slavery*, p. 229.

40 Miller, *The Problem of Slavery as History*. See chapter 1. On replacing debt-bondsmen by foreign slaves: M.I. Finley, 'The Emergence of a Slave Society', in D.A. Pargas and F. Roşu, eds., *Critical Readings on Global Slavery*, vol. 1 (Leiden, 2017), pp. 58–89. Debate about whether already the Judaic sect of the Essenes referred to this passage to claim that slavery was contrary to God's will: M. Meltzer, *Slavery: A World History* (New York, 1993), pp. i, 44–45, 93–96. Contra: D. Brion Davis, 'Review of Islam and the Abolition of Slavery by William Gervase Clarence-Smith (New York 2006)', *American Historical Review*, 112, 4 (2007), pp. 1134–1135; H. Grieser and N. Priesching, eds., *Theologie und Sklaverei von der Antike bis in die frühe Neuzeit* (Hildesheim, Zürich and New York, 2016).

41 *Biblia sirech knigi Vetchago i Novago Zaveta po iazyku slovensku*: 'Propovedati plennikom proshchenie'. Identical in the Moscow Bible, 1663. *Slovar' XI–XVII vv.*: 'Dati proshchenie' – to liberate (*osvobodit'*). '*Propovedati*' – 'to proclaim' may be understood as a stronger version of 'to give'/'dati' in this context and is taken for granted in the translation of the Bible. Even the generic meaning of '*proshchenie*' – 'pardon, forgiveness' (of capture, debt) conveys the same meaning. The official Bible editions until the 1740s have largely the same text, as they were based on the Gennadii Bible of 1499 which in turn took the Latin Vulgate as textual basis for all books that had not been translated before: The Elisabeth edition of 1751, published during the years before the conquest of Crimea, is based on a new translation ordered by Peter I. It changed this passage to: '*plennikom otpushchenie*', further clarifying that it means liberation. It is central for the significance of this text that the translators used '*plenniki*' – captives in the sense of those captured by foreign or heterodox slavers. It does not apply to peasants and serfs. Variant translations in the old Slavonic bible texts could be perceived to strengthen master's power, as 1 Corinth 7,20–24. Note the context is a letter on matrimony and sexuality. Debates ensued in the 1840s and 1850s: I. Paperno, 'The Liberation of the Serfs As a Cultural Symbol', *Russian Review*, 50, 4 (1991), pp. 417–436, here pp. 419–420. Likewise, '*slepym prozrenie*' – 'eyesight for the blind' instead of '*uznikam – otkrytie temnitsy*' – 'for prisoners the opening of the dark cell' [in which they are locked] is a variant reading corrected in late nineteenth century editions: *Bibliia ili knigi sviashchennago pisaniia Vetkhago i Novago Zaveta v russkom perevode s parallel'nymi mestami* (Sanktpeterburg, 1904 [1875]).

7   instead of disgrace
you will rejoice in your inheritance [. . .]^42

Since the introduction in Moscow of the ritual of crowning and anointing, God's anointed had been the tsar, who was now all the more obliged to liberate and ransom captives and slaves. The year of mercy hardly meant merely an ephemeral 'Good Year',[43] since the more salient point is the liberation of all slaves after seven times seven years (Lev 25: 35–55), obliging even foreign potentates. Those mourning in exile are led home to Zion, where great joy and rule over formerly powerful peoples await them. This cycle is historic wishful thinking. A group defined by covenant, religious or dynastic boundaries now finds itself in a dependent position, now it rules.[44] Moreover, it is an apt expression for a newly founded counter dependency zone allowing for enserfment, which still lives under the threat of reverting into a slaving zone:[45] *plennik* is the captive, primarily someone captured by foreign or heterodox slavers; in this context it was not applicable to peasants or serfs living in Russia. Isaiah 61 was therefore a fitting image for Moscow's aspirations to imperial rule over their former masters, the Tatar middle Volga, in the late 1540s and 1550s, when the murals were painted.

The central figure in the vault, surrounded by the quote from Isaiah, Jesus Christ Immanuel represented as the Ancient of Days, is an iconographic equation adopted from Byzantium. It underscores the cyclical unity of salvific history in which exile and redemption alternate by representing Jesus Christ. This applies even more so to the precursor figure of Immanuel, usually interpreted by Christians as an oblique allusion to Jesus Christ – as an old, white-haired man. This equation is derived from an apocryphal biblical book ascribed to Enoch, which was often cited in Muscovy.[46] In the same spirit, the passage from the contemporary Hundred Chapters Synod of 1551, mentioned above, regarding the obligation to ransom refers to Enoch, as does the law code of 1649.

---

42 *Biblia sirech knigi Vetchago i Novago Zaveta po iazyku slovensku*: Dkh~ gdn~ na mne, egozhe radi pomazamia. Blagovestiti nishchim posla mia, istseliti s"krushenyia serdtsem, propovedati plennikom proshchenie i slepym prozrenie. Nareshchi leto gne~ blgo~ izvoleno i dn'~ bezdaniia. Outeshiti vsia plachiushchaa, dati plachiushchim siona slavu v"mesto pepela, pomazanie veselyia alchiushchim, oukrasheniia slave za dukh ounyniia. Inarek~usia rodove pravdy, nasluzhenie gne~ v"slavu. I s"zizhdutsia putynia vechnyia, zapustevshiia prezhe v"zd~vignut, obnoviat grady poustevshaiavrody. I priidut inorodnii pasushche ovtsa tvoia, i inoplemennitsy ratai tvoi, i vinogradnitsy. Vyzhenarechetesia zhertsy gni~, i slugi bzhiia~. Krepost' iazyk poiast', v"bogatstve ikh oudivitesia. Sitse zemliu svoiu vtoritse naslediat', i veselie vechnoe nad glavoiu ikh.
43 Cf. Kämpfer, '"Rußland an der Schwelle zur Neuzeit"', pp. 508–512.
44 See chapters 2 and 6.
45 Fynn-Paul, 'Introduction. Slaving Zones in Global History'; Fynn-Paul, 'Empire, Monotheism and Slavery in the Greater Mediterranean Region from Antiquity to the Early Modern Era'.
46 C. Böttrich, *Das slavische Henochbuch* (Gütersloh, 1996), pp. 40–47.

The second passage quoted in the New Year missal, Psalm 74, explicitly mentions the connection of the annual cycle, salvific history including Exodus ('you separated the sea'), and ransom ('the nation you purchased'). Though the ritual was probably not open to the general public, these quotes are indicative of the views held by the boyar elite who had the privilege to always access the Kremlin; some were still residing within its walls. The quotes were immediately accessible to anyone who had even a passing education in reading and writing, as the psalms are part of the reading exercises in the primer, the *Azbuka*:[47]

Psalm 74[48]
1   O God, why have you rejected us forever?
    Why does your anger smoulder against the sheep of your pasture?
2   Remember the nation you purchased (*stiazhal*; RUSV) long ago,
    the people of your inheritance whom you redeemed (*iskupil*)[49] —
    Mount Zion, where you dwelt.
3   Turn your steps toward these everlasting ruins,
    all this destruction the enemy has brought on the sanctuary.
8   They said in their hearts, "We will crush them completely!"
    They burned every place where God was worshiped in the land.
10   How long will the enemy mock you, God?
    Will the foe revile your name forever?
12   But God is my King from long ago;
    he brings salvation on the earth.
13   It was you who split open the sea by your power;
    you broke the heads of the monster in the waters.
14   It was you who crushed the heads of Leviathan
    and gave it as food to the people [the exiled Israelites; C.W.].[50]
15   It was you who opened up springs and streams; [. . .]
16   The day is yours, and yours also the night;
    you established the sun and moon.
17   It was you who set all the boundaries of the earth;
    you made both summer and winter.
18   Remember how the enemy has mocked you, Lord,
    how foolish people have reviled your name.

---

47 V.P. Bogdanov, *Ot azbuki Ivana Fedorova do sovremennogo bukvaria* (Moskva, 1974). I am grateful to C. Soldat for reminding of this nexus.
48 The basic translation is the New International Version; where appropriate, the transcription of the Ostroh Bible is added in brackets.
49 *Biblia sirech knigi Vetchago i Novago Zaveta po iazyku slovensku*. 'pomiani soim tvoi, izhe stiazhal isperva, izbavil esi zhezl dostoianiia tvoego'.
50 'Bog zhe tsar nash prezhde vek, sodela spasenie posrede zemlia. Ty outverdil esi siloiu more. Ty sterl esi glavy smiem v vode. Ty sokrushil esi glavu smievu, dal esi togo vrashno liudem'. Ibid.

19   Do not hand over the life of your dove to wild beasts;
     do not forget the lives of your afflicted people forever.
21   Do not let the oppressed retreat in disgrace;
     may the poor and needy praise your name.

The historical motif of the downfall and deliverance of Israel and Jerusalem in this is integral to the annual cycle and the history of creation. The choice of these texts makes clear that the serenity of late Muscovite textual and imagery sources is entwined with an eschatological view, which looks back and forth seeing destruction and exile. However, it never loses sight of the liberating, saving, and redeeming presence of the Old Testament God assumed to be concerned for the welfare of his 'slaves'.

These entwined notions are obvious even where a clear difference between liberation and salvation is maintained. Thus, Ivan IV, when he spoke to metropolitan Makarii, motivated his campaign against Kazan in 1549 using the religiously charged term *rabota*. Normally, *rab* is used in the sense of slave of God. However, here it refers to both Egyptian and to contemporary Kazanian slavery:

> Pray with all of your Holy Synod that [. . .] Christ sends mercy and grants liberation from Kazan slavery (*rabota*) to all Christians despite our sins and ignorance. We may be sinful, but nevertheless His creation. So, to avoid His holy name being soiled by our sins he should liberate (*izbavit*) poor Christianity, which is being tortured by the *bezsermeny*, just as the Lord has redeemed (*iskupi*) them by his honourable blood.[51]

The motif of the *besermeny* is ubiquitous in Muscovite texts. It is ambiguously invoked in this passage in a context of ransom, liberation and salvific history meaning Tatars, Muslims and Mongol-Tatar tax collectors. The term may refer here to origin as well as to the custom then notorious in Eurasia to compensate for tax arrears by enslaving kin. In Northeastern Rus' this practice had led to rebellions in 1262.[52] *Besermeny* thus underscores the language of the slave market and the claim of the monarch.

The old Russian idea that Tatar raids had to be accepted as God's punishment for sins is rejected in Ivan's speech. God or rather Christ saves Christians transcendentally from sin in the hereafter. However, as he is present in his creation, he also immanently liberates them from worldly slavery. Significantly, slavery is no longer expiation for sins, but itself now appears reprehensible. This idea is remarkable in the Muscovite context and, as mentioned above, similar to later Protestant abolitionist views that reject slavery. Nevertheless, it was spread at best indirectly beyond the in-group of the Russian Orthodox.[53]

It is instructive to confront these ideas with the most advanced concepts of their time in terms of what we today consider human rights. They may be found in concepts

---

51 Tikhomirov, *Letopisets nachala tsarstva*, p. 60.
52 Langer, 'Slavery in the Appanage Era', p. 119; A. Zimin, *Kholopy na Rusi* (Moskva, 1973), p. 272.
53 Clarence-Smith, *Islam and the Abolition of Slavery*, p. 229. For more on this question, see chapters 1 and 6.

of a similar level and at a proximate time in respective societies. In the southern German Great Peasant War of 1525, the pressing needs of defence from Ottoman inroads encountered in the neighbouring Austrian borderlands were not present. Yet, the former was influenced by ideas which had gained currency in the latter areas.[54] The territorialisation of power, an increasing level of taxation and duties, and the levelling of the once multifarious medieval status of peasants and craftsmen created for a short time even more explosive conditions. These developments resulted in the occupation of many cities and castles by mixed peasant and burgher troops. Fifty delegates from the territories of the Swabian League convened in Memmingen and devised a Federal Order and the Twelve Articles. 12,000 copies were printed, an astonishingly large number at the time, and distributed all over Germany.

Already the preamble of the Twelve Articles makes clear how the peasants connected belief and rebellion, taking Moses as an example for their rising:

> [. . .] it follows that the peasants in their articles demand such Gospel for teaching and living [and] do not want to be called disobeying and rebellious. [. . .] Who wants to dispute his Majesty [God]? Did he not answer the Children of Israel crying to him and freed them from the hand of pharaoh, does he not want to deliver his people to this day? Yes, he will release them![55]

In the first two articles, the rebels demand in the Austrian vein that their priest be elected and deposed at their instigation, teach the Gospel in the vernacular and that the tithe predominantly be used for his upkeep. The third article again explicitly refers to the language of redemption and the slave market to demand liberty in theological terms:

> It has been practice so far that we have been held as villains, which is pitiful, since Christ redeemed (*erlößt und erkaufet*) all of us with his precious bloodshed, the shepherd as well as the highest, no one excluded. Therefore, scripture teaches that we are and want to be free.[56]

They explain further that they wanted to live within the Ten Commandments and 'peacefully' obey the authority elected or set by God 'in all decent and Christian things'. The following articles leave no doubt in detail as well as in spirit that they wished to ameliorate strong asymmetric dependency, or at least put barriers in the

---

54 On the grounding of the southern German ideas of the Great Peasant War in developments in the Austrian borderlands, see chapter 5. A. Niederstätter, *Das Jahrhundert der Mitte: An der Wende vom Mittelalter zur Neuzeit* (Wien, 1996), pp. 123–132.
55 G. Franz, ed., *Quellen zur Geschichte des Bauernkrieges* (Darmstadt, 1963), p. 175. On Martin Luther's refusal to accept a political interpretation, further debates on 'Christian freedom' and serfdom and on practice well into the seventeenth century, see: L. Scholz, 'Leibeigenschaft rechtfertigen: Kontroversen um Ursprung und Legitimität der Leibeigenschaft im Wildfangstreit', *Zeitschrift für Historische Forschung*, 45, 1 (2018), pp. 41–81, esp. p. 67.
56 Ibid., pp. 175–176.

path of more requirements from masters. They based their demand on this understanding of the Bible as a yardstick for interpreting and disputing set rules.[57]

In this forcefully expressed demand to limit arbitrary demands of landlords – albeit one limited by the rules of Christian decency and obedience – they most clearly differed from Muscovite sources. Realities were different there in the sixteenth century, when serfdom was not even firmly established, but still in the process of formation until 1649.[58] Moreover, the federal, representative spirit of authority of the Swabian peasants and burghers is replaced in the Muscovite sources with sheer sovereignty. The frontier spirit is as palpable in the Muscovite demand for sovereignty as in the Austrian version, both of which faced imminent raids. Nevertheless, the Twelve Articles launch their demands on similar theological premises as some of the contemporary Muscovite sources. As mentioned above, the latter turn away from an understanding that slavery was punishment for sin towards one of entitlement to liberation or redemption from captivity of at least a limited group, formed at the kernel by the Russian Orthodox community. The transmission of the ideas of the Great Peasant War is very patchy, if it existed at all until human rights were formulated in the context of the natural law tradition and the Atlantic Revolutions. Therefore, differences should neither be neglected nor overestimated, particularly where and insofar as they were a function of various and ephemeral environmental, military, and political factors.[59]

The Blessed Host

The icon 'Blessed Host of the Heavenly Tsar' [Fig. 1] is closely related in time to the Kazan campaign. It was prominently displayed near the tsar's throne in the main church of the Moscow Kremlin, the Dormition Cathedral. Recently analyse pertinently focuses on the military aspect of its message.[60] However, there is another side to it that is just as prominent: the depiction of martyrs. The imagery of the icon focuses on mounted people with halos moving from a burning city to the Heavenly Jerusalem. In the long scholarly debate about this central icon, the mounted warriors have been variously identified with leading historical figures. However, I. Kochetkov and others have rightly objected that most of the figures on this icon are just nameless warrior-saints,

---

[57] Ibid., pp. 175–179. P. Blickle, *Unruhen in der ständischen Gesellschaft: 1300–1800* (München, 2012), pp. 28–33.
[58] See Introduction.
[59] As discussed in chapter 6, apart from the Reformation it was the universities that influenced the worldview of peasants in Western Europe, while plans to establish a university in Muscovy were delayed until the Petrine era.
[60] D. Rowland, 'Biblical Military Imagery in the Political Culture of Early Modern Russia: The Blessed Host of the Heavenly Tsar', in M. Flier and D. Rowland, eds., *Medieval Russian Culture*, vol. 2 (Berkeley and Los Angeles, 1994), pp. 182–212.

without princely insignia or clear identification, apart from very few specified historical figures. Therefore, the icon likely depicts a contemporary event, the return of Ivan IV's army from the conquest of Kazan to Moscow, shown as Heavenly Jerusalem.[61]

The title, derived from a seventeenth-century description of the icon, refers to two biblical sources, Daniel 12 and Revelation 19.[62] In Daniel's vision, the Archangel Michael leads the heavenly host against an unnamed king:

> At that time [grand prince][63] Michael shall stand up, who standeth for the children of thy people, and there shall be a time of trouble such as never was [. . .]; and at that time thy people shall be delivered.[64] (Dan 12:1)

Deliverance from slavery or captivity as a theme connects this biblical subtext underlying the icon with the passage from Revelation and with Muscovite texts of the period.[65] In Rev 19, Christ mounted on a white horse leads an army, which is conventionally seen as an army of martyrs, against the forces of evil at Armageddon. Rowland notes that in the icon, angels holding martyr crowns fly to distinguish the fallen;[66] however, there are no obviously dead, mutilated or ailing bodies on the icon, only apparently healthy, militarized figures with haloes.

By the same token any realistic depiction cannot be expected with regard to captives, either, who cannot be shown fettered after their release. The inscription on a second, possibly later, icon of the same type refers again to Rev 19 and to the *stikhira* for martyrs sung during morning service commencing on Saturdays.[67] In Muscovite texts closely related to the events depicted, as well as in captives' narratives, the figure of the 'martyr', another translation of the 'tormented (*muchennik*)', is the captive who stood firm to Orthodox belief. He did not succumb to the temptations and ordeal

---

[61] I.A. Kochetkov, 'K istolkovanii ikony "Tserkov voinstvuiushchaia" ("Blagoslovenno voinstvo nebesnogo tsaria")', *Trudy otdela drevnerusskoi literatury*, 38 (1985), pp. 185–209; Rowland, 'Biblical Military Imagery in the Political Culture of Early Modern Russia', p. 186. There is some dispute about evidence for the attribution of the city in the fiery pool, an element from the Book of Revelations. However, none of the evidence excludes identification on the historical level with Kazan. The rugged terrain under the feet and hooves of all three columns indicates historical time rather than the visionary world of Revelations. Overall, eschatological and redemptive motifs hold a balance and complement each other on this icon.
[62] V.I. Antonov and N.E. Mneva, *Katalog drevnerusskoi zhivopisi XI-nachala XVIII vv.*, vol. 2 (Moskva, 1963), p. 131; Rowland, 'Biblical Military Imagery in the Political Culture of Early Modern Russia', p. 186.
[63] *Biblia sirech knigi vetchago i novago Zaveta po iazyku slovensku*: King James Bible translates 'Michael, the great prince'.
[64] 'I v to vremia spustsia liudie tvoi vsi' Ibid.
[65] The crucial bit is in Tikhomirov, *Letopisets nachala tsarstva*, pp. 82, 89.
[66] Rowland, 'Biblical Military Imagery in the Political Culture of Early Modern Russia', p. 187.
[67] Kochetkov, 'K istolkovanii ikony "Tserkov voinstvuiushchaia" (Blagoslovenno voinstvo nebesnogo tsaria)', p. 209.

Fig. 1: Icon 'Blessed Host of the Heavenly Tsar', 1550s, inv. nr. 6141, with permission of Tretyakovskaia Galereia.

suffered at the hands of the captors, trying to sway him to convert to Islam.[68] In the 'Chronicle of the Beginning of Tsardom', Ivan asks Makarii to implore

> Christ [. . .] to liberate poor Christendom from Kazan slavery [. . .] [where they were] tormented by the Muslims.[69]

The point here is not an alternative interpretation of the 'Blessed Host', but a redemptive one that complements the military reading Rowland rightly proposes: Makarii in his letter reveals the prospect of entering heaven due to military valour.[70] Redemption in an earthly sense is conditional on 'suffering torments' in captivity in the 1649 code of laws stipulating that returning captives are to be liberated from tax obligations or service to their master; masters even had to manumit their wife and children.[71]

Metropolitan Makarii supported Ivan's general commemoration of 1548, which put captives on an equal footing with the fallen. Though it was dedicated to princes and boyars, it addressed the entire 'Christ–loving army', clerics of all ranks and all Orthodox Christians collectively as 'all Orthodox Christians killed by foreigners on the battlefield or led into captivity'.[72] Note the equal treatment of captives and soldiers fallen in combat with foreigners, who are memorialized in the same way. One of the events commemorated on this day in special church services was the first, unsuccessful campaign against Kazan in 1547–48.[73]

Contemporary official sources and chronicles on the Kazan campaign point out repeatedly that liberated Russian captives and slaves were 'martyrs', that is, 'tormented' (*muchennye*). Among the earliest examples is metropolitan Makarii's second letter to Ivan IV and his 'Christ–loving host' at Sviiazhsk on the eve of the escalade of Kazan:

> [. . .] it is befitting for thee, O pious tsar Ivan, [. . .] to struggle [. . .] for all Orthodox Christians, innocently led into captivity, kidnapped and tormented by the [Kazanians] with every possible calamity and defiled by various passions.[74]

---

68 Captives' narratives, for example in Rossiiskii Gosudarstvennyi Arkhiv Drevnikh Aktov (hereafter: RGADA), f. 210 d. 609 ll. 121, 122, 125; ibid. d. 808 l. 37. On the background of this formula, see chapter 6.
69 Tikhomirov, *Letopisets nachala tsarstva*, p. 60.
70 Ibid., pp. 82, 89.
71 Hellie, *The Muscovite Law Code (Ulozhenie) of 1649*, XIX §33 (p. 159) and XX §34 (p. 172).
72 L. Steindorff, *Memoria in Altrußland: Untersuchungen zu den Formen christlicher Totensorge* (Stuttgart, 1994), p. 76. *Akty, sobrannye v biblotekakh i arkhivakh Rossiiskoi imperii Arkheograficheskoiu ekspeditsieiu Imperatorskoi Akademii Nauk*, vol. 1: *1294–1598* (Sanktpeterburg, 1836), p. 208 n. 219. Cf. I.V. Dergacheva, *Stanovlenie povestvovatel'nykh nachal v drevnerusskoi literature XV-XVII vekov (na materiale sinodika)* (München, 1990), p. 26.
73 M.E. Bychkova, *Sostav klassa feodalov Rossii v XVI v.: Istoriko-genealogicheskoe issledovanie* (Moskva, 1986), p. 168. Cf. Steindorff, *Memoria in Altrußland*, chapter 7, "Sinodik für die Gefallenen".
74 *Akty istoricheskie, sobrannye i izdannye arkheograficheskoiu kommissieiu*, vol. 1: *1334–1598* (Sanktpeterburg, 1841), pp. 290–296. It was incorporated into the 'Chronicle of the Beginning of Tsardom': Tikhomirov, *Letopisets nachala tsarstva*, pp. 86–90. See also Pelenski, *Russia and Kazan*, pp. 194–213.

Liberated captives who had stood firm in their belief deserved the martyr's crown and were likened to warriors by military garb. This links the icon 'Blessed Host of the Heavenly Tsar' to the literary texts about the tsar's deliverance of slaves in Kazan. On the icon, the Heavenly Jerusalem of salvation history therefore symbolizes Moscow, the Second Jerusalem, where the earthly captives worthy of redemption and their military liberators head.

Muscovites consciously mixed the history of salvation and the fate of captives. Eschatological motives, often misunderstood as exclusively concerned with the imminent last days of the world were actually often seen in the perspective of the 'small' eschatology, which evolves in our days, on an everyday level.[75] Studying Muscovite maps and icons, Russian millenarianism is characterised, in some works, by a greater continuity between paradise and external world than in the Latin West and, in other works, by catastrophic expectations. Orthodoxy is rife with second chances.[76] Looking at slaves as well as campaigning in the steppe and against Kazan, this meant that seemingly unambiguous millenarian symbols like the cross and religiously determined icons like the 'Blessed Host' could convey the earthly purpose of liberating Russian captives. Accordingly the military connotations were legitimate, too. The actions of the tsar had a place in salvation history, but Muscovites were less concerned about which place exactly. After being quite clear that he was most concerned for the captives' plight in his speech to the boyars in April 1551, Ivan IV in the guise of the shepherd appeals to Christ:

> [. . .] the wicked Kazan Tatars have no other means of idling than by tormenting the bodies of Your abandoned slaves and by defiling Your holy name. As the prophet says: Not for us, Lord, not for us, but for the glory of your name lead us onto the path of salvation and let me strive for your holy name and for the Christendom which you have entrusted to me. [. . .] I cannot suffer the doom of [Orthodox] Christendom since it has been entrusted to me by my Christ.[77]

Focus on the torments of captive Orthodox Christians united the present perceived in terms of redemption from captivity with the history of salvation, the military symbols and the heavenly Jerusalem on the icon 'Blessed Host'.

---

[75] L. Steindorff, 'Review of Pod znakom kontsa vremeni: Ocherki russkoi religioznosti kontsa XIV– nachala XVI vv. by A. I. Alekseev (Sankt-Peterburg 2002), *Jahrbücher für Geschichte Osteuropas*, 53, 1 (2005), pp. 113–114.
[76] Kivelson, *Cartographies of Tsardom*.
[77] Tikhomirov, *Letopisets nachala tsarstva*, p. 73.

Chapter 4
Spreading Liberation Ideas

Muscovite sources are definite about the political obligations and rights of rulers and subjects.[1] As the preceding chapters have shown, this was true with respect to the liberation of slaves. This chapter and the next will focus on further categories of sources and aim to flesh out the views of those beyond the elite, of ordinary servitors and Muscovites in general. It is usually difficult to find extensive sources for the early modern period that allow us to reliably assess the views of the general population. It might be presumptuous to expect a better situation in Muscovy. However, there are indications of a more broadly shared concern for the well-being of captives and for expectations about the behaviour of rulers relating to them. The sources closest to these groups include public events such as rituals and clerical theatre, and popular saint's lives. The symbolism of texts, rituals and icons requires some knowledge about the wider discourse to determine its meanings.

Baptism and crossing the Red Sea

Prominent among the imagery in the Blessed Host icon is the motif of trees pouring from the Heavenly Jerusalem onto earth, where in a grove a spring feeds a river along which a multitude of trees grow into the barren steppe, alongside the path of the host. Imaginatively, these trees at times seem to blend with the bodies and wings of the angels who bear the martyr crowns. Overall, this is an obvious alteration of the text of the Book of Revelation, which places water and fruit trees squarely within the Heavenly Jerusalem. Iconography thus suggests a link between martyrs, trees, and water and, it should be added in the light of what has been said above, liberated slaves.

The aftermath of the conquest of Kazan saw special efforts to adapt salvific history to illustrating the telos of Muscovy in liberating slaves. Interpolations inserted into existing stories increased the weight of slave liberation in redemptive history, especially in the 'Royal Book of Degrees', and these are closely related to the imagery of water and wood. The 'Book of Degrees' was presumably composed to teach the offspring of the tsar to rule the realm and a handful of copies were disseminated to monastic centres around the realm.[2] It is usually ascribed to metropolitan Afanasii

---

1 See e.g.: S. Bogatyrev, *The Sovereign and His Counsellors* (Saarijärvi, 2000).
2 N.S. Kollmann, 'On Advising Princes in Early Modern Russia: Literacy and Performance', in A. Kleimola and G. Lenhoff, eds., *The Book of Royal Degrees and the Genesis of Russian Historical Consciousness/"Stepennaia kniga tsarskogo rodosloviia" i genezis russkago istoricheskogo soznaniia* (Bloomington IN, 2011), pp. 341–348.

Open Access. © 2022 the author(s), published by De Gruyter. This work is licensed under the Creative Commons Attribution-NonCommercial-NoDerivatives 4.0 International License.
https://doi.org/10.1515/9783110696431-005

(1564–66), who followed Makarii in Moscow and signed one of the earliest copies. Research on the oldest manuscript, which was recently found in Tomsk, as well as internal evidence have led to an array of opinions whereby the 'Book of Degrees' is dated to either the mid-1550s or the early 1560s. Some contend that the text only stabilized under metropolitan Filip (1566–68), while the late Edward Keenan put it in a different context, that it took its final shape during the rule of Boris Godunov, the regent and authority behind Tsar Fedor Ivanovich, in the years after Ivan IV's death in 1584.[3] However, intra-textual evidence on dating the 'Book of Degrees' requires more attention than it has been given so far. As will be shown below, it contains many of the details of the Biblical Exodus inscribed in the murals of the Golden Hall throne- and anterooms of Ivan IV, and adds slavery-related details to the sources copied. However, it barely mentions Joseph, whose extensive slave career from sale and incarceration to the very top of Egyptian society fills two walls in Fedor Ivanovich's and Boris Godunov's newly painted throne room, the Palace of Facets.[4] These diverging foci align with the majority of attempts to date the 'Book of Degrees' within the years immediately after the fall of Kazan.

Gail Lenhoff has shown that the 'Royal Book of Degrees' inner structure builds towards the fulfilment of Rus' and Muscovite history in the reign of Ivan IV and the conquest of the Tatar capital on the Volga.[5] Beyond this ground-breaking observation, a close reading and textual comparison reveals an internal view that stresses liberation from foreign slavery as the aim of Muscovy, which was fulfilled by Ivan IV. In comparing the origins of prominent founding stories, such as the lengthy account of the baptism of Kievan Rus' in the 'Tale of Bygone Years', to its putative copy in the 'Book of Degrees', a series of interpolations stands out.[6] They reflect the motives inscribed in this text as they twist the story in a peculiar way.

The narrative structure of the story about the baptism of Rus' applies salvific history in the speech delivered by the Greek Orthodox 'philosopher' from Makedonia to Great Prince Vladimir of Kyiv. The speech, which is followed by a dialogue or interrogation, is the most elaborate endeavour to sway Rus' to Greek Orthodoxy rather than to

---

[3] E.L. Keenan, 'The Stepennaia Kniga and the Godunovian Renaissance', in A. Kleimola and G. Lenhoff, eds., *The Book of Royal Degrees and the Genesis of Russian Historical Consciousness/ "Stepennaia kniga tsarskogo rodosloviia" i genezis russkago istoricheskogo soznaniia* (Bloomington IN, 2011), pp. 69–80; S. Bogatyrev, 'The Book of Degrees of the Royal Genealogy: The Stabilization of the Text and the Argument from Silence', in A. Kleimola and G. Lenhoff, eds., *The Book of Royal Degrees and the Genesis of Russian Historical Consciousness/"Stepennaia kniga tsarskogo rodosloviia" i genezis russkago istoricheskogo soznaniia* (Bloomington IN, 2011), pp. 51–68. See, however, chapter 2 on recent watermark analysis placing the Tomsk ms. in the 1550s.
[4] A. Nasibova, B. Kuznetsov and B. Groshnikov, eds., *Granovitaia palata Moskovskogo Kremlia: The Faceted Chamber in the Moscow Kremlin* (Leningrad, 1978).
[5] Lenhoff, 'Politics and Form in the Stepennaia Kniga'.
[6] On interpreting interpolations: Ostrowski, 'Dressing a Wolf in Sheep's Clothing'.

any neighbouring faith, such as the Muslim, Hebrew and Latin communities. The 'philosopher', or missionary starts with the creation of the world, briefly covering the main Biblical themes and ending with Pentecost. The following interrogation settles the main themes and questions on Vladimir's mind: they revolve around the axis of the fall of Adam and Eve from paradise and humanity's redemption, marked by intermediary elements of the legend of the wood and water which connect paradise, Golgotha and the earthly redemptive or militarily liberating efforts of the rule of Ivan IV.[7] The connection of religious salvation to the latest events in this line is enhanced by the interpolations which will be discussed in detail below.

From the time of the Rus' principalities onwards, the comprehensive story of the Exodus of the Israelite slaves from Egypt was available to readers and audiences in the '*Stepennaia kniga* (Royal Book of Degrees)' and the texts from which it borrowed. The interpolations strengthen this aspect of the Biblical narrative. The speech of the philosopher who recommends Orthodox Christianity as the appropriate faith for Rus' to grand prince Vladimir, which starts on page 248, is copied and slightly rephrased but remains almost unchanged from earlier chronicles. It sums up God's motivation for leading the Israelites out of Egypt as follows:

> The [Israelites] lived for 400 years in Egypt [where] their tribe spread and multiplied but the Egyptians forced them to do slave work (*porabotisha*) after Joseph's and Jacob's death and the Egyptians mistreated them in slavery.[8]

Moses as baby is saved from the fate of the Hebrew new-borns by the love of a princess and the 'tsar', i.e. pharaoh. During the reign of his successor, the envy of the boyars and the experience of oppression of another Israelite by an Egyptian, whom Moses then kills, finally drive him into exile. Two quick sentences on his further life follow, then the archangel Gabriel appears and tells him the whole story of the world crammed in one sentence, followed by a note that he told Moses 'all wisdom'. In the next sentence God in the burning bush tells him about his intention to liberate the Israelite slaves:

> I have seen the poor treatment of those people in Egypt and will lead them out of this land. Go to pharaoh, the *tsar'* of Egypt, and tell him: "Let Israel go (*ispusti*) [. . .]"[9]

One more page (255) is spent entirely on the process of liberation: the redeeming plagues and the rescue from Israel's oppressors through Moses, the instrument of God, who parted the Red Sea with his staff while their persecutors perished in the floods. This is followed closely by the account of how the bitter water of Marah in the Sinai desert was sweetened by the touch of the wood, and how God fed the

---

[7] Pokrovskii and Lenhoff, *Stepennaia kniga tsarskogo rodosloviia po drevneishim spiskam*, pp. 247–265.
[8] Ibid., pp. 254–255.
[9] Ibid., p. 254. Cf. the broadly similar terms in this passage used in earlier variants: *Ipat'evskaia letopis'* (S.-Peterburg, 1908), p. 58.

faltering, starving former slaves with manna to make them forget Egypt's fleshpots.[10] Another page covers the Ten Commandments. The conquest of the Promised Land by Joshua (in Russian, Jesus son of Nun) and the story of the *tsars* [kings] of Israel starting on page 257 gives way to the prophets presaging the descent of Christ to humanity right up to page 260. The New Testament to the descent of the Holy Spirit at Pentecost is summarized on the remaining pages until 264. Summing up the speech of the philosopher, Exodus is one of only a few heavily emphasized subjects in this choice of texts, providing relevant clues for the prefiguration of Christ's ordeal. Slavery is mentioned a number of times, as it is in earlier chronicles.[11]

Next, Vladimir wants to better understand the 'unspeakable secrets' he has just heard and asks theologically more systematic questions:

> Because of which sin did the unfathomable God will to be born by woman and why was He crucified on the wood, He whom all ethereal powers fear? And what kind of purification did the Sinless [Jesus] need, when He was baptised [by John the Forerunner; CW] in the water?[12]

The background to the extensive interpolations in the following account of the baptism of Vladimir and then of the Rus' is summed up and prefigured in the answer of the philosopher. He stresses the circular view of salvific history: driven from paradise by woman's gullibility, he says, humanity will be saved by the Son of God born by woman. The salvific role of the wood will be discussed in the following section. On account of the water and the baptism, the answer is that it renews life just as the flood took away sinful humanity except for Noah's kin, so today water washes away human sins. Within this circularity, redemption is at work and cannot be disentangled from both its worldly and its ethereal meanings, as the 'philosopher' continues:

> This is why the Hebrews were purified in the sea of the wicked custom of Egypt, since the water was from the very beginning. In the Beginning, it is said, the Spirit of God hovered over the water, and so today baptism is by water and Spirit.[13]

Water as the prefiguration of baptism and concomitant of Wisdom, the philosopher explains here, overcomes the bad habits of slave life in Egypt.

The philosopher continues to explain how water triggered the conquest of the Promised Land. Gideon led the Israelites against the Midianites when the latter had returned as instruments of God to enslave the Israelites and punish them for their relapse into polytheism. Before Gideon found resolve for this endeavour, he tested the angel of the Lord who brought God's request. Since it seemed extraordinary that he should succeed in leading the Israelites against the more numerous Midianites, he

---

10 Pokrovskii and Lenhoff, *Stepennaia kniga tsarskogo rodosloviia po drevneishim spiskam*, pp. 254–255.
11 *Ipat'evskaia letopis'*, pp. 81–82.
12 Pokrovskii and Lenhoff *Stepennaia kniga tsarskogo rodosloviia po drevneishim spiskam*, p. 264.
13 Ibid., p. 265. Already in *Ipat'evskaia letopis'*, p. 65.

required as a sign that dew should fall exclusively on the fleece he put on the earth, and not on the ground around it. The next day, he required the opposite. The anti-Judaic 'philosopher' symbolically explains the positive result both times: earlier, the Jews enjoyed the water of Exodus from slavery and the gentiles – the Egyptians – lived in drought; whereas after baptism, this relation reversed: renewal is effected by water. In the context of the preceding explanations, this kills several birds with one stone: the conquest of the Promised Land is linked to the salvific history of water, baptism effects the difference between the Promised Land of the Jews and the promised land of Rus' – or at least its flourishing; and baptism is represented as a root cause for overcoming the bad habit of slaving in the service of another power.

Since the philosopher has spoken convincingly, Vladimir calls on his boyars and they decide to send envoys to all neighbouring faiths. Earlier chronicles share the stress on the joy of the Greek tsar, the great honour in which they were received in Constantinople, and how they marvelled at the bright and sumptuous festival in the impressive cathedral of Sophia that was quickly organised for their benefit.[14] In the 'Book of Royal Degrees', the reason for the Greeks' enthusiastic greeting is that the latter hope to

> change [Rus'] slave raids (*plenenia*) against us into love for us as they recognize the mercy of holy baptism.[15]

This reasoning is based on the preceding explanations of the redemptive role played by water and baptism. It is an interpolation entirely new to the 'Book of Degrees', which is not found in the older Ipat'ev chronicle dated to the 1420s, nor in the direct source of the surrounding text, the early sixteenth century Nikon chronicle.[16]

This intention of saving the Greeks from the slave raids of Rus' is restated more clearly in the following story of Vladimir's conquest of Korsun' (Chersonesos) and his request to marry the emperor's sister Anna after his baptism. As she opposes the proposal of the 'heathen' Vladimir, the Byzantine emperor tells her that she will be involved in stopping slave raids:

> You will be the instrument of God for saving your heathen husband and converting the Rus' land to Orthodoxy. You will save the Greek land from vicious warfare *and unmerciful slave raids* and killing. Look, sister, how many wicked deeds Rus' have done to the Greeks, how often they fought wars *[and] how many were led away into slavery* (v plen raskhishchakhu) [. . .][17]

---

[14] *Ipat'evskaia letopis'*, p. 66; A.F. Bychkov, ed., *Letopisnyi sbornik, imenuemyi Patriarsheiu ili Nikonovskoiu letopis'iu*, vol. 1 (Sankt Peterburg, 1882), 52.

[15] Pokrovskii and Lenhoff, *Stepennaia kniga tsarskogo rodosloviia po drevneishim spiskam*, p. 270.

[16] Cf. D.S. Likhachev and D.M. Bulanin, eds., *Slovar' knizhnikov i knizhnosti drevnei Rusi*, vol. 2: *Vtoraia polovina XIV – XVI v.*, pt. 1: *A – K* (Leningrad, 1989), p. 75. Cf. Bychkov, *Letopisnyi sbornik, imenuemyi Patriarsheiu ili Nikonovskoiu letopis'iu*, vol. 1, p. 53 and the 'Chronicle of Bygone Years': *Lavrent'evskaia letopis'*, vol. 1: *Povest' vremennykh let* (Leningrad, 1926–1928), p. 108.

[17] Pokrovskii and Lenhoff, *Stepennaia kniga tsarskogo rodosloviia po drevneishim spiskam*, p. 276. Interpolations in italics.

The emperor's motive of preventing slave raids is, again, entirely an interpolation compared to the Ipat'ev chronicle, which merely says: '[your marriage] will save the Greek land from cruel warfare (*rati*)'.[18] A century later, in the Nikon chronicle, slow changes had taken place which mark the accelerating evolution of ideology between the 1530s and the 1550s–60s. Although the alliance with the Crimean Tatars had been broken, the Nikon chronile still notes ambiguously: '[your marriage] will save the Greek land from cruel slavery (*raboty*)'.[19]

The 'Book of Degrees' aims to portray Vladimir as a new Moses, focusing on water. In preparation of the following baptism of Rus', another extensive interpolation has Vladimir wishing to perform a symbolical feat of liberation, although it also whitewashes an obvious theft of relics:

> Just as Moses [who] led Israel out of slavery (*raboty*) in Egypt took with him the bones of Joseph the Most-Beautiful [which had been buried in the waters of the Nile], so Vladimir, when he left Chersonesos wanted to lead the New Israel out of [the city], out of the reach of the enslaving monstrous idol worshippers (*ot raboty kumirobesia*). [Therefore, he, too,] took the relics of the great holy martyr St Clement, the pope of Rome and disciple of St Peter, whom the impious emperor Trajan put in custody in Chersonesos.[20]

Accordingly, St Clement had baptised almost the whole population of the Crimean Peninsula but when the end of his life came, his holy relics were thrown into the water by order of the 'impious and dishonourable' governor using an anchor to fix them under water; like the remains of the Biblical Joseph. However, once a year the water parts and there is a dry path leading to his relics and to the 'crystal church which had wondrously sprung up above them'.[21] This is likened to the New Israel story in the same paragraph and to the earlier summary of Exodus detailing the partition of the Red Sea. By comparison, the main source of the 'Book of Degrees', the 'Nikon Chronicle', like earlier chronicles barely mentions St Clement's relics, let alone Joseph's, or, for that matter, Moses and slavery.[22]

---

18 *Ipat'evskaia letopis'*, p. 68. Cf. the 'Chronicle of Bygone Years' in *Lavrent'evskaia letopis'*, vol. 1: *Povest' vremennykh let*, p. 110; F. Butler, *Enlightener of Rus': The Image of Vladimir Sviatoslavich Across the Centuries* (Bloomington IN, 2002), pp. 42–43.
19 Cf. Bychkov, *Letopisnyi sbornik, imenuemyi Patriarsheiu ili Nikonovskoiu letopis'iu*, vol. 1, p. 54.
20 Pokrovskii and Lenhoff, *Stepennaia kniga tsarskogo rodosloviia po drevneishim spiskam*, pp.289–290.
21 Ibid. On Moses and Joseph cf. chapters 2, 5 and 6. On the adjective '*nechestivyi*' adding another layer of redemptive prefiguration, see chapter 6. The events alluded to are part of an inner Byzantine power struggle, in which Vladimir sided with the emperor Basilius II: A. Poppe, *Kak byla kreshchena Rus'* (Moscow, 1989), pp. 202–204; R.C. Martin, ed., *Encyclopedia of Islam and the Muslim World*, vol. 2: *L–Z* (Farmington Hills MI, 2016), entry 'Rus'.
22 Bychkov, *Letopisnyi sbornik, imenuemyi Patriarsheiu ili Nikonovskoiu letopis'iu*, vol. 1, p. 54. D.G. Ostrowski, *The Povest' Vremennykh Let: An Interlinear Collation and Paradosis* (Cambridge MA, 2003), p. 116 l. 10; *Ipat'evskaia letopis'*, p. 72.

'*Ot raboty kumirobesia*' in the context of its time and of the source means slave raiders, referring to Egypt, although in this passage they are otherwise not expressly addressed. The Greeks give the 'Korsun peninsula' to Vladimir

> not so much for the marriage of the Byzantine princess, but because of the mercy shown by the baptism of Rus'.[23]

Just before the mercy of God saving from slave raids is mentioned again, Vladimir obtains 'the celestial tsardom, the ulterior city on the hill, Jerusalem'.[24]

One page down, just after the collective baptism of the Kievan Rus', the meaning of baptism as analogy of water and liberation is impressed again on readers. It is a passage interpolated into what was in the Nikon Chronicle still only Vladimir's traditional Orthodox speech emphasizing victory over the enemy's sly designs:[25]

> So they all went out of the water, their soul and body enlightened, happily extolling and praising Christ God, who saved them just as old Israel was saved from slavery at the hand of Moses [. L]ikewise today the New Israel, the Rus' people [are saved from slavery] through Vladimir's hand, the sovereign equal to the apostles.[26]

The 'Royal Book of Degrees' employs interpolations into the source texts to express a new emphasis in its worldview. It closely aligns baptism with the redemptive or ransom theory of atonement. While these additions do not add any new concepts previously unknown to Christianity, they stress particular messages in Biblical and Rus' history as it was related before. The writers of the 1560s changed the founding narrative of Rus' and Muscovite Orthodoxy, the baptism of the Rus'. The new text impresses on the reader that from the very beginning of Rus' history, its purpose was the liberation of slaves and the foundation of an empire built on such a legitimation. It was fulfilled and completed by Ivan IV.[27]

Starting in the late 1540s, after Ivan's inauguration as tsar and during his campaigns against Kazan, a renewed emphasis on the early Christian redemptive or ransom interpretation of salvific history appears in Muscovite sources. It allows to see Muscovy as New Israel on its way to liberating the slaves from the Tatars under Ivan IV in analogy to the Biblical Exodus from Egypt in an extended dynastic narrative since great prince Vladimir's baptism of Rus'. The 1560s 'Book of Degrees' fully develops this theory. It is implicitly or partly formulated in earlier sources form the 1540s onwards, such as the murals of the Golden Palace, the rituals and texts of the New Year's ceremony, or the 'Chronicle of the Beginning of Tsardom' and the chronicles copying it. These sources stress the prefiguration of Moses to Christ and Vladimir of Kyiv to Ivan

---

23 Pokrovskii and Lenhoff, *Stepennaia kniga tsarskogo rodosloviia po drevneishim spiskam*, p. 288.
24 Ibid., p. 288.
25 Bychkov, *Letopisnyi sbornik, imenuemyi Patriarsheiu ili Nikonovskoiu letopis'iu*, vol. 1, pp. 57–58.
26 Pokrovskii and Lenhoff, *Stepennaia kniga tsarskogo rodosloviia po drevneishim spiskam*, p. 294.
27 On later copies, see Butler, *Enlightener of Rus'*, p. 100.

IV in their roles as redeemers, on the salvific or this-worldly level respectively. Therefore, the sacralisation of the tsar in the 'Book of Degrees' and elsewhere was closely related to Ivan's role as ransom agent and liberator of captives and slaves.

The True Cross and purification by water

An important symbol in the composition of the 'Blessed Host' icon mentioned above, the cross, was central to the oath of loyalty delivered by the whole population, including peasants, to the grand prince since 1547 the tsar of Muscovy. It was an oath performed on a Bible, called 'kissing the cross'.[28] The 1649 code of laws stipulates that false cross-kissing is to be punished by excommunication, and possibly by cutting out the tongue. It expressly combines this-worldly and otherworldly aspects of redemption, tying it to the solemnity of the oath:

> The Cross was given to Christians for consecration and enlightenment and to expel enemies seen and unseen. For that reason, it behoves Orthodox Christians to revere the holy cross with faith and truth and purity; and to kiss the honourable[29] cross with fear and trepidation and a clear conscience.[30]

It will be shown below that the sign of the cross referred to the liberation of captives. As discussed in Chapter 2, contemporary sources attributed the conquest of Kazan, from where the army depicted on the 'Blessed Host' icon is shown returning, to fulfilling the duty to liberate slaves. In the first sentence of Ivan IV's speech announcing the campaign of 1552, the Kazanians are called 'enemies of the cross', after just previously their deceit has been exposed namely their alleged failure to manumit all Russian slaves as agreed and sworn.[31] However, as Muslims the Tatars swore on a copy of the Qur'an, not the Bible covered by the cross.[32] Metropolitan Makarii in his speech during tsar Ivan's and the army's triumphant entry into the capital spelled out that the power of the cross signified redemption and how it contributed to liberation:

> [Y]our enemies the dishonourable tsars [khans] of Kazan and oath-breaking Kazan Tatars have captured the Orthodox people of the cross (*krestiian*) and scattered them over the face of the earth. Since you have liberated the stolen herd from slavery (*ot raboty*) [. . .] and [since] they had been captured and tortured in many ways and suffered from [the Tatars] [. . .] God has shown mercy: He gave to you the city of Kazan and all the adjoining lands and slew the

---

28 Y. Mikhailova and D. Prestel, 'Cross Kissing: Keeping One's Word in Twelfth-Century Rus'', *The Slavic Review*, 70, 1 (2011), pp. 1–22; H.W. Dewey and A.M. Kleimola, 'Promise and Perfidy in Old Russian Cross-Kissing', *Canadian Slavic Studies*, 3 (1968), pp. 327–341.
29 Hellie translated 'venerable' Cf. chapter 6.
30 Hellie, *The Muscovite Law Code (Ulozhenie) of 1649*, pp. 99–100.
31 Tikhomirov, *Letopisets nachala tsarstva*, pp. 72–73.
32 Khodarkovsky, *Russia's Steppe Frontier*.

dragon[33] nesting in it, which viciously devoured us, with the power of the cross and your agency, pious and honourable tsar he has ousted these dishonourable [Tatars], instilled compassion, set up[34] the life-giving cross, restored the holy church and delivered through your tsar's hand many [Orthodox] Christians from slavery (*raboty*).[35]

In another speech during the preparations for the 1552 campaign, Ivan exhorts the metropolitan and all clerics to pray in the Cathedral of the Annunciation and

> consecrate water with all relics and the cross of the life-giving wood, at which was crucified our Lord Christ, to release our human kin from hellish torments.[36]

In the context of liberation rhetoric of the 'Chronicle of the Beginning of Tsardom' and the explicit purpose of these prayers, the torments are those suffered by slaves who are perceived to live in conditions like hell, rather than in transcendental hell. This is corroborated by statements, placed just after the conquest, about the hell-like qualities of Kazan under the khans.[37]

The life-giving wood alludes to the 'Legend of the True Cross', or the holy wood, handed down in Russian sources in both the legend of the same title and, more extensively, in the widely copied 'Life of Moses'. In the 1550s metropolitan Makarii included it in his 'Great Reading Menaion', all-embracing collection of holy texts. The Russian version unmistakably identifies the wood used by Moses to transform the bitter water of the source at Marah into potable water, thereby saving the Israelite fugitives from slavery in the desert, with the cross of Christ. Moses says:

> Just like this wood sweetens the water, so the blood of the crucified hallows this wood. For just like the wood makes the bitter water of Marah potable, the cross of Christ sweetens the bitterness of heathen unbelieve.[38]

---

33 The Tatar khan of Kazan, along with his supporters among the city's population, are labelled as enemies and slavers.
34 Setting up the life-giving cross refers to the Orthodox feast itself linked to liberation of captives.
35 Tikhomirov, *Letopisets nachala tsarstva*, p. 114. Original interspersed with praise for Ivan's piety and honour (*chest*) and the feats of Byzantine emperor Constantine and the dynasty since St Vladimir.
36 Ibid., p. 75. See also F. Kämpfer, ed., *Historie vom Zartum Kasan (Kasaner Chronist)* (Graz, 1969), p. 259.
37 Tikhomirov, *Letopisets nachala tsarstva*, p. 87; Volkova, *Kazanskaia Istoriia*, chapters 17 and 23.
38 M.V. Rozhdestvenskaia, *Zhitie proroka Moiseia: Vstuplenie i kommentarii*, Elektronnaia biblioteka IRLI RAN, 2006–2011, (http://lib.pushkinskijdom.ru/Default.aspx?tabid=4917 [accessed 24 Mar. 2017]); A.A. Alekseev, 'Russko-evreiskie literaturnye sviazi do XV v.', in A. Alekseev, W. Moskovich and S. Shvarzband, eds., *Jews and Slavs*, vol. 1 (Sankt Petersburg, 1993), pp. 44–75; M. Taube, 'On the Slavic Life of Moses and Its Hebrew Sources', in A. Alekseev, W. Moskovich and S. Shvarzband, eds., *Jews and Slavs*, vol. 1 (Jerusalem, 1993), pp. 84–119. However, the Russian version of the Legend of the Cross sees the wood of Marah made into the cross of the unrepentant thief crucified with Jesus: M.D. Kagan-Tarkovskoi, 'Slovo o krestnom dreve: Podgotovka teksta, perevod i kommentarii', http://lib.pushkinskij dom.ru/Default.aspx?tabid=4928 (accessed 19 Dec. 2020). Overall, this is a story compiled from various apocryphal sources about the reunification of the parts of the tree of paradise in Golgotha.

This episode explains why the wood of the cross was named 'the cross of the life-giving wood' in contexts of liberation propaganda, as it saves the liberated slaves from dying of thirst, making sure that they will reach their destination in the promised land (*svoboda*).³⁹ Moreover, it is part of an extended analogy of the Exodus from Egyptian slavery and the Immaculate Conception, whereby the waters drowning pharaoh's army as if there was never a dry path beneath the sea is the analogy of the birth canal of the virgin mother of God that closed as if there never had been a birth. The more abstract sense of these analogies is that saving the Israelites from slavery – with slavery seen as expiation of sin – prefigures Christ saving the world from sin by giving himself as ransom, in the ransom theory of salvation. Significantly, the episode at Marah and two episodes in which Moses and Aaron used their staffs during Exodus – likewise considered part of the history of the wood of the cross – were part of the murals in the anteroom of the Golden Palace.⁴⁰ This underlines the importance of these closely interlaced ideas about the purifying power of water, the wood of the cross, and liberation from slavery for the worldview during Ivan IV's reign.

The 'Legend of the True Cross', popular in Latin Christianity as well as in Orthodoxy due to its Bogomil origins, is a form of this-worldly salvation history that focuses on the story of the wood of the tree in paradise from which Eve plucked the apple. Some of it ended up in the roof of Solomon's temple, a passage which may be read as boosting Moscow's claim as Second Jerusalem. A portion appears during the Exodus, when Moses satisfied the thirsty and seditious former slaves in the Sinai desert by putting down twigs in cruciform to make the bitter waters of Marah sweet. The legend predicts at this point that the saviour will be crucified on the Holy Wood, highlighting the unity of salvation history, liberation from slavery and salvation in the afterlife. Moses' staff has also been handed down the generations since the expulsion from paradise, and sometimes gets mixed up with the Holy Wood. It performs various miracles during the Exodus, among them the parting of the Red Sea and striking water from a rock; Aaron transforms it into a snake to impress pharaoh and force him to release the slaves: scenes also featuring in the vault of the Golden Palace's anteroom.⁴¹ For John of Damascus, one of the seven ecumenical church fathers accepted in Orthodoxy, the

---

39 In the middle of the sixteenth century, *svoboda* meant the ability to return to one's home and family. This sense was preserved in the eighteenth century. Smolarz, 'Speaking about Freedom and Dependency'. The 1649 code of laws adds another interpretation, considerably closer to contemporary views: returning captives were to be liberated (*svobodit*) from tax obligations if they had been inscribed to the taxable town people, or set free from the pretensions of former masters if they were dependents or slaves (*kholopy*): R. Hellie, *The Muscovite Law Code (Ulozhenie) of 1649*, XIX §33 (p. 159) and XX §34 (p. 172). See chapter 3, footnote 86.
40 K.K. Lopialo, 'K primernoi rekonstruktsii rospisi svodov Zolotoi palaty', in O.I. Podobedova, ed., *Moskovskaia shkola zhivopisi pri Ivane IV. Raboty v Mosk. Kremle 40-kh-70-kh godov XVI v* (Moskva, 1972), pp. 193–200; Appendix; Zabelin, *Materialy dlia istorii, arkheologii i statistiki goroda Moskvy*, p. 1252.
41 Podobedova, *Moskovskaia shkola zhivopisi pri Ivane IV. Raboty v Mosk. Kremle 40-kh-70-kh godov XVI v*, app. Zabelin, *Materialy dlia istorii, arkheologii i statistiki goroda Moskvy*, pp. 1238–1255.

tree of life in paradise and the staffs of Joseph and Moses in the Old Testament prefigure the cross, bringing the gift of life to the liberated slaves according to the classical or ransom theory of atonement.[42]

The religious discourse of Muscovy therefore corroborates the reading that the cross is called 'life–giving' in the sources concerning the Kazan campaign in the context of liberating captives. In case anybody missed the significance of the dual aspects of redemption by the cross in this world and the hereafter, an interpolation was placed in the Russian version of the 'Life of Moses' after the miracle of Aaron turning his staff into snakes. Interpolations were often used to clarify the meaning of a passage. This one has the bishop of Cyprus turn a snake into a coin for redeeming (*vykup*) a debt slave, thereby discharging the duty of his position to ransom. He redeems a poor man whom a merchant threatens to sell into slavery imminently.[43] The Muscovite 'Legend of the True Cross' thus relates salvific history with a strong emphasis on the Exodus, including scenes ranging from slavery to the miraculous redeeming of a bondsman.

The 'Legend' in its entirety was not part of the mural programme in the Kremlin's Golden Palace. However, the scenes relating to the Exodus were important enough for the Muscovite elite to be included in the central representational space of tsardom, the antechamber of the throne room, where courtiers and all those waiting for an audience cooled their heels before meeting the tsar. The scenes covered more than half of the panels of the second tier in the cupola; the rest of the tier was dedicated to the conquest of the Promised Land, biblical Canaan, by the former slaves. All scenes were accompanied by an explanation in Church Slavonic for those who could read, but the pictorial programme was self-explanatory for anyone who attended church services.[44] By the end of the sixteenth century, redemption superseded the military connotations of the New Israel. Shown in the central place of the Muscovite empire, liberation from slavery in scenes from Exodus and the tale of Joseph were an essential part of the stories that identified and represented Muscovy as a New Israel, especially where they touched upon the Legend of the True Cross.

In the post-Crucifixion parts of the Legend as it was handed down in the Russian tradition, the True Cross and the Holy Wood are connected in several ways to

---

42 P.I. Damaskin, ed., *Tochnoe izlozhenie pravoslavnoi very* (St Petersburg, 1894), pp. 213–216. *Nastol'naia kniga sviashchennosluzhitelia*, vol. 6 (Moscow, 1988), p. 177. 'Life-giving cross' for example in Tikhomirov, *Letopisets nachala tsarstva*, p. 75.

43 Rozhdestvenskaia, *Zhitie proroka Moiseia*; B. Baert, *Heritage of Holy Wood: The Legend of the True Cross in Text and Image* (Leiden, 2004), p. 10. On textual history, see Rozhdestvenskaia, *Zhitie proroka Moiseia* and Taube, 'On the Slavic Life of Moses and Its Hebrew Sources'; Alekseev, 'Russko-evreiskie literaturnye sviazi do XV v.'.

44 K.K. Lopialo, 'K primernoi rekonstruktsiia rospisi svodov Zolotoi palaty Kremlevskogo dvortsa i ee monumental'noi zhivopisi', in O.I. Podobedova, ed., *Moskovskaia shkola zhivopisi pri Ivane IV. Raboty v Mosk. Kremle 40-kh–70-kh godov XVI v* (Moskva, 1972), pp. 193–200 (Appendix); Flier, 'Golden Hall Iconography and the Makarian Initiative'.

deliverance from captivity. Centuries after Christ's redemption of humankind at the cross which had been made of the Holy Wood, the empress Helena, mother of Constantine the Great, found the buried cross in Jerusalem in the fourth century and brought one of its constituent parts to Constantinople.[45] The orally transmitted 'Great Sacred Song' bears out a particular meaning of being buried alive in this way: St George is buried by the Crimean khan and is 'resurrected' years later to release his mother.[46] The implications of this image are borne out by slaves in the Crimea and elsewhere who were sometimes kept overnight in covered pits on which guards slept, to prevent elopement or rebellion.[47] Moreover, the 'Chronicle of the Beginning of Tsardom' notes this practice as an attempt by the Kazanians to circumvent Ivan IV's prohibition of keeping slaves by hiding them underground.[48]

St George was himself a former captive and essential element of the 'Blessed Host' icon, which assembles redeemed and redeeming martyrs, former captives, and saints.[49] In the 'Great Sacred Song' St George finally returns to his 'native' cathedral, where he liberates his imprisoned mother, Holy Wisdom, the personification of the parish, thus fulfilling the promise of redemption. On his way, he addresses three women shepherds, captives of the khan, and urges them to flee and return home.[50] Burial and resurrection, particularly on the great Orthodox church holiday of the Resurrection of the Cross which commemorates Helena's search for the Cross, implied redemption from slavery.

Another part of the True Cross was captured by the Sassanid emperor Khosrow II as he conquered Jerusalem, who presented it to his wife in 605; the legends conveniently forget that she was a Christian. In the year 628, the Byzantine emperor Heraclius defeated Khosrow and returned the 'liberated' cross to Jerusalem. This part of the cross was later carried by the crusader kingdoms as a battle standard until it was finally lost in battle. The Constantinopolitan section was broken into many pieces and divided among the Latin crusaders during the sack of Constantinople in 1204. The splinters were relics that sanctified a large number of 'true crosses' throughout Latin Christianity and to a lesser degree also in the Orthodox world, among others in Muscovy.[51]

The intervening middle Byzantine era was characterised by the rise of Islam and slave raids from Crete. The Jerusalemite feast day of the Exaltation of the Cross was given an ecumenical makeover in Constantinople, which integrated the return

---

[45] Baert, *Heritage of Holy Wood*. Elevation of the Cross on Sept. 27: Russkaia pravoslavnaia tserkov', *Mineia obshchaia s prazdnichnoi* (Moskva, 1650).
[46] M.S. Vladyshevskaia, 'Sviatoi Georgii i gnostitsizm: Semantika imen v predaniiakh o sv. Georgii', in F.B. Uspenskii, ed., *Imenoslov: Zametki po istoricheskoi semantike imeni* (Moskva, 2003), pp. 70–102.
[47] Sanin, *Otnosheniia Rossii i Ukrainy s Krymskim Khanstvom v seredine XVII veka*, pp. 195–196.
[48] Boeck, 'Identity as Commodity'; Tikhomirov, *Letopisets nachala tsarstva*, p. 68.
[49] Rowland, Biblical Military Imagery in the Political Culture of Early Modern Russia, p. 189.
[50] Vladyshevskaia, 'Sviatoi Georgii i gnostitsizm', p. 86.
[51] Baert, *Heritage of Holy Wood*.

of the cross from Persia in 628, 'liberated' by imperator Heraclius.[52] Readings were introduced into the missal printed in Moscow in 1650 that hinted at this sense, which were retained until the late Muscovite period:

> Oh come ye Godloving all, to see the noble cross which has been brought to us, we will praise our one deliverer, God, crucified on the wood of the cross, do not scorn us. The bitterness was once sweetened by Moses, delivering Israel by forming a cross. [. . .] God our Tsar once created salvation upon the earth. Moses overcame the Amalekites when he stood on a hill stretching out his arms in the form of a cross, signifying the passion of Christ. [. . .] Moses prefigured you, he stretched out his hands on the hill, overcame Amalek the tormentors. The noble cross is [. . .] for every righteous [man] the saviour. [. . .]

Reading from Exodus[53]

22 Then Moses led Israel from the Red Sea and they went into the Desert of Shur. For three days they travelled in the desert without finding water. 23 When they came to Marah, they could not drink its water because it was bitter. That is why the place is called Marah. 24 So the people grumbled against Moses, saying, "What are we to drink?" 25 Then Moses cried out to the Lord, and the Lord showed him a piece of wood. He threw it into the water, and the water became fit to drink. There the Lord issued a ruling and instruction for them and put them to the test. 26 He said, "If you listen carefully to the Lord your God and do what is right in his eyes, if you pay attention to his commands and keep all his decrees, I will not bring on you any of the diseases I brought on the Egyptians, for I am the Lord, who heals you".

Reading from Isaiah[54]

11 Your gates will always stand open, they will never be shut, day or night, so that people may bring you the wealth of the nations— their kings led in triumphal procession. 12 For the nation or kingdom that will not serve you will perish; it will be utterly ruined. 13 The glory of Lebanon will come to you, the juniper, the fir and the cypress together, to adorn my sanctuary; and I will glorify the place for my feet. 14 The children of your oppressors will come bowing before you; all who despise you will bow down at your feet and will call you the City of the Lord of Israel, Zion [. . .] and the God of Israel has redeemed you. 16 [. . . T]he God of Israel redeemed you *with the cross*.[55]

---

52 K. Onasch, *Lexikon Liturgie und Kunst der Ostkirche unter Berücksichtigung der alten Kirche* (Berlin, 1993), p. 224.
53 2.Mose 15 translation: New International Version (NIV), edited according to the *Minieia*. The intervening lecture from Proverbs 3 is germane to the moral aspect.
54 Jes. 60,11–16 translation: NIV, edited according to the *Minieia*.
55 Russkaia pravoslavnaia tserkov', *Mineia obshchaia s prazdnichnoi*, [Exaltation of the Cross]: p. SNIzh 'Priidete bogoliubyvi vsi, kresta chestnago voznosima vidiashche, vozvelichim koupno, i slavu dadim, edinomu izbaviteliu bogu, vzyvaiushche, raspiisia na dreve krestnem, ne prezri moliashchikhsia nas. Gorest' drevle oslazhdaia Moisei, izbavi Izrailia, obrazom krest propisouia. [. . .] Bog zhe tsar nash prezhde vek sodela spasenie posrede zemli. Egda Amalika, Moisei pobezhdashe, na vysotu routse imyn, krestoobrazno, znamenashe Khristovu strast' prechistuiu. [. . .] Moisei proobrazuia tia, routse proster na vysotu, pobezhdashe Amalika muchitelia, kreste chestnyi vernym pokhvalo, stradaltsem outverzhenie, apostolom oukrashenie, prayednym vozbranniche, vsem prepodobnym spasiteliu'.
p. SIzhF 'Ot iskhoda chtenie

The motif of liberation and redemption is repeated several times on the following pages of the missal to impress its significance on the parishioners and trace the history of the wood of the cross:

> Moses had made the sign of the cross before he divided the Red Sea by his stave so Israel could crossit [on the bottom]. When he turned, [the water] hit pharaoh and his chariots.[56]

The 'bitter' curse of Adam and Eve was, in a manner of speaking, the basis of enslaving all nations around Israel, whereas the covenant during Exodus had lifted it for Israel. Christians therefore had to explain why they were exempt, too. The cross provided the vehicle of both transcendental redemption and this-worldly liberation during Exodus:

> He lifted the ancient deadly bitterness [the curse], for the Lord [Christ] abolished it by [using] the cross. This is why he also sweetened the bitter water of Marah by the wood, prefiguring the force of the cross.[57]

The readings and the canon reprinted in the 1650 version of the missal of the Exaltation of the Cross reinforce the Legend of the Cross, or of its Holy Wood, where it relates to slavery and redemption, especially the Exodus. In this way, it openly connects redemption both in this world and in the afterlife. Up to 1682, the missal was

---

    Siat Moisei syny Izrailevy ot moria Chermnago, i vede ikh v pustynia Sir. I idiakhu tri dni v pustyni, i ne obretakhu vody, dabysha pili. Priidosha v Merru i nemozhakhu piti vody ot Merry, gorka bo be. Sego radi narechesia imia mestu tomu, gorest'. I roptakhu liudie na Moiseia, glagoliushi chto piem. I vozopi Moisei k bogu, i pokaza gospod emou drevo, i vlozhi ei v vodu i sladka byst voda [. . .]'
    p. SKs 'Ot prorochestva Isaina chtenie
    Otverzutsia vrata tvoia Ierusalime, vynu den' i noshch, i nezatvoriatsia vvesti k tebe silu iazyk, i tsari ikh vedomy. Iazytsy bo i tsarie izhe ne poslushaiut tebe, pogibnut. I iazytsy zapusteniem zapusteiut. I slava Livanova k tebe priidet, s kiparisom i pevgom i kedrom vkoupe, proslaviti mesto sviatoe me, i mesto nogu moeiu proslavliu. I poidut k tebe boiashchesia, synove smirivshikh tia, i prognevavshikh tia, i pokloniatsia ne meste stopy nogu tvoeiu, vsi prognevavshi tia. I narecheshi sia grad Sion, sviatogo Izraileva tsaria nashego. [. . .] i izbavliai tia bog izrailev. [. . .]
    I izbavliai tia Bog Izrailev. [. . .] pravoslavnykh liudei tvoikh rog voznesi, chestnago kresta tvoego vozdvizheniem Khriste. Chestnago kresta Khriste detel' proobraziv Moisei, pobedi protivnago Amalika v pustyni Sinaistei'.
    p. SKsI 'Egozhe drevle Moisei proobrazova soboiu, Amalika nizlozhiv muchitelia
    Spasi gospodi liudi svoia, i blagoslovi dostoianie svoei, pobedy blagovernomu tsariu nashemu nasoprotivnyia daruia, i svoia sokhraniaia krestom liudi'.
56 Russkaia pravoslavnaia tserkov', *Minieia obshtaia s prazdnichnoi*, p. SKsD: 'Kresta nachertav Moisei, v priam zhezlom Chermnoe preseche, Izrailiu prokhodiashchu. Tozhe obrashch' na Faraona s kolesnitsami oudariv'.
57 Russkaia pravoslavnaia tserkov', *Minieia obshtaia s prazdnichnoi*, pp. KsI-KsIzhe: 'I gorest' drevniuiu ostavl' oubistvenuiu, gospodi krestom do kontsa potrebil esi. Sego radi i drevom osladi, drevle gorest' vod merrskikh, proobrazhdaia krestnuiu detel'.

to be read in almost all parishes.[58] It was a defining holiday of the Russian Orthodox Church, underscoring the redemptive political culture of the realm.

The salvific associations of redemption from slavery in the legends of the True Cross and the Holy Wood are central to interpreting Muscovite political culture. Promoted by tsar Aleksei, the cult of the True Cross became widespread in Muscovy.[59] Muscovites customarily swore 'on the cross', which was usually found on the cover of the bible. Someone who broke an oath consequently was called a *krestoprestupnik*, a 'criminal of the cross'. The same applies to those who actually swore on a copy of the Qur'an, for example the Kazanians; so Tatars who hid slaves in 1551/52 despite their oath to release them, were called 'enemies of the cross', recalling the purpose of the cross, redemption. When the betrayal of the Kazanians was 'discovered', Ivan IV addressed his prayers to the Mother of God, the great miracle workers and to God:

> [Ivan] never thought about anything else than the peace and calm of Christians. Those enemies of your cross, the evil Kazanians have no other thoughts for us, but to steal the bodies of your orphaned slaves.[60]

Enemies of the cross were imagined as transferring people from the tsar's patronage to Kazanian or generally Muslim slavery by theft. According to the 'Chronicle of the Beginning of Tsardom', these considerations led to the decision to punish and conquer Kazan: 'For if Christ looks at our unwavering truthfulness, he will release us from [them] all'.[61]

According to the 'History of Kazan', after the conquest the city was ceremonially 'cleaned' from the impurity of slavery, its streets copiously sprinkled with holy water that had been consecrated by crosses after carrying them around the walls.[62] The use of crosses for consecrating holy water is related to redemption from slavery by the Russian version of the Legend of the Cross. As mentioned above, it relates how Moses uses the Holy Wood to form a cross from two twigs to turn bitter water into sweet during the Exodus. The contrast to this purification is clear: Kazan is compared to Egypt and Babylon; in the 'praise' of the city of Kazan, hellish images of flowing liquids abound:

---

[58] N. Uspenskii, 'Chin Vozdvizheniia Kresta (Istoriko-liturgicheskii ocherk)', *Zhurnal Moskovskogo Patriarkhiia*, 9 (1954), pp. 55–56.

[59] I. Thyrêt, 'The Cult of the True Cross in Muscovy and Its Reception in the Center and the Regions', in A. Kappeler, ed., *Die Geschichte Russlands im 16. und 17. Jahrhundert aus der Perspektive seiner Regionen* (Wiesbaden, 2004), pp. 236–258.

[60] Tikhomirov, *Letopisets nachala tsarstva*, p. 73. Again, 'rab' may indicate the biblical 'slave of God' to oblige him, but the speech focuses on earthly bodies.

[61] Ibid.

[62] Kämpfer, *Historie vom Zartum Kasan (Kasaner Chronist)*, p. 161.

> Russian blood boiled in your streets and tears like streams flowed and you were overflowing with horrors and impurities.[63]

In a later passage, the text extols the tsar as liberator with full-bodied claims that 'the frequent barbarian raids stopped' after conquest; it compares him to Moses.[64]

Likewise, the 'Chronicle of the Beginning of Tsardom' revels in the final conquest of Kazan, employing cross symbolism and praising the liberation of captives. The tsar's cousin, prince Volodimir Andreevich, the boyars and commanders

> praised the tsar for his new tsardom Kazan. [. . .] "You are in truth our heavenly intercessor in affliction from the ungodly Hagarians;[65] by your agency the poor Christians (*krestiiany*) are liberated for all eternity and the unclean place is cleansed by grace".[66]

The cross is then carried by the victorious tsar and his entourage into the conquered city, to the khan's palace. In the palace, the commanders and all Orthodox people hail the tsar, remembering that before, Christians suffered 'many injustices' in this place as slaves:

> And they saw the life-giving cross and the Orthodox tsar in the deserted ignominy of Kazan. [In the times] before [us], the impious and dishonourable unbeliever tsars [i.e. khans] held court in this palace, where much Christian blood was spilled, and the people of the cross suffered many injustices. However, today in this place the righteous sun shines, the life-giving wood itself, [which is] the life-giving cross and the icon of Christ Our Lord.[67]

In its promise of liberation, there is a different emphasis than the prevailing Orthodox dictionary interpretation which stresses patient suffering: 'Cross – in Christian moral theology all physical privations, sufferings et c., which should be born without transgressing religious rules, in the name of Christ'.[68]

Similar associations are behind the description of the cross procession during the foundation of Sviiazhsk in the 'Chronicle of the Beginning of Tsardom'. It connects Sviiazhsk with liberation from slavery already in the intra-textual title at the start of the report about Ivan IV's campaigns against Kazan.[69] Muscovite forces founded the fortress on a mountain top near the centre of Kazan territory right after a successful raid on Kazan's suburbs that 'liberated many Rus' captives'.[70] After

---

63 Ibid., p. 163. Correspondingly, a city in a burning pool appears on the right of the icon The Blessed Host of the Heavenly Tsar.
64 Pelenski, *Russia and Kazan*, pp. 119–120, see also pp. 73, 75–77, 96–97.
65 See chapter 6.
66 Tikhomirov, *Letopisets nachala tsarstva*, p. 109.
67 Ibid.
68 *Polnyi pravoslavnyi bogoslovskii entsiklopedicheskii slovar'* v 2 t, vol. 2 (Sankt-Peterburg, 1913), p. 2464.
69 Pelenski, *Russia and Kazan*, p. 205; Tikhomirov, *Letopisets nachala tsarstva*, p. 59. See chapter 2 for the quote.
70 Tikhomirov, *Letopisets nachala tsarstva*, p. 61.

retiring from the city, they met the main army led by Moscow's Chinggisid candidate to the Kazan throne, Shah Ali, at Sviiazhsk mountain, and they

> jumped out of the boat, started to clear the forest, sang religious songs, sanctified water and walked along the [planned] wall with crosses.[71]

As a result of this foundation, the neighbouring mountain Cheremis, former allies of Kazan, submit to Ivan IV, whose conditions a few lines further down stress that 'they must not keep any Rus' captives, all are to be liberated'.[72] All elements of symbolic action and demands of the local people in this chronicle entry are linked to the liberation of captives.

Makarii's speech during the victory celebrations in Moscow, briefly cited at the start of this discussion of the meaning of the cross, employs even more profusely the liberating symbolism of the cross, as a kind of summary of the whole campaign:

> The grace of God shines on you [, o tsar,] even more [than on your predecessors Dmitrii Donskoi and Aleksandr Nevskii]: He gave [to you] the tsar's [khan's] capital, Kazan and all its environs [. . .], and raised the life-giving cross and re-erected the Holy Church and with your tsar's hand delivered many captive people of the cross [*krest'iany*: Christians] from slavery. Christ Our Lord saw your current efforts and works for His holy name[73] and for [the benefit of] the Christ-named flock which was entrusted to you by His all-powerful hand, He filled you with will of the heart and fulfilled your wish, giving you victory over the enemies of the cross.[74]

The purpose of victory and the raising of the cross in Kazan is unambiguously stated as delivering the people of the cross from captivity. The rhetoric mode of addition underscores the identification of the resurrected cross with the re-established community of believers and the deliverance of captives. The underlying ransom theory of atonement serves to combine the characterization of Kazanians as oath-breaking enemies of the cross with that of slavers. In the following passage Makarii repeats his praise for Ivan for liberating the slaves by embedding this-worldly cross imagery within layers of motifs of captivity and liberation at the instigation of the crucified:

> With God's help you have mercifully delivered us from the slave raids of the barbarians and destroyed their abodes to the very foundations, and you have liberated our poor captured brothers from slavery.[75] Together with our liberated brothers we tell you: be happy, merciful tsar, and joyful, for Christ has instigated all this, our guiding shepherd.[76]

---

71 Ibid., p. 62.
72 Ibid.
73 This passage is preceded by meditations on how the fate of Christian slaves disparages the honour of God's name: cf. chapter 2.
74 Tikhomirov, *Letopisets nachala tsarstva*, pp. 114–115.
75 'izbavi nas ot nakhozhdeniia [. . .] i bednuiu bratiiu nashiu plenenuiu ot raboty svobodi'.
76 Tikhomirov, *Letopisets nachala tsarstva*, pp. 114–115.

In the following paragraph, the entry of Ivan into the city and the Kremlin highlights the life-giving cross worn 'around his neck and bosom', and the way he humbly walked behind the cross. Ivan's enactment was solemnly repeated during the Palm Sunday ceremony, as the tsar went on foot from the cathedral of the Ascension in the Kremlin to the new Trinity Cathedral of the Intercession of the Most Holy Theotokos on the Moat, now commonly called St Basil's on Red Square. He led the metropolitan's horse, which was disguised as an ass, while the mounted bishop brandished a golden cross. Among the innovations in Ivan's time was a full-sized tree carried on two sledges.[77] It was difficult to miss its significance, given the many readings on trees to which Muscovites were treated, which they painted on maps and icons symbolically filling the land with plenty and promising security from slave raiding. The fruit made to hang from it, which along with the branches were distributed among attendants after the procession, may allude to the fruits of the trees in paradise, in the Heavenly Jerusalem, or to the icon of the dynastic and clerical tree of the Muscovite tsardom. St Basil's Cathedral in turn was founded to commemorate the conquest of Kazan. It was commonly known as Jerusalem and one of its chapels was dedicated to the New Jerusalem.[78] Emphasis placed on the symbol of the cross and its wood assimilated the Palm Sunday ceremony to the liberating (in this life) and salvific aspects (in the afterlife) of the Legend of the Cross. The procession was so important for Muscovites that when the Poles occupying the Kremlin during the Time of Troubles cancelled it as an aberration in 1611, a popular rising forced them to allow its re-enactment.

The implications for the history of Russian consciousness are more wide-reaching than the official sources adduced so far suggest. The starting point is again the icon 'Blessed Host of the Heavenly Tsar'. On the left, Moscow as Second Jerusalem is surrounded by several protective circles, symbols of wisdom.[79] Very untypical for these spheres, which are frequently found on Muscovite maps, they are open below the Mother of God; trees spill from this breach into the Rus' land. In a fascinating and fresh interpretation, Valerie Kivelson has recently shown that the plenitude of trees on Muscovite maps derived from their use on icons. These frequently preserved maps

---

[77] M.S. Flier, 'The Iconography of Royal Procession: Ivan the Terrible and the Muscovite Palm Sunday Ritual', in H. Duchhardt, R.A. Jackson and D. Sturdy, eds., *European Monarchy: Its Evolution and Practice from Roman Antiquity to Modern Times* (Stuttgart, 1992), pp. 109–125; M.S. Flier, 'Breaking the Code: The Image of the Tsar in the Muscovite Palm Sunday Ritual', in M. Flier and D. Rowland, eds., *Medieval Russian Culture*, vol. 2 (Berkeley and Los Angeles, 1994), pp. 213–242. Other possible interpretations of the tree, such as linked to Muscovite icons of the entry into Jerusalem are not mutually exclusive with this association of security from slaving. In fact both are closely related expressions of the underlying concept of redemption.
[78] A. Batalov, *Sobor Pokrova Bogorodicy na Rvu: Istorija i ikonografija architektury* (Moskva, 2016), pp. 336–411.
[79] On the circles, or spheres, see chapter 6. On symbolising 'protection', see S.U. Remezov's Siberian oeuvre in Kivelson, *Cartographies of Tsardom*.

were drawn by or for local gentry to be presented in courts of law to support claims in landed property litigation suits against neighbours. Abundant trees appear on these maps, sketched for wholly secular purposes, where such a multitude cannot be derived from pragmatic concerns alone, as they do not add information in the suits. They symbolise a joyous vision of the position of Muscovites in God's world, projecting this optimism into the secular present. There is nothing to add or subtract from this: Kivelson offers alternate explanations of the tree in terms of millenarian expectations, and as trees of paradise spilling onto earth.[80]

Well-documented as this reading is presented, the icon bears out a complementary interpretation: as already mentioned, the Theotokos – the Mother of God who gave birth to Christ – and an infant Christ present martyr's crowns to both military heroes and to formerly tormented and now liberated captives. Trees symbolize redemption from slavery; therefore, they spill onto earth, symbolising protection that allows the 'filling of the Russian land with human settlements', as the 'History of Kazan' ends after Kazan's purification by the holy wood of the cross.[81] Moreover, the symbolism of the planting of trees is explained in the well-known text from Isaiah cited during the New Year Ceremony which asks for the liberation of captives:

1	The [. . .] Lord has anointed me
	to [. . .] proclaim liberation for the captives [. . .]
3	and provide for those who grieve in Zion [. . .]
	They will be called oaks of righteousness,
	a planting of the Lord [. . .]
4	They [. . .] will renew the ruined cities
	that have been devastated for generations.
7	instead of disgrace
	you will rejoice in your inheritance. [. . .][82]

So, the oaks of righteousness spilling from Heavenly Jerusalem on the icon 'Blessed Host' during the return from conquered Kazan are the liberated people who settle the Muscovite land of promise.

Such a reading is supported by Russian governors who ordered crosses to be carved into the palisades of wooden fortresses set up at the rivers Mius' and Orel along the steppe frontier in 1571. It was a sign of redemption rather than exclusively

---

80 Ibid., pp. 113–116. On continuing cultural contexts of afforestation in the nineteenth and twentieth centuries which promised to make the steppes more 'Russian' and familiar, see D. Moon, *The Plough that Broke the Steppes: Agriculture and Environment on Russia's Grasslands, 1700–1914* (Oxford, 2013). Moon devotes considerable space to settlers' and explorers' initial impressions of the steppes, finding that over and over they described them first and foremost as 'treeless'. This effect may be observed on seventeenth century maps, too.
81 *Istoriia o Kazanskom tsarstve: Kazanskii letopisets* (St Petersburg, 1903), p. 176.
82 See last chapter (The New Year Ceremony) for the full text.

of acquisition, implying that the territory north of the as yet fragile and porous border from now on belonged to Russia.[83] In frontier areas, governors were mostly from the same gentry stratum as the makers of landholding maps or those who ordered them; therefore, associations of wood with the Legend of the Cross were at hand. Moreover, the date just months after the last great sack of Moscow by the Crimean khan Devlet Girei, who led up to 150,000 Muscovites into slavery as the chronicle alleged,[84] and just before the defeat of Crimean forces in the following year, suggests that the crosses referred to the defence against and intelligence about slave raids that these fortresses provided. The task of advance outposts such as the one on the Mius was to serve as bases for regular steppe sentinels who observed Tatar troop movements and warned of raids in advance, enabling Muscovite forces to respond in a timely fashion. It was precisely the fortified Arzamas line, set up as a reaction to increased slave raids after the conquests of Kazan and Astrakhan, that made the only tangible social and political difference to the lands conquered by Muscovy on the middle Volga, shielding them from the steppe and providing a lasting Muscovite military and administrative presence.[85] Similarly, it is unlikely that Peter the Great founded the Holy Cross fortress in northern Dagestan to introduce the idea of re-Christianization of the Caucasus.[86] The first attempt to evangelize among the local population was not made until 1744, when the government decided to send a mission to the Ossetians. This mission had to be kept secret: the Senate instructed the Synod to send only Georgian priests instead of Russians, and to give them no written instructions. In this way, they hoped to avoid any suspicion of missionary intent on the part of the Ottoman or Persian governments. It is more likely that Peter I had, decades earlier, intended this fortress to interrupt the transport of slaves in the busy trade corridor skirting the Northern Caucasus. The purpose of the name may have been propagandistic, citing the redemptive power of the cross.[87]

To sum up, the abundant property litigation maps drawn locally and ordered by members of the provincial gentry in the last decades of the seventeenth century offer access to their sponsors' consciousness. They expected the earthly redemption of slaves as much as in the afterlife. This part of the population's point of view might not necessarily be represented by the lofty imagery of the Kremlin churches and palaces.

---

[83] A.I. Filiushkin, 'Problema genezisa Rossiiskoi imperii', in I. Gerasimov et al., eds., *Novaia Imperskaia istoriia postsovetskogo prostranstva* (Kazan', 2004), pp. 375–408, here p. 398.

[84] Davies, *Warfare, State and Society on the Black Sea Steppe, 1500–1700*, p. 20.

[85] Romaniello, *The Elusive Empire*, pp. 38–49.

[86] M. Khodarkovsky, 'Of Christianity, Enlightenment, and Colonialism: Russia in the North Caucasus, 1550–1800', *Journal of Modern History*, 71, 2 (1999), pp. 394–430, here pp. 412–413.

[87] On this trade and Russian abolition of the slave trade, see Kurtynova-D'Herlugnan, *The Tsar's Abolitionists*.

The 'Book of Royal Degrees', compiled in the years between 1560 and 1563, offers a closely related take on the image of the tree. It starts with a preface exhibiting the text's view of the tsardom's history. The organizing theme is the 'family tree' of the grand princes, which draws on several theological associations. They provide clues to the book's structure in degrees or generations of the ruling dynasty and the role of liberation from captivity in Rus' and in the destiny of its ruling house:

> A tale of the holy piety of Russia's rulers and their holy seed [. . .]; a book of degrees of the royal genealogy, which was [manifest] in the piety of the divinely–affirmed sceptre-holders who shone forth in the Russian land, who were from God, like trees of paradise, planted by the rivers of water, watered by Orthodoxy, and nurtured with divine wisdom and grace. [They] shone forth with divine glory like a garden: luxuriant, and with beautiful foliage and blessed flowers; fruitful and ripe and exuding a divine fragrance; great and tall, and with many noble offshoots, extending like bright branches, growing through virtues pleasing to God. And many from its root and its branches through diverse labours, as on golden steps, erected a ladder, which ascends to heaven and does not falter, securing for themselves and for those who came after them unhindered access to God.[88]

The context to this elaborate image is Jacob's dream in Genesis 28, which was adopted in the correspondence between Ivan and the exiled prince Andrei Kurbskii as well as in Kurbskii's 'counter history' of Ivan's reign. At the top of a ladder reaching to heaven the Lord appears: he promises that Jacob and his descendants will own the land where he sleeps, and that they will flourish and multiply because they have His blessing.[89] As has been shown, for the compilers of the 'Royal Book of Degrees' the Muscovites are a chosen people on the path to salvation in the afterlife and redemption from captivity in this life, as well as expansion into the lands of the former slavers.[90] The tree is the metaphorical ladder, its wood provides fortification both physically and figuratively towards this aim, inscribing the dynasty into the history of redemption.

A broad variety of sources such as Russian Orthodox elucidations of the sign of the cross, official documents, icons and local maps, provide windows on widespread sixteenth and seventeenth century perceptions. They support the conclusion that redemption from slavery was closely linked to Muscovite renditions of the Legend of the True Cross, the image of the holy wood and the oath of loyalty to the sovereign.

---

88 P.G. Vasenko, ed., *Kniga stepennaia tsarskogo rodosloviia* (Sankt Peterburg, 1908), p. 5; translation in Lenhoff, 'The Construction of Russian History in Stepennaia Kniga', p. 38.
89 Lenhoff, 'The Construction of Russian History in Stepennaia Kniga', p. 40.
90 Vasenko, *Kniga stepennaia tsarskogo rodosloviia*, pp. 17–18 (Ol'ga's life), 65, 89, 133 (step 1), 168 (step 2), 239 (step 6), 354 (step 11), 395 (step 12), 433, 439–440 (step 13), 562–563 (step 15: missive of 'bishop Vassian Rylo'), 590 (step 16), 636–637, 644, 646 (step 17).

Delivering saints

The vitae of some of the most widely venerated Muscovite saints feature extensive and intricate stories about their feats delivering captives.

St Sergius

St Sergius was thought of as intercessor with the Mother of God protecting Muscovite towns against Tatar attacks; he was seen as the main prop of the dynasty.[91] His connection to the theme of liberating slaves developed slowly, starting in the 1550s. The most plainly stated expression is provided in the 'History of Kazan'. Overall, this text is a literary reformulation of earlier accounts which clarify Sergei's role and its implications. In the chapter entitled: 'On the bell-ringing at that place' – future Sviiazhsk – 'and on the miracle wrought by Sergei and his apparition', the text states that the chapel dedicated to Sergei in the new monastery at Sviiazhsk became the site of many miracles:

> At the grave the blind were healed [. . .] he exorcised demons and liberated [many people] from captivity in Kazan [. . .] by the present of divine mercy. [. . .] All recognized that it indicated he irrevocably wanted to live in Sviiazhsk, to protect his city and all people who lived in it from the Barbarians.[92]

As previously mentioned, the 'History of Kazan' is but one of a multitude of texts influenced by or, in most other cases, copying the 'Chronicle of the Beginning of Tsardom'. This is particularly the case regarding St Sergius' connection to liberating captives. These texts emphasize the role of the Muscovite saint in delivering slaves. When Ivan IV arrived in Sviiazhsk on 13 August 1552 to prepare the final onslaught on Kazan, boyars met him at the gates and led him to the new church. The tsar prayed to Sergius' icon 'for assistance and the deliverance (*izbavleniia*) of Christians from pagan captivity'.[93] *Izbavleniia* also translates as salvation, which is equally tenable but obscures the plurivalent and liberating aspect in favour of the more commonly recognized reference to the afterlife, although here the latter is hardly dominant.[94]

St Sergius is present in the 'Chronicle' and its copies at every stage of the conquest. In most cases it is the wider context of the campaign and rhetoric implying

---

91 D.B. Miller, *Saint Sergius of Radonezh, His Trinity Monastery and the Formation of the Russian Identity* (DeKalb IL, 2010); P. Gonneau, *À l'aube de la Russie muscovite: Serge de Radonège et André Roublev. Légendes et images (XIVe-XVIIe siècles)* (Paris, 2007).
92 Kämpfer, *Historie vom Zartum Kasan (Kasaner Chronist)*, pp. 121–123.
93 Tikhomirov, *Letopisets nachala tsarstva*, p. 94; Miller, *Saint Sergius of Radonezh, His Trinity Monastery and the Formation of the Russian Identity*, p. 102.
94 See chapter 3.

that by his miraculous intervention he wanted to protect and liberate captives. However, one more episode clearly expresses this impetus: it is when Ivan visited the Trinity monastery of Sergius on his return from conquered Kazan to make a triumphal entry into Moscow. He prostrated himself at the saint's tomb, wept profusely and gave thanks to God, the Mother of God and the great saints. Then he thanked the current metropolitan, the abbot Ioasaf, and the brothers for their sacrifices and prayers for a victory at Kazan. In return, the clerics emphasize the liberation of captives as their main motive:

> They bow to the earth tearfully to the lord [thanking] for the deliverance (*o izbavlenie*) of the Christians.[95]

This connection between the commemoration of Sergius and the liberation of slaves was devised and launched in the 1550s by bookmen labouring in the close vicinity of Aleksei Adashev, the tsar's advisor, the organiser of the Kazan campaign and administrator, with gentry background – perhaps Adashev himself was behind it.[96] The difference of these texts to clerics writing at the behest of the tsar, the metropolitan and the abbot of the influential St Sergius monastery could hardly be greater. In two narratives written during the short lifespan of Ivan's firstborn son Dmitrii, between October 1552 and June or July 1553,[97] bookmen at the St Sergius monastery sought to stress the influence of the saint as intercessor with the Mother of God on behalf of the tsar and Orthodox Christians. Although they had all the information available, as they were themselves eyewitnesses and spoke directly to the tsar during his visit at the monastery, they offered only a brief overview of events, concentrating on the prayers offered to St Sergius. In these prayers there is not a single mention of captives, slaves, or liberation even in connection with New Israel tropes, such as pharaoh or Joshua.[98]

Just how firmly focused these monks were on the interests of their flourishing monastery, the largest economic enterprise of the country, is palpable where they actually mentioned slaves.[99] At the opening of the first document, they cite almost literally the passage from the start of the Sviiazhsk narrative in the 'Chronicle of the Beginning of Tsardom' where Ivan IV motivates the campaign, albeit with some indicative changes. The dependency of this document on the 'Chronicle' has been challenged, and most of the text is quite different, with little overlap. However, the

---

95 Miller, *Saint Sergius of Radonezh, His Trinity Monastery and the Formation of the Russian Identity*, p. 102; Tikhomirov, *Letopisets nachala tsarstva*, p. 112.
96 On Adashev, see chapter 2.
97 A.N. Nasonov, 'Novye istochniki po istorii Kazanskogo "vziatiia"', *Arkheograficheskii ezhegodnik za 1960 god* (1962), pp. 3–26, here p. 6.
98 Ibid., esp. p. 12.
99 Miller, *Saint Sergius of Radonezh, His Trinity Monastery and the Formation of the Russian Identity*.

spirit and literal argument of this initial sequence is so obviously one of a kind with the 'Chronicle' that it is hard not to conclude that some degree of copying took place, if only in this instance:

> When [tsar Ivan] had seen the captured Christians and much Christian bloodshed and how many churches were empty [he asked] who perpetrated such insufferable ills? As I say, this bad was done by the godless Kazan Saracens.[100]

The next sentence already simply omits one crucial term – here in italics. The next omitted half-sentence only serves to reinforce the impression that liberation was at the centre of the argument:

> Our tsar's pious soul could not suffer to see Christians in such distress, *in captivity* (v plenu), and said to himself as follows: "The merciful God appointed me to this Orthodox land and all its people as tsar and shepherd, leader and ruler, for me to rule and keep His people unperturbed in Orthodoxy, to graze them without harm and keep any hardship from them. *Lord, help me and liberate* (izbavi) *your captured slaves from pagan hands*. Indeed, the good shepherd lays down his soul for his sheep.[101]

In the chronicle, the tsar's soliloquy ends here. The narrative from the St Sergius monastery, however, continues after 'keep any hardship from them' to make its point:

> Since the tsar is from God, they should fear me and obey me in every regard, for God, and not the people, has invested me with rule over them and with the tsardom.[102]

This interpretation of the tsar's power as God-given 'and not from man' to defend His people demands unconditional obedience instead of promising liberation to the slaves. It comes across as the bookish view of monks, which contrasts with the text of the 'Chronicle'. The St Sergius narrative further reinforces this impression of absolute power by a slight allusion to the captivity theme in the next few sentences, demonstrating the discursive relevance of liberation despite the monks' intentions:

> The tsar was asked by someone whence he acquired these prerogatives: "Since we, your lowly subjects ([ni]shchie tvoi), cannot understand your tsar's words", and they received the answer: "Understand the power of my words: as I see how Christians are captured by the sword and slain, so I will campaign for them with my army, as it is said: a good shepherd lays down his soul for his sheep".[103]

---

100 Nasonov, 'Novye istochniki po istorii Kazanskogo "vziatiia"', p. 8; Tikhomirov, *Letopisets nachala tsarstva*, p. 59.
101 Nasonov, 'Novye istochniki po istorii Kazanskogo "vziatiia"', p. 8; Tikhomirov, *Letopisets nachala tsarstva*, p. 60.
102 Nasonov, 'Novye istochniki po istorii Kazanskogo "vziatiia"', p. 8.
103 Ibid.

But while captivity as a theme is woven into the text, it is simultaneously de-emphasized by adding 'by the sword and slain', which makes captivity a mere transitory state on the road to destruction. The monks' treatment of the theme of slave raids underpins the difference in perception of the tsar's rule and heterodox rulers.

A. Nasonov was right to point out that this is rich material characterizing the development of political views; he fittingly observed that the St Sergius narrative in no way indicates any advice given to or sought by the tsar – except for the tsar's stern rebuke – unlike the account in the much more influential 'Chronicle'. Unsurprisingly, in the 1960s Soviet Union Nasonov went no further than this.[104] However, the 'Chronicle', emphasizing the role of Adashev, leaves no doubt as to the existence of the habit of advice-giving, as do scores of other sources,[105] though rarely in such controversial style as in these two which appear engaged in lively debate cross-referenced by textual borrowings. For the monks, unconditional support for the prerogatives of the ruler meant an increased likelihood of generous donations. It is significant that these questions about the limitations of advice vs limitations to the tsar's power were expressed so straightforwardly in the St Sergius narrative, while inadvertently underlining the relevance of liberation from slavery. Muscovites in their particular frontier situation were exposed to slave raids.[106] Nevertheless, for them it was well in the range of the thinkable to apply ideas of liberation to common situations and internal issues of governance. It has therefore become widely acknowledged that autocracy in internal relations in Muscovy was a façade covering the de-facto power of the elite.[107] The monks resisted such an approach and consequently de-emphasized liberation in favour of traditional protection from attacks.

For Muscovite worldviews it is therefore significant that gentry and chancellery officials did not go as far as the monks in emphasizing the unbridled authority of the tsar.

St Nicholas

St Nicholas of Myra is called the 'Russian God (*Russkii bog*)' in a great variety of sources, stressing the saint's exceptional prevalence throughout all social groups in

---

104 Ibid., p. 7.
105 Rowland, 'The Problem of Advice in Muscovite Tales about the Time of Troubles'; D. Rowland, 'Did Muscovite Literary Ideology Place Limits on the Power of the Tsar?', *The Russian Review*, 49, 2 (1990), pp. 125–155.
106 On the movable church of St Sergius during the reign of Fedor Ivanovich, see chapter 6.
107 D. Ostrowski, 'The Façade of Legitimacy: Exchange of Power and Authority in Early Modern Russia', *Comparative Studies in Society and History*, 44, 3 (2002), pp. 534–563; R.E. Martin, *A Bride for the Tsar: Bride-Shows and Marriage Politics in Early Modern Russia* (DeKalb IL, 2012); Kollmann, *The Russian Empire 1450–1801*.

Russia.[108] Extensive coverage of his involvement in redeeming captives and liberating slaves therefore met with a receptive audience.

Many Muscovites saw St Nicholas as one of the foremost heavenly helpers in the liberation of captives. The compilers of the 'History of Kazan' ascribed an important role to Nicholas appearing in soldiers' dreams during the night before the crucial day and spurring them to attack.[109] As shown in chapter two, the campaign is justified by liberating captives. In the 'Royal Book of Degrees', directly after the main scene parallelizing the Exodus of the Israelite slaves from Egypt and the conquest of Kazan depicted as liberation of slaves, St Nicholas appears to a warrior in his dream and orders to use the cross to consecrate water and purify the city. The symbolism of the ritual is thus defined by the significance of water and baptism to the liberation of slaves.[110] Under the year 1559, a mounted St Nicholas appears in the church of the steppe frontier town of Dedilov. He tells people that the 'dishonourable tax collectors (*busurmane*), the pagan Tatars, boiling with rage, prepare to attack your city and many Christian places'. But they are not to fear anything as he will protect them. At the same time, it is said, two Crimean Tatars wished to serve the tsar and told him news about the Crimean khan's plans to attack Muscovy, which are subsequently thwarted.[111]

In the 'Chronicle of the Beginning of Tsardom', St Nicholas makes a more modest appearance among other wonderworkers, archangels and saints in the encouraging letter by metropolitan Makarii to Ivan IV. However, the text implores St Nicholas to help the army

> without fail to fight for Orthodox Christians who have been captured and taken away and tortured and defiled by manifold passions.[112]

This lead was taken up elsewhere: according to 'Kurbskii's' *History of Ivan IV*, written either after prince Kurbskii's death in the seventeenth century or in the sixteenth century in his scriptorium in Lithuania,[113] God

> manifested by night to men of merit and clear conscience certain visions of the taking of the Muslim town, urging the army on to this and, I think, avenging the incalculable and long-lasting [. . .] slavery.[114]

---

108 B.A. Uspenskii, *Filologicheskie razyskaniia v oblasti slavianskikh drevnostei (Relikti iasychestva v vostochnoslavianskom kul'te Nikolaia Mirlikiiskogo)* (Moskva, 1982), pp. 119–122; M. Stößl, ed., *Verbotene Bilder: Heiligenfiguren in Russland* (München, 2006), p. 63.
109 Kämpfer, *Historie vom Zartum Kasan (Kasaner Chronist)*, pp. 223–225; Cf. Pelenski, *Russia and Kazan*, p. 212.
110 Pokrovskii, *The Book of Degrees of the Royal Genealogy*, pp. 365–366.
111 Ibid., p. 401.
112 Tikhomirov, *Letopisets nachala tsarstva*, p. 87. The intervening passage repeats this accusation using a more symbolic language and starts with a call for the help of archangel Michael.
113 K.I. Erusalimskii, *Sbornik Kurbskogo: Issledovanie knizhnoi kul'tury*, vol. 1 (Moskva, 2009).
114 Translation: Pelenski, *Russia and Kazan*, p. 212; J.L.I. Fennell, ed., *A. M. Kurbsky's History of Ivan IV* (Cambridge, 1965), p. 55.

The Tobolsk cossack, architect and chronicler Semen U. Remezov, writing at the turn of the eighteenth century, justified the conquest of Siberia in his 'History of Siberia' by portraying the khan as a slaver. In two scenes, St Nicholas takes centre stage and spurs Ermak's cossacks to action, telling them they should 'observe all virtues in loving your brother', using quotes from the 'Letter to the Ugra' and the 'Chronicle of the Beginning of Tsardom'.[115] According to the 1649 law code as well as canon law, these virtues included the paying of ransom: 'Do not be stingy with gold and silver for your brother, but redeem him'.[116] Remezov's family had a track record in ransoming.[117] Thus, there is a tendency in the seventeenth century accounts of the conquest of Kazan and in other documents to see in St Nicholas a redeemer from slavery.

This interpretation emerges in petitions in the 1670s to the Military Chancellery by redeemed slaves who had returned to Moscow, in a rare case of ordinary Muscovites expressing religious preferences. Reacting to numerous requests,[118] Tsar Fedor Alekseevich in a decree dated March 1678 ordered icon painters in the Kremlin to copy 300 icons measuring 27 centimetres each, and make them available in the Military Chancellery to returning captives.[119] Upon their safe return from captivity or slavery after they had prayed to the saints or made a pledge, the captives were unable to fulfil their promise, and applied to the Military Chancellery. Most of these petitions just asked for an icon, but some petitioners had clear ideas. Out of eight such requests that specify the desired type of the icon, five name St Nicholas.[120]

When Trofim Agafonov syn Pereverzev, a local servitor from the southern fortress town of Oboian' on the river Psël, which blocked the Tatar road, dedicated himself to St Nicholas, he had spent sixteen years in captivity in Crimea. His short narrative, which is limited to essentials, gives the view of a causal relation between liberation and the interagency of the saint:

> I was captured and taken to Crimea where I lived in captivity for sixteen years and this current year, 1676, I dragged myself out of captivity, but it occurred due to the promise I had given to St Nicholas of Mozhaisk, the miracle worker.[121]

While the *modus operandi* indicated by '*is polonu vybrel*' is reminiscent of the stories of people who dragged themselves out of the swamp by their own hair, this tension

---

115 S.U. Remezov, *Remezovskaia letopis': Sluzhebnaia chertezhnaia kniga* (Tobol'sk, 2006), pp. 190–192, 230.
116 Hellie, *The Muscovite Law Code (Ulozhenie) of 1649*, chapter VIII, art. 1.
117 L.A. Gol'denberg, *Izograf zemli sibirskoi: Zhizn' i trudy Semena Remezova* (Magadan, 1990), pp. 84–85.
118 RGADA f. 210 no. 791, ll. 1–59.
119 Ibid., l. 60.
120 RGADA f. 210 no. 791 (1677–78), ll. 46–102.
121 RGADA f. 210 no. 791, l. 48. A *syn boyarskii*. See chapter 5 for the concept of interagency, particularly with symbolic agents.

is resolved by reference to St Nicholas. Indeed, one of the most widely disseminated Russian legends about St Nicholas is the tale of the miraculous saving of Basilios from captivity after a Saracen raid during a local pilgrimage dedicated to St Nicholas. His parents despair, and it takes three years until they regain trust in St Nicholas. However, after they resolve to invocate the saint he immediately restores their son to his parents' house in Asia Minor, still holding the cup which he was ordered to serve the emir of Crete.[122] Pereverzev's allusion to miraculous transportation from place to place may obscure some truth less palatable to the Muscovite clerks on how he returned. Nevertheless, the plot does show some basic familiarity with expectations drawing on Eastern Slavic miracle stories about St Nicholas.

Pereverzev's instruction may have been oral as he asked the professional scribe to sign the petition, but the spread of saint's *vitae* occurred in an environment characterised by secondary orality. In other words, people trusted the written word more than the merely spoken.[123] As David B. Miller just demonstrated, the donors to the famous Trinity St Sergius monastery, who lived all over Muscovy, and all those who had business transactions with this wealthy monastery, were overwhelmingly literate for practical purposes and called on literate witnesses to sign deeds. That they preferred literate witnesses, who were often the same people, implies that there were plenty of illiterate ones, but also the esteem in which the literate were held.[124] The donors were likely those who were receptive to the spread of saint's lives beyond the clerical world, if such a divide can be upheld at all. Sophisticated theological treatises were rare in Muscovy, and most of the chronicles and lives of saints were written in a language comprehensible to those who could read business Russian.[125]

Far from being merely traditional, the saints' cults of late Muscovy were appreciably adaptive to current needs and events. Some became more widely available during the sixteenth to seventeenth centuries. This particularly applies to the cult of St

---

122 A.P. Boguslawski, *The Vitae of St. Nicholas and His Hagiographical Icons in Russia* (PhD dissertation, University of Kansas, 1982), pp. 96–98. Editions: I.I. Sreznevskii, *Svedeniia i zametki o maloizvestnykh i neizvestnykh pamiatnikakh: I–XL* (Sanktpeterburg, 1867); *Velikaia Mineia Chet'ia mesiatsa dekabria 6 den', ottsa nashego Nikolaia chudotvortsa, arkhiepiskopa Mirlikiiskago* (Moskva, 1901), pp. 3–8; *Velikaia Minei Chet'ii sobrannyia vserossiiskim mitropolitom Makariem*, vol. 7: *Dekabr' 6–17* (Moskva, 1907), pp. 582–589; A. Leonid, *Posmertnyia chudesa sviatitelia Nikolaia arkhiepiskopa Myr-Likiiskago, chudotvortsa: Pamiatnik drevnei russkoi pis'mennosti XI veka: Trud Efrema, episkopa pereiaslavskago* (Sankt-Peterburg, 1888), here pp. 3–9; A.I. Ponomarev, ed., *Pamiatniki drevnei russkoi tserkovno-uchitel'noi literatury*, vol. 2: *Slaviano-russkii prolog,*, pt. 1: *Sentyabr'-dekabr'* (Sankt-Peterburg, 1896), pp. 62–65; *Russkaia staropechatnaia literatura (XVI –pervaia chetvert' XVIII v.)* (Moskva, 1978), pp. 206–207.
123 W. Ong, *Orality and Literacy: The Technologizing of the Word* (New York, 1982); Witzenrath. 'Literacy and Orality in the Eurasian Frontier', p. 65.
124 Miller, *Saint Sergius of Radonezh, His Trinity Monastery and the Formation of the Russian Identity*, pp. 239–243, 250.
125 Witzenrath, 'Literacy and Orality in the Eurasian Frontier'; Miller, *Saint Sergius of Radonezh, His Trinity Monastery and the Formation of the Russian Identity*, p. 242.

Nicholas; most available Muscovite copies of his life were made from the middle of the sixteenth century onwards, when the cult of St Nicholas of Mozhaisk became popular in Muscovy after an intervention by Makarii, then archbishop of Novgorod and former abbot in Pskov. His sculpture [fig. 2], typically holding a raised sword, is outwardly reminiscent of the Latin protector of towns Roland who was not a saint, but mainly recalls the sword which the saint, appearing out of nowhere miraculously purloins from the executioner of innocent captives in several texts widespread in Muscovy: *Vita of Nicholas the Sionite, Slovo pokhvalno, Vita according to Metaphrastes, Prolog, Miracle of the Presbyter, Miracle of Petro the Scholar*.[126]

Fig. 2: 'St Nicholas of Mozhaisk', seventeenth century, Russia, inv. nr. 116-ДРС, with permission of Arkhangelsk District Museum.

The petitioners for icons who had returned from slavery mentioned above specified the local palladiums of St Nicholas of Mozhaisk and of Zaraisk, which are well-documented in wood-carving, a form of veneration which the Orthodox church did not fully appreciate. The extraordinary spread of these statues in the second half of the sixteenth century is, therefore, a sign of their popular appeal.[127] In these sculptures, St Nicholas

---

[126] Boguslawski, *The Vitae of St. Nicholas and His Hagiographical Icons in Russia*, pp. 70, 78, 137, 190.
[127] Stößl, *Verbotene Bilder*. S.U. Remezov sketched St Nicholas with raised sword in the Mozhaisk fashion: Remezov, *Remezovskaia letopis'*, pp. 230, 236.

clenches a sword in one hand and a model of a town or church in the other. Therefore, these icons were first seen as a palladium protecting a town, one of the many functions of the saint in Russia. However, some of the less obvious features of the saintly figure concern the question how these changes to the saint's iconographic representation occurred. Dmitrii Donskoi (1350–1389) had dedicated a tower of the Kremlin wall to Nicholas, a defensive ring of walled Nicholas-monasteries was built around Moscow and there was at least one early local icon of Nicholas – without the feature of the sword – in Zaraisk in the steppe frontier principality of Riazan'. Nevertheless, the first evidence of a widespread, popular cult dates to the high period of slaving, the second half of the sixteenth and especially the seventeenth century, when the wooden, armed sculpture of St Nicholas of Mozhaisk – a small town on the steppe border just one hundred kilometres west of Moscow which was formerly Lithuanian – made its way first to the northern, Novgorod lands, then spread across Muscovy.[128]

Based on Nikol'skii's count at the time of his research, there were 605 manuscript copies of the saint's life and single miracle legends – in some cases these were included in more comprehensive lives – copied during the mid-sixteenth to seventeenth centuries, out of a total of 720 since the beginning of Eastern Slavic literature. Among these manuscripts, 360 were directly connected to the theme of 'Saracen' raids, captivity and liberation. The stories' titles were as follows: *Pamiat' na prenesenie*, *Vita Nicolai Sionitae*, *Vita per Metaphrasten*, *Periodoi Nikolaou*, *Thauma de Basilio*, *Thauma de Presbytero*, *Thauma de Petro scholario*, Saracen miracle, *Thauma de patriarcha*, Polovtsian miracle. Another 178 did not include this subject, but included unjust captivity in Christian Constantinople and Myra: *Slovo pokhvalno*, Prolog, *Thauma de 3-s Christ*. The frequency of liberation themes in the copies supports the interpretation that Pereverzev's claim, i.e. that it was St Nicholas 'of Mozhaisk' who set him free, places the petitioner well within contemporary Muscovite discourse.

This calculation is based on Boguslawski's figures, but not on his categorization of the texts; I have re-evaluated the stories based on a close reading of his descriptions and discussions given for each text.[129] These numbers will have to be updated continuously, since new copies have already been found. In 1997, Russian researchers counted the impressive number of more than 800 manuscripts. According to Krutova, there was no church in Russia without an icon of St Nicholas, and

---

128 G.V. Sidorenko, 'Die frühesten Skulpturen des christlichen Rußland: Berittene und bewaffnete Heilige als Beschützer der Stadt und Befreier vom Tatarenjoch', in M. Stößl, ed., *Verbotene Bilder: Heiligenfiguren in Russland* (München, 2006), pp. 95–106. On the possible relevance of a Finnic prototype, cf. S. Bogatyrev, 'The Heavenly Host and the Sword of Truth: Apocalyptic Imagery in Ivan IV's Muscovy', in V. Kivelson, M. Flier, N.S. Kollmann and K. Petrone, eds., *The New Muscovite Cultural History: A Collection in Honor of Daniel B. Rowland* (Bloomington IN, 2009), pp. 77–90, here 84–85 n. 29.
129 Boguslawski, *The Vitae of St. Nicholas and His Hagiographical Icons in Russia*, p. 137. See N.V. Pak, *Zhitiinye pamiatniki o Nikolae Mirlikiiskom v russkoi knizhnosti XI–XVII vv.* (PhD dissertation, University Sankt-Petersburg, 2000).

no archive without at least one manuscript that relates a miracle by the saint. Since during Soviet times it was impossible to research the lives of the saint, even at the time of writing there is no full list of copies of his life.¹³⁰ However, given the vast prevalence of captivity themes in the count, it is unlikely that the basic tendencies outlined above will have to be reversed decisively.

The most prevalent of these texts was the 'Translation of the Relics of Our Holy Father Nicholas, Bishop of Myra, to Bari' with a total count of 142 copies, out of which nine date from the fifteenth century, three from the turn of the century, 72 from the middle of the sixteenth and another 55 from the following century. Again, the creation of the manuscripts inclines heavily towards the period in which liberation from slavery became an official ideology. The compilers aimed to cater to the needs of Muscovite readers; they mention the grand princes Vsevolod Iaroslavich and Vladimir Monomakh, and bring the events closer to home. The Prologue in its 1910 edition adds an explanation for the translation of Nicholas' relics, which occurred in 1087, putting it down to the insecurity due to the raids of the 'dishonest Sons of Hagar'.¹³¹ The recent publication of the long redaction of the life, based on Metaphraste's standard work, is unequivocal about the reasons for the translation:

> At that time [. . .] the people of Ismail¹³² overran the Greek lands [. . .] killing men everywhere and capturing their wives and children.¹³³

Moreover, the readings for the second holiday consecrated to St Nicholas, 9 May, which honoured the translation of the relics, privilege liberation from captivity on the first page that explains why the saint was important:

> With [his wisdom and powers of the soul] he overcomes heresy and is victorious in battle against the false intrigues of the dragon, and everywhere he appears quickly to help those in need: he liberates captives.¹³⁴

The 360 copies of his life directly connected to the theme of Saracen raids, captivity and liberation, contain the following further details: in *Periodoi Nikolaou*, copied 78 times in later Muscovy, the last part is an invocation to St Nicholas to save the Russian sons and daughters from the coercion of pagans (*poganykh nasiliia*).¹³⁵ In the

---

130 M.S. Krutova, *Sviatitel' Nikolai Chudotvorets v drevnerusskoi pis'mennosti* (Moskva, 1997), p. 113. Further recent literature on St Nikolai's Eastern Slavic lives: V.V. Kalugin, "Zhitie sviatitelia Nikolaia Mirlikiiskogo" v agiograficheskom svode Andreia Kurbskogo (Moskva, 2003), p. 8.
131 Boguslawski, *The Vitae of St. Nicholas and His Hagiographical Icons in Russia*, pp. 137, 147–148.
132 See chapter 6 (Hagarites).
133 Krutova, *Sviatitel' Nikolai Chudotvorets v drevnerusskoi pis'mennosti*, p. 52.
134 Ibid., p. 51. My translation. An enumeration of further boons follows. Moreover, his *akathistos* in the liturgy cites his powers of liberating captives in the 6ᵗʰ and 10ᵗʰ ikos. My thanks go to Marianne Stößl for reminding.
135 Boguslawski, *The Vitae of St. Nicholas and His Hagiographical Icons in Russia*, p. 54.

Miracle of Basilius, the son of a wealthy admirer of the saint is captured during a raid along with others. The Saracens divide the spoils, send Basilius to the emir of Crete, sell some of the captives and put others in prison. Because of his beauty, Basilius ends up personally serving the emir. As already mentioned, the saint accomplishes one of his immediate, space-transcending actions when he saves Basilius at the behest of his parents.[136] In the Miracle of the Presbyter, the 'Saracen' raid and selection scenes reappear, but the focus has shifted to saving those put to the sword. The protagonist of the Miracle of Peter the Scholar is returned to Saracen captivity because he does not live up to his pledge to St Nicholas, but he mends his ways and is finally liberated to a monk's life.

These individual stories, from the Miracle of Basilius to the Polovtsian Miracle,[137] were usually inserted after the main text of the Vita Nicolai Sionitae, which in its original version omitted the subject of liberation from captivity, though it speaks of help to those unjustly executed.[138] St Nicholas of Sion is actually another person, frequently mistaken for St Nicholas of Myra. The abbot of Sion was little connected to Myra and did not conform to the ideal image of the bishop in Byzantium.

Since the Arab conquests had shaken Eastern Roman power in the Mediterranean, it had fallen to the Christian community and ultimately the bishop to care for captives. Conversely, in the Roman Empire at its zenith captives generally lost their status as citizens, as well as all property. In Byzantium it was the bishop who was first obliged to redeem captive parishioners, in reaction to Arab intruders selling captives into slavery. It was only from 745 on that Byzantines and Arabs exchanged captives. Therefore, East Rome reconsidered early Roman Republican norms that disenfranchised those who had fallen into foreign captivity. Byzantine norms upheld citizen rights and limited the debt former captives had to reimburse by bonded labour.[139] The Muscovite compilers added these altogether sixteen stories to the confusing life of St Nicholas the Sionite, six of which were directly concerned with

---

[136] Ibid., pp. 96–98, 100; Krutova, *Sviatitel' Nikolai Chudotvorets v drevnerusskoi pis'mennosti*, pp. 58–62.
[137] See chapter 6.
[138] Boguslawski, *The Vitae of St. Nicholas and His Hagiographical Icons in Russia*, pp. 88–89, 118–121, 188.
[139] Y. Rotman, 'Byzance face à l'Islam arabe, VIIe–Xe siècle: D'un droit territorial à l'identité par la foi', *Annales Histoire, Sciences Sociales*, 60, 4 (2005), pp. 767–788. I am thankful to Julia Hillner for providing hints to literature on earlier ransom activities by bishops in Italy and Provence as a spin-off of debates during the course 'Transcultural Comparison' within the Master in Dependency and Slavery Studies at BCDSS: K. Sessa, 'Ursa's Return: Captivity, Remarriage and the Domestic Authority of Roman Bishops in Fifth-Century Italy', *Journal of Early Christian Studies*, 19, 3, 2011, pp. 401–432; C. Rapp, *Holy Bishops in Late Antiquity: The Nature of Christian Leadership in an Age of Transition* (Berkeley and Los Angeles 2005), pp. 228–232 on care of captives; W. Klingshirn, 'Charity and Power: Caesarius of Arles and the Ransoming of Captives in Sub-Roman Gaul', *Journal of Roman Studies*, 75 (1985), pp. 183–203.

captivity in foreign countries and another two with unjust captivity. They tried in this way to assimilate the life of the Sionite to that of the ideal bishop St Nicholas of Myra, which is especially telling for the esteem of ransom obligations of the bishop.

Less apparent signs of Nicholas' connection to ransom are the three spheres and three stripes found on *omophoria* on icons of the saint painted mainly during the sixteenth century.[140] Three spheres are the sign of pawnbrokers and Nicholas' principal attribute, signifying the three bags of money awarded to the daughters of a debt bondsman as recompense – or alternatively, the three Byzantine officials unjustly accused of treason liberated by him; thus Nicholas became the patron saint of prisoners.[141] The bishop wears the *omophorion* across his shoulders, symbolizing the Lamb of God, which was sacrificed to ward off the Angel of Death who pursued the Egyptians during the night before Exodus, and the incarnation of Christ who redeemed human sin.

So, the renewed, popular cult of St Nicholas, like other religious features of changing imperial culture, referred to protection, liberation of captives, ransom – and, of course, to fertility and renewal in the agricultural sphere. It is mere speculation whether this was the basis of the original veneration; however, evidence of the saint-redeemer earlier than the reign of Ivan III is tenuous and scarce, with the exclusion of Dmitrii Donskoi's dedications. Therefore, the link between conquest and ransom, between defence and redemption, is at least as strong as in the miracle of the icon of St Nicholas – among a few other icons mentioned – which according to all extant chronicle versions 'burst in flames' and frightened off the defenders. As such, it became the means of success during Ivan IV's 1558 siege of Narva, another 'Orthodox Rus'' town that had been 'captured' by infidels, according to the chronicles, although in this case it was Protestants, Latins and even some apostate Orthodox were involved.[142]

---

140 Sidorenko, 'Die frühesten Skulpturen des christlichen Rußland', p. 97; T.M. Kol'tsova, 'Die Holzskulptur des Achangel'sker Nordens', in M. Stößl, ed., *Verbotene Bilder: Heiligenfiguren in Russland* (München, 2006), pp. 129–145, here pp. 135–142. The original fifteenth-century Mozhaisk sculpture is without paint and spheres, although three panels are carved into the forward end of the *omophorion*.
141 F. Lanzi and G. Lanzi, *Saints and Their Symbols: Recognizing Saints in Art and in Popular Images* (Collegeville MN, 2004), p. 113. Acc. to *Nastol'naia kniga sviashchennosluzhitelia*, http://www.magister.msk.ru/library/bible/comment/nkss/nkss17.htm (accessed 19 Aug. 2021), neither spheres nor three lines are required on the *omophorion*'s frontal end, and they are less prevalent today, while, to the best of my knowledge, there are no contemporary examples of spheres.
142 M.P. Romaniello, *Conquest, Colonization and Orthodoxy. Muscovy and Kazan', 1552–1682* (MA thesis, Ohio State University, 1998), p. 41. See also P. Bushkovitch, *Religion and Society in Russia: The Sixteenth and Seventeenth Centuries* (New York, 1992), pp. 106–107.

St George and the dragon

St George was pronounced the 'helper' of St Nicholas, although he appeared in his own capacity as liberator from slavery.[143] This image was connected to his status as miraculous saviour from the menace of legendary dragons. In some saint stories, he acts as Nicholas' helper who opens the door of the prison for the imprisoned guards in the 'Miracle of the Saracen'. St Nicholas liberated a captive 'Saracen' in Crete who implored him to do so, but the uninvolved prison guards were held responsible by his Christian captors. When the former prisoner returns at the helm of a Muslim fleet, reveals his identity and negotiates with the Christians from Crete, St George meanwhile frees the guards.[144] Such tales show that the saints prefer Christian Orthodoxy as a religion, but help all captives.

St George is central to Russian iconography as part of the city of Moscow's arms and those of the Russian Empire – although in the latter case the figure is supposed to be a mounted warrior. The symbol of Kazan is the dragon.[145] A drawing from the manuscript of the 'History of Kazan' explores this myth: Ivan as a horseman in the manner of St George kills a figure trampled under his horse's hooves which an inscription identifies as 'Ediger, impious *tsar*' [khan] of Kazan'.[146] In the 'History', this symbolic relation is narratively transformed. First, the story presents the location of the city as the former lair of a dragon, until it is killed by a wizard. In chapter seven, 'About the Origin of the Kazan Tsardom, the Local Riches and the Dragon's Lair', the legend is then compared to Tatar rule in Kazan on the grounds of captives taken:

> Just as before the ferocious dragon [. . .] had [his] lair in this place, [so afterwards] an infidel tsar assumed the rule in this city: because of his impiety and dishonour (*nechestiia*) he was filled with great anger, lighting up like fire, like a dragon, in fury against the Christians, and burning like fire and terrifying with flaming lips, he kidnapped and devoured like sheep the humble Russian people living in all [settlements] in the neighbourhood of Kazan, and he expelled thence the Russians – the autochthonous [people] (*Rus'-tozemtsa*) – and devastated this land for three years [. . .][147]

---

[143] Special thanks to Marianne Stößl for raising awareness of L. Kretzenbacher, 'Bischof Nikolaus von Myra als reitender Knabenretter', in L. Kretzenbacher, ed., *Griechische Reiterheilige als Gefangenenretter: Bilder zu mittelalterlichen Legenden um Georgios, Demetrios und Nikolaos* (Wien, 1983), pp. 57–78.
[144] Boguslawski, *The Vitae of St. Nicholas and His Hagiographical Icons in Russia*, pp. 81–82, 106–108. For more on this type of liberation of Muslims tale, see chapter 6.
[145] The dragon (*zilant*) as symbol of Kazan is interpreted ambivalently and sometimes controversially, as fitting the overlap between the European, Persian and East Asian cultural spheres, where dragons appear on alternating ends of the moral scale: R.A. Mustafin, *Ozero Kaban: Istoriko-dokumental'noe povestvovanie* (Kazan', 1989). It is often represented as more of a cockatrice, with bird's body, chicken legs, red wings and a snake's tail.
[146] M. Cherniavsky, *Tsar and People: Studies in Russian Myths* (New Haven CT, 1961), plate 3.
[147] Trans. and the full text on the Kazan dragons in Pelenski, *Russia and Kazan*, p. 120; Volkova, *Kazanskaia Istoriia* (modern Russian trans.).

Rus'-tozemtsa for Pelenski proved the nationalist character of this text, redoubled with the dubious claim of medieval Russian settlement in the area of the Kazan khanate. However, ethnos and confession are aligned in this text. It mentions sheep and invokes in religious terms the protective obligation of the tsar – the good shepherd – towards captive co-religionists. Therefore, the national argument Pelenski identified in this text is obscure. The argument is about imperial monarchical rather than national legitimacy, in terms of the counter dependency zone.

The dragon as a symbol for slavers is emphasized three times in the 'Chronicle of the Beginning of Tsardom': first in metropolitan Makarii's letter to Ivan during the decisive campaign of 1552:

> [You] should wage war for your holy church and all Orthodox Christians who have been captured unjustly and enslaved and tortured by all kinds of maltreatment and defiled by manifold passions [. . .] We are always savaged by the haughty dragon, the all-cunning fiendish devil, who sends the heathen foes to fight us, the Crimean khans and their supporters, the Crimean and Kazan Tatars.[148]

The inhabitants of Nizhnyi Novgorod received the tsar after the conquest and praise him:

> Give him many years of life, merciful God, for he liberated us from those poisonous dragons, from whom we have suffered evil for many years.[149]

In Moscow, the 'Chronicle' has the metropolitan Makarii ceremonially address Ivan IV during his triumphal entry:

> The greatest mercy of God has come upon you, o tsar: he gave to you the capital city Kazan with all its land and with the same clemency destroyed the dragons that nested and hid there in their lairs [. . .] and liberated by your tsar's hand many enslaved Christians (*ot raboty izbavi*).[150]

Dragons and serpents that snatch and devour humans are found in an illustration of Remezov's 'History of Siberia', a narrative justifying conquest in which he early on exposes the khan of Sibir as a polygamous slaver. There is a very small, beardless, youthful St George present in this image who fearlessly slays a small dragon and does not seek shelter behind the walls of the town as the soldiers do.[151] The text cites the prophecy of Isaiah 14 about the reversal of the Babylonian captivity, which begins with the words, 'They will take captive their former captors, and rule over those who oppressed them'. (Isa 14:2.) Moreover, Remezov cites verse 29, along with other verses of Isaiah, comparing the Babylonians and slavers in general to dragons and serpents:

---

148 Tikhomirov, *Letopisets nachala tsarstva*, pp. 86–87.
149 Ibid., p. 111.
150 Ibid., p. 114.
151 Remezov, *Remezovskaia letopis'*, pp. 113, 136.

Ermak and his cossacks fulfilled the prophecy of Isaiah, which concerns Kuchum [the khan of Sibir]. For it says: What I presage, it will come to pass. Do not be merry, you foreigners all, for your flowering will soon come to an end; from the seed of the dragon springs a breed of vipers, and the fruit will be a winged dragon. The low will be rescued by the Lord and the unfortunate will relax in security; God extirpates your kin and root, viper. They fanfare the town's gates [as the walls in Jericho; CW] and the enemy's fortresses will be taken. Like smoke he approaches from the north, and there is no power opposing him.[152]

Remezov may have got his fondness for this 'smoke from the north' passage in Isaiah from the Swedish officers held as prisoners of war at Tobolsk, who frequented him:[153] this prophecy was dear to partisans of the Swedish king in Germany during the Thirty Years War.[154]

In Muscovy, the subtlety was that St George did not just slay the dragon, but, as above, appeared as a liberator of slaves. In one story lifted from a petition, the merchant Evstafii Kostiantinov from the town of Ianin in Rumelia had fallen foul of the followers of Aslan Pasha, and as a consequence underwent a judiciary nightmare. To be able to claim ransom from coreligionists in Muscovy, he had to overcome the border regime, where each post feigned not to understand and sent him to another, and finally to a monastery. As they did not turn him away at once, they felt uneasy, but nevertheless determined. When all attempts had failed, he was returned to Rumelia. After a six-day journey he was waiting for the ferry to cross the river Dnipro at Kyiv. That night he claimed he was approached by a man he identified as St George mounted on a horse. The horseman transported him miraculously to the Sevsk border post again during the same night, whence he travelled concealed among herdsmen taking 'sheep' to Moscow:

> From Kyiv they [with his nephew] went to Putivl but they were not allowed to continue to Moscow [. . .] but told to go to the Svinskoi monastery with a sealed letter, but there they were returned to Putivl whence they were sent back to the [Polish-]Lithuanian border. So they travelled six days to Kyiv and arrived at the ferry across the Dnepr [. . .] [but] had to spend the night waiting. That night a horseman rode up to them and sat them both behind him and dropped them at Putivl in that very one night. He said not to pause and go on to Moscow directly. He Ostashka [determined] that the miracle worker St George had offered his mercy to them. No ordinary man could have done such a feat. From Putivl they went with a flock of sheep driven by merchants to be sold on the market. It took them five weeks; while they asked for alms along the way. Once they will have collected alms in Moscow, they will return to *Tsargrad* [Istanbul] to ransom their captives.[155]

---

152 Ibid.
153 Gol'denberg, *Izograf zemli sibirskoi*.
154 W. Schmidt-Biggemann, 'Apokalypse und Millenarismus im Dreißigjährigen Krieg', in K. Bußmann and H. Schilling, eds., *1648: Krieg und Frieden in Europa, Katalog der Ausstellung in Münster and Osnabrück 24. Okt. 1998–17. Jan. 1999, Textband I: Politik, Religion, Recht und Gesellschaft* (Osnabrück, 1999), pp. 259–263.
155 RGADA f. 52, 1640, No. 1, 15 October, pp. 1–3 (petition). For an analysis of his account, the patriarchs' recommendations and the reports see C. Witzenrath, 'Agency in Muscovite Archives:

Usually, miraculous transfer through time and space were the preserve of St Nicholas; this mythical power might have been acquired by St George through association. However, the journey with the sheep was not devoid of religious significance either. As seen above, Muscovite rulers claimed to deliver their 'flock of Christian sheep' especially from captivity, and Kostiantinov aspired to the same benefit. He justified his forced entry into Moscow by virtuously playing on the symbolic keyboard of liberation from slavery. Such symbolic capital had real effects, even, as in this case, unintended ones.

Theatre and liberation

While theatre in the modern sense was rejected as pagan in the early and mid-Muscovite periods, liturgical drama retained a significant role in public life. The Christian churches had long employed dramatization as a means of reaching the illiterate population, and it was consequently used for transporting the image of the New Israel redeemed from slavery.

On the fringes of Christianity, where local languages significantly diverged from the sacred Latin texts of the mass, liturgical drama conveyed the Christian message in the early times.[156] There was less need for it in Russia, since Church Slavonic was, if slightly outlandish as it derived from south Slavic dialects, still close to the vernacular. This did not exclude the use of liturgical drama as an educational tool. Religious drama was once considered un-Orthodox as it was believed to be less developed than in the West; however, this was mainly due to romantic nationalist efforts to portray Orthodoxy as opposed to Latin church culture, where liturgical plays had been common since the middle ages.[157] Marina Swoboda has recently refuted this notion, reminding us that such plays were performed in Constantinople before the iconoclastic episode.[158] Moreover, Christian and particularly Orthodox liturgy is generally characterised by elements of 'theatrical' performance within the confines of a specific liturgical ceremony; these include personification, positional symbolism, subtle gestures, movements, songs, silence, garments, explicit changes in locality and condensation of time through implicit concurrent layers with multiple meanings: the altar represents

---

Trans-Ottoman Slaves Negotiating the Moscow Administration', in S. Conermann and G. Şen, eds., *Slaves and Slave Agency in the Ottoman Empire* (Göttingen, 2020), pp. 87–129.
156 K. Young, *The Drama of the Medieval Church*, vol. 1 (Oxford, 1933).
157 B.N. Aseev, *Russkii dramaticheskii teatr XVII–XVIII vekov* (Moskva, 1958), p. 30; I.N. Dmitriev and E.G. Kholodov, eds., *Istoriia russkogo dramaticheskogo teatra*, vol. 1 (Moskva, 1977); B.V. Varneke, *Istoriia russkogo teatra 17–19 vekov* (Moskva, 1939); M. Tereshina and N.N. Evreinov, *Istoriia russkogo teatra: Illiustrirovannoe izdanie* (Moskva, 2011).
158 G. La Piana, 'The Byzantine Theatre', *Speculum*, 11, 2 (1936), pp. 171–211, here p. 210.

Jerusalem, or the room of the Last Supper, the Cross, the Tomb, the heavenly Jerusalem, the Garden of Paradise, etc.[159]

Despite its general Byzantine inheritance, Muscovy reinvented the grander liturgical plays, as there were few models – late Byzantium and especially the Greek Orthodox Church under the Ottomans was too impoverished for exuberant staging; the same is applicable to medieval Rus'. Muscovy did so most likely under the influence of the Latin West, since this occurred in the first instance in late fifteenth-century Novgorod, sharpening its identity vis-a-vis Moscow.[160] However, its susceptibility to this genre may be connected with the role of clerics travelling to the tsar's court from the south during Muscovy's 'second Byzantine period', when they sought refuge and alms in the only remaining territory under an Orthodox ruler.[161]

Among the central enactments in the church calendar the New Year Ceremony and the Furnace Play took important places both in public and church life; they were connected in various ways to the conquest of Kazan and redemption from slavery. This is particularly clear in the case of the Furnace Play, which was available in contemporary printed liturgies and evidently conducted in several cities, particularly in Moscow, Novgorod and Vologda.[162] Despite attempts by nineteenth-century scholars to trace the performance of the play back to Kievan times, in fact the Furnace Play formed part of Russian church liturgy for a surprisingly brief time. Extant copies of the play and the occasions when it was mentioned occur only between the mid-sixteenth and mid-seventeenth centuries. The first copy might date to the reign of Vasilii Ivanovich (1505–33), however, his name mentioned in the play is reliable for dating purposes only as terminus post-quem. The first incontrovertible reference to the ceremony was made in 1548 in Novgorod, and the latest in 1654 in Moscow;[163] thus, at

---

159 M. Swoboda, 'The Furnace Play and the Development of Liturgical Drama in Russia', *Russian Review*, 61, 2 (2002), pp. 220–234, here p. 220; C.C. Schnusenberg, *The Relationship Between the Church and the Theatre* (Lanham MD, 1988), p. 93.
160 Swoboda, 'The Furnace Play and the Development of Liturgical Drama in Russia', pp. 220–234; Flier, 'Breaking the Code', p. 227.
161 Kraft, *Moskaus griechisches Jahrhundert*; Chrissidis, *An Academy at the Court of the Tsars*.
162 The English traveler Giles Fletcher reports that it was conducted "by every local bishop": G. Fletcher, *Of the Rus' Commonwealth* (Ithaca NY, 1966), pp. 141–142; Swoboda, 'The Furnace Play and the Development of Liturgical Drama in Russia', p. 221; A. Spitsyn, 'Peshchnoe deistvo i khaldeiskaia peshch', *Zapiski: Russkoe arkheologicheskoe obshchestvo*, 12 (1901), pp. 95–209; K.T. Nikol'skii, *O sluzhbakh Russkoi tserkvi, byvshikh v prezhnikh pechatnykh bogosluzhebnykh knigakh* (Sankt Peterburg, 1885).
163 Swoboda, 'The Furnace Play and the Development of Liturgical Drama in Russia', pp. 221, 224; A.A. Dmitrievskii, 'Chin peshchnogo deistva: Istoriko-arheologicheskii etiud', *Vizantiiskii vremennik*, 1, 3–4 (1894), pp. 553–600; E.E. Golubinskii, *Istoriia Russkoi Tserkvi*, vol. 3 (Moskva, 1998 [1911]); N. Krasnosel'tsev, 'Chin peshchnogo deistva: Zamechania i popravki k stat'e M. Savinova', *Russkii filologicheskii vestnik*, 26 (1891), pp. 117–123, here p. 120; Spitsyn, 'Peshchnoe deistvo i khaldeiskaia peshch', pp. 115–136; Nikol'skii, *O sluzhbakh Russkoi tserkvi, byvshikh v prezhnikh pechatnykh bogosluzhebnykh knigakh*, p. 174.

least the starting date and the subsequent popularisation of the play broadly coincide with the onset of Muscovite imperial culture after the conquest of Kazan.

In the Byzantine Empire and Novgorod, the play commemorated the refusal of three young Jewish men who had been chosen as officials by the Babylonian king Nebuchadnezzar II and consequently had to pay reverence to an 'idol', a statue of the king, but failed to comply. As officials in the empire's provinces, they thereby failed in their oath of allegiance. Subsequently they were cast in the burning furnace from which they were miraculously delivered. The mode of transfer is characteristic of the tense but close relations between Novgorod and Moscow in the sixteenth century, as well as the divergent focus of the latter which included the steppe. Metropolitan Makarii, who as erstwhile bishop of Novgorod had been exposed to the western influences represented in the city's customs, not only transferred this play to Moscow, but profoundly changed it in the process.

Compared to the Muscovite version of the furnace play, the Byzantine one was much closer to the Book of Daniel; the verses from that biblical book contained in it concentrate on resistance to idolatry. Characteristic for time-honoured historiographical notions about Russian culture, Marina Swoboda, who uncovered long-neglected continuities in the Russian tradition of theatre, overlooked the import of these changes, although she acknowledged their significance; she sees in them a generical, 'stronger message of an overwhelming and omnipresent Creator'.[164]

The Muscovite version of the play added two songs which set the tone for the whole play. This was reduced to the bare action at the furnace, omitting the idol which might distract from the new focus on the wider context of the furnace episode: Babylonian captivity. When the Chaldeans, soldiers of the foreign tsar, had threatened the boys with fire and thrown stag-horn clubmoss (lycopodium) powder, a flammable swamp-grass, the play continued with Psalm 136 (137):

> 1 By the rivers of Babylon we sat and wept when we remembered Zion. [. . .]
> 3 for there our captors asked us for songs, our tormentors demanded songs of joy; they said, Sing us one of the songs of Zion!'

The redemptive emphasis of the Psalm was increased by adding the following canticle: 'Blessed be the God of Shadrach, Meshach, and Abednego [the three slaves], who has sent his angel and delivered his servants who trusted in him' (Daniel 3:28). The Book of Daniel itself focuses on idolatry and not on the wider context of captivity in Babylon. Given that the 'youths (*otroki*)', a term that can also mean slave, were officials of Nebuchadnezzar in the biblical tradition, the Muscovite version distorted the sense of Daniel, which concentrates on observing monotheism. After

---

[164] Swoboda, 'The Furnace Play and the Development of Liturgical Drama in Russia', p. 225.

this short quotation, the deacon lowered the image of an angel into the 'furnace', which was lit by candles, the Chaldeans fell to their knees, and the image was lifted above the furnace.[165]

Nebuchadnezzar was mentioned in a similar context of the New Israel, rebutting enslavement in a text that spread widely in sixteenth and seventeenth Muscovy, the 'Tale about Queen Dinara'. The story about a legendary Georgian warrior queen who defeats the attacking Persian shah mentions during the announcement of victory and the spoils taken from her challenger that he is a descendant of Nebuchadnezzar. Dinara spurs on her warriors:

> Friends and brethren! I want to lay down my life ('head') before you do [. . .] for all Orthodox people of our kingdom. If you will the same as I do, God shall speedily help us. If you refuse, may God [. . .] turn you over to slavery and robbery, as happened to the Israelites!

The last threat refers to the destruction of the temple of Jerusalem by Nebuchadnezzar II and the Babylonian captivity of Israel (Jer. 20:4–5). The 'Tale about Queen Dinara' exists in various hagiographic, heroic and rhetoric versions. It was included in the miscellanies collecting legends about the miracles of the Mother of God and, among other miscellanies of military and historical content, often accompanies the Russian Chronograph.[166] To mention Nebuchadnezzar in Muscovy therefore retrieved the topoi of captivity, liberation, and the New Israel.

The Moscow liturgy printed in 1650 is outspoken about the frame of reference within which to place the captive youths. It features a song entitled, 'I am singing a song for the three slave boys (*otroki*) and for [prophet] Daniel the Great, created by Feofan', who appears to have been a Muscovite cleric:

> We are singing the praise of God our redeemer, who has led the people of Israel fleeing Egypt's evils, crossing the water as if on dry ground.[167]

These lines place the fiery furnace ritual plainly within the framework of Muscovy as the New Israel being led out of captivity, as a special instance of resistance to slavery.

The message of redemption from captivity, which goes beyond deliverance from having one's faith repressed, is further reinforced in the Muscovite church play, which added the Chaldeans as guards, a detail unknown in the Byzantine version. It made captivity immediately visible to spectators, as the Chaldeans led the captives to and from the furnace and the priest. The way in which the Chaldeans were presented differed markedly between the Novgorod and Moscow versions. In the Novgorod text, there is a dialogue in simple, local language between the boys

---

[165] Ibid., p. 221.
[166] N.S. Demkova, *Divnaia i muzhestvennaia povest' o khrabrosti i mudrosti tselomudrennoi devitsy Dinary tsaritsy, docheri Iverskogo tsaria Aleksandra*, http://lib.pushkinskijdom.ru/Default.aspx?tabid=5084 (accessed 23 June 2020). For further detail, see chapter 6.
[167] Russkaia pravoslavnaia tserkov'. *Mineia obshchaia s prazdnichnoi*, p. 306.

and the Chaldeans, who become overawed by the intervention of the angel. In Moscow, this dialogue was omitted, but the Chaldeans contributed some of the most popular and significant episodes of the play, which due to the participation of the patriarch and attendance of the tsar became more elaborate.[168]

At the same time, reports by foreign travellers suggest that the play's liturgical character declined noticeably, a development that was emphasized by the participation of Chaldeans in festivities outside of the church. Adam Olearius noted in 1630:

> Chaldeans was the name given [. . .] to certain dissolute people who each year received the Patriarch's permission, for a period of eight days before Christmas until the Day of the Three Saintly Kings [Epiphany], to run about the streets with special fireworks.[169]

In the late 1500s, Giles Fletcher similarly describes the furnace play in his account of Russian church ceremonies:

> Another pageant they have [. . .] the week before the nativity of Christ, when every bishop in his cathedral church setteth forth a show of the three children in the oven, where the Angel is made to come flying from the roof of the church with great admiration of the lookers on, and many terrible flashes of fire are made with resin and gunpowder by the Chaldeans, as they call them that run about the town all the twelve days, disguised in their players' coats, and make much good sport for the honour of the bishop's pageant. At Moscow, the Emperor himself and the Empress never fail to be at it, though it be but the same matter played every year.[170]

Fletcher's zealous Protestantism and scorn for the elaborate and gilded Orthodox ceremonies have to be considered in assessing this source. Nevertheless, his portrayal of the Chaldeans' behaviour corresponds with that by Olearius: the Chaldeans emerge as performers reminiscent of *skomorokhi* or *riazhenye*, street entertainers dressed in various costumes. Their negative appeal was heightened by their outlandish attire and boisterous conduct. The church account books reveal that *skomorokhi* were routinely engaged by the church to perform the part of the Chaldeans during the staging of the Furnace Play; perhaps the Muscovite version of the Chaldeans' part required acting techniques not possessed by church officials or the congregation at large. Even though the Chaldeans were not always played by the 'professional' *skomorokhi*, the performers resembled them in their outrageous behaviour.[171] The evil, negative, devilish image attributed to the Chaldeans, an attribute of slavers discussed above, made it necessary for the church authorities to assign the performance of their role to outsiders and not to respectable members of the church community. This was especially true if the 'actors' were *skomorokhi*, who were already identified as the country's underclass.

The shift from a restricted and prescribed liturgical ceremony conducted within the controlled enclosure of the church, into the unlimited expanse of the city, has

---

168 Swoboda, 'The Furnace Play and the Development of Liturgical Drama in Russia', p. 229.
169 A. Olearius, *The Travels of Olearius in Seventeenth-Century Russia* (Stanford CA, 1976), p. 241.
170 Fletcher, *Of the Rus' Commonwealth*, pp. 141–142.
171 Spitsyn, 'Peshchnoe deistvo i khaldeiskaia peshch', pp. 115–136.

led to characterising the event as carnivalized.¹⁷² This was an important factor in the eventual demise of the furnace play, which was no more mentioned after mid-century, due to the great Moscow rising in 1648–9 followed by an edict of tsar Aleksei Mikhailovich proscribing the activities of *skomorokhi*.¹⁷³

Some qualifications are necessary: carnivalization does not explain the specific form of popular activities associated with the furnace play, a question Swoboda does not touch. As she notes, the normal laws of reality are suspended during the celebrations; the carnival world is situated between reality and unreality. In carnival the entire idea of performance is invalidated as the division between the performer and the spectator disappears. According to Mikhail Bakhtin, participants at the carnival 'live it'; they are submerged into a world 'counterpoised to the all-powerful socio-hierarchical relationship of non-carnival life'.¹⁷⁴ However, the Furnace Play was popularized and enriched in the 1550s to suit the participation of tsar and metropolitan, and it still contained important formal, liturgical elements. These traits make it improbable that carnivalization is applicable to the acts of the Chaldeans – although it would have been a perfect reason for the eventual demise of the play.

Olearius' and Fletcher's description of the popular and possibly unruly fireworks of the Chaldeans is given a different spin by the 'Vita of Grigorii Neronov', although it may have been written decades after the event:

> 'In the year 1620, the young man Neronov, also named Ioann, came to the city of Vologda during the celebration of the birth of Christ and His holy appearance, when the days were named sacred [. . .] During those days, more than in any other times, foolish people usually were gathering for their devilish games. They were covering their faces with various horrible masks made in the devil's image'.¹⁷⁵

Even taking into account the sentiment of Neronov, who became an ardent Old Believer and an outspoken antagonist of all street performances, this description is corroborated by the decrees banning the *skomorokhi* and street plays in 1648. The employment of *skomorokhi* had been common practice within the tsar's household and those of the boyars.¹⁷⁶ However, with the succession of tsar Aleksei in 1648 the entire character of court entertainment changed. Aleksei exhibited a preference for a more spiritual life than his predecessors.¹⁷⁷ Under Aleksei, the so-called Zealots of Piety, a group mainly of parish

---

172 Swoboda, 'The Furnace Play and the Development of Liturgical Drama in Russia', p. 230.
173 R. Zguta, *Russian Minstrels: A History of the Skomorokhi* (Philadelphia, 1978), pp. 45–80; Swoboda, 'The Furnace Play and the Development of Liturgical Drama in Russia', p. 231.
174 M. Bakhtin, *Problems of Dostoevsky's Poetics* (Minneapolis, 1984), pp. 122–123.
175 Spitsyn, 'Peshchnoe deistvo i khaldeiskaia peshch', p. 136.
176 I. Zabelin, *Domashnii byt russkikh tsarei v XVI i XVII stoletiiakh*, vol. 1 (Moskva, 1990), pp. 283–288.
177 P. Longworth, *Alexis: Tsar of all the Russias* (London, 1984); R.N. Bain, *The First Romanovs (1613–1725): A History of Muscovite Civilisation and the Rise of Modern Russia under Peter the Great and His Forerunners* (London, 1905); J.T. Fuhrmann, *Tsar Alexis: His Reign and His Russia* (Gulf Breeze FL, 1981).

clergy, gained some influence upon the tsar. Two decrees banning the *skomorokhi* appeared in 1648, signed by the tsar. The first, 'On the Correction of Morals and the Abolition of Superstition', accused *skomorokhi* of drunkenness, staging 'devilish games' and performing 'diabolic rituals'. The second, 'Concerning *Koliada, Usen*', and Other Popular Games' of 24 December 1648, focused specifically on 'pagan' rituals related to the celebration of Christmas and New Year's Day – the noisy revels of the Chaldeans happened during this period. *Skomorokhi* were ordered to abandon their performances, their musical instruments were destroyed, and the population was instructed to expel them from the cities, towns, and villages.[178] Apart from the domestic political situation in the mid-1600s, the banning of *skomorokhi* may be related to the Muscovite state's attempt to reinvent itself ideologically. The collapse of Constantinople had made Moscow the political centre of the Orthodox Church. The church of Constantinople, as well as those of Bulgaria and Serbia under the rule of the Muslim Ottomans, looked to independent Moscow not only for political but also for spiritual guidance. However, the deviations which crept into Russian church services and the general deterioration of Orthodox norms and standards, such as tolerance toward the *skomorokhi*, were plainly evident. The general move toward a more regal style of conduct for the court and for the church service left no place for street performers, or an even indirect association with them. It is therefore conceivable that the affiliation of the Furnace Play with the noisy, visual, and in some ways 'pagan' acts described by Fletcher, Olearius, and Neronov's Vita, struck a chord unwelcome to authorities by the mid-century.

The 'devilish' character of the Chaldeans' public performances has to be considered separately: In metropolitan Makarii's letter to Ivan IV and his host on the eve of the conquest of Kazan, he derided the Tatars as the agents of the 'dragon (*zmii*), the cunning enemy [who burnt the land and captured Christians], the devil (*diavol*)', asking that God send the Archangel Michael and other 'incorporeal powers' to help the Muscovite army, just as Michael had helped Joshua against the Canaanites at Jericho, or Gideon against the Midianites, during the conquest of the Promised Land by the biblical ex-slaves.[179] Makarii had been behind the transferral of the play from Novgorod and the accompanying changes, one of which was the extensive fireworks, the demonic character of the public performances after the Furnace Play that was at the heart of the criticism in the mid-1600s. However, for about a century it had stressed the theme of redemption from slavery inherent in all changes to the liturgical play in its Muscovite version.

---

178 Zguta, *Russian Minstrels*, pp. 45–80. According to V. Vsevolodskii-Gemgross, *Russkii teatr ot istokov do serediny XVIII v.* (Moskva, 1957) campaigns and laws against *skomorokhi* were related to their participation in the disturbances of 1648; however, this was one of several reasons for the persecution of street performers.

179 Rowland, 'Biblical Military Imagery in the Political Culture of Early Modern Russia', p. 188; *Akty istoricheskie, sobrannye i izdannye arkheograficheskoiu kommissieiu*, pp. 290–296; Tikhomirov, *Letopisets nachala tsarstva*, pp. 86–90.

The discontinuation of the Furnace Play as part of the church liturgy did not altogether erase the memory of its performance. About twenty years later, in the 1670s, Simeon Polotskii wrote a play for tsar Aleksei's court theatre, the 'Tragedy about the Tsar Nebuchadnezzar, about the Golden Idol and the Three Youths who Did Not Burn in the Furnace'. There is no reason to translate *otrok* here as slave. All previous additions to the biblical text that referred to the New Israel and Exodus imagery had been removed. The play contained only one remark about God who liberates the three youths not only from the furnace but from Nebuchadnezzar, who is portrayed as a – now remorseful – false, unbelieving and tyrannical tsar in contrast to Aleksei.[180] Thus, the former furnace play a decade after the rebellion of 1648/49 had to do without any of the popular and once customary elements hinting at liberation; instead, it attributes resistance only to unbelief, exonerating the Muscovite tsar. At court level, the entanglement of Muscovites with a political culture that included the theme of liberation from slavery was now avoidable and outmoded.

The popular saint's lives that centred on ransom and the miraculous liberation of slaves, the imagery of the property litigation maps, the context of the Muscovite cross-kissing oath and the wide attention enjoyed by the church plays in the streets of Moscow all show that ideas about liberation from slavery and of Moscow as a Second Israel leaving slavery were widespread far beyond the tiny elite in the capital. It is generally difficult to gauge the ideas held by ordinary people, especially if they could not read. Nevertheless, the noisy, visual and fiery public display connected to the liturgical Furnace Play was hard to ignore in wooden Moscow, and it enjoyed much broader support in the population than the Novgorod variant, which lacks the themes of liberation from slavery and the New Israel ostentatiously displayed in Moscow until the middle of the seventeenth century.

---

180 Swoboda, 'The Furnace Play and the Development of Liturgical Drama in Russia', p. 233; S. Polotskii, *Izbrannye sochineniia* (Moskva, 1953), pp. 189–202, 254.

Chapter 5
Slavery, Ransom and Loyalty in Muscovy

Legitimacy has been an important concept in recent studies on Muscovy, however it tends to prefer a top-down rather than a bottom-up perspective. Loyalty as a research perspective privileges the opposite. It presupposes legitimacy of the ruler and recalls the multitude of reasons among different groups and people to accept a given ruler as legitimate, so that their orders should normally be followed. While there may be grounds not to follow those orders, it is important to understand why people preferred to accept and follow them, without having to be forced into submission. Recent sociological and anthropological studies have advanced the hypothesis that any loyalty relation is principally oriented towards reciprocity. This perspective looks through the prism of the political-moral economy which takes into account the quid pro quo expected by subjects in return for compliance.[1] An important question derived from these more theoretical considerations is: what were returning slaves expected to deliver in order to be considered loyal?

There are three major types of sources on loyalty beyond the elite in Muscovy: oaths, petitions in general, and the special category of petition that will be discussed in this chapter: petitions for compensation for ransom and captivity.[2] They are peculiar sources for several reasons: the petitioners state their loyalty forthrightly – although they use different words. These captives had spent time outside the immediate sphere of influence of the tsar, usually quite a long time. Many were sold in Black Sea ports or slave markets in the Caucasus or Central Asia, to owners who might reside even farther away. In most cases, the captives actively decided to return to Muscovy out of loyalty to the tsar.

This begs the question what the captives did while they lived with their masters, usually in Muslim households: did they give up their loyalty to the tsar and their hope to return, did they try to integrate into the societies into which they had been brought? At the very least, such were the questions on the minds of contemporaries in England, the Habsburg lands or Italy, when they were confronted with slaves who returned from beyond the Mediterranean or the Ottoman Empire after many years. As scholars who

---

[1] N. Buschmann and K.B. Murr, '"Treue" als Forschungskonzept? Begriffliche und methodische Sondierungen', in N. Buschmann and K.B. Murr, eds., *Treue: Politische Loyalität und militärische Gefolgschaft in der Moderne* (Göttingen, 2008), pp. 11–35, here p. 31; M. Schulze Wessel, '"Loyalität" als geschichtlicher Grundbegriff und Forschungskonzept: Zur Einleitung', in M. Schulze Wessel, ed., *Loyalitäten in der Tschechoslowakischen Republik 1918–1938: Politische, nationale und kulturelle Zugehörigkeiten* (München, 2004), pp. 1–22, here pp. 10–11; M. Weber, *Wirtschaft und Gesellschaft: Grundriß der verstehenden Soziologie*, vol. 1 (Tübingen, 1976), p. 16.
[2] A.M. Kleimola, 'The Duty to Denounce in Muscovite Russia', *Slavic Review*, 31, 4 (1972), pp. 759–779.

Open Access. © 2022 the author(s), published by De Gruyter. This work is licensed under the Creative Commons Attribution-NonCommercial-NoDerivatives 4.0 International License.
https://doi.org/10.1515/9783110696431-006

compared narratives of slavery from these areas with those from Muscovy rightly noted, the latter are laconic and contain few of the detail that one finds in their Western counterparts. These were written to satisfy the curiosity of a partly academic public, often for publication, and they answered to increasingly elaborate questionnaires developed by the budding science of ethnology. Only a few longer Muscovite accounts of captivity have been analysed, and their structure and contents are in some respects different from those in the early modern Atlantic and Mediterranean areas.[3]

Using loyalty as a heuristic principle, rather than a comparison of genres, allows us to focus on the similarities between these accounts, which go beyond the superficial form of the narrative and its immediate contents; they may be found more easily accessible in the functions these narratives performed in their own societies, which lived under quite different conditions, in continental Eastern Europe and on the Atlantic rim respectively.[4]

To speak about slavery and loyalty in Muscovy immediately raises the historiographical spectre of the identification of boyars and other high-born subjects as 'slaves of the tsar'.[5] Instead of engaging further in the interpretation of Russian terms that are sometimes considered equivalents of 'slave', as many historians and travellers have done before, what is necessary instead is a quick look at the term used in translation. Any superficial glance at a history of slavery tells us that 'slave', as well as German *Sklave*, French *esclave* and Arabic *esqaliba*, for solid historical reasons derives from the ethnonym 'Slav' and its equivalents.[6] Similarly, *saracen* and other ethnonyms were at certain times used instead of 'slave', using a different term according to the exigencies of war and politics, for a captive sold on to buyers. So historians should beware of a simple, reductionist translation as it risks an oxymoron: 'Boyars were Slavs of the tsar'.

The alternative interpretation, i.e. that boyars were captives of the tsar, or otherwise strongly asymmetrical dependents has been questioned in recent debates about the character of the relation between the tsar and the boyars in Muscovy as well as their institutional forerunners in Scandinavia.[7] While the tsar and an oligarchy of

---

3 Davies, 'The Prisoner's Tale'.
4 Ostrowski, 'The End of Muscovy'; D. Christian, *A History of Russia, Central Asia and Mongolia* (Oxford and Malden MA, 1998), p. xxi.
5 M. Poe, 'What Did Russians Mean When They Called Themselves "Slaves of the Tsar"?', *Slavic Review*, 57, 3 (1998), pp. 585–608.
6 Oxford English Dictionary, *'slave, n.1 (and adj.)'*, https://www.oed.com/view/Entry/181477 (accessed 6 Nov. 2015); J. Heers, *Esclaves et domestiques au Moyen Âge dans le monde méditerranéen* (Paris, 1996); J.P. Maher, *The Indo-European Origin of Some Slavic Grammatical Categories: Substantives in -jb,-ja, -je, -jane/-jahъ* (PhD dissertation, Indiana University, 1965).
7 S. Brink, *Lord and Lady – Bryti and Deigja: Some Historical and Etymological Aspects of Family, Patronage and Slavery in Early Scandinavia and Anglo-Saxon England* (London, 2008); S. Brink, 'Slavery in the Viking Age', in S. Brink and N.S. Price, eds., *The Viking World* (London and New York, 2008), pp. 49–56.

boyars tended to have greater influence in politics, in general the political system was one of a variety of monarch-in-council forms of rule found all over Eurasia, Europe and Northern Africa.[8] Moreover, Muscovite nobles sold and bequeathed their lands, and so were less dependent than has been previously believed.[9] The boyars did not exclusively judge their peers in court cases; the tsar reserved the last judgement, marking Muscovy at one extreme on a possible scale of monarch-in-council rule. The vestiges of earlier advisory bodies involving larger parts of the population than a tiny oligarchy were no longer convoked in the second half of the seventeenth century. However, these are differences of degree, rather than quality, compared to various European territories.

Iurii Krizhanich, the seventeenth-century itinerant Croatian monk and author of the *Politika*, a work that commented on Muscovite policy options, already remarked on this topic:

> To be tsar is to serve God, but to be slave (*kholop*) of the tsar of one's own people, this is honourable and is actually a kind of freedom.

It is less well known that this sentence continues:

> 'however, to serve the tsar or ruler of another people is dishonourable slavery (*pozornoe rabstvo*) and a great misfortune'.[10]

Krizhanich combined a Latin education with first-hand insights into Muscovite dealings as he was among the few foreign observers who spoke the language. His observations stress the competitive character of loyalty and slavery in the trans-Ottoman area. Nevertheless, these quotes have often been interpreted along lines established by the romantic and early nationalist Slavophiles in the nineteenth century, favouring a simple model according to which boyars were subservient.[11]

Recent scholarly work on the tsars and their subjects tend to emphasize more reciprocal relations. The gentry was attached to regional groups which helped to further legal disputes in regional and Moscow chancelleries,[12] they entertained and

---

[8] D. Sneath, *The Headless State: Aristocratic Orders, Kinship Society, and Misrepresentations of Nomadic Inner Asia* (New York, 2007); Atwood, 'Ulus emirs, Keshig Elders, Signatures, and Marriage Partners'; Woodworth, 'The Birth of the Captive Autocracy'; Ostrowski, 'Muscovite Adaptation of Steppe Political Institutions'.

[9] Hammond, *State Service in Sixteenth Century Novgorod*; C. Peach and S. Vertovec, eds., *Islam in Europe: The Politics of Religion and Community* (London and New York, 1997); J. Martin, 'From Fathers to Sons? Property and Inheritance Rights of Pomeshchiki in 16th-Century Muscovy', in G. Szvák and I. Tiumentsev, eds., *Rusistika Ruslana Skrynnikova: Sbornik statej pamjati professora R. G. Skrynnikova* (Budapešt, 2011), pp. 68–75.

[10] L.M. Mordukhovich, 'Iz rukopis'nogo nasledstva Iu. Krizhanicha', *Istoricheskii arkhiv*, 1 (1958), pp 154–189, here p. 185.

[11] R. Pipes, *Rußland vor der Revolution: Staat und Gesellschaft im Zarenreich* (München, 1977).

[12] Kivelson, *Cartographies of Tsardom*.

defended a concept of personal and royal honour,[13] and important methods used to enhance the power of the tsar derived from nascent European absolutism via the Lithuanian Statutes.[14] Angela Rustemeyer's investigation of a supposedly predominantly repressive mechanism, the inquisitional litigation *slovo i delo gosudarevy* or *lèse majesté*, turned up evidence for a widespread loyal disposition toward the tsar. Although there were critical voices as well, this concurs with findings for Siberia.[15]

On a structural level, the closest similarities in handling the cases of a monarch's blemished honour occurred in areas in which the Habsburg Empire was most similar to Muscovy and even to Siberia: in their frontier areas open to the Ottoman Empire, to the Tatars and the steppe. It is no coincidence that slave raids across the steppe between 1475 and 1700 yielded great numbers of slaves sold at markets in Crimea, Central Asia and, following trade routes through the Caucasus, distant places such as Aleppo.[16] Eastern Europe from the Caucasus to Poland–Lithuania was second as a source of slaves only to sub-Saharan Africa in terms of numbers between 1475 and 1694.[17] In frontier areas beset by slave raids or uncontrolled cross-border activity such as smuggling or raiding from the Habsburg Empire to Siberia, an increasingly intrusive state treated cases of defection and insubordination from the second half of the sixteenth century onwards as treason, connecting them with the honour of the emperor and repressing them severely.[18] Significantly, the connection between treason and defence of the land from the 'Turkish menace' in the Habsburg frontier was first made in the late fifteenth century by peasant covenanters. They targeted nobles and priests who supposedly sold out to the Ottomans, abusing the special tax collected to fight the Turks. Only with a time lag coinciding with the Great Peasant Wars which caused an unwillingness to arm ordinary people, did the emperor and other rulers in the second half of the sixteenth century include this line of argument in the *Landesdefension*, a call-to-arms of able-bodied and willing men. By then they used the 'Turkish menace' to suppress peasants and

---

13 Kollmann, *By Honor Bound*.
14 A. Rustemeyer, *Dissens und Ehre: Majestätsverbrechen in Russland (1600–1800)* (Wiesbaden, 2006).
15 Witzenrath, *Cossacks and the Russian Empire, 1598–1725*.
16 I. Wilkinson, 'The Problem of Suffering as a Problem for Sociology', *Medical Sociology Online*, 1, 1 (2006); C. Wilkins, 'A Demographic Profile of Slaves in Early Ottoman Aleppo', in C. Witzenrath, ed., *Eurasian Slavery, Ransom and Abolition in World History, 1200–1860* (Farnham, Surrey, 2015), pp. 221–246.
17 See Introduction. İnalcık, *An Economic and Social History of the Ottoman Empire*, pp. 32–37; Fisher, 'Muscovy and the Black Sea Slave Trade', p. 579; Novosel'skij, *Bor'ba Moskovskogo gosudarstva s tatarami v pervoj polovine XVII veka*, p. 436; Sanin, *Otnosheniia Rossii i Ukrainy s Krymskim Khanstvom v seredine XVII veka*, p. 243; Kołodziejczyk, 'Slave Hunting and Slave Redemption as a Business Enterprise', p. 151; Kizilov, 'Slave Trade in the Early Modern Crimea from the Perspective of Christian, Muslim, and Jewish sources', pp. 6–7.
18 Rustemeyer, *Dissens und Ehre*; Dávid and Fodor, *Ransom Slavery along the Ottoman Borders*.

dismiss militias that showed any sign of resistance. Soon, these militias became part of the conflicts between various confessions, a less effective but cheaper and therefore mushrooming part of the military landscape.[19] Moreover, imperial tax-collectors exploited such feelings deep in the German lands as they funded broadsheets advertising the atrocities of Turks to make taxpayers compliant.[20]

While the conditions in the Habsburg Empire's frontiers in the east were severe, they were unlike those of Muscovy and, even more so, Inner Eurasia,[21] not least in that there are no or very few documents concerning the views of peasants. In many ways this virtual absence is connected to overall conditions in Muscovy. At least until the 1630s, all peripheral areas of Muscovy with few exclusions must be regarded as frontiers in the sense that there were no clear border lines established beyond possession of fortified places, so that they could be invaded or crossed unnoticed by small groups, offering fertile grounds for slave raids, brigandage and smuggling.[22] Since the dynasty did not intermarry with those to the west and south up to the early eighteenth century, losses of manpower by migration or raids across borders were absolute losses, rather than a re-shuffling of demography among territories one might at least potentially possess.[23] While areas around Moscow were largely safe from outside raids by the mid-seventeenth century, many peripheral regions were not: Moscow's Siberian possessions remained a string of fortresses with some pockets of settlement until the Siberian fortified line was built between 1720 and 1760.[24] Although Muscovy and its cossack proxies engaged in external slave raids to some extent, it would be a definite exaggeration to say that overall gains and losses were even, as recent investigations of the Mediterranean Muslim-Christian frontiers have extrapolated for that particular region.[25] On balance, then, Muscovy and much more so, Ruthenia, lost population due to slave raids. Michael Khodarkovsky has even suggested that stalling urban development was caused by losses across this frontier and

---

19 Rustemeyer, *Dissens und Ehre*, pp. 232–234.
20 A. Kappeler, *Ivan Groznyj im Spiegel der ausländischen Druckschriften seiner Zeit* (Bern and Frankfurt am Main, 1972).
21 Ostrowski, 'The End of Muscovy'; Christian, *A History of Russia, Central Asia and Mongolia*, p. xxi.
22 Davies, *Warfare, State and Society on the Black Sea Steppe, 1500–1700*. Early fortified lines existed south of Kazan': Romaniello, *The Elusive Empire*.
23 Rustemeyer, *Dissens und Ehre*.
24 I.V. Naumov and D. Collins, eds.,, *The History of Siberia* (London, 2006), p. 87; M.O. Akishin, *Rossiiskii absoliutizm i upravlenie Sibiri XVIII veka: Struktura i sostav gosudarstvennogo apparata* (Novosibirsk, 2003), p. 9.
25 J. Korpela, '" . . . And They Took Countless Captives": Finnic Captives and the East European Slave Trade during the Middle Ages', in C. Witzenrath, ed., *Eurasian Slavery, Ransom and Abolition in World History, 1200–1860* (Farnham, Surrey, 2015), pp. 171–190; Davies, *Warfare, State and Society on the Black Sea Steppe, 1500–1700*; S. Bono, *Schiavi musulmani nell'Italia moderna: Galeotti, vu' cumprà', domestici* (Napoli, 1999).

by the drain on finances and resources due to ransom, building and maintaining border protections.²⁶

Urban development was linked to general levels of education and literacy even in the countryside, which lagged behind to the east of Western Hungary and Poland-Lithuania. In Italy and France and some other parts of Europe, an abundance of impoverished law students led to access to professional legal advice for peasants, who successfully fought in court against demands from landlords.²⁷ Peasants in the frontier areas who formed *coniurationes* to fight both the Turks and suspicious nobles, therefore, had both the means to leave documentary traces and wealth that they wanted to keep from both parties. On one level, the unavailability of information on peasant views about slave raids in Muscovy and how they defined loyalty is down to a lack of peasant literacy, and partly to the greater extent of raids themselves and their indirect consequences such as lower levels of education, as well as the reaction of Moscow in terms of expensive fortifications, tributes and ransom.

It is therefore unsurprising that applying *lèse majesté* to suppress rebels found in the Habsburg-Ottoman frontier are found in Muscovy as a whole. However, in peripheral areas they are few and late – in the eighteenth century – in the south, but more common in Siberia, where levels of literacy permitted such high-brow approaches to privileged avenues of litigation already in the seventeenth century.²⁸

Significant and common to the Habsburg and Muscovite frontiers, however, is the aspect of political theology that was present in the Austrian *coniurationes* and, in a different form, the *Landesdefension*. The peasant *coniurationes* demanded the right to appoint their priest and tied various sacraments to partaking in the defence of the land against the Ottoman armies and Tatar raids. In their view, the state was constituted from the communal level and legitimated by providing protection against raids. The *coniuratio* soon lost out when their peasant army confronted an actual Ottoman army, and was further discredited during the chain of Great Peasant Wars in the first decades of the sixteenth century.²⁹ The idea that loyalty was owed to someone who provided protection from slave raids lived on in the *Landesdefension* with a changed social focus from the second half of the sixteenth century. To limit the exorbitant costs of standing or mercenary armies, rulers agreed to train subjects to form militias, starting in Inner

---

26 Khodarkovsky, *Russia's Steppe Frontier*.
27 Overview of scholarship: C. Witzenrath, 'Literacy and Orality in the Eurasian Frontier: Imperial Culture and Space in Seventeenth-Century Siberia and Russia', *The Slavonic and East European Review*, 87, 1 (2009), pp. 53–77. A connection with low-born rebels is detectable in the writings of the Upper Rhine Revolutionary, a lawyer trained in Italy who collected the demands of the peasants in the early sixteenth century: Niederstätter, *Das Jahrhundert der Mitte*, p. 129. On the general background of the Austrian and German rebellions and conditions of peasant life, see idem, pp. 108–116, 123.
28 V.A. Aleksandrov and N.N. Pokrovskii, *Vlast' i obshchestvo: Sibir' v XVII v* (Novosibirsk, 1991); Rustemeyer, *Dissens und Ehre*.
29 Niederstätter, *Das Jahrhundert der Mitte*, pp. 123–132.

Austria due to the proximity of the Ottomans.[30] While the nobility was back in positions of command in the militia, the religious aspects of the now disbanded *coniuratio* were adapted to enhance the position of the ruler. The defence of the land by these new militias was propagated as a religious duty, even as a 'citizen's obligation', but this helped to persecute peasant resistance and rebellion as treason.[31]

Loyalty and fidelity in political use are secularised theological terms. Even John Locke in his 1685 'Letter on Tolerance' considered loyalty without belief in God void. As a corollary of this view, atheism dissolves all the bonds of society.[32] Constitutive, therefore, is the biblical conception of loyalty and fidelity: the relation between humans and God is established by the covenant which they concluded. Reciprocity is part and parcel of this relation, although it remains asymmetrical – God remains true to his promise to save the people irrespective of their actions.[33] Political theology in this sense was promoted in the early phase of Ivan IV's reign, before and after the conquest of Kazan. Usually the metropolitan of Moscow, Makarii, is held responsible for this, but one of the best sources on these campaigns, the 'Chronicle of the Beginning of Tsardom', was clearly penned by someone close to Aleksei Adashev, if not by this trusted adviser of Ivan IV himself, who as administrator organised the Kazan' campaigns. The 'Chronicle' insists repeatedly on the strong link between the tsar's legitimacy and liberation from captivity. At the beginning of the text about the campaigns against Kazan during the 1550s, Ivan is portrayed intimately, musing about the liberation of captives in religious terms:

> Tsar [. . .] Ivan [. . .] saw the captivity of Christians, streams of Christian blood and numerous holy churches destroyed, which are insupportable evils [. . .] at the hands of the Kazanians. [. . .] The honourable soul of our tsar, chosen by God, could not bear these tribulations of Christianity in captivity, and he said to himself: "Merciful God [!] By the prayers of your pure mother, by those of the saints and our Russian miracle workers I was put before these Orthodox lands and all people as tsar and shepherd, leader and ruler, to rule these people steadfastly according to Orthodoxy, guard them from all ills and all hardships befalling them. Lord, help me and redeem [*izbavi*] your captured slaves (*plennykh rab*)[34] from the heathens. For he is truly the good shepherd, who gives his soul for [his] sheep.[35]

---

30 Styria, Carinthia, Carniola, and the Littoral. W. Schulze, 'Die deutschen Landesdefensionen im 16. und 17. Jahrhundert', in J. Kunisch, ed., *Staatsverfassung und Heeresverfassung in der europäischen Geschichte der frühen Neuzeit* (Berlin, 1986), pp. 129–149, here pp. 136–137.
31 Rustemeyer, *Dissens und Ehre*, p. 233; W. Schulze, *Landesdefension und Staatsbildung: Studien zum Kriegswesen des innerösterreichischen Territorialstaates (1564–1619)* (Wien, 1973), p. 198.
32 J. Locke and J. Ebbinghaus, *Ein Brief über Toleranz: Englisch-Deutsch* (Hamburg, 1957), p. 94.
33 C. Schmitt, *Politische Theologie* (München, 1922), p. 35. Schulze Wessel, '"Loyalität" als geschichtlicher Grundbegriff und Forschungskonzept', pp. 3–4.
34 'Slave' here refers to the biblical reference of the believer to themselves in their covenant with God, whereas 'captured' underlines the notion of worldly captivity.
35 Tikhomirov, *Letopisets nachala tsarstva*, pp. 59–60. See chapter 2.

The reciprocity of obligations and terms in this political theology of redemption is established in metropolitan Makarii's letter. After a short, initial invocation he starts to implore the Muscovite army to do their best during the impending, decisive assault on Kazan:

> [W]e pray for [. . .] the whole Christ-loving army of the Orthodox people, who battle for honour, and for the current campaign, [so that they may] stand up with God's help and your valiant intercession, o tsar [. . .] against your foes, the godless Kazan Tatars, your traitors and deserters, who have always spilled innocent Christian blood [. . .] And therefore it befits you and [. . .] your whole Christ-loving army to raise arms with God's help for [. . .] all Orthodox Christians who were led into captivity not by their own fault, and [who were] robbed and tormented by them and defiled by manifold passions.[36]

Makarii continues to motivate the soldiers by evoking images of captivity and liberation, referring to Joshua and the fall of Jericho. He implores the army to behave virtuously, eschew temptation and be cunning in battle in order to win their empire, which he promises quoting Isaiah 45 about the liberation of Israel from Babylonian captivity by the armies of the Persian king Cyrus. Lazarus von Schwendi, who first advocated the *Landesdefension* in districts of Inner Austria that suffered frequent slave raids, similarly exhorted the nobles to bethink them of their martial virtues. However, in the tradition of criticism of nobles they appear as effeminate weaklings in splendid clothes instead of armour, who are no longer capable, let alone willing, to fight. Consequently, merit and tax reductions must be given to those who fight, be they commoners or nobles.[37]

Makarii could rely on the martial values of the Muscovite nobility, although the rank-and-file often barely made a living while frequently fighting on two fronts in the same year; for many, the costs of service to the tsar were higher than the returns.[38] From his musings about Muscovy as the New Israel and about the necessary morals, Makarii jumps a few centuries of salvation history to find a New Testament parallel closer to the image of the Christ-emulating ruler who liberates his flock, the image we encountered at the start of the 'Chronicle's narrative about the defining, Muscovite conquest of Kazan:

> And if anyone from among the Orthodox Christians should suffer grievously during this strife for the holy Church [. . .] and for the multitude of the Orthodox people, and survive, they will truly cleanse themselves through their spilled blood from earlier sin and [. . .] they will not only receive from God tangible benefits in this life, added lifespan and painless living, but also will receive remuneration in the future life [the afterlife]. If anyone [. . .] suffers death for [. . .] Orthodox Christianity and for the plenitude of Orthodox people, they will be redeemed by Christ from the torments of hell by His honourable blood, and [therefore] measure up to

---

36 Ibid., pp. 87–88.
37 Schulze, 'Die deutschen Landesdefensionen im 16. und 17. Jahrhundert', pp. 143–144.
38 On the *pomeshchiki* army, see Frost, *The Northern Wars*, pp. 9–11, 81–87.

Christ's word: "Greater love hath no man than this, that a man lay down his soul for his brother".[39]

This last text, liberally adapted from John 15 who means Christ, was originally applied to the Byzantine bishop's duty to ransom captives evolving from the ninth century.[40] The bishop's obligation to care for his flock was transferred to the ruler in the 'Letter to the Ugra', which was written by disciples of the Roman cardinal and the exiled Greek Orthodox metropolitan of Niceae, Bessarion. These scholars had accompanied Ivan III's wife Sofiia Palaiologina to Moscow. She herself had been taught in Bessarion's Roman palace-academy, which helped her to start the Italian Renaissance by translating Greek texts. Bessarion promoted the common defence from the Ottomans against the inner divisions of European rulers, a task that took more than his lifetime to see results.[41] The convergence of these transfers in European renaissance thought, Byzantine tradition and Muscovite religious and political ideas adds to the commonalities of the frontiers, although no connection is known between Bessarion's ideas and those of the Inner Austrian peasants.

The main message of Makarii beyond military values and ample remuneration is in the symbolic reciprocity of the tsar's and the soldiers' obligations. Loyalty is measured by the rod of liberating captives. Sacrifice for the sake of redeeming captives and saving the church equals the deeds of Christ, entitles to redemption in the hereafter and unites ruler and loyal subjects in what is seen as the highest form of love, martyrdom by dying in battle. Makarii's jump through salvation history summarizes Muscovite interpretations of it as one in which the New Israel, or Muscovy, is liberated from Tatar captivity by the tsar as the new Moses and redeemed by Christ's vicar on earth to gain empire and allegiance of the pagans and Muslims.

Beyond this mainly military virtue, the elite was at pains to portray subjects and Orthodox slaves in Muslim areas, justly or not, as loyal to the cause of Orthodoxy and liberation. The 'Martyrdom of Ivan', by all appearances invented by order of Makarii in 1551 or 1552 and included among his collection of authoritative documents, the 'Great Reading Menaion', underscores this interpretation: the slave 'Ivan' from Nizhnii Novgorod is beheaded in Kazan by his master, the khan's uncle, for refusing to convert to Islam. However, he miraculously manages to put his head back on his neck at night, walks away – unintentionally reminiscent of Klaus Störtebecker's execution narrative – and finally saves himself from slavery by reaching

---

39 Tikhomirov, *Letopisets nachala tsarstva*, pp. 86–89. This quote still adorns modern day books on military chaplaincy: R.L. Dilenschneider, n.t., in D.L. Bergen, ed., *The Sword of the Lord: Military Chaplains from the First to the Twenty-First Century* (Notre Dame IN, 2004), exchanges 'life' for 'soul'.
40 Rotman, *Byzantine Slavery and the Mediterranean World*, pp. 50, 177.
41 Pliukhanova, "'Poslanie na Ugru" i vopros o proiskhozhdenii moskovskoi imperskoi ideologii', p. 465. For background, see chapter 2.

the tsar's army. He dies a martyr's death after a night of preparation for the afterlife in the security of a Muscovite town.⁴²

So martyrdom was not restricted to the tsar's soldiers but could be extended to captives. The icon 'Church Militant', or 'Blessed Host of the Heavenly Tsar', which was painted shortly after the conquest of Kazan' and placed by the tsar's throne, shows an army returning victoriously from a burning city to the Heavenly Jerusalem, where they receive martyrs' crowns, may well have been seen as containing the '60,000' – meaning a large number in premodern parlance – former slaves at Kazan who had reported to the tsar's army commanders.⁴³ This interpretation is consistent with the illustrations in the throne room's anteroom, where Joshua led former slaves to the Promised Land, or, as inscriptions state, the 'mountain and the plain', citing the chronicle description of the Kazan khanate.⁴⁴

Simeon Polotskii, the Kiev-educated teacher of Tsar Aleksei Mikhailovich's children, wrote a poem explaining martyrdom in which he referred to the obligations of the ruler to care for their subjects, especially captives. In Polotskii's poem, in the Baroque style, slaves suffer at the hand of an illicit ruler for whom the care for his subjects and slaves is less important than his curiosity and striving for knowledge, symbolized by an apple.⁴⁵ Polotskii changed the Latin original to include a line saying that the three young men – or slaves, depending on translation⁴⁶ – were 'of the honourable lineage', in other words, the Muscovite New Israel.

An earlier reference to interpreting slaves as martyrs is found in Iosif of Volok Lamskii's 'Enlightener':

> 'This is why it is proper to bow and serve bodily, but not spiritually, and to do them the honour due to the tsar, but not that due to God, as the Lord says: give to Caesar what is Caesar's and to God what is God's. As you thus bow and serve, you beware from the loss of your soul, but you learn from it the fear of God: for the Tsar is God's servant, for man [he is] pardon and punishment. But if the tsar, who had to rule the people, begins to rule of his own – there will be evil passions and sins, rapacity and violence, falsehood and deceit, and worst of all, unbelief and blasphemy, in this way the tsar is not God's servant, but a Devil; [he is] not a tsar, but a tormentor. Such a tsar is, because of his wickedness, not called a tsar by our Lord Jesus Christ, but a fox: go, he said, tell that fox. And the prophet says: the tsar who is overbearing will die, and his ways will be dark. The three young men were not obedient to the commands of the tsar Nebuchadnezzar, but called him a lawless enemy and a vile apostate, and the most wicked on earth. And you will not obey such a tsar or prince and not serve him, who leads you

---

42 Pelenski, *Russia and Kazan*, pp. 276–278; Miller, 'The Velikie Minei Chetii and the Stepennaia Kniga of Metropolitan Makarii and the Origins of Russian National Consciousness', pp. 263–382, here p. 301.
43 Tikhomirov, *Letopisets nachala tsarstva*, p. 66.
44 Kochetkov, 'K istolkovanii ikony "Tserkov voinstvuiushchaia"', p. 206; Zabelin, *Domashnii byt russkikh tsarei v XVI i XVII stoletiiakh*, pp. 155–156.
45 S. Polotskii and A. Hippisley, eds., *Vertograd mnogocvětnyj*, vol. 2 (Köln, 1999), p. 385.
46 M. Fasmer and O.N. Trubachev, eds., *Etimologicheskii slovar' russkogo iazyka* (Moskva, 1971), pp. 172–173.

into dishonour and wickedness, even if he tortures and threatens with death. To this testify the prophets and apostles, and all martyrs, for they were killed by impious and dishonoured tsars, but did not fulfil their commands. This is the way in which to serve tsars and princes'.[47]

Iosif explains how prophets deal properly with such an evil – and unbelieving – tsar by resisting him, but this cannot be the exclusive model for mere humans. Thus, to 'beware of the loss of your soul' by serving outwardly but not inwardly, or spiritually, is a proper way to deal with captivity. Zakhariia Kopystensky in *Palinodia*, the 1621 rejoinder to P. Skarga's and L. Krevza's earlier theological attacks against Orthodoxy, took this a step further. Skarga and Krevza had accused Orthodoxy of being a church in captivity, which they presented as proof that God's grace had been withdrawn from it. Kopystensky turned this argument on its head by insisting on the central tenets of Christianity:

> The Grace of God remain[s] in the holy Eastern Church that is bodily enslaved. [. . .]
>
> Just as [. . .] Jerusalem was ruled by pagans in the era of the Old Testament, so it has now been ruled for many years by the ungodly Turks. This holy city and the [. . .] shrine of the resurrection [. . .] have all been defiled by the many kinds of iniquities perpetrated by the Turks. Nevertheless, the grace of [. . .] our Saviour [. . .] has remained in Jerusalem. [. . .] cities populated by good people holding the right faith become defiled when the faithful residing in them desert the pious and Orthodox faith [. . .] and take up customs and manners of life that are loathsome to God and base in all respects [. . .] But as long as they hold firmly to the pious and genuine faith in Christ God and suffer with constancy [. . .] the diverse tribulations which the ungodly pagans and the evil and accursed heretics contrive against them, their cities resemble those towers in which the holy martyrs [of the persecuted early church] were once incarcerated. [This is] [. . .] in accordance with the words of Jesus our Lord: "Blessed are they who are expelled for righteousness's sake, for theirs is the kingdom of heaven".[48]

In the conflict with the Uniates[49] in Poland-Lithuania, Kopystens'kyj represents the Orthodox Church as uniquely suited to life on the frontier and in the captivity of the church and its people. He seeks to show that faithful and patient suffering in captivity produces the preconditions of redemption both in this life and the next – a soteriological argument derived from the language of the slave market.[50] Captivity is even seen as a hothouse of liberation, providing an 'armour of spiritual warfare'.

---

47 I. Volotskii, *Prosvetitel' ili oblichenie eresizhidovsvuiushchikh: Tvorenie prepodobnago ottsa nashego Iosifa, igumena Volotskago* (Kazan', 1896), pp. 286–288. Trans. in C. Soldat, 'The Limits of Muscovite Autocracy: The Relations between the Grand Prince and the Boyars in the Light of Iosif Volotskii's Prosvetitel', *Cahiers du monde russe*, 46, 1–2 (2005), pp. 265–276, here pp. 270–271.
48 Koropeckyj, R., and B. Struminsky (eds.), *Lev Krevza's "A Defense of Church Unity" and Zaxarija Kopystens'kyjs "Palinodia"* (Cambridge MA, 1995), pp. 606–607.
49 Orthodox Ruthenian bishops who agreed to the Union of Brest in 1596 formed the Uniate Church. They retained Orthodox ritual and accepted the authority of the pope.
50 D. Peterson, ed., *Where Wrath and Mercy Meet: Proclaiming the Atonement Today. Papers from the Fourth Oak Hill College Annual School of Theology* (Carlisle, 2001), vol. 1, chapters 1–2; L. Morris, *The Apostolic Preaching of the Cross* (London, 1965), p. 27; Cf. J.D.G. Dunn, *Word Biblical Commentary*,

There are thus two acceptable modes of dealing with captivity in Orthodoxy – either to fight the Turks boldly and bravely; or to suffer in bodily captivity, give the emperor his due, live by Moses' law and abide in the grace of God and the Orthodox faith.

Petitions by returning slaves and captives

Tatars

Before addressing the petitions by captives who returned to Muscovy, I would like to draw attention to the situation and indeed the plight of some of the Tatar captives in Muscovy. Hans-Heinrich Nolte has recently noted that they were often treated without much regard, and that specifically the Russian Orthodox Church did not protect them as co-religionists, a primary defence of most Orthodox *kholopy*.[51] It is true that captured Tatars who were appropriated by boyars were sometimes abused, compared to the standards for the treatment of *kholopy*.[52]

Sudak Basary's case shows that such poor treatment even of the most defenceless was not unconditionally accepted, but depended on the position of the master in wider society. He petitioned to be transferred from the Moscow court of Vasilii Vasil'evich Golitsyn, the favourite and most powerful boyar during Sofiia Alekseevna's regency, to the prison of Sevsk. It is obvious that nobody could have deprived Golitsyn of his slave as long as he was the most powerful man in Muscovy. When Basary's case was heard in October 1689, Golitsyn had been overthrown just a month earlier – he was still addressed as boyar, a rank he lost weeks later.[53] His Tatar slave seized the opportunity to bring his case to the attention of the victorious Naryshkin clan. Basary claimed that he had lived in poverty and had not been fed appropriately, which was the main and absolute obligation of any *kholop*'s master.[54] Vasilii Golitsyn's foes may actually have used this case to advance the process of his downfall and loss of the rank of boyar, leading to his exile in the Russian North, considering the timing. It was noted that Basary had been sent to Golitsyn's

---

vol. 38A: *Romans 1–8* (Dallas, 1988), pp. 169, 179–180; D. Moo, *The Wycliffe Exegetical Commentary*, vol. 1: *Romans 1–8* (Chicago, 1991), pp. 229–230.
51 H.-H. Nolte, 'Iasyry: Non-Orthodox Slaves in Pre-Petrine Russia', in C. Witzenrath, ed., *Eurasian Slavery, Ransom and Abolition in World History, 1200–1860* (Farnham, Surrey, 2015), pp. 247–264.
52 Hellie, *Slavery in Russia, 1450–1725*; A. Stanziani, 'Serfs, Slaves, or Wage Earners? The Legal Status of Labour in Russia from a Comparative Perspective, from the Sixteenth to the Nineteenth Century', *Journal of Global History*, 3, 2 (2008), pp. 183–202.
53 L. Hughes, 'Sophia, Regent of Russia', *History Today*, 32, 7 (1982), pp. 10–15, here p. 15; L. Hughes, *Sophia, Regent of Russia: 1657–1704* (New Haven CT, 1990).
54 Hellie, *Slavery in Russia, 1450–1725*, pp. 126–129; A. Stanziani, *Bondage: Labor and Rights in Eurasia from the Sixteenth to the Early Twentieth Centuries* (New York, 2014).

court without ever having been interrogated by any chancellery, as was the rule for captives, making sure the information they provided was duly used. He did not want to be baptised, as he had wife and children in Crimea to return to; Golitsyn was impelled to confirm that he never was. Finally, V.V. Golitsyn's successor Tikhon N. Streshnev, head of the Naryshkin clan, decided in Basary's favour, who was sent to Sevsk prison 'where my Tatar brethren sit'.[55] There he was available for an exchange, for the benefit of all Muscovite captives abroad and their families. This case encapsulates the relativity of the position of foreign captives in Muscovy, but also the considerable weight of the rights of Muscovite captives that often helped to open a window towards release for Tatar captives, which was more accessible in Sevsk.

Sevsk functioned as the main prison for Tatars and Turks. In 1692, 122 Crimean and Nogai Tatars were held there, as well as Wallachian and 'Turkish' captives.[56] Many petitioners who sought Tatar captives to exchange for themselves or their relatives at one point or another addressed Sevsk. This central facility had been set up to make tracing simpler and exchanges less costly. It served as a model for similar institutions in the Ottoman Empire, where the need for exchange was more keenly felt when the empire reached its nadir in 1683 and the once great flow of captives from the outside world became a trickle.[57] Sevsk is an example of Muscovy's attempts to turn its lowly position in the pecking order of empires into a strength by paying close attention to the needs of captives and slaves.

In the same vein, Muscovite legislation sought to advance the interests of captives. The *Ulozhenie* code of laws of 1649, which collected and confirmed earlier rules, made provision for a captives' tax:

> [. . .] so that no one will be omitted from that cash levy because such ransoming is a common act of mercy. The pious tsar and all Orthodox Christians will receive great recompense from God, as the righteous Enoch said: "Do not spare gold and silver for your brother, but redeem him, and you will receive a hundred–fold from God".[58]

Both the Hundred Chapters Synod of 1551 and the *Ulozhenie* citing it verbatim emphasize that these ideas were widely distributed among the population: until the early nineteenth century, the 1649 Law Code was the only code of law, and the only basic collection of laws commonly available in all provincial courts, printed in its

---

[55] RGADA f. 210 d. 1435, ll. 274–278.
[56] RGADA f. 210 d. 1453, l. 304.
[57] On Ottoman prisons and evolution from slavery to prisoner of war: W. Smiley, 'Abolishing Bondage: A "Barbarous Law"? Capture and Liberation in the Russo-Habsburg-Ottoman War of 1787–1792', in C. Witzenrath, ed., *Eurasian Slavery, Ransom and Abolition in World History, 1200–1860* (Farnham, Surrey, 2015), pp. 323–334. See now: Smiley, *From Slaves to Prisoners of War*.
[58] Hellie, *The Muscovite Law Code (Ulozhenie) of 1649*, p. 17; Hecker, 'Die Christenpflicht als Rechtsnorm', p. 156.

first edition with the remarkable press run of 2,400 copies.[59] Moreover, it was the last law of Russia owing its existence to a dual process of law making rather than autocratic fiat: it was codified by a commission of boyars in reaction to the great 1648–49 Moscow rebellion, including much of the chancellery law of preceding decades.[60]

Petitions for recompense come in two varieties: some are very pragmatic and secular, while many others include some sort of reference to religious notions. As noted above, these ideas are far from the elaborate references to biblical stories in the narratives of captives who sought to justify themselves in the Habsburg Empire or in England. Mostly they just quote or allude to these ideas almost obliquely, yet unmistakably:

> The widow Ovdot'ia Poluianova, daughter of Ivan Zakharevskii bows [. . .] I, your slave (*raba*), was eight years in captivity in the Turkish lands and my children, my two sons Ivan and Petr, remained in Sivesk [Sevsk] as poor and helpless beggars [since] the Crimean people destroyed my house completely and now I die of hunger and go from house to house begging [. . .] as my children do. Merciful ruler, o tsar [. . .] show your mercy on me your slave (*raba*), a poor and helpless captive, give my children tax exemptions as God tells you.[61]

Ovdot'ia received a mandate that recapitulated her petition and ordered the 'local head' to

> grant a tax exemption to the widow Ovdot'ia for her endurance in captivity and to her children according to local best knowledge (*naskol'ko dovedettsa*).[62]

In the draft, the supervisor deleted the addition 'according to your judgement', confirming Ovdot'ia's right to receive exemption. There was no attempt to confirm Ovdot'ia's statement at the Moscow archival level, something that was done with male military petitioners, presumably because there were no records. The wording suggests that her plea and expectation of reciprocity was granted because of the male children she had raised. Widows could retain control of conditional service lands if they provided for requisite soldiers and male children who would one day take over. Nevertheless, the exemption was granted on the grounds of 'her endurance in captivity', affording her a martyr-like status although she had only dared to claim the care of the ruler for the 'slave (*raba*)' according to the covenant with God. Petitions from returning female slaves are very rarely preserved in the archives. This was due to the conditions in their place of captivity, to attachment to children conceived in their new places, to return journeys even more arduous and dangerous for

---

59 Art. 'Ulozhenie', in J. Millar, ed., *Encyclopedia of Russian History* (London, 2004), pp. 828–831.
60 Schmidt, *Sozialkontrolle in Moskau*.
61 Rossiiskii Gosudarstvennyi Arkhiv Drevnikh Aktov (RGADA) f. 210 d. 232 ll. 147–148.
62 RGADA f. 210 d. 232 ll. 149.

them than for men, to impediments such as slavers hunting fled captives, and to the often less than favourable place in their old Muscovite lives – or a dependent position in a household, where they might or might not be socially secure but could not hope to improve. All of these forms of dependency could mean, among other things, that many saw no reason to go to Moscow to petition and undergo an interview.[63]

The typical petition of a returning captive who had been a military servitor of the tsar included a section detailing his services and the moment and the way in which he was captured. Coincidence with a battle during which captives were taken or a narrative that stressed the sudden and forcible manner of capture helped the claim. In most cases, such details were checked against existing records and the chancellery clerks came up with either confirmation, or they might find that archival records had been destroyed due to the exigencies of war. If no corroboration was found and the claim seemed dubious or, as in the case of a Polish soldier who had been stranded in Moscow after leaving slavery through the Caucasus route, the claim was left without remuneration. To be able to claim compensation was linked to loyal service or at least the ability to claim such loyalty, or simply a formal ability to claim Orthodoxy or subjecthood, irrespective of how actual behaviour in captivity had evolved. Those who successfully claimed loyalty could expect not only compensation, but also to be reinstated in their service ranks, providing a livelihood. Like trust, loyalty reduces social complexity: this was an essential function of it from both the perspectives of the giver of loyalty and the ruler.[64]

However, the former slaves brought to Moscow in 1686 by the emissary of the khan of Khiva, Abraim Bek Asvebekov, were accepted without even checking their backgrounds. They were two mounted musketeers, a townsman and a Tatar military servitor, Biik Bekaev from Kazan, who had been captured 'in various parts in the Kalmyk steppe' and sold on to Khiva, where they had recently 'been liberated'. Probably to avoid repercussions in foreign relations, and because they had arrived from an almost inaccessible place, they received compensation for 'their endurance of captivity'.[65] Overall, this was the most common of religious descriptions, often self-ascribed in petitions.

A slightly more articulate version of this claim to a martyr-like status is the expression used by the Sevsk servitor Perfil' Iurev. Moreover, in tune with most petitions by military servitors, he detailed the length of his service, his commanding boyar and his

---

[63] Lavrov, 'Captivity, Slavery and Gender'; Lavrov, 'Rapatriement, genre et mobilité sociale'. For more on women's lives in captivity, see the Introduction.
[64] Schulze Wessel, '"Loyalität" als geschichtlicher Grundbegriff und Forschungskonzept', pp. 11–12; R. Richter and E. Furubotn, *Neue Institutionenökonomik: Eine Einführung und kritische Würdigung* (Tübingen, 1996), p. 176.
[65] RGADA f. 210 d. 617 l. 5.

last assignment, adding that he had been injured during his capture. He continued, 'In captivity I, your *kholop*, endured all kinds of misery and torments'. It is unclear on this one-leaf record why he was granted exemptions without verification, but he had added that his wife had married again and lived with her new husband, a soldier at Iurev's former court. In June 1685, he was granted exemption from field and town service 'for this enslavement as a captive (*polonnoe porab[-oshchenii]*)'.[66] Originating from the same area and giving the same command, position and date of capture on the same day in the chancellery, the petition by Aksip Riazhskii raises the question whether they had swapped their stories, but this must have occurred to the clerks, too. Their stories were similar down to individual phrases, but the difference was in the resolution and in one detail: Riazhskii's homestead had been destroyed, it was 'empty', and his wife had remarried and gone to live in an unknown place. He had not suffered wounds, but 'in captivity I endured all kinds of misery and torments'. He was granted a tax exemption for three years 'due to his endurance of captivity'.[67] Similarities in handwriting indicate that both had consulted the same public secretary and that the same clerk had heard both cases. Still, in resolution the clerk used different phrases and decisions.

In these and many other cases, to return from slavery or more short-term captivity was all that was expected from ordinary people for compensation. As the code of laws suggests, it applied to rank-and-file servitors as well as to peasants, however unequally and few of the latter appeared in the Moscow military list chancellery. One Martyn Ermolaev, a peasant of Ignat'ii Ivanov from the village of Pokhotinnyi in Pereiaslavl Riazan' district, was summarily allowed compensation 'for leaving [captivity] and for enduring slavery'.[68] There was no petition, perhaps because he returned from Khiva with the tsar's emissary Vasilii Daudov, who had great difficulty to find slaves whom he was allowed to deliver from a country that was well protected by deserts and steppe.[69]

While peasants and Tatars serving the tsar were allowed into the simpler category of those who endured captivity, some of the military men were more forthright in claiming martyr status. Thus, in the account given by the governor of Rylsk of a written petition delivered to his office by Makarii Lavrent'ev son Samoilov, from Chernigov, who had served with the boyar V.B. Sheremetev, we find the expression 'in captivity he was tormented bodily for a long time' from 1661/62 to 16 December 1677, when he 'left captivity in Rylsk and lay ill for a long time in Rylsk'.[70] Considering the statements of Kopystenskyi and Iosif of Volok Lamskii cited above, the expression stressed that they had preferred lesser status and conditions in favour of avoiding conversion. The governor granted passage to Moscow, where Makarii

---

[66] RGADA f. 210 d. 609 ll. 121–121 ob.
[67] RGADA f. 210 d. 609 ll. 122–122ob.
[68] RGADA f. 210 d. 808 l. 40.
[69] Burton, *The Bukharans*; A. Burton, *Bukharan Trade, 1558–1718* (Bloomington IN, 1993).
[70] RGADA f. 210 d. 808 ll. 37–38.

Samoilov asked to convert his compensation of cloth into a monetary award, citing his debts, 'for my endurance in captivity and for my escape'. It was granted by the military list chancellery for the amount of 1 rouble 16 *altyn* 4 *dengi*.[71]

The same expression was used by Aleksei Martynov son Elagin from Solovetsk, who applied for an icon submitting that

> I suffered torment for many years on the galley [. . .] give compensation for my needy endurance of captivity.[72]

Similarly, in 1680/1681 one Ivan Nikolev asked in Kiev for ransom for his brother Samoilo, who had been captured in 1679/1680, saying 'I have been tormented bodily' as a captive among the Belgorod Tatars; he received relief.[73] Thus they confirmed the Orthodox view that it was more important to survive and preserve Orthodoxy in thought and soul than by outwardly serving the tsar in captivity.

Some former captives had to explain themselves in more words, as their conditions and lives were open to interpretation. The military servitor, 'captive and returnee from Khiva' Fedot Ivanov had to explain himself, but not his name, which could indicate a convert. He arrived in Moscow in 1676/77 with his son Mamet after more than thirty years in captivity:

> I endured all kinds of hardship and I did not leave the Orthodox Christian faith, because I memorised the fear of God and the oath [cross kissing.] I was married against my will to a Tatar woman and had a son with her and I have led this son out with me to Moscow and he has more than twenty years of age now[. H]e wanted to leave Islam and was baptized in the Orthodox Christian faith. Those of our brethren who left captivity have received your tsar's icon [. . .] give it to me and my son, the convert.[74]

Fedot and Mamet were awarded an icon each, although much of their story is shrouded in silence. They appeared in Moscow out of nowhere. Considering how difficult, if not virtually impossible, it was to traverse the Turkmen, 'Kirgiz' [i.e. Kazakh] or Kalmyk steppe in those days, there is more than a little detail lacking in this account. Fedot's wife might have died before he left and his Khivan master's rationale for letting him go is less than obvious: why manumit them and allow them to go if Mamet was raised in the Islamic faith? Punishment for apostasy was among the most hotly debated subjects in Islamic jurisprudence. While Islamic clerics mostly agreed to disagree about the death penalty, Central Asia was not an area renowned for lenience.[75] Fedot and Mamet might have cleverly avowed to Muslim nomads along the way that they were coreligionists, but not all nomads were

---

71 RGADA f. 210 d. 808 ll. 38ob–39.
72 RGADA f. 210 d. 791 ll. 85–85ob.
73 RGADA f. 52, 18 June 1686 No. 9 l. 1.
74 RGADA f. 210 d. 791 ll. 65–65ob.
75 Clarence-Smith, *Islam and the Abolition of Slavery*, p. 42.

Muslims – the Kalmyks were Buddhists and many Kazakhs did not appear to care too much. Moreover, Turkmens are known for claiming that the career of the prophet Joseph demonstrated that captives benefited from being sold, so that it was allowed to enslave Muslims despite the fervent exhortations of the mullahs.[76] Still, it was impossible to ask more than their story from these two self-styled returnees, who required icons to show that officialdom had accepted their Orthodox credentials. In this need for acceptance they were quite similar to the more elaborate captives' narratives further west, including the added detail of life in captivity.

The use of devoutness to overplay episodes in captivity that seemed to threaten loyalty is also evident in the petition of Vasilii Vasil'ev *syn* Polozov, who was captured at Iablonov while serving under town governor B.A. Repnin, and returned during the reign of Fedor. The account of his captivity covers only a fifth of the petition; it is very laconic and vague: he was at the sultan's court but did not convert; he was sentenced and pardoned to serve on a galley. After shipwreck, the rest is a mix of miracle story and pilgrimage narrative, which B.L. Davies considers was very likely invented.[77] O.A. Belobrova noted that this part, which covers all the notable biblical sites where Polozov claimed to have passed himself off as a Turk, is entirely traditional and stereotypical.[78] Polozov had to explain how he ended up in Persia, a friendly power, where two envoys of the tsar picked him up. He used models available to him to conform to the expectations of society and especially of the court, but the models in Muscovy were unlikely to be academic as in Britain or elsewhere. The lack of universities explains some of the differences between Russian captive narratives and, on the other hand, Western and Southern European ones. The latter were often more detailed on conditions in captivity, using detailed questionnaires compiled by early ethnographers. Tsar Fedor's pious demeanour inspired some people to come forward with their stories of individual devotion during captivity and the quest to return. Since there was always the threat of a stint of re-education in a monastery, petitioners were wise to stress their loyalty to Orthodox precepts, especially under such a devout ruler.[79]

It would be a mistake to limit religious motifs in returning captives' petitions to Fedor's short reign, as other Romanov rulers were no less devout, although the martial qualities of e.g. Aleksei Mikhailovich were more pronounced. Yet during Aleksei's reign the Greek Kostiantinov appeared in Moscow with an unlikely story of collecting alms to ransom his relatives in Rumelia. To explain how he had passed

---

[76] C. Letourneau, *L'évolution de l'esclavage dans les diverses races humaines* (Paris, 1897), p. 226.
[77] Davies, 'The Prisoner's Tale'.
[78] O.A. Belobrova, 'Cherty zhanra khozhdenii v nekotorykh drevnerusskikh pis'mennykh pamiatnikakh XVII veka', *Trudy Otdela drevnerusskoi literatury*, 27 (1972), pp. 257–272.
[79] Rowland, 'Did Muscovite Literary Ideology Place Limits on the Power of the Tsar?'; Aleksandr S. Lavrov, 'Voennyi plen i rabstvo na granitsakh Osmanskoi imperii i Rossiiskogo gosudarstva v 17 – nachale 18 veka', *DHI Moskau: Vorträge zum 18. Jahrhundert*, 5 (2010), paragraph 15–16.

the border posts, who had turned him down, he cited supernatural aid by holy wonderworkers.[80]

Recommendations from Greek religious authorities under Ottoman rule were used in particular cases. Some were uncommon, like that of Kostiantinov, who used the recommendation to confirm his story of suppression and enslavement by Turkish superiors. Even though by his early death he had only collected part of the sum of 700 roubles required, reliance on clerics and the Muscovite ransom institutions increased his interagency. The concept of agency has often been invoked in slavery studies.[81] However, in view of recent critique of this notion[82] I understand agency not merely in terms of more or less violent opposition or resistance, but rather as the chance to act within relations of asymmetrical dependency.[83] Therefore, agency is approached here using the concept of *inter*agency, which emphasizes that individual agency relies on relations to other actors.[84] When captives and slaves came up to the tsar or the patriarchs, they were still in a position of asymmetric dependency, which nonetheless increased their interagency. However, conversion to Islam might serve the same purpose, although it precluded the return option. As Polozov's use of the holy sites and Kostiantinov citing supernatural help confirms, such interagency might also rely on imagined and real relations to inanimate and symbolic objects.[85]

In the case of Petr Andreianov *syn* Tatarinov, it was his very high profile that exposed him to doubts. He submitted a petition in 1677 in which he claimed that he did not receive his rightful salary although he had been appointed two years earlier by Tsar Fedor's father Aleksei as translator in the Foreign Chancellery. His special services to Aleksei were made possible by his high-ranking position at the court in

---

80 See chapter 4.
81 E.P. Thompson, *The Making of the English Working Class* (New York, 1963); A. Gell, *Art and Agency: An Anthropological Theory* (Oxford, 2007); B. Latour, *Reassembling the Social: An Introduction to Actor-Network-Theory* (Oxford, 2005); K. Frank, 'Agency', *Anthropological Theory*, 6, 3 (2006), pp. 281–302; M. Holzinger, *Natur als sozialer Akteur: Realismus und Konstruktivismus in der Wissenschafts- und Gesellschaftstheorie* (Opladen, 2004).
82 J.D. Needell, 'The Abolition of the Brazilian Slave Trade in 1850: Historiography, Slave Agency and Statesmanship', *Journal of Latin American Studies*, 33, 4 (2001), pp. 681–711; W. Johnson, 'On Agency', *Journal of Social History*, 37, 1 (2003), pp. 113–124.
83 M. Machado, 'Slavery and Social Movements in Nineteenth-Century Brazil: Slave Strategies and Abolition in São Paulo', *Review (Fernand Braudel Center)*, 34, 1–2 (2011), pp. 163–191; S.B. Schwartz, 'Denounced by Lévi Strauss: CLAH Luncheon Address', *The Americas*, 59, 1 (2002), pp. 1–8.
84 V. Despret, 'From Secret Agents to Interagency', *History and Theory*, 52, 4 (2013), pp. 29–44; D.G. Shaw, 'The Torturer's Horse: Agency and Animals in History', *History and Theory*, 52, 4 (2013), pp. 146–167; J. Schiel, I. Schürch and A. Steinbrecher, 'Von Sklaven, Pferden und Hunden: Trialog über den Nutzen aktueller Agency-Debatten für die Sozialgeschichte', in C. Arni, M. Leimgruber and S. Teuscher, eds., *Neue Beiträge zur Sozialgeschichte/Nouvelles contributions à l'histoire sociale* (Zürich, 2017), pp. 17–48.
85 Latour, *Reassembling the Social*; D.J. Haraway, *The Companion Species Manifesto: Dogs, People, and Significant Otherness* (Chicago, 2003).

Istanbul, where he attended 'to foreign affairs in the proximity of the Turkish sultan and the vizier', as he put it. His main motive, to secure his salary two years after starting to work in the Chancellery and after the inauguration of the present tsar, is palpable in the petition where he quotes his regular income in Istanbul, 40 roubles per month plus 300 per annum. It serves the same purpose that he professes to Orthodox commandments in an even more elaborate way than others:

> I have served you and your father for more than twenty years and was taken captive [. . .] in 1660 at Chiudnovo [. . .] with [. . .] Vasilii B. Sheremetev [. . .] to Crimea and was sold to the Turkish lands. In captivity I tormented my body among the Hagar people for seventeen years.[86]

The category 'Sons of Hagar' was often used generically for Muslims; however, in many sources such as those about the conquest of Kazan and in the murals of the Palace of Facets they appear as slave traders. In the Palace of Facets they are shown to sell biblical Joseph to Egypt, long before Islam appeared. They were seen as the disowned but manumitted sons of Abraham's slave Hagar in a circular worldview that oscillates between owning slaves and being conquered.[87] Continuing from the point about his Istanbul salary, Tatarinov states:

> this was well known to the Holiest Ecumenical Patriarch and all Greeks and Your emissaries [in Istanbul]. I declared myself to the Patriarchs, remembering the holy and Orthodox Christian faith and your, o ruler, cross-kissing oath and my nature, not wishing to serve the Muslims and leaving behind my considerable possessions and everything, fully confirming all news and taking with me many letters from the sultan's foreign office. [The patriarchs] gave me advice and letters of recommendation which I took to Moscow in 1675 [. . .] and your father [. . .] [personally] interviewed me more than once about all these affairs [. . .] and I gave full evidence for all my claims [. . .][88]

Even in hindsight Tatarinov took pains to portray himself not only as outstandingly useful, but as someone who, appropriate to his status, knew well how to apply Orthodox precepts.

The account of his services is actually more detailed and refers to letters and strategic plans about hetman of the Zaporizhian Host Petro Doroshenko. After the partition of Ukraine in the Treaty of Andrusovo between Russia and Poland, Doroshenko became an Ottoman partisan during the Polish-Ottoman war in Ruthenia (1672–1676) and helped to extend Ottoman rule to the Dnipro. His policies caused discontent among the cossacks leading to the election of a counter hetman who

---

[86] RGADA f. 159 op. 2 d. 1732 l. 1.
[87] For details, see excurse 'Sons of Hagar' in chapter 6. Clarence-Smith, *Islam and the Abolition of Slavery*, p. 24. A. Kazhdan, 'The Concept of Freedom (*eleutheria*) and Slavery (*duleia*) in Byzantium', in G. Makdisi, ed., *La notion de liberté au Moyen Age Islam, Byzance, Occident* (Paris, 1985), pp. 215–226, here pp. 218–219; Hellie, *Slavery in Russia, 1450–1725*, pp. 73–74. On the cyclical view of enslavement, liberation and domination: Tikhomirov, *Vologodsko-permskii letopisets*, p. 271.
[88] RGADA f. 159 op. 2 d. 1732 l. 1.

sought support in Muscovy. Doroshenko was captured by Muscovite forces in 1676 when they took his capital Chyhyryn.[89]

Tatarinov confidently highlighted tsar Aleksei's endorsement of his loyalty:

> I gave him the clearest evidence about all my declarations since I was privy to the sultan's and vizier's very secrets, and he the great ruler, seeing my truthful service to you, o great ruler, with his own holy mouth declared that my services do not fail, and granted me gentry status on the Moscow list [. . .][90]

Archival research confirmed his claims. He had been granted a grain income of 2256 quarters.

One detail carefully omitted by Tatarinov in his petition for remuneration has great significance for the conditions for elite slaves in the Ottoman Empire, and for his choice to return. As in the cases of some other slave-returnees, his master, the Sultan's Greek translator Panagiotis, had died before his return. Tatarinov had served as Panagiotis' chamberlain and was privy to all military and foreign affairs.[91] Panagiotis Nikosias Mamonas was a Greek from Chios who had studied medicine in Padova, the first to be named *başterkümân* or Grand Dragoman in 1669, the highest rank of translator and interpreter at the Sublime Porte. He had shown his utility to the Ottoman dynasty during successful negotiations at the end of the Cretan war.[92] Starting with Panagiotis, the Grand Dragoman's tasks were at least potentially political, and they had a direct bearing on diplomacy, as the Ottoman dynasts avoided the use of languages other than Turkish and those holy to Islam.[93] Together, the Tatar convert – or descendant of a convert – to Russian Orthodoxy and the Greek educated at an Italian university covered wide areas relevant to the high office of translation and diplomacy.

The translations of the patriarchs' letters confirmed Tatarinov's points and his devotion to Orthodoxy and the tsar. As a loyal Orthodox believer, he had signally helped in law cases 'unjustly' imputing the patriarch of Alexandria, Paisii.[94] The death of Tatarinov's master left him without patronage, the only resource on which

---

[89] H. İnalcık and S. Faroqhi, eds., *An Economic and Social History of the Ottoman Empire* (Cambridge, 2004), p. 428; Davies, 'The Second Chigirin Campaign (1678)'.
[90] Ibid.
[91] RGADA f. 159 op. 2 d. 1732 l. 2.
[92] G. Veinstein, 'L'administration ottomane et le problème des interprètes', in B. Marino, ed., *Études sur les villes du Proche-Orient XVIe–XIXe siècles: Hommage à André Raymond* (Damascus, 2001), pp. 65–79, here p. 66.
[93] B. Lewis, *From Babel to Dragomans: Interpreting the Middle East* (New York, 2004), p. 25; J. Ulbert and G. Le Bouëdec, '"Les drogmans des consulats", la fonction consulaire à l'époque moderne: L'affirmation d'une institution économique et politique (1500–1800)', in A. Gautier and M. de Testa, eds., *Drogmans, diplomates et ressortissants européens auprès de la porte ottomane* (Istanbul, 2013), pp. 13–30, here pp. 19–21; J. Matuz, 'Die Pfortendolmetscher zur Herrschaftszeit Süleymans des Prächtigen', *Südost-Forschungen*, 34 (1975), pp. 26–60, here pp. 27–41.
[94] RGADA f. 159 op. 2 d. 1732 l. 3.

to count in court intrigues as well as in Ottoman society at large. Enslavement had cut the social ties with which he had grown up. They had been re-attached to the new entity, Panagiot's household which commanded his entire loyalty, thereby extending its social, political and economic capabilities.[95] Unlike earlier translators at the Sublime Porte during the reign of Suleyman the Magnificent, Panagiot's elevated role at court and in diplomacy rendered conversion unnecessary, so he and his slave remained Orthodox.[96] However, this tied the former slave Tatarinov upon his manumission even more closely to the patronage relationship to his late master. His choice to return to Muscovy was therefore not only, as he stated, due to his unfaltering loyalty, but also conditioned by drastic changes in his life. Not all the evidence of loyalty was evoked only after the fact; as the patriarchs' recommendations imply, he did indeed entertain at least a working relation with several of the patriarchs, providing for all contingencies. Moreover, he seems to have lived the life of a proper Orthodox Christian throughout.

The intricately interwoven lives of captives and residents of the Ottoman Empire are further illustrated by the story of one 'khadzhi Ivanov', who first appeared in Moscow in 1686. Mikhail Ivanov, a Christian Arab from Jerusalem, showed letters of recommendation from the patriarchs to collect ransom money for his family, as some foreigners attempted, who were attracted by the tsar's generosity to captives. He explained that a Greek who had moved to Jerusalem had manumitted a female slave from Muscovy upon his death. The woman decided to stay and converted, whereupon the pasha demanded her two sons from their Orthodox teacher, Ivanov's brother Georgii. Conflicts within the family may be inferred, although the sources are silent on this aspect. It is possible that this lessened Ivanov's appeal in the eyes of Muscovites.[97]

The teacher resolved to save them for Christianity and had them tonsured, for which he incurred a fine of 500 Leeuwendaalder. He could only pay 300 up front and had to pawn his family. To find the ransom, he travelled first to Astrakhan, received another recommendation from the local metropolitan and some money which allowed him to go on to Moscow. At the chancellery, he received 50 roubles compensation and a *zbornaia pamiat*, a document which allowed him to collect further alms for ransom.

---

95 Toledano, 'Enslavement in the Ottoman Empire in the Early Modern Period', pp. 34–38. See M. Kunt, 'Ethnic-Regional (Cins) Solidarity in the Seventeenth-Century Ottoman Establishment', *International Journal of Middle East Studies*, 5, 3 (1974), pp. 233–239, here pp. 237–238; Wilkins, 'A Demographic Profile of Slaves in Early Ottoman Aleppo'.
96 Matuz, 'Die Pfortendolmetscher zur Herrschaftszeit Süleymans des Prächtigen'.
97 For more detail on these family conflicts and reasons for conversion of the former slave: C. Witzenrath, 'Negotiating Early Modern Transottoman Slaving Zones: An Arab in Moscow', in E. Toledano and S. Conermann, eds., *What is Global about Global Enslavement? Crossing Time-Space Divides*, Tel Aviv, forthcoming 2022.

However, one year later he reappeared, claiming that he had lived in poverty, bought only one caftan for himself and sent the entire sum he had received to Jerusalem with the emissary of the patriarch. Scarcely more than another 47 roubles in alms had been given to him, and now, he said, his wife had died in captivity and his house taken by the Turks. He asked to be accepted into the service of the tsar. The chancellery checked for comparable cases but obviously mistrusted Ivanov. It merely paid him three roubles and, this time, banned him from Moscow.[98] A good, heart-warming story of embattled Orthodoxy competently told and the right recommendations from clerics could go far in ransom affairs of foreigners in Moscow. Nevertheless, there was already an abundance of ransom seekers in Moscow. Doubts about the loyalty of foreigners were quickly at hand, especially if they seemed contradictory and appeared of little use. Eligibility for ransom, therefore, was not stable with respect to both ethnic background and faith. As intersectional approaches underline, several status markers interacted to determine the actual position of a person.[99]

Conclusion

Returning captives in any but the lowest ranks needed to demonstrate loyalty according to their capabilities. Ransom compensation and restoration to former ranks depended on such demonstrations. Whereas early modern and modern statements of loyalty usually only had consequences for one's position in the community, they had direct, palpable and essential meaning for former slaves returning to Muscovy.[100]

Returning slaves relied on loyalty as an institution that seemingly transcended time, space, and social and cultural differences of Muscovy and the society in which they had been captives. Recent sociological approaches to institutional analysis highlight that institutions are mechanisms consisting of concepts, patterns of behaviour and symbolic representations of their aims. This can be conveyed in any institutionally regulated action, in words, gestures and material signs. What usually, even in scientific vocabulary, is called an institution is on closer examination an organization or a form of interaction, in which the visibility of its order is put centre-stage: a church, state, family and kinship, educational establishments, sometimes also large-scale enterprises.[101]

---

98 RGADA f. 159 d. 3248, 1686 noiabr, ll. 1–8; ibid., d. 3470 7 oktiabria–28 dekabria 1687, ll. 1–13.
99 M. Bähr and F. Kühnel, eds., *Verschränkte Ungleichheit: Praktiken der Intersektionalität in der Frühen Neuzeit* (Berlin, 2018); A. Griesebner and S. Hehenberger, 'Intersektionalität: Ein brauchbares Konzept für die Geschichtswissenschaften?', in V. Kallenberg, J. Meyer and J.M. Müller, eds., *Intersectionality und Kritik: Neue Perspektiven für alte Fragen* (Wiesbaden, 2013), pp. 105–124.
100 Cf. Schulze Wessel, '"Loyalität" als geschichtlicher Grundbegriff und Forschungskonzept', p. 11.
101 K.-S. Rehberg, 'Institutionenwandel und Funktionsveränderung des Symbolischen', in G. Göhler, ed., *Institutionenwandel* (Opladen, 1997), pp. 94–118.

It is true that organizations cannot exist without institutional mechanisms. However, institutional mechanisms can exist without organizations; for example in the etiquette governing letter-writing, the socially elaborated norms and symbols of romantic love or heightened forms of friendship. On the other hand, to codify and make even these norms controllable by specialists, an organization can be established, as in the eighteenth-century German 'friendship alliances' (Freundschaftsbünde). The same was true for the Muscovite chancelleries controlling the norms of loyalty. Thus an institutional mechanism can be sustained as mere conventions, requiring a social base but not a permanent organization.[102]

Loyalty for captives was just that – conventions that could only be claimed and controlled in hindsight, in the Moscow chancelleries. Returnees had to polish their convoluted lives according to Moscow's requirements. In most cases, this meant omitting any dubious details, for which there could be many occasions. In a way, the motivation to return could be sufficient proof of loyalty in itself, since the cosmopolitan Ottoman Empire was hugely attractive to most captives, and upward social mobility strongly developed among slaves, although not without certain pitfalls. In particular the loss of patronage due to the death of an owner could be a strong spur to return to Muscovy. Moreover, some slaves were – despite contrary customary expectations – persistently sold on without manumission and they often had to carry out menial duties. Galley slaves also often wished to return to Muscovy, since they had little perspective in the Ottoman Empire and many were military men who returned to their previous service. Their principal way of proving their loyalty was therefore to recite their services to the tsar and explain how they had succumbed to captivity. These were the two main characteristics checked by the chancellery who decided about reinstatement, compensation and, in a few cases, promotion for having undergone captivity.

Captives aimed to demonstrate their persisting adherence to Orthodoxy during captivity, either in thought or in deed, in order to stress their loyalty to the tsar. Those who occupied relatively high positions in the Muscovite service hierarchy – even more so if they had served in exalted position in Istanbul – and especially educated persons had to elaborate on religion and the Orthodox view of the duties of proper captives, however low in this regard their profile was allowed to have been during captivity. Various expressions of religious credentials fell in line with or at least alluded to Russian Orthodox and general Orthodox theories of how captives should behave. This trend peaked during the reign of Fedor Alekseevich, but such

---

102 G. Göhler, 'Wie verändern sich Institutionen?', in G. Göhler, ed., *Institutionenwandel* (Opladen, 1997), pp. 21–56; E. Stölting, 'Wandel und Kontinuität der Institutionen: Rußland – Sowjetunion – Rußland', in G. Göhler, ed., *Institutionenwandel* (Opladen, 1997), pp. 181–203; H. Duchhardt and G. Melville, eds., *Im Spannungsfeld von Recht und Ritual* (Köln, 1997); B. Schimmelpfennig, 'Das Papsttum im Mittelalter: Eine Institution?', in G. Melville, ed., *Institutionen und Geschichte: Theoretische Aspekte und mittelalterliche Befunde* (Köln, 1992), pp. 209–229. For a summary of institutionality: Witzenrath, *Cossacks and the Russian Empire, 1598–1725*, 'Introduction'.

dispositions may be spotted throughout the Muscovite period. From at least the reign of Ivan IV, the obligation of the tsar to ransom all Orthodox believers and especially his military servitors had become a major aspect of reciprocity in relations with loyal subjects; the *Ulozhenie* of 1649 codified this in secular, dual[103] law, but in religious terms copied from the Hundred Chapters Synod (1551).[104] So reciprocity and a sense of entitlement based on proven loyalty were much more important elements in the relation between tsar and loyal subjects than admitted in accounts that take autocracy as a form of government at face value, and which depict the tsar as ruling unrestrictedly and tyrannically; however, Muscovy was chronically under-governed, or lightly governed.[105]

This did not mean that returnees entered a balanced relation of mutual dependency. They were entitled to tax exemption and liberated from the obligation to stay with their fellow local tax payers.[106] Nevertheless, the local context was the most frequently stressed aspect in their petitions. Contact to the central chancelleries was a special opportunity to forge new alliances for life. In terms of interagency, this meant more social relations and a decreased dependency on one form, the local context. Yet since these relations radiated like the spokes of a wheel into the depths of the empire, each returnee increased the tsar's interagency and therefore overall dependency in the population on the person with most social relations in the counter dependency zone.

Some slaves purposely kept all options open, or lived in conditions which allowed them to adhere to an Orthodox way of life. Overall, most stayed in the Ottoman Empire after manumission, although their precise motivations are difficult to gauge due to many overlapping motivations, and the daunting obstacles to a safe return and to making a living. The institutional mechanism of loyalty to the tsar afforded additional options for interagency to them, even as it lay dormant. However, some discovered that their means of life in Muscovy had been acquired by others and their relatives or spouses no longer cared.

---

103 A boyar commission codified the *Ulozhenie* reacting to the great Moscow rebellion of 1648–9 and included basics of chancellery law, rules set autonomously in the chancelleries: Schmidt, *Sozialkontrolle in Moskau*; Brown, 'How Muscovy Governed'.
104 Hecker, 'Die Christenpflicht als Rechtsnorm'.
105 Frost, *The Northern Wars*, p. 10. Kollmann, *The Russian Empire 1450–1801*, p. 160.
106 Hellie, *The Muscovite Law Code (Ulozhenie) of 1649*, 159, art. 33, 172, art. 34.

Chapter 6
Slavery and Empire

The preceding chapters showed representations of slavery and liberation in political culture, and the ways in which Muscovites interacted with them. During the middle Muscovite period, such representations increasingly shaped the worldview of wider sections of the population. The Orthodox religious imagery inherent in these ideas of liberation might indicate that their scope was limited to Orthodoxy, in which the Christian flock closed in on itself, closed ranks against dangerous external slavers, excluded nomads and Muslims. However, this was not what happened. Muscovy employed large numbers of mounted Tatar warriors in its armies, and the conquest of Kazan would not have been feasible without the active participation of Tatar princes of the first rank, and many Tatar warriors serving the Muscovite tsar.[1] Muscovy depended heavily on Tatar military and leadership during some of its wars.[2] Some Tatars achieved high status, and many were able to redeem themselves through service and retained some of their status over several generations during the century after the conquest. Although they lost some land to monasteries and Russian landowners in the middle Volga region, and often found themselves moved to the new Arzamas steppe fortress line in the south, most towns remained predominantly Tatar, or Chuvash, or Mari or, in any case, non-Russian in ethnic terms.[3] Moreover, the very activities associated with ransoming demanded the involvement of Tatars. They communicated throughout inner Eurasia in their own language in a context foreign to Orthodox Muscovites, in order to find captives and slaves and negotiate with their masters. This chapter will, on the one hand, trace this socio-cultural context of ransoming and liberation from captivity, and on the other, investigate the symbolical means of communicating across cultural and religious boundaries for the sake of ransoming and empire-building. The question is whether and by what means such practices and ideologies contributed to the power of Muscovy's rulers.

The increasing focus on the religious dimension in Muscovite political language has just begun to make early attempts to formulate policies and symbolical strategies of empire accessible to researchers.[4] Writers in the 1960s preferred national

---

[1] P. Gonneau, 'Guerre et chevalerie au pays des Tatars: L'or, les esclaves, les femmes et les paladins dans "l'Histoire de Kazan"', *Russian History*, 42, 1 (2015), pp. 49–63.
[2] Martin, 'Tatars in the Muscovite Army during the Livonian War'.
[3] Romaniello, *The Elusive Empire*, pp. 117–205.
[4] Kollmann, *The Russian Empire 1450–1801*. There is still a prevailing tendency to exclude Muscovy from accounts of imperial ideologies: Semyonov, 'How Five Empires Shaped the World and How this Process Shaped those Empires'. Semyonov and Kumar have raised awareness of the central place of imperial ideologies in empires' functions: Kumar, *Visions of Empire*. See chapter 1 for discussion of these topics.

interpretations, which, however, were severely criticized and do not fit the period, which was marked by the growth and takeover of empire.[5] They emphasized the inability of Muscovites to communicate their ideas of unconditional, permanent allegiance to a steppe environment that seemed to adhere to diametrically opposed ideas, i.e. conditional, ephemeral alliances.[6] However, Muscovy was part of this cultural environment of the steppe and Eurasia as much as it was part of Europe or the post-Byzantine area of cultural influence; in fact, the Byzantine Empire itself had participated in the wider steppe environment, hybridising its own institutions.[7] The growing Muscovite empire needed a language which allowed it to distinguish between supporters and foes regardless of their cultural and ethnic background, and to tie them to their promises.[8] This was particularly true for the chasm between Orthodoxy and Islam, as maintained and perceived mainly by the claim to exclusive truth on the part of clerics and religions.[9] This claim was important to establish, organise and perpetuate the counter dependency zone, which relied on religious props to bolster political will for implementing its rules.[10]

For centuries, Muscovy had sustained relations with the Muslim south and east; during the Time of Troubles of the early seventeenth century, the middle Volga Tatars, conquered half a century ago, already supported Moscow by its own standards.[11] When Muscovy increasingly came to rely on Tatar cavalry, and dominated whole Muslim societies, an integrative language of empire was in demand that 'provided telos and coherence to the imperial polity and [. . .] made sense of relations in imperial space'.[12]

This chapter investigates how Muscovite writers and artists in literary and documentary sources reached out to the new, heterodox subjects of the tsar. Sources range from individual petitions, chronicles and murals to stories about saints and comments on religious abstractions included in central cultural texts and representative murals. Muscovite criteria for inclusion or at least association and alliance were framed in terms of slavery, ransom and liberation.

---

5 Imperial ideology was exclusively seen as justifying the takeover of one nation of the territory of another: Pelenski, *Russia and Kazan*; Kämpfer, *Die Eroberung von Kasan 1552 als Gegenstand der zeitgenössischen russischen Historiographie.*
6 Keenan, 'Muscovy and Kazan".
7 Ostrowski, *Muscovy and the Mongols*; Neumann and Wigen, *The Steppe Tradition in International Relations.*
8 Khodarkovsky, *Russia's Steppe Frontier*; Rakhimzianov, *Moskva i tatarskii mir.*
9 Ostrowski, 'The Mongols and Rus".
10 See chapter 1.
11 Romaniello, *The Elusive Empire.*
12 Semyonov, 'How Five Empires Shaped the World and How this Process Shaped those Empires', p. 47.

Intermediaries

In the late fifteenth and sixteenth centuries, the largest group of Muslims within Muscovy and the city of Moscow were Tatars. From various local extractions, their ancestors had either lived in Moscow for centuries, or they had come from Kazan, Crimea, Astrakhan and Siberia; some were Nogai. They served in the grand princes' and tsars' armies or as interpreters, translators and mediators in negotiations with eastern and southern neighbours. The influx was considerable: at the turn of the seventeenth century, about 60 Chinggisid princes lived within Muscovy's confines; including kin and retainers, their number reached the thousands.[13] Interpreters were instrumental to the tsar in ransoming slaves; some at least made a conscious show of loyalty. In 1633, the Tatar interpreter Mustofa Tevkelev accompanied the tsar's envoys Afonasei Pronchishchev and Tikhon Bormosov to Istanbul. The vizier Azdem Magmed offered him a position in the sultan's services and reproved him for helping the enemies of the believers. Tevkelev turned down the offer:

> [I]n Tsargrad [Istanbul] [. . .] the vizier Azdem Magmed pasha told him, the interpreter Mustofa, many times that they were of the same faith and that he should leave the tsar to serve the sultan. He promised him a large salary and great honour just like it was granted to himself, the vizier [. . .] The interpreter Mustofa did not agree in any way and told the vizier [. . .] that he was truly the eternal natural servant (*kholop*) of his Lord the Tsar's Highness as did his grandfather and father and all his kin and clan faithfully and truly without betrayal.[14]

In the words of the envoys, Tevkelev proudly answered the 'very astonished' vizier's questions about why there were '1060' Muslim Tatars serving the tsar:

> There is no obstruction to their faith, they receive generous salary, plots of land and daily upkeep from His Highness the Tsar, and in their Muslim law they live according to their own determination and there is no pressure to convert.[15]

This experience was not shared by all Tatars and Muslims in Muscovy – particularly those who lived in Muscovite households as slaves found it difficult to retain their

---

13 J. Martin, 'Religious Ideology and Chronicle Depictions of Muslims in 16th-Century Muscovy', in V. Kivelson, M. Flier, N.S. Kollmann and K. Petrone, eds., *The New Muscovite Cultural History: A Collection in Honor of Daniel B. Rowland* (Bloomington IN, 2009), pp. 285–299, here pp. 290–292; Ostrowski. *Muscovy and the Mongols*, p. 56; D.G. Ostrowski, 'Troop Mobilization by the Muscovite Grand Princes (1313–1533)', in E. Lohr and M. Poe, eds., *The Military and Society in Russia, 1450–1917* (Leiden, 2002), pp. 19–40, here pp. 38–39; A.L. Khoroshkevich, *Rus' i Krym: Ot soiuza k protivostoianiiu: Konets XV–nachalo XVI vv.* (Moskva, 2001), pp. 297–307.
14 RGADA f. 159 op. 2 No. 453, ll. 114–115.
15 RGADA f. 159 op. 2 No. 453, ll. 105–116.

faith.[16] Nevertheless, until the 1680s it conforms to the general pattern of tolerance, or simply ignorance and generosity towards those of other faiths, despite an Orthodox fear of contamination by 'impure food'.[17] The Tevkelevs indeed went on to serve as interpreters throughout the seventeenth century.[18]

At the same time, Tatars were among the main political enemies of Muscovy. Until the early sixteenth century, the adversary was the Great *Ulus*, or Great Horde, along the northern shores of the Caspian Sea. When Muscovy became more powerful and the Great *Ulus* declined, alliances changed and from 1521 on a former ally, the Crimean Tatar khanate, became Moscow's main enemy in the south and east, trying to limit the scope of Muscovite power and influence in Eurasia.[19]

To distinguish between friends and foes was complicated, especially in terms of recognition on a symbolic level in a multi-faith environment. Which set of values would prevail? How best to have connections with another ruler without compromising one's allegiance to the tsar? Such decisions were influenced not only by considerations of kinship, tradition, and material benefits, but also by bridges built between culturally coded discourses and deliberate attempts to gain moral capital. How to represent a Muslim Tatar in a chronicle entry, a court sentence, a report, or a petition? In keeping with the role of interpreters in ransoming negotiations, Tevkelev went as far as appropriating the Orthodox Christian martyr's topos:[20]

> [His kin] lay down their heads for his Tsar's Highness. He, Mustofa, wants to serve his Highness the Tsar with all of his life and does not want to become a traitor because he already receives a large amount of salary and needs no more.[21]

So Tevkelev used an image trans-confessionally denoting commitment to the cause of liberating captives, 'laying down one's soul [head]', to signify his loyalty and faithful service, which was being compromised by the constant offers of a position in Istanbul.

---

16 Nolte, 'Iasyry'; D.Z. Khairetdinov and D.V. Mukhetdinov, eds., *Islam v Moskve: Entsiklopedicheskii slovar'* (Nizhnii Novgorod, 2008). Cf. the mixed experiences of the Kazan Tatars: Romaniello, *The Elusive Empire*.
17 Kappeler, *The Russian Empire*; D.Z. Khairetdinov, *Musul'manskaia obshchina Moskvy v XIV – nachale XX veka* (Nizhnii Novgorod, 2002); L.I. Rozenberg, 'Tatary v Moskve XVII-serediny XIX vekov', in I.I. Krupnik, ed., *Etnicheskie gruppy v gorodakh evropeiskoi chasti SSSR: Formirovanie, rasselenie, dinamika kul'tury* (Moskva, 1987), pp. 16–26; H.-H. Nolte, *Religiöse Toleranz in Rußland: 1600–1725* (PhD dissertation, University of Göttingen, 1969).
18 Entry: 'Tevkelev' in Khairetdinov and Mukhetdinov, *Islam v Moskve*.
19 Arens and Klein, 'Das frühneuzeitliche Krimkhanat zwischen Orient und Okzident'; D. Klein, ed., *The Crimean Khanate between East and West (15th–18th century)* (Wiesbaden, 2012); V. Ostapchuk, 'Long-Range Campaigns of the Crimean Khanate in the Mid-Sixteenth Century', *Journal of Turkish Studies*, 29 (2004), pp. 75–99.
20 First in the *Letter to the Ugra*, discussed in chapter 2.
21 RGADA 159 op. 2 No. 453, ll. 114–115.

This and similar dispositions add a peculiar twist to the way the treatment of Tatars living within the borders of Muscovy is categorized. While earlier historians maintained that in the chronicles, if not in the chancelleries and normal life, Tatars were treated as enemies, recent contributors detect Tatars whose immense contributions to Muscovite campaigns and administration could not be ignored even by monks. During the first two centuries after the Mongols established their empire, the Russian Orthodox Church had maintained a positive view of Tatars, as the Mongol and Byzantine Empires were allies and the Church enjoyed privileges under the Mongol emperors. From the mid-fifteenth century, this view of the Tatars changed. Crimean ports and the northern shore of the Black Sea had been conquered by the Ottomans by the 1470s, the post-Mongolian order slowly disintegrated, and slave raids and the slave trade resurged. Chroniclers turned to negative rhetoric, using terms like 'impious and dishonourable (*nechestivyi*)',[22] 'oath-breaking',[23] or 'accursed Sons of Hagar'[24] for Moscow's political enemies,[25] whom they depicted as slavers.

In later Muscovy, most chronicles did not mention Tatars in Muscovite service at all, except very briefly in cases when their contribution was essential for a particular event. More extensive accounts were devoted to those who converted to Christianity.[26] Beyond these two main ways of depicting Tatars, Janet Martin noticed only one case that the chronicles up to the late sixteenth century reported in detail: the Chinggisid prince Shah Ali was extraordinarily important for Ivan IV's campaigns, especially the conquest of Kazan. Twice khan of Kazan and at Kasimov in Russian territory, he had served the tsar throughout his life.[27] However, none of the two approaches above apply to him: he was no Muslim convert. His career was described in detail for the first time in the 'Chronicle of the Beginning of Tsardom' – and then in all subsequent chronicles.[28] As mentioned above, this chronicle was written outside the usual monastic environment, in the chancelleries. It is therefore much closer to depictions of Tatars in documentary sources, as Tevkelev. J. Martin sums up:

> The chroniclers of "Letopisets nachala tsarstva" and "Tsarstvennaia kniga" thus offered a third option for reconciling the profundity of Orthodox ideology with the reality of Muslims functioning in influential roles in Muscovy. They portrayed Shah Ali as absolutely contrite, dependent, and subservient in relation to the grand prince. They thus articulated the characteristics and qualities

---

22 Discussed below.
23 See chapter 2.
24 See below.
25 Martin, 'Religious Ideology and Chronicle Depictions of Muslims in 16th-Century Muscovy'.
26 Ostrowski, 'The Mongols and Rus'"; cf. Janet Martin above.
27 See chapter 2. The debate on the status of Kasimov is summarized in D.M. Iskhakov, *Tiurko-tatarskie gosudarstva XV–XVI vv.* (Kazan', 2004) and B.R. Rakhimzyanov, 'The Debatable Questions of the Early Kasimov Khanate (1437–1462), *Russian History* 37, 2 (2010), pp. 83–101.
28 Martin, 'Religious Ideology and Chronicle Depictions of Muslims in 16th-Century Muscovy', pp. 287–289, 292–299.

that would make a Muslim Tatar acceptable or tolerable in Muscovy. A Muslim Tatar would have to be, like Shah Ali, loyal, obedient, and subservient.[29]

However, this image of single-minded obedience is challenged to a considerable degree during a decisive, almost cathartic moment in the 'Chronicle's' story about the conquest of Kazan: when Shah Ali, who had been banned by the previous tsar and forgiven by Ivan IV, is within an inch of losing the tsar's favour once again.[30] These two episodes are closely related, as both are motivated by campaign needs that are legitimised by the liberation of Muscovite slaves from Kazan. In the second episode, during Shah Ali's second reign as khan of Kazan, he and Ivan's representative in the city, prince Dmitrii Fedorovich, discuss honour and heterodox allegiance. While Tevkelev's statement is linked to honour as faithful service and, because of his office, to ransom, Shah Ali was confronted directly with the tsar's obligation to liberate the slaves held, as Moscow claimed, in Kazan:

> "You [Shah Ali] know yourself how much dishonour (*bezchestie*) and losses our tsar suffered from Kazan. Even now they keep Christian captives and lie about their oaths; even many Kasimov Tatars [subjects of the tsar; C.W.], who arrived with you, keep unwilling (*nevolnye*) Christian captives, as you know. In future, Kazanians will behave just like that. How do you reckon our Lord will endure this, seeing Christianity enslaved? When you, Lord, were enthroned in Kazan by the boyar of the grand prince, prince Iurii Golitsyn, the whole land [Kazan Tatars] swore an oath that they will deliver all captives, yet they have not released even one. The [tsar] must stand in for his Christianity, as God may help him. Lord, if the [tsar] does not defend (*stati* [. . .] *za*) the captives, then our [tsar] must answer to God for them.

The khan rejoined:

> If you don't return the mountainous [right] bank [of the Volga; which Ivan IV had held on to after occupation in 1551], how can I live in Kazan facing their hostility. I will have to flee to the tsar and grand prince.

Prince Dmitrii replied: 'If you flee to the [tsar], strengthen the city with Russian [soldiers]'.

They exchanged further arguments. Then the khan said:

> I am a Muslim, I do not want to abandon [*stati na*, literally: rise against] my faith, but I also do not want to be disloyal to my Lord the Tsar and Grand Prince. There is nowhere to go from here, so I will head to the tsar and grand prince. Give me, prince Dmitrii, whatever can be spared as an addition to my allowance Kasimov, so the Grand Prince will not lose me. I will hang the traitors [in Kazan] and make the canons and harquebus unusable. Then, the lord [Ivan IV] may arrive himself and decide about their betrayal whatever he may with God's help. Yet I cannot let Russians into town'.

The khan swore an oath according to his faith about his promise.[31]

---

29 Ibid., p. 298.
30 Ibid., pp. 295, 297–298.
31 Four preceding citations: Tikhomirov, *Letopisets nachala tsarstva*, p. 69.

The khan repeats the term '*stati*', adding '*na veru* (apostasy)' which delineates the dilemma he faces between his two allegiances. During this crisis described at length in both the 'Chronicle' and the 'History of Kazan', Shah Ali's loyalty to the tsar and responsibility for slaves finally won out. If the khan cannot be described as directly and morally responsible for the liberation of Orthodox and Muscovite slaves, he was still bound to this endeavour by allegiance to the tsar and the oath of the Kazanians. Shah Ali is won back to the side of the tsar by the tsar's unwavering care for the slaves, which is presented as an issue on which no compromise is possible.

Nevertheless, Shah Ali appears as a man of integrity and honour in every respect, which includes his faith: he declines to let Muscovite troops into the city. He only agrees to mete out justice to the traitors and to render useless the guns that have been appropriated from the Muscovites – which he deems acceptable for a Muslim ruler and befitting his loyalty to the tsar. In the conception of the 'Chronicle', the two-sided loyalty of the Orthodox tsar's heterodox supporter to, on the one hand, his fellow believers and, on the other, to the tsar, links the imperial effort to build a multi-faith state and the overarching Orthodox obligation to redeem slaves, which motivates the formation of empire.

Honour and empire

As the above episode about Shah Ali indicates, honour is one of the most discussed notions in Muscovite sources in general.[32] This is particularly true with regard to Muslim Tatars. Dishonourable (*nechestivye*) – and 'peaceless' – Tatars mostly lived outside the realm, and they raided it for slaves or were otherwise unreliable. Since '*nechestivyi*' is used without much qualification for heterodox outsiders, it is often translated as 'impious' according to the model of '*blagochestivyi*', a direct translation from the Greek for 'pious', as in 'pious tsar'. '*Blago-*' enhances the positive impression of a term. Moreover, impiety implies outsider status if it is not mitigated by some other qualification. According to the requirements of redemption discussed in chapter three, the pious were to be ransomed and liberated and the impious, the heathen outsiders, to be enslaved. A reason for ignoring central tenets of Islam, therefore, was to mark Muslim slavers as outsiders eligible for enslavement.

The common root of these terms, which also occurs in '*bezchestie* (dishonour, shame)', is '*chest*' (honour)'. In pre-Muscovite times, '*chest*'' either expressed clerical godliness or military glory.[33] Fifteenth-century law codes applied '*chest*'' to matters of reputation. The piety and honour of the tsar are ambiguously related to liberating slaves and captives:

---

32 Kollmann, *By Honor Bound*.
33 Ibid., pp. 33–34, 36.

> The pious (*blagochestivaia*) soul of our highly honourable (*blagochestivyi*) Tsar, chosen by God, could not bear these tribulations of Christianity in captivity, and he said to himself: "Merciful God [!] [. . .] I was put before these Orthodox lands and all people as tsar and shepherd, leader and ruler, to rule these people steadfastly according to Orthodoxy, guard them from all ills and all hardships. Lord, help me and redeem (*izbavi*) your captured slaves (*plennykh rab*) from the heathens. For he is truly a good shepherd who gives his soul for [his] sheep".[34]

Both the honour and the piety of the tsar are characterised in terms of the liberation of slaves in the triumphal entry into Moscow in 1552:

> Countless people stood along both sides of the roads meeting the Lord, from the river Iauza to town and within the Kremlin, young and old shouted loudly, and there was nothing to be heard but "Many years to the pious and honourable (*blagochestivomu*) tsar, victorious over the barbarians and liberator of Christians".[35]

The dynasty's piety and honour are addressed in the 'Book of Degrees' in the account of how the pagan slave raider, grand prince Vladimir of Kyiv was to be saved for a Christian afterlife by his future wife, the sister of the emperor of Constantinople. This account was interpolated into older versions of the text in the 1560s.[36] When Vladimir first announced his intention to be baptized and marry Anna in 988, the emperor's sister was taken aback, since she was 'pious and sensible':

> It is better for me to die here [in Constantinople] a spinster, rather than to rule in heathen lands with an unbeliever (*nevernyi*) spouse.[37]

The emperor convinced her 'in a long and consoling speech' to marry Vladimir and live among his pagan subjects to save the Greeks from Rus' slave raids. It was all a matter of living piously and doing the right, honourable deed to help save Greek slaves from the clutches of godless, barbarians as the double linchpin of tsardom, or empire:

> Take heed, our esteemed sister, since if today you save your impious and dishonourable (*nechestivyi*) husband, God will convert the Rus' land to Orthodoxy. This will liberate the Greek land from [. . .] merciless slave raids [. . .] Look, sister, the evil done to the Greeks by Rus', [. . .] how many are sold into slavery.[38]

---

34 Tikhomirov, *Letopisets nachala tsarstva*, pp. 59–60.
35 Ibid., p. 112.
36 On this and further interpolations, cf. chapter 3. Butler, *Enlightener of Rus'*, pp. 92–100.
37 Pokrovskii and Lenhoff, *Stepennaia kniga tsarskogo rodosloviia po drevneishim spiskam*, p. 275. 'Heathen' and 'unbeliever' are terms often used in Scandinavian sagas and chronicles since the fourteenth century for the king's enemies, among them Rus' and Finns said to have 'captured women and children and pillaged' at a time of Swedish-Rus' competition: S. Jakobsson, 'The Schism that Never Was: Old Norse Views on Byzantium and Russia', Byzantinoslavica, 66, 1–2 (2008), pp. 173–188, here pp. 185–186.
38 Ibid., pp. 275–276.

As a model of Orthodoxy for captives taken from the budding Muscovite multi-faith empire of the sixteenth century, the emperor thus expresses the view that Orthodox people can live piously in a marriage with a recently converted person, if it will save Christians from enslavement. Her husband Vladimir, the future Orthodox grand prince, appears as a model for Tatars to emulate, or as a standard for acceptable, honourable, loyal and heterodox outsiders.

Although Russian Orthodox sensibilities did not allow for a direct declaration in the clerically inspired 'Book of Royal Degrees' that Vladimir and Anna could be seen as Orthodox reinterpretations of the Tatar and Central Asian Muslim role models Joseph and Zulaykha, the parallels and influences of these conversion-cum-captive stories are hard to miss.[39] The text contains subtle hints, at least for readers who knew Joseph and Zulaykha: the interpolations in the following episode highlight the similarities between the bones of St Clement brought from Kherson to Kyiv by Vladimir and the remains of Joseph carried by the Israelites as they left slavery in Egypt. Just to underscore the message, liberation from slavery and the New Israel are mentioned.[40]

Two inversions of gender roles as a mark of the Muscovite imperial style are notable, first, in the Christ-like redeeming posture of Anna, who ransoms Kherson and Constantinople by offering up herself. It is another take on the recurring theme of ambiguous redemption in the afterlife and this world, derived from the language of the slave market.

Second, Anna is the captive who converts her heathen captor-husband Vladimir, whereas in the Muslim variants of the Joseph story, the husband of the non-Muslim Zulaykha is the slave owner, and the Muslim slave Joseph converts her. In re-interpreting Anna's role, the 'Book of Royal Degrees' manages to avoid the motive of justifying slavery as a vehicle of upward social mobility. It is latent in the story of Joseph and Zulaykha, and it was also exploited by slave-raiding Turkmens as justification for not abiding by the *ulama*'s rule not to enslave Muslims.[41]

There are discursive elements in these links between intercultural texts, and good reasons why the writers of the 'Book of Degrees' might have placed them deliberately. Nevertheless, in a religious culture claiming the moral higher ground over its competitors, such links could not be admitted openly. Any discursive operation that takes inspiration from texts from the other side of the religious boundary, or that reaches out to it, must of necessity be concealed. If such an operation did indeed take place, it cannot for these reasons be proven more conclusively in principle and practice. After all, direct citation from 'Joseph and Zulaykha' would have

---

39 See below.
40 Pokrovskii and Lenhoff, *Stepennaia kniga tsarskogo rodosloviia po drevneishim spiskam*, p. 294. For the text, see chapter 3.
41 See below.

diminished the integrative effect of this story, especially on Tatars: its reinterpretative effect builds on subtle shifts of focus, not on open debate.

Once baptised, Vladimir's Rus' attracts and subdues foreigners, but those who are not conquered by his newfound piety do so for special reason: the Bulgars immutably stick to their heathen 'dishonest and lying ways' of slave raiding throughout the centuries. Jumping forward through centuries in the midst of Vladimir's vita, this serves as justification of conquering Kazan in the present time, conveniently glossing over the transition from Bulgars to Tatars:

> Ivan [IV] Vasilevich, Vladimir's kinsman after 17 generations [the 17 degrees of the 'Book of Degrees'], finally moved against them, destroyed all their heathen [i.e. Muslim] sanctuaries along with their guile and their towns, and liberated innumerable Christian captives.[42]

The appropriation of Kyivan history and the genealogy of Riurikids in the 'Book of Degrees' by the Muscovite Empire is closely linked to the ideology of liberating slaves.[43] This aligns the book's narrative, genealogy, and the history of Rus' principalities to the dual purpose of integrating the multi-faith empire by an ideology of liberating slaves, and of justifying the conquest of Kazan.

The sensibilities of the 'History of Kazan' are closer to Kazan Tatar worldviews, while maintaining a pro-Moscow stance overall. Doubts about the authenticity of the claim placed at the beginning of this account now appear alleviated. The unknown author narrates his enslavement by the Kazanians, about his personal bond to the khan, how he served the khan as a chronicler and, in this capacity, gathered personal recollections and evidence of Tatar history. Brief autobiographical elements such as this are common in Ottoman literature, some appear at the opening of a text, as in this case.[44] This intra-textual evidence supports the claim of an early origin of this text, although no copies contemporary to events exist.[45] However, we

---

42 Pokrovskii and Lenhoff, *Stepennaia kniga tsarskogo rodosloviia po drevneishim spiskam*, p. 308.
43 On this genealogical link, see Lenhoff, 'The Construction of Russian History in Stepennaia Kniga'.
44 C. Kafadar, 'Self and Others: The Diary of a Dervish in Seventeenth Century Istanbul and First-Person Narratives in Ottoman Literature', *Studia Islamica*, 69 (1989), pp. 121–150. Special thanks to the auditory of the 18th Otto Spiess memorial lecture and especially to Selim Karahasanoglu, who allowed discussing this topic. A similar, though straightforward anti-Islamic case: N. Iskander, *Povest' o vziatii Tsargrada*, http://lib.pushkinskijdom.ru/Default.aspx?tabid=5059 (accessed 5 Sep. 2021); cf. Keenan, 'Coming to Grips with the Kazanskaya Istoriya, p. 150.
45 Cf. Kämpfer, *Die Eroberung von Kasan 1552 als Gegenstand der zeitgenössischen russischen Historiographie*, p. 137; Keenan, 'Coming to Grips with the Kazanskaya Istoriya'. For a recent comprehensive overview of the textual history covering newly discovered copies, versions and a new genealogical schematic: L.A. Dubrovina, 'Predislovie k izdaniiu 2000 g.', in A.D. Koshelev, ed., *Istoriia o Kazanskom tsarstve: Kazanskii letopisets* (Moskva, 2000), pp. IV–XXVII; L.A. Dubrovina, *Istoriia o Kazanskom tsarstve (Kazanskii letopisets): Spiski i klassifikatsiia tekstov* (Kiev, 1989). On the basis of 270 known manuscripts Dubrovina concludes that no extant protograph of the three

cannot simply assume an underlying eyewitness quality since the text appears at least reworked fundamentally in the seventeenth century. The sources of many details and especially of Tatar cultural elements are in the Nogai and Crimean foreign affairs archive in Moscow, which was accessible to members of the Ambassadorial Chancellery.[46] As we have seen, among them worked Tatar translators and interpreters. The elements of a Tatar consciousness, albeit laced with Muscovite values, may therefore be identified as very close to Tatar. In fact, this can be read as a uniquely extensive, Muscovite Tatar-style captivity narrative that became constitutive of the early Muscovite imperial worldview. Its literary value contributes to its appeal. Consequently, the 'History' does not shy away from attributing honour to the heterodox. Even Muslims and those not subservient to Moscow can be honourable if they treat the captive grand prince with an eye to Orthodox precepts:

> Mamotiak [son of the founder of Kazan] [. . .] led the captured Grand Prince Vasilii [II] Vasil'evich in 1445 away to his place at Kazan and kept him for fourteen months, but not in prison, and honourably put him at the same table with himself [. . .] He did not sully Vasilii by the food of unbelievers, but ordered that he be served only with honourable (*chestnyi*) Rus' food.[47]

The 'History of Kazan' praises Shah Ali in the same way that Tevkelev had attributed to himself, trans-confessionally, the Orthodox Christian martyr image. It thus diverges from the picture drawn in the 'Chronicle of the Beginning of Tsardom', which largely abstains from comments on Shah Ali's worldview. This adds to the peculiar position of the 'History', perched uneasily between Tatar and Muscovite views – note the authorial perspective anxious to justify itself:

> Khan Shah Ali was highly versed in the art of war and valiant, like no other khan who served the tsar [. . .] and he took care and suffered for the Christians all his life to the end. No one shall judge me for reproving my fellow-believers and praising heathen barbarians![48]

Pierre Gonneau has shown insightfully that the codex of chivalry informs the 'History of Kazan'; Shah Ali is presented as a role model.[49] However, he excels in this passage, entitled 'Eulogy to Shah Ali' in yet another, related discipline. He conforms to the model of the sovereign who liberates and ransoms his subjects, applying himself with all his means and even his life. It is the model followed by Tevkelev, so it is hardly exclusive to chivalry.

---

versions was compiled before 1584, although they relate to an assumed, authorial text which originated earlier than that.
46 Keenan, 'Coming to Grips with the Kazanskaya Istoriya', pp. 170–182.
47 'Kazanskaia istoriia', in *Pamiatniki literatury Drevnei Rusi*, vol. 7: *Seredina XVI veka* (Moskva, 1985), p. 327.
48 'Kazanskaia istoriia' in Ibid., p. 492.
49 Gonneau, 'Guerre et chevalerie au pays des Tatars', p. 61.

Honour offered or promised to Tatars along with presents, pay, plots of land and rulership over towns is a recurring phenomenon in the 'History of Kazan'.[50] It was backed up by the practice of employing Tatars in the service of the Muscovite grand princes, where they could rise to very exalted positions. Shah Ali, a Muslim, went on to lead the Muscovite army in the Baltic during the early period of the Livonian War.[51] Simeon Bekbulatovich was even raised to the Muscovite throne, if only formally and controversially.[52] Such rhetoric and practices became part of the conciliatory approach cultivated in the decades after the conquest when Muscovy, badly shaken by rebellions, tried to integrate the middle Volga Tatars.[53]

The rhetoric of honour and liberation that is applied to Tatars in the 'History of Kazan' occurs trans-confessionally. It applies communal values of Russian Orthodoxy without requiring conversion. This was unusual in standard, monastic chronicle depictions of Tatars, and points to the particular position of the 'History' with regard to them, while it closely follows actual practice.[54]

Honour gained by avoiding captivity or redeeming slaves as a common strategy of imperial rhetoric is reiterated by the Muscovite 'Tale about Queen Dinara', which is set in a semi-mythical Georgia. The 'wise' Queen Dinara – modelled on both legendary and historical accounts of two separate Georgian queens, Tamara and Dinara – calls on the Georgian elite to stand up for the Mother of God and not to allow themselves to fall into slavery at the hands of the Persians, in language reminiscent of the 'Letter to the Ugra'.[55]

The rhetorical equation of the defeat of the Israelites by Nebuchadnezzar II and the elite of Georgia draws on similar images in Muscovite imperial culture, symbolically uniting the two Orthodox realms in a common effort of liberation from slavery. There is some uncertainty about the date of the lost original; however, the quote from the 'Tale' appears in the murals of the Golden Palace and in Ivan IV's speech

---

50 G.N. Moiseeva and V.P. Adrianova-Peretts, eds., *Kazanskaia istoriia* (Moskva, 1954), pp. 65–66, 97–100, 144–145; Kämpfer, *Historie vom Zartum Kasan (Kasaner Chronist)*, pp. 80–82, 143–145, 228–230.
51 Martin, 'Tatars in the Muscovite Army during the Livonian War'.
52 D.G. Ostrowski, 'The Extraordinary Career of Tsarevich Kudai Kul/Peter in the Context of Relations between Muscovy and Kazan'', in J. Duzinkiewicz, M. Popovych, V. Verstiuk and N. Yakovenko, eds., *States, Societies, Cultures: East and West* (New York, 2004), pp. 697–719; J. Martin, 'Simeon Bekbulatovich and Steppe Politics: Some Thoughts on Donald Ostrowski's Interpretation of the Tsar's Remarkable Career', *Russian History*, 39, 3 (2012), pp. 331–338; Martin, 'Tatars in the Muscovite Army during the Livonian War'.
53 Kappeler, *The Russian Empire*; Romaniello, *The Elusive Empire*.
54 Ostrowski, *Muscovy and the Mongols*, pp. 164–168.
55 *Divnaia povest muzhestvena o khrabrosti i mudrosti tselomudrenyia devitsa, Dinary tsaritsy, dshcheri iverskago tsaria Aleksandra: Podgotovka teksta, perevod i kommentarii N.S. Demkovoi*, http://lib.pushkinskijdom.ru/Default.aspx?tabid=5084 (accessed 6 Sep. 2018). For more detail, see chapter 4.

calling for the final attack in the 'History of Kazan'.[56] In the second half of the sixteenth century the 'Tale' circulated widely; it was cited in the secular 'Russian Chronograph' and occurred in a wealth of different versions in the collections containing the life of the Mother of God.[57] Moreover, this imbued the old protective legends about the Mother of God with new meaning. The fictional adjustment of Georgian history to post-1552 Muscovite imperial rhetoric went as far as to claim, almost in an ironical twist – which may have been lost on any but the very Muscovite elite – in the last lines of the 'Tale' that Georgians lived henceforth 'ruled by no-one (*nikimzhe obladaemi*)', i.e. by no foreign or heterodox ruler, taking tribute from the Persians, in a version of the promised land. In reality, Muscovite influence in Georgia never went as far as de-facto guaranteeing the integrity of the Georgian kingdoms. Nevertheless, the dissemination of the 'Tale' demonstrates once more the versatility of imperial rhetoric of honour and liberation, subsuming all kinds of people deemed loyal subjects of the tsar.[58]

Saints' lives

Stories about Orthodox saints liberating captives might be suspected of excluding heterodox or even non-ethnic Russians. Whether due to the state's policies or the Russian Orthodox Church's interests in the middle Volga, where many monasteries competed for the local workforce with Russian landowners, in fact such exclusions were blurred in a significant number of stories.

M.P. Romaniello revisited the issue of saints' lives and miracle stories in the middle Volga and came to the conclusion that a change occurred around the time of the conquest, when an earlier portrayal of life in the frontier as rough and perilous, which included stories about miraculous liberation from captivity, yielded to stories about exemplary lifestyles of exclusively Orthodox believers.[59] However, there are more stories about liberation from captivity not specifically mentioning or originating in the middle Volga region that in various ways involve heterodox and non-Russian characters.

---

56 Zabelin, *Domashnii byt russkikh tsarei v XVI i XVII stoletiiakh*, p. 178.
57 M.N. Speranskii, 'Povest' o Dinare v russkoi pis'mennosti', *Izvestiia Otdeleniia russkogo iazyka i slovesnosti Akademii Nauk*, 31 (1926), pp. 43–92; *Divnaia povest muzhestvena o khrabrosti i mudrosti tselomudrenyia devitsa, Dinary tsaritsy, dshcheri iverskago tsaria Aleksandra*.
58 Cf. W.E.D. Allen, ed., *Russian Embassies to the Georgian Kings, 1589–1605* (Cambridge, 1970); R.G. Suny, *The Making of the Georgian Nation* (Bloomington IN, 1988).
59 Romaniello, *The Elusive Empire*, pp. 130–136.

Saving heterodox subjects

Less well-known miracle stories about St Nicholas are still revealing for the Muscovite stance toward empire. Until we know more, the low number of available copies for these texts might have to be explained by nationalist predilections in later centuries. Add to this the blind spots of nineteenth-century editors and a late imperial aversion to mixing Orthodox Christian precepts with heterodoxy. These stories invert the familiar schemata previously outlined, putting those usually portrayed as captors in the position of the captive, albeit not quite in that of a victim.[60]

The Saracen miracle, with twenty copies altogether and nine in late Muscovy, only survives in Eastern Slavonic, whether in translation or original. Since the Mediterranean setting might have been copied from other captivity miracle stories, any prejudice is excluded. Significantly, it puts the Saracen in the position of protagonist and captive, who thus becomes a hero inviting identification. From the prison on Cyprus a Saracen captive mysteriously disappears, and his guards are arrested in his stead. After a while, a Saracen fleet appears, but when the Cypriotes send out their own fleet to battle, a small craft leaves the ships of the arrivals and the rower asks them where the Saracen prisoner is. He reveals himself and explains that he overheard a conversation among the guards about St Nicholas liberating captives and resolved to try it himself. Although the prisoner is a Muslim, St Nicholas immediately set him free, a feat which ultimately convinces him to convert. Meanwhile, the guards' chains are broken by St George, pronounced 'a helper of St Nicholas'.[61] This is an example of the stories about conversion following miraculous rescues. Its focus on captivity made it particularly fitting for the steppe 'sport', which often left raiders in the position of captives.[62]

This story was specially revised for the first print edition of St Nicholas' vita in 1641, in which it was positioned third after the legend of miraculous rescue of one Vasilii from Cretan captivity. Irina Makeeva rightly notes that it is indicative that the main theme of the story, liberation of a Muslim and his conversion, remained unchanged while the confusing marginal participation of St George in a miracle otherwise attributed to the then hugely popular St Nicholas was eliminated.[63]

---

[60] See also below for Shah Ali inverting these roles several times and calling 'the Russian saints' for help in captivity.

[61] Boguslawski, *The Vitae of St. Nicholas and His Hagiographical Icons in Russia*, pp. 106–108. See chapter 4 on St George. I.I. Makeeva, 'Chudesa Nikolaia Chudotvortsa o saratsine v russkoi pis'mennosti', *Trudy Otdela drevnerusskoi literatury*, 60 (2009), pp. 3–28.

[62] B.J. Boeck, *Shifting Boundaries on the Don Steppe Frontier: Cossacks, Empires and Nomads to 1739* (PhD dissertation, Harvard University, 2002), p. 45 (61); M. Hrushevs'kyi, V.A. Smolii and P.S. Sokhan', *Istoriia Ukraïny-Rusy*, vol. 7 (Kyïv, 1991–2000), pp. 81, 99.

[63] Makeeva, 'Chudesa Nikolaia Chudotvortsa o saratsine v russkoi pis'mennosti', p. 27.

A different inversion occurs in the miracle of the Polovtsian. A captive in Kyiv, the Polovtsian makes an oath in front of the icon of St Nicholas to pay his ransom after he is freed. However, he thinks little of the pledge, and when back home in the steppe he tries to forget. St Nicholas violently forces him to heed it by invisibly mocking him in front of his fellow Polovtsians. While the victim is one of those often seen in the opposite role as raider and slaver, St Nicholas' part is to intimidate him by one of his surprising, space-transcending appearances.[64] The fact that nine out of eleven copies in Nikol'skii's count originate from late Muscovy reflects growing Muscovite confidence relative to the new subject peoples, and an appreciation of serving debts.[65] Where St Nicholas helps heterodox captives in his Russian Orthodox lives, the task is to integrate them and ultimately to ensure the superiority of Christianity despite tolerance for their faith. Moreover, the motif of debt to St Nicholas established by liberation is common to both stories and founds a new narrative in which former enemies were integrated into the budding empire in a dependent position, even in distant places.[66]

Adding to these motifs of imperial ideology attached to St Nicholas, the Tobolsk military servitor, architect and chronicler Semen U. Remezov at the turn to the eighteenth century justified the conquest of Siberia in his 'History of Siberia' by portraying the khan as a slaver. In two scenes, St Nicholas takes centre stage and spurs Ermak's cossacks to action, emphasizing that they should 'observe all virtues in loving your brother', in the very words used in the 'Letter to the Ugra' and the 'Chronicle of the Beginning of Tsardom'.[67] According to the 1649 law code as well as canon law, these virtues included paying ransom: 'Do not be stingy with gold and silver for your brother, but redeem him'.[68] Remezov's family had a track record of ransoming Tatars.[69]

Sarı Saltuk and St Nicholas: transcendental agents of empire

The Ottoman *homme des lettres* Evliyah Çelebi, a perceptive traveller and good read, recognized in his writings the importance of St Nicholas as an agent of empire and expansion. Many of St Nicholas' transcultural, trans-confessional, ambiguous and at times mocking approaches and appeals are mirrored in the legends attributed to Sarı Saltuk, the Bektaşi Sufi order's saintly hero who died in 1298. Like the cult of

---

64 Boguslawski, *The Vitae of St. Nicholas and His Hagiographical Icons in Russia*, pp. 118–121.
65 On conversion and missionary policies, see M. Khodarkovsky, '"Not by Word Alone": Missionary Policies and Religious Conversion in Early Modern Russia', *Comparative Studies in Society and History*, 38, 2 (1996), pp. 267–293.
66 On power overcoming distance: C. Witzenrath, 'Orthodoxe Kirche und Fernmacht: Das Moskauer Reich, die Kosaken und die Gründung des Bischofssitzes von Tobolsk und Sibirien 1620–1625', in S. Rau and C. Hochmuth, eds., *Machträume der Frühneuzeitlichen Stadt* (Konstanz, 2006), pp. 309–333.
67 Remezov, *Remezovskaia letopis'*, vol. 1, pp. 190–192, 230.
68 Hellie, *The Muscovite Law Code (Ulozhenie) of 1649*, chapter VIII, art. 1.
69 Gol'denberg, *Izograf zemli Sibirskoi*, pp. 84–85.

St Nicholas of Mozhaisk, Sarı Saltuk's veneration survived in the late middle ages in the steppe frontier, in Northern Rumelia and the Qipchak steppe, now part of Romania. Some attribute to Sarı a Tatar origin from Crimea, more frequently Central Asia. Unlike those about St Nicholas, legends about Sarı, a Sufi dervish, sometimes hint that his religious disputes might end with killing the 'unbeliever'. Sarı Saltuk was first accepted by sultans as a Sunni dispenser of the faith. However, Suleyman sought to delineate Sunni Islam and ordered a legal opinion that designated Sarı as a heretic. Nevertheless, Evliyah in the 1660s took the risk of defending and attributing new stories to him. Remarkably, these new stories picked up the lead that had had Sarı Saltuk kill monks or other clerics and, taking their appearance, convert further Christians to Islam, exploiting asymmetric dependency on clerical figures.

Evliyah in his *Travels* as a novelty attributed to Sarı specifically the killing of St Nicholas as bishop in Gdansk. He claims that Sarı Saltuk in St Nicholas' clothes converted many Polish Christians, who became the Lipka Tatars. In Muscovy, Evliyah insists, he took the same appearance, and this was why there were Tatars living in Muscovy. These Tatar groups exist; however, Evliyah appropriated their genesis in these legends, making them compatible with claims of Ottoman superiority.[70]

The degree to which these legends reflected increased trans-imperial communication has just been revealed in the research project 'Transottomanica'.[71] Evliyah's time was characterized by increasing tensions and exchanges between Ottomans, Poland-Lithuania and Muscovy over control of the Pontic steppe, with a host of local actors to be won over. Evliyah's modelling of Sarı Saltuk on the appearance of St Nicholas interacts with the episcopal saint's frontier legends of liberating captives. This is underlined by another type of legend: Again, Evliyah relates that Sarı, reminiscent of Nikolai's helper St George, had killed a dragon to liberate the emperor's two daughters.[72] Moreover, he released an Orthodox Christian from Frankish, 'Latin', captivity on condition that they convert.[73]

In short, Evliyah's Sarı Saltuk in the guise of St Nicholas – except for the more active, even violent missionary streak – engaged from an Ottoman perspective in broadly similar activities as did St Nicholas and his helper and fellow transcendental and translocal imperial agent St George in Muscovite lives: sponsoring imperial values and worldviews. The risk Evliyah took in promoting a saint designated a

---

[70] S. Rohdewald, 'Sarı Saltuk im osmanischen Rumelien, der Rus' und Polen-Litauen: Zugänge zu einer transosmanischen religiösen Erinnerungsfigur (14.–20. Jh.)', in K. Jobst and D. Hüchtker, eds., *Heilig: Transkulturelle Verehrungskulte vom Mittelalter bis in die Gegenwart* (Göttingen, 2017), pp. 67–98.
[71] H.-J. Bömelburg and S. Rohdewald, 'Polen-Litauen als Teil transosmanischer Verflechtungen', in S. Rohdewald, S. Conermann and A. Fuess, eds., *Transottomanica: Osteuropäisch-osmanisch-persische Mobilitätsdynamiken: Perspektiven und Forschungsstand* (Göttingen, 2019), pp. 169–190.
[72] C.J. Jireček, *Geschichte der Bulgaren* (Prag, 1876), p. 536.
[73] H.T. Norris, *Popular Sufism in Eastern Europe: Sufi Brotherhoods and the Dialogue with Christianity and "Heterodoxy"* (New York, 2006), p. 59.

heretic shows that this insightful, cosmopolitan observer took St Nicholas' legends about liberating slaves and captives very seriously as a tool of Muscovite expansion against the background of increasing trans-imperial cultural interconnections and tensions and as a transcendental relation increasing slaves' interagency.

Joseph the Beautiful

The stories of 'Joseph the Beautiful' and 'Joseph and Zulaykha' are in many ways common to Turkic, Iranian, Georgian and Slavic literatures and oral lore. The various versions mark the shared cultural codes and experiences of slavery and monotheism as well as the degree to which these experiences differed. Apart from the Biblical and Qur'anic versions of these stories, there are the Central Asian, middle Volga and Russian adaptations, some of which differ quite drastically in taking into account local habits and needs. These literary stories became popular again in the eighteenth and nineteenth century, when they saw many print editions in Tatar and served to proselytize in the Muslim drive for spreading Islam in the steppe and the middle Volga.[74] On the Russian side, the originally Greek story about *Iosif Prekrasnyi* (Joseph the Most Beautiful) still appeared in the local songs collected in the nineteenth century.[75] While any attempt to trace such oral lore to earlier centuries is fraught with methodological problems, the similarities of their narratives to the Biblical story are reminiscent of the murals in the Kremlin's second throne room in the Palace of Facets, first painted in the 1590s and described in detail by the icon painter Simon Ushakov and undersecretary Nikolai Klement'ev in 1672.[76] The extant Central Asian and middle Volga versions are centuries older and, according to the record of manuscript copies, were already fairly widely disseminated by the sixteenth and seventeenth centuries.[77]

The 'Life of Joseph', which denounces the practice of selling relatives into slavery, forms the programme of the murals in the second throne room of the Kremlin. It is the story of a Jew treacherously sold into slavery by kin, who rises in the

---

[74] A. Kefeli, 'The Tale of Joseph and Zulaykha on the Volga Frontier: The Struggle for Gender, Religious, and National Identity in Imperial and Postrevolutionary Russia', *Slavic Review*, 70, 2 (2011), pp. 373–398.
[75] See for example T.G. Ivanova, S.N. Azbelev and I.I. Marchenko, eds., *Belomorskie stariny i dukhovnye stikhi: Sobranie A.V. Markova* (St Petersburg, 2002), pp. 164–166, 727–730.
[76] Nasibova, Kuznetsov and Groshnikov, *Granovitaia palata Moskovskogo Kremlia*; D.B. Rowland, 'Architecture and Dynasty: Boris Godunov's Uses of Architecture, 1584–1606', in J. Cracraft and D.B. Rowland, eds., *Architectures of Russian Identity: 1500 to the Present* (Ithaca NY, 2003), pp. 34–47, here 44–45.
[77] The current count of known copies of Kul 'Ali's *Kyssa-i Iusuf* runs at 333: K.F. Islamov, 'K probleme izucheniia kopii rukopisi "Kyssa-i Iusuf" Kul 'Ali', *Vestnik Kazanskogo gosudarstennogo universiteta kul'tury i iskusstv*, 1 (2014), pp. 146–150.

Egyptian hierarchy to become the first minister of pharaoh. He predicts seven lean years, takes precautionary grain stocking measures and purchases debt bonds from anyone in need of food relief. When his brothers arrive driven by famine, they do not recognize him and he puts them to a test. However, he uses his position to release and symbolically redeem his captive brothers. The illustrated, circular story of a slave who enslaved his masters and liberated his kin might have helped to integrate Tatars and those of the Russian Orthodox who were captured and rose in heterodox service but contemplated returning to Muscovy.

In the Palace of Facets, which was furnished with this elaborate cycle of wall paintings in the late sixteenth century under tsar Fedor and his regent Boris Godunov, the life of Joseph replaced the military Exodus scenes of the Golden Palace.[78] However, in the 1670s, when the icon painter and head of the Imperial Icon Painting Workshop in the Kremlin Armory, Simon Ushakov, described the partly-decayed murals of the Golden Palace, knowledge about the context was still available. He noted Joseph's appearance in the scene of the crossing the Red Sea: 'among [the sons of Israel following Moses] people carry the sarcophagus of Joseph the Beautiful'.[79] There was always a context of liberation to the story of Joseph the Beautiful in Muscovy.

Beyond the story of Joseph sold as a slave in Egypt, the murals of the Palace of Facets show tsar Fedor Ivanovich as the last tsar in a long genealogical line, together with his chief advisor, Boris Godunov; he appears with his court dignitaries in an especially sumptuous robe. This provides a clue for dating the paintings, which are generally accepted to have originated during the 1590s.[80] Nevertheless, the question remains to what degree the paintings we know give an account of the original frescos. In 1882, master artists from Palekh restored the paintings in the throne room of the Palace of Facets according to the description made in 1672 by Ushakov. They obviously did so according to their own visions and the styles of the era but closely adhered to the description, especially in terms of content.

There are two interpretations of the sources related to these descriptions and restorations. The majoritarian is sceptical about the unchanged survival of the frescos until their description. However, new sources have led to a re-interpretation of the source material which points to the survival of the sixteenth century murals. According to a decree of tsar Aleksei Mikhailovich, the murals of the Palace of Facets were in a bad state as early as 1663 and required restoration. However, this decree was not acted upon until in 1668 Simon Ushakov prepared a tender for renovating the interior

---

[78] Zabelin, *Materialy dlia istorii, arkheologii i statistiki goroda Moskvy*, pp. 1255–1271; Nasibova, Kuznetsov and Groshnikov, *Granovitaia palata Moskovskogo Kremlia*, pp. 11–12; Rowland, 'Biblical Military Imagery in the Political Culture of Early Modern Russia', p. 195.
[79] Zabelin, *Materialy dlia istorii, arkheologii i statistiki goroda Moskvy*, p. 1252.
[80] N.E. Mneva, Zhivopis' kontsa XVI-nachala XVII veka, in I.E. Grabar' et al., eds., *Istoriia russkogo iskusstva*, vol. 3 (Moskva, 1955), pp. 635–642, here p. 636.

of the Palace of Facets which, again, was never executed due to bad weather and other works. In 1672 there was still the intention to rescue the murals, and Ushakov wrote the surviving protocol. The wider range of documents on the renovation of the Palace of Facets studied by E.M. Kozlitina confirms the former minority opinion that the 1672 description is in fact the old picture programme of the sixteenth century and does not delineate, as most historians had claimed following Zabelin, new wall paintings of 1668, which were never painted. The Muscovite seventeenth century in general was careful to preserve murals, as these documents and further examples show. In the early autumn of 1667, citing a great number of artists needed for this effort, Ushakov wrote:

> The Great Sovereign may decree that the Palace of Facets shall be repainted in the best manner, better than before or just like before, [however] in this short remaining time it cannot be done by any means until October when the cold period begins and wall painting applied in this time will not last.[81]

Ushakov prevailed. Renovations of the churches of the Archangel Michael and the Cathedral of the Dormition of the Mother of God were likewise preceded by careful sketches taken from the wall paintings under tsars Mikhail and Aleksei.[82] A wide range of documents point toward continuity in the seventeenth century. The murals painted during Fedor Ivanovich and Boris Godunov's reigns in the 1590s were most likely visible well after 1672, when they were recorded and, after their repair, even into Peter's reign. The scenes were then covered by plaster and tapestry according to the new European fashion, most likely in Peter I's reign.

Typical traits of the version of Joseph's story in the Palace of Facets comprise an emphasis on slavery and redemption, as well as its circularity. Two murals show 'Ishmaelites', ascribing to them Joseph's redemption from the well into which his envious brothers had thrown him. Notably, the murals celebrate the faked 'death' of Joseph, with which the brothers covered up the fact of the sale when they showed Joseph's ornate robe smeared with blood to their father Jacob. Slavery as social death is a subject explored long before Orlando Patterson's pathbreaking and now controversial book.[83] The murals of the Palace of Facets seize on this theme, dedicating a whole image to the issue of slavery, death and kin:

> Gen 39:26 (RSV, NIV): 'Judah said to his brothers, "What will we gain if we kill our brother and cover up his blood? [27] Come, let's sell him to the Ishmaelites and not lay our hands on him; after all, he is our brother, our own flesh and blood". His brothers agreed'.

---

81 E.M. Kozlitina, 'Dokumenty XVII veka po istorii Granovitoi palaty Moskovskogo Kremlia', *Materialy i issledovanja*, 1 (1973), pp. 95–110.
82 I.N. Dmitriev, 'Stenopis' Arkhangel'skogo sobora Moskovskogo Kremlia', in V.N. Lazarev, O.N. Podobedova and V.V. Kostochkin, eds., *Drevnerusskoe iskusstvo: XVII vek*, vol. 2 (Moskva, 1964), pp. 138–159, here p. 141.
83 Patterson, *Slavery and Social Death*.

The resemblance of enslavement to social death and ransom are the subject of these murals, and re-attachment to a foreign society is the theme of the following. The next mural shows the 'Ishmaelites', already closely associated to the slave trade, selling Joseph in Egypt to Potiphar. His wife appears in several murals as an evil and egotistic temptress; upon her testimony Joseph is thrown in the dungeon. After his liberation, as a result of his wise ability to interpret dreams and rise to power, he redeems his brothers from poverty.

Since his divine premonitions helped to overcome the seven bad harvests, collecting grain and disbursing it manifest another close similarity to, on the one hand, the Josephs of the Bible and in the Palace of Facets and, on the other, Godunov, who tried to overcome the baleful effects of unprecedentedly bad harvests during the Time of Troubles by distributing stocked grain and money.[84] The Palace of Facets storyline culminates in a double mural paralleling Joseph and Godunov. The latter appears as first among equals among the advisers to tsar Fedor, whose imaginative exaltation barely covers Godunov's ambition. Meanwhile, just above, Joseph and pharaoh together receive the adulation of their subjects saved from drought and starvation: a double image of good government directed by wise counsel.[85] Since the connected stories of the slave Joseph and the rising Godunov justify debt bondage and, implicitly, dislocation of Tatars by saving the population from famine and slave raids, one might be forgiven for speaking of an ambivalent legacy. It combined legitimation by liberation with legitimating enserfment in the counter dependency zone. At the outset, enserfment differed from slaving by preserving the communal and kinship links often seen during the premodern period as the main guarantee against the initial deracination, loss of rights, and often forced mobility associated with enslavement.[86] Godunov's own record in this regard is not entirely straightforward: he mixed measures which can be seen as enforcing enserfment as a way of tying peasants to their land with others that relaxed such a regime. The aim of both was to strengthen the government's clout and defence against slave raids.[87]

Boris Godunov's reign is, furthermore, lauded for his efforts to further the liberation from slavery in the 'Life of Fedor Ivanovich', which inscribed the activities of

---

[84] A.P. Pavlov, 'Fedor Ivanovich and Boris Godunov (1584–1605)', in M. Perrie, ed., *Cambridge History of Russia*, vol. 1: *From early Rus' to 1689* (Cambridge, 2006), pp. 264–285, here pp. 281–282.

[85] Nasibova, Kuznetsov and Groshnikov, *Granovitaia palata Moskovskogo Kremlia*. Cf. F. Kämpfer, *Das russische Herrscherbild von den Anfängen bis zu Peter dem Großen: Studien zur Entwicklung politischer Ikonographie im byzantinischen Kulturkreis* (Recklinghausen, 1978), pp. 98–99. On the trope of wise advice to the tsar, see Rowland, 'The Problem of Advice in Muscovite Tales about the Time of Troubles'; Bogatyrev, *The Sovereign and His Counsellors*; H. Rüß, *Herren und Diener: Die soziale Mentalität des russischen Adels, 9.–17. Jahrhundert* (Köln, 1994).

[86] Finley, 'The Emergence of a Slave Society'. For details, see Introduction.

[87] Pavlov, 'Fedor Ivanovich and Boris Godunov (1584–1605)', pp. 273–274.

Godunov as rising regent to the life of the pious, but largely inactive tsar. As the Crimean khan Gazy Girei attacks Muscovy with a large ('150,000 strong') army in 1591 and futilely assaults Moscow's recently reconstructed battlements, Fedor acts like Moses and 'arms the army' but confines himself to praying, while Godunov 'beatified by wisdom' leads the army. Beyond the allusions to and comparisons with the Exodus, the claim that the Crimeans 'left by the wayside numerous captives taken in villages in the vicinity of the capital city as they were chased off'[88] could not fail to locate this story squarely within the – by this time well-known – narrative of liberation from slavery. So did the claim that occurred early on in the chronicle entry on the raids of that year that the Crimean Tatars 'attacked Great *Rosiia* and [. . .] slave-raided many of the honourable tsar Fedor Ivanovich's towns and great villages'.[89]

Moreover, Godunov's wooden church of St Sergius, which he had had purpose-built for the campaign, is associated to the portable Israelite tabernacle during Exodus. Just a few lines further down, saving Moscow from the Crimean khan is compared to the feat of discouraging Temir-Aksak, an episode already assimilated into the Muscovite narrative of the liberation from slavery of the New Israel during the 1550s and 1560s.[90]

If the late Edward Keenan's single vote was right in attributing the 'Stepennaia kniga' to the Godunov era,[91] then everything that has been said above about the Exodus narrative within this text directly relates to the immediate historical context of the murals in the Palace of Facets. This liberatory streak in the 'Godunovian Renaissance'[92] is further corroborated by the great building programme of Boris' reign, which notably encompassed many important new fortresses along the steppe border, like Belgorod, Tsarev-Borisov, Elets, Voronezh and Livny, as well as the string of fortifications along the river Volga between Kazan and Astrakhan aligning with Boris' anti-slave raid policy.[93]

The murals of the life of Joseph in the Palace of Facets are contextualised in the specific wording of the description of Fedor's and Boris Godunov's reactions to Crimean attacks and raids which cite issues of slavery and liberation. Godunov's self-representation as descendant of noble Tatar ancestry – a Chinggisid, albeit a converted one who had arrived already in the early fourteenth century –[94]

---

88 PSRL 14, pt. 1 (Zhitie tsaria i velikogo kniazia Fedora Ivanovicha), p. 14.
89 PSRL 14, pt. 1, p. 11.
90 PSRL 14, pt. 1, p. 12; Lenhoff, 'The Tale of Tamerlane in the Royal Book of Degrees'.
91 Keenan, 'The Stepennaia Kniga and the Godunovian Renaissance'.
92 The term was coined by E. Keenan.
93 Pavlov, 'Fedor Ivanovich and Boris Godunov (1584–1605)'; Rowland, 'Architecture and Dynasty'.
94 A frequent observation among Muscovite nobles. Chet Murza/Zakhariia, identified as an ancestor of Boris Godunov, is said to have arrived in this period: see Ostrowski, *Muscovy and the Mongols*, p. 56; Ostrowski, 'Troop Mobilization by the Muscovite Grand Princes (1313–1533)', p. 37. For doubts about this version of Godunov's ancestry – but not about the fact of his claim: S.B. Veselovskii, *Issledovaniia po istorii klassa sluzhilykh zemlevladel'tsev* (Moskva, 1969), pp. 162–164; Martin, 'Religious Ideology and Chronicle Depictions of Muslims in 16th-Century Muscovy', p. 289.

places him in a predicament not unlike that of Shah Ali:[95] an outsider who made it to the highest rank, underpinning his claim to power by liberating slaves, just like Joseph the Beautiful. That he tied the peasants more closely to the soil and so deprived them of free movement was not regarded as an obstacle to this image by the landlords, an in-group who naturally saw themselves as ineligible for slaving – in fact, they saw it as a boon.

A Tatar point of view on Joseph

Tatars might look at the murals from particular angles. The *Qïssa-yï Yusuf* (Tale of Joseph) is a thirteenth-century version of the story that differs in important ways from the mainstream of Biblical and Qur'anic narratives, especially as it carves out an equal role for a female character, Zulaykha, while recognizably remaining the same story. Written in Qipchak-Oghuz Turkish by the Volga Bulgar poet Qul 'Ali (born c. 1183), this story became widely disseminated long before printed books took hold in the nineteenth century, with over 200 manuscript copies found so far.[96]

Equal humanity and access to the divine granted to women are traits partly in common with another version of the Joseph and Zulaykha story, by the fifteenth century Turk writer al-Rabghuzi, which he completed in 1311. Unlike earlier Arabic expansions of the literary subject matter or the Biblical and Qur'anic sources, these authors did not reduce Zulaykha to the role of the depraved temptress. Qul 'Ali portrayed her as a kind of female St Cyril, with a divinely inspired dream of Joseph which she had as an innocent child. God's angel guarded her virginity in this version, even in marriage. Rabghuzi, in contrast, at the outset casts her as adulterous and tainted temptress, who does not really love Joseph and tells lies about him. This accords with Rabghuzi's negative views of women and reflects debates in the wider Muslim world about women's place in society and the story of Joseph and Zulaykha in particular.[97] Nevertheless, after her rejection by Joseph Zulaykha finds his god and dedicates herself to God's service. When Joseph later on discovers his love for Zulaykha, she initially rejects him because of her newfound faith. The following happy ending reunites the lovers. It is in keeping with Sufi practice, which requires temporary rather than life-long abstinence to advance along the path of experiencing the divine:[98]

---

95 J. Martin, 'Multiethnicity in Muscovy: A Consideration of Christian and Muslim Tatars in the 1550s–1580s', *Journal of Early Modern History*, 5, 1 (2001), pp. 1–23; Martin, 'Tatars in the Muscovite Army during the Livonian War'.
96 M. Usmanov, 'Kauryi kaləm ezennən', *Archeograf iazmalary (Arkheograficheskie zapiski)*, 1994, p. 64.
97 Kefeli, 'The Tale of Joseph and Zulaykha on the Volga Frontier', p. 384.
98 Ibid., esp. p. 385.

Oh, Joseph, I loved you and lost my heart to you. When you did not look at me, . . . I turned to my Lord the Creator . . . He united me with you whom I love so intensely . . . How could I not serve Him?[99]

As Agnes Kefeli notes, to the Tatars living under Russian rule in the sixteenth century this story provided a paradigm of how to live as good Muslim in a non-Muslim state. Joseph, sold to a heterodox land, had continued proselytizing for his faith – even in prison – and had eventually risen to power.[100]

In turn, this had implications for Muscovy. Literate Tatars and those who had heard about the story of Joseph and Zulaykha would approach the murals in the Palace of Facets with this set of ideas, making them – inadvertently or by design – an invitation to advance in the service of the tsar. Remarkably, the Muscovite emphasis on redemption in this view appears as part of a trans-confessional Eurasian discourse in which Muscovites and Turkmens occupied opposite extremes. Turkmens, who supplemented the meagre rewards of nomad life by raiding, were known to claim that the career of Joseph demonstrates that slaving was not despicable, as it leads to advancement in life. Nevertheless, they additionally required their Muslim victims to claim they were heretics, to evade *shariah*-inspired reprisals against enslaving Muslims.[101]

By contrast, the Kremlin murals emphasized that Ishmaelites sold Joseph into slavery – although they also ransomed him from death in the well. The culprits are his kin-selling brothers who envy his excellency. Finally, Joseph demonstrates his quality as an inspiring leader by forgiving his brothers on behalf of the innocent Benjamin, and redeems them from imminent hunger and slavery.[102] In terms of how Joseph's story was seen among the Tatars, the Muscovite story thus stresses a different kind of transformation, which was not even conversion to Christianity. According to the murals, the qualifying traits of a foreigner able to rise in Muscovite services were the ability to liberate others from slavery and to save subjects from starvation. Moreover, the nameless female character, Potiphar's wife, remains clearly heathen without access to the – monotheistic or otherwise – divine, without personal traits beyond lust or any development of character:[103] this might have been read as a denunciation of cross-confessional marriage among slaves.[104]

---

99 Rabġūzī, Nāṣir ad-Dīn Ibn Burhān ad-Dīn, H. Boeschoten and J. O'Kane, *Al-Rabghūzī, The Stories of the Prophets: Qiṣaṣ al-Anbiyā': An Eastern Turkish Version* (Leiden, 2015); Kefeli, 'The Tale of Joseph and Zulaykha on the Volga Frontier', p. 373.
100 Kefeli, 'The Tale of Joseph and Zulaykha on the Volga Frontier', p. 376.
101 Letourneau, *L'évolution de l'esclavage dans les diverses races humaines*, p. 226; Clarence-Smith, *Islam and the Abolition of Slavery*, pp. 43–44. Regardless whether this nineteenth-century traveller was correct, it coincides with the positive stance taken by *mamluk* soldiers traded to Egypt: see Introduction.
102 Zabelin, *Materialy dlia istorii, arkheologii i statistiki goroda Moskvy*, pp. 1263, 1270–1271; Nasibova, Kuznetsov and Groshnikov, *Granovitaia palata Moskovskogo Kremlia*.
103 Zabelin, *Materialy dlia istorii, arkheologii i statistiki goroda Moskvy*, p. 1264.
104 Cf. metropolitan Makariiʻs letters as discussed in chapter 2, which are similarly decrying sexual relations between former slaves and liberators as a danger to Orthodoxy.

'Sons of Hagar'

The Ishmaelites appear twice in the Palace of Facets murals of the Joseph story. In the Old Testament, they are the descendants of Hagar, the female slave of the prophet Abraham who took the place of his wife Sarah during her infertility and produced offspring, Ismael, later disinherited. The 'Sons of Hagar' are a frequent trope in Muscovite sources, usually denoting nomadic Muslims of the steppe, or nomads. However, in many – especially sixteenth-century – sources they take on further connotations, particularly of slavers. This has led to some confusion. Pelenski claimed that the following quote proved the 'religious motivation' of the conquest of Kazan:

> And you, lord, god-crowned, with God's help, have destroyed the ungodly and dishonourable sons of Hagar and liberated Orthodox Christians from slavery and captivity.[105]

Even the seemingly religious part of the statement in this source about the destruction of Ishmaelites calls attention to their being slavers. In many sources such as those about the conquest of Kazan and in the murals in the throne room of the Palace of Facets they appear as slave traders, who sell Joseph to Egypt, set over a millennium before Islam.[106] They were seen as the disowned but manumitted sons of Abraham's slave Hagar in a circular worldview that oscillates between owning slaves, being conquered and enslaved.[107]

Not only in Muscovite sources does 'Sons of Hagar' refer to the legendary descent of Muhammad and the Arabs from Ismail, and ultimately his mother Hagar, Abraham's slave concubine.[108] The biblical terms Hagarites and Ishmaelites were incorporated into Arabic genealogical systems as part of the larger Jewish influence on early Islamic culture.[109] Such ideas are documented in scholarly Islamic works and in oral lore of the Hagar legend.[110] Inheritance through female descent was of secondary importance, but not disregarded by Arabs.[111] A tradition associated with Muhammed

---

[105] Pelenski, *Russia and Kazan*, p. 292.
[106] Nasibova, Kuznetsov and Groshnikov, *Granovitaia palata Moskovskogo Kremlia*; Zabelin, *Materialy dlia istorii, arkheologii i statistiki goroda Moskvy*, p. 1263.
[107] Nasibova, Kuznetsov and Groshnikov, *Granovitaia palata Moskovskogo Kremlia*; Clarence-Smith, *Islam and the Abolition of Slavery*, p. 24; Kazhdan, 'The Concept of Freedom (*eleutheria*) and Slavery (*duleia*) in Byzantium', pp. 218–219; Hellie, *Slavery in Russia, 1450–1725*, pp. 73–74. On the cyclical view of enslavement, liberation and domination: Tikhomirov, *Vologodsko-permskii letopisets*, p. 271 and chapter 2.
[108] Crone and Cook, *Hagarism*, p. 121.
[109] I. Eph'al, '"Ishmael" and "Arab(s)": A Transformation of Ethnological Terms', *Journal of Near Eastern Studies*, 35, 4 (1976), pp. 225–235, here pp. 234–235.
[110] Clarence-Smith, *Islam and the Abolition of Slavery*, p. 24. The remainder of the paragraph is based on this and I. Goldziher, *Muslim Studies*, vol. 1 (London, 1967), pp. 116–119.
[111] Hodgson, *The Venture of Islam*, vol. 1, p. 259.

the prophet – a *hadith*, one of the pillars of Islam – tells how the patriarch Ibrahim (Abraham), at the instigation of his free wife Sarah, renounced Hagar.[112] Folk traditions embellished Hagar's misfortunes in the desert with her son Isma'il (Ismael), who is seen as the progenitor of the Arabs.[113] The Qur'an (2:125–7) states that Isma'il and Ibrahim founded Mecca and built the revered Ka'ba shrine.[114] To overcome bias against the caliphs born of slave mothers, Muslim scholars stressed that the Quraysh, Muhammed's own tribe, descended from Hagar, the concubine, while the reviled Jews were of Sarah's lineage, the free woman.[115] Military slaves took Isma'il as one of their 'exemplars'.[116]

The history of the identification of Arabs, later Turks and ultimately the Polovtsy/Cuman and Tatars, with the descendants of Hagar and Ishmael is complicated and based on many misunderstandings. The general mode is to identify contemporary people whose origin is uncertain with ethnonyms in the books which, from the Christian point of view, signify barbaric mores, nomadism and heterodoxy. Identification of steppe peoples as Ishmaelites first occurred after the 1096 raid of Kyiv by the Polovtsy in a specifically Rus' phase of the term's transmission, following a well-known Greek source, pseudo-Methodius. During the raids of the 1220s–1240s, Rus' clerics applied the term and its corollary with apocalyptic significance to the as yet unknown Tatars. In this form it found its way to Western Europe by diplomatic contacts and fugitives' reports. Although it denoted 'barbaric' customs and a general anti-Christian posture – despite the proximity of the Orthodox church and the Mongol Empire, which occurred shortly after – the connotation of slavery and especially liberation would be far-fetched in these texts.[117]

New interpretations of the expression 'Sons of Hagar' occurred in the sixteenth century. The example of Abraham's first wife Sarah, who according to the biblical book of Genesis allowed polygamy to produce an heir, was held in contempt in Muscovy as a carnal solution to the problem of royal infertility and dynastic continuity. This is demonstrated by the tale in the ecclesiastical Pafnut'ev Borovskii chronicle about the alleged spiritual fecundity of the childless *tsaritsa* Solomoniia,

---

112 N. Awde, *Women in Islam: An Anthology from the Qurān and Ḥadīths* (Richmond, Surrey, 2000), p. 143.
113 M. Ruthven, *Islam in the World* (New York, 2000), pp. 13–19.
114 Hodgson, *The Venture of Islam*, vol. 1, p. 279.
115 Goldziher, *Muslim Studies*, vol.1, pp. 116–119.
116 B. Walker, *Foundations of Islam: The Making of a World Faith* (London, 1998), p. 335.
117 Chekin, 'The Godless Ishmaelites'; Jackson, 'The Testimony of the Russian "Archbishop" Peter Concerning the Mongols (1244/5)'; Laushkin, 'Nasledniki praottsa Izmaila i bibleiskaia mozaika v letopisnykh izvestiiakh o Polovtsakh'. On the contrived interpretation of the obscure origins of the term 'Saracen' by medieval Christians connoting the supposed attempt of the Arabs to hide their origin from Hagar, the 'bondswoman' and posing as descendants of Sarah, the free wife: D.F. Graf and M. O'Connor, 'The Origin of the Term Saracen and the Rawwafa Inscriptions', *Byzantine Studies/Etudes byzantines*, 4 (1977), pp. 52–66, here p. 60.

whom tsar Vasilii III divorced in 1526. The 'Tale' was composed in the 1540s at metropolitan Daniil's court. It claims that she asked for divorce to devote herself to ascetic life as a nun:

> For the Christ-loving [Solomoniia] did not imitate Sarah but Anna, the wife of Joachim, the man of God. For Sarah because of her infertility ordered Abraham to take Hagar, his slave, [as his concubine to produce an heir], but Anna untied the knot of her infertility through fasting and prayer, and conceived the Virgin Mary in her womb, and by this act gave birth to the immaterial light, the queen. The pious and Christ-loving grand princess and nun Sofiia [Solomoniia's 'model' and wife of Ivan III; C.W.] did not untie the knot of the infertility of her womb, but she betrothed herself in faith to Christ, the bridegroom.[118]

In typical Muscovite fashion, this text has more to tell implicitly and in context of other Muscovite sources than at first appears. To denounce Sarah not only emphasizes *tsaritsa* Solomoniia's piety, a traditional epithet of Kremlin rulers and their spouses; in other words, a clear rejection of power forming gender roles. The implied frontal attack on the 'Sons of Hagar'[119] was easily grasped: it targets Ottoman marriage patterns, due to which rulers were often the sons of formerly enslaved mothers.[120]

Intently or not, Muscovites might have missed the point that concubines became legal wives after giving birth to an heir. The ambiguous position of slave concubines who became mothers of their master's son and consequently, due to Islamic law, were manumitted to become wives of their former masters and sometimes regents was known in East Slavic lore. In the epic poem 'Marusia Boguslavka', the captive heroine liberates Slavic prisoners from the dungeon using the khan's key. Nevertheless, as his wife and mother of their son she cannot or will not abscond with them. This fact is coded in the – from the point of view of the Ruthenians and Muscovy – euphemistic quote: 'I have already been spoilt by the luxuries'.[121]

The Tobolsk cossack officer, historian and architect Semen U. Remezov wrote and sketched at the turn of the eighteenth century a complex history of the conquest of Siberia. He connected 'Sons of Hagar'[122] to slavery and polygamy, thereby

---

118 I. Thyrêt, '"Blessed is the Tsaritsa's Womb": The Myth of Miraculous Birth and Royal Motherhood in Muscovite Russia', *Russian Review*, 53, 4 (1994), pp. 479–496, here p. 488.
119 Hagar (Hajar) and Ismael are esteemed in Islamic tradition, as examples of dignity in adversity: exiling them is seen as a test of Ibrahim's obedience to God's commands: A. Schussmann, 'The Legitimacy and Nature of Mawid al-Nabī (Analysis of a Fatwā)', *Islamic Law and Society*, 5, 2 (1998), pp. 214–234, here p. 218. According to Genesis, Abraham was distressed at Sarah's demand to divorce Hagar and freed her and her son; thus, claims to his inheritance were invalidated (Gen 21:14–21).
120 Cf. Introduction. Toledano, *As if Silent and Absent*, p. 43.
121 V. Antonovich and M. Dragomanov, *Istoricheskiia pesni malorusskago naroda s obiasneniiami Vl. Antonovicha i M. Dragomanova*, vol. 1 (Kiev, 1874), No. 46: Marusia Boguslavka osvobozhdaet kozakov iz turetskoi nevoli (Duma) (Zapisal v Zen'kovsk. u. Poltavskoi gubernii A. Metlinskii).
122 Remezov, *Remezovskaia letopis'*, p. 10 (14).

denouncing the victims of Ermak's invasion. He lived in a world that combined the influences of Swedish prisoners of war who lived in Tobolsk, information from local Tatars to whom he talked, and both Siberian and Muscovite tradition. In a storyline rife with redemptive imagery such as the biblical column of fire accompanying the Israelites along their way out of Egypt through the Red Sea, the khan of Sibir's end was neigh and the Muscovite Christian empire presaged. In this context, his relations to women and slaves from Rus' are depicted as corollary justification:[123]

> Kuchum was of the Muslim faith (*very basurmanskie*), bowed to idols and prayed in a filthy fashion. He lived without [canon] law (*bezakonno*) since he was not ashamed – as did other Sons of Hagar, too – to possess 100 women and also [according to the images, underage] girls, as many as he wanted. The all-seeing God put a quick end to his rule. [. . .] The next year [. . .] he married the daughter of the Kazanian khan Murat and took along with her [. . .] Rus' captives to the river Sibir, where he was well-respected.[124]

Due to their custom of enslaving, Remezov insinuates, the Siberian 'Sons of Hagar' can be subjugated. The Byzantine church used the argument of descent from Hagar to legitimise enslavement of 'obdurate' Muslims as a 'natural' consequence, although the Church recommended that converts be manumitted.[125] While there is no overt communication with Muslims in almost all of these instances, the usages of the term '*agariane*' along with the closely aligned 'Ishmaelites' are among the most frequent Muscovite pejorative references to Muslims. They betray a good deal of otherwise hardly noticeable, intimate if superficial knowledge of slavery and its complex justifications in Islam from a rather practical, yet mostly derogatory point of view.

A reading of 'Sons of Hagar' referring to slavery and liberation is uppermost in the 'Chronicle of the Beginning of Tsardom', when Volodimir Andreevich, boyars and military leaders praise Ivan for the conquest of Kazan and the concomitant liberation of slaves:

> Remain, o sovereign, in good health for many years to come in your God-given tsardom of Kazan. You are verily our intercessor with God against the godless Hagarites. Through your agency today Christians are liberated (*svobozhiaiutsia*) forever and the dishonourable place is purified by mercy.[126]

The conquest and accompanying liberation of slaves in the view of the elite confirmed the image of the tsar as intercessor for slaves. Meanwhile the routed Tatars were framed in the image of 'Sons of Hagar' as living in an unclean or rather shameful place which the Muscovites forcefully 'cleansed' by liberating the 'poor Christian' slaves,

---

123 Ibid., p. 52 (60).
124 Ibid., pp. 132–133.
125 Ibid., p. 224. Kazhdan, 'The Concept of Freedom (*eleutheria*) and Slavery (*duleia*) in Byzantium', pp. 218–219. Hellie, *Slavery in Russia, 1450–1725*, pp. 73–74.
126 Tikhomirov, *Letopisets nachala tsarstva*, p. 109.

spilling much Muslim blood and deporting the remainder of Kazan Tatars. The tsar calls the city dishonourable or impious because the 'Sons of Hagar' stole Christians and broke their oaths. Liberation from slavery justifies conquest in this speech.

'Sons of Hagar' are mentioned several times in the 'Chronicle'. Ivan IV's speech during the review makes it clear that the first meaning of 'Sons of Hagar' refers to its basis in difference of belief. Nevertheless, the rousing aspect of using this term is in liberation from slavery, as he continues immediately:

> Sons of Hagar they are as they have no God [. . .] The time is upon us bravely to affirm the holy Trinity and [help] our brotherly Orthodox Christians.[127]

Ivan points out the basis for the assertion that Tatars unlawfully acquired Orthodox Christians as slaves – whether all of these slaves were Christians is questionable, nevertheless this is the tsar's argument. In any case, they were not to keep their slaves as Muslims should not be allowed to hold Christian slaves.[128] The fact that he mentions the Trinity as a point of inter-faith polemics in this context actually invalidates the religious argument, since it implies that they 'have a God'. Prince Volodimir Andreevich's answer to Ivan IV's later speech about the benefits of liberating Christian slaves loosely and rather traditionally uses the words 'those godless Sons of Hagar'.[129]

Finally, metropolitan Makarii, an authority on questions of faith, reaffirms the image of the 'Sons of Hagar' as dishonourable slave raiders during the victorious tsar's entry into the capital:

> God effected these miracles, showing His glory to you, honourable tsar and giving you splendid victories over the dishonourable Crimean Tatar khan and rescuing us, His Christ-named flock from the raids of the foreign Hagarians by your agency, our lord. You, our lord, with the aid of [. . .] all of the Christ-loving army's great works fighting manfully for honour with God's help and protection, you, o tsar, have campaigned like a good tsar against your enemies the dishonourable tsars [khans] and oath-breaking Kazanian Tatars, who [. . .] enslaved Orthodox Christians (*v plen raskhishchaia*) and scattered them over the face of the whole earth. You, honourable tsar strong in battle put your steadfast hope and faith in almighty God and showed great works and strength of the soul. You have increased the talent given to you and liberated from slavery the flock that was robbed from your pasture (*raskhishchenoe stado* [. . .] *svobodit' ot raboty)*'.[130]

The Crimean and Kazanian 'foreign' Tatars are Hagarites specifically for breaking their oaths by robbing and enslaving Christians.

The specific interpretation of 'Sons of Hagar' as slavers was spread by the previously mentioned *tsaritsa* Sofiia Palaiologina (c. 1440/49–1503),[131] the niece of

---

127 Ibid., p. 82.
128 Kivelson, 'Bitter Slavery and Pious Servitude'.
129 Tikhomirov, *Letopisets nachala tsarstva*, p. 96.
130 Ibid., p. 114.
131 I. de Madariaga, *Ivan the Terrible: First Tsar of Russia* (New Haven CT, 2005).

the last Byzantine emperor and wife of Ivan III, and her entourage. It helped to stabilise the precarious dynastic position of the *tsaritsa* in general, as well as her personal situation as an outsider and, later, a disgraced person. The interpretation they gave to the expression 'Sons of Hagar' in the 'Letter to the Ugra' is in keeping with her mission of proselytizing the Muscovites for common campaigns with Latin rulers against the Ottomans:[132]

> [W]hen the old sons of Ismail had sinned before God he enslaved them to foreigners; once they had atoned, he saved them from foreign slavery and enslaved the foreigners to them.[133]

Such a cyclical view was conducive to integrating steppe nomads into the Muscovite Empire, as they could imagine themselves and their families as former and future masters according to the vicissitudes of as yet unknown historical future and despite the apparent glass ceiling of enthronisation of Chinggisids as serious rulers of Muscovy.[134]

Moreover, according to the same passage, the 'sly and proud Egyptian pharaoh' was 'the pagan son of Ismail', which makes this a very specifically redemptive story of social mobility, obliquely referencing the Mamluk dynasty, which recruited military slaves. This implicit explanation of Islamic state and military power based on slavery, the slave trade and slave raids is summary and in this form no longer appealing to the social science-trained modern eye. Nevertheless, it expressly links Biblical themes concerning slavery, even Egyptian slavery, to the term Hagarites, in the very sentence following the above quote on their enslavement and redemption:

> [The Israelites] did likewise, when they were slaves in Egypt, and the Lord liberated them from Egyptian slavery (*rabota*) by the agency of Moses.[135]

While the 'Letter to the Ugra' does not go as far as identifying Muslims with Jews, it attributes an exodus from slavery to Muslims which is seen similar to the Old Testament Exodus from Egyptian slavery, and as such qualifies them to rule over slaves. It was a reworking of the Byzantine sources used by Patricia Crone and Michael Cook in an attempt to base the early history of Islam on outsider sources, which is now as such discredited among scholars of Islam.[136] Crone's former reading of these sources interpreted the Hijra to Medina as an exodus movement of a Jewish tribe

---

132 On the 'Letter to the Ugra', see chapter 2.
133 Tikhomirov, *Vologodsko-permskii letopisets*, p. 271.
134 D. Ostrowski, 'Simeon Bekbulatovich's Remarkable Career as Tatar Khan, Grand Prince of Rus', and Monastic Elder', *Russian History*, 39, 3 (2012), pp. 269–299; C.J. Halperin, 'Simeon Bekbulatovich and Mongol Influence on Ivan IV's Muscovy', *Russian History*, 39, 3 (2012), pp. 306–330; Martin, 'Simeon Bekbulatovich and Steppe Politics'.
135 Tikhomirov, *Vologodsko-permskii letopisets*, p. 271.
136 A. Neuwirth, 'Structural, Linguistic and Literary Features', in J.D. McAuliffe, ed., *The Cambridge Companion to the Qur'ān* (Cambridge, 2006), pp. 97–114, here pp. 100–101.

towards the Promised Land. They conquered Jerusalem and later sought to distance themselves from Jews and Christians to defend their possession and invented Islam for the purpose.[137] On the background of Islamic sources and the fact that Inner Arabia was a terra incognita to the Byzantines of the period, these interpretations are highly speculative, but point to open questions in historiography. Finally, they summarize early outsiders' ideas about Islam which partly re-appear in the 'Letter to the Ugra'.[138] The very tendency in the outsider, heterodox sources on early Islam – as well as in the Muscovite texts about the 'Sons of Hagar' quoted above – to erase differences between the monotheistic faiths is relevant to the argument that Muscovites along with their post-Byzantine teachers tried to set up a device to connect Christianity and Islam by using the idiom of liberation from slavery.

The very few voices that survived from inside of Kazan's walls tend to show there was a battle for the higher moral ground going on, or more precisely competition for the moral capital of liberation and liberty.[139] In some cases, Tatars even used Muscovite terminology. Thus, the Muscovite envoy to the Nogai Tatars reported after the conquest of Kazan that they believed they would become subservient to the Moscow tsar, too:

> Our books say that all Muslim rulers will serve (*porabotaiut*) the lord of Moscow.[140]

Another envoy reported about the letter written by a Nogai *mirza* who supported Moscow. He replied to the Ottoman sultan's demand to back the cause of Islam facing the Muscovite Christians:

> In our Muslim books it is written that those years have come, the years of the Moscow tsar Ivan. His hand is high over the Muslims.[141]

These statements align with comments in one of the accounts of the conquest, the 'History of Kazan' which, as mentioned above, was written from an insider's view. The anonymous author, or his alter ego, a self-acknowledged, former favoured slave of the khan, came to live in Muscovy after the conquest. In many passages his

---

137 Crone and Cook, *Hagarism*.
138 See also Patricia Crone's summary of the debate: P. Crone (2008), *What Do We Actually Know about Mohammed?* 10.06.2008, https://www.opendemocracy.net/faith-europe_islam/mohammed_3866.jsp (accessed 10 June 2020).
139 For the concept of moral capital and liberation, cf. Brown, *Moral Capital*; Kane, *The Politics of Moral Capital*.
140 S.M. Solov'ev, *Istoriia Rossii s drevneishikh vremen*, vol. 3, pt. 6 (Moskva, 1959–1966), p. 488; Kämpfer, *Die Eroberung von Kasan 1552 als Gegenstand der zeitgenössischen russischen Historiographie*, p. 150.
141 M. D'iakonov, *Vlast' moskovskikh gosudarei* (Sanktpeterburg, 1889), p. 63; G.Z. Kuntsevich, *Istoriia o kazanskom tsarstve ili Kazanskii letopisets*, S.-Peterburg, 1905, p. 385; Kämpfer, 'Die Eroberung von Kasan', p. 150.

point of view is anti-Muscovite, as one would expect from someone who had lived a privileged life in Kazan.[142]

He is in a good position to express the worldview of Kazan's defenders; however, he does so in order to refute it. It cannot be excluded that the following quote may have been tendentiously changed. In any case, the contrast to Muscovite statements is what counts in the context of the narrative of the 'History'. When the first ominous signs of imminent doom appear, a vocal group rejects submission:

> Do we really want to become subjects of the Muscovite ruler, his princes and commanders, who always fear us? Th[e latter] indeed suits them, it is ours to rule and collect tribute from them as before. For they have sworn submission to our tsars and paid tribute. So, from the beginning we are their masters and they are our slaves. How dare our slaves (*raby*) and how are they even capable to resist us, their masters, since they have been vanquished by us so many times? We have never been dominated by anyone except our tsars. Yet, even in his service we remain free: we go wherever we want. Where we live, we serve according to our freedom. We are not accustomed to live in great unfreedom (*nevolia*), as they do under [Ivan IV] in Moscow, suffering greatly.[143]

The author had no qualms about denouncing Kazanian Tatars according to the preconceptions shared by Muscovite writers. Hagar's sons are depicted as living by the sword and by robbery at least twice in the 'History of Kazan'.[144] Chapter 23 immediately follows the first indictment and focuses on the Kazanian Tatars enslaving the Rus' people. Thus, it is impressed on the reader that the habit of the 'Sons of Hagar' of living by the sword means enslavement for countless people from Muscovy. The message of these lines in their context is: unlimited Tatar freedom means enslavement for Muscovites.

How fractured such groups were is made abundantly clear in the same chapter when the readiness of Shah Ali to accept the throne of Kazan is praised, although he knew that for him it meant 'sure captivity and even death'. Yet, as instrument of taking care of Orthodox captives, he overlooks the treachery of Kazanians who advise Ivan. He obeys the tsar's order, and thereby demonstrates the futility of Ivan's attempts to assuage them. The 'History' tersely restates an extreme form of worldview of this counter-dependency zone combining strong asymmetrical dependency and liberation from the perceived wilfulness of foreigners: 'Unfreedom (*nevolia*) is capable of so much more than unlimited freedom (*volia*)!'[145]

---

142 Kämpfer, 'Die Eroberung von Kasan', pp. 155–161.
143 Kämpfer, *Historie vom Zartum Kasan (Kasaner Chronist)*, p. 146; Volkova, *Kazanskaia Istoriia*, chapter 30.
144 Volkova, *Kazanskaia Istoriia*, chs. 22, 101; Moiseeva and Adrianova-Peretts, *Kazanskaia istoriia*, 75, 176.
145 Volkova, *Kazanskaia Istoriia*, chapter 23.

Wisdom, empire and liberation

Wisdom has been recognized as a central principle of Muscovite political culture and philosophy of law, yet as representing slavery, empire and inter-confessional relations it could actually have attracted closer scrutiny.[146] Wisdom is connected to many strands of transculturally accessible topoi and therefore deserves attention. The biblical Books of Wisdom as sources of this ideology had already aligned the belief in one God with the heterodox environment: they were written mostly late in the Old Testament era, during the Persian and Hellenistic imperial periods. Their notions and terms were conceived under the influence of the pantocratic, i.e. almighty, and ethnically inclusive images of God prevalent in these cultures. The biblical Books of Wisdom 'humanize' monotheism by re-interpreting the wrathful, punishing and violent God of the older parts of the Hebrew Bible – who liberates to take possession of his people – as mainly benevolent and merciful; or, they mediate between these two images as in the book of Job: God punishes apparently without cause, testing Job's faith to the very point of desperation, but finally he is saved.[147]

Wisdom was among the main principles according to which the grand prince and tsar was judged; it subsumed to be righteous, just and law-abiding, and to deliver captives and slaves.[148] When thousands of slaves in Kazan are set free in 1551 according to Moscow's conditions for peace, the 'Chronicle of the Beginning of Tsardom' praises Ivan:

> Today the Christian people were liberated by the mercy of God and by the wisdom of our ruler, the Orthodox tsar.[149]

---

146 Rowland, 'The Problem of Advice in Muscovite Tales about the Time of Troubles'; Bogatyrev, *The Sovereign and His Counsellors*; S. Bogatyrev, 'Battle for Divine Wisdom: The Rhetoric of Ivan IV's Campaign Against Polotsk', in E. Lohr and M. Poe, eds., *The Military and Society in Russia, 1450–1917* (Leiden, 2002), pp. 325–363; P. Hunt, 'The Wisdom Iconography of Light: The Genesis, Meaning and Iconographic Realization of a Symbol', *Byzantinoslavica*, 67 (2009), pp. 55–118.

147 M. Witte, '"Barmherzigkeit und Zorn Gottes" im Alten Testament am Beispiel des Buchs Jesus Sirach', in R.G. Kratz and H. Spieckermann, eds., *Divine Wrath and Divine Mercy in the World of Antiquity* (Tübingen, 2008), pp. 176–202; M. Witte, 'Vom El Schaddaj zum Pantokrator: Ein Überblick zur israelitisch-jüdischen Religionsgeschichte', in J.F. Diehl and M. Witte, eds., *Studien zur Hebräischen Bibel und ihrer Nachgeschichte: Beiträge der 32. Internationalen Ökumenischen Konferenz der Hebräischlehrenden, Frankfurt am Main 2009* (Kamen, 2011), pp. 211–256; M. Witte, *Von der Weisheit des Glaubens an den einen Gott* (2013), https://www.perlentaucher.de/essay/von-der-weisheit-des-glaubens-an-den-einen-gott.html (accessed 11 May 2022).

148 Rowland, 'The Problem of Advice in Muscovite Tales about the Time of Troubles'; I. Thyrêt, *Between God and Tsar: Religious Symbolism and the Royal Women of Muscovite Russia* (DeKalb IL, 2001). Cf. C. Witzenrath, 'Sophia – Divine Wisdom, and Justice in Seventeenth-Century Russia', *Cahiers du monde russe*, 50, 2–3 (2009), pp. 409–429.

149 Tikhomirov, *Letopisets nachala tsarstva*, p. 66.

Likewise, the 'Book of Royal Degrees', written in the 1560s to edify and educate the tsar's heir, sets apart the liberation of the captives at Kazan as a major achievement of the campaign and evidence of the tsar's wisdom. Moreover, it was copied to replace lost or omitted chapters in the 'History of Kazan', which became particularly widespread in the seventeenth century.[150] The 'wise' tsar is portrayed as 'winning the hearts and minds' of people living in the former khanate and in Siberia, to use twenty-first century propagandistic language:

> All other Kazanian people [Tatars, Cheremis and Mordvins], who live in the lands near the city, the land of Kazan as well as the land of Sibir, seeing God's great power in the feats of the wise tsar, ceased their enmity to approach him in prayer. They submitted by throwing themselves onto the ground before him, gave themselves up and begged for his mercy for breaking their oaths [of delivering the captives] many times. The ruler showed his grace to his new subjects and told them to serve him, and they were sent back to their homes unharmed. [. . .] Ivan had made an effort for the flock of the word [i.e., the Christians; CW] entrusted to him by God: he had gained a praiseworthy victory over the enemies, returned the Christian slaves from among the heathens [Muslims and animists] and wisely set up the tsardom of Kazan, given to him by God.[151]

There is no dedicated theoretical literature in Muscovy and usually no definitions. Therefore, calling the tsar 'wise' twice at the start and the end of this passage is a strong way of saying that the actions narrated indicate what the epithet means. '*Slovesnye ovtsy*' (speaking sheep) refers to the vita of Cyril, who adapted the Greek alphabet to meet the needs of Slavic speakers and thus developed the predecessor of Cyrillic script, Glagolitic, which made the Word of the Bible intelligible to the Slavic tongue. His vita portrays Cyril as lover of Wisdom, who tells his father about a dream in which he chose to marry a girl called Sophia.[152]

The 'Chronicle of the Beginning of Tsardom' uses epithets related to Wisdom to enhance Ivan's praise at the close of the campaign: Faith, Hope and Charity, or, in the Russian text, *liubov* (Love, *agape*) are the daughters of St Sophia the Roman martyr who are revered in Orthodoxy.[153] Extolled by St Paul in 1 Kor. 13, these are standard Christian principles[154] with particular application in Eurasia. In Semen U. Remezov's detailed Siberian coat of arms at the turn of the eighteenth century, these three appear as allegoric figures positioned on columns above the pictures of local Russian, Tatar,

---

150 Dubrovina, *Istoriia o Kazanskom tsarstve (Kazanskii letopisets)*; T.F. Volkova, *Slovar knizhnikov i knizhnosti Drevnei Rusi: Kazanskaia istoriia*.
151 N.N. Pokrovskii and G. Lenhoff, eds., *Stepennaia kniga tsarskogo rodosloviia po drevneishim spiskam: Teksty i kommentarii: Stepeni XI–XVII – prilozheniia – ukazateli* (Moskva, 2008), p. 371. Enemies and Muslims engaging in slaving are denounced as 'heathens'.
152 The extended *vita of Constantine (Kirill)*: *Zhitiia Kirilla i Mefodiia*, Moskva, 1986.
153 Tikhomirov, *Letopisets nachala tsarstva*, pp. 59, 63, 76, 89, 90, 96, 114, 115; O.B. Strakhov, *The Byzantine Culture in Muscovite Rus': The Case of Evfimii Chudovskii (1620–1705)* (Köln, 1998), p. 224.
154 A.I. Filiushkin, 'Religioznyi faktor v russkoi vneshnei politike XVI veka: Ksenofobiia, tolerantnost' ili pragmatizm?', in L. Steindorff, ed., *Religion und Integration im Moskauer Russland: Konzepte und Praktiken, Potentiale und Grenzen 14.–17. Jahrhundert* (Wiesbaden, 2010), pp. 145–180.

Samoyed and *Obdarinets* ethnic subjects of the tsar in Siberia, along with the personification of Justice on the fourth column.[155] Justice and law were among the main subjects covered by the over-arching concern for the ruler's wisdom; in his own writings, Remezov subsumed to this the customary law of Siberia's people.[156]

Remezov appears to have appreciated the implications of St Paul's lines, specifically about the long-suffering nature of charity, as towards the end of his life he was still paying the debts his father had engendered by ransoming people who were clearly neither Orthodox nor Russian. The Remezovs took seriously the obligation to redeem the tsar's subjects stipulated in the code of laws. Ulian Remezov went as envoy to the Mongols. During his mission to Devlet-Girei,[157] to Lauzan-*taisha* and to the powerful Oirat Ablai-*taisha*[158] in 1660, Ulian succeeded in peace negotiations. He agreed to the request of 31 Tatar *iasak*[159]-payers of the tsar from the Barabinsk steppe to ransom them and convoyed them back to Tara on his own camels, buying expensive extra foodstuffs from the Kalmyks. Ulian was memorialized by a street named after him in the upper town of Tobolsk, just opposite the governor's palace. However, neither the ransomed Tatars nor Russian officials seemed to repay the debts he had incurred to redeem them. More than four decades later, his son Semen Ulianovich Remezov wrote a complaint: he was still paying off the debt and expected compensation.[160] While Moscow might disagree with some of the ideas entertained by Muscovites, with some of the interpretations of the law code – which did neither explicitly mention nor exclude non-Orthodox people as 'brothers' – this episode illustrates the ways in which these guidelines informed how Muscovites made sense of their actions in imperial space and relations.

Charity and faith as attributes of the wise ruler in Russian sources were expected to direct the actions of Ivan IV in Kazan. Metropolitan Makarii, often seen as the epitome of Muscovy's crusading, anti-Tatar ideologists,[161] congratulated his tsar for virtuous accomplishments subsumed by wisdom and proven by the liberation of

---

155 Kivelson, *Cartographies of Tsardom*, p. 169 fig. 6.7.
156 Ibid.; Witzenrath, 'Sophia – Divine Wisdom, and Justice in Seventeenth-Century Russia'.
157 On the debate and contradictory sources about the origins of the Girei dynasty, see A. Ibraim, 'Predki Geraev: Istoricheskie versii i fakty', *Tiurkologicheskie publikatsii*, http://turkolog.narod.ru/info/I139.htm. See also http://turkology.tk/library/139. See M. Ivanics, 'Die Şirin: Abstammung und Aufstieg einer Sippe in der Steppe', in D. Klein, ed., *The Crimean Khanate Between East and West (15th–18th Century)* (Wiesbaden, 2012), pp. 27–44.
158 West Mongol prince.
159 Tax paid by native peoples as a privilege, stemming from Mongol times.
160 Gol'denberg, *Izograf zemli sibirskoi*, pp. 84–85.
161 Martin, 'Multiethnicity in Muscovy', pp. 2–4; Miller, 'The Velikie Minei Chetii and the Stepennaia Kniga of Metropolitan Makarii and the Origins of Russian National Consciousness', pp. 294–301; Pelenski, *Russia and Kazan*, pp. 194–204. Janet Martin has realigned this view with more diverse characterizations of Tatars, while the characterization of Makarii remains unchanged: Martin, 'Religious Ideology and Chronicle Depictions of Muslims in 16th-Century Muscovy', p. 286.

slaves. Citing the need to liberate the slaves, he justified and called for a severe approach to Kazan:

> You, o tsar, have risen as behoves a tsar against your enemies the impious and dishonourable tsars and oath-breaking Kazan Tatars, who have [. . .] captured Orthodox Christians and scattered them across the face of the whole earth. And you, strong in battle as is worthy of a tsar, have put your unfaltering hope and faith in God Almighty, showing great works and efforts and undertaking to multiply the talents received [by] liberating your captured flock from slavery. The Lord saw your unwavering faith and purity and truthful love and your wise consideration (*razsuzhenie blagorazsudnoe*), your courage and valour and your readiness to give your soul for [. . .] those led into slavery, tortured by [Kazan Tatars] by all means and abused with manifold passions, and due to your faith and unheard-of efforts God [. . .] gave you the city and the tsardom of Kazan.[162]

These instructions for empire-building subscribe to a supra-ethnic principle which includes those whom imperial propaganda considers secure. However, it excludes those regarded as attackers and enslavers of its subjects.

This view is cross-referenced in the text. During the campaign to found Sviiazhsk in 1551, the tsar treated servitors and auxiliaries extraordinarily well and spent huge sums on provisions and salaries, so that all his servitors and the new allies among Kazan's former subjects would be fully satisfied. Such disbursements were unheard of in earlier chronicles and needed explanation. The authors of the 'Chronicle' noted that liberating and protecting his people from slave raids by such means was a mark of the ruler's wisdom. They reiterate the supra-ethnic principle conflicting with an often-assumed crusading spirit in this period:

> In earlier chronicles, we do not find records about such expenditure, which the ruler extends to all of his soldiers and those who have recently arrived [i.e. Tatars and further ethnic groups]. God may invest him to have mercy on the Christian people and redeem them from Barbarian assaults and liberate the[m] forever from the Tatars.[163]

The following lines combine Ivan's love for his subjects as an attribute of wisdom and a means of winning favour with the conquered, with direct military action to discourage and cow the Kazanians. Liberation of his subjects from slavery as a condition of alliance inspired auxiliaries to follow the tsar. This is then summed up in a straightforward, firm instruction for how to establish rule in a multi-cultural empire:

> As the[people from the] mountainous, western bank of the Volga saw [tsar Ivan's] love and generosity and how he cared every waking hour for the people God had entrusted to him, they all became weary, [sought] to strive for God and for him the lord, while the neighbours feared him. [. . .] [Soon] the Kazanians in town and villages saw that the mountainous side firmly supported the sovereign [. . .][164]

---

162 Tikhomirov, *Letopisets nachala tsarstva*, p. 114.
163 Ibid., p. 63.
164 Ibid.

This is followed by a description of how the tsar's army cut off the city. Military success, the tsar's generosity towards auxiliary troops and his ostentatious compassion for the slaves he claimed as his subjects led to disunity among the Kazanian Tatars and those sent from Crimea to help and rule them. The 'Chronicle' asserts that this imperial strategy was followed by Tatar defections to Moscow.

Another version of imperial sensibilities is offered by the 'History of Kazan'. As mentioned above, Frank Kämpfer highlighted the layer of pro-Kazanian, at times even anti-Russian, consciousness in this text.[165] Right at the start it states that it was written by a former slave and favourite of the khan, who entered Muscovite service just in time. It is reasonable to assume that there was an original, written or oral, relation which subsequently was embellished by writers and copyists. They placed the primary emphasis on Muscovite views while retaining the rather vivid descriptions of Tatar personalities from a Tatar or near Tatar point of view. Kämpfer assumed an intentionally abridged version that later became widespread in Muscovy as portions of the original had been replaced and amended with excerpts from the 'Book of Royal Degrees' about the events of the 1552 conquest. However, it is unlikely that the many staunchly pro-Tatar aspects of earlier chapters should have survived such a conscious falsification alongside pro-Muscovite episodes. It is more plausible that some parts of the early versions – only five copies of early versions survived – were lost or became unavailable, and were replaced by readily accessible sources.[166] Even in the early versions, the 'History' does not waste much effort vindicating the purported author's deeds as a slave beyond lip service, but signs up to the main thrust of Muscovite interpretation and justification of the conquest. Tellingly, the Kazanians are shown as intrepid defenders of their independence who nevertheless appear as unreliable traitors.[167] This paradoxical combination allows the author to remind Muscovites of the ideological battle for moral capital:[168] the Tatars use a language of liberty, whereas the Muscovites speak of liberation. When the text presents the first ominous signs of Muscovite attack and the Tatar haruspices advise to surrender to the tsar, the leaders of Kazan reply:

> Do we really want to be subjects of Moscow's ruler, [. . .] We have never been ruled by anyone but our khan. Even in his service we are free (*volny esmia v sebe*): we go wherever we want.

---

[165] Kämpfer, *Die Eroberung von Kasan 1552 als Gegenstand der zeitgenössischen russischen Historiographie*, p. 149.
[166] 'Kniga stepennaia', in Volkova, *Slovar knizhnikov i knizhnosti Drevnei Rusi*.
[167] Volkova, *Kazanskaia Istoriia*, chapter 15; Kämpfer, *Historie vom Zartum Kasan (Kasaner Chronist)*, p. 91; G.Z. Kuntsevich, ed., *Istoriia o Kazanskom tsarstve* (Sankt Peterburg, 1903), p. 40; Volkova, *Kazanskaia Istoriia*, chapter 20; Kämpfer, *Historie vom Zartum Kasan (Kasaner Chronist)*, p. 105; Kuntsevich, *Istoriia o Kazanskom tsarstve*, p. 50.
[168] Brown, *Moral Capital*; Kane, *The Politics of Moral Capital*.

> Where we live, we serve in our freedom. We are not suited to lack freedom, such as the life people live in Moscow, who endure great grief from [Ivan IV].[169]

This is an expression of 'steppe politics', as E. Keenan called contemporary ideas about allegiance east and south of Muscovy, which the latter aimed to overcome. Alliances could be repealed as soon as conditions changed and allegiances outside the closer kin group were considered revocable.[170] This view may have been laced here with the Muscovite view, which called for a permanent hierarchy, but whether such a view inhered in the original text or is a later attribution remains a matter of conjecture in the absence of compatible Tatar sources.

The Muscovite cyclical model of slavery and mastery mentioned above reads almost like a reply to this – Kazanian Tatars might not be masters any more, but there is a chance that they might again become masters or slavers one day.[171] Similar ideas are evident in the well-known lament of Suyum-bike, widow of khan Safa Girei, on her way into Muscovite captivity, as well as in the Muscovite commander's reply:

> Woe betides! To whom should I entrust my sorrows in Moscow? [. . .] To the Kazanians? Yet they have delivered me despite their oath. [. . .] I was once your wife, o khan, now I am a bitter captive. Ruler I was called of a whole khanate, now I am a miserable slave.[172]

Note the denunciation of the Kazanians as traitors to their own khan who serve Muscovite ends, despite the thrust of Suyum-bike's speech, which is to decry sorrowful captivity. The Muscovite commander, however, tries to placate her by promising she would not suffer dishonour, but that the tsar will receive her and allow her to live as an esteemed ruler over many towns. This reply blunted the edge of Kazanian aspirations to the moral capital of liberty and, to some degree, explains how the author could get away with pro-Kazanian sentiments.

Earlier in the text, Shah Ali is in mortal danger, trapped in his palace and heavily guarded by the anti-Moscow faction in Kazan. That is when it becomes glaringly obvious that the condition for him to be saved, liberated and accepted back in Muscovy is that he would hand over '100,000' Christian slaves:[173] He was

> alone in Kazan, in 1546, not like a khan, but like a captive, seized and tightly watched. They did not allow him anywhere out of town. When he saw his great, inescapable calamity of the Kazanians it grieved him and he wailed and secretly asked God according to his belief, and he

---

169 Moiseeva and Adrianova-Peretts, *Kazanskaia istoriia*, pp. 89–90; Kämpfer, *Historie vom Zartum Kasan (Kasaner Chronist)*, p. 146. See above for the whole quote.
170 Keenan, 'Muscovy and Kazan'; E.L. Keenan, *Muscovy and Kazan', 1445–1552: A Study in Steppe Politics* (PhD dissertation, Harvard University, 1965).
171 See chapter 2. At the time, the historical, conclusive loss of freedom could hardly be presaged.
172 Kämpfer, *Historie vom Zartum Kasan (Kasaner Chronist)*, pp. 143–145.
173 Ibid., p. 139.

called on the Russian saints and considered how to get liberated (*osvoboditisia*) from this senseless death. Instead of a khan's power he showed meekness to them, he was obedient and did not object in any way to their orders. [. . .] However, the death of a tsar usually does not occur without God's will [. . .] God put mercy for the khan (*tsar*) into the heart of the great prince Chiura Narykov, the ruler of all Kazan, because of Shah Ali righteously suffered (*pravednye stradaniia*) for the Christians.[174]

The term *stradaniia* refers to Christ's passion, exalting the Muslim Chinggisid who calls on the Christian saints. This trans-confessional openness of Muscovite redemption ideology and saints' cults demonstrates again the intended inclusiveness of imperial culture to those who harboured doubts about heterodoxy or who, like Shah Ali, served the tsar by faithfully liberating and ransoming Orthodox slaves.

Light symbolism

The criterion of liberating and ransoming slaves allowed the inclusion of those who supported the tsar's agenda, while excluding enemies and those regarded as malevolent, irrespective of ethnic and confessional affiliations. While it was transferred from internal relations and expectations to cover allies and trans-confessional brokers, other concepts are more obviously transcultural in origin – i.e. rooted in more than one culture.

This is particularly so in the case of the light symbolism of wisdom. The 'History of Kazan' recounts how Shah Ali as khan of Kazan fell into captivity of the faction opposing Muscovy. He was still nominally khan and used his remaining, ceremonial duties to mollify and mislead his detractors. After four nights of celebrations which he himself had organised to put them to sleep, Shah Ali escaped:

> [he] rode out of Kazan with the Muscovite military leaders, overjoyed to get away from Kazan's grief, like a child is born to the light or like a dead man escaping hell.[175]

Hell was a metaphor for prison and captivity, as any Orthodox who attended mass and religious plays during the Feast of the Resurrection of Christ could tell.[176] Moreover, sunlight and hell are opposed in contexts of slave liberation in the 'Chronicle of the Beginning of Tsardom'.[177] These connotations underline the importance of the light and

---

[174] Ibid., pp. 107–108; Volkova, *Kazanskaia Istoriia*, chapter 25.

[175] Moiseeva and Adrianova-Peretts, *Kazanskaia istoriia*, p. 108; 'Kazanskaia Istoriia', in *Pamiatniki literatury Drevnei Rusi*, pp. 300–624, here p. 434; Kämpfer, *Historie vom Zartum Kasan (Kasaner Chronist)*, p. 161.

[176] P. Lewin, *Ukrainian Drama and Theater in the Seventeenth and Eighteenth Centuries* (Toronto, 2008); I.R. Makaryk, *About the Harrowing of Hell = Slovo o zbureniu pekla: A Seventeenth-Century Ukrainian Play in its European Context* (Ottawa, 1989).

[177] Tikhomirov, *Letopisets nachala tsarstva*, p. 87.

birth metaphors for deliverance.[178] We can exclude alternative readings such as that he was enlightened by Christian Orthodoxy, since Shah Ali never converted. This interpretation remains valid although some church writers such as the priest and advisor of Ivan IV, Sil'vestr, used the light metaphor to praise the conversion of Tatar dignitaries and their sons after the conquest.[179]

Light could not only emanate from the Christian god, it was also characteristic of wisdom as a strongly trans-confessional concept which, moreover, was closely wedded to both imperial integration and the liberation of slaves. The 'History of Kazan', despite its ambivalence regarding allegiance, again sets the mark in a reply by Nogai nobles to the Ottoman sultan's urge to fight the enemies of Muslims in 1551, following peace conditions stipulating the handing over Kazan's slaves and cession of the mountainous riverbank:

> For our own as well as the Christian books say that in the latter years all peoples will be united and will be in the one Christian faith and under the rule of the people who confess this faith, which is the [. . .] Russian faith, shining among all our dark faiths like the most sparkling sun.[180]

Eschatological ideas among Muslim people in Muscovy's neighbourhood that argue for submitting to the tsar are attested elsewhere in the sixteenth century, and by Ottoman sources, too.[181]

Darkness is wedded to slavery in a key chapter of the 'History of Kazan', the lament about Kazan, and to slave raids into Muscovy. Placed just between the introductory portrait of young tsar Ivan IV and his compassionate prayer for slaves in the next chapter, it suggests rather than claims its programmatic status. The chapter suitably ends in a comparison of Muscovite slaves in Kazan to the Israelites in Egypt:

> Kazanian Saracens [i.e. Tatars] and Cheremis took Orthodox Christians captive on every day. O sun, why do you not darken and stop shining! [. . .] The Kazanians took the Russian captives into their homes, deceived and forced them to convert to Islam. Many unwisely allowed themselves to be led astray and became Muslims: some did this due to terror, fearing torture and being sold into slavery. Alas! Bitterness came over us from those: I do not understand how they [renegades] went awry, how their mind was darkened, but they behaved worse to Christians than barbarians and more evilly than Cheremis. Those who did not accept their faith were killed, others were kept in ropes, like logs, and sold to foreign traders in the market place, to heathens [i.e. Muslims] like themselves, to far-away foreign countries, so that they all perished without hope of escape. Since the Kazanians feared to keep many Russian men without

---

178 Cf. 'Kazanskaia Istoriia' in *Pamiatniki literatury Drevnei Rusi*, pp. 410–411.
179 D.P. Golokhvastov, 'Blagoveshchenskii ierei Sil'vestr i ego pisaniia', *Chteniia v imperatorskom obshchestve istorii i drevnostei rossiiskikh pri Moskovskom universitete*, 1 (1874), pp. 1–110, here p. 91.
180 'Kazanskaia Istoriia', in *Pamiatniki literatury Drevnei Rusi*, pp. 422–423; Volkova, *Kazanskaia Istoriia*, pp. 91–92.
181 Kämpfer, *Die Eroberung von Kasan 1552 als Gegenstand der zeitgenössischen russischen Historiographie*, pp. 150–152.

> conversion in Kazan and its lands, they left only women and girls and young boys, to ensure that Kazan did not fill with Russians in growing numbers, like the Israelites in Egypt, nor that Russians became stronger and started to tread the Kazanians underfoot.[182]

Slavery and slave raiding are likened to the darkened mind, to the sun of wisdom not shining. The rising empire of Muscovy is built on the perception of dire oppression by the Tatar slavers, as the comparison to Israel in Egypt intimates. This kind of confident imperial certainty compensated for the very real and extreme stretching of Muscovite power during the rest of the sixteenth century. As Matthew Romaniello has recently shown, the khanate of Kazan was only superficially pacified during these decades of recurring rebellions. It was only during the Time of Troubles in the early seventeenth century that middle Volga Tatars actively took part in restoring the tsar in Moscow as they faced Polish rule.[183]

As a rebuff to Kazanian nostalgia and perceived unruliness, the 'Book of Degrees', which was written in the aftermath of the conquest, in the rebellious 1560s, took to very lofty and abstract metaphors of rule over the rising empire, again using solar and wisdom images:

> [P]eople in Kazan, and those living in neighbouring countries, the whole land of Kazan and of Sibir saw the great God's power, acting vicariously through the hand of the tsar made wise by God (*bogomudryi*). Rather than [Ivan IV] making enemies by fighting, they came praying and threw themselves to the ground and submitted to the mercy of the Orthodox tsar. They accepted their faults and asked forgiveness for breaking their oath [of delivering slaves] so often. The lord mercifully pardoned those who had submitted, told them to serve him and sent them back to their homes. [. . .] Thereby the god-sent victor, god-crowned tsar had accomplished a great feat for his flock of speaking sheep, whom God had entrusted to him: he had won a praiseworthy victory over the enemies and returned the Christian captives from the pagan Tatars, and he wisely (*blagorazumno*) set up the tsardom of Kazan given to him by God, as he saw fit. [. . .] [H]e returned to the ruling city of Moscow, carrying a shining and glorious victory and was met by everybody with great joy. Everybody thanked the victor, gave him presents and bowed. Joy enlightened all beyond the shining sun.[184]

Heterodox Tatars are represented as seeing the hand of God, then peacefully submitting to the victor. The wise tsar pardons after punishment and accepts their vows although they broke their oaths, and lets them return to their homes unharmed – but only after delivering the Christian slaves. Submission and the liberation of Orthodox Christian captives cause enlightenment shining 'beyond the sun', which includes heterodox subjects within the realm who serve the tsar and help to liberate Orthodox slaves.

---

182 'Kazanskaia Istoriia', in *Pamiatniki literatury Drevnei Rusi*, pp. 368–369. Volkova, *Kazanskaia Istoriia*, pp. 49–51.
183 Romaniello, *The Elusive Empire*.
184 Pokrovskii and Lenhoff, *Stepennaia kniga tsarskogo rodosloviia po drevneishim spiskam*, p. 371.

The inclusive sun imagery of wisdom, which is so tangible in the 'Royal Book of Degrees', has a long pedigree, which goes back to the beginnings of Roman Christianity. In the canonical report about the victory of the Roman emperor Constantine over his rival, the cross appears in the sun. According to Maria Pliukhanova, who has investigated solar imagery as a sign of centrality, there was no particular context attached to these images in the Muscovite texts.[185] Adding to the wider context of the significance of liberation of slaves to the symbolism of the cross mentioned above, the 'Chronicle of the Beginning of Tsardom' gives reason to pause. It identifies the signs of the sun, the cross and liberation from slavery as it relates the final conquest of Kazan. The tsar's cousin prince Volodimir Andreevich, the boiars and commanders

> praised the tsar for his new tsardom Kazan. [. . .] "You are in truth our heavenly intercessor in affliction by the ungodly Hagarians. By your agency the poor Christians (*krestiiany*, lit. people of the cross) are liberated for all eternity and the unclean place is cleaned by grace".[186]

Next, khan Shah Ali praises Ivan. In contrast to the previous 'dishonourable *tsary*' of Kazan, he is addressed as '*blagochestivyi*' tsar. Only in context of the liberation of Orthodox slaves could a Muslim ruler be called 'most honourable', an epithet otherwise connoting piety and usually restricted to the Muscovite tsar. Shah Ali is extolled in the spirit of the counter dependency zone, as a Tatar Muslim ruler serving the Muscovite tsar to liberate Christian slaves. The procession solemnizing the defeat progresses into the conquered city, to the khan's palace, where the commanders and all Orthodox people hail the tsar:

> They saw the life-giving cross and the Orthodox tsar in the deserted ignominy of Kazan. Before [him], the impious and dishonourable tsars had held court in this palace, where much Christian blood had been spilled and the people of the cross suffered many injustices. However, today in this place the righteous sun shines, the life-giving wood itself, the life-giving cross.[187]

A Muslim Tatar prince, Shah Ali hesitated but found a way to reconcile claims to loyalty attached to his roles as Muslim leader and subject of the Moscow tsar. During the initial victory celebration at Kazan, he vocally accepts the tsar's legitimate conquest while not commenting on the symbolism of the speeches and procession. He attended the ceremony designed to include him.

This approach to loyalty rephrases the perspective first put forward by the 'Letter to the Ugra'. Muscovy never accepted that Chinggisids were mere robber barons, as the 'Letter' claimed, which released Ivan III from sworn loyalty to the Khan. Metropolitan Makarii nevertheless endorsed the document by including it in his Great Reading Menaion. In the medieval period, Rus' princes had taken oaths by kissing

---

185 M. Pliukhanova, *Siuzhety i simvoly Moskovskogo gosudarstva* (Sankt-Peterburg, 1995), p. 134.
186 Tikhomirov, *Letopisets nachala tsarstva*, p. 109.
187 Ibid. On the wood of the cross in redemption and ransom analogies, see chapter 3.

the cross, either to make a common stand against the steppe people or to unite with them to fight one of their own ranks, true to the form of a slaving zone.[188] However, these were mutual oaths. Discussions of oaths in relations to Tatars in the mid-sixteenth century already focus exclusively on Tatar subjects who take an oath without receiving a reciprocal oath from the tsar.[189] Within these ramifications, Shah Ali proved his honour and the loyal fulfilment of his oath by helping to liberate Muscovite slaves in Kazan. The oath, once a sign of mutuality allowing for slaving, had become an obligation to deliver Muscovite captives and serve the tsar.

Within this imperial imagery, the 'Book of Royal Degrees' comments on the applicability of the sun metaphor to all countries and all people:

> Just as the sun, which God has created in the sky, does not shine in one place only, but lights up in turn the whole earth und enlightens with its rays all lands, so the icon of the Mother of God effects its miracles and cures not in one place, but enlightens and delivers from calamity and cures ills in the whole world.[190]

The seemingly bulky solar and cross symbolism in these quotes is informed by the prefiguration of Ivan IV by Constantine. Although the mother of the Roman emperor Constantine the Great had been a Christian, he himself was baptized only on his death bed, which became an acceptable practice for Christian rulers. For him the solar cult of Sol Invictus was a convenient way of turning towards monotheism without compromising his links to the Roman priesthood and believers in the pagan gods. By this intermediary device, he side-stepped full commitment to the new faith until the approach of death.[191] Perceptively, he claimed to have seen 'a cross of light in the heavens, above the sun'[192] foretelling his victory before the decisive battle at the Milvian Bridge against his rival. His mother Helena was already a Christian when she travelled to Palestine, where it was claimed she found the wood of the cross of Christ. Her excavation aimed to recover the dynasty's reputation after scandal had shaken the court. While Ivan IV was often named a new Constantine, the solar imagery inherited from the Roman emperor helped to include heterodox subjects in the new empire, just as it survived in Muslim imagery of the ruler's relation to subjects.[193]

---

188 N. Mika, 'Siły chestnogo kresta: Krzyż i praktyka jego całowania na Rusi w obliczu zagrożenia i´ najazdów tatarskich (do końca XV wieku)', in I. Danilevskyy et al., eds., *Religions and Beliefs of Rus' (9th–16th centuries)* (Krakow, 2018), pp. 365–384.
189 Cf. Khodarkovsky, *Russia's Steppe Frontier*, pp. 51–56.
190 Pokrovskii and Lenhoff, *Stepennaia kniga tsarskogo rodosloviia po drevneishim spiskam*, p. 89.
191 N. Lenski, 'Evoking the Pagan Past: "Instinctu Divinitatis" and Constantine's Capture of Rome', *Journal of Late Antiquity*, 1, 2 (2008), pp. 204–257, here p. 214.
192 Eusebius Pamphilius, *Church History, Life of Constantine, Oration in Praise of Constantine*, ch. XXVIII: Translated and commented by Philip Schaff, https://www.ccel.org/ccel/schaff/npnf201.iv.vi.i.xxviii.html (accessed 19 July 2017).
193 On solar imagery in world religions, see M. Eliade, 'Spirit, Light, and Seed', *History of Religions*, 11, 1 (1971), pp. 1–30.

Ivan as 'New' Constantine referenced St Vladimir the second Constantine, whose baptism of Rus', as mentioned above, was interpreted in the 'Book of Royal Degrees' as an end to slave raids on Byzantium.[194] An ecclesiastical source from the 1560s, 'In Praise of Ivan IV and His Host for the Victory Against the Kazanian Tatars', underlines the imperial theme which praises the New Constantine Ivan IV for ending the Kazanian slave raids:

> The sovereign emulated the ancient and apostle-like tsars Constantine and Vladimir, since they shattered the idols and strengthened piety. Similarly, you, o sovereign, God-crowned tsar, have dispersed the ungodly Sons of Hagar and liberated Orthodox Christians from slavery and captivity.[195]

Ungodly 'Sons of Hagar' are portrayed as those Tatars and Muslims who did not submit to the Muscovite tsar, engaging instead in slaving directed against Muscovy. The link between the various Constantines in this quote characteristically expresses the preoccupations of the ransom theory of salvation: shattering idols is equated to liberating slaves. It was a fitting propagandistic image for this early imperial period of rebellions in the middle Volga.[196]

Muscovites displayed a sense of these connections between ostensibly unrelated faiths in Muscovite cultural artefacts and texts which were discursively interrelated yet did not necessarily give away trans-confessional content to a passive, uninitiated bystander, such as an Orthodox commoner. In the Golden Palace, Ivan's throne room, the sun, moon and stars appear as part of the cosmogony.[197] In several Muscovite texts these are the signs of the divine among the neighbouring pagans or those conquered. The 'Tale of Petr, Tsarevich of the Horde' tells about the early entry of a Mongol prince into the service of the prince of Rostov. He converted to Christianity as he began to entertain doubts about the religion of the Horde rulers, who 'venerate the sun, the moon, the stars and fire'. The 'Tale's' earliest known manuscript copies can be traced to the second third of the sixteenth century; its origins prior to that period are mired in speculation, as is the actual existence of its eponymous hero.[198] The so-called charter (*iarlik*) of the Tatar khan Akhmat to Ivan III, a forgery, says that the former comes to capture Muscovites

---

194 On the epithet 'New Constantine' and St Vladimir, see Khunchukashvili, 'Die heiligen Städte als eschatologische Legitimationssymbole der Zarenmacht unter den Rjurikiden', 138 n. 33.
195 Cited acc. Pelenski, *Russia and Kazan*, p. 292 n. 9: 'Porevnoval esi gosudar prezhnim sviatym i ravno apostolom tsarem Konstantinu i Vladimeru, jakozh ubo oni idoly poprasha i blagochestie utverdisha. Tako i ty, gosudar', bogovenchanyi tsariu, bozhieiu pomoshchiiu, bezbozhnykh agarian potrebi i pravoslavnykh krestiian ot raboty i pleneniia svobodi'.
196 Romaniello, *The Elusive Empire*.
197 Flier, 'Golden Hall Iconography and the Makarian Initiative', p. 68.
198 Pelenski, *Russia and Kazan*, pp. 257–258; 'Zhitie tsarevicha Petra', *Pravoslavnii sobesednik*, 3 (1859), pp. 360–375, here p. 361; Ostrowski, 'The Extraordinary Career of Tsarevich Kudai Kul/Peter in the Context of Relations between Muscovy and Kazan''.

but is repelled. He is said to have worshipped the sun, moon and stars, although he was a Muslim.[199]

Such representations of Muscovy's heterodox neighbours were often empirically inaccurate or outdated. Nevertheless, they are germane to trans-confessional issues at the heart of Muscovite representations of the new imperial culture. In Persian and Ottoman culture, the relations of the ruler and his subjects including, particularly, slaves, were often imagined in solar and light imagery. Hierarchies appeared as concentric circles of light, an image reused on Remezov's maps of Tobolsk and Siberia, with the regional capital city at the centre.[200] The Ottoman idea of the ruler as immovable mover was expressed in such images as a moth, which represented a subject or a slave who sought the light of the ruler's candle to which it ultimately succumbed, without any fault by the ruler himself.[201] The ruler's or master's divine light of wisdom and the obligatory limitless love or loyalty of his subjects or disciples who could not know such wisdom were expressed in these images.[202]

The monastic movement of Hesychasm brought such light imagery to Muscovite attention in the fifteenth century in its Jesus Prayer, which connects the pneuma and the experience of various light phenomena.[203]

Love and wisdom in propaganda

Love, or charity, which implicitly marked the tsar as a victorious deliverer from slavery, was one of the available labels for allies in steppe and foreign relations in general.[204] Moreover, it was used to probe into internal relations of neighbouring countries. In 1643, ambassador Gribov, a merchant fluent in eastern languages, arrived in Bukhara on tsar Mikhail Romanov's orders to promote the release of Muscovite slaves. He particularly targeted renegades in high positions at the Khwarazmian court, such as one Lazarev, a minor noble from Muscovy. Tsar Michael ordered Gribov to take Lazarev aside

---

199 Halperin, *The Tatar Yoke*, pp. 187–188.
200 On the various interpretations of this imagery, see B.A. Ergene, 'On Ottoman Justice: Interpretations in Conflict (1600–1800)', *Islamic Law and Society*, 8, 1 (2001), pp. 52–87. Applied to Sufism: J.-L. Michon, 'Introduction', in J.-L. Michon and R. Gaetani, eds., *Sufism: Love and Wisdom* (Bloomington IN, 2006; Kivelson, *Cartographies of Tsardom*.
201 W. Andrews, *Poetry's Voice, Society's Song: Ottoman Lyric Poetry* (Seattle, 1985).
202 Such imagery fit the *padishah* as strong military leader of earlier Ottoman centuries just as well as the recluse behind palace doors often encountered in the eighteenth century, who was side-lined and left in the dark about current government business by a strong elite. I am grateful to Yusuf Karabicak for sharing this insight.
203 Miller, *Saint Sergius of Radonezh, His Trinity Monastery and the Formation of the Russian Identity*, p. 52.
204 Filiushkin, 'Religioznyi faktor v russkoi vneshnei politike XVI veka'; Sanin, *Otnosheniia Rossii i Ukrainy s Krymskim Khanstvom v seredine XVII veka*, pp. 185, 188.

and promise him that he would be held in great esteem if he returned.[205] More such cases include Gavril Pavlov, the slave of the khan of Bukhara (*chelovek*, 'man') 'of Russian extraction' who bought Lev Stepanov, son of a peasant from Kostroma district, and released him.[206] Tsar Michael heard that many slaves had been held in Bukhara for years, even decades, tortured, starved and ill-treated. Gribov explained to khan Nadir Muhammad that many formally manumitted slaves were unable to leave because the return voyage on their own through the desert was too dangerous, because the warlike Turkmens might not bother whether the manumitted carried proper letters or not. The tsar requested the khan to order a search for Muscovite slaves and deliver them to the envoy, whether they had been released or were still in bondage; in return, the khan would obtain the tsar's 'love and friendship'. Faced with this general request, the khan was at pains to clarify that only manumitted slaves who had worked off the price they had fetched could be delivered to the envoy and return to Muscovy. Due to the distance and intervening territories, the khan explained, there were no actual war captives from Muscovy in Bukhara. This he would order for the sake of 'love'.

This obvious rebuff did not stop Gribov, who contacted high-ranking dignitaries at the Bukharan court, asked for their help in searching for the captives and having them manumitted. In exchange, he offered the promise of stipends from the tsar for good services in this cause. He used the khan's request for more gerfalcons from Moscow to reiterate his point: If Nadir Muhammad 'showed his love' by searching for the captives in Bukhara and other towns and helping to send them back, his wishes would be heard.[207] Despite the promise of highly sought-after gerfalcons, there was little incentive for the Bukharan khan to let the Russians leave. He showed disdain by a revealing comparison: he would not let the Russian slaves go, manumitted or not, before the tsar released all Muslims living near Astrakhan. This meant the Nogai Tatars and was aimed at their allegiance to the tsar, which was actually a mainly voluntary relationship with some mutual degree of independence based on trade relations.[208]

This was a veiled dig at Moscow's geopolitical positions and possible imperial aims – although, or rather because, current power relations meant Russia did not penetrate Central Asia for another two hundred years. However, this offence might have been motivated by something else, a cultural misunderstanding open to manipulation of transcultural symbolical resources of legitimacy. Muscovite and Central Asian Muslim notions differed starkly in this regard, at least in theory. In Muscovy,

---

[205] Burton, 'Russian Slaves in Seventeenth-Century Bukhara', pp. 353–354.
[206] A.N. Samoilovich, ed., *Materialy po istorii Uzbekskoi, Tadzhikskoi i Turkmenskoi SSR: Torgovlia s Moskovskim gosudarstvom i mezhdunarodnoe polozhenie Srednei Azii v XVI–XVII vv.*, vol. 3: *Materialy po istorii narodov SSSR* (Leningrad, 1932), p. 391.
[207] Burton, 'Russian Slaves in Seventeenth-Century Bukhara', pp. 353–354.
[208] Khodarkovsky, *Russia's Steppe Frontier*; Burton, 'Russian Slaves in Seventeenth-Century Bukhara', p. 354.

the ruler or master was traditionally obliged to show love and charity to retainers and even slaves.[209] Central Asian, Persian and Ottoman political philosophy, however, approached the question of loyalty from a quite different angle. Islamic moral law required the ruler and believers to show charity, especially by giving alms. Moreover, there were many instances in which Muslim rulers ransomed retainers.[210] Nevertheless, the power of the ruler, especially the Ottoman sultan, was built on the support of elite slaves. They enjoyed many privileges and great power but submitted to the sultan more readily than Turkish and local dignitaries, not least because they could not bequeath possessions until manumitted. Consequently, they were not obliged to kin and clans, whose social ties constituted the fabric of Ottoman and Turk oasis societies and the power relations between local and elite dignitaries in the capital as well as at court. In principle and typically in practice, slaves in the entourage of the sultan increased the latter's personal power.[211]

The idea of love was among further reflections on these social relations in Ottoman belles-lettres, such as the already mentioned interpretation of the descent of Mohammed from Isma'il and Hagar. At least in court-centred poems, the ideal slave (*qul*) owed unconditional, self-sacrificing love to the ruler, his master, who was imagined as a disinterested beloved – disinterested, because the sultan was obliged to be neutral in personal affinities towards his manifold subjects. The sultan as the master in a one-sided love relationship is portrayed in Ottoman poetry as the 'unmoved mover': he inspires love but is not required to participate in the emotional situation. Andrews claims that this pattern, epitomized by distinctive Ottoman metaphors like the moth and the candle – where the candle signifies the master – reflects the 'official' definition of the relationship between the sovereign and his military 'slaves': personal, affective loyalty is expected irrespective of the actions of the object of loyalty, i.e. the sultan. The rewards and punishments that ultimately derive from the 'unmoved mover' are not meant to reflect any objective principle of justice, since the authority of the ruler is considered to be totally independent of any kind of obligation towards his slaves.[212] Such ideas were also widespread in treatises on *hikmet*, the wisdom of the ruler, and in much of Persian philosophy, to which the former was indebted.[213] Such concepts were distinctive, but need to be considered in a wider social context – especially with regard to non-slaves; while even slaves had more rights than proposed by this imperial ideology, which sought to symbolically place various categories of subjects at the same distance.[214]

---

[209] Rüß, *Herren und Diener*; Hellie, *Slavery in Russia, 1450–1725*.
[210] Ivanics, 'Enslavement, Slave Labour and Treatment of Captives in the Crimean Khanate', p. 199.
[211] Miller, *The Problem of Slavery as History*.
[212] Ergene, 'On Ottoman Justice', pp. 64, 87; Andrews, *Poetry's Voice, Society's Song*, pp. 89–108.
[213] P. Crone, *God's rule: Government and Islam* (New York, 2004).
[214] Cf. Introduction.

Muscovite writers took up such transcultural concepts as early as the sixteenth century, at the time of the conquest of Kazan and in the following decades. Thus, the 'Book of Royal Degrees' greatly expanded the role of the philosopher (*filosof*) which it borrowed from the 'Tale of Bygone Years'. In the long but summary relation of the origin of the world and early Biblical history, the story of the Exodus once again stands out by its many details. Moses, whom pharaoh, the 'tsar, saw and started to love', was thus saved by the love of the ruler from the 'oppressive slavery' into which his people had fallen, and from certain death – in contrast to the purported role of the sultan. Baby Moses inspires love, as a good Muscovite ruler would, redeeming a faithless pharaoh who served the defenceless infant. Nevertheless, he flees into the desert as he cannot watch his own people oppressed and killed without trying to defend them. An angel teaches him everything the philosopher has told Vladimir so far, summarized in key words comprising the history of the world, adding:

> and [he taught Moses] every kind of wisdom. Then God appeared to him in the Burning Bush and said: "I see the misfortunes of my people in Egypt and I will lead them out of those lands. Go to pharaoh, the Egyptian *tsar*, and tell him: 'Let Israel go, or the punishment of God will be upon you within three days'. If he does not obey, I will hit him with My miracles".[215]

Already before Moses put this order in action it is thus established that wisdom is the precondition of liberating slaves, the epithet of a good ruler.

References to wisdom that could make Muscovy more accessible to Muslim Tatars or explain transcultural contacts to the Orthodox population, appear especially late in the seventeenth century, when Muscovy and the Ottoman Empire for the first time directly competed for what is now Ukraine in major wars. The Muscovite court eulogist of Ruthenian extraction, Simeon Polotskii, was educated in Kyiv and so exposed to Western influences in the Polish–Lithuanian Commonwealth. He used Russian Orthodox topoi of liberation from slavery to denounce the sultan:

> Torment (*Muchitel'stvo*)
>
> Makhmet the Ottoman, sultan of *Tsargrad* [Constantinople],
> went down into the garden with three slave boys (*otroki*),
> which was beautifully laid out (*uteshna*), to enjoy himself;
> only with the apple he fell in love
> on some tree; he spared it and left.
> Then the slave furtively approached
> and greedily devoured it;
> the sultan returned to the tree before the hour,
> and saw so much. The fruit had gone,
> the three slave boys of the honourable people
> incurred his evil wrath, and he asked them terribly,

---

[215] Pokrovskii and Lenhoff, *Stepennaia kniga tsarskogo rodosloviia po drevneishim spiskam*, pp. 253–254.

> Who among them put the apple in his stomach.
> Anxiously they denied any part taken
> swearing terrible oaths.
> The sultan ferociously ordered to cut open
> the bellies, knowing that within was the tree's fruit.
> The first is taken, the stomach dissected
> and there in his intestines he views the apple
> Not even digested. So was allay'd
> the terrible rage of the beast.
> Oh, how nefarious! He valued the apple
> more than those youngsters. He lost his wit![216]

One of Polotskii's sources for the *Vertograd* was Jacobus de Voragine's *Legenda Aurea* in Matthias Faber's Latin version.[217] Polotskii heavily reworked this model, apart from putting it in verse. Some terms stand out, for example the apple becomes the tree's fruit and *cedrum* a 'tree', thus allowing the mention of 'tree' three times in this poem, which in Muscovite Orthodoxy rings bells, as mentioned above, about redemption. The Russian version of the 'Legend of the Cross' and the holy wood as context of the motif of the apple tree refocuses this poem to the subjects of slavery and mistreatment by non-Orthodox masters.

Otrok translates as both a boy and, as a secondary meaning, servant or slave. The latter is preferable in this context, especially due to the addition that they were 'of the most honourable people', in other words, Muscovites; as opposed to the dishonourable captors in a closely related context such as the fiery furnace play.[218] This reference is necessary here despite Polotskii's abhorrence of the New Israel theme, as otherwise a Muscovite audience would miss the significance of the whole episode – the poem is located clearly outside of Muscovy, so there cannot be any mistaking the sultan for the tsar.

Whether *um* (reason, wit) means wisdom, which the sultan lacks, is subject to interpretation. However, the general context indicates the obligations of the ruler, and specifically a lack of meekness and care for his subjects. Polotskii was very

---

216 Polotskii and Hippisley, *Vertograd mnogocvětnyj*, vol. 2, pp. 385–386.
217 Ibid., p. 625.: 'Taken from Faber, Dominica 5 Post Pentecosten, No. 7 "De malis effectibus irae", sect. 1 "Praecipitantia": "S. Iacobus in epist. sua c.1. [James 1.19–20] admonet, ut *sit omnis homo tardus ad iram. Ira enim viri iustitiam Dei non operator*, inquit. Sane non operator, sed per fas et nefas iniustitiam potius, quod etiam exemplo Mahumetis Ottomani Turcarum regis discere possumus. 'Hic enim nostra aetate, Campofulgosus l. 9. c. 2. cum in hortis, quos Constantinopoli in deliciis habebat, deesse pomum in arbore cedro, quod Paulo ante inapexerat, animadvertisset; arbitrates procul dubio unum e tribus pueris, quos secum habebat, pomum decerpsisset, quod in horto preater eos alius nullus fuerat; quia quilibet illorum se pomum decersisse negabat, iussit ut ferro eorum corpora aperirentur, et nisi in primi cuius apertum fut pectus stomach fuisset inventum, dubium non erat, quia ad omnes ipsos ea poena transiret'. Quis hic non videt praecipitantis irae saevitiam patier et iniustitiam.'".
218 See the section on the fiery furnace ritual and Russkaia pravoslavnaia tserkov', *Mineia obshchaia s prazdnichnoi*, p. 306.

much an author of the Baroque, but he also drew on more traditional sources; he may have used this alienation intentionally. In any case, it is an allusion to the Paradise story as well as to the crossing of the Red Sea, which in the biblical Book of Wisdom (*Kniga Premudrosti*) is parted by the wisdom of God.[219]

Moreover, Polotskii's twist to Faber's texts draws on the Russian imperial theme of the paradise garden, generally a context of the *Vertograd*. S.U. Remezov explicated the links of the garden metaphor extensively, explaining that the lions lying down with the lambs embodied the various people in and around his Siberia.[220] As a particular innovation, Remezov's 'Atlas of Siberia' features a thematic map – among the first of its kind worldwide – outlining areas inhabited by ethnic groups. He assigned to semi-nomadic people a territory to which many might otherwise only aspire in petitions and very hands-on ways.[221] The tree in the centre of Remezov's paradise sketch, as in Polotskii's '*Muchitelstvo* (Torment)', refers to the Legend of the Cross. As mentioned above, it liberates the captives and symbolically subjects the dragons, who only a few pages earlier were marked as an allegory of oppressors and slavers and identified with Kuchum and his Tatars, to the new imperial tranquillity.[222] The topicality of liberation from slavery in this context is underlined by the slightly altered text of the 'Prophecy About the Defeat of the Foreigners by the Christians' in the Old Testament. It is the 'satirical poem about the King of Babylon', or, in Russian, 'victory song' over the tyrant, oppressor and enslaver, who 'did not release his captives' [Is 14:17].[223] The liberation of the formerly enslaved and enslavement of the former masters is several times stressed in the biblical text, and very hard to miss:

> The Lord shall give thee rest from thy sorrow and from thy fear and from the hard bondage (*rabstvo*) wherein thou wast enslaved [*porabosheno*].[224]   (Is 14:3)

From among a multitude of possible quotes, Remezov cites:

> "God will save the poor, and the wretched will rest in safety [. . .] the fortresses of the foreigners will be taken. Like smoke from the north he comes up and there is no force that withstands him". And this prophecy will entirely come true for the Turks.[225]

Thereby, the tree becomes the distinguishing detail in a common Muslim and Orthodox topos of the paradise garden in which the ruler needs wise advice to make

---

219 Pliukhanova, '"Poslanie na Ugru" i vopros o proiskhozhdenii moskovskoi imperskoi ideologii', p. 484 (Cf. PSRL 20 pp. 343–344).
220 Remezov, *Remezovskaia letopis'*, [120] 151.
221 S.U. Remezov, *Chertezhnaia kniga Sibiri* (Moskva, 2003); Kivelson, *Cartographies of Tsardom*.
222 Remezov, *Remezovskaia letopis'*, [113] 136.
223 'I plenenykh ne razreshi' *Biblia sirech knigi Vetchago i Novago Zaveta po iazyku slovensku*.
224 'I budet v toi den' g~ ot boleznii iarosti tvoeia, i ot raboty zhestokiia, eiuzhe rabotaste im'. Ibid.
225 Remezov, *Remezovskaia letopis'*, [113] 136.

the 'wolf walk together with the lamb', rejecting enslavement by non-Orthodox masters or at least those who did not subject to the tsar of Moscow.

This imagery of paradise as a place in which there are no more slave raids is evoked by the inscriptions and carvings on the tsar's throne or pew in the Cathedral of the Dormition – the misnamed 'Throne of Monomakh'. Michael Flier has investigated the semiotics of the pew in detail, noting that the panels are remarkable for their absence of typically Christian scenes, such as lives of saints or Christ's passion. This makes the imagery of paradise stand out.[226] The inscription says that God will not withhold His mercy from the ruler anymore:

> I will give you what you did not ask for, glory and riches, and nations will yield to you. If your iniquity appears, I will chasten you, [but] I will not take my mercy away from you.[227]

Earlier, removing God's mercy would have signified punishment for sins by Tatar slave raids. As shown in chapter three, the 'Chronicle of the Beginning of Tsardom' is the earliest source that invokes a right to safety from slave raids in Muscovy, against this previous interpretation of slavery. Thus, paradise is the place of plenty where there are no more slave raids, or which is defended effectively from slave raids. From the little evidence we have, Michael Flier concluded the pew was dedicated on 1 September 1551, the first day of the New Year during which, as mentioned above, an elaborate church ritual announced a new era of liberating slaves.[228] This date was weeks after the oaths given by the Kazanians to release all Muscovite slaves, time to carve the inscriptions of the pew.[229] In 1551 the Hundred Chapters Church Council promulgated rules which prominently included the obligation of the tsar and the believers to ransom captives.[230] In the icon known as Church Militant, or 'The Blessed Host of the Heavenly Tsar', placed on the wall just beside the pew, the trees flowing into the land from the Heavenly Jerusalem or Moscow indicate the return of the slaves after liberation from Kazan.[231] Moreover, the New Year ritual's emphasis on a new era resonates with the rhetoric of the August 13, 1551 peace, after which the 'Chronicle of the Beginning of Tsardom' announces a new era of liberating slaves and safety from slave raids.[232] It was only in September, after the dedication of the pew, that news from Kazan reported the breaking of the oath and the release of only some of the

---

[226] M.S. Flier, 'The Throne of Monomakh: Ivan the Terrible and the Architectonics of Destiny', in J. Cracraft and D.B. Rowland, eds., *Architectures of Russian Identity: 1500 to the Present* (Ithaca NY, 2003), pp. 21–33.
[227] Ibid., p. 31.
[228] Ibid., pp. 30–33.
[229] Tikhomirov, *Letopisets nachala tsarstva*, pp. 65–66.
[230] See chapter 5.
[231] See above. Kochetkov, 'K istolkovaniiu ikony "Tserkov' voinstvuiushchaia" (Blagoslovenno voinstvo nebesnogo tsaria)'; Rowland, 'Biblical Military Imagery in the Political Culture of Early Modern Russia'.
[232] Tikhomirov, *Letopisets nachala tsarstva*, p. 66. See chapters 2 and 3.

captives.²³³ During the period in which the pew was carved it seemed assured that the Kazanian Tatars acknowledged the tsar's retainer on the Kazan throne and the conditions imposed in 1550. In the garden of paradise carved into the panels of the pew, therefore, Tatars followed the rules that in symbolical terms connected the tree of paradise to the earthly redemption of slaves.

Advising the ruler is seen as the main task of courtiers in the eleventh century 'Wisdom of Royal Glory *(Kutadgu Bilig)*' by Yūsuf Khāṣṣ Hājib, generally illustrative of the traditions of Inner Asian rulership of the Turk people.²³⁴ Hājib's Central Asian ruler is 'imperfect', and so needs the wise counsel of chosen subjects, while the ideal Ottoman and Sassanid ruler can afford to be arbitrary because of his genius. However, in reality, Ottoman rulers, despite the support of their *qul* elite slaves in government, faced the delaying tactics of their subjects, the *re'aya*.²³⁵ Remezov stresses that good counsel means drawing on various sources of common or customary law,²³⁶ an interpretation of wise statecraft that avows Hājib's affirmation of traditional, customary law.²³⁷ However, this went beyond Polotskii, who was more oriented towards the tsar. Both refer to wisdom to denounce the sultan and the steppe rulers. Thus, the state of perfect imperial tranquillity affirms Central Asian traditions and draws upon a common ideal of Persian philosophy, the paradise garden. In order to turn this trans-confessional image into moral capital to be used in the contemporary Russo-Turkish war, Polotskii's poem denounces the Ottoman sultan as a raging beast and slaveholder who rejects the wise ruler's obligations in favour of knowledge derived from the apple of paradise or, more mundanely, the sweet life. It thus confirms to the general image of just service to the Orthodox ruler, as opposed to unjust slavery under heterodox rulers.²³⁸

The net effect is that traditional Inner Asian political culture is reflected in the approach by Remezov, who was actively involved with the tsar's new subject polities in Siberia. Meanwhile Polotskii, remote from Central Asia and more preoccupied with the Ottomans because of his own life story, denounced the sultan as a remorseless slave master. On the other hand, in Polotskii's clerical head and given the western influences he had imbibed, relations between higher, celestial and lower, human wisdom turn sour: the former is identified as good, the latter as base and evil and there is no connection between them. Humans are advised to strive for

---

233 Ibid., p. 67.
234 A. Schimmel, 'Review of Wisdom of Royal Glory (Kutadgu Bilig) by Yūsuf Khāss Hājib. A Turco-Islamic Mirror for Princes edited by Robert Dankoff (Chicago 1983)', *Journal of the American Oriental Society*, 105, 2 (1985), pp. 356–357, here p. 356. On Mongol statecraft, cf. above.
235 Ergene, 'On Ottoman Justice', p. 63; Yūsuf Khāss Hājib and R. Dankoff, *Wisdom of Royal Glory (Kutadgu Bilig): A Turko-Islamic Mirror for Princes* (Chicago, 1983), p. 66.
236 Remezov, *Remezovskaia letopis'*, [121] 152.
237 Ergene, 'On Ottoman Justice', p. 63; Yūsuf Khāss Hājib and Dankoff, *Wisdom of Royal Glory (Kutadgu Bilig)*, pp. 53–54, 218.
238 Kivelson, 'Bitter Slavery and Pious Servitude'.

God's wisdom, however inaccessible, and therefore in need of intercession.[239] This underlines the power of the Orthodox ruler in the counter dependency zone and shelters them against the corrosive forces of an interpretation of redemption which aims at alleviating internal social or political tensions.

A sixteenth-century Muscovite version of these trans-confessional interrelations of love, wisdom and liberation from slavery is accessible in the early chapters of the 'History of Kazan'. These chapters cover the pre-history of the ultimate conquest of 1552. They survive in the more than 200 extant copies of seventeenth-century versions that omitted the last fifty chapters of the original.[240]

The Kazanian moral capital of liberty is expressed in these texts by exploiting the liberation from slavery to justify conquest and nominally unlimited monarchical rule. At the same time, the leading characters are described as loving friends in a very emotional, direct and personal relationship as it was imagined in monarchy.[241] In this way, the praise of Shah Ali's service and his rewards are instrumental in defining Muscovite imperial culture as a reply to the enslavement of Orthodox Christian people:[242]

> Upon Shah Ali's approach the grand prince [Vasilii III] could not sit for joy. He left his palace quickly and received [the khan] on the stairway, without guile, not like a slave (*rab*) but like a brother and beloved friend. They flung their arms around each other's necks and cried for a long time, all the boyars present cried, too. Then they took each other's hands and went into the palace. The grand prince was comforted about Shah Ali's well-being and his arrival, desisted from wailing and crying and cheered up. He gave great reward to the [former] Khan Shah Ali for not having been misled to betray him when he faced the sword, even bitter death and the jaws of hell. Yet, he was kin to those barbarians, shared their language and faith. Khan Shah Ali deserves great accolade since he did not strive to rule according to his own will; he did not refuse being called a slave; he did not even refuse to die for the love of the autocrat [sovereign (*samoderzhets*)] to him. The unbeliever barbarian (*varvar*) did this more diligently than we believers did. It behoves us to marvel at his inner strength, his discretion and truthful service.[243]

The 'History' chose the solution of emotional personal relation to the conundrum of trans-confessional love between master and slave. The strong imagined asymmetry in these relations and Shah Ali's readiness to die 'for the love of the autocrat' is foiled by the reliance of the grand prince on Shah Ali's rank as Chingissid.[244] Moreover, the

---

239 'Mudrost'', in Polotskii and Hippisley, *Vertograd mnogocvětnyj*, vol. 2, pp. 373–379.
240 'Vstuplenie', in Volkova, *Kazanskaia Istoriia*.
241 J.C. Miller, 'History as a Problem of Slaving' in A. P. Damian and F. Roşu, eds., *Critical Readings on Global Slavery*, vol. 1 (Leiden, 2017), pp. 201–248, at p. 230.
242 On Kazanian slave raids prior to this event: Davies, *Warfare, State and Society on the Black Sea Steppe, 1500–1700*, chapter 1; Golokhvastov, 'Blagoveshchenskii ierei Sil'vestr i ego pisaniia'; Kämpfer, *Historie vom Zartum Kasan (Kasaner Chronist)*, pp. 56–59, 62, 70.
243 Moiseeva and Adrianova-Peretts, *Kazanskaia istoriia*, p. 66; Kämpfer, *Historie vom Zartum Kasan (Kasaner Chronist)*, pp. 80–82.
244 Rakhimzyanov, 'The Muslim Tatars of Muscovy and Lithuania'; Rakhimzianov, *Moskva i tatarskii mir*.

typically Muscovite obligation to generosity on the part of the grand prince in both material and affectionate terms occurs in the 'History' against a backdrop of complete failure and collapse caused by the unreasonable suspicion of Muscovites three generations earlier. The capture of grand prince Vasilii the Blind in 1445 is explained as the result of 'bitter advice', and the distrust between settled, agricultural Muscovites and Tatar nomads. They are represented by advisors as wolves and sheep that are socially alienated in mutual suspicion,

> since wolves and sheep neither eat together, nor do they rest or settle. The heart of one is wounded by fear, since one of them will die.[245]

This dualistic incompatibility of wolf and sheep was integral to Muscovite[246] as well as to Central Asian political culture. Yusuf Khass Hajib's goal was to instruct the ruler in his duties thanks to which 'the wolf walked together with the lamb' (line 460), a formula always used in classical Persian literature for the just ruler.[247] Remezov's 'History of Siberia' contains an idealizing sketch of an imperial paradise depicting all kinds of animals, including several peaceful dragons that usually signify slavers in Muscovite use.[248]

Tracing the Muscovite outreach mode of imperial visions of liberating captives to heterodox and non-ethnic Russians has demonstrated that they seemed to operate with little in the way of theory or ideology, at least not in the way that those educated in post-Enlightenment sensibilities might expect. However, in the absence or unavailability of such universalisms, Muscovites did not simply resign to ethnic or religious exclusivism. Given the claims of clerics and imams about the exclusive truth of their faiths, the underlying narrative in Qur'an and Bible about liberation, slave careers, and building a polity was most usable for intermediary empire builders. Muscovites alluded to common traditions without acknowledging the commonalities – for example, the various stories about Joseph in Russian Orthodox and Central Asian or Mid-Volga Muslim traditions. When Muslims and Tatars heard about or glanced at the images in the Palace of Facets, these might seem to invite interpretations of Joseph as a prophet of Islam, but also committed to redeem captives. Orthodox Christians primarily saw the Russian stories about Beautiful Joseph. Similarly divergent and shifting interpretations might be at work in saints' vitae and wisdom imagery drawing the attention of Muslim bystanders; even the exceptionally knowledgeable Ottoman traveller reacted viciously to their appeal, to the

---

245 Moiseeva and Adrianova-Peretts, *Kazanskaia istoriia*, pp. 49–51.
246 See esp. chapters 4 on St George and 3 on redemption.
247 Schimmel, 'Review of Wisdom of Royal Glory (Kutadgu Bilig) by Yūsuf Khāss Hājib', p. 356.
248 Remezov, *Remezovskaia letopis'*, p. 233. On p. 226, Remezov shows dragons beleaguering Ermak's cossacks in a town, snatching bodies. The text identifies the Turks – in the context of his *History*, that is the Tatars – with the neighbouring people of the Israelites in Isaiah's prophecy about liberation and rule over former oppressors.

point of taking personal risks. Better evidence of such strategies can hardly be expected, as they straddled mutually exclusive communities of faith. Explicit reference to stories working in both faiths risked the wrath of the guardians of truth. Speaking about Bernard Porter's critique of imperial visions due to the lack of awareness of British people about their empire in a later age, Kumar notes: 'The whole point about ideology [. . .] is that it is disguised, that we are the last people to know that it is working on us. The structures of ideology [. . .] operate mostly "behind our back"'.[249]

---

[249] Kumar, *Visions of Empire*, p. 321. Cited according to Semyonov, 'How Five Empires Shaped the World and How this Process Shaped those Empires', p. 47.

Conclusion

Recent contributions have stressed that the Muscovite Empire in the sixteenth and seventeenth centuries consciously managed difference, and emphasized it by staging its rule over distinct regions. This book shows that the elite deliberately applied transethnic, transcultural and trans-religious rules and categories of enslavement and liberation, separating the loyal from the inimical. Beyond ex-post analytical descriptions of Muscovy as empire and contemporary emphasis on the particular, this expresses an imperial consciousness articulating the parts. Moreover, by applying such distinguishing categories Muscovite rulers answered to a certain degree to needs expressed in the population.

A wide range of key sources from the sixteenth and seventeenth centuries reflect a pervasive rhetoric and imagery of ransom, the liberation of slaves, and protection from slave raids, which needs contextualisation. Muscovite rulers, the church, and governments of the sixteenth and seventeenth centuries catered to widespread sensibilities and needs that demanded protection from slave raids and liberation from captivity and slavery in foreign lands or under heterodox masters. These are attested by petitions that ask for compensation for ransom payments and for reintegration, as well as by a wide array of sources ranging from popular saints' vitae, rituals, commemorations of the dead and captives to local property litigation maps and theatrical performances both in churches and in the streets. These observations neatly fulfil the requirements of a counter dependency zone where religious and secular rules proscribe the enslavement of certain groups, and there is the political intention to implement these rules.

Many people from Eastern Europe and Western Eurasia who were sold by slave raiders and traders to the Ottoman Empire, Central Asia, and other far off regions found opportunities to improve their lives within their new societies. Among the majority who did not return were many captured women, who decided to stay either because they did not expect better conditions back in Muscovy, because they had formed new social relations in the Ottoman Empire or beyond, including caring for offspring; fewer opportunities for ransom and earning manumission, or because of the harshness and distance of travel. However, knowledge about opportunities for social mobility beyond the steppe does not seem to have been common among Muscovites. Several factors mitigated their interest in proclaiming and spreading this knowledge. The initial act of enslavement, the raid, remained violent and dangerous for those spared, killed, and the victims herded off against their will. There are few signs of people migrating from Muscovy on their own accord to be enslaved. Such occasions remained exclusions or hinged on specific conditions such as prior captivity and marriage in their new place of living or disappointment by family members in Muscovy.

Evidence points to prevailing opinions held within Muscovy being to the contrary. Petitions of returning slaves along with investigations conducted in the chancelleries, the plenitude of stories from the widely distributed and popular vitae of saints about the liberation of captives, eulogies and laudatory speeches, as well as public events with wide appeal all exude a myth of liberation among large sections of the Muscovite population. In Muscovy, where most people beyond the narrow circles of scribes, courtly elites, and some local gentry were illiterate, these are the best available sources to gauge the views of the wider population. They hardly allow us to generalize about the worldviews held among peasants. However, some of the media listed were accessible to wide strata of the illiterate urban population, and more generally to parishioners. Reports underline the popular appeal of rituals and events of the counter dependency zone, even though foreign observers were generally ignorant about their significance. Most petitioners returning from captivity used at least a few words pertaining to Orthodox views of ransom obligations to express the pain they endured in captivity. Some asked for an icon of St Nicholas from the chancellery or already carried one that depicted the revered ransoming miracle worker. Insight into the views of ordinary people may also be gained in the Siberian petitions and chronicles written by town cossacks. Often themselves deported or seeking a fortune, the Siberian cossacks gained much from service and trade and enjoyed extensive opportunities for negotiating with the Moscow government. Nevertheless, they upheld the final authority of the tsar, as decisions reached them often after many months.[1] One of their officers, the polymath Semen Ulianovich Remezov, applied the redemptive models of the conquest of Kazan to the conquest of Siberia.

Adding to negative views of slavery abroad, those who were not captured remembered violence and severance from relatives and friends. Those who returned were rarely those who had done well in their new or temporary places of living. This presented a selection of experiences that was not amenable to words of admiration about conditions in captivity – nor would they have been heard. Widely distributed law codes and canon law backed up and institutionalized ransom, along with price lists for redeeming slaves.[2] The political culture of liberation obliged the tsar and the faithful to redeem their 'brothers', to fight for liberating them abroad, and to secure the steppe frontier.

Such an assessment cannot be dismissed by pointing to continuing practices of strong asymmetric dependency in Muscovy, the enslavement of foreign captives in Muscovy as well as the evolving enserfment of broad parts of the rural population. The counter dependency zone allowed for such exclusions from the generalised rule that people could not be enslaved. The stress on liberation as a return home rather than emphatic freedom in the modern sense continued into the eighteenth century, epitomizing the notion that security from slave raids legitimized internal strong asymmetric dependency. It relied on a premodern view of the fact that all

---

1 Witzenrath, *Cossacks and the Russian Empire, 1598–1725*.
2 On ransom payments and practices, see Boeck, 'Identity as Commodity'.

human societies include important building blocks of strong asymmetrical dependency.³ Even in Europe the picture was patchy. The idea that anti-slaving policies should apply to all humans alike started late, with the Enlightenment.

Earlier, religious borders were far more incisive. In combination with dedicated policy they might define who was to be ransomed and who could be enslaved, as in the case of the Orthodox, which affected Ukrainian and Muscovite slaves in Renaissance southern Europe.⁴ The demand for protection from slave raids was evident, and it was sensible for governments to provide for it. The degree to which government complied depended on a host of factors and circumstances. The pull of early modern labour markets reached far beyond political, religious, and cultural boundaries. Nevertheless, migration across the steppe was rarely voluntary given the perils of travel, hard-to-navigate cultural boundaries, and the exclusive definitions of non-enslavable in-groups, such as in many Muslim areas. Slave raids filled this void of transaction. Their effects could be devastating on distant neighbours of prospering areas in the Mediterranean and Middle East. Slaving zones lost labour and lived with the uncertainty of impending violence that slowed development and engendered trauma, while a few profited from the trade. They suffered from internal divisions deepened by mutual slave raids and human trade to supply external labour markets. This was exacerbated by the military power of steppe nomads, whose superiority in pitched battle continued into the eighteenth century.

From the second half of the fourteenth century trade flows along the steppe branches of the Silk Road were increasingly affected by breakdown of authority within the fluid nomadic political organization. Muscovy benefitted from these changes by opening new trading routes through Siberia to China and via the Volga to Persia and India. Despite the horse trade of nomads with Muscovy and further settled societies, the steppe itself gradually descended into slaving area conditions. Steppe nomads had been enslaving each other according to the changing fortunes of warfare since Tamerlane's raids on the lower Volga cities in the 1390s. The urban base of the *Ulus* of Jochi (aka the 'Golden Horde') around the lower Volga decayed since the late fourteenth century.⁵ Some nomads mounted slave raids on sedentary neighbours to supplement their meagre income from nomadic pastoralism. It was these dire conditions of recurring and increasing instability in the steppe, trade impediments, and the resultant slave raids that prompted the introduction of the New Israel worldview in Muscovy. Such a

---

3 R. Stichweh, 'A Theory of Asymmetrical Dependency: Sociological and Historical Considerations', *Beyond Slavery and Freedom: Opening Up New Fields. Cluster of Excellence Opening Conference, Bonn, November 6–7, 2019.*
4 W.G. Clarence-Smith and D. Eltis, 'White Servitude', in D. Eltis and S.L. Engerman, eds., *The Cambridge World History of Slavery*, vol. 3: *AD 1420–AD 1804* (Cambridge, 2011), pp. 132–160, here p. 140.
5 A.V. Pachkalov, *Srednevekovye goroda nizhnego Povolzh'ia i severnogo Kavkaza* (Moskva, 2018). *Orda* means ruler's tent in Tatar.

worldview supported the competition for trade routes to China and further parts of Asia between the steppe and the northern river systems. Its focal point became the conquest of Kazan due to the increased requirements for mobilization and the quelling of rebellions in the middle Volga region for decades to come.

A combination of religious rules and political organization provided the means for stabilizing extended slaving zones such as the Rus' principalities in the late medieval, post-Mongol period. Resulting no-slaving areas, such as in Muscovy, often started with a limited group circumscribed by religious rules and political boundaries being immune from enslavement or strong asymmetric dependency, especially from outsiders. In the Muscovite case, more precisely described as a counter dependency zone, Orthodox landowners might legitimately enserf peasants to provide for military forces to intercept slave raids. Orthodox masters cohabiting with their dependents were perceived differently from a Muslim doing the same thing, since the dependents might succumb to cultural influences. However, in the sixteenth and seventeenth centuries this tendency took a back seat to the general trend of treating Orthodox and Non-Orthodox landowners alike.[6] However, if the state needed fugitive peasants to man the new fortified steppe lines, claims from their former masters could be disregarded, despite their gentry status. As long as the counter dependency zone needed their fighting services, even heterodox nobles were allowed to rule over Orthodox populations in Muscovy's steppe frontier appanage fiefdoms of Romanov, Kashira, Iur'ev-Pol'skii, Serpukhov, Khotun', Zvenigorod, Surozhik, Andreev Gorodok Kamennyi, Novgorod-on-Oka, and the khanate Kasimov. In these towns and extended fiefdoms there lived a considerable Russian Orthodox population served locally by a Russian administration. However, supervision of the administration headed by an Orthodox governor, the last word in decisions, plus court fees and revenues, belonged to Muslim Chinggisid princes installed by the grand prince, albeit on an intermittent basis.[7] This was the founding moment of the multi-faith empire. It was largely co-terminus with the counter dependency relation, a special form of no-slaving zone in which enserfment of the religious in-group

---

6 A. Belyakov, 'Serving Tatars: Legal Status, Number and Economic Features', in R. Khakimov, I. Gilyazov and B. Izmaylov, eds., *The History of the Tatars since Ancient Times*, vol. 5: *Tatars in Russia (Second Half of the 16–18th Centuries)* (Kazan, 2017 [Russian: 2014]), pp. 224–232, here pp. 224–226; A. Nogmanov, 'Incorporation of Tatars into the Russian Legal Space in the Latter Half of the 16–First Half of 17th Centuries', in R. Khakimov, I. Gilyazov and B. Izmaylov, eds., *The History of the Tatars since Ancient Times*, vol. 5: *Tatars in Russia (Second Half of the 16–18th Centuries)* (Kazan, 2017 [Russian: 2014]), pp. 140–155; A. Nogmanov, 'The Tatar Population in the Russian Legislation in the Latter Half of the 17th Century', in R. Khakimov, I. Gilyazov and B. Izmaylov, eds., *The History of the Tatars since Ancient Times*, vol. 5: *Tatars in Russia (Second Half of the 16–18th Centuries)* (Kazan, 2017 [Russian: 2014]), pp. 156–178.

7 Rakhimzianov, *Moskva i tatarskii mir*, pp. 144–170. Similar zones along the steppe rim existed in Iran: K. Matin, 'Uneven and Combined Development in World History: The International Relations of State-formation in Premodern Iran', *European Journal of International Relations*, 13, 3 (2007), pp. 419–447.

and strict hierarchies were allowed to cater for military 'liberators', defence, and redemption efforts. At variance with but not against the internal logic of many no-slaving zones, this was a rule expressed in Orthodox terms of redemption. Its benefit was conditionally extended to heterodox retainers, stressing the relational rather than community-based character.

Rebels on the steppe boundary like the Bashkirs, who at one point had loyally defended their section of the fortified lines, could be turned over to allied nomads for raiding. Likewise, those in the middle Volga who did not observe the peace 'mercifully' offered by tsar Ivan IV after the conquest of Kazan were subjected to devastating raids by Tatar and Cheremissian supporters side by side with Muscovites during the rebellious decades. Monasteries were located where they would block access to Kazan to insurgents, establishing gradients of dependency among the rural population. Monasteries could offer better conditions to peasants and *iasak* tribute payers than the smaller *pomest'e* estates distributed to the gentry, who were constantly on campaign provisioning themselves from meagre revenues.[8] In what amounted to an imperial method of rule, the slaving zone was the 'stick' of governance, and the 'carrot' was the counter dependency relation.

It was a matter of evolving perspective: what started as defensive and redemptive action soon became an expansionary euphemism, as early as the conquest of Kazan. The threat of slave raids nonetheless remained serious during the Muscovite period, at times overshadowing other concerns and leading to the construction of the hugely expensive protective steppe lines. These fortified lines instantly became tools of expansion and growing internal asymmetric dependency as they controlled the flow of labour. In the symbolic realm, the tsar was portrayed as bishop defending his flock against metaphorical wolves, or as Moses leading the New Israelites out of Egyptian or Kazanian slavery; alternatively into the new promised land that was the middle Volga. In this way he became sacralised, anointed like the kings of Israel, and gained status and power.[9] The asymmetric dependency of his subjects was conveyed in Biblical imagery of the slaves of God who had been liberated from slavery in Egypt because and only in so far as they committed to the one and only God. By extension, this signified transposition of dependency to the king of the New Israel, in the Russian Bible translation the *tsar'*. Monotheism and monarchy both used redemptory rhetoric to squeeze out competitors in the Eurasian labour markets. At the same time, they reached out to former agents and hierarchs of decaying Eurasian empires. They worked hand in hand

---

[8] A. Bakhtin and B. Khamidullin, 'Political History of the Kazan Khanate', in I. Mirgaleev and R. Khakimov, eds., *The History of the Tatars since Ancient Times*, vol. 4: *Tatar States (15–18th Centuries)* (Kazan, 2017 [Russian: 2014]), pp. 288–358, here pp. 346–357.
[9] Since a 1561 update to the crowning ceremony: M. Obolenskii, ed., *Sobornaia gramota dukhovenstva pravoslavnoi vostochnoi tserkvi, utverzhdaiushchaia san tsaria za velikim kniazem Ioannom IV Vasil'evichem, 1561* (Moskva, 1850), p. 33. However, the first prince of Moscow to be anointed was Dmitrii Ivanovich in 1498, see chapter 2.

to legitimize the strict hierarchy, which increasingly weighed on the populace as both the empire and the associated transaction costs expanded.[10]

This religious-political language sought to maintain a distance from Islam and alternative Christian confessions, to prevent its failure to serve as a crystal nucleus of counter dependency relations. Group-related emotive qualities, even demonization of the enemy, were central to initial mobilization; they were part of the package of the counter dependency zone, not separate ideas in distinct phases. Muscovy thrived by occupying the commando heights, the sedentary trading emporia of the steppe frontier, and the precondition was death or deportation of previous city dwellers unless they proved loyal.[11]

However, there was a need to collaborate toward the same goal with Tatars, and increasingly also with other groups on the frontiers of the growing empire. This meant that Muscovy could not simply remain an exclusively ethnic Russian or Orthodox state. The career of the Biblical and Qur'anic Joseph from slave to pharaoh's steward, as well as other symbolic devices, was used to build bridges with local cultures in inner Eurasia and to welcome warriors, nobles, and translators. Ethnic and religious groups were expected to fracture along the lines of redemptive language and trade affiliations. St Nicholas liberated Orthodox captives, but in some stories also nomads and Muslims, whose loyalty was thereby won or strengthened. The great Ottoman traveller and observer, Evliya Çelebi, confirmed the appeal of such trans-Ottoman stories in the steppe frontier by contesting them, precariously making up a fanciful counter narrative. Muslim Tatar translators serving the Ambassadors' Chancellery portrayed themselves in the Christian image as martyrs for the cause of slave liberation. Loyalty required from all subjects in the counter dependency zone was expressed in terms of liberating or manumitting slaves kept by disloyal outsiders.

The counter dependency zone provided an Orthodox face to a norm present in both Europe and the steppe: recidivist 'hardened' traitors to the cause of liberating Orthodox slaves could be extirpated. During the expansion, the Mongol Empire had even punished resistance to its initial conquest by wholesale destruction, dispersal, and sale into slavery. Ivan IV was portrayed as acting like Chinggis Khan in Kazan, but as if through a veil that was opaque on the Orthodox side: the king of the New Israel, the tsar, could be perceived as the khan on the other side. Muscovite diplomats manipulated and employed the language of the steppe even in Russian translation; they could

---

10 Cf. V. Kivelson, *Desperate Magic: The Moral Economy of Witchcraft in Seventeenth-Century Russia* (Ithaca NY, 2013).

11 The focal point of these, in both symbolical and real terms, was Kazan, as aptly observed by the trans-Ottoman traveller, soldier, and later supporter of Muscovy, Ivan Peresvetov, or by the writer with access to the tsar's inner circle who re-worked his petition. I.S. Peresvetov and A.A. Zimin, *Sochineniia I. Peresvetova* (Moskva, 1956), p. 167. Izmaylov, 'Conquest of the Middle Volga Region and Sociopolitical Consequences. §1. Conquest of Kazan', p. 60.

tell.¹² The counter dependency zone required observance of its religious rules, while it was paramount for Muscovite diplomats until the early 1520s to delay decisions not commensurate with current Tatar practices. It was the complex interplay of realpolitik and symbolical acts that counted in Muscovite-steppe relations even thereafter, and the symbolism of the counter dependency zone provided orientation. As such, it was not so much direct Tatar cultural heritage, which did not extend beyond the tiny elite, but continued practical inclusion into the steppe world of diplomacy, raids, and trade that made the Muscovite Empire more tolerant in treating its heterodox groups, and so different in religious and cultural terms from maritime colonial empires.¹³

Religion imagined a community, a flock to be protected by its shepherd, who in Muscovy was the tsar. As such, it is a facilitating ingredient of the no-slaving zone. It did not form a nation in Muscovy. Instead, the borders of community were malleable according to the needs of empire which could include heterodox people serving the purpose of liberating, ransoming or exchanging prisoners and slaves. To achieve the same purpose some heterodox or peripheral people enjoyed privileges temporarily exceeding those of the religiously defined in-group. Therefore, beyond the narrow Russian Orthodox community it is better to speak of imagined and renegotiable counter dependency relations.

Orthodoxy offered options for agency to dependent people as they attempted to return from slavery or to prevent double suffering in overlapping slaving zones.¹⁴ State laws provide for the manumission of formerly bonded or enserfed captives who returned from foreign lands; their wives and children were automatically manumitted, too. Doubtful loyalty, even if paired with questionable roots, could be masked by a demonstration of piety enhanced by good deeds towards the aims of the counter dependency zone. Some of these options came with the price of continuing or deepening asymmetric dependency. These counter dependency relations were based on the imagined personal relation to the tsar extending beyond the bounded counter dependency zone.

Meanwhile, the agency of the Russian Orthodox Church was both restricted and enjoyed certain openings. It accepted restrictions to proselytizing, to confessionalization, and to the privileges of heterodox believers in the service of the tsar and the counter dependency zone, even service relations of its own followers to heterodox masters. Confessionalization was an ambiguous state-building strategy, as it risked losing connections with Eastern Orthodox Churches in the Ottoman Empire. Moreover, it threatened the veiled symbolic contacts with the Muslim cultures of inner

---

12 Keenan, 'Muscovy and Kazan'.
13 Kivelson, *Cartographies of Tsardom*; Cf. Neumann and Wigen, *The Steppe Tradition in International Relations* for emphasis on the varying extent, frequency and intensity of steppe-sedentary cultural hybridisations in Europe and Russia.
14 S. Conermann and G. Şen, eds., *Slaves and Slave Agency in the Ottoman Empire* (Göttingen, 2020).

Eurasia. However, the specific climatic and counter dependency conditions of early and middle Muscovy also meant a relative lack of means to foster literacy and erudition as prerequisites of elite theological distinction and confessionalization at parish level. Yet the Russian Orthodox Church cast a vast network of churches and monasteries over far-flung territories of cohabitation with heterodox beliefs. Streams of Orthodox clerics and petitioners from the Ottoman Empire who sought alms or ransom collection entitlements in Moscow and the concomitant cultural transfers were not yet a sign of Muscovite hegemony. However, they increased the agency of the Muscovite Empire and its Church, as well as the diversity of cultural influences in trans-Ottoman spaces.

Outlook

In early modern Russian Orthodoxy, a frequently conservative outlook coincided with emphasis on the early Christian ransom theory of salvation, a low effectiveness of proselytization, and more often than not 'tolerant' relations with adherents of heterodox creeds, as long as they were loyal to the tsar. While these findings contrast with areas in western and southern Europe, it might be instructive to compare them with conditions in the Ottoman Empire. A conservative outlook, moreover, correlates with the continuing integration of trans-Ottoman areas and often Muslim steppe peoples. The fact of growing Russian strength made driving out Muslims – as opposed to integrating them – a viable option following the annexation of Crimea in 1783, with its strong trans-maritime cultural and trade relations.[15]

Christian re-traditionalization of the symbols and rituals of this-worldly redemption was in the mid-1500s as forward-looking a movement as any reform. However, it had long-lasting after effects by transcendentally entrenching in Russian Orthodoxy and the Slavophiles a mistrust towards the emerging West, as well as a misguided reliance on 'Holy Russia' and the enduring popularity of the tsar. It was perhaps harder in the long term to sustain an optimistic outlook in a steppe environment in which modernizing agricultural security meant fortification and hiding behind now largely forgotten walls than in the maritime empires. Their physical manifestation of power, the oceangoing ship, can still be associated with exploration. The symbol of power of the steppe fortification line was the tsar and his or her centralised façade of power. The power of maritime empires was symbolized by the ship and the joint stock company distributing the burden of liability within society. It is important to note that in practice, such roles were much less binarily distributed among the maritime empires and Russia. Moreover, in practice

---

15 K. O'Neill, *Claiming Crimea: A History of Catherine the Great's Southern Empire* (New Haven CT, 2017).

they meant no less asymmetric dependency within each empire, whether maritime or land-locked, of which the Middle Passage is a graphic reminder. Nevertheless, the institutions, symbols, and connected rituals of autocracy and evolving democracy had their own respective weight and intrinsic logic.

Despite the weighty secondary effects of strong internal asymmetric dependency, as well as the end of Tatar liberties and increasingly, privileges, there remained an ambivalent, oddly liberationist air about Muscovite imperial culture. Adapted to Polish relations during the Time of Troubles, it worked well in overcoming Polish-Lithuanian occupation and attraction to the latter's republican constitutionalism. Moreover, Orthodox retrenchment against Polish-Lithuanian Catholicism was no hindrance to Tatar participation in restoring the tsar in 1612, attesting the multi-cultural appeal of the underlying concept of liberation and stopping slave raids.[16]

During the second half of the seventeenth century, however, a liberationist political culture proved dangerous enough to the evolving, still insecure counter dependency empire. Muscovite imperial culture was gradually diluted and abandoned by the elites in the decades after the town rebellions of 1648/1649. Popular rituals and theatrical enactments like the fiery furnace were abandoned, and later, edited versions lacked the former liberationist zest and apparent popular appeal. The New Israel murals in the Kremlin were covered up under Peter I after refurbishment in the 1670s and the palace was demolished in the eighteenth century; historiography remains silent on any traces of the Exodus rhetoric in later centuries. Growing serfdom and its strains on the social fabric may have contributed to this trend in a more favourable external environment. In the late nineteenth and the twentieth centuries, historians of the state school and Russian nationalists widely portrayed Muscovy the state as the 'Third Rome', competing with the British Empire's propagandistic claim to Roman heritage. This theme was then used, especially after the Second World War, by Western commentators to portray Soviet visions as essentially expansionist Muscovite eschatology in a new, communist guise. Had the Muscovite cultural pattern not fallen into oblivion, the 'Third Rome' with its feeble basis in the sources would not have allowed such distortion, since it was hardly used in official documents pertaining to state concerns. The relatively few Muscovite expressions of this concept involve the church in its relations to the state rather than the state on its own; or they are sectarian. In the sixteenth-century versions, they fit well with the incipient focus on preserving the unity of Muscovite Orthodoxy in the face of widespread slave raids. Muscovites usually stressed that an eschatological level of redemption at the second coming of Christ was prefigured in historical liberation, strengthening the religious function that helped to focus the counter dependency zone. The Russian synods edition of the Bible of 1875 tellingly changed the Septuagint translation of Isaiah 61.1 to the post-emancipation version,

---

16 Gruber, *Orthodox Russia in Crisis*; Witzenrath, 'Versklavung, Befreiung und Legitimität im Moskauer Reich'.

'proclaim [...] release from dark cells for prisoners (*uznikam otkrytie temnitsy*)'.[17] This change in the part of the prophet's speech applicable to serfs underscores the paternal character of asymmetrical dependency widespread during the decades before the Emancipation of the 1860s. The Empire reinvented itself under Peter I as European, by then already a fashionable declaration. But its previous worldview had been no less European in origin, given a less 'Europeanized' world on the threshold of the early modern period.[18]

Certain elements of Muscovite imperial worldview survived and were applied in changing conditions in the eighteenth and early nineteenth centuries.[19] The 1649 law code contained the requirement to redeem captives, effective until the early nineteenth century. Greeks in conflict with the Ottoman Empire in the early nineteenth century capitalized on these religiously justified rules.[20] Peter was faulted for turning members of the Russian elite into citizens of the world, since at the same time they ceased in vital respects to be 'citizens of Russia'.[21] However, Petrine ideologues were only too well aware of the problem. In a landmark of the creation of the Petrine myth, archbishop Feofan Prokopovich in his funeral oration for his ruler not only claimed that he had 'given birth' to Russia. A typically Muscovite cast of Old Testament and Byzantine character models followed, reinterpreted to fit the new ways. Moses stood out since he was described as the law-giver, not the liberator.[22] Catherine II laid claim to Byzantine and Greek heritage in ways Muscovite rulers had rejected, as an active geopolitical assertion. She used the image of the garden and its landscape as propagandistic imagery of imperial harmony embracing traditions of her Muslim subjects.[23] Yet celebrating her

---

17 Translated using the congenial terms of the New International Version of the Bible. In the variant ancient Slavic reading: 'eyesight to the blind'.
18 On Petrine mass deportations to Azov: B.J. Boeck, 'Calculating the Casualties of Forced Labor: Azov as the Harbinger of Petrine Policies', in M.S. Flier et al., eds., *Seeing Muscovy Anew: Politics – Institutions – Culture: Essays in Honor of Nancy Shields Kollmann* (Bloomington IN, 2017), pp. 275–284. However, deportations were common in many empires at the time, among them European.
19 Kollmann, *The Russian Empire 1450–1801*, p. 276.
20 L.J. Frary, 'Slaves of the Sultan: Russian Ransoming of Christian Captives during the Greek Revolution (1821–1830)', in L.J. Frary and M. Kozelsky, eds., *Russian-Ottoman Borderlands: The Eastern Question Reconsidered* (Madison WI, 2014), pp. 101–130.
21 R. Pipes, ed., *Karamzins Memoir on Ancient and Modern Russia* (New York, 1966), p. 124, cited after L. Hughes, 'Petrine Russia', in A. Gleason, ed., *A Companion to Russian History* (Malden MA, 2009), pp. 165–179, here p. 167.
22 F. Prokopovich, 'Funeral Oration', in L.J. Oliva, ed., *Peter the Great* (Englewood Cliffs NJ, 1970), pp. 78–81, cited acc. Hughes. 'Petrine Russia', p. 173. On imperial culture in the eighteenth century, see now R. Vulpius, *Die Geburt des russländischen Imperiums: Herrschaftskonzepte und -praktiken im 18. Jahrhundert* (Wien, Köln and Weimar, 2020).
23 S.L. Baehr, *The Paradise Myth in Eighteenth Century Russia: Utopian Patterns in Early Secular Russian Literature and Culture* (Stanford CA, 1991); K. O'Neill, 'Constructing Russian Identity in the Imperial Borderland. Architecture, Islam, and the Transformation of the Crimean Landscape', *Ab Imperio*, 2 (2006), pp. 163–192.

victory over the Ottoman fleet at Chesme, Turkish captives appeared on a large painting laying flags at the foot of Peter I's mounted statue. Given her origin as German princess and her perpetual need for legitimation, Catherine thus hinted at Petrine and Muscovite traditions of defending the realm against steppe raids and the Ottomans. It was, in fact, a geopolitical inversion of Muscovite precedent, given that the great Blessed Host icon adorning Ivan IV's throne shows liberated Muscovite martyr captives returning to New Jerusalem. Another related law in the 1649 code allowed for those who returned from captivity to be manumitted from serfdom. Some still used this rule to rid themselves of unwanted landowner control in the 1820s.[24] The extensive use in the modern Russian Synodal Bible edition of the term 'to redeem (*iskupit'*)' and its derivatives in both this-worldly and transcendent senses give pause to those researching continuities.

Serfdom slowly faded beginning with the annexation of the Crimean Peninsula in 1783, the hub of the slave trade.[25] In the 1840s and 1850s, debates about serfdom among Westernizers, Slavophiles and clerics centred on the ransom theory of atonement. Serfdom was portrayed as slavery and, hence, a sin in Christian terms now broadly in tune with Atlantic abolition movements.[26] Finally, defeat in the Crimean War against European powers accustomed to anti-slavery rhetoric set an end to serfdom.[27] Petitioners captured or enslaved in Central Asia and the Caucasus still applied for ransom during the nineteenth century.[28] The Russian Empire retained elements of Muscovite redemptive imperial culture that elevated the status and image of the tsar and propagated the counter dependency zone, but tried to abandon more ambiguous traits that landowning elites might regard as potentially conducive to rebellion.

---

24 Brower and Layton, 'Liberation through Captivity'.
25 According to J. Czajewski, Russian peasants fled in large enough numbers to incite the Empire to raid Polish territories and kidnap people, claiming they were recovering fugitives: J. Czajewski, 'Zbiegostwo ludności Rosji w granice Rzeczypospolitej', *Pro Memoria journal*, 6, 15 (2004), pp. 24–27. This would extend the dependency zone in a peculiar, activist way.
26 Paperno, 'The Liberation of the Serfs As a Cultural Symbol'.
27 P.B. Brown, 'Russian Serfdom's Demise and Russia's Conquest of the Crimean Khanate and the Northern Black Sea Littoral: Was There a Link?', in C. Witzenrath, ed., *Eurasian Slavery, Ransom and Abolition in World History, 1200–1860* (Farnham, Surrey, 2015), pp. 335–366. Precisely the role of propaganda in this war needs elucidation; there are now first results which the author could not evaluate due to restrictions in the reading rooms during the Covid-19 pandemic.
28 Smolarz, 'Speaking about Freedom and Dependency'; Kurtynova-D'Herlugnan, *The Tsar's Abolitionists*.

Bibliography

Abdyl-Latif, Shertnaia gramota byvshago Kazanskogo tsaria Abdyl-Latifa velikomu kniaziu Vasiliiu Ioannovichu po pozhalovanii emu goroda Iur'eva. 1508 dekabria 29, *Zapiski Odesskogo Obshchestva Istorii i Drevnostei*, N 5 (1863), pp. 399–401.

Abrahamowicz, Z. (ed.), *Księga podróży Ewliji Czelebiego*. Warszawa, Książka i Wiedza, 1969.

Adamovsky, E., Euro-Orientalism and the Making of the Concept of Eastern Europe in France, 1810–1880, *The Journal of Modern History*, N 77, 3, 2005, pp. 591–628.

Agafonov, N., *Kazan' i kazantsy: Arkheologiia, istoriia, etnografiia, byt religioznyi, domashnii i obshchestvennyi, biografii, vospominaniia, memuary, pis'ma, predaniia, legendy, skazaniia starozhilov, genealogiia, nravy, obychai, pamiatniki, iskusstvo, kul'tura, prosvieshchenie, literatura, poeziia, bibliografiia, bytovye miestnye bellestristicheskie ocherki, etiudy i prochie materialy iz kazanskoi zhizni*. Kazan', 2 vols., Tipo-Litogr. I.S. Perova, 1906/1907.

Akishin, M.O., *Rossiiskii absoliutizm i upravlenie Sibiri XVIII veka: Struktura i sostav gosudarstvennogo apparata*. Novosibirsk, Drevlekhranilishche, 2003.

Akty istoricheskie, sobrannye i izdannye arkheograficheskoiu kommissieiu. Vol. 1: *1334–1598*. Sanktpeterburg, Tipografiia Ekspeditsii zagotovleniia Gosudarstvennykh bumag, 1841.

Akty, sobrannye v bibliotekakh i arkhivakh Rossiiskoi Imperii arkheograficheskoiu ekspeditsieiu Imperatorskoi Akademii Nauk. Vol. 1: 1294–1598. Sanktpeterburg, Tipografiia II Otd. Sobstv. E.I.V. Kants.,1836.

Aleksandrov, V.A., and N.N. Pokrovskii, *Vlast' i obshchestvo: Sibir' v XVII v*. Novosibirsk, Nauka, 1991.

Alekseev, A.A., Russko-evreiskie literaturnye sviazi do XV v., In: A. Alekseev, W. Moskovich and S. Shvarzband (eds.), *Jews and Slavs*. Vol. 1. Sankt Petersburg, Nauka, 1993, pp. 44–75.

Alekseev, I.G., Moskovskie gorozhanie v 1480 g. i pobeda na Ugre, In: I. Froianov (ed.), *Genezis i razvitie feodalizma v Rossii: Problemy social'noj i klassovoj bor'by: Mevuzovskij sbornik*. Leningrad, Izdatel'stvo Leningradskogo universiteta, 1985, pp. 118–119.

Allen, W.E.D. (ed.), *Russian Embassies to the Georgian Kings, 1589–1605*. Cambridge, Cambridge University Press, 1970.

Andrews, W., *Poetry's Voice, Society's Song: Ottoman Lyric Poetry*. Seattle, University of Washington Press, 1985.

Anstey, R., Review of The Problem of Slavery in the Age of Revolution, 1770–1823 by David Brion Davis, Oxford 1999, *The English Historical Review*, N 91, 358 (1976), pp. 141–148.

Antonov, V.I., and N.E. Mneva, *Katalog drevnerusskoi zhivopisi XI-nachala XVIII vv*. Vol. 2. Moskva, Iskusstvo, 1963.

Antonovich, V., and M. Dragomanov, *Istoricheskiia pesni malorusskago naroda s ob"iasneniiami Vl. Antonovicha i M. Dragomanova*. Vol. 1. Kiev, Tipografiia M.P. Fritsa, 1874.

Arens, M., and D. Klein, Neues Forschungsprojekt am Ungarischen Institut München: "Das frühneuzeitliche Krimkhanat zwischen Orient und Okzident: Dependenzen und autonome Entwicklungsmöglichkeiten an der Schnittstelle zwischen orthodoxer, lateinischer und muslimischer Welt", *Ungarn-Jahrbuch*, N 27 (2004), pp. 492–498.

Aseev, B.N., *Russkii dramaticheskii teatr XVII–XVIII vekov*. Moskva, Iskusstvo, 1958.

Atwood, C., Ulus Emirs, Keshig Elders, Signatures, and Marriage Partners: The Evolution of a Classic Mongol Institution, In: D. Sneath (ed.), *Imperial Statecraft, Political Forms and Techniques of Governance in Inner Asia, Sixth-Twentieth Centuries*. Bellingham WA, Western Washington University, 2006, pp. 141–173.

Aust, M., *Die Schatten des Imperiums: Russland seit 1991*. München, C.H. Beck, 2019.

Awde, N., *Women in Islam: An Anthology from the Qurān and Ḥadīths*. Richmond, Surrey, Curzon, 2000.

Ayalon, D., *L'esclavage du Mamelouk*. Vol. 1. Jerusalem, Israel Oriental Society, 1951.
Baehr, S.L., *The Paradise Myth in Eighteenth Century Russia: Utopian Patterns in Early Secular Russian Literature and Culture*. Stanford CA, Stanford University Press, 1991.
Bähr, M., and F. Kühnel (eds.), *Verschränkte Ungleichheit: Praktiken der Intersektionalität in der Frühen Neuzeit*. Berlin, Duncker&Humblot, 2018.
Baert, B., *Heritage of Holy Wood: The Legend of the True Cross in Text and Image*. Leiden, Brill, 2004.
Bain, R.N., *The First Romanovs (1613–1725): A History of Moscovite Civilisation and the Rise of Modern Russia under Peter the Great and His Forerunners*. London, Archibald Constable & Co., 1905.
Bakhtin, A., and B. Khamidullin, Political History of the Kazan Khanate, In: I. Mirgaleev and R. Khakimov (eds.), *The History of the Tatars since Ancient Times*. Vol. 4: *Tatar States (15–18th Centuries)*. Kazan, Sh. Marjani Institute of History, 2017 [Russian: 2014], pp. 288–358.
Bakhtin, M., *Problems of Dostoevsky's Poetics*. Minneapolis, University of Minnesota Press, 1984.
Barker, H., *Egyptian and Italian Merchants in the Black Sea Slave Trade, 1260–1500*. PhD dissertation, Columbia University, 2014.
Barkey, K., *Empire of Difference: The Ottomans in Comparative Perspective*. Cambridge, Cambridge University Press, 2009.
Barkhudarov, S.G. et al. (eds.), *Slovar' russkogo iazyka XI–XVII vv.*, 31+3 vols., Moskva, Nauka et al., 1975–[2020; incomplete].
Barrett, T.M., *At the Edge of Empire: The Terek Cossacks and the North Caucasus Frontier, 1700–1860*. Boulder CO, Westview Press, 1999.
Batalov, A., *Sobor Pokrova Bogorodicy na Rvu: Istorija i ikonografija architektury*. Moskva, Izdatel'skij dom "Lingva-F", 2016.
Bazilevich, K.V., *Vneshniaia politika russkogo tsentralizovannogo gosudarstva: Vtoraia polovina XV veka*. Moskva, Izdatel'stvo Moskovskogo universiteta, 1952.
Begunov, I.K., *Pamiatnik russkoi literatury XIII veka "Slovo o pogibeli Russkoi Zemli"*. Moskva, Nauka, 1965.
Beilinson, O., Review of The Russian Empire 1450–1801 by Nancy Kollmann, Oxford 2017, *Review in History*, Review no. 2120, https://reviews.history.ac.uk/review/2120 (accessed 6 Sep. 2019).
Belobrova, O.A., Cherty zhanra khozhdenii v nekotorykh drevnerusskikh pis'mennykh pamiatnikakh XVII veka, *Trudy Otdela drevnerusskoi literatury*, N 27, 1972, pp. 257–272.
Belyakov, A., Serving Tatars: Legal Status, Number and Economic Features, In: R. Khakimov, I. Gilyazov and B. Izmaylov (eds.), *The History of the Tatars since Ancient Times*. Vol. 5: *Tatars in Russia (Second Half of the 16–18th Centuries)*. Kazan, Sh. Marjani Institute of History, 2017 [Russian: 2014], pp. 224–232.
Bentley, J.H., Early Modern Europe and the Early Modern World, In: C.H. Parker and J.H. Bentley (eds.), *Between the Middle Ages and Modernity: Individual and Community in the Early Modern World*. Lanham MD, Rowman & Littlefield, 2006, pp. 13–31.
Bibliia ili knigi sviashchennago pisaniia Vetkhago i Novago Zaveta v russkom perevode s parallel'nymi mestami. Sanktpeterburg, Synodal'naia Tipografiia, 1904 [1875].
Biblia sirech knigi Vetchago i Novago Zaveta po iazyku slovensku. Ostrog, Ivan Fedorov, 1581.
Billington, J.H., *The Icon and the Axe: An Interpretive History of Russian Culture*. London, Weidenfeld & Nicolson, 1966.
Blickle, P., *Unruhen in der ständischen Gesellschaft: 1300–1800*. München, Oldenbourg, 2012.
Boeck, B.J., *Shifting Boundaries on the Don Steppe Frontier: Cossacks, Empires and Nomads to 1739*. PhD dissertation, Harvard University, 2002.

Boeck, B.J., Containment vs. Colonization: Muscovite Approaches to Settling the Steppe, In: N.B. Breyfogle, A.M. Schrader and W. Sunderland (eds.), *Peopling the Russian Periphery: Borderland Colonization in Eurasian History*. London, Routledge, 2007, pp. 41–60.

Boeck, B.J., Identity as Commodity: Tournaments of Value in the Tatar Ransom Business, *Russian History*, N 35, 3–4, 2008, pp. 259–266.

Boeck, B.J., *Imperial Boundaries: Cossack Communities and Empire-Building in the Age of Peter the Great*. Cambridge, Cambridge University Press, 2009.

Boeck, B.J., Calculating the Casualties of Forced Labor: Azov as the Harbinger of Petrine Policies, In: M.S. Flier et al. (eds.), *Seeing Muscovy Anew: Politics – Institutions – Culture. Essays in Honor of Nancy Shields Kollmann*. Bloomington IN, Slavica, 2017, pp. 275–284.

Bogatyrev, S., *The Sovereign and his Counsellors*. Saarijärvi, The Finnish Academy Sciences and Letters, 2000.

Bogatyrev, S., Battle for Divine Wisdom: The Rhetoric of Ivan IV's Campaign Against Polotsk, In: E. Lohr and M. Poe (eds.), *The Military and Society in Russia, 1450–1917*. Leiden, Brill, 2002, pp. 325–363.

Bogatyrev, S., Localism and Integration in Muscovy, In: S. Bogatyrev (ed.), *Russia Takes Shape: Patterns of Integration from the Middle Ages to the Present*. Helsinki, Finnish Academy of Science and Letters, 2005, pp. 59–127.

Bogatyrev, S., Ivan IV (1533–1584), In: M. Perrie (ed.), *Cambridge History of Russia*. Vol. 1: *From Early Rus' to 1689*. Cambridge, Cambridge University Press, 2006, pp. 240–263.

Bogatyrev, S., The Heavenly Host and the Sword of Truth: Apocalyptic Imagery in Ivan IV's Muscovy, In: V. Kivelson, M. Flier, N. Kollmann and K. Petrone (eds.), *The New Muscovite Cultural History: A Collection in Honor of Daniel B. Rowland*. Bloomington IN, Slavica, 2009, pp. 77–90.

Bogatyrev, S., The Book of Degrees of the Royal Genealogy: The Stabilization of the Text and the Argument from Silence, In: A. Kleimola and G. Lenhoff (eds.), *The Book of Royal Degrees and the Genesis of Russian Historical Consciousness/"Stepennaia kniga tsarskogo rodosloviia" i genezis russkago istoricheskogo soznaniia*. Bloomington IN, Slavica, 2011, pp. 51–68.

Bogdanov, V.P., *Ot azbuki Ivana Fedorova do sovremennogo bukvaria*. Moskva, Prosveshchenie, 1974.

Boguslawski, A.P., *The Vitae of St. Nicholas and His Hagiographical Icons in Russia*. PhD dissertation, University of Kansas, 1982.

Bömelburg, H.-J., and S. Rohdewald, Polen-Litauen als Teil transosmanischer Verflechtungen, In: S. Rohdewald, S. Conermann and A. Fuess (eds.), *Transottomanica: Osteuropäisch-osmanisch-persische Mobilitätsdynamiken: Perspektiven und Forschungsstand*. Göttingen, V&R unipress, 2019, pp. 169–190.

Bono, S., *Schiavi musulmani nell'Italia moderna: Galeotti, vu' cumprà', domestici*. Napoli, Edizioni Scientifiche Italiane, 1999.

Böttrich, C., *Das slavische Henochbuch*. Gütersloh, Gütersloher Verlagshaus, 1996.

Brink, S., *Lord and Lady – Bryti and Deigja: Some Historical and Etymological Aspects of Family, Patronage and Slavery in Early Scandinavia and Anglo-Saxon England*. London: Viking Society for Northern Research, 2008.

Brink, S., Slavery in the Viking Age, In S. Brink and N.S. Price (eds.), *The Viking World*. London and, New York, Routledge, 2008, pp. 49–56.

Brion Davis, D., Review of Islam and the Abolition of Slavery by W.G. Clarence-Smith, New York 2006, *American Historical Review*, N 112, 4, 2007, pp. 1134–1135.

Broekmann, T., *Rigor iustitiae: Herrschaft, Recht und Terror im normannisch-staufischen Süden (1050–1250)*. Darmstadt, Wissenschaftliche Buchgesellschaft, 2005.

Broniewski, M., Opisanie Kryma (Tartariae Descriptio), *Zapiski Odesskogo obshchestva istorii i drevnostei*, N 6, 1867, pp. 333–367.

Brower, D., and S. Layton, Liberation through Captivity, *Kritika*, N 6, 2, 2005, pp. 259–279.

Brown, C.L., *Moral Capital: Foundations of British Abolitionism*. Chapel Hill, University of North Carolina Press, 2006.

Brown, P.B., How Muscovy Governed: Seventeenth-Century Russian Central Administration, *Russian History*, N 36, 4, 2009, pp. 459–529.

Brown, P.B, Russian Serfdom's Demise and Russia's Conquest of the Crimean Khanate and the Northern Black Sea Littoral: Was There a Link?, In: C. Witzenrath (ed.), *Eurasian Slavery, Ransom and Abolition in World History, 1200–1860*. Farnham, Surrey, Ashgate, 2015, pp. 335–366.

Brunschvig, R., 'Abd, In: P. Bearman et al. (eds.), *Encyclopedia of Islam*. Leiden, Brill, 1960, pp. 24–40.

Burbank, J., and F. Cooper, *Empires in World History: Power and the Politics of Difference*. Princeton NJ, Princeton University Press, 2010.

Burton, A., *Bukharan Trade, 1558–1718*. Bloomington IN, Indiana University Research Institute for Inner Asian Studies, 1993.

Burton, A., *The Bukharans: A Dynastic, Diplomatic and Commercial History, 1550–1702*. Richmond, Surrey, Curzon, 1997.

Burton, A., Russian Slaves in Seventeenth-Century Bukhara, In T. Atabaki and J. O'Kane (eds.), *Post-Soviet Central Asia*. London, I.B. Tauris, 1998, pp. 345–365.

Buschmann, N., and K.B. Murr, "Treue" als Forschungskonzept? Begriffliche und methodische Sondierungen, In: N. Buschmann and K.B. Murr (eds.), *Treue: Politische Loyalität und militärische Gefolgschaft in der Moderne*. Göttingen, Vandenhoeck & Ruprecht, 2008, pp. 11–35.

Bushkovitch, P., *Religion and Society in Russia: The Sixteenth and Seventeenth Centuries*. New York, Oxford University Press, 1992.

Bushkovitch, P., Review of Tretii Rim: Istoki i evoliutsiia russkoi srednevekovoi kontseptsii (XV–XVI vv.) by N.V. Sinitsyna, Moscow 1998, *Kritika*, N 1, 2, 2008, pp. 391–399.

Butler, F., *Enlightener of Rus': The Image of Vladimir Sviatoslavich Across the Centuries*. Bloomington IN, Slavica, 2002.

Bychkov, A.F. (ed.), *Letopisnyi sbornik, imenuemyi Patriarsheiu ili Nikonovskoiu letopis'iu*. Vol. 1. Sankt Peterburg, 1882.

Bychkov, A.F. (ed.), *Letopisnyi sbornik, imenuemyi Patriarsheiu ili Nikonovskoiu letopis'iu*. Vol. 2. Sanktpeterburg, 1885.

Bychkova, M.E., *Sostav klassa feodalov Rossii v XVI v.: Istoriko-genealogicheskoe issledovanie*. Moskva, Nauka, 1986.

Cerman, M., "Serfdom" and Slavery in European History since the Middle Ages: Identifying Common Aspects for Future Research. Contribution to the Final Round Table, In: S. Cavaciocchi (ed.), *Schiavitù e servaggio nell'economia europea, secc. XI–XVIII/Serfdom and Slavery in the European Economy, 11th–18th Centuries*. Firenze, Firenze University Press, 2014, pp. 665–676.

Chaev, N.S., "Moskva-tretii Rim" v politicheskoi praktike moskovskogo pravitel'stva XVI v., *Istoricheskie zapiski*, N 17, 1945, pp. 3–23.

Chekin, L.S., The Godless Ishmaelites: The Image of the Steppe in Eleventh-Thirteenth-Century Rus', *Russian History*, N 19, 1–4, 1992, pp. 9–28.

Cherepnin, L.V., *Obrazovanie russkogo tsentralizovannogo gosudarstva v XIV–XV vekakh: Ocherki sotsial'no-ėkonomicheskoi i politicheskoi istorii Rusi*. Moskva, Izdatel'stvo sotsial'no-ekonomicheskoi literatury, 1960.

Cherepnin, L.V., and S.V. Bakhrushin (eds.), *Dukhovnye i dogovornye gramoty velikikh i udel'nykh kniazei XIV–XVI vv.* Moskva and Leningrad, Izdatel'stvo Akademii Nauk SSSR, 1950.

Cherniavsky, M., *Tsar and People: Studies in Russian Myths*. New Haven CT, Yale University Press, 1961.

Chitty, N., L. Ji, G.D. Rawnsley and C. Hayden (eds.), *The Routledge Handbook of Soft Power*. London, Routledge, 2017.

Chrissidis, N.A., *An Academy at the Court of the Tsars: Greek Scholars and Jesuit Education in Early Modern Russia*. DeKalb IL, Northern Illinois University Press, 2016.

Christian, D., *A History of Russia, Central Asia and Mongolia*. 2 Vols. Oxford, Blackwell, 1998–2017.

Clarence-Smith, W.G., *Islam and the Abolition of Slavery*. London, C. Hurst & Co., 2006.

Clarence-Smith, W.G., and D. Eltis, White Servitude, In: D. Eltis and S.L. Engerman (eds.), *The Cambridge World History of Slavery*. Vol. 3: *AD 1420–AD 1804*. Cambridge, Cambridge University Press, 2011, pp. 132–160.

Colley, L., *Captives: Britain, Empire and the World, 1600–1850*. London, Jonathan Cape, 2002.

Conermann, S., Review of Slaving Zones: Cultural Identities, Ideologies, and Institutions in the Evolution of Global Slavery, edited by Jeff Fynn-Paul and Damian Alan Pargas, Leiden 2018, *sehepunkte*, N 19, 1, 2019.

Conermann, S., A. Fuess and S. Rohdewald (eds.), *Transottomanica: Osteuropäisch-osmanisch-persische Mobilitätsdynamiken: Perspektiven und Forschungsstand*. Göttingen, V&R unipress, 2019.

Conermann, S., and G. Şen (eds.), *Slaves and Slave Agency in the Ottoman Empire Ottoman Studies*. Göttingen, V&R unipress, 2020.

Crone, P., *Slaves on Horses: The Evolution of the Islamic Polity*. Cambridge and New York, Cambridge University Press, 1980.

Crone, P., *God's Rule: Government and Islam*. New York, Columbia University Press, 2004.

Crone, P., What Do We Actually Know about Mohammed?, 10.06.2008, https://www.opendemocracy.net/faith-europe_islam/mohammed_3866.jsp (accessed 10 June 2020).

Crone, P., and M. Cook, *Hagarism: The Making of the Islamic World*. Cambridge, Cambridge University Press, 1977.

Cumming, D. (ed.), *The Country of the Turkomans: An Anthology of Exploration from the Royal Geographical Society*. London, Oguz Press, 1977.

Czajewski, J., Zbiegostwo ludności Rosji w granice Rzeczypospolitej, *Pro Memoria*, N 6, 15, 2004, pp. 24–27.

Damaskin, P.I. (ed.), *Tochnoe izlozhenie pravoslavnoi very*. St Petersburg, Synodal'naia Tipografiia, 1894.

Danilevskii, I., Bibliia i povest' vremennykh let (k probleme interpretatsii letopisnykh tekstov), *Otechestvennaia istoriia*, N 1, 1993, pp. 78–94.

Dankoff, R. (ed.), *An Ottoman Traveller: Selections from the Book of Travels of Evliya Çelebi*. London, Eland, 2011.

Dávid, G., and P. Fodor (eds.), *Ransom Slavery along the Ottoman Borders: Early Fifteenth– Early Eighteenth Centuries*. Leiden, Brill, 2007.

David-Fox, M., P. Holquist and M. Martin (eds.), *Orientalism and Empire in Russia*. Bloomington IN, Slavica, 2006.

Davies, B.L., The Politics of Give and Take: Kormlenie as Service Remuneration and Generalized Exchange 1488–1726, In: A.M. Kleimola and G.D. Lenhoff (eds.), *Culture and Identity in Muscovy, 1359–1584*. Moscow, "ITZ-Garant", 1997, pp. 39–67.

Davies, B., The Second Chigirin Campaign (1678): Late Muscovite Military Power in Transition, In: E. Lohr (ed.), *The Military and Society in Russia: 1450–1917*. Leiden, Brill, 2002, pp. 97–118.

Davies, B.L., *Warfare, State and Society on the Black Sea Steppe, 1500–1700*. London, Routledge, 2007.

Davies, B.L., The Prisoner's Tale: Russian Captivity Narratives and Changing Muscovite Perceptions of the Ottoman-Tatar Dar-Al-Islam, In: C. Witzenrath (ed.), *Eurasian Slavery, Ransom and Abolition in World History, 1200–1860*. Farnham, Surrey, Ashgate, 2015, pp. 279–294.

Davis, D.B., *The Problem of Slavery in Western Culture*. Ithaca NY, Oxford University Press, 1988 [1966].

Demarest, B.A., *The Cross and Salvation: The Doctrine of Salvation*. Wheaton IL, Crossway Books, 1997.

Demkova, N.S., *Divnaia i muzhestvennaia povest' o khrabrosti i mudrosti tselomudrennoi devitsy Dinary tsaritsy, docheri Iverskogo tsaria Aleksandra*, http://lib.pushkinskijdom.ru/Default.aspx?tabid=5084 (accessed 23 June 2020).

Dennison, T., *The Institutional Framework of Russian Serfdom*. Cambridge, Cambridge University Press, 2011.

Dergacheva, I.V., *Stanovlenie povestvotatel'nykh nachal v drevnrusskoi literature XV–XVII vekov (na materiale sinodika)*. München, O. Sagner, 1990.

Despret, V., From Secret Agents to Interagency, *History and Theory*, N 52, 4, 2013, pp. 29–44.

Dewey, H.W., and A.M. Kleimola, Promise and Perfidy in Old Russian Cross-Kissing, *Canadian Slavic Studies*, N 2, 1968, pp. 327–341.

Dewey, H.W., and A.M. Kleimola, From the Kinship Group to Every Man His Brother's Keeper: Collective Responsibility in Pre-Petrine Russia, *Jahrbücher für Geschichte Osteuropas*, N 30, 3, 1982, pp. 321–335.

D'iakonov, M.D., *Vlast' moskovskikh gosudarei*. Sanktpeterburg, I.N. Skorokhodov, 1889.

Dilenschneider, R.L., n.t. In: D. Bergen (ed.), *The Sword of the Lord: Military Chaplains from the First to the Twenty-First Century*. Notre Dame, University of Notre Dame Press, 2004, p. i.

Divnaia povest muzhestvena o khrabrosti i mudrosti tselomudrenyia devitsa, Dinary tsaritsy, dshcheri iverskago tsaria Aleksandra: Podgotovka teksta, perevod i kommentarii N.S. Demkovoi, http://lib.pushkinskijdom.ru/Default.aspx?tabid=5084 (accessed 6 Sep. 2018).

Dmitriev, I.N., Stenopis' Arkhangel'skogo sobora Moskovskogo Kremlia, In: V.N. Lazarev, O.N. Podobedova and V.V. Kostochkin (eds.), *Drevnerusskoe iskusstvo: XVII vek*. Vol. 2. Moskva, Nauka, 1964, pp. 138–159.

Dmitriev, I.N., and E.G. Kholodov (eds.), *Istoriia russkogo dramaticheskogo teatra*. Vol. 1. Moskva, Iskustvo, 1977.

Dmitriev, M.V., Predstavleniia o "russkom" v kul'ture Moskovskoi Rusi XVI veka, In: *Obshchestvo, gosudarstvo, verkhovnaia vlast' v Rossii v srednie veka i rannee novoe vremia v kontekste istorii Evropy i Azii (X–XVIII stoletiia): Mezhdunarodnaia konferentsia, posviashchennaia 100-letiiu so dnia rozhdeniia akademika L.V. Cherepnina. Moskva, 30 noiabria–2 dekabria 2005 g*. Moskva, n.p., 2005, pp. 182–187.

Dmitrievskii, A.A., Chin peshchnogo deistva: Istoriko-arheologicheskii etiud", *Vizantiiskii vremennik*, N 1, 3–4, 1894, pp. 553–600.

Dubrovina, L.A., *Istoriia o Kazanskom tsarstve (Kazanskii letopisets): Spiski i klassifikatsiia tekstov*. Kiev, Naukova dumka, 1989.

Dubrovina, L.A., Predislovie k izdaniiu 2000 g., In: A.D. Koshelev (ed.), *Istoriia o Kazanskom tsarstve: Kazanskii letopisets*. Moskva, Iazyki russkoi kul'tury, 2000, pp. IV–XXVII.

Duchhardt, H., and G. Melville (eds.), *Im Spannungsfeld von Recht und Ritual*. Köln, Böhlau, 1997.

Dunn, J.D.G., *Word Biblical Commentary*. Vol. 38A: *Romans 1–8*. Dallas, Word Books, 1988.

Dunning, C. S. L., *Russia's First Civil War: The Time of Troubles and the Founding of the Romanov Dynasty*. University Park PA, Pennsylvania State University Press, 2001.

Efimov, N. I., *Rus'–novyi Izrail': Teokraticheskaia ideologiia svoezemnago pravoslaviia v do-Petrovskoi pis'mennosti*. Kazan' and Urzhum, Tipografiia F.P. Okisheva, 1912.

Elbashir, A.E., *The United States, Slavery and the Slave Trade in the Nile Valley*. Lanham MD, University Press of America, 1983.

Eliade, M., Spirit, Light, and Seed, *History of Religions*, N 11, 1, 1971, pp. 1–30.

Eltis, D., and S.L. Engerman, Dependence, Servility, and Coerced Labor in Time and Space, In: D. Eltis and S.L. Engerman (eds.), *The Cambridge World History of Slavery*. Vol. 3: *AD 1420–AD 1804*. Cambridge, Cambridge University Press, 2011, pp. 1–21.

Elwahed, A.A., *Contribution à une théorie sociologique de l'esclavage: Étude des situations génératrices de l'esclavage avec app. sur l'esclavage de la femme et bibliographie crit.* Paris, Mechelinck, 1931.

Eph'al, I., "Ishmael" and "Arab(s)": A Transformation of Ethnological Terms, *Journal of Near Eastern Studies*, N 35, 4, 1976, pp. 225–235.

Erdem, Y.H., *Slavery in the Ottoman Empire and its Demise, 1800–1909*. Basingstoke, Palgrave Macmillan, 1996.

Ergene, B.A., On Ottoman Justice: Interpretations in Conflict (1600–1800), *Islamic Law and Society*, N 8, 1, 2001, pp. 52–87.

Erusalimskii, K.I., *Sbornik Kurbskogo: Issledovanie knizhnoi kul'tury*. Vol. 1. Moskva, Znak, 2009.

Etkind, A., *Internal Colonization: Russia's Imperial Experience*. Cambridge, Polity Press, 2011.

Eusebius Pamphilius, *Church History, Life of Constantine, Oration in Praise of Constantine, ch. XXVIII: Translated and commented by Philip Schaff*, https://www.ccel.org/ccel/schaff/npnf201.iv.vi.i.xxviii.html (accessed 19 July 2017).

Fasmer, M., and O.N. Trubachev (eds.), *Etimologicheskii slovar' russkogo iazyka*. Moskva, Progress, 1971.

Fedotov, G.P., Rußland und die Freiheit, *Merkur*, N 5, 40, 1951, pp. 505–523.

Fels, E. (ed.), *Power in the 21st Century: International Security and International Political Economy in a Changing World*. Berlin, Springer, 2012.

Fennell, J.L.I. (ed.), *Prince A. M. Kurbsky's History of Ivan IV*. Cambridge: Cambrige University Press, 1965.

Fennell, J.L.I., *Ivan the Great of Moscow*. New York, St. Martin's Press, 1961.

Figes, O., *A People's Tragedy: The Russian Revolution 1891–1924*. London, Jonathan Cape, 1996.

Filiushkin, A.I., Problema genezisa Rossiiskoi imperii, In: I. Gerasimov et al. (eds.), *Novaia Imperskaia istoriia postsovetskogo prostranstva*. Kazan', Tsentr Issledovanii Natsionalizma i Imperii, 2004, pp. 375–408.

Filiushkin, A.I., Religioznyi faktor v russkoi vneshnei politike XVI veka: Ksenofobiia, tolerantnost' ili pragmatizm?, In: L. Steindorff (ed.), *Religion und Integration im Moskauer Russland: Konzepte und Praktiken, Potentiale und Grenzen 14.–17. Jahrhundert*. Wiesbaden, Harrassowitz Verlag, 2010, pp. 145–180.

Fine, J.V.A., The Mucovite Dynastic Crisis of 1497–1502, *Canadian Slavonic Papers/Revue Canadienne des Slavistes*, N 8, 1966, pp. 198–215.

Finley, M.I., The Emergence of a Slave Society, In: D.A. Pargas and F. Roşu (eds.), *Critical Readings on Global Slavery*. Vol. 1. Leiden, Brill, 2017, pp. 58–89.

Fisher, A., Muscovy and the Black Sea Slave Trade, *Canadian-American Slavic Studies*, N 6, 4, 1972, pp. 575–594.

Fisher, A., Chattel Slavery in the Ottoman Empire, *Slavery and Abolition*, N 1, 1, 1980, pp. 25–45.

Fletcher, G., *Of the Rus' Commonwealth*. Ithaca NY, Cornell University Press, 1966.

Flier, M.S., The Iconography of Royal Procession: Ivan the Terrible and the Muscovite Palm Sunday Ritual, In: H. Duchhardt, R.A. Jackson and D. Sturdy (eds.), *European Monarchy: Its Evolution and Practice from Roman Antiquity to Modern Times*. Stuttgart, Franz Steiner Verlag, 1992, pp. 109–125.

Flier, M.S., Breaking the Code: The Image of the Tsar in the Muscovite Palm Sunday Ritual, In: M. Flier and D. Rowland (eds.), *Medieval Russian Culture*. Vol. 2. Berkeley and Los Angeles, University of California Press, 1994, pp. 213–242.

Flier, M.S., The Throne of Monomakh: Ivan the Terrible and the Architectonics of Destiny, In: J. Cracraft and D.B. Rowland (eds.), *Architectures of Russian Identity: 1500 to the Present*. Ithaca NY, Cornell University Press, 2003, pp. 21–33.

Flier, M.S., Political Ideas and Ritual, In: M. Perrie (ed.), *Cambridge History of Russia*. Vol. 1: *From Early Rus' to 1689*. Cambridge, Cambridge University Press, 2006, pp. 387–408.

Flier, M.S., Golden Hall Iconography and the Makarian Initiative, In: V. Kivelson, M. Flier, N. Kollmann and K. Petrone (eds.), *The New Muscovite Cultural History: A Collection in Honor of Daniel B. Rowland*. Bloomington IN, Slavica, 2009, pp. 63–76.

Floria, B.N., Greki-emigranty v Russkom gosudarstve vtoroi poloviny XV-nachala XVI v.: Politicheskaia i kul'turnaia deiatel'nost', In: P. Rusev (ed.), *Rusko-balkanski kulturni vrazki prez srednevekovieto*. Sofiia, Bulgarian Academy of Sciences Press, 1982, pp. 122–138.

Florovsky, G., *Ways of Russian Theology*. Vol. 1. Belmont MA, Nordland Publishing Company, 1966.

Fontaine, J.M., *Slave Trading in the British Isles and the Czech Lands, 7th–11th Centuries*. PhD dissertation, King's College, 2017.

Forsyth, J., *A History of the Peoples of Siberia: Russia's North Asian Colony 1581–1990*. Cambridge, Cambridge University Press, 1992.

Frank, K., Agency, *Anthropological Theory*, N 6, 3, 2006, pp. 281–302.

Franz, G. (ed.), *Quellen zur Geschichte des Bauernkrieges*. Darmstadt, Wissenschaftliche Buchgesellschaft, 1963.

Frary, L.J., Slaves of the Sultan: Russian Ransoming of Christian Captives during the Greek Revolution (1821–1830), In: L.J. Frary and M. Kozelsky (eds.), *Russian-Ottoman Borderlands: The Eastern Question Reconsidered*. Madison WI, The University of Wisconsin Press, 2014, pp. 101–130.

Freedman, P., and M. Bourin (eds.), *Forms of Servitude in Northern and Central Europe*. Turnhout, Brepols, 2005.

Freitag, U., and A. v. Oppen, Translocality: An Approach to Connection and Transfer in Regional Studies, in: U. Freitag and A. v. Oppen (eds.), *Translocality – the Study of Globalising Phenomena from a Southern Perspective*. Leiden, Brill, 2010, pp. 1–21.

Frost, R.I., *The Northern Wars: War, State, and Society in Northeastern Europe, 1558–1721*. Harlow, Longman, 2000.

Fuess, A., Handel und Waren, In: S. Conermann, A. Fuess and S. Rohdewald (eds.), *Transottomanica: Osteuropäisch-osmanisch-persische Mobilitätsdynamiken*. Göttingen, V&R unipress, 2019, pp. 105–134.

Fuhrmann, J.T., *Tsar Alexis: His Reign and His Russia*. Gulf Breeze FL, Academic International Press, 1981.

Fynn-Paul, J., Tartars in Spain: Renaissance Slavery in the Catalan City of Manresa, c. 1408, *Journal of Medieval History*, N 34, 4, 2008, pp. 347–359.

Fynn-Paul, J., Empire, Monotheism and Slavery in the Greater Mediterranean Region from Antiquity to the Early Modern Era, *Past & Present*, N 205, 1, 2009, pp. 3–40.

Fynn-Paul, J., Introduction: Slaving Zones in Global History: The Evolution of a Concept, In: J. Fynn-Paul and D.A. Pargas (eds.), *Slaving Zones: Cultural Identities, Ideologies, and Institutions in the Evolution of Global Slavery*. Leiden, Brill, 2018, pp. 1–19.

Fynn-Paul, J., and D.A. Pargas (eds.), *Slaving Zones: Cultural Identities, Ideologies, and Institutions in the Evolution of Global Slavery*. Leiden, Brill, 2018.

Ganelin, I.S., Ob umeniii chitat' raznochteniia, *Trudy Otdela drevnerusskoi literatury*, N 16, 1960, 637–638.
Garlick, J., *The Impact of China's Belt and Road Initiative: From Asia to Europe*. London, Routledge, 2020.
Gell, A., *Art and Agency: An Anthropological Theory*. Oxford, Clarendon Press, 2007.
Gervaise, N., *An Historical Description of the Kingdom of Macasar in the East Indies*. Farnborough, Hants Gregg International, 1971.
Geyer, D., Die Idee der Freiheit in der osteuropäischen Geschichte, In: D. Geyer (ed.), *Europäische Perspektiven der Perestrojka*. Tübingen, Francke Verlag, 1991, pp. 9–22.
Giliazov, I., Islam i pravoslavie v Srednem Povolzh'e posle 1552, In: A. Kappeler (ed.), *Die Geschichte Russlands im 16. und 17. Jahrhundert aus der Perspektive seiner Regionen*. Wiesbaden, Harrassowitz, 2004, pp. 310–321.
Glancy, J.A., Slavery and the Rise of Christianity, In: K. Bradley and P. Cartledge (eds.), *The Cambridge World History of Slavery*. Vol. 1: *The Ancient Mediterranean World*. Cambridge, Cambridge University Press, 2011, pp. 456–481.
Glancy, J.A., "To Serve Them All the More": Christian Slaveholders and Christian Slaves in Antiquity, In: J. Fynn-Paul and D.A. Pargas (eds.), *Slaving Zones: Cultural Identities, Ideologies, and Institutions in the Evolution of Global Slavery*. Leiden, Brill, 2018, pp. 23–49.
Göhler, G., Wie verändern sich Institutionen? In: G. Göhler (ed.), *Institutionenwandel*. Opladen, Westdeutscher Verlag, 1997, pp. 21–56.
Gol'denberg, L.A., *Izograf zemli sibirskoi: Zhizn' i trudy Semena Remezova*. Magadan, Magadanskoe knizhnoe izdatel'stvo, 1990.
Golden, P.B., *An Introduction to the History of the Turkic Peoples: Ethnogenesis and State Formation in Medieval and Early Modern Eurasia and the Middle East*. Wiesbaden, Harrassowitz, 1992.
Goldziher, I., *Muslim Studies*. Vol. 1. London, George Allen & Unwin, 1967.
Golokhvastov, D.P., Blagoveshchenskii ierei Sil'vestr i ego pisaniia, *Chteniia v Imperatorskom obshchestve istorii i drevnostei rossiiskikh pri Moskovskom universitete*, N 1, 1874, pp. 1–110.
Golubinskii, E.E., *Istoriia Russkoi Tserkvi*. Vol. 3. Moskva, Krutitskoe Patriarshee Podvor'e, 1998.
Goncharov, S., Moskau neues Jerusalem (Moskva, novyj Ierusalim), In: N. Franz (ed.), *Lexikon der russischen Kultur*. Darmstadt, Wissenschaftliche Buchgesellschaft, 2002.
Gonneau, P., *À l'aube de la Russie muscovite: Serge de Radonège et André Roublev: Légendes et images (XIVe–XVIIe siècles)*. Paris, Institut d'Etudes Slaves, 2007.
Gonneau, P., Guerre et chevalerie au pays des Tatars: L'or, les esclaves, les femmes et les paladins dans l'Histoire de Kazan', *Russian History*, N 42, 1, 2015, pp. 49–63.
Gorskaia, N.A., *Krest'ianstvo v periody rannego i razvitogo feodalizma*. Vol. 2. Moscow, Nauka, 1990.
Graf, D.F., and M. O'Connor, The Origin of the Term Saracen and the Rawwafa Inscriptions, *Byzantine Studies/Etudes byzantines*, N 4, 1977, pp. 52–66.
Griesebner, A., and S. Hehenberger, Intersektionalität: Ein brauchbares Konzept für die Geschichtswissenschaften?, In: V. Kallenberg, J. Meyer and J. Müller (eds.), *Intersectionality und Kritik: Neue Perspektiven für alte Fragen*. Wiesbaden, Springer, 2013, pp. 105–124.
Grieser, H., and N. Priesching (eds.), *Theologie und Sklaverei von der Antike bis in die frühe Neuzeit*. Hildesheim, Zürich and New York, Georg Olms Verlag, 2016.
Gruber, I., *Orthodox Russia in Crisis: Church and Nation in the Time of Troubles*. DeKalb IL, Northern Illinois University Press, 2012.
Güneş-Yağcı, Z., The Black Sea Slave Trade According to the Istanbul Port Customs Register, 1606–1607, In: C. Witzenrath (ed.), *Eurasian Slavery, Ransom and Abolition in World History, 1200–1860*. Farnham, Surrey, Ashgate, 2015, pp. 207–220.

Hagen, M., "Volju nevolja učit" – Die russische Freiheit, In: M. Hagen (ed.), *Die Russische Freiheit: Wege in ein paradoxes Thema*. Stuttgart, Franz Steiner Verlag, 2002, pp. 9–22.

Halperin, C.J., The East Slavic Response to the Mongol Conquest, *Archivum Eurasiae Medii Aevi*, N 10, 1998–1999, pp. 98–117.

Halperin, C., Paradigms of the Image of the Mongols in Medieval Russia, In: V. Rabatzii, A. Pozzi, P. Geier and J. Krueger (eds.), *The Early Mongols: Language, Culture and History. Studies in Honor of Igor de Rachewiltz on the Occasion of his 80th Birthday*. Bloomington IN, Denis Sinor Institute for Inner Asian Studies, 2009, pp. 53–62.

Halperin, C.J., *The Tatar Yoke: The Image of the Mongols in Medieval Russia*. Bloomington IN, Slavica, 2009.

Halperin, C.J., *Stepennaia kniga* on the Reign of Ivan IV: Omissions from Degree 17, *The Slavonic and East European Review*, N 89, 1, 2011, pp. 56–75.

Halperin, C.J., Simeon Bekbulatovich and Mongol Influence on Ivan IV's Muscovy, *Russian History*, N 39, 3, 2012, pp. 306–330.

Hamilton, C. and S.G. Grady, *The Hedayah, or Guide: A Commentary on the Mussulman Laws*. London: W.H. Allen, 1870.

Hammond, V.E., *State Service in Sixteenth Century Novgorod: The First Century of the Pomestie System*. Lanham MD, University Press of America, 2009.

Haraway, D.J., *The Companion Species Manifesto: Dogs, People, and Significant Otherness*. Chicago, Prickly Paradigm Press, 2003.

Hastings, A., Holy Lands and Their Political Consequences, *Nations and Nationalism*, N 9, 1, 2003, pp. 29–54.

Hausteiner, E., Selbstvergleich und Selbstbehauptung: Die historische Imagination imperialer Eliten, In: H. Münkler and E. Hausteiner (eds.), *Die Legitimation von Imperien: Strategien und Motive im 19. und 20. Jahrhundert*. Frankfurt am Main and New York, Campus Verlag, 2012, pp. 15–33.

Hausteiner, E., *Greater than Rome: Neubestimmungen britischer Imperialität 1870–1914*. Frankfurt am Main, Campus, 2015.

Hecker, H., Die Christenpflicht als Rechtsnorm: Der Loskauf der Gefangenen im Uloženie von 1649, In: U. Halbach (ed.), *Geschichte Altrusslands in der Begriffswelt ihrer Quellen: Festschrift zum 70. Geburtstag von Günter Stökl*. Wiesbaden, Franz Steiner Verlag, 1986, pp. 154–163.

Heers, J., *Esclaves et domestiques au Moyen Âge dans le monde méditerranéen*. Paris, Hachette, 1996.

Hellie, R., *Enserfment and Military Change in Muscovy*. Chicago, University of Chicago Press, 1971.

Hellie, R., *Slavery in Russia, 1450–1725*. Chicago, University of Chicago Press, 1982.

Hellie, R., *The Muscovite Law Code (Ulozhenie) of 1649*. Vol. 1. Irvine CA, C. Schlacks Jr, 1988.

Hellie, R., Slavery, In: P.W. Goetz, R. MacHenry, J.E. Safra and D. Hoiberg (eds.), *The New Encyclopaedia Britannica*. Vol. 27, Chicago and London, Encyclopaedia Britannica, 1993, pp. 288–300.

Hellie, R., The Economy, Trade and Serfdom, In: M. Perrie (ed.), *Cambridge History of Russia*. Vol. 1: *From Early Rus' to 1689*. Cambridge, Cambridge University Press, 2006, pp. 539–558.

Hildermeier, M., *Geschichte Russlands: Vom Mittelalter bis zur Oktoberrevolution*. München, C.H. Beck, 2016.

Hoch, S.L., *Serfdom and Social Control in Nineteenth Century Russia: Petrovskoe a Village in Tambov*. Ann Arbor, University Microfilms International, 1983.

Hodgson, M., *The Venture of Islam*. Vol. 2: *The Expansion of Islam in the Middle Periods*. Chicago, University of Chicago Press, 1974.

Holzinger, M., *Natur als sozialer Akteur: Realismus und Konstruktivismus in der Wissenschafts- und Gesellschaftstheorie*. Opladen, Leske & Budrich, 2004.

Hopkins, B.D., Race, Sex and Slavery: "Forced Labour" in Central Asia and Afghanistan in the Early Nineteenth Century, *Modern Asian Studies*, N 42, 4, 2008, pp. 629–671.

Hrushevs'kyi, M., V.A. Smolii and P.S. Sokhan', *Istoriia Ukraïny-Rusy*. Vol. 7. Kyïv, Naukova dumka, 1991–2000.

Hughes, L., Sophia, Regent of Russia, *History Today*, N 32, 7, 1982, pp. 10–15.

Hughes, L., *Sophia, Regent of Russia: 1657–1704*. New Haven CT, Yale University Press, 1990.

Hughes, L., Petrine Russia, In: A. Gleason (ed.), *A Companion to Russian History*. Malden MA, Blackwell, 2009, pp. 165–179.

Hughes, T.M., *A Dictionary of Islam: Being a Cyclopaedia of the Doctrines, Rites, Ceremonies, and Customs, Together With the Technical and Theological Terms, of the Muhammadan Religion*. London, W.H. Allen, 1885.

Hunt, P., The Wisdom Iconography of Light: The Genesis, Meaning and Iconographic Realization of a Symbol, *Byzantinoslavica*, N 67, 2009, pp. 55–118.

Hunwick, J.O., *Sharī'a in Songhay: The Replies of al-Maghīlī to the Questions of Askia al-Ḥājj Muḥammad*. Oxford, Oxford University Press, 1985.

Hunwick, J., Black Africans in the Mediterranean World: Introduction to a Neglected Aspect of the African Diaspora, In: E. Savage (ed.), *The Human Commodity: Perspectives of the Trans-Saharan Slave Trade*. London, Routledge, 1992, pp. 5–38.

Hunwick, J., and E.T. Powell, *The African Diaspora in the Mediterranean Lands of Islam*. Princeton NJ, Markus Wiener, 2002.

Hurwitz, E., Metropolitan Hilarion's Sermon on Law and Grace: Historical Consciousness in Kievan Rus', *Russian History*, N 7, 1, 1980, pp. 322–333.

İnalcık, H. (ed.), *An Economic and Social History of the Ottoman Empire*. Cambridge, Cambridge University Press, 1997.

İnalcık, H., and S. Faroqhi (eds.), *An Economic and Social History of the Ottoman Empire*. Cambridge, Cambridge University Press, 2004.

Ipat'evskaia letopis'. S.-Peterburg, Arkheograficheskaia kommissiia AN SSSR, 1908.

Iskander, N., *Povest' o vziatii Tsargrada*, http://lib.pushkinskijdom.ru/Default.aspx?tabid=5059 (accessed 5 Sep. 2021).

Iskhakov, D.M., *Tiurko-tatarskie gosudarstva XV–XVI vv*. Kazan', Institut istorii im. Sh. Mardzhani An RT, 2004.

Islamov, K.F., K probleme izucheniia kopii rukopisi "Kyssa-i Iusuf" Kul 'Ali, *Vestnik Kazanskogo gosudarstennogo universiteta kul'tury i iskusstv*, N 1, 2014, pp. 146–150.

Israel, J., *The Dutch Republic: Its Rise, Greatness, and Fall 1477–1806*. Oxford, Clarendon Press, 1995.

Istoriia o Kazanskom tsarstve: Kazanskii letopisets. St Petersburg, 1903.

Ivanics, M., Enslavement, Slave Labour and Treatment of Captives in the Crimean Khanate, In: G. Dávid and P. Fodor (eds.), *Ransom Slavery Along the Ottoman Borders, Early Fifteenth – Early Eighteenth Centuries*. Leiden, Brill, 2007, pp. 193–220.

Ivanics, M., Die Şirin: Abstammung und Aufstieg einer Sippe in der Steppe, In: D. Klein (ed.), *The Crimean Khanate Between East and West (15th–18th Century)*. Wiesbaden, Harrassowitz, 2012, pp. 27–44.

Ivanova, T.G., S.N. Azbelev and I.I. Marchenko (eds.), *Belomorskie stariny i dukhovnye stikhi: Sobranie A.V. Markova*. St. Petersburg, Dmitrii Bulanin, 2002.

Izmaylov, I., Conquest of the Middle Volga Region and Sociopolitical Consequences. §1. Conquest of Kazan: Reasons, Course, Consequences, In: R. Khakimov, I. Gilyazov and B. Izmaylov (eds.), *The History of the Tatars since Ancient Times*. Vol. 5: *Tatars in Russia (Second Half of the 16–18th Centuries)*. Kazan, Sh. Marjani Institute of History, 2017 [Russian: 2014], pp. 60–70.

Jackson, P., The Testimony of the Russian "Archbishop" Peter Concerning the Mongols (1244/5): Precious Intelligence or Timely Disinformation?, *Journal of the Royal Asiatic Society*, N 26, 1–2, 2016, pp. 65–77.

Jakobsson, S., The Schism that Never Was: Old Norse Views on Byzantium and Russia, *Byzantinoslavica*, N 66, 1–2, 2008, pp. 173–188.

Jersild, A., *Orientalism and Empire*. Montreal, McGill-Queen University Press, 2002.

Jireček, C.J., *Geschichte der Bulgaren*. Prag, Tempsky, 1876.

Johnson, W., On Agency, *Journal of Social History*, N 37, 1, 2003, pp. 113–124.

Jomier, J., *Pour connaître l'Islam*. Paris, Cerf, 1988.

Judson, P.M., *The Habsburg Empire: A New History*. Cambridge MA, Harvard University Press, 2016.

Kafadar, C., Self and Others: The Diary of a Dervish in Seventeenth Century Istanbul and First-Person Narratives in Ottoman Literature, *Studia Islamica*, N 69, 1989, pp. 121–150.

Kagan-Tarkovskoi, M.D., 'Slovo o krestnom dreve: Podgotovka teksta, perevod i kommentarii', http://lib.pushkinskijdom.ru/Default.aspx?tabid=4928 (accessed 19 Dec. 2020).

Kalugin, V.V., *"Zhitie sviatitelia Nikolaia Mirlikiiskogo" v agiograficheskom svode Andreia Kurbskogo*. Moskva, Iazyki slavianskoi kul'tury, 2003.

Kämpfer, F., *Die Eroberung von Kasan 1552 als Gegenstand der zeitgenössischen russischen Historiographie*, Wiesbaden, Harrassowitz, 1969.

Kämpfer, F. (ed.), *Historie vom Zartum Kasan (Kasaner Chronist)*. Graz, Styria, 1969.

Kämpfer, F., "Rußland an der Schwelle zur Neuzeit": Kunst, Ideologie und historisches Bewußtsein unter Ivan Groznyj, *Jahrbücher für Geschichte Osteuropas*, N 23, 4, 1975, pp. 504–524.

Kämpfer, F., *Das russische Herrscherbild von den Anfängen bis zu Peter dem Großen: Studien zur Entwicklung politischer Ikonographie im byzantinischen Kulturkreis*. Recklinghausen, Bongers, 1978.

Kämpfer, F., Die Lehre vom Dritten Rom – pivotal moment, historiographische Folklore?, *Jahrbücher für Geschichte Osteuropas*, N 49, 3, 2001, pp. 430–441.

Kane, J., *The Politics of Moral Capital*. Cambridge and New York, Cambridge University Press, 2001.

Kappeler, A., *Ivan Groznyj im Spiegel der ausländischen Druckschriften seiner Zeit*. Bern and Frankfurt am Main, Peter Lang, 1972.

Kappeler, A., *Russland als Vielvölkerreich*. München, C.H. Beck, 1992.

Kappeler, A., *The Russian Empire: A Multiethnic History*. Harlow and New York, Longman, 2001 [German: 1992].

Kazhdan, A., The Concept of Freedom (*eleutheria*) and Slavery (*duleia*) in Byzantium, In: G. Makdisi (ed.), *La notion de liberté au Moyen Age: Islam, Byzance, Occident*. Paris, Société d'Édition Les Belles Lettres, 1985, pp. 215–226.

Keenan, E.L., Coming to Grips with the Kazanskaya Istoriya: Some Observations on Old Answers and New Questions, *Annals of the Ukrainian Academy of Arts and Sciences in the U.S.*, N 11, 1–2, 1964, pp. 143–183.

Keenan, E.L., *Muscovy and Kazan', 1445–1552: A Study in Steppe Politics*. PhD dissertation, Harvard University, 1965.

Keenan, E.L., Muscovy and Kazan': Some Introductory Remarks on the Patterns of Steppe Diplomacy, *Slavic Review*, N 26, 4, 1967, pp. 548–558.

Keenan, E.L., Review of Russia and Kazan: Conquest and Imperial Ideology (1438–1560s) by J. Pelenski, The Hague 1974, *Slavic Review*, N 34, 3, 1975, pp. 585–588.

Keenan, E.L., The *Stepennaia Kniga* and the Godunovian Renaissance, In: A. Kleimola and G. Lenhoff (eds.), *The Book of Royal Degrees and the Genesis of Russian Historical Consciousness/"Stepennaia kniga tsarskogo rodosloviia" i genezis russkago istoricheskogo soznaniia*. Bloomington IN, Slavica, 2011, pp. 69–80.

Kefeli, A., The Tale of Joseph and Zulaykha on the Volga Frontier: The Struggle for Gender, Religious, and National Identity in Imperial and Postrevolutionary Russia, *Slavic Review*, N 70, 2, 2011, pp. 373–398.

Kennedy, H.N., Review of Byzantium: The Decline and Fall by J.J. Norwich, London 1995, *The New York Times Book Review*, 7 January, 1996.

Khairetdinov, D.Z., *Musul'manskaia obshchina Moskvy v XIV– nachale XX veka*. Nizhnii Novgorod, Medina, 2002.

Khairetdinov, D.Z., and D.V. Mukhetdinov (eds.), *Islam v Moskve: Entsiklopedicheskii slovar'*. Nizhnii Novgorod, Medina, 2008.

Khakimov, R., I. Gilyazov and B. Izmaylov (eds.), *The History of the Tatars since Ancient Times. Vol. 5: Tatars in Russia (Second Half of the 16–18th Centuries)*. Kazan, Sh. Marjani Institute of History, 2017 [Russian: 2014].

Khitrov, D., Tributary Labour in the Russian Empire in the Eighteenth Century: Factors in Development, *International Review of Social History*, 61, S24, 2016, pp. 49–70.

Khodarkovsky, M., "Not by Word Alone": Missionary Policies and Religious Conversion in Early Modern Russia, *Comparative Studies in Society and History*, N 38, 2, 1996, pp. 267–293.

Khodarkovsky, M., Of Christianity, Enlightenment, and Colonialism: Russia in the North Caucasus, 1550–1800, *Journal of Modern History*, N 71, 2, 1999, pp. 394–430.

Khodarkovsky, M., *Russia's Steppe Frontier: The Making of a Colonial Empire, 1500–1800*. Bloomington IN, Indiana University Press, 2002.

Khodarkovsky, M., *Bitter Choices: Loyalty and Betrayal in the Russian Conquest of the North Caucasus*. Ithaca NY, Cornell University Press, 2011.

Khoroshkevich, A.L., *Rus' i Krym: Ot soiuza k protivostoianiiu: Konets XV–nachalo XVI vv*. Moskva, Editorial URSS, 2001.

Khudiakov, M.G., *Ocherki po istorii Kazanskogo khanstva*. Moskva, INSAN, 1991.

Khunchukashvili, D., Die heiligen Städte als eschatologische Legitimationssymbole der Zarenmacht unter den Rjurikiden, In: D. Ordubadi and D. Dahlmann (eds.), *Die 'Alleinherrschaft' der russischen Zaren in der 'Zeit der Wirren' in transkultureller Perspektive*. Göttingen, V&R unipress, 2021, pp. 129–158.

Kivelson, V.A., *Autocracy in the Provinces: The Muscovite Gentry and Political Culture in the Seventeenth Century*. Stanford CA, Stanford University Press, 1996.

Kivelson, V., Bitter Slavery and Pious Servitude: Muscovite Freedom and its Critics. In: R.O. Crummey (ed.), *Russische und ukrainische Geschichte vom 16.–18. Jahrhundert*. Wiesbaden, Harrassowitz, 2001, pp. 110–119.

Kivelson, V., *Cartographies of Tsardom: The Land and its Meanings in Seventeenth-Century Russia*. Ithaca NY, Cornell University Press, 2006.

Kivelson, V., *Desperate Magic: The Moral Economy of Witchcraft in Seventeenth-Century Russia*. Ithaca NY, Cornell University Press, 2013.

Kivelson, V.A., Diskussion: Papers of a Conference Complementing the New Edition of the "Stepennaia Kniga", *Jahrbücher für Geschichte Osteuropas*, N 61, 3, 2013, pp. 444–446.

Kivelson, V.A., and R.G. Suny, *Russia's Empires*. New York and Oxford, Oxford University Press, 2017.

Kizilov, M., Slave Trade in the Early Modern Crimea from the Perspective of Christian, Muslim, and Jewish Sources, *Journal for Early Modern History*, N 11, 1–2, 2007, pp. 1–31.

Kleimola, A.M., The Duty to Denounce in Muscovite Russia, *Slavic Review*, N 31, 4, 1972, pp. 759–779.

Kleimola, A., and G. Lenhoff (eds.), *The Book of Royal Degrees and the Genesis of Russian Historical Consciousness/"Stepennaia kniga tsarskogo rodosloviia" i genezis russkago istoricheskogo soznaniia*. Bloomington IN, Slavica, 2011.

Klein, D. (ed.), *The Crimean Khanate between East and West (15th–18th century)*. Wiesbaden, Harrassowitz, 2012.

Klingshirn, W., Charity and Power: Caesarius of Arles and the Ransoming of Captives in Sub-Roman Gaul, *Journal of Roman Studies*, N 75, 1985, pp. 183–203.

Kloss, B.M., *Nikonovskii svod i russkie letopisi XVI–XVII vekov*. Moskva, Nauka, 1980.

Kloss, B.M. (ed.), *L'vovskaia letopis'*. Moskva, Iazyki slavianskoi kul'tury, 2005.

Kloss, B.M. Predislovie, In *Letopisets nachala tsarstva tsaria i velikogo kniazia Ivana Vasil'evicha – Aleksandro-Nevskaia letopis' – Lebedevskaia letopis'*. Moskva, Znak, 2009, pp. V–VI.

Kloss, B.M., and V.D. Nazarov, Rasskazy o likvidatsii ordynskogo iga na Rusi v letopisanii kontsa XV v., In: O.I. Podobedova (ed.), *Drevne-russkoe iskusstvo XIV–XV vv*. Moskva, Nauka, 1984, pp. 283–313.

Kniga slova izbrannyia sviatykh otets o poklonenii i o chesti sviatykh ikon. Moskva, [Pechatnyi dvor], 1642.

Kochetkov, I.A., K istolkovanii ikony "Tserkov voinstvuiushchaia" ("Blagoslovenno voinstvo nebesnogo tsaria"), *Trudy Otdela drevnerusskoi literatury*, N 38, 1985, pp. 185–209.

Kolchin, P., *Unfree Labor: American Slavery and Russian Serfdom*. Cambridge MA, Harvard University Press, 1987.

Kollmann, N.S., *By Honor Bound: State and Society in Early Modern Russia*. Ithaca NY, Cornell University Press, 1999.

Kollmann, N.S., On Advising Princes in Early Modern Russia: Literacy and Performance, In: A. Kleimola and G. Lenhoff (eds.), *The Book of Royal Degrees and the Genesis of Russian Historical Consciousness/"Stepennaia kniga tsarskogo rodosloviia" i genezis russkago istoricheskogo soznaniia*. Bloomington IN, Slavica, 2011, pp. 341–348.

Kollmann, N.S., *The Russian Empire 1450–1801*. Oxford, Oxford University Press, 2017.

Kollmann, N.S., and K. Petrone (eds.), *The New Muscovite Cultural History: A Collection in Honor of Daniel B. Rowland*. Bloomington IN, Slavica, 2009.

Kołodziejczyk, D., Slave Hunting and Slave Redemption as a Business Enterprise: The Northern Black Sea Region in the Sixteenth to Seventeenth Centuries, *Oriente Moderno*, N 25, 86, 1, 2006, pp. 149–159.

Kołodziejczyk, D., *The Crimean Khanate and Poland-Lithuania: International Diplomacy on the European Periphery (15th–18th Century): A Study of Peace Treaties Followed by Annotated Documents*. Leiden, Brill, 2011.

Kol'tsova, T.M., Die Holzskulptur des Achangel'sker Nordens, In: M. Stößl (ed.), *Verbotene Bilder: Heiligenfiguren in Russland*. München, Hirmer, 2006, pp. 129–145.

Konstantinou, E., *Der Beitrag der byzantinischen Gelehrten zur abendländischen Renaissance des 14. und 15. Jahrhunderts*. Frankfurt am Main, Peter Lang, 2006.

Korpela, J., ". . . And They Took Countless Captives": Finnic Captives and the East European Slave Trade during the Middle Ages, In: C. Witzenrath (ed.), *Eurasian Slavery, Ransom and Abolition in World History, 1200–1860*. Farnham, Surrey, Ashgate, 2015, pp. 171–190.

Kozlitina, E.M., Dokumenty XVII veka po istorii Granovitoi palaty Moskovskogo Kremlia, *Materialy i issledovanja gosudarstvennyh muzeev Moskovskogo Kremlia*, N 1, 1973, pp. 95–110.

Kraft, E., *Moskaus griechisches Jahrhundert: Russisch-griechische Beziehungen und metabyzantinischer Einfluss 1619–1694*. Stuttgart, Franz Steiner Verlag, 1995.

Krasnosel'tsev, N., Chin peshchnogo deistva: Zamechania i popravki k stat'e M. Savinova, *Russkii filologicheskii vestnik*, N 26, 1891, pp. 117–123.

Kretzenbacher, L., Bischof Nikolaus von Myra als reitender Knabenretter, In: L. Kretzenbacher (ed.), *Griechische Reiterheilige als Gefangenenretter: Bilder zu mittelalterlichen Legenden um Georgios, Demetrios und Nikolaos*. Wien, Verlag der Österreichischen Akademie der Wissenschaften, 1983, pp. 57–78.

Koropeckyj, R., and B. Struminsky (eds.), *Lev Krevza's "A Defense of Church Unity" and Zaxarija Kopystens'kyj's "Palinodia"*. Cambridge MA, Harvard University Press, 1995.

Królikowska-Jedlińska, N., The Role of Circassian Slaves in the Foreign and Domestic Policy of the Crimean Khanate in the Early Modern Period, In: S. Conermann and G. Şen (eds.), *Slaves and Slave Agency in the Ottoman Empire Ottoman Studies*. Göttingen, V&R unipress, 2020, pp. 355–372.

Krom, M., Review of The Russian Empire 1450–1801 by N. Shields Kollmann, Oxford 2017, *Ab Imperio*, N 4, 2017, pp. 295–302.

Krutova, M.S., *Sviatitel' Nikolai Chudotvorets v drevnerusskoi pis'mennosti*. Moskva, Martis, 1997.

Kudriavtsev, I.M., "Poslanie na Ugru" Vassiiana Rylo kak pamiatnik publitsistiki XV v, *Trudy Otdela drevnerusskoi literatury*, N 8, 1951, pp. 158–186.

Kudriavtsev, I.M., "Ugorshchina" v pamiatnikakh drevnerusskoi literatury: Letopisnye povesti o nashestvii Akhmata i ikh literaturnaia istoriia, In: Institut mirovoi literatury imeni A.M. Gor'kogo (ed.), *Issledovaniia i materialy po drevnerusskoi literature*. Vol. 1. Moskva, Izdatel'stvo Akademii Nauk, 1961, pp. 23–67.

Kumar, K., *Visions of Empire: How Five Imperial Regimes Shaped the World*. Princeton NJ, Princeton University Press, 2017.

Kunt, M., Ethnic–Regional (*Cins*) Solidarity in the Seventeenth-Century Ottoman Establishment, *International Journal of Middle East Studies*, N 5, 3, 1974, pp. 233–239.

Kuntsevich, G.Z. (ed.), *Istoriia o Kazanskom tsarstve*. Sankt Peterburg, Tipografiia I.N. Skorokhodova, 1903.

Kuntsevich, G.Z., *Istoriia o kazanskom tsarstve ili Kazanskii letopisets*, S.-Peterburg, Tip. I.N. Skorokhodova, 1905.

Kurtynova-D'Herlugnan, L., *The Tsar's Abolitionists: The Slave Trade in the Caucasus and its Suppression*. Leiden, Brill, 2010.

La Piana, G., The Byzantine Theatre, *Speculum*, N 11, 2, 1936, pp. 171–211.

Lang, D.M., *The Last Years of the Georgian Monarchy, 1658–1832*. New York, Columbia University Press, 1957.

Langer, L.N., Slavery in the Appanage Era: Rus' and the Mongols, In: C. Witzenrath (ed.), *Eurasian Slavery, Ransom and Abolition in World History, 1200–1860*. Farnham, Surrey, Ashgate, 2015, pp. 145–170.

Lanzi, F., and G. Lanzi, *Saints and Their Symbols: Recognizing Saints in Art and in Popular Images*. Collegeville MN, Liturgical Press, 2004.

Latour, B., *Reassembling the Social: An Introduction to Actor-Network-Theory*. Oxford, Oxford University Press, 2005.

Laushkin, A.V., Nasledniki praottsa Izmaila i bibleiskaia mozaika v letopisnykh izvestiiakh o Polovtsakh, *Drevniaia Rus': Voprosy medievistiki*, N 4, 54, 2013, pp. 76–86.

Lavrent'evskaia letopis'. Vol. 1: *Povest' vremennykh let*. Leningrad, Arkheograficheskaia kommissiia AN SSSR, 1926–1928.

Lavrov, A.S., Voennyi plen i rabstvo na granitsakh Osmanskoi imperii i Rossiiskogo gosudarstva v 17 – nachale 18 veka, *DHI Moskau: Vorträge zum 18. Jahrhundert*, N 5, 2010, paragraph 15–16.

Lavrov, A., Captivity, Slavery and Gender: Muscovite Female Captives in the Crimean Khanate and in the Ottoman Empire, In: C. Witzenrath (ed.), *Eurasian Slavery, Ransom and Abolition in World History, 1200–1860*. Farnham, Surrey, Ashgate, 2015, pp. 309–319.

Lavrov, A., Rapatriement, genre et mobilité sociale: La liste des captifs rapatriés de Crimée par Timofej Hotunskij (1649), *Cahiers du monde russe*, N 57, 2–3, 2016, pp. 667–685.

Law, J., On the Methods of Long-Distance Control: Vessels, Navigation and the Portuguese Route to India, In: J. Law (ed.), *Power, Action and Belief: A New Sociology of Knowledge?* London, Routledge, 1986, pp. 234–263.

LeDonne, J.P., Poltava and the Geopolitics of Western Eurasia, *Harvard Ukrainian Studies*, N 31, 1–4, 2009–2010, pp. 177–191.
Lenhoff, G., The Tale of Tamerlane in the *Royal Book of Degrees*, In: G. Svak (ed.), *Mesto Rossii v Evrazii/The Place of Russia in Eurasia*. Budapest, Magyar Ruszisztikai Intezet, 2001, pp. 121–129.
Lenhoff, G., The Construction of Russian History in *Stepennaia Kniga*, *Revue des études slaves*, N 76, 1, 2005, pp. 31–50.
Lenhoff, G., Politics and Form in the *Stepennaia Kniga*, In: G. Lenhoff and A. Kleimola (eds.), *The Book of Royal Degrees and the Genesis of Russian Historical Consciousness/"Stepennaia kniga tsarskogo rodosloviia" i genezis russkago istoricheskogo soznaniia*. Bloomington IN, Slavica, 2011, pp. 157–174.
Lenhoff, G., Neue Literatur zur "Stepennaja kniga": Current Research on the *Stepennaja kniga*: Consensus, Controversies, Questions, *Jahrbücher für Geschichte Osteuropas*, N 61, 3, 2013, pp. 438–443.
Lenski, N., Evoking the Pagan Past: "Instinctu Divinitatis" and Constantine's Capture of Rome, *Journal of Late Antiquity*, N 1, 2, 2008, pp. 204–257.
Leonid, A., *Posmertnyia chudesa sviatitelia Nikolaia arkhiepiskopa Myr-Likiiskago, chudotvortsa: Pamiatnik drevnei russkoi pis'mennosti XI veka: Trud Efrema, episkopa pereiaslavskago'*. Sankt-Peterburg, Izdatel'stvo Obshchestvo lyubitelia drevnei russkoi pis'mennosti, 1888.
Letourneau, C., *L'évolution de l'esclavage dans les diverses races humaines*. Paris, Vigot, 1897.
Levi, S., India, Russia and the Eighteenth-Century Transformation of the Central Asia Caravan Trade, *Journal of the Economic and Social History of the Orient*, N 42, 4, 1999, pp. 519–548.
Levi, S.C., Hindus beyond the Hindu-Kush: Indians in the Central Asian Slave Trade, *Journal of the Royal Asiatic Society*, N 12, 3, 2002, pp. 277–288.
Levin, E., Muscovy and Its Mythologies: Pre-Petrine History in the Past Decade, *Kritika: Explorations in Russian and Eurasian History*, N 12, 4, 2011, pp. 773–788.
Lewin, P., *Ukrainian Drama and Theater in the Seventeenth and Eighteenth Centuries*. Toronto, Canadian Institute of Ukrainian Studies Press, 2008.
Lewis, B., *From Babel to Dragomans: Interpreting the Middle East*. New York, Oxford University Press, 2004.
Likhachev, D.S., *Russkie letopisi i ikh kul'turno-istoricheskoe znachenie*. Moskva, Izdatel'stvo Akademii Nauk SSSR, 1970.
Likhachev, D., and D. Bulanin (eds.), *Slovar' knizhnikov i knizhnosti drevnei Rusi*. Vol. 2: *Vtoraia polovina XIV–XVI v.*, Pt. 1: *A–K*. Leningrad, Nauka, 1988.
Likhachev, D.S., and D.M. Bulanin (eds.), *Slovar' knizhnikov i knizhnosti drevnei Rusi*. Vol. 2: *Vtoraia polovina XIV–XVI v.*, Pt. 2: *L–Ja*. Leningrad, Nauka, 1988.
Locke, J., and J. Ebbinghaus, *Ein Brief über Toleranz: Englisch-Deutsch*. Hamburg, Meiner, 1957.
Longworth, P., *Alexis: Tsar of all the Russias*. London, Martin Secker & Warburg Ltd, 1984.
Lopialo, K.K., K primernoi rekonstruktsii rospisi svodov Zolotoi palaty, In: O. Podobedova (ed.), *Moskovskaia shkola zhivopisi pri Ivane IV. Raboty v Mosk. Kremle 40-kh-70-kh godov XVI v.* Moskva, Nauka, 1972, pp. 193–200; Appendix.
Lur'e, I.S., Novonaidennyi rasskaz o "stoianii na Ugre", *Trudy Otdela drevnerusskoi literatury*, N 18, 1962, pp. 289–293.
Lur'e, I.S., *Obshcherusskie letopisi XIV–XV vv.* Leningrad, Nauka, 1976.
Lur'e, I.S., Genealogicheskaia skhema letopisei XI-XVI vv., vkliuchennykh v "Slovar' knizhnikov i knizhnosti Drevnei Rusi", *Trudy Otdela drevnerusskoi literatury*, N 40, 1985, pp. 190–205.
Lur'e, I.S., *Dve istorii Rusi XV veka: Rannie i pozdnie, nezavisimye i ofitsial'nye letopisi ob obrazovanii Moskovskogo gosudarstva*. Sankt-Peterburg, Bulanin, 1994.

Machado, M., Slavery and Social Movements in Nineteenth-Century Brazil: Slave Strategies and Abolition in São Paulo, *Review (Fernand Braudel Center)*, N 34, 1–2, 2011, pp. 163–191.
de Madariaga, I., *Ivan the Terrible: First Tsar of Russia*. New Haven CT, Yale University Press, 2005.
Magocsi, P.R., *A History of Ukraine: The Land and Its Peoples*. Toronto, University of Toronto Press, 2010.
Maher, J.P., *The Indo-European Origin of Some Slavic Grammatical Categories: Substantives in -jb,-ja, -je, -jane/-jahъ*. PhD dissertation, Indiana University, 1965.
Majerczak, R., Le mouridisme au Caucase, *Revue du Monde Musulman*, N 20, 1912, pp. 162–241.
Makaryk, I.R., *About the Harrowing of Hell = Slovo o zbureniu pekla: A Seventeenth-Century Ukrainian Play in its European Context*. Ottawa, Dovehouse Editions, 1989.
Makeeva, I.I., Chudesa Nikolaia Chudotvortsa o saratsine v russkoi pis'mennosti, *Trudy Otdela drevnerusskoi literatury*, N 60, 2009, pp. 3–28.
Man'kov, A.G., *Ulozhenie 1649 goda: Kodeks feodal'nogo prava Rossii*. Leningrad, Nauka, 1980.
Martin, J., Multiethnicity in Muscovy: A Consideration of Christian and Muslim Tatars in the 1550s–1580s, *Journal of Early Modern History*, N 5, 1, 2001, pp. 1–23.
Martin, J., Tatars in the Muscovite Army during the Livonian War, In: E. Lohr and M. Poe (eds.), *The Military and Society in Russia, 1450–1917*. Leiden, Brill, 2002, pp. 365–388.
Martin, J., *Medieval Russia: 980–1584*. Cambridge, Cambridge University Press, 2007.
Martin, J., Religious Ideology and Chronicle Depictions of Muslims in 16th-Century Muscovy, In: V. Kivelson, K. Petrone, N. Shields Kollmann and M.S. Flier (eds.), *The New Muscovite Cultural History: A Collection in Honor of Daniel B. Rowland*. Bloomingston IN, Slavica, 2009, pp. 285–299.
Martin, J., From Fathers to Sons? Property and Inheritance Rights of Pomeshchiki in 16th-Century Muscovy, In: G. Szvák and I. Tiumentsev (eds.), *Rusistika Ruslana Skrynnikova: Sbornik statej pamjati professora R. G. Skrynnikova*. Budapešt, Russica Pannonicana, 2011, pp. 68–75.
Martin, J., Simeon Bekbulatovich and Steppe Politics: Some Thoughts on Donald Ostrowski's Interpretation of the Tsar's Remarkable Career, *Russian History*, N 39, 3, 2012, pp. 331–338.
Martin, R.C. (ed.), *Encyclopedia of Islam and the Muslim World*. Vol. 2: L–Z. Farmington Hills MI, Macmillan Reference USA, 2016.
Martin, R.E., *A Bride for the Tsar: Bride-Shows and Marriage Politics in Early Modern Russia*. DeKalb IL, Northern Illinois University Press, 2012.
Matin, K., Uneven and Combined Development in World History: The International Relations of State-Formation in Premodern Iran, *European Journal of International Relations*, N 13, 3, 2007, pp. 419–447.
Matuz, J., Die Pfortendolmetscher zur Herrschaftszeit Süleymans des Prächtigen, *Südost-Forschungen*, N 34, 1975, pp. 26–60.
Mauss, M., *The Gift: Forms and Functions of Exchange in Archaic Societies*. London, Cohen & West, 1954.
McNeill, W.H., *Europe's Steppe Frontier, 1500–1808*. Chicago, University of Chicago Press, 1964.
Meltzer, M., *Slavery: A World History*. New York, Da Capo Press, 1993.
Metlinskii, A. (ed.), Marusia Boguslavska osvobozhdaet kozakov iz turetskoi nevoli (Duma) (Zapisal v Zen'kovsk. u. Poltavskoi gubernii A. Metlinskii), In: V. Antonovich and M. Dragomanov, *Istoricheskiia pesni malorusskago naroda s ob"iasneniiami Vl. Antonovicha i M. Dragomanova*. Vol. 1. Kiev, 1874, No. 46.
Michon, J.-L., Introduction, In: J.-L. Michon and R. Gaetani (eds.), *Sufism: Love and Wisdom*. Bloomington IN, World Wisdom Books, 2006.
Mika, N., Siły chestnogo kresta: Krzyż i praktyka jego całowania na Rusi w obliczu zagrożenia i' najazdów tatarskich (do końca XV wieku), In: Igor Danilevskyy et al. (eds.), *Religions and*

Beliefs of Rus' (9th–16th centuries). Krakow, Towarzystwo Wydawnicze "Historia Iagiellonica", 2018, pp. 365–384.

Mikhailov, V., *Adventures of Michailow: A Russian Captive among the Kalmucs*. Bloomington IN, The Mongolia Society, 1996.

Mikhailova, Y., and D. Prestel, Cross Kissing: Keeping One's Word in Twelfth-Century Rus', *The Slavic Review*, N 70, 1, 2011, pp. 1–22.

Millar, J. (ed.), *Encyclopedia of Russian History*. London, Thomson-Gale, 2004.

Miller, D.B., *The Velikie Minei Chetii and the Stepennaia Kniga of Metropolitan Makarii and the Origins of Russian National Consciousness*. Wiesbaden, Harrassowitz, 1979.

Miller, D.B., The Viskovatyi Affair of 1553–54: Official Art, the Emergence of Autocracy, and the Disintegration of Medieval Russian Culture, *Russian History*, N 8, 3, 1981, pp. 293–332.

Miller, D.B., *Saint Sergius of Radonezh, His Trinity Monastery and the Formation of the Russian Identity*. DeKalb IL, Northern Illinois University Press, 2010.

Miller, J.C., *The Problem of Slavery as History: A Global Approach*. New Haven CT, Yale University Press, 2012.

Miller, J.C., History as a Problem of Slaving, In: A.P. Damian and F. Roşu (eds.), *Critical Readings on Global Slavery*. Vol. 1. Leiden, Brill, 2017, pp. 201–248.

Mirgaleev, I., and R. Khakimov (eds.), *The History of the Tatars since Ancient Times*. Vol. 4: *Tatar States (15–18th Centuries)*. Kazan, Sh. Marjani Institute of History, 2017 [Russian: 2014].

Miura, T., and J.E. Philips, *Slave Elites in the Middle East and Africa: A Comparative Study*. London, Keegan Paul International, 2000.

Mneva, N.E., Zhivopis' kontsa XVI-nachala XVII veka, In: I.E. Grabar' et al. (eds.), *Istoriia russkogo iskusstva*. Vol. 3. Moskva, Izdatel'stvo Akademii Nauk SSSR, 1955, pp. 635–642.

Mohler, L., *Kardinal Bessarion als Theologe, Humanist und Staatsmann: Funde und Forschungen*. Paderborn, Schöningh, 1967.

Moiseeva, G.N., and V.P. Adrianova-Peretts (eds.), *Kazanskaia istoriia*. Moskva, Izdatel'stvo Akademii Nauk, 1954.

Monahan, E., *The Merchants of Siberia: Trade in Early Modern Eurasia*. Ithaca NY, Cornell University Press, 2016.

de Montesquieu, C.-L., and P. Vernière, *Lettres persanes*. Paris, Garnier, 1960.

Moo, D., *The Wycliffe Exegetical Commentary*. Vol. 1: *Romans 1–8*. Chicago, Moody Publishers, 1991.

Moon, D., *The Russian Peasantry, 1600–1930: The World the Peasants Made*. London and New York, Longman, 1999.

Moon, D., *The Plough that Broke the Steppes: Agriculture and Environment on Russia's Grasslands, 1700–1914*. Oxford, Oxford University Press, 2013.

Mordukhovich, L.M., Iz rukopis'nogo nasledstva Iu. Krizhanicha, *Istoricheskii arkhiv*, N 1, 1958, pp. 154–189.

Morgan, J.L., *Reckoning with Slavery: Gender, Kinship, and Capitalism in the Early Black Atlantic*. Durham, Duke University Press, 2021.

Morozov, V.V., *Litsevoi svod v kontekste otechestvennogo letopisaniia XVI veka*. Moscow, Indrik, 2005.

Morris, L., *The Apostolic Preaching of the Cross*. London, Tyndale Press, 1965.

Motyl, A.J., *Imperial Ends: The Decay, Collapse, and Revival of Empires*. New York, Columbia University Press, 2001.

Munkh-Erdene, L., The Rise of the Chinggisid Dynasty: Pre-Modern Eurasian Political Order and Culture at a Glance, *International Journal of Asian Studies*, N 15, 1, 2018, pp. 39–84.

Murdock, G., *Calvinism on the Frontier, 1600–1660: International Calvinism and the Reformed Church in Hungary and Transylvania*. New York, Clarendon Press, 2000.

Mustafin, R.A., *Ozero Kaban: Istoriko-dokumental'noe povestvovanie*. Kazan', Tatar. Kn. Izdatel'stvo, 1989.

Nasibova, A., B. Kuznetsov and B. Groshnikov (eds.), *Granovitaia palata Moskovskogo Kremlia: The Faceted Chamber in the Moscow Kremlin*. Leningrad, Avrora, 1978.

Nasonov, A.N., Novye istochniki po istorii Kazanskogo "vziatiia", *Arkheograficheskii ezhegodnik za 1960 god*, 1962, pp. 3–26.

Nasonov, A.N., *Istoriia russkogo letopisaniia XI – nachala XVIII veka: Ocherki i issledovaniia*. Moskva, Nauka, 1969.

Nastol'naia kniga sviashchennosluzhitelia. Vol. 6. Moscow, Moskovskaia Patriarkhiia, 1988.

Naumov, I.V., and D. Collins (eds.), *The History of Siberia*. London, Routledge, 2006.

Needell, J.D., The Abolition of the Brazilian Slave Trade in 1850: Historiography, Slave Agency and Statesmanship, *Journal of Latin American Studies*, N 33, 4, 2001, pp. 681–711.

Negrov, A.I., *Biblical Interpretation in the Russian Orthodox Church: A Historical and Hermeneutical Perspective*. Tübingen, Mohr Siebeck, 2008.

Neumann, I.B., and E. Wigen, *The Steppe Tradition in International Relations: Russians, Turks and European State Building 4000 BCE–2018 CE*. Cambridge, Cambridge University Press, 2018.

Neuwirth, A., Structural, Linguistic and Literary Features, In: J. McAuliffe (ed.), *The Cambridge Companion to the Qur'ān*. Cambridge, Cambridge University Press, 2006, pp. 97–114.

Niederstätter, A., *Das Jahrhundert der Mitte: An der Wende vom Mittelalter zur Neuzeit*. Wien, Ueberreuter, 1996.

Nikol'skii, K.T., *O sluzhbakh Russkoi tserkvi, byvshikh v prezhnikh pechatnykh bogosluzhebnykh knigakh*. Sankt Peterburg, Tipografiia Tovarishchestva Obshchestvennaia Pol'za, 1885.

Nitsche, P., *Grossfürst und Thronfolger: Die Nachfolgepolitik der Moskauer Herrscher bis zum Ende des Rjurikidenhauses*. Köln, Böhlau, 1972.

Nogmanov, A., Incorporation of Tatars into the Russian Legal Space in the Latter Half of the 16 – First Half of 17th Centuries, In: R. Khakimov, I. Gilyazov and B. Izmaylov (eds.), *The History of the Tatars since Ancient Times*. Vol. 5: *Tatars in Russia (Second Half of the 16–18th Centuries)*. Kazan, Sh. Marjani Institute of History, 2017 [Russian: 2014], pp. 140–155.

Nogmanov, A., The Tatar Population in the Russian Legislation in the Latter Half of the 17th Century, In: R. Khakimov, I. Gilyazov and B. Izmaylov (eds.), *The History of the Tatars since Ancient Times*. Vol. 5: *Tatars in Russia (Second Half of the 16–18th Centuries)*. Kazan, Sh. Marjani Institute of History, 2017 [Russian: 2014], pp. 156–178.

Nolte, H.-H., *Religiöse Toleranz in Rußland: 1600–1725*. PhD dissertation, University of Göttingen, 1969.

Nolte, H.-H., Iasyry: Non-Orthodox Slaves in Pre-Petrine Russia, In: C. Witzenrath (ed.), *Eurasian Slavery, Ransom and Abolition in World History, 1200–1860*. Farnham, Surrey, Ashgate, 2015, pp. 247–264.

Norris, H.T., *Popular Sufism in Eastern Europe: Sufi Brotherhoods and the Dialogue with Christianity and "Heterodoxy"*. New York, Routledge, 2006.

Novosel'skij, A.A., *Bor'ba Moskovskogo gosudarstva s tatarami v pervoj polovine XVII veka*. Moskva, Akademiia Nauk SSSR, 1948.

Nye, J.S., *Soft Power: The Means to Success in World Politics*. New York, Public Affairs, 2004.

O'Neill, K., *Claiming Crimea: A History of Catherine the Great's Southern Empire*. New Haven CT, Yale University Press, 2017.

O'Neill, K., Constructing Russian Identity in the Imperial Borderland: Architecture, Islam, and the Transformation of the Crimean Landscape, *Ab Imperio*, N 2, 2006, pp. 163–192.

Obolenskii, M. (ed.), *Sobornaia gramota dukhovenstva pravoslavnoi vostochnoi tserkvi, utverzhdaiushchaia san tsaria za velikim kniazem Ioannom IV Vasil'evichem, 1561*. Moskva, Sinodal'naia Tipografiia, 1850.

Olearius, A., *The Travels of Olearius in Seventeenth-Century Russia*. Stanford CA, Stanford University Press, 1976.

Onasch, K., *Lexikon Liturgie und Kunst der Ostkirche unter Berücksichtigung der alten Kirche*. Berlin, Buchverlag Union, 1993.

Ong, W., *Orality and Literacy: The Technologizing of the Word*. New York, Methuen 1982.

Ostapchuk, V., The Human Landscape of the Ottoman Black Sea in the Face of the Cossack Naval Raids, *Oriente Moderno*, N 81, 1, 2001, pp. 23–95.

Ostapchuk, V., Long-Range Campaigns of the Crimean Khanate in the Mid-Sixteenth Century, *Journal of Turkish Studies*, N 29, 2004, pp. 75–99.

Ostrowski, D., Early *Pomest'e* Grants as a Historical Source, *Oxford Slavonic Papers*, N 33, 2000, pp. 36–63.

Ostrowski, D.G., *Muscovy and the Mongols: Cross-Cultural Influences on the Steppe Frontier, 1304–1589*. Cambridge, Cambridge University Press, 1998.

Ostrowski, D., Muscovite Adaptation of Steppe Political Institutions, *Kritika*, N 1, 2, 2000, pp. 267–304.

Ostrowski, D., The Façade of Legitimacy: Exchange of Power and Authority in Early Modern Russia, *Comparative Studies in Society and History*, N 44, 3, 2002, pp. 534–563.

Ostrowski, D.G., Troop Mobilization by the Muscovite Grand Princes (1313–1533), In: E. Lohr and M. Poe (eds.), *The Military and Society in Russia, 1450–1917*. Leiden, Brill, 2002, pp. 19–40.

Ostrowski, D.G., The Extraordinary Career of Tsarevich Kudai Kul/Peter in the Context of Relations between Muscovy and Kazan', In: J. Duzinkiewicz, M. Popovych, V. Verstiuk and N. Yakovenko (eds.), *States, Societies, Cultures, East and West*. New York, Ross Publishing, 2004, pp. 697–719.

Ostrowski, D., "Moscow the Third Rome" as Historical Ghost, In: S.T. Brooks (ed.), *Byzantium: Faith and Power (1261–1557): Perspectives on Late Byzantine Art and Culture*. New York, Metropolitan Museum of Art, 2007, pp. 170–179.

Ostrowski, D., The Mongols and Rus': Eight Paradigms, In: A. Gleason (ed.), *A Companion to Russian History*. Malden MA, Blackwell, 2009, pp. 66–86.

Ostrowski, D., The End of Muscovy: The Case for ca. 1800, *Slavic Review*, N 69, 2, 2010, pp. 426–438.

Ostrowski, D., Simeon Bekbulatovich's Remarkable Career as Tatar Khan, Grand Prince of Rus', and Monastic Elder, *Russian History*, N 39, 3, 2012, pp. 269–299.

Ostrowski, D., Dressing a Wolf in Sheep's Clothing: Toward Understanding the Composition of the "Life of Alexander Nevskii", *Russian History*, N 40, 1, 2013, pp. 41–67.

Ostrowski, D., Towards the Integration of Early Modern Rus' into World History, In: C. Witzenrath (ed.), *Eurasian Slavery, Ransom and Abolition in World History, 1200–1860*. Farnham, Surrey, Ashgate, 2015, pp. 105–143.

Ostrowski, D.G., *The Povest' Vremennykh Let: An Interlinear Collation and Paradosis*. Cambridge MA, Harvard University Press, 2003.

Pachkalov, A.V., *Srednevekovye goroda nizhnego Povolzh'ia i severnogo Kavkaza*. Moskva, Knorus, 2018.

Pak, N.V., *Zhitiinye pamiatniki o Nikolae Mirlikiiskom v russkoi knizhnosti XI–XVII vv*. PhD dissertation, University Sankt-Petersburg, 2000.

Pamiatniki literatury Drevnei Rusi. Vol. 7: *Seredina XVI veka*. Moskva, Khudozhestvennaia Literatura, 1985.

Paperno, I., The Liberation of the Serfs as a Cultural Symbol, *Russian Review*, N 50, 4, 1991, pp. 417–436.

Papoulia, B.D., *Ursprung und Wesen der "Knabenlese" im Osmanischen Reich*. München, Oldenbourg, 1963.
Papp, S., Die Inaugurationen der Krimkhane durch die Hohe Pforte (16.–18. Jahrhundert), In: D. Klein (ed.), *The Crimean Khanate between East and West (15th–18th century)*. Wiesbaden, Harrassowitz, 2012, pp. 75–90.
Patterson, O., *Slavery and Social Death: A Comparative Study*. Cambridge MA, Harvard University Press, 1982.
Pavlov, A.P., Fedor Ivanovich and Boris Godunov (1584–1605), In: M. Perrie (ed.), *Cambridge History of Russia*. Vol. 1: *From Early Rus' to 1689*. Cambridge, Cambridge University Press, 2006, pp. 264–285.
Pavlov, A.P., and M. Perrie, *Ivan the Terrible*. London, Routledge, 2003.
Pavlov, P.N., Deistvitel'naia rol' arkhiepiskopa Vassiana v sobytiiakh 1480 g., *Uchenye zapiski Krasnoiarskogo pedagogicheskogo instituta*, N 4, 1, 1955, pp. 202–212.
Peabody, S., Slavery, Freedom, and the Law in the Atlantic World, In: D. Eltis and S. Engerman (eds.), *The Cambridge World History of Slavery*. Vol. 3: *AD 1420–AD 1804*. Cambridge, Cambridge University Press, 2011, pp. 594–630.
Peach, C., and S. Vertovec (eds.), *Islam in Europe: The Politics of Religion and Community*. London and New York, Palgrave Macmillan, 1997.
Peirce, L.P., *The Imperial Harem: Women and Sovereignty in the Ottoman Empire*. New York, Oxford University Press, 1993.
Peirce, L.P., *Empress of the East: How a European Slave Girl Became Queen of the Ottoman Empire*. New York, Basic Books, 2017.
Pelenski, J., *Russia and Kazan: Conquest and Imperial Ideology (1438–1560s)*. The Hague, Mouton, 1974.
Penrose, G.L., Inner Asian Influences on the Earliest Russo-Chinese Trade and Diplomatic Contacts, *Russian History*, N 19, 1–4, 1992, pp. 361–392.
Peresvetov, I.S., and A.A. Zimin, *Sochineniia I. Peresvetova*. Moskva, Izdatel'stvo Akademii Nauk SSSR, 1956.
Perrie, M. (ed.), *Cambridge History of Russia*. Vol. 1: *From Early Rus' to 1689*. Cambridge, Cambridge University Press, 2006.
Peterson, D. (ed.), *Where Wrath and Mercy Meet: Proclaiming the Atonement Today. Papers from the Fourth Oak Hill College Annual School of Theology*. Carlisle, Paternoster Press, 2001.
Pipes, D., *Slave Soldiers and Islam*. New Haven CT, Yale University Press, 1981.
Pipes, R. (ed.), *Karamzins Memoir on Ancient and Modern Russia*. New York, Athenaeum, 1966.
Pipes, R., *Rußland vor der Revolution: Staat und Gesellschaft im Zarenreich*. München, C.H. Beck, 1977.
Pitirim, mitropolit Volokolamskogo i Jur'evskogo (ed.), *Simfoniia ili slovar'-ukazatel' k Sviashchennomu Pisaniiu Vetkhogo i Novogo Zaveta*. Vol. 2. Moskva, Russkaia pravoslavnaia tserkov, 1988.
Pliukhanova, M., *Siuzhety i simvoly Moskovskogo gosudarstva*. Sankt-Peterburg, Akropol', 1995.
Pliukhanova, M.B., "Poslanie na Ugru" i vopros o proiskhozhdenii moskovskoi imperskoi ideologii, *Trudy Otdela drevnerusskoi literatury*, N 61, 2010, pp. 452–488.
Podhorodecki, L., *Chanat Krymski i jego stosunki z Polska w XV-XVIII w*. Warszawa, Książka i Wiedza, 1987.
Podobedova, O.I. (ed.), *Moskovskaia shkola zhivopisi pri Ivane IV: Raboty v Moskovskom Kremle 40-kh–70-kh godov XVI v*. Moskva, Nauka, 1972.
Podskalsky, G., *Von Photios zu Bessarion: Der Vorrang humanistisch geprägter Theologie in Byzanz und deren bleibende Bedeutung*. Wiesbaden, Harrassowitz, 2003.

Poe, M., What Did Russians Mean When They Called Themselves "Slaves of the Tsar"?, *Slavic Review*, N 57, 3, 1998, pp. 585–608.

Poe, M., Moscow the Third Rome: The Origins and Transformations of a "Pivotal Moment", *Jahrbūcher fūr Geschichte Osteuropas*, N 49, 3, 2001, pp. 412–429.

Pokrovskii, N.N. and G. Lenhoff (eds.), *The Book of Degrees of the Royal Genealogy: A Critical Edition Based on the Oldest Known Manuscripts. Texts and Commentary*. 2 Vols. Moskva, Iazyki slavianskoi kul'tury, 2007–2008.

Polnyi pravoslavnyi bogoslovskii entsiklopedicheskii slovar' v 2 tomach. Vol. 2. Sankt-Peterburg, P.P. Soikina, 1913.

Polotskii, S., *Izbrannye sochineniia*. Moskva, Akademia Nauk SSSR, 1953.

Polotskii, S., and A. Hippisley (eds.), *Vertograd mnogocvětnyj*. Vol. 2. Köln, Böhlau, 1999.

Ponomarev, A.I. (ed.), *Pamiatniki drevnei russkoi tserkovno-uchitel'noi literatury*. Vol. 2: *Slaviano-russkii prolog*. Pt. 1: *Sentyabr'-dekabr'*. Sankt-Peterburg, Tipografia S. Dobrodeeva, 1896.

Poppe, A., *Kak byla kreshchena Rus'*. Moscow, Politizdat, 1989.

Poslanie na Ugru Vassiana Rylo: Podgotovka teksta E.I. Vaneevoi, perevod O.P. Likhachevoi, kommentarii Ia.S. Lur'e, http://lib.pushkinskijdom.ru/Default.aspx?tabid=5070 (accessed 7 Sep. 2018).

Prestel, D., Creating Redemptive History: The Role of the Kievan Caves Monastery in the *Stepennaia Kniga*, In: G. Lenhoff (ed.), *The Book of Royal Degrees and the Genesis of Russian Historical Consciousness/"Stepennaia kniga tsarskogo rodosloviia" i genezis russkago istoricheskogo soznaniia*. Bloomington IN, Slavica, 2011, pp. 97–110.

Prior, C.W., Hebraism and the Problem of Church and State in England, 1642–1660, *The Seventeenth Century*, N 28, 1, 2013, pp. 37–61.

Prokopovich, F., Funeral Oration, In: L. Oliva (ed.), *Peter the Great*. Englewood Cliffs NJ, Prentice-Hall, 1970, pp. 78–81.

Pskovskiia i sofiskiia letopisi. Sanktpeterburg, Ed. Pratsa, 1851.

Raba, J., Moscow – the Third Rome or the New Jerusalem. In: Osteuropa-Institut (ed.), *Beiträge zur 7. Internationalen Konferenz zur Geschichte des Kiever und Moskauer Reiches*. Wiesbaden, Harrassowitz, 1995, pp. 297–308.

Rabġūzī, Nāṣir ad-Dīn Ibn Burhān ad-Dīn, H. Boeschoten and J. O'Kane, *Al-Rabghūzī, The Stories of the Prophets: Qiṣaṣ al-Anbiyā': An Eastern Turkish Version*. Leiden, Brill, 2015.

Rakhimzianov, B.R., *Moskva i tatarskii mir: Sotrudnichestvo i protivostoianie v ėpochu peremen, XV-XVI vv*. St Peterburg, Evraziia, 2016.

Rakhimzyanov, B., The Muslim Tatars of Muscovy and Lithuania: Some Introductory Remarks, In: B.J. Boeck (ed.), *Dubitando: Studies in History and Culture in Honor of Donald Ostrowski*. Bloomington IN, Slavica, 2012, pp. 117–128.

Rakhimzyanov, B.R., 'The Debatable Questions of the Early Kasimov Khanate (1437–1462), *Russian History* N 37, 2, 2010, pp. 83–101.

Ramelli, I., *Social Justice and the Legitimacy of Slavery: The Role of Philosophical Asceticism from Ancient Judaism to Late Antiquity*. Oxford, Oxford University Press, 2016.

Rapoport, D.C., Moses, Charisma, and Covenant, *The Western Political Quarterly*, N 32, 2, 1979, pp. 123–143.

Rapp, C., *Holy Bishops in Late Antiquity: The Nature of Christian Leadership in an Age of Transition*. Berkeley and Los Angeles, University of California Press, 2005.

Rehberg, K.-S., Institutionenwandel und Funktionsveränderung des Symbolischen, In: G. Göhler (ed.), *Institutionenwandel*. Opladen, Westdeutscher Verlag, 1997, pp. 94–118.

Remezov, S.U., *Chertezhnaia kniga Sibiri*. Moskva, FGUP PKO Kartografiia, 2003.

Remezov, S.U., *Remezovskaia letopis': Sluzhebnaia chertezhnaia kniga*. Tobol'sk, Fond Vozrozhdenie Tobolska, 2006.

Richter, R., and E. Furubotn, *Neue Institutionenökonomik: Eine Einführung und kritische Würdigung*. Tübingen, Mohr Siebeck, 1996.

Rieber, A.J., *The Struggle for the Eurasian Borderlands: From the Rise of Early Modern Empires to the End of the First World War*. Cambridge, Cambridge University Press, 2014.

Rio, A., *Slavery after Rome, 500–1100*. Oxford and New York, Oxford University Press, 2017.

Robertson, C.C., and M.A. Klein (eds.), *Women and Slavery in Africa*. Madison, University of Wisconsin Press, 1983.

Rohdewald, S., Sarı Saltuk im osmanischen Rumelien, der Rus' und Polen-Litauen: Zugänge zu einer transosmanischen religiösen Erinnerungsfigur (14.–20. Jh.), In: K. Jobst and D. Hüchtker (eds.), *Heilig: Transkulturelle Verehrungskulte vom Mittelalter bis in die Gegenwart*. Göttingen, Wallstein Verlag, 2017, pp. 67–98.

Romanchuk, R., The Reception of the Judaizer Corpus in Ruthenia and Muscovy: A Case Study of the Logic of Al-Ghazzali, the "Cipher in Squares," and the Laodicean Epistle. In: V.V. Ivanov and J. Verkholantsev (eds.), *Speculum Slaviae Orientalis: Muscovy, Ruthenia and Lithuania in the Late Middle Ages*. Moscow, Novoe izdatel'stvo, 2005, pp. 144–165.

Romaniello, M.P., *Conquest, Colonization and Orthodoxy: Muscovy and Kazan', 1552–1682*. MA thesis, Ohio State University, 1998.

Romaniello, M.P., *The Elusive Empire: Kazan and the Creation of Russia, 1552–1671*. Madison WI, University of Wisconsin Press, 2012.

Rossabi, M., The "Decline" of the Central Asian Caravan Trade, In: J.D. Tracy (ed.), *The Rise of Merchant Empires: Long Distance Trade in the Early Modern World 1350–1750*. Cambridge, Cambridge University Press, 1991, pp. 351–370.

Rotman, Y., Byzance face à l'Islam arabe, VIIe-Xe siècle: D'un droit territorial à l'identité par la foi, *Annales Histoire, Sciences Sociales*, N 60, 4, 2005, pp. 767–788.

Rotman, Y., *Byzantine Slavery and the Mediterranean World*. Cambridge MA, Harvard College, 2009.

Rowland, D., The Problem of Advice in Muscovite Tales about the Time of Troubles, *Russian History*, N 6, 2, 1979, pp. 259–283.

Rowland, D., Did Muscovite Literary Ideology Place Limits on the Power of the Tsar?, *The Russian Review*, N 49, 2, 1990, pp. 125–155.

Rowland, D., Biblical Military Imagery in the Political Culture of Early Modern Russia: The Blessed Host of the Heavenly Tsar, In: M. Flier and D. Rowland (eds.), *Medieval Russian Culture*. Vol. 2. Berkeley and Los Angeles, University of California Press, 1994, pp. 182–212.

Rowland, D., Moscow – the Third Rome or the New Israel?, *Russian Review*, N 55, 4, 1996, pp. 591–614.

Rowland, D.B., Architecture and Dynasty: Boris Godunov's Uses of Architecture, 1584–1606, In: J. Cracraft and D.B. Rowland (eds.), *Architectures of Russian Identity: 1500 to the Present*. Ithaca NY, Cornell University Press, 2003, pp. 34–47.

Rozanov, S.P. (ed.), *Polnoe sobranie russkikh letopisei*. Vol. 24: *Tipografskaia letopis'*. Petrograd, 1921.

Rozenberg, L.I., Tatary v Moskve XVII-serediny XIX vekov, In: I.I. Krupnik (ed.), *Etnicheskie gruppy v gorodakh evropeiskoi chasti SSSR: Formirovanie, rasselenie, dinamika kul'tury*. Moskva, Moskovskii filial Geogragicheskogo obshchestva SSSR, 1987, pp. 16–26.

Rozhdestvenskaia, M., *Zhitie proroka Moiseia: Vstuplenie i komentarii*, Elektronnaia biblioteka IRLI RAN, 2006–2011, http://lib.pushkinskijdom.ru/Default.aspx?tabid=4917 (accessed 24 Mar. 2017).

Rüß, H., *Herren und Diener: Die soziale Mentalität des russischen Adels, 9.–17. Jahrhundert.* Köln, Böhlau, 1994.

Russkaia pravoslavnaia tserkov', *Mineia obshchaia s prazdnichnoi.* Moskva, Pechatnyi dvor', 1650.

Russkaia staropechatnaia literatura (XVI – pervaia chetvert' XVIII v.). Moskva, Nauka, 1978.

Rustemeyer, A., Szlachta, Bauern und Majestätsverbrechen in Smolensk 1654–1764, In: A. Kappeler (ed.), *Die Geschichte des Moskauer Reiches im 16. und 17. Jahrhundert aus der Perspektive seiner Regionen.* Wiesbaden, Harrassowitz, 2004, pp. 137–158.

Rustemeyer, A., *Dissens und Ehre: Majestätsverbrechen in Russland (1600–1800).* Wiesbaden, Harrassowitz, 2006.

Ruthven, M., *Islam in the World.* New York, Oxford University Press, 2000.

Said, E.W., *Orientalism.* New York, Pantheon Books, 1978.

Samoilovich, A.N. (ed.), *Materialy po istorii Uzbekskoi, Tadzhikskoi i Turkmenskoi SSR: Torgovlia s Moskovskim gosudarstvom i mezhdunarodnoe polozhenie Srednei Azii v XVI–XVII vv.* Vol. 3: *Materialy po istorii narodov SSSR.* Leningrad, Izdatel'stvo Akademii Nauk SSSR, 1932.

Sanin, G.A., *Otnosheniia Rossii i Ukrainy s Krymskim Khanstvom v seredine XVII veka.* Moskva, Nauka, 1987.

Schaeder, H., *Moskau das dritte Rom: Studien zur Geschichte der politischen Theorien in der slavischen Welt.* Darmstadt, Hermann Gentner Verlag, 1957.

Schiel, J., Sklaven, In: M. Borgolte (ed.), *Migrationen im Mittelalter: Ein Handbuch.* Berlin, De Gruyter, 2014, pp. 251–265.

Schiel, J., I. Schürch and A. Steinbrecher, Von Sklaven, Pferden und Hunden: Trialog über den Nutzen aktueller Agency-Debatten für die Sozialgeschichte, In: C. Arni, M. Leimgruber and S. Teuscher (eds.), *Neue Beiträge zur Sozialgeschichte/Nouvelles contributions à l'histoire sociale.* Zürich, Chronos, 2017, pp. 17–48.

Schimmel, A., Review of Wisdom of Royal Glory (Kutadgu Bilig) by Yūsuf Khāss Hājib: A Turco-Islamic Mirror for Princes, edited by R. Dankoff, Chicago 1983, *Journal of the American Oriental Society*, N 105, 2, 1985, pp. 356–357.

Schimmelpenninck van der Oye, D., *Russian Orientalism: Asia in the Russian Mind from Peter the Great to the Emigration.* New Haven CT, Yale University Press, 2010.

Schimmelpfennig, B., Das Papsttum im Mittelalter: Eine Institution?, In: G. Melville (ed.), *Institutionen und Geschichte: Theoretische Aspekte und mittelalterliche Befunde.* Köln, Böhlau, 1992, pp. 209–229.

Schmidt, C., *Sozialkontrolle in Moskau: Justiz, Kriminalität und Leibeigenschaft 1649–1785.* Stuttgart, Franz Steiner Verlag, 1996.

Schmidt, C., *Leibeigenschaft im Ostseeraum: Versuch einer Typologie.* Köln, Böhlau, 1997.

Schmidt, C., Freiheit in Russland: Eine begriffshistorische Spurensuche, *Jahrbücher für Geschichte Osteuropas*, N 55, 2, 2007, pp. 264–275.

Schmidt-Biggemann, W., Apokalypse und Millenarismus im Dreißigjährigen Krieg, In: K. Bußmann and H. Schilling (eds.), *1648: Krieg und Frieden in Europa, Katalog der Ausstellung in Münster and Osnabrück 24. Okt. 1998–17. Jan. 1999. Textband I: Politik, Religion, Recht und Gesellschaft.* Osnabrück, Veranstaltungsgesellschaft 350 Jahre Westfälischer Friede mbH, 1999, pp. 259–263.

Schmitt, C., *Politische Theologie.* München, Duncker & Humblot, 1922.

Schneider, I., *Kinderverkauf und Schuldknechtschaft: Untersuchungen zur frühen Phase des islamischen Rechts.* Habilitation, Universität Köln, 1996.

Schnusenberg, C.C., *The Relationship between the Church and the Theatre.* Lanham MD, University Press of America, 1988.

Scholz, L., Leibeigenschaft rechtfertigen: Kontroversen um Ursprung und Legitimität der Leibeigenschaft im Wildfangstreit, *Zeitschrift für Historische Forschung*, N 45, 1, 2018, pp. 41–81.

Schulze, W., *Landesdefension und Staatsbildung: Studien zum Kriegswesen des innerösterreichischen Territorialstaates (1564–1619)*. Wien, Böhlau, 1973.

Schulze, W., Die deutschen Landesdefensionen im 16. und 17. Jahrhundert, In: J. Kunisch (ed.), *Staatsverfassung und Heeresverfassung in der europäischen Geschichte der frühen Neuzeit*. Berlin, Duncker & Humblot, 1986, pp. 129–149.

Schulze Wessel, M., "Loyalität" als geschichtlicher Grundbegriff und Forschungskonzept: Zur Einleitung, In: M. Schulze Wessel (ed.), *Loyalitäten in der Tschechoslowakischen Republik 1918–1938: Politische, nationale und kulturelle Zugehörigkeiten*. München, Oldenbourg, 2004, pp. 1–22.

Schussmann, A., The Legitimacy and Nature of Mawid al-Nabī (Analysis of a Fatwā), *Islamic Law and Society*, N 5, 2, 1998, pp. 214–234.

Schwartz, S., Denounced by Lévi Strauss: CLAH Luncheon Address, *The Americas*, N 59, 1, 2002, pp. 1–8.

Semyonov, A., How Five Empires Shaped the World and How this Process Shaped those Empires, *Ab Imperio*, N 4, 2017, pp. 27–51.

Serbina, K.N. (ed.), *Letopisnyi svod 1518 (Uvarovskaia)*. Moskva and Leningrad, Izdatel'stvo Akademii Nauk SSSR, 1962.

Sessa, K., Ursa's Return: Captivity, Remarriage and the Domestic Authority of Roman Bishops in Fifth-Century Italy. *Journal of Early Christian Studies*, N 19, 3, 2011, pp. 401–432.

Shakhmatov, A.A., *Razbor sochineniia I.A. Tikhomirova "Obozrenie letopisnykh svodov Rusi Severo-Vostochnoi"*. Sanktpeterburg, 1899.

Shakhmatov, A.A., Ermolinskaia letopis' i Rostovskii vladychnyi svod, *Izvestiia otdeleniia russkago iazyka i slovestnosti imperatorskoi Akademii Nauk*, N 9, 1, 1904, pp. 366–423.

Shakhmatov, A.A., and M.D. Priselkov, *Obozrenie russkikh letopisnykh svodov XIV–XVI vv*. Moskva and Leningrad, Izdatel'stvo Akademii Nauk SSSR, 1938.

Shaw, D.G., The Torturer's Horse: Agency and Animals in History, *History and Theory*, N 52, 4, 2013, pp. 146–167.

Sidorenko, G.V., Die frühesten Skulpturen des christlichen Rußland: Berittene und bewaffnete Heilige als Beschützer der Stadt und Befreier vom Tatarenjoch, In: M. Stößl (ed.), *Verbotene Bilder: Heiligenfiguren in Russland*. München, Hirmer, 2006, pp. 95–106.

Smiley, W., Abolishing Bondage: A "Barbarous Law"?: Capture and Liberation in the Russo-Habsburg-Ottoman War of 1787–1792, In: C. Witzenrath (ed.), *Eurasian Slavery, Ransom and Abolition in World History, 1200–1860*. Farnham, Surrey, Ashgate, 2015, pp. 323–334.

Smiley, W., *From Slaves to Prisoners of War: The Ottoman Empire, Russia and International Law*. Oxford, Oxford University Press, 2018.

Smirnov, P., *Chelobitnaia dvorian i detei boiarskikh vsekh gorodov v pervoi polovine 17 veka*. Moskva, Sinodal'naia Tipografia, 1915.

Smolarz, E., Speaking about Freedom and Dependency: Representations and Experiences of Russian Enslaved Captives in Central Asia in the First Half of the 19th Century, *Journal of Global Slavery*, N 2, 1–2, 2017, pp. 44–71.

Sneath, D., *The Headless State: Aristocratic Orders, Kinship Society, and Misrepresentations of Nomadic Inner Asia*. New York, Columbia University Press, 2007.

Sobers Khan, N., *Slaves Without Shackles: Forced Labour and Manumission in the Galata Court Registers, 1560–1572*. Berlin, Klaus Schwarz Verlag, 2015.

Soldat, C., The Limits of Muscovite Autocracy: The Relations between the Grand Prince and the Boyars in the Light of Iosif Volotskii's Prosvetitel, *Cahiers du monde russe*, N 46, 1–2, 2005, pp. 265–276.

Solov'ev, S.M., *Istoriia Rossii s drevneishikh vremen*. Moskva, Izdal'stvo sotsial'no-ekonomicheskoi literatury, 1959–1966.

Spaulding, J., Slavery, Land Tenure, and Social Class in the Northern Turkish Sudan, *International Journal of African Historical Studies*, N 15, 1, 1982, pp. 1–20.

Speranski, M.N., Sentiabr'skaia mineia-chetia do-Makar'evskago sostava, *Sbornik otdeleniia russkago iazyka i slovesnosti Imperatorskoi Akademii Nauk*, N 64, 4, 1896, pp. 1–23.

Speranskii, M.N., Povest' o Dinare v russkoi pis'mennosti, *Izvestiia Otdeleniia russkogo iazyka i slovesnosti Akademii Nauk*, N 31, 1926, pp. 43–92.

Spitsyn, A., Peshchnoe deistvo i khaldeiskaia peshch, *Zapiski: Russkoe arkheologicheskoe obshchestvo*, N 12, 1901, pp. 95–209.

Sreznevskii, I.I., *Svedeniia i zametki o maloizvestnykh i neizvestnykh pamiatnikakh: I-XL*. Sanktpeterburg, Tipografia Imperatorskoi Akademii Nauk, 1867.

Stanziani, A., Serfs, Slaves, or Wage Earners?: The Legal Status of Labour in Russia from a Comparative Perspective, from the Sixteenth to the Nineteenth Century, *Journal of Global History*, N 3, 2, 2008, pp. 183–202.

Stanziani, A., *Bâtisseurs d'empires: Russie, Chine et Inde à la croisée des mondes, XVe-XIXe siècle*. Paris, Raisons d'agir, 2012.

Stanziani, A., *Bondage: Labor and Rights in Eurasia from the Sixteenth to the Early Twentieth Centuries*. New York, Berghahn, 2014.

Stearns, P.N., M. Adas, S.B. Schwartz and M.J. Gilbert (eds.), *World Civilizations: The Global Experience*. Boston, Pearson, 2011.

Steindorff, L., *Memoria in Altrußland: Untersuchungen zu den Formen christlicher Totensorge*. Stuttgart, Franz Steiner Verlag, 1994.

Steindorff, L., Review of Pod znakom kontsa vremeni: Ocherki russkoi religioznosti kontsa XIV – nachala XVI vv. by A. I. Alekseev, Sankt-Peterburg 2002, *Jahrbücher für Geschichte Osteuropas*, N 53, 1, 2005, pp. 113–114.

Stevens, C.B., *Russia's Wars of Emergence, 1460–1730*. Harlow, Pearson, 2007.

Stichweh, R., How Do Divided Societies Come About? Persistent Inequalities, Pervasive Asymmetrical Dependencies, and Sociocultural Polarization as Divisive Forces in Contemporary Society, *Global Perspectives*, N 2, 1, 2021.

Stökl, G., Review of The Velikie Minei Chetii and the Stepennaia Kniga of Metropolitan Makarii and the Origins of Russian National Consciousness by David B. Miller, Wiesbaden 1979, *Jahrbücher für Geschichte Osteuropas*, N 29, 2, 1981, pp. 264–266.

Stölting, E., Wandel und Kontinuität der Institutionen: Rußland – Sowjetunion – Rußland, In: G. Göhler (ed.), *Institutionenwandel*. Opladen, Westdeutscher Verlag, 1997, pp. 181–203.

Stößl, M. (ed.), *Verbotene Bilder: Heiligenfiguren in Russland*. München, Hirmer, 2006.

Strakhov, O.B., *The Byzantine Culture in Muscovite Rus': The Case of Evfimii Chudovskii (1620–1705)*. Köln, Böhlau, 1998.

Stupperich, R., Kiev – das zweite Jerusalem: Ein Beitrag zur Geschichte des ukrainisch-russischen Nationalbewusstseins, *Zeitschrift für slavische Philologie*, N 12, 3–4, 1935, pp. 332–354.

Sunderland, W., *Taming the Wild Field: Colonization and Empire on the Russian Steppe*. Ithaca NY, Cornell, 2004.

Suny, R.G., *The Making of the Georgian Nation*. Bloomington IN, Indiana University Press, 1988.

Swoboda, M., The Furnace Play and the Development of Liturgical Drama in Russia, *Russian Review*, N 61, 2, 2002, pp. 220–234.

Tatishchev, V.N., *Istoriia rossiiskaia v semi tomakh*. Vol. 5. Moskva and Leningrad, Izdatel'stvo Akademii Nauk SSSR, 1965.

Taube, M., On the Slavic Life of Moses and Its Hebrew Sources, In: A. Alekseev, W. Moskovich and S. Shvarzband (eds.), *Jews and Slavs*. Vol. 1. Jerusalem, Nauka, 1993, pp. 84–119.

Tereshina, M., and N.N. Evreinov, *Istoriia russkogo teatra: Illiustrirovannoe izdanie*. Moskva, Ėksmo, 2011.

Thompson, E.P., *The Making of the English Working Class*. New York, Vintage, 1963.

Thomson, F.J., The Intellectual Difference between Muscovy and Ruthenia in the Seventeenth Century: The Case of the Slavonic Translations and the Reception of the Pseudo-Constantinian Constitution (Donatio Constantini), *Slavica Gandensia*, N 22, 1995, pp. 63–107.

Thomson, F.J., The Slavonic Translation of the Old Testament, In: J. Krašovec (ed.), *The Interpretation of the Bible: The International Symposium in Slovenia*. Sheffield, Sheffield Academic Press, 1998, pp. 605–920.

Thyrêt, I., "Blessed is the Tsaritsa's Womb": The Myth of Miraculous Birth and Royal Motherhood in Muscovite Russia, *Russian Review*, N 53, 4, 1994, pp. 479–496.

Thyrêt, I., *Between God and Tsar: Religious Symbolism and the Royal Women of Muscovite Russia*. DeKalb IL., Northern Illinois University Press, 2001.

Thyrêt, I., The Cult of the True Cross in Muscovy and Its Reception in the Center and the Regions, In: A. Kappeler (ed.), *Die Geschichte Russlands im 16. und 17. Jahrhundert aus der Perspektive seiner Regionen*. Wiesbaden, Harrassowitz, 2004, pp. 236–258.

Tikhomirov, M.N. (ed.), *Polnoe sobranie russkikh letopisei*. Vol. 26: *Vologodsko-Permskaia letopis'*. Moskva and Leningrad, Nauka, 1959.

Tikhomirov, M.N. (ed.), *Vologodsko-permskii letopisets*. Moskva and Leningrad, Izdatel'stvo Akademii Nauk SSSR, 1959.

Tikhomirov, M.N. (ed.), *Letopisets nachala tsarstva*. Moskva, Izdatel'stvo Nauka, 1965.

Toledano, E., *Slavery and Abolition in the Ottoman Middle East*. Seattle, University of Washington Press, 1998.

Toledano, E., *As if Silent and Absent: Bonds of Enslavement in the Islamic Middle East*. New Haven CT, Yale University Press, 2007.

Toledano, E., Enslavement in the Ottoman Empire in the Early Modern Period, In: D. Eltis and S. Engerman (eds.), *The Cambridge World History of Slavery*. Vol. 3: *AD 1420–AD 1804*. Cambridge, Cambridge University Press, 2011, pp. 25–46.

Tolz, V., Orientalism, Nationalism, and Ethnic Diversity in Late Imperial Russia, *The Historical Journal*, N 48, 1, 2005, pp. 127–150.

Tsurkan, R.K., *Slavianskii perevod Biblii: Proiskhozhdenie, istoriiāteksta i vazhneishie izdaniiā*. Sankt Peterburg, Kolo, 2001.

Ulbert, J., and G. Le Bouëdec, "Les drogmans des consulats", la fonction consulaire à l'époque moderne: L'affirmation d'une institution économique et politique (1500–1800), In: A. Gautier and M. de Testa (eds.), *Drogmans, diplomates et ressortissants européens auprès de la porte ottomane*. Istanbul, Isis Press, 2013, pp. 13–30.

Usachev, A.J., *Stepennaia kniga i drevnerusskaia knizhnost' vremeni mitropolita Makariia*. Moskva, Al'ians-Arkheo, 2009.

Usmanov, M., Kauryi kaləm ezennən, *Archeograf iazmalary (Arkheograficheskie zapiski)*, p. 64.

Uspenskii, B.A., *Filologicheskie razyskaniia v oblasti slavianskikh drevnostei (Relikti iasychestva v vostochnoslavianskom kul'te Nikolaia Mirlikiiskogo)*. Moskva, Izdatel'stvo Moskovskogo universiteta, 1982.

Uspenskii, B.A., and V.M. Zhivov, Tsar and God: Semiotic Aspects of the Sacralization of the Monarch in Russia, In: B. Uspenskii, V. Zhivov and M. Levitt (eds.), *"Tsar and God" and Other Essays in Russian Cultural Semiotics*. Boston, Academic Studies Press, 2012, pp. 1–112.

Uspenskii, N., 'Chin Vozdvizheniia Kresta (Istoriko-liturgicheskii ocherk)', *Zhurnal Moskovskogo Patriarkhiia*, N 9, 1954, pp. 49–57.

Varneke, B.V., *Istoriia russkogo teatra 17–19 vekov*. Moskva, Iskusstvo, 1939.

Vasenko, P.G. (ed.), *Kniga stepennaia tsarskogo rodosloviia*. Sankt Peterburg, 1908.

Veinstein, G., L'administration ottomane et le problème des interprètes, In: B. Marino (ed.), *Études sur les villes du Proche-Orient XVIe-XIXe siècles: Hommage à André Raymond*. Damascus, Presses de l'Ifpo, 2001, pp. 65–79.

Vel'iaminov-Zernov, V.V., *Izsledovanie o Kasimovskikh tsariach i tsarevichakh*. Pt. 1. Sankt-Peterburg, Tipografia Imperatorskoi Akademii Nauk, 1863.

Velikaia Minei Chet'ii sobrannyia vserossiiskim mitropolitom Makariem. Vol. 7: *Dekabr' 6–17)*. Moskva, 1907.

Velikaia Mineia Chet'ia mesiatsa dekabria 6 den', ottsa nashego Nikolaia chudotvortsa, arkhiepiskopa Mirlikiiskago. Moskva, 1901.

Veselovskii, S.B., *Issledovaniia po istorii klassa sluzhilykh zemlevladel'tsev*. Moskva, Nauka, 1969.

Vladyshevskaia, M.S., Sviatoi Georgii i gnostitsizm: Semantika imen v predaniiakh o sv. Georgii, In: F.B. Uspenskii (ed.), *Imenoslov: Zametki po istoricheskoi semantike imeni*. Moskva, Indrik, 2003, pp. 70–102.

Vlassopoulos, K., Does Slavery Have a History? The Consequences of a Global Approach, *Journal of Global Slavery*, N 1, 1, 2016, pp. 5–27.

Vodovozov, N.V., *Istoriia drevnei russkoi literatury*. Moskva, Prosveshchenie, 1966.

Volkova, T.F., and I.A. Evseeva, Kazanskaia Istoriia, In: L.A. Dmitrieva and D.S. Likhacheva (eds.), *Pamiatniki literatury drevnei rusi*. Vol. 7: *Seredina XVI veka*. Moskva, Khudozhestvennaia Literatura, 1985, pp. 300–565.

Volkova, T. F., Kazanskaia istoriia, In: *Slovar' knizhnikov i knizhnosti drevnei Rusi* 2006 http://lib.pushkinskijdom.ru/Default.aspx?tabid=4006 (accessed 29 Aug. 2017).

Volkova, T.F., *Kazanskaia Istoriia*, n.y., http://www.pushkinskijdom.ru/Default.aspx?tabid=5148 (accessed 8 July 2017).

Volotskii, I., *Prosvetitel' ili oblichenie eresizhidovsvuiushchikh: Tvorenie prepodobnago ottsa nashego Iosifa, igumena Volotskago*. Kazan', Tipo-Litografiia Imperatorskogo Universiteta, 1896.

von Mallinckrodt, R., There Are No Slaves in Prussia?, In: E. Rosenhaft and F. Brahm (eds.), *Slavery Hinterland: Transatlantic Slavery in Continental Europe, 1680–1850*. Woodbridge, Boydell & Brewer, 2016, pp. 109–131.

Vozgrin, V.E., *Istoriia krymskikh tatar: Ocherki ėtnicheskoi istorii korennogo naseleniia Kryma*. Vol. 1. Simferopol', Krymuchpedgiz, 2013.

Vsevolodskii-Gemgross, V., *Russkii teatr ot istokov do serediny XVIII v*. Moskva, Izdatel'stvo Akademii Nauk SSSR, 1957.

Vulpius, R., *Die Geburt des russländischen Imperiums: Herrschaftskonzepte und -praktiken im 18. Jahrhundert*. Wien, Köln and Weimar, Böhlau, 2020.

Walker, B., *Foundations of Islam: The Making of a World Faith*. London, Peter Owen, 1998.

Ware III, R.T., Slavery in Islamic Africa, 1400–1800, In: D. Eltis and S. Engerman (eds.), *The Cambridge World History of Slavery*. Vol. 3: *AD 1420–AD 1804*. Cambridge, Cambridge University Press, 2011, pp. 47–80.

Weber, D., *Erzählliteratur: Schriftwerk, Kunstwerk, Erzählwerk*. Göttingen, Vandenhoeck & Ruprecht, 1998.

Weber, M., *Wirtschaft und Gesellschaft: Grundriß der verstehenden Soziologie*. Vol. 1. Tübingen, Mohr Siebeck, 1976.

de Wet, C.L., *The Unbound God: Slavery and the Formation of Early Christian Thought*. London and New York, Routledge, 2018.

Wilkins, C., A Demographic Profile of Slaves in Early Ottoman Aleppo, In: C. Witzenrath (ed.), *Eurasian Slavery, Ransom and Abolition in World* History, *1200–1860*. Farnham, Surrey, Ashgate, 2015, pp. 221–246.

Wilkinson, I., The Problem of Suffering as a Problem for Sociology, *Medical Sociology Online*, N 1, 1, 2006, pp. 45–47.

Williams, B.G., *The Crimean Tatars: The Diaspora Experience and the Forging of a Nation*. Leiden, Brill, 2001.

Wimmer, E., and J. Henning, *Novgorod – ein Tor zum Westen?: Die Übersetzungstätigkeit am Hofe des Novgoroder Erzbischofs Gennadij in ihrem historischen Kontext (um 1500)*. Hamburg, Verlag Dr. Kovač, 2005.

Wink, A., *Al-Hind: The Making of the Indo-Islamic World*. Vol. 2. Leiden, Brill, 2003.

Winnebeck, J., O. Sutter, A. Hermann, C. Antweiler and S. Conermann, *On Asymmetrical Dependency*. Bonn, Bonn Center for Dependency and Slavery Studies, 2021, https://www.dependency.uni-bonn.de/images/pdf-files/bcdss_cp_1-_on-asymmetrical-dependency.pdf (accessed 9 May 2022).

Wirtschafter, E.K., *Russia's Age of Serfdom 1649–1861*. Malden MA, Blackwell, 2008.

Witte, M., "Barmherzigkeit und Zorn Gottes" im Alten Testament am Beispiel des Buchs Jesus Sirach, In: R.G. Kratz and H. Spieckermann (eds.), *Divine Wrath and Divine Mercy in the World of Antiquity*. Tübingen, Mohr Siebeck, 2008, pp. 176–202.

Witte, M., Vom El Schaddaj zum Pantokrator: Ein Überblick zur israelitisch-jüdischen Religionsgeschichte, In: J.F. Diehl and M. Witte (eds.), *Studien zur Hebräischen Bibel und ihrer Nachgeschichte: Beiträge der 32. Internationalen Ökumenischen Konferenz der Hebräischlehrenden, Frankfurt am Main 2009*. Kamen, Verlag Hartmut Spenner, 2011, pp. 211–256.

Witte, M., *Von der Weisheit des Glaubens an den einen Gott*, 2013, https://www.perlentaucher.de/essay/von-der-weisheit-des-glaubens-an-den-einen-gott.html (accessed 11 May 2022).

Wittram, R., Das Freiheitsproblem in der russischen inneren Geschichte, *Jahrbücher für Geschichte Osteuropas*, N 2, 4, 1954, pp. 369–386.

Witzenrath, W., 'Negotiating Early Modern Transottoman Slaving Zones: An Arab in Moscow', in: E. Toledano and S. Conermann (eds.), *What is Global about Global Enslavement? Crossing Time-Space Divide*. Tel Aviv, forthcoming 2022.

Witzenrath, C., Sklavenbefreiung, Loskauf und Religion im Moskauer Reich, In: H. Grieser and N. Priesching (eds.), *Gefangenenloskauf im Mittelmeerraum: Ein interreligiöser Vergleich*. Hildesheim, Georg Olms, 2015, pp. 287–310.

Witzenrath, C., Orthodoxe Kirche und Fernmacht: Das Moskauer Reich, Kosaken und die Gründung des Bischofssitzes von Tobolsk und Sibirien 1620–1625, In: C. Hochmuth and S. Rau (eds.), *Machträume der frühneuzeitlichen Stadt*. Konstanz, UVK, 2006, pp. 309–332.

Witzenrath, C., *Cossacks and the Russian Empire, 1598–1725: Manipulation, Rebellion and Expansion into Siberia*. London and New York, Routledge, 2007.

Witzenrath, C., Literacy and Orality in the Eurasian Frontier: Imperial Culture and Space in Seventeenth-Century Siberia and Russia, *The Slavonic and East European Review*, N 87, 1, 2009, pp. 53–77.

Witzenrath, C., Sophia – Divine Wisdom, and Justice in Seventeenth-Century Russia, *Cahiers du monde russe*, N 50, 2–3, 2009, pp. 409–429.

Witzenrath, C., Introduction: Slavery in Medieval and Early Modern Eurasia: An Overview of the Russian and Ottoman Empires and Central Asia, In: C. Witzenrath (ed.), *Eurasian Slavery, Ransom and Abolition in World* History, *1200–1860*. Farnham, Surrey, Ashgate, 2015, pp. 1–77.

Witzenrath, C., The Conquest of Kazan' as Place of Remembering the Liberation of Slaves in Sixteenth- and Seventeenth-Century Muscovy, In: C. Witzenrath (ed.), *Eurasian Slavery,*

Ransom and Abolition in World History, 1200–1860. Farnham, Surrey, Ashgate, 2015, pp. 295–308.

Witzenrath, C., Agency in Muscovite Archives: Trans-Ottoman Slaves Negotiating the Moscow Administration, In: S. Conermann and G. Şen (eds.), *Slaves and Slave Agency in the Ottoman Empire Ottoman Studies*. Göttingen, V&R unipress, 2020, pp. 87–129.

Witzenrath, C., Versklavung, Befreiung und Legitimität im Moskauer Reich: Avraamij Palicyn und die "Zeit der Wirren", In: D. Ordubadi and D. Dahlmann (eds.), *Die "Alleinherrschaft" der russischen Zaren in der "Zeit der Wirren" in transkultureller Perspektive*. Göttingen, V&R unipress, 2021, pp. 13–44.

Woodworth, C., The Birth of the Captive Autocracy: Moscow, 1432, *Journal for Early Modern History*, N 13, 1, 2009, pp. 49–69.

Young, K., *The Drama of the Medieval Church*. Vol. 1. Oxford, Clarendon Press, 1933.

Yūsuf Khāss Hājib and R. Dankoff, *Wisdom of Royal Glory (Kutadgu Bilig): A Turko-Islamic Mirror for Princes*. Chicago, University of Chicago Press, 1983.

Zabelin, I.E., *Materialy dlia istorii, arkheologii i statistiki goroda Moskvy*. Vol. 1. Moskva, Mosk. Gor. Duma, 1884.

Zabelin, I., *Domashnii byt russkikh tsarei v XVI i XVII stoletiiakh*. Vol. 1. Moskva, Kniga, 1990.

Zguta, R., *Russian Minstrels: A History of the Skomorokhi*. Philadelphia, University of Pennsylvania Press, 1978.

Zhitie tsarevicha Petra, *Pravoslavnii sobesednik*, N 3, 1859, pp. 360–375.

Zhitiia Kirilla i Mefodiia. Moskva, Kniga, 1986.

Zimin, A., *I.S. Peresvetov i ego sovremenniki: Ocherki po istorii russkoi obshchestvenno-politicheskoi mysli serediny xvi veka*. Moskva, Izdatel'stvo Akademii Nauk SSSR, 1958.

Zimin, A.A., *Kholopy na Rusi*. Moskva, Nauka, 1973.

Index

Abd-al-Latif 79
Ablai, *taisha* 226
abolition 104
abuse 101–102, 179, 227
academic 185
academic public 169
Adam and Eve 126, 137
Adashev, Aleksei 83, 146, 148, 174
administration 9, 25, 39, 43, 78, 108, 197, 250
– agents 10, 12
– mid-managerial level 102
Afanasii, metropolitan 124
Africa 4–5, 14, 27, 29, 35, 43–45, 170–171
Agafonov syn Pereverzev, Trofim 150
agency
– as concept 186
– inter- 12, 150, 186, 192, 209
– of dependent people 253
– of peasants 10
– of slaves 18
– of the church 254
Akhmat, khan 57, 73, 77, 235
Alekseevich, Fedor 150, 191
Alekseevna, Sofiia 179
Aleppo 30, 171
alliance 91, 196
– conditional, ephemeral 194
– Crimean khanate 26, 43, 69, 72, 80
– Moldova 75
– steppe 72
– Tatars 76
al-Rabghuzi 214
Amalekites 97, 136
Anna, sister of the Byzantine emperor 128, 201
anointment 77, 115, 142, 251
apocalypse 47, 108, 217
– sects 109
apostasy 199
– apostate 82, 90, 156, 177
Arab 15
– Christian 189
– conquests 155
– descent from Hagarites 216–217
– *esqaliba* 169
– Inner Arabia 222
– literature 214
– proverb 17–18

archive 102, 154, 181, 203
artillerymen 107
Aslan Pasha 159
ass 141
Astrakhan 27, 189
– annexation 8, 28, 91, 143
– Muslims decended from 195
Asvebekov, Abraim Bek 182
Atlantic 7, 44, 104, *see also* trade, triangular Atlantic
– abolition movements 257
– revolutions 119
– slave trade 5
attachment 18, 65, 181, 212
Austria 118–119, 173
– Inner 174–176
authority 9, 27, 80, 104, 118–119, 125, 148, 220, 238, 248–249
autobiographical elements 202
autochthonous 157
autocracy 51–52, 148, 192, 255
– promise of liberation 101
azbuka 116

Bakhtin, Mikhail 165
baptism 128, 130, 149
– Rus' 50, 125, 127, 131, 235
– saves from slaving 128
Basary, Sudak 180
Bashkirs 38, 251
Basilios 151
Batu, khan 26, 57, 69, 71
begging 181, 225
Bekaev, Biik 182
Bekbulatovich, Simeon 32, 204
Belgorod 39, 184, 213
Belozero 73–74, 76–77
Belozersk monastery 73–74, 77
Berdiaev, Nikolai 47
besermeny 39, 117, 149
Bessarion, Basilius (Vasilii Vissarion) 72, 78, 80, 82, 176
Bible 131, 245
– as yardstick 119
– Elisabeth translation 114
– Gennadii translation 45, 76, 114
– new perspectives 104

– Russian translation 251
– Slavonic variant translations 114
– Vulgate 114
bishop 156, 164
– arch- 99
– bishopric 73
– care for captives 155
– of Cyprus 134
– of Novgorod 162
– Orthodox Ruthenian 178
– redeeming captives 82
– role in ransom 156, 176
– transfer to ruler 77, 100, 112
– tsar's secular likeness 101, 251
Black Sea 5, 34, 44, 168, 197
– steppe 29
'Blessed Host of the Heavenly Tsar' 141, 177, 242
bodily 177–179, 183–184
Book of Revelation 109, 120, 124
'Book of Royal Degrees' 49, 55, 81, 85–86, 126, 128, 144, 201, 213, 225, 228, 235, 239
– date 85
border fortifications 11
Borovskii, Pafnut'ev 217
boundary 5, 9, 42, 116
– communication across 193
– cultural 193, 249
– dynastic 115
– political 250
– religious 34, 115, 193, 201, 249
– steppe 251
bow 62–63, 100–101, 136, 146, 177, 181, 219, 232
boyar 63
– captives 31
– commission 107, 181
– competing clans 32
– elite 104, 116
– in court 170
– obligation 64
– relation to tsar 169
– role 52
brother 79, 226, 248
Bukhara 20, 237
Bulgars 202
burning bush 126, 239
Byzantine 26, 45, 84, 93, 135, 155–156, 161–163, 176, 194, 221–222, 256

– bishop 82, 176
– church 219
– emperor 27, 72, 128, 132, 135, 221
– heritage 3, 256
– influence in Muscovy 72
– literature 45
– post-Byzantine influence 161
– princess 130
– renaissance 45
Byzantium 80, 115, 155, 235

campaigns
– Crimean 79
captive 21, 88, 96, 155, 182, 213
– equal to fallen 122
– exchange 21, 31, 155, 180
– innocent 82, 95, 122, 152
– liberated 95, 139
– returned 30, 79, 92–93, 152, 159, 168, 182, 225, 237, 248, 257
– tax 107, 180
– torture 95, 122, 123, 132, 136, 177, 183–184, 239
captivity 174, 178
– endurance 183, 198, 229
– narrative 120, 154, 169, 182, 185, 203, 213
career 125, 185
Carib 35
carnivalized 165
Caspian Sea 5, 196
Cathedral of the Annunciation 81, 132
Caucasus 5, 12, 20–22, 28–29, 40, 43, 88, 143, 168, 171, 182, 257
Çelebi, Evliyah 209
Central Asia 7, 13–14, 16, 20, 28, 30, 35, 41, 51, 70, 168, 171, 184, 201, 208–209, 237, 243, 245, 247, 257
Chaldeans 166
chamberlain 188
chancellery 181, 189, 191–192
chancellery Russian 151
charity 225–226, 236, 238
Cheremis 37, 62, 92, 140, 225, 231, 251
Chernigov 183
child 63, 97, 154
– foster 21
– levy 21
– manumission 253
– of concubine 15

– slave 22
Chinggis Khan 51, 91, 252
Chingissid 69, 79, 92, 244
Chios 188
Chiudnovo 187
chivalry 203
chosen people 105, 144
Christianity
– superiority 207
Christ-like 201
'Chronicle of the Beginning of Tsardom' 55, 132, 135, 150, 158, 174, 207
– narrative 57
chronicles 56, 62, 69, 71, 73–75, 84, 128, 130, 156, 197, 227
church
– privileges under Tatars 197
– views of Tatars 48
Church Fathers 45, 112, 133
Church Slavonic 62, 106, 110, 134, 160
citizenship 35, 155, 256
clerics 190, 194, 208
– clerical party 81
– views 27, 69
climatic zone 5
column of fire 219
commemoration 122
community 140
comparison 172
compensation 168, 182–184, 189–191, 226, 247
concubine 16, 19, 217–218
conquest 4, 143, see also liberation
– dynastic 101
– justification 57, 150, 158, 202, 207, 220, 244
– legitimation 84, 233
– Mongol 56
– motivations 49, 54, 216
– political language 53
Constantine 101, 132, 135, 233–235
Constantinople 44, 49, 128, 135–136, 153, 160, 200–201, 239
– conquest 1453 72, 75, 166
– sack 1204 135
conversion 183, 186, 189, 201, 204, 206, 215, 231–232
– forced 108
corsair 7, 17
cossacks 8–9, 13, 22, 30, 40, 52, 107, 172, 187

– Tatars 79
court case 170
creation 76, 81, 109, 117, 126
– God's presence 26, 76, 109, 117
Crete 135, 157
– emir 151, 155
Crimea 8, 32, 60, 63, 67, 88, 129, 135, 150, 171, 180, 197, 213, 254, 257
– khanate 26, 43, 62, 69, 72, 80, 92, 95, 135, 143, 149, 158, 196, 213
cross 123, 137, 139, 142–143, 149, 233–234
– captive people of 140
– carry into Kazan 139
– carved into palisade 142
– enemies of 131, 138, 140
– Holy Cross Fortress 143
– honourable 131
– Jesus Christ death as a ransom 110
– kissing 7, 131, 167, 184, 187, 234
– life-giving 98, 132, 134, 139–140, 233
– oath 131, 138, 167, 184, 187, 234
– procession 139
– Resurrection of 135–137
– sign 137–138, 144
– 'True' 132, 135, 138
crusade 72, 135
– Latin 135
crusading 25, 108, 227
cyclical thinking (timelines) 221

Dagestan 143
Daniel 120, 163
Daudov, Vasilii 183
debate 148
debt 4, 11, 19, 156, 184, 207, 226, 238, see also dependency, strong asymmetrical
– bondage 4, 111, 210, 212
– limit 155
– slavery 39, 114, 134
deliverance 146
dependency 3, 11, 26, 118, 182, 192, 248–249, 254, 256
– continuum 3
– counter dependency zone 7, 82, 89, 96, 115, 158, 192, 194, 212, 223, 233, 244, 257
– role of insiders 94
– cyclical 115, 221, 229
– mutual 192
– strong asymmetrical 52, 94, 186, 208, 223

deportation 108, 212, 252, 256
diplomats 83
– Muscovite 3, 253
– papal 3
disciple 72, 129, 176, 236
discrimination 26
disgrace 89, 94, 115, 117, 142, 221
dispersal 99, 252
distance 20, 237, 247
disunity 228
Dmitriev, Iurii 51
Donskoi, Dmitrii 51, 101, 140, 153, 156
Doroshenko, Petro 188
dragon 98, 154, 166, 208
– Kazan 55, 132
– lair 157
– symbol for slavers 158, 241, 245
dry path 76, 129, 133

Ediger-Mahmet, khan 95–96, 157
education 13, 78, 116, 160, 173, 190
– Latin 170
– reeducation 185
Elagin, Aleksei Martynov son 184
Elena of Moldova 75
eligibility
– enslavement 24, 34–35, 199, 214
– ransom 190
elite 103, 116
emancipation 19, 106, 256
empire 35, 175, 227
– agent of 207
– British 104, 246, 255
– Byzantine 77, 106, 162, 194, 197
– early 39
– gunpowder 7–8, 14, 57
– Habsburg 5, 45, 168, 172, 181
– hub-and-spoke model 25
– Mongol 26, 28–29, 41, 43, 45, 197, 217, 252
– Ottoman 3–4, 6, 12, 15, 22, 24, 28–31, 44, 57, 79, 168, 171, 180, 188–189, 191–192, 239, 247, 253–254, 256
– Roman 2–3, 47, 93, 101, 110, 155, 233–234, 255
– Russian 2, 5–6, 25, 42, 107, 157, 257
– Spanish 35, 91
Enbars, Kazan mirza 63
'Enlightener' 177
Enoch 107, 115, 180

enslavement as establishing suzerainty 57
Ermak 150, 159, 207, 219, 245
Ermolaev, Martyn 183
escape 21, 88, 184, 232
eschatology 49, 54, 104, 109, 117, 123, 231, 255
– psychosis 108
– 'small' 123
ethnic 7, 34, 40, 190, 193, 205, 224, 230, 245, 252
– group 3, 37, 40, 108, 227, 241
– imperial 24
– marker 35
– multi- 5
– trans- 227, 247
ethnology 169
Eurasia 4–5, 6, 10, 27, 29, 44–45, 47, 52, 117, 170, 194, 196, 215, 225, 247, 251
– inner 3, 5–7, 15, 34–35, 172, 193, 252, 254
Europe 15, 34, 50
evangelicalism 104
excommunication 94, 131
exile 46, 51, 91, 117, 126, 144, 176, 179
Exodus 65, 67, 70, 76, 84, 93, 101, 109, 116, 128–129, 133, 136, 156, 210, 213, 221, 239
expansion 1, 4, 48, 207, 251
– European 44
– Mongol 252
– Muscovite 52, 67, 144, 209, 255
– Ottoman 4
– Russian 2, 38

favour (tsar) 198
Fedorovich, Dmitrii 198
Filip, metropolitan 125
Final Judgement 108–109
foreign affairs 187–188, 203
– chancellery 107, 187
foreign policy 32, 78, 84
fortified line (*zaseka*) 38–39, 43, 251
– Arzamas 143, 193
– Belgorod 213
– Siberia 172
freedom 20, 223, 248
– as norm 19
– autocracy 51
– of movement 214
frontier 9, 12, 36, 45, 148, 173, 176, 252
– Islamic 8
– legends 208

- life-style 178, 205
- steppe 10, 31, 33, 142, 208, 248, 250, 252
- town 39, 64, 149
- zone 5, 32, 40, 143, 171

galley 30, 44, 184–185, 191
- rower 30, 44, 206
gatekeeper 107
gender 16, 35, 127, 181, 184, 201, 217–218
- boy 232
- girl 232
- spinster 200
- temptress 212, 214
genealogy 25, 85, 144, 202, 210, 216
Genoese 34
gentry 38, 52, 143, 146, 148, 170, 188, 250–251
- local 109, 142, 248
Georgia 21, 143, 163, 204–205, 209
Gerontii, metropolitan 73
Girei 7, 79, 226
- Devlet 143, 226
- Gazy 213
- Mengli 79
- Safa 229
- Utemesh 63
Godunov, Boris (tsar) 12, 32, 125, 214
Golden Horde see Ulus of Jochi
- cities 249
- *orda* 249
Golitsyn, Iurii Mikhailovich 64, 89, 198
Golitsyn, Vasilii Vasil'evich 179–180
Grand Dragoman 188
grand prince
- installed by khan 57
'Great Reading Menaion' 84, 132, 176, 233
'Great Sacred Song' 135
Great *Ulus* 68, 196
Greek Orthodox clerics 3
gunner 107

Hagar 59, 84, 100, 154, 187, 197, 235, 238
Hagarites (Sons of Hagar) 65, 98
hardened heart 70
Helena, empress 135, 234
hell 111, 132, 175, 230, 244
- hellish 132, 138
Heraclius, emperor 136
Herberstein, Sigmund von 43, 75

heresy 75, 108, 154
heuristic principle 169
High Bank 63–64, 88, 90
'History of Kazan' 55, 66, 102, 138, 142, 145, 149, 157, 199, 202, 205, 223, 225, 228, 232, 244
'History of Siberia' 150, 158, 207, 245
honour 94, 100, 171, 198, 203, 205
household 9, 182, 195
- captives 63
- elite 16
- extended 14
- in Islamic law 17
- Muslim 168
- slaves 15, 22
- tsar's 165
human rights 117–119
humility 96
Hundred Chapters Synod 81, 115, 180, 192
Hungary 173

Ianin (Ioannina, Epirus) 159
iasak 40, 61, 226, 251
icon 124, 184
Immanuel 115–116
imperial culture 79, 156, 162, 204, 230, 236, 244, 255, 257
- 'silent' 82, 106
- ideology 2, 27, 194, 207, 238
- Is 61 113
- tranquillity 241, 243
- worldview 4, 27, 203, 256
imperial
- crisis 2, 32, 49, 51, 79, 199
- durability 2
- historiography 2, 27
- mission 2
- nation 38
- repertoires 1
imperialism 106
'In Praise of Ivan IV and His Host for the Victory Against the Kazan Tatars' 59
inauguration 86, 130, 187
incarnation 109, 156
inclusive 3, 26, 224, 230, 233
India 6–7, 20, 28, 44, 249
inheritance 33, 84, 115–116, 142, 161, 216, 238
institution 14, 19
- hybrid 194

– institutionalisation 52, 248
– mechanism 191–192
integration 19, 25, 168, 204, 207, 210, 221, 231, 254
– disintegration 41–42, 57, 197
– language 194
– reintegration 247
intermarriage 31, 172
interpolation 71, 77, 124–130, 134, 167, 200–201, 206, 228, 235
intersectional approach 190
interview 7, 182, 187
Ioasaf, metropolitan 98, 146
Ireland 91
Irenaeus of Lyons 112
Isaiah 97, 111, 115, 136, 142, 159, 175, 245, 255
Ishmael/Ismailsons of see Hagarites
iskuplenie 107, 110
Islam 187, 199, 221
Istanbul 17, 22, 29–30, 44, 83, 159, 187, 191, 195–196
Iur'ev 79
Iurev, Perfil' 183
Ivan III 26, 68, 70, 72, 75, 78–79, 112, 156, 176, 218, 221, 233, 235
Ivan IV 20, 23, 32, 37, 54, 58–59, 64, 72, 81–89, 91–92, 102, 117, 120–123, 130–131, 133, 135, 138, 140, 145–149, 156, 158, 166, 174, 192, 197–198, 205, 220, 223, 226, 229, 231–236, 251–252, 257
Ivan the Younger 75
Ivanov, Fedot 185
– Mamet 185
Ivanov, Mikhail 190
Ivanovich, Dmitrii
– coronation 251
Ivanovich, Fedor (tsar) 32, 125, 213

Jew 18, 22, 71, 80, 111, 128, 162, 209, 217, 222
John of Damascus 133
Joseph (Old Testament) 125–126, 129, 134, 185, 187, 201
Joshua 55, 77, 127, 146, 166, 175, 177
judiciary 159

Kalmyk 38, 182, 184–185, 226
Kamaia-*murza* 96
Kämpfer, Frank 54, 58, 99, 228

karachi bey 88
Kashira 79, 250
Kasimov 32, 61, 91, 198, 250
Kazakh 184–185
Kazan 65, 92, 140, 175, 198, 202
– High Bank 86, 89, 227
khan 91, 98, 159, 198
Khiva 20, 184
kholopy 39, 133, 170, 179, 183, 195
Khosrow II 135
kidnap 37, 55, 123, 157, 257
Kievan Rus' 125, 130
kinship 35, 190, 196, 212
Konstiantinov, Evstafii 160, 186
Kopystensky, Zakhariia 178–179, 183
Kremlin's Cathedral Square 113
Krevza, L. 178
Krizhanich, Iurii 170
Kurbskii, Andrei 81, 144, 149
Kyiv 41, 49, 159, 201–202, 217, 239

Landesdefension 171, 173, 175
Latin West 123, 161
law code 39, 107, 115, 150, 180, 199, 207, 226, 248, 256
– chancellery 107
– dual process of law making 107, 181
– sharia 13, 15, 17, 215, 218
– *ulozhenie* 107, 180–181, 192
'Legend of the True Cross' 134, 144
legitimation 92, 100, 130, 212
Lenhoff, Gail 49, 125
lèse majesté 171, 173
'Letter of the Three Patriarchs' 76, 78
Leviticus 97
liberate 62, 81, 86, 117, 200
liberation 76, 83, 89–90, 93, 96, 102, 110, 115, 125, 146, 167, 178, 198, 205, 220, 232
– biblical 113
– command 89
– de-emphasized 82, 148
– implementation 63
– innate right 83, 86
– isolated ideology 69
– *izbaviti* 81, 117
– omitted 147, 155
– peace condition 57
– purpose of empire 202, 253
– remaining captives 63

– returning slaves from tax 39, 122, 181, 183, 192
liberty 62, 65
– in maritime empires 5
'Life of Fedor Ivanovich' 212
'Life of Moses' 132, 134
literacy 13, 173, 254
liturgy 154, 161, 164–165, 167
– liturgical drama 160
– printed 161, 163
Locke, John 174
Lord's speech of mercy 63, 86
loyalty
– hindsight 191

Machiavelli 91
Makarii, archbishop of Novgorod, metropolitan 48, 54, 56, 61, 65, 70, 72, 80–84, 89–90, 99–101, 111, 113, 117, 121–123, 125, 131–132, 140, 149, 152, 158, 162, 166, 174–177, 183, 215, 220, 226, 233
mamluk 22, 215, 221
Mamotiak 203
manumission 63, 95, 122, 131, 184, 192, 216, 219, 237–238
– without 191
Marah 113, 126, 132–133, 136–137
Mari 193
Maria Palaeologina 74
market capitalization 41
marriage 72, 74, 129–130, 201, 214–215, 218, 247
martyr 123, 177–178, 181, 203, 225, *see also* torture
– crown 123, 124, 142, 177
– topos 196
'Martyrdom of Ivan' 176
'Marusia Boguslavskaia' 218
master 11, 16–17, 30, 101, 122, 179, 193, 210, 218, 223, 241, 244, 250
– heterodox 109, 253
Mediterranean 8, 13–14, 20, 22, 155, 168–169, 172, 206, 249
– eastern 44–45
– Greater 34, 41
– Ottoman 28
meekness 230, 240

mercy 61–63, 77, 93, 96–97, 100, 107, 115, 117, 128, 130–131, 145, 158–159, 180–181, 219, 224–225, 227, 230, 232, 242
Midianites 93, 127, 166
migration 11, 38, 172, 249
– Greek Orthodox clerics 45, 72, 125
– out- 11, 42
Mikhailovich, Aleksei (tsar) 165, 177, 185, 210
Military Chancellery 150
militia 172–174
miracle 58, 99–100, 108, 133–134, 145, 151–157, 163, 185, 205–207, 220, 234, 239
– cult 46
– worker 60, 138, 150, 159, 174, 248
mission 25, 126, 143, 208, 221
mistreatment 15, 126, 240
mobilisation 99
mobility 4, 36, 65
– deprivation of 87
– forced 212
– limiting 10
– social 14–15, 191, 201, 221, 247
monarchy 39, 111–112, 244, 251
monastery 73–74, 77, 98, 145–147, 151, 153, 159, 185
Mongol 23, 26, 33, 38, 43, 45, 48, 51, 56, 68, 91, 96, 106, 117, 197, 226, 235, 243, 250
– Oirat 8
Mongols
– Oirat 226
monotheism 13–14, 22, 34, 93, 111, 162, 209, 215, 222, 224, 234, 251
moral capital 80, 86–87, 89, 196, 222, 229, 243
Mordvins 37, 225
Moses 50, 65, 77, 83, 85, 93–94, 97, 113, 118, 126, 129–130, 132–133, 136–139, 179, 213, 221, 239, 251, 256
– new 47, 96, 129, 176
Mother of God 133, 138, 142, 146, 163, 204–205, 211, 234
Mozhaisk 153, 208
multi-cultural 227, 255
murals (Golden Palace) 6, 55, 113, 115, 125, 130, 133–134, 187, 194, 205, 209–216, 255
musketeer 23, 64, 107, 182
Muslim 13, 15–16, 19, 21–22, 72, 185, 187, 200, 206, 217, 219

narrative 6, 58, 64, 67, 73–77, 84, 99, 102, 110, 125–126, 146–150, 158, 169, 175–176, 185, 202–207, 213, 223, 245, 252
– addition 140
– cathartic moment 198
– climax 57, 95
– dramatization 160
– dynastic 130
– founding 130
– plot 151
– reinterpetation 202
– subtle shifts 202
– transformation 157
Narva 156
Naryshkin 179–180
nationalism 24, 106
– ethno- 38
nationalist 48, 105, 158, 160, 170, 206, 255
Nebuchadnezzar 163, 167, 177, 204
Netherlands 28, 91
nevolia 87, 223
Nevskii, Aleksandr 101, 140
– vita 71
new era 64, 67
New Israel 1, 6, 56, 58, 67, 72, 78, 86, 94, 96, 102, 104, 106, 131, 134, 146, 160, 163, 167, 177, 201, 213, 240, 253, 255
– new quality 56
New Jerusalem 49, 109, 141, 257
– St Basil's on Red Square 141
New Year 113, 116, 130, 142, 161, 166, 242
Newfoundland 7
Nikolev, Ivan 184
nomad
– warfare 249
nomads 4, 13, 21, 29–30, 37–39, 71, 87, 92, 106, 184, 193, 215–216, 221, 245, 249, 251–252
– federations 27
– pastoral 249
– semi- 37–38, 241
norm 9, 91, 155, 191, 252
– *cimar* 91
– freedom as 19
– Mongol 91
– Orthodox 166
– sharia 15

no-slaving zone 6, 25, 33–36, 40, 61, 74, 101, 117, 250, 253
Novgorod 46, 48, 72, 76–77, 84, 102, 153, 162–164, 167
Nur-Sultan 79

oath 63, 69, 79, 86–88, 96, 131, 162, 168, 198, 207
– breaking 100, 197, 225
– mutual 234
objects
– inanimate 186
– symbolic 186
Oboian' 150
Olearius, Adam 164
omophorion 156
oppressors 126, 136, 241, 245
orality
– secondary orality 151
Orientalism 80
Orthodoxy 184, 187, 189
– food 196
– model 201
– Russian 138
– second chances 122
Ossetians 143
otkup 106
otroki 162, 239
Ottoman 118, 143, 189, 202, *see also* empire, Ottoman
– literature 202
outlaw 79
outsider 199, 214, 221
outsiders 20, 94, 164, 199, 201, 222, 250, 252

Palace of Facets 125, 187, 209–213, 215–216, 245
Palaeolog, Andrei 74
Palekh 210
Palinodia 178
Palm Sunday 141
Panagiotis Nikosias Mamonas 188
pantocratic 224
pardon 114, 177, 185, 232
parishioner 137, 155, 248
patriarchs 72, 159, 164, 186–190, 217
patronage 22, 33, 138, 189, 191
pawnbroker 156

peasant 131, 183, 237
- covenanters 173
- Great Peasant Wars 171
Persia 6, 20, 29, 35, 57, 136, 143, 157, 163, 175, 185, 224, 236, 238, 243, 245, 249
Peter I [the Great] 4, 6, 25, 114, 143, 211, 255–257
petition 150, 159, 168, 180–182, 186, 194, 196, 241, 247–248, 252
Petrine 106, 119, 256–257
- continuities 6
- divide 6
pharaoh 69, 77, 95, 113, 118, 126, 133, 137, 146, 210, 212, 221, 239, 252
- hardened 70, 85, 96
Phinehas 93
piety 95, 132, 144, 199–200, 202, 218, 233, 235, 253
- impiety 157, 199
pit 88, 135
pleniti 69
Poland-Lithuania 29, 32, 42, 106, 173, 178, 208
Polish occupation of the Kremlin 141, 255
political culture
- steppe politics 80, 87, 90–91
Polotskii, Simeon 167, 177
Polotsky, Simeon 239
Polozov, Vasilii Vasil'ev syn 185–186
Poluianova, Ovdot'ia 181
polygamy 158, 217–218
polytheism 94, 127
pragmatism 108
precedent 91, 108–109, 257
prefiguration 49, 65, 127, 129–130, 234
prison 111, 155, 157, 179–180, 203, 206, 215, 230
prisoner of war 23, 180
Promised Land 50, 55, 77, 85, 113, 127–128, 133–134, 166, 205, 222
- Kazan 177, 251
property 9, 52, 114, 155
- litigation maps 109, 143, 167, 247
Protestant 45, 113, 117, 156
Psalm 74 116
public secretary 183
purification 127, 138, 142
Putivl 159

qarachi beys 51
'Qïssa-yï Yusuf' 214
qul 238, 243
Qul 'Ali 214
Qur'an 17–20, 21, 22, 23, 209, 214, 217, 245, 252
- oath 131, 138

rab /raba 96, 117, 181
rabota 56, 101, 117, 221–222, 241
race 5, 34–35
rank restoration 190
ransom 97, 107, 110, 116–117, 133–134, 150, 167, 173, 189, 193, 203, 207, 226, 238
- compensation 106, 168
- Tatars 207
rebellion 86, 117–118, 135, 204, 235
reception 46–47, 80, 83, 94, 151
reciprocity 168, 170, 175–176, 181, 192, 234
recommendation 72, 93, 159, 186–187, 189–190
Red Sea 77, 113, 124, 126, 129, 133, 136–137, 210, 219, 241
- steppe as 70
redemption 105, 110, 122, 126, 143, 166, 211
- ambiguous 109, 201
- as ransom 110, 248
- as resurrection 97, 135
- cyclical salvation 115
- entitlement to 81, 119, 176
- generalisation 105
- Jesus as prisoner 110
- path to salvation 100, 144
- ransom theory 109, 133
- ransom 100
- salvation history 54, 109, 115, 133
- slave market as salvation 109, 111–112, 118, 201
- triumph 109
Reformation 119
religion 1, 14, 26, 28, 35, 40, 54, 60, 94, 157, 191, 194, 235, 253
religious duty 174
Remezov, Semen Ulianovich 94, 141, 150, 152, 158–159, 207, 218–219, 225–226, 236, 241, 243, 245, 248
Remezov, Ulian 226
Renaissance 26, 36, 67, 72, 78, 84, 176, 213, 249

renegade 231, 236
resistance 18, 162–163, 167, 172, 174, 186, 252
retribution 20, 91
return from captivity 150
Riazan' 41, 153, 183
right of conquest 63, 86
Riurikids 202
Roman Empire
– Republican norm 155
Romania 34, 208
ruler
– election 96
– in council 52, 170
Rumelia 159, 185, 208
Rus' principalities 33, 57, 71, 126, 202, 250
Ruthenians 30, 42, 106, 110, 178, 218, 239
Rylsk 183

sacralisation 104, 131, 251
Safavid 29, 41
salary 186–187, 195–196
salvation *see* redemption
Samoilov, Makarii Lavrent'ev son 183–184
Sarı Saltuk 208
saviour 98, 103, 105, 107, 133, 136, 157, 178
Scott, Thomas 105
'Secret History of the Mongols' 91
sentinels 143
serf 8–9, 22, 34, 37–40, 114–115, 256
– enserfment 6, 11, 25, 28, 36–37, 115, 212, 248, 250, 253
– flight 9
serpent 98, 113, 158
service 53, 64, 89, 175, 190, 215, 237, 253
Sevsk 159, 179–182
Shah Ali /khan of Kazan 61–64, 67, 86–92, 140, 197–199, 203–204, 214, 223, 229–231, 233–234, 244
shatter zone 35
sheep 159
Sheremetev, Vasilii B. 183, 187
Shirin
– -Muralev 88
– -Teginia 51
Siberia 171–173, 225
– khanate (Sibir') 158–159, 219
Sil'vestr 231
Sibir 219
Silk Roads 27–29, 249

– northern 44
– through Siberia 28
sin 100, 110, 114, 117, 119, 127, 133, 156, 175, 257
– 'not by their own fault' 175
Sinai desert 94, 113, 116, 126, 133
Skarga, P. 178
skomorokhi 166
slave raid 57, 200, 202, 235, 242
– protection 11, 129, 143, 249
slave
– boy 163, 239
– Christian 8, 140, 220, 225, 229, 232–233
– confiscation 64
– consort 30
– demand for 14, 35, 57, 61
– elite 15, 22, 188, 238, 243
– elopement 135
– female 15–16, 17, 20, 181, 189, 216
– girl 30
– Gypsy 34
– labour 14, 20
– market language 109, 117, 178, 201
– military 8, 15, 217, 221
– mother 19
– rebellion 135
– sale 8, 17, 33, 37
– 'slave of God' 96, 117, 138
– 'slavish' habits 75
– 'slaves of the tsar' 169
– trade 13, 65–66, 101, 104, 187, 212, 215–216
slaver 89, 150, 216
slavery
– contrary to God's will 114
– impurity 138
– sale into 134, 155, 252
– sale of relatives into 209
– unjust 158, 243
slaving 99–100, 127, 158, 218–219, 223
– beneficiaries 57
– biological metaphor 89, 93, 95–96, 126
– overcome 128
– prohibited to heterodox subjects 89
slaving zone 33, 48, 59, 61, 79, 91, 115, 234, 249–251, 253
– 'long-term' 34
Slavophiles 170, 254, 257
slovo i delo gosudarevy 171

Sofiia (Zoe) Palaiologina 27, 72–73
– accusations 74
– Greek entourage 176, 220
Sol Invictus 234
Solov'ev, Vladimir 47
Solovetsk 184
soteriology 109, 178
sovereignty 68, 87, 119
space
– dialogic 38
– economic 4
– imperial 1, 194, 226
– representational 134
– -transcending 155, 160, 190, 207
sphere
– protective 141
– sign of pawnbroker 156
St Basil's 141
St George 157–160, 206, 208
St Nicholas 156, 160, 209, 248, 252
– life 156
– manuscripts 154
– of Myra 148, 156
– of Sion 155
– stories 155
St Sergius 98, 145–148, 151, 213
St Sophia 225
Stepanov, Lev 237
steppe 124, 193
– Barabinsk 226
– Kalmyk 182
– Pontic 208
– Qipchak 208
– 'sport' 206
stigma 35
Streshnev, Tikhon N. 180
subjects 34, 90, 182
– heterodox 194
– loyal 236
submission 168, 223
sun 98, 116, 139, 230–236
suzerainty 29, 41, 56, 60, 68, 87
Sviiazhsk 58, 63, 65, 90, 92, 99, 123, 139, 145–147, 227
– signs at 66, 145
svoboda 133
svobozhdati 62
Swabian League 118

sword 93, 147–148, 152–153, 155, 223, 244
– right of the 89

'Tale about Queen Dinara' 163, 204
'Tale of Bygone Years' 125, 239
'Tale of Petr, Tsarevich of the Horde' 235
'Tale of the Battle with Mamai' 56
Tamerlane (Amir Timur or Timur the Lame, Temir Aksak) 70, 85, 249
Tatar 7, 74, 179, 182, 184, 193, 195, 203, 225, 227, *see also* translator, Tatar
– convert 188
– Crimean 62
– Kazan 228
– Muscovite 203
– road 150
Tatarinov, Petr Andreianov *syn* 186–189
tax 10, 22, 36, 39–41, 61, 66, 171, 180
– collector *see besermeny*
– exemption 4, 181
– khan's 66
– liberation from 133
– -payer 40, 114, 172
– reduction 175
– sell kin for arrears 117
teleology 2
terror 91, 108–109, 231
Tevkelev, Mustofa 195–198, 203
'The Book of Royal Degrees' 70
theatre 1, 7, 124, 167
– court 167
– liturgical 164
theocracy 1, 50
Third Rome 48, 255
– nineteenth century 47–48
Time of Troubles 7, 12, 25, 32, 141, 194, 212, 232, 255
'*Tipografskii* chronicle' 73
Tobolsk 207, 219, 226, 236
tolerance 45, 80, 166, 196, 207, 253–254
Tomsk 85, 125
tonsure 189
torture 21, 81, 95, 101, 117, 131, 149, 158, 178, 227, 231, 237
trade 5–6, 9, 13, 21, 24, 27–29, 31, 33–35, 44–45, 143, 231, 237, 247–250, 252–254
– Caucasus 28, 143, 171
– Egypt 44

– grain 44
– horse 249
– human 249, *see also* slave trade
– Livonia 28
– transcontinental 28–29, 31, 43
– triangular Atlantic 44
'Tragedy about the Tsar Nebuchadnezzar . . .' 167
traitor 74, 82, 91, 95–96, 175, 196, 198–199, 228–229, 252
Trakhaniot the Younger, George 75
trans
– -confessional 196, 203–204, 207, 215, 230–231, 235–236, 243–244
– -cultural 4, 207, 209, 224, 230, 237, 239, 247
– -imperial 23, 208–209
– -maritime 254
– -Ottoman 7, 170, 252, 254
– -religious 247
transfer 45, 77, 80, 84, 100, 112, 138, 162, 166, 176, 179, 230
– cultural 50, 72, 254
– legitimacy 31
– through space and time 160
translator 114, 186, 188–189, 252
– Greek 78, 188
– Tatar 195, 203, 252, *see also* Tatar interpreter
tribute 12, 21, 38–40, 43, 74, 173, 205, 223, 251
Trinity St Sergii 98
tsar
– as khan or basileus 23
– as shepherd 59–60, 101, 112, 122, 147, 158, 174, 200, 253
– Christ-emulating 175
– false 167
– obligation 82, 85, 100, 124, 158, 177, 192, 198, 226, 238, 240, 242–243
– title 32, 60, 69
– tyrannical 167, 192
– unbeliever 139, 167, 178
tsar' 32, 69, 90, 92, 98, 126, 157, 251
tsaritsa 27, 74, 83, 217–218, 220–221
Turkmens 7, 16, 21, 30, 184–185, 201, 215, 237
Twelve Articles 119

Ugra 68, 75, 84
– battle 74
– 'Stand on the Ugra River' 56

Ugra, letter to 25–27, 60, 67, 69–71, 73, 76–79, 82, 84, 100, 112, 150, 176, 204, 207, 221–222, 233
– gap in tradition 73
– liberation 69
Ukraine 12, 29, 40, 43, 46, 187, 239
ulus see Tatars
Ulus of Jochi *see* Golden Horde
union of Christian churches 72
Union of Florence 75
universalism 3, 245
university 12, 46, 119, 185, 188
– Padova 188
urbanization 12, 39
Ushakov, Simon 209–211

Vasilii II the Blind 203, 245
Vasilii III Ivanovich 73, 75–76, 79, 161, 218, 244
Vassian Rylo 68–70, 73–76, 84, 144
Vereia 74–75
vernacular 118, 160, 163
violence 32, 89, 177, 249
'Vita of Grigorii Neronov' 165
vizier 187–188, 195
Vladimir of Kyiv, grand prince 125, 130, 200
Volga 27–28, 44, 61, 65, 125, 213, 249
– lower 8, 29, 249
– middle 27, 29, 32–33, 37, 43, 52, 58, 89, 92, 99, 115, 143, 193–194, 204–205, 209, 235, 250–251
– mountainous right bank 198
– Tatars 28
volia 65, 223
Volodimir Andreevich Staritsky 97
Vologda 161, 165
Vologda-Perm chronicle 73, 77
Volok Lamskii, Iosif of 178, 183
Vsevolozh 51

westernizing 106, 257
widow 15, 32, 79, 181, 229
Wilberforce 105
wisdom 126–127, 154, 213, 224–226, 236, 239–240, 243–245
– book of 241
– books of 224
– divine 113, 144, 241, 244
– holy 135

- light as symbol 230–231, 236
- ruler 66, 224–227, 238
- sun imagery 232–233
- symbols of 141
Wisdom of Salomon 76
witness 146, 203
- biased 17
- literate 151
wood 9, 124, 126–127, 132, 136–137, 142–144, 152, 234, 240
- cypress 136
- fir 136
- Holy 132–135, 137–138
- juniper 136
- life-giving 132–133, 139, 233
- live-giving 98
- oak 142
- Palm Sunday 141, *see also* Palm Sunday
- planting 142, 144
- spilling 141–142
- staff 133
- tree (in paradise) 124, 133
workforce 9, 14, 37, 40, 205
worldview 6–7, 24, 27, 33–34, 94, 97, 102, 119, 130, 133, 143, 193, 203, 248–249, 256

- circular 187, 216
- coherent 37, 39
- expression of 223
- extreme 223
- imperial 27, 208, 256
- Kazan Tatar 202
- monarchical 41
- Muscovite 1, 3, 6, 48, 53, 67, 148, 256
- paucity of sources 6
- transcultural 4
writer 78, 130, 193, 201, 214, 228
- ecclesiastical 48, 231
- Hebrew 94
- Muscovite 67, 91, 194, 223, 239
writers
- Muscovite 59

'Year of the Lord's Favour' 111, 115
'yoke of slavery' 57
Yūsuf Khāṣṣ Hājib 243

Zaraisk 153
zbornaia pamiat 189
Zulaykha 201, 214–215

www.ingramcontent.com/pod-product-compliance
Lightning Source LLC
Chambersburg PA
CBHW080911170426
43201CB00017B/2286